Somewhere Over the Rainbow is a Place Called San Francisco...

Put on your Ruby Slippers & Celebrate Pride '97 in San Francisco!
June 28 & 29, 1997
Saturday & Sunday

Events all week before the Celebration!:
Films, culture, art, entertainment,
politics, and parties, parties, parties!

*For information about the
Largest Pride Celebration
on this side of the Rainbow:*

call 415/864-FREE Fax: 415/864-5889
email: sfpride@aol.com

DINAH
SHORE
WEEKEND
PALM SPRINGS

MARCH 27-30, 1997

Produced by JOANI WEIR PRODUCTIONS
POM POM PRODUCTIONS
KLUB BANSHEE

Photos by LINVIL

LIVE CELEBRITY ENTERTAINMENT • COMEDY SHOW

POOL PARTIES • DANCE PARTIES

TENNIS COURTS • VOLLEYBALL • GOLF PACKAGES

CASUAL AND FINE DINING • SHOPPING

CONTESTS WITH AMAZING GIVEAWAYS

The Ultimate Hotel & Entertainment Package at the All Inclusive

DOUBLE TREE RESORT

Book today to ensure availability
For hotel and party ticket Information Call

310.281.7358

A GREAT VACATION FOR COUPLES AS WELL AS SINGLES

EVERYTHING YOU WILL NEED OR WANT CAN BE FOUND AT
THE DOUBLE TREE RESORT...JUST FLY IN...THEN PARK AND PLAY

TRULY A SPRING GETAWAY WEEKEND
TO GET THE WINTER BLOOD FLOWING

You've been asking for it...

DAMRON ATLAS

A TOUR & TRAVEL LLP

DAMRON ATLAS

WORLD TRAVEL

A Full Service Travel Agency

- offices nationwide
- great rates on airfare
- cruises & tours
- groups & special events
- fully accredited IATA agency

WORLD TRAVEL

TOLLFREE 1·888·907·9771
310·670·6991

Damron Accommodations

Now you'll always have a home away from home! The first and only **full-color guide** to gay-friendly B&Bs, inns, hotels and other accommodations in North America, Europe and Australia. Most listings include **color photographs** and a comprehensive description. Sophisticated travellers will appreciate the handy multiple **cross-referenced index**.

Over 400 pages.   Only **$18.95**

To order, call **(800) 462-6654**
or turn to the Damron Mail Order Section
on pages 22-23

Outside the U.S., call **(415) 255-0404**

Mail: Damron Mail Order
PO Box 422458,
San Francisco, CA 94142

*please include $5 shipping fee
plus $1 for each additional item*

The only lesbian & gay atlas is the perfect companion to the *Address Book* and the *Women's Traveller!* This attractive full-color guide features **more than 125 maps** with color-coded dots that pinpoint lesbian & gay bars, accommodations and bookstores in **over 60 cities** and resorts in the U.S. and Canada. Unmapped listings cover restaurants, cafes, gyms, travel agencies, publications

Damron Road Atlas

and more. "Info boxes" detail major annual gay events, local tourist attractions, transit, weather, best views of the city, and directions from the airport.

Over 300 pages.

Only **$14.95**

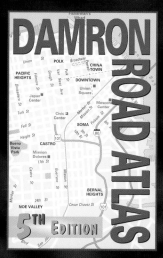

Damron Mail Order

Women's Traveller..$11.95 ....

Women's Traveller T-Shirt   M-L-XL

(size_____). $14.00 ....

(XXL_____)... $20.00 ....

Special Combo
Women's Traveller & T-Shirt (any size)

(size _____) $20.00 ....

Damron Tank Top   M-L-XL

(size_____) ..$14.00 ....

Damron Accommodations ....$18.95 ....

Damron Address Book................................$14.95 ....

Damron Road Atlas ....$14.95 ....

Names T-Shirt M-L-XL (size _____) $15.00 ....

Best Guide To Amsterdam.........................$18.95 ....

Betty & Pansy's SF Review ....$ 9.95 ....

G'Day Guide ....$14.95 ....

Damron Mail Order Catalog ....   Free ....

Subtotal   ....

CA Residents add 8.25% sales tax   ....

postage & handling - add $4.00 + $1.00 per item   ....

overnight delivery add $15.00   ....

Total ....

Call: 1-800-462-6654 or 415-255-0404

Visa • Mastercard • Amex

Or Send Check or Money Order To:
Damron Company
PO Box 422458 • San Francisco, CA 94142-2458

Orders processed as received.
Please allow 4-8 weeks for check clearing and delivery.
Send no cash or postage stamps. No C.O.D. orders.

Women's Traveller T-Shirt
Damron Tank Top
100% heavyweight cotton

Betty & Pansy's
Severe Queer Review
San Francisco

Names Project
T-Shirt
100% cotton - pre-shrunk

Best Guide Amsterdam

G'Day Guide
(Australia accommodations)

Enter the Women's

PROVINCETOWN

Enjoy the New England charm of

GABRIEL'S

(See ad on pg. 264)

Sweepstakes Rules

Responsibility: Damron Company assumes no responsibility for any delay, loss or accident caused by fault or negligence of any hotel, transportation company or local operator rendering any part of tour services, nor for any damage or inconvenience caused by late air travel. Damron Company shall not be responsible for any expense caused by loss or damage of personal items including but not limited to luggage and its contents.

Deadline: Entries must be received by June 15, 1997.

Prize: 4 nights lodging in Provincetown, Massachusetts. Airfare not included.

Drawing: Prize Winner will be determined by random drawing on June 20, 1997 from all entries received. Prize winners will be notified by mail and/or phone.

Eligibility: Open to anyone over 18 years of age, except employees of Damron Company, their affiliates and agencies or employees and agents for the resorts participating in these sweepstakes. Void where prohibited or restricted by law. All federal, state and local laws apply.

No purchase necessary. One entry per person. Complete entry form and mail to the Damron Company.

Traveller **Sweepstakes**

WIN!
4 NIGHTS

accommodations for
two in the friendly
coastal resort town
of Provincetown.

Clip-and-mail this coupon

Welcome to the 8th edition of the *Damron Women's Traveller*, the word on the lesbian lifestyle in North America. This year we are featuring city overviews by our readers and are very excited about opening up our pages to the community we serve. I have asked one of my editors to do the same: to share her view of the *Women's Traveller* in her own words. I would like to thank you for choosing the *Women's Traveller* and invite you to send us new information for the next edition. If we choose to include it and have not already discovered it during our research, we will send you a complimentary copy.

On a personal note, I would like to dedicate this issue to my mother for all of her support, acceptance and belief in me (see the photo of us with my distinguished brother, Edward, at the Names Project Quilt Fundraiser).

—*Gina M. Gatta*

In the short time since I started working on the *Women's Traveller*, I have been amazed by the number of women-oriented events and adventures there are to enjoy, and it has been a challenge and a real pleasure for me to find them and bring them to you. With the thousands of listings in the *Women's Traveller*, I hope that we can inspire the wanderer in you, and that you will use the book as a starting point to create your own adventures. Whether it's a day-trip to a nearby town, a white-water rafting excursion, or a tour across the country, the information here should spark your curiosity and motivate you to visit places you've never been. We want you to see and celebrate for yourself the diversity of our community.

Finally, we can't stress enough how important your feedback is. You, the correspondent in the field, contribute immensely to the content of the *Women's Traveller*.

Keep in touch. Send in those essays and any other information you'd like to share with our readers, and remember that your participation will help keep the *Damron Women's Traveller* the nation's best-selling women's travel guide.

—*Erika O'Connor*
Editor, Women's Traveller

DAMRON WOMEN'S TRAVELLER

is produced by

Publisher **Damron Company**

President & Editor-in-Chief
Gina M. Gatta

Managing Editor **Ian Philips**

Editors **Drew K. Campbell**
Beth Rabena Carr
Erika O'Connor

Art Director **Kathleen Pratt**

Advertising Director **David Howley**

Account Executive **Gillian Francis**

Photography **Rebecca McBride**

Board of Directors

Executive Director **Edward Gatta, Jr.**

Chairman **Mikal Shively**

Secretary **Louise Mock**

Mail: PO Box 422458, San Francisco, CA 94142
Email: DamronCo@aol.com
Web: http://www.damron.com/
Fax: (415) 703-9049
Phone: (415) 255-0404
Copyright © 1997 Damron Company Inc.
Printed in Hong Kong

NATIONAL RESOURCES

AIDS/HIV

National AIDS/HIV Hotlines
[800] 342-2437 • [800] 243-7889(TTY)
[800] 344-7432 (en español)

Sexual Health Information Line
[613] 563-2437 (Canada)

CANCER

Cancer Information Service
[800] 422-6237

HATE CRIMES

National Hate Crimes Hotline
[800] 347-4283

YOUTH SERVICES

Hetrick-Martin Institute
[212] 674-2400 (TTY)

LYRIC (Lavendar Youth Recreation/Information Center)
[415] 863-3636
[800] 246-7743 (outside San Francisco)

CHEMICAL DEPENDENCY

Pride Institute
[800] 547-7433

LEGAL RIGHTS

Lambda Legal Defense Fund
[212] 995-8585 (New York City, NY)

National Gay/Lesbian Task Force
[202] 332-6483 (Washington, DC)
[202] 332-6219 (TTY)

TRAVEL

International Gay Travel Association
(IGTA)
[800] 448-8550

TRAVELLER CODES

▲ - This symbol precedes the listing of an establishment that has a display advertisement.

Popular - So they say.

Mostly Women - 80%-90% lesbian.

Mostly Gay Men - Women are welcome.

Lesbians/Gay Men - 60%/40% or 40%/60% mix.

Gay Friendly - Queer folk are definitely welcome but are rarely the ones hosting the party.

Neighborhood Bar - Regulars and local flavor, often has a pool table.

Dancing/DJ - Usually has a DJ at least Fri & Sat .

Transgender-friendly - Transsexuals, cross-dressers, & other transgendered people welcome.

Live Shows - From piano bar to drag queens and dancers.

Multi-racial - Our favorite kind of clientele. We love a variety of colors.

Wheelchair Access - Including restrooms.

Beer/Wine - Beer and/or wine. No hard liquor served.

Private Clubs - Mostly in the South where it's the only way to keep a liquor license. Call the bar before you go out and tell them you're visiting. They will advise you of their policy regarding membership. Private clubs usually have set-ups so you can BYOB.

IGTA - International Gay Travel Association member (please support our industry).

TABLE of CONTENTS

TABLE OF CONTENTS

ALABAMA

Auburn (334)

BOOKSTORES & RETAIL SHOPS

Etc. 125 N. College St. • 821-0080 • noon-6pm, clsd Sun • general • wheelchair access

Birmingham (205)

INFO LINES & SERVICES

AA Gay/Lesbian 933-8964 • 8pm Wed, 11am Sat, 6pm Sun

Common Ground 5117 1st Ave. N. (Covenant MCC) • 599-3363/836-0300 • meets 3rd & 4th Fri • coffeehouse for youthful gays & lesbians

Lambda Resource Center 205 32nd St. S. • 326-8600 • info line 6pm-10pm Mon-Sat • library • drop-in coffeehouse

Lesbian Support Group 798-3938 • 2pm 1st Sun at MCC

BARS

22nd Street Jazz Cafe 710 22nd St. S. • 252-0407 • clsd Sun-Tue • gay-friendly • call for events • alternative night Wed • live shows • food served

Bill's Club 208 N. 23rd St. • 254-8634 • 6pm-4am Wed-Sat, from 5pm Sun, clsd Mon-Tues • mostly women • dancing/DJ • live shows • karaoke • wheelchair access

Club 21 117-1/2 21st St. N. • 322-0469 • 10pm-4am Th-Sat • gay-friendly • mostly African-American • dancing/DJ • live shows

Mikatam 3719 3rd Ave. S. • 592-0790 • 3pm-? • mostly men • dancing/DJ • wheelchair access • patio

Misconceptions Tavern 600 32nd St. S. • 322-1210 • mostly men • food served • videos

The Quest Club 416 24th St. S. • 251-4313 • 24hrs daily • lesbians/gay men • DJ Tue-Sun • patio • wheelchair access

Southside Pub 2830 7th Ave. S. • 324-0997 • 3pm-midnight Sun-Wed, til 2am Th, til 3am Fri-Sat • gay-friendly • also a restaurant

RESTAURANTS & CAFES

Anthony's 2131 7th Ave. S. • 324-1215 • lunch 11am-2:30pm weekdays, dinner 5pm-11pm Mon-Sat, clsd Sun • lesbians/gay men • some veggie • full bar • wheelchair access • $6-15

BOOKSTORES & RETAIL SHOPS

Lodestar Books 2020-B 11th Ave. S. • 939-3356 • 10am-6pm, 1pm-5pm Sun • lesbi-gay/feminist • wheelchair access

Planet Muzica 731 29th St. S. • 254-9303 • 12pm-8pm Mon-Th, til 9pm Fri-Sat, 1pm-6pm Sun • lesbigay gifts • videos • magazines

TRAVEL & TOUR OPERATORS

A World of Travel 2101 Civic Center Blvd. • 458-8888/(800) 458-3597

Exotic Travel 1406 17th St. S. • 930-0911/(800) 414-7015 • IGTA

Village Travel 1929 Cahaba Rd. • 870-4866/(800) 999-2899 • IGTA

SPIRITUAL GROUPS

BCC (Birmingham Community Church) PO Box 130221, 35233 • 933-7305 • Bible study 7pm Tue • services 7pm Sat • gospel singing 2nd Sat

Covenant MCC 5117 1st Ave. N. • 599-3363 • 11am & 7pm Sun

Integrity/Alabama PO Box 530785, 35253-0785 • 871-1815 • 6pm 4th Sun

PUBLICATIONS

Alabama Forum 205 S. 32nd St. Ste. 216 • 328-9228

The Rainbow Pages PO Box 36784, 35236 • 425-2286/985-5609 • annual business & organization guide

EROTICA

Alabama Adult Books 901 5th Ave. N. • 322-7323 • 24hrs

Birmingham Adult Books 7610 1st Ave. N. • 836-1580 • 24hrs

The Downtown Bookstore 2731 8th Ave. N. • 328-5525

Dothan (334)

BARS

Chuckie Bee's 134-A Foster St. • 794-0230 • 9pm-6am Th-Sun • lesbians/gay men • dancing/DJ • live shows

Huntsville (205)

INFO LINES & SERVICES

GALOP (Gay/Lesbian Org. of Professionals) PO Box 914, 35804 • 517-6127 • meets 4th Th • call for events

Pink Triangle Alliance 539-4235 • 9am-9pm • resource & info line

Bars

Upscale 2021 Golf Rd. • 883-8884 • 8pm-2am Fri-Sat, 6pm-2am Sun • lesbians/gay men • dancing/DJ • call for events • patio • 'Alabama's largest gay dance complex' • wheelchair access

Vieux Carre 1204 Posey • 534-5970 • 7pm-2am, from 4pm Sun • lesbians/gay men • neighborhood bar • karaoke Tue • country/western Wed • DJ Fri-Sat • shows Sun • patio • wheelchair access

Bookstores & Retail Shops

Rainbow's Ltd. 4321 University Dr. Ste. 400-B, rear • 722-9220 • 11am-9pm Mon-Sat, 1pm-6pm Sun, clsd Tue • lesbigay • wheelchair access

Spiritual Groups

MCC 3015 Sparkman Dr. NW • 851-6914 • 11am & 6pm Sun, 7pm Wed

Mobile (334)

Info Lines & Services

Pink Triangle AA Group 3100 Cottage Hill Rd. #100 • 438-1679 • 8pm Sat

Bars

B-Bob's 6157 Airport Blvd. #201 • 341-0102 • 5pm til ? • lesbians/gay men • dancing/DJ • private club • wheelchair access

Gabriel's Downtown 55 S. Joachim St. • 432-4900 • 5pm - ? • mostly gay men • videos • private club

Golden Rod 219 Conti • 433-9175 • 9am-?, 24hrs wknds • lesbians/gay men • private club

Outer Limits 7 S. Joachim St. • 433-3262 • 24hrs • lesbians/gay men • dancing/DJ • live shows • food served • private club

Society Lounge 51 S. Conception • 433-9141 • noon-? • popular • lesbians/gay men • dancing/DJ • live shows • private club • wheelchair access

Zippers 215 Conti St. • 433-7436 • 4pm-? • mostly gay men • neighborhood bar • private club

Spiritual Groups

Cornerstone MCC 2201 Gov't St. • 476-4621 • 11am & 7pm Sun

Montgomery (334)

Info Lines & Services

Montgomery Institute PO Box 3361, 36109 • 244-9623 • transgender info line • contact Christine Marshall

Accommodations

Lattice Inn B&B 1414 S. Hull St. • 832-9931 • gay-friendly • full brkfst • swimming • $55-75

Bars

Hojons 215 N. Court St. • 269-9672 • 8pm-?, til 2am Sat, clsd Sun-Mon • popular • lesbians/gay men • dancing/DJ • live shows • private club

Jimmy Mac's 211 Lee St. • 264-5933 • 7pm-2am • lesbians/gay men • dancing/DJ • private club

Travel & Tour Operators

Alabama Bureau of Tourism & Travel PO Box 4309, 36103 • 242-4169/(800) 252-2262

Spiritual Groups

MCC 5290 Vaughn (Unitarian Church) • 279-7894 • 5:30pm Sun

Tuscaloosa (205)

Info Lines & Services

Gay/Lesbian/Bisexual Alliance UA Ferguson Student Center, 3rd flr. • 348-7210

Tuscaloosa Lesbian Coalition PO Box 6085, 35486-6085 • 333-8227 • meets 1st Sat 8pm • call for location

Bars

Michael's 2201 6th St. • 758-9223 • 6:30pm-?, clsd Sun • lesbians/gay men • dancing/DJ • live shows

Rumors 5479 Jug Factory Rd. E. • 752-0499 • 8pm-? Wed-Sat • live shows

Bookstores & Retail Shops

Illusions 519 College Park • 349-5725 • 11am-5:45pm • alternative

ALASKA

Anchorage   (907)

INFO LINES & SERVICES

AA Gay/Lesbian 1231 W. 27th Ave. • 272-2312 • 7pm Mon, Th, Fri & Sun

Anchorage Gay/Lesbian Helpline PO Box 200070, 99520 • 258-4777 • 6pm-11pm Wed-Sun

The Berdache Society PO Box 92381, 99509-2381 • transgender group

Gay Teens 3201 Turnigan St. (Unitarian Church) • 688-3906 • 4pm-6pm Sat • contact Liz

Women's Resource Center 111 W. 9th St. • 276-0528 • 8:30am-5pm Mon-Fri • one-on-one counseling & referrals

ACCOMMODATIONS

Arctic Feather B&B 211 W. Cook • 277-3862 • lesbians/gay men • 5 min. to downtown • nice view

Aurora Winds Resort B&B 7501 Upper O'Malley • 346-2533 • lesbians/gay men • on a hillside above Anchorage

Cheney Lake B&B 6333 Colgate Dr. • 337-4391 • gay-friendly • lesbian-run • $65-85

The Pink Whale Guesthouse 3627 Randolph St. • 563-2684 • gay-friendly • self-serve kitchen • smokefree • kids ok • women-owned/run

Rose-Beth's B&B 337-6779 • mostly women

BARS

Blue Moon 530 E. 5th Ave. • 277-0441 • 2pm-2:30am, from 3pm wknds • lesbians/gay men • live shows • DJ on wknds • pool table • dinner & Sun brunch • plenty veggie • $12-26 • wheelchair access

O'Brady's Burgers & Brew 6901 E. Tudor Rd. • 338-1080 • 10am-midnight • gay-friendly • some veggie

Raven 618 Gambell • 276-9672 • 11am-2:30am • lesbians/gay men • neighborhood bar • wheelchair access

▲ **The Wave** 3103 Spenard Rd. • 561-9283 • 6pm-2:30am, clsd Sun-Tue (seasonal) • gay-friendly • dancing/DJ • live shows • theme nights • videos • more gay Sat • espresso bar upstairs (year-round) • wheelchair access

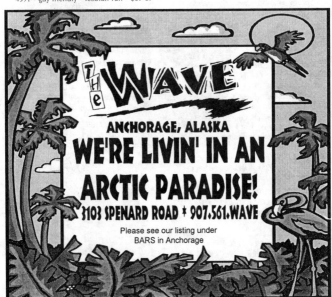

THE WAVE

ANCHORAGE, ALASKA

WE'RE LIVIN' IN AN

ARCTIC PARADISE!

3103 SPENARD ROAD ★ 907.561.WAVE

Please see our listing under
BARS in Anchorage

BOOKSTORES & RETAIL SHOPS
Cyrano's Bookstore & Cafe 413 'D' St. • 274-2599 • 10am-10pm • live shows • food served • beer/wine

TRAVEL & TOUR OPERATORS
Apollo 1207 West 47th Ave. • 561-0661/(800) 770-0661 • IGTA

Triangle Tours 733 W. 4th Ave. Ste. 817 • 786-3707/(800) 779-3701 • IGTA

SPIRITUAL GROUPS
Lamb of God MCC PO Box 142095, 99514 • 258-5266 • 11am & 7pm Sun, 7pm Wed

Unitarian Universalist Fellowship 3201 Turnigan St. • 248-3737 • 9am & 10:30am Sun

PUBLICATIONS
Anchorage Press PO Box 241841, 99524-1841 • 561-7737 • alternative paper • arts & entertainment listings

Identity Northview PO Box 200070, 99520 • 258-4777 • newsletter • also sponsors 4th Fri potluck

EROTICA
La Sex Shoppe/Ace's 305 W. Dimond Blvd. • 522-1987 • 24hrs

Chugiak

INFO LINES & SERVICES
Alaskan Tpeople PO Box 670349, 99567-0349 • transgender group

Fairbanks   (907)

INFO LINES & SERVICES
Lesbian/Gay Info Line 458-8288 • 5:30pm-8pm

ACCOMMODATIONS
Alta's B&B 5132 Haystack Mtn. Rd. • 389-2582/457-0246 • lesbians/gay men • log home above the Chatanika River • full brkfst • $50-100

Billie's Backpackers Hostel 2895 Mack Rd. • 457-2034 • gay-friendly • hostel & campsites • kids ok • food served • women-run • $15-20

Crabtree Guest House 724 College Rd. • 451-6501 • mostly gay men • shared baths • kitchens • kids ok

▲ **Fairbanks Hotel** 517 3rd Ave., Box Q, 99701 • 456-6411/(888) 329-4685 • gay-friendly • $55-95

Bars
Palace Saloon Alaskaland • 456-5960 •
7pm-10pm, til 3am Fri-Sat (seasonal) •
gay-friendly • dancing/DJ • live shows •
mainly tourists • more gay after 11pm

Homer   (907)

Accommodations
Island Watch B&B PO Box 1394, 99603 •
235-2265 • gay-friendly • also cabins • full
brkfst • kitchens • smokefree • kids/pets
ok • wheelchair access • women-
owned/run • $75-100/double

Travel & Tour Operators
Alaska Fishing Charters PO Box 2807,
99603 • 235-6468/(800) 478-7777 • deluxe
cabin cruiser for big-game fishing (halibut)

Juneau   (907)

Info Lines & Services
Women's Prerogative KTO 104.3 & 103.1
FM • 586-1670 • 9pm Wed • women's
music

Accommodations
Pearson's Pond Luxury Inn 4541 Sawa Cir.
• 789-3772 • gay-friendly • $69-165

Restaurants & Cafes
Inn at the Summit Waterfront Cafe 455 S.
Franklin St. • 586-2050 • 5pm-10pm • full
bar • $15-38

Travel & Tour Operators
Alaska Tourism Marketing Council PO
Box 110801, 99811 • 465-2010 • ask for
vacation planner
Women Sail Alaska PO Box 20348, 99802 •
463-3372 • custom charters • whale watching • women-owned/run

Ketchikan   (907)

Accommodations
Millar Street House PO Box 7281, 99901 •
225-1258/(800) 287-1607 • gay-friendly •
also kayak tours

Seward   (907)

Accommodations
Sauerdough Lodging 225 4th Ave. • 224-
8946 • gay-friendly • $125-210

ARIZONA

Bisbee (520)

BARS

St. Elmo's 36 Brewery Gulch Ave. • 432-5578 • 10am-1am • gay-friendly • live bands Fri-Sat

Cottonwood (520)

ACCOMMODATIONS

Mustang B&B 4257 Mustang Dr. • 646-5929 • lesbians/gay men • full brkfst • one RV hookup • movie theater • $45-65

Flagstaff (520)

ACCOMMODATIONS

Hotel Monte Vista 100 N. San Francisco St. • 779-6971/(800) 545-3068 • gay-friendly • historic lodging circa 1927 • food served • full bar • cafe • $25-120

Piñon Country Cottage 5339 Parsons Ranch Rd. • 526-4797 • mostly women • cabin • $65

BARS

Charlie's 23 N. Leroux • 779-1919 • 11am-1am, Sun brunch • gay-friendly • food served • some veggie • patio • wheelchair access • $7-14

The Depot 26 S. San Francisco St. • 773-9550 • 3:30pm-1am • gay-friendly • dancing/DJ • live shows • patio • wheelchair access

Monte Vista Lounge 100 N. San Francisco St. • 779-6971 • 10am-1am, cafe from 6am • gay-friendly • live shows • some veggie

BOOKSTORES & RETAIL SHOPS

Aradia Books 116 W. Cottage • 779-3817 • 10:30am-5:30pm, clsd Sun • lesbian/feminist • wheelchair access • women-owned/run

Kingman (520)

ACCOMMODATIONS

Kings Inn Best Western 2930 E. Andy Devine • 753-6101/(800) 528-1234 • gay-friendly • swimming • non-smoking rms. avail. • food served • bakery on premises

Mesa (602)

TRAVEL & TOUR OPERATORS

Executive Tour Associates PO Box 42151, 85274-2151 • 898-0098/(800) 382-1113 • IGTA

EROTICA

Castle Boutique 8315 E. Apache Trail • 986-6114 • 24hrs

Phoenix (602)

INFO LINES & SERVICES

AA Lambda Club 2622 N. 16th St. • 264-1341 • 6pm & 8pm

Camelback Business & Professional Assoc. PO Box 2097, 85001 • 225-8444

Lesbian Resource Project 3136 N. 3rd Ave. • 266-5542/266-5797 • call for events • many social/educational groups

Lesbian/Gay Community Switchboard 3136 N. 3rd Ave. • 234-2752 also TDD • 10am-10pm (volunteers permitting)

Valley of the Sun Gay/Lesbian Center 3136 N. 3rd Ave. • 265-7283

Valley One In Ten 3136 N. 3rd Ave. • 264-5437 • 7pm Wed • youth group • HIV peer education

ACCOMMODATIONS

Arizona B&B 274-1474/(800) 974-1474 • reservation service

Arrowzona 'Private' Casitas PO Box 11253, Glendale, 85318 • 561-1200/(800) 266-7829 • lesbians/gay men • 2-rm B&B in private home • hot tub • IGTA • $69-199

Be My Guest B&B 893-6663 • women only • swimming • great location

Bed & Breakfast Inn Arizona PO Box 11253, Glendale, 85318 • 561-0335/(800) 266-7829 • gay-friendly • $45-295

Larry's B&B 502 W. Claremont Ave. • 249-2974 • mostly gay men • B&B-private home • full brkfst • swimming • hot tub • nudity • $45-65

Mom's B&B 5903 W. Cortez, Glendale • 979-2869 • women only • swimming • available for outdoor weddings/commitment ceremonies • wheelchair access • women-owned/run • $65-85

Stewart's B&B 1319 E. Hayward • 861-2500 • mostly gay men • leather-friendly • nudity • wheelchair access • $55-95

Westways Resort PO Box 5550, Carefree, 85377 • 488-1110 • lesbians/gay men • swimming • IGTA

Windsor Cottage B&B 62 W. Windsor • 264-6309 • lesbians/gay men • 2 English Tudor-style cottages • swimming • nudity • patio • gay-owned/run • $65-115

BARS

307 Lounge 222 E. Roosevelt • 252-0001 • 6am-1am • Sun brunch from 10am • mostly gay men • neighborhood bar • transgender-friendly • live shows • food served • wheelchair access

Ain't Nobody's Bizness 3031 E. Indian School #7 • 224-9977 • 2pm-1am • lesbians/gay men • dancing/DJ • complimentary food Fri-Sat • wheelchair access

Apollos 5749 N. 7th St. • 277-9373 • 8am-1am, from 10am Sun • mostly gay men • neighborhood bar • karaoke • darts • wheelchair access

Cash Inn 2140 E. McDowell Rd. • 244-9943 • 6pm-1am, from 3pm Sun, clsd Mon-Tue • lesbians/gay men • dancing/DJ • country/western • wheelchair access

Country Club Bar & Grill 4428 N. 7th Ave. • 264-4553 • 11am-1am • lesbians/gay men • dancing/DJ • country/western • karaoke • food served • patio • wheelchair access

Desert Rose 4301 N. 7th Ave. • 265-3233 • 11am-1am • women only • country/western • live shows • food served • wheelchair access • women-owned/run

The Eagle 4531 N. 7th St. • 285-0833 • 3pm-1am, from 1pm Sun • mostly gay men • leather • pub appetizers • sports bar

Foster's 4343 N. 7th Ave. • 263-8313 • 4pm-1am • lesbians/gay men • dancing/DJ • leather • wheelchair access • 'Trash Disco' Sun • leather-friendly

Harley's 155 155 W. Camelback Rd. • 274-8505 • noon-1am • lesbians/gay men • dancing/DJ • also 'The Cell' in back • mostly gay men • leather

Incognito Lounge 2424 E. Thomas Rd. • 955-9805 • 2pm-1am, til 3am Fri-Sat, clsd Mon • popular • mostly women • dancing/DJ • live bands • wheelchair access

J.C.'s Fun One Lounge 5542 N. 43rd Ave., Glendale • 939-0528 • 11am-1am • lesbians/gay men • dancing/DJ • live shows • wheelchair access

Phoenix (602)

WHERE THE GIRLS ARE: Everywhere. Phoenix doesn't have one section of town where lesbians hang out, but the area between 5th Ave.-32nd St., and Camelback-Thomas streets does contain most of the women's bars.

LESBIGAY PRIDE: June: 352-7165.

ANNUAL EVENTS: August - Dog Days of Summer: 266-5542. 3-day lesbian cultural extravaganza. September - Women's Music Festival: 266-5542. October - AIDS Walk: 265-3300.

CITY INFO: 254-6500. Arizona Office of Tourism: 230-7733/ (800) 842-8257.

ATTRACTIONS: Castles & Coasters Park on Black Canyon Fwy. & Peoria. Phoenix Zoo and Desert Botanical Garden in Papago Park.

BEST VIEW: South Mountain Park at sunset, watching the city lights come on.

WEATHER: Beautifully mild and comfortable (60°-80°) October through March or April, hot (90°-100°+) in summer. August brings the rainy season (severe monsoon storms) with flash flooding.

TRANSIT: Yellow Cab: 252-5252. Super Shuttle: 244-9000. Phoenix Transit: 253-5000.

Phoenix

*C*an't stand another cloudy day? Sick of spending your summers in a fog bank and your winters in a snowdrift? Try this sunny getaway known as the Valley of the Sun.

Here the winters are warm and the summers sizzle. And each day ends with a dramatic desert sunset.

The people of Phoenix have perfected many ways to soak up the incredible sunshine. Some do it as they hike or horseback ride along the many trails along Squaw Peak (off Lincoln Dr.) or Camelback Mountain. Some do it by the pool or on the golf course or tennis court. Some do it as they hover over the valley in a hot air balloon.

Some do it between galleries as they enjoy the popular Thursday night Art Walk along Main St., Marshall Way and 5th Ave. in Scottsdale. Others do it dashing from the car to the Scottsdale Galleria or Fashion Square. Still others get sun in the car on the half-hour trip north to Rawhide (563-1880—admission is free!), Arizona's real live western town and Native American village, gunfights, hayrides and all.*

What do lesbians do in Phoenix? Pretty much the same things, but usually in couples. Couples will feel free to enjoy themselves at one of the three women-only B&Bs in town. The single lesbian traveller searching for another to share her journeys with should try one of the friendly women's bars in town: **Desert Rose** or **Incognito Lounge**. Phoenix also has a large sober women's community, and its own AA club house. And many lesbians just like to get away from it all on camping, fishing, or hiking trips.

*Driving in the Arizona desert during the summer can be dangerous. Always carry a few gallons of water in your vehicle, check all fluids in your car before you leave, and frequently during your trip.

Marlys' 15615 N. Cave Creek Rd. • 867-2463 • 3pm-1am • lesbians/gay men • neighborhood bar • live bands • food served

The Metro 4102 E. Thomas Rd. • 224-9471/224-9457 • mostly gay men • 3-level dance floor • Wed women's night, 'Cat Walk' • dancing/DJ • leather • live shows • patio • wheelchair access

Nasty's 3108 E. McDowell Rd. • 267-8707 • noon-1am • lesbians/gay men • sports bar • dancing/DJ • wheelchair access

Options Restaurant & Media Bar 5111 N. 7th St. • 263-5776 • 11am-1am • lesbians/gay men • internet access • talent shows • piano bar • bistro • some veggie • wheelchair access • $9-17

Pookie's Cafe 4540 N. 7th St. • 277-2121 • noon-midnight, kitchen til 11pm • lesbians/gay men • Sun brunch • live shows • $5-7

Trax 1724 E. McDowell • 254-0231 • 6am-1am, til 3am Fri-Sat • popular • mostly men • dancing/DJ • alternative • leather • wheelchair access

Winks 5707 N. 7th St. • 265-9002 • 11am-1am • popular • lesbians/gay men • live shows • piano bar • lunch & Sun brunch served • wheelchair access • $5-9

RESTAURANTS & CAFES

Alexi's 3550 N. Central • 279-0982 • clsd Sun • intercont'l • full bar • patio • $6-9

AZ-88 7535 E. Scottsdale Mall • 994-5576 • 11am-11pm • upscale American • some veggie • $8-15

Azz Jazz 1906 E. Camelback Rd. • 263-8482 • 5pm-10pm, til 1am wknds, clsd Mon • Argentinian • live shows • full bar • wheelchair access • $10-15

Deceptions 5025 N. 7th Ave. • 274-6275 • 11am-1am, til 3am wknds, kitchen open til midnight • late-night brkfst wknds • some veggie • live shows • full bar • wheelchair access • $3-9

Eddie's Grill 4747 N. 7th St. • 241-1188 • lunch & dinner, clsd Sun • full bar • some veggie • patio • wheelchair access • $10-18

Katz's Deli 5144 N. Central • 277-8814 • 7am-3pm, til 7:30pm Tue-Fri • some veggie • $5

GYMS & HEALTH CLUBS

Beauvais Fitness Center 1301 E. University • 921-9551 • gay-friendly

BOOKSTORES & RETAIL SHOPS

Obelisk the Bookstore 24 W. Camelback Ste. A • 266-2665 • 10am-10pm, noon-8pm Sun • lesbigay • wheelchair access

Sexy Styles 2104 W. Camelback Rd. • 242-2886 • 11am-7pm, til 6pm Fri-Sat, clsd Sun • wigs • leather • lingerie • shoes up to size 14

Tuff Stuff 1714 E. McDowell Rd. • 254-9651 • 10am-6pm, til 4pm Sat, clsd Sun-Mon • leather shop

Unique on Central 4700 N. Central Ave. #105 • 279-9691 • 10am-8pm • cards & gifts • wheelchair access

TRAVEL & TOUR OPERATORS

All About Destinations Gallery Three Plaza, 3819 N. 3rd St. • 277-2703/(800) 375-2703 • IGTA

Arizona Office of Tourism 230-7733/(800) 842-8257

FirsTravel Ltd. 5150 N. 7th St. • 265-0666/(800) 669-8885 • IGTA

TGI Travel Agency 5540 W. Glendale Ave. #A-102, Glendale • 939-1445/(800) 289-2172 • IGTA

SPIRITUAL GROUPS

Augustana Lutheran Church 2604 N. 14th St. • 265-8400 • 10:30am Sun

Casa de Cristo Evangelical Church 1029 E. Turney • 265-2831 • 8:45am,10am & 6:30pm Sun

Community Church of Hope 502 W. Camelback (Ramada Inn) • 234-2180 • 10am Sun • independent Christian church & counseling center

Lutherans Concerned PO Box 7519, 85011 • 870-3611

MCC Gentle Shepherd 5150 N. 16th St. • 285-9020 • 9am & 11am Sun

PUBLICATIONS

Echo Magazine PO Box 16630, 85011-6630 • 266-0550

Greater Phoenix Women's Yellow Pages 4425 N. Saddlebag Tr. • 945-5000

Western Express PO Box 5317, 85010-5317 • 254-1324

EROTICA

The Barn 5021 W. Indian School Rd. • 245-3008 • 24hrs

Castle Boutique 300 E. Camelback • 266-3348 • 24hrs • also 5501 E. Washington • 231-9837 • 8802 N. Black Canyon Fwy • 995-1641

International Bookstore 3640 E. Thomas Rd. • 955-2000 • 24hrs

Pleasure Palace 1524 E. Van Buren • 262-9942 • 24hrs

Prescott (520)

Accommodations

A Woman's Space PO Box 12048, 86304 • 717-2977 • gay-friendly • full brkfst • kids/pets ok • massage avail. • women-owned/run • $65

Scottsdale (602)

Bars

B.S. West 7125 5th Ave. (pedestrian mall) • 945-9028 • 1pm-1am • lesbians/gay men • dancing/DJ • videos • Sun BBQ • wheelchair access

The Works 7223 E. 2nd St. • 946-4141 • 10pm-3am Wed-Sat • popular • mostly gay men • dancing/DJ • alternative • live shows • videos • call for events • wheelchair access

Restaurants & Cafes

Malee's 7131 E. Main • 947-6042 • Thai • plenty veggie • $12-20

Travel & Tour Operators

Dolphin Travel Services 10632-B N. Scottsdale Rd. • 998-9191/(800) 847-2835 • IGTA

Welcome Aboard 7744 E. Northland Dr. • 596-6787 • IGTA

Erotica

Zorba's Adult Book Shop 2924 N. Scottsdale Rd. • 941-9891 • 24hrs

Sedona (520)

Accommodations

Huff & Puff Straw Bale Inn PO Box 406, Rimrock, 86335 • 567-9066 • lesbians/gay men • kids ok • pets by arr. • tours avail. • near Montezuma's Well • solar powered • wheelchair access • women-owned/run • $50-70

Iris Garden Inn 390 Jordan Rd. • 282-2552 • gay-friendly • motel • $55-119

Paradise Ranch 135 Kachina Dr. • 282-9769 • women only • guesthouse • kitchens • women-owned/run • $85-125

Sedona Artist Guest Suite B&B PO Box 2130, 86335 • 204-2966 • gay-friendly • $75-85

Tempe (602)

Bookstores & Retail Shops

Changing Hands 414 S. Mill • 966-0203 • 10am-9pm, til 10pm Fri-Sat, noon-5pm Sun • general • lesbigay section

Spiritual Groups

Dignity/Integrity 2222 S. Price Rd. • 222-8664 • 6pm Sat • call for info

Erotica

Modern World 1812 E. Apache • 967-9052 • 24hrs

Tucson (520)

Info Lines & Services

AA Gay/Lesbian 624-4183 • many meetings • call for info

Wingspan Community Center 422 N. 4th Ave. • 624-1779 • lesbigay & youth info • lesbigay AA • library • call for events

Womyn's Third Friday Coffeehouse 4831 E. 22nd (Unitarian Church) • 748-1551 • 8pm-midnight 3rd Fri

Accommodations

Casa Alegre B&B Inn 316 E. Speedway Blvd. • 628-1800/628-5654 • gay-friendly • 1915 craftsman-style bungalow • full brkfst • hot tub • swimming • kids ok by arr. • patio • $70-105

Casa Tierra Adobe B&B Inn 11155 W. Calle Pima • 578-3058 • gay-friendly • full brkfst • hot tub • smokefree • kids age 3+ ok • patio • 30 min. outside Tucson • $85-95

Catalina Park Inn 309 E. 1st St. • 792-4541/(800) 792-4885 • gay-friendly • full brkfst • smokefree • kids 10+ okay • $50-115

Elysian Grove Market B&B 400 W. Simpson • 628-1522 • gay-friendly • renovated historic adobe building w/garden • full brkfst • kitchen in suite • $75

Hacienda del Sol Guest Ranch Resort 5601 N. Hacienda del Sol Rd. • 299-1501 • gay-friendly

Hotel Congress 311 E. Congress • 622-8848/(800) 722-8848 • gay-friendly • food served • $28-50

Montecito House PO Box 42352, 85733 • 795-7592 • gay-friendly • kids ok by arr. • $35-40

Natural B&B 3150 E. Presidio Rd. • 881-4582 • lesbians/gay men • full brkfst • smokefree • kids ok • massage avail. • $65

Tucson

"Yeah, but it's dry heat!"

Whether you believe that or know better, you won't need much clothing, and the locals are used to seeing skin. Bring your SPF 160 sun lotion, a good pair of shades, and prepare for a great time. You'll see the rainbow everywhere, but mainly around shops on 4th Ave., the downtown Arts District, and residences in the Armory Park Historic neighborhood (the annual homes tour might as well be called the who's who of home-owning homos).

Downtown is where you'll find such gay-friendly establishments as **Cafe Magritte**, **B&B Cafe** at the Temple of Music & Art, the **Grill on Congress**, and **Hydra**, purveyor of fine BDSM gear. At night, grab a beer in the **Tap Room** or **Cup Cafe** in the Hotel, and boogie to retro, alternative sounds in the **Club Congress**, where Tucson's first cybercafe is in the works. In addition to some of the better-known bars like **It's Nobody's Bizness** and **IBT's** (recently voted Best Gay Bar by the Tucson Weekly), check out **The Graduate**, which sometimes features fun for all in the form of jello-wrestling contests.

Just a few blocks notheast is 4th Ave., where you'll find queer businesses standing strong between sports bars. In addition to gay-owned hair and skin care salons, real estate offices, restaurants, and retail stores, you'll find **Wingspan**, the lesbigay community center, and **Antigone Books**, arguably the best women's bookstore in the Southwest. Also check out the new, très lavender women's bookstore in N. Oracle, **Girlfriends**; they also feature acoustic music now and then.

West of Tucson, near the famed Desert Museum is a women's community called Adobe Land. For general outdoor hilarity, Tucson's gay softball league can't be beat.

Lesbigay spirituality and healing groups abound, as do Latina, discussion, writers, and readers groups. For films, try the Loft or Catalina theaters and The Screening Room or one of the three film festivals.

When you're done with the entertainment, and the temperature at midnight has dropped its usual 30 or 40 degrees, settle in at one or the many gay-owned or gay-friendly B&Bs.

Oh, yes, one last thing: the winter weather is perfect.

—By Karen Falkenstrom

(See back section on how to submit an essay about your favorite city.)

2nd Runner Up

Suncatcher B&B 105 N. Avenida Javelina • (800) 835-8012 • gay-friendly • full brkfst • hot tub • swimming • nudity • smokefree • kids ok • on 4 acres • wheelchair access

▲ **Tortuga Roja B&B** 2800 E. River Rd. • 577-6822/(800) 467-6822 • lesbians/gay men • hot tub • swimming • nudity • smokefree • kids ok in cottage • wheelchair access • IGTA • $50-95

BARS

Ain't Nobody's Bizness 2900 E. Broadway Ste. #118 • 318-4838 • 2pm-1am • mostly women • dancing/DJ • wheelchair access

Atlantis 2201 N. Oracle • 318-9068 • gay-friendly • dancing/DJ • live shows • food served

Congress Tap Room 311 E. Congress (inside Hotel Congress) • 622-8848 • 11am-1am • dance club from 9pm • gay-friendly • alternative • live bands • theme nights

The Fineline 101 W. Drachman • 882-4953 • 6pm-1am, til 4am Fri-Sat • gay-friendly • dancing/DJ • 18+

Hours 3455 E. Grant • 327-3390 • noon-1am • popular • lesbians/gay men • neighborhood bar • dancing/DJ • country/western (Wed-Sun) • patio • wheelchair access

IBT's (It's About Time) 616 N. 4th Ave. • 882-3053 • noon-1am • lesbians/gay men • dancing/DJ • live shows • wheelchair access

Stonewall Eagle 2921 1st Ave. • 624-8805 • noon-1am • Stonewall from 9pm • dancing/DJ • leather • patio • wheelchair access

RESTAURANTS & CAFES

Cafe Magritte 254 E. Congress • 884-8004

Cafe Quebec 121 E. Broadway • 798-3552

The Grill on Congress 100 E. Congress • 623-7621

Stacia's Bakery Café 3022 E. Broadway • 325-5549 • 7am-5:30pm Mon-Fri, 8am-4:30pm Sat, clsd Sun • low-fat baked goods • gourmet lunch menu • gay-owned/run

BOOKSTORES & RETAIL SHOPS

Antigone Books 411 N. 4th Ave. • 792-3715 • 10am-6pm, til 5pm Sat, noon-5pm Sun • lesbigay/feminist • wheelchair access

TORTUGA ROJA
BED & BREAKFAST

2800 EAST RIVER ROAD
TUCSON, ARIZONA 85718
(520) 577-6822 • (800) 467-6822

Girlfriends 3540 N. Oracle Rd #126 • 888-4475 • noon-11pm, til 9pm Sun, clsd Mon • lesbian bookstore & cafe • occasional acoustic music • wheelchair access

TRAVEL & TOUR OPERATORS
Arizona Travel Center 2502 E. Grant Rd. • 323-3250/(800) 553-5471 • IGTA

SPIRITUAL GROUPS
Cornerstone Fellowship 2902 N. Geronimo • 622-4626 • 10:30am Sun • 7pm Wed Bible Study
MCC 3269 N. Mountain Ave. • 292-9151 • 10:45am Sun, 7pm Wed

PUBLICATIONS
The Observer PO Box 50733, 85703 • 622-7176

EROTICA
The Bookstore Southwest 5754 E. Speedway Blvd. • 790-1550
Caesar's Bookstore 2540 N. Oracle Rd. • 622-9479
Hydra 145 E. Congress • 791-3711 • SM gear

Yuma (520)
EROTICA
Bargain Box 408 E. 16th St. • 782-6742 • 24hrs

ARKANSAS

Conway
INFO LINES & SERVICES
U of Central Arkansas Gay/Lesbian Student Union PO Box 7006, 72032

Crossett (501)
RESTAURANTS & CAFES
Pig Trail Cafe Rte. 16, east of Elkins • 643-3307 • 6am-9pm • popular • American/Mexican • under $5

Eureka Springs (501)
ACCOMMODATIONS
Arbour Glen Victorian Inn B&B 7 Lema • 253-9010/(800) 515-4536 • gay-friendly • historic Victorian home • full brkfst • jacuzzis • fireplaces • kids ok • $75-125
Cedarberry Cottage B&B 3 Kings Hwy. • 253-6115/(800) 590-2424 • gay-friendly • full brkfst • kids ok • $69-89
Cliff Cottage B&B Inn 42 Armstrong St. • 253-7409/(800) 799-7409 • gay-friendly • suites & guestrooms in 1892 'Painted Lady' • full brkfst • Victorian picnic lunches • cruises • massage • women-owned/run • $99-140
Crescent Dragonwagon's Dairy Hollow House B&B 516 Spring St. • 253-7444/(800) 562-8650 • gay-friendly • full brkfst • hot tub • special occasion dining • call for dates
Dixie Cottage 2 Prospect • 253-7553 • gay-friendly
The Gardener's Cottage c/o 11 Singleton • 253-9111/(800) 833-3394 • gay-friendly • seasonal • private cottage on wooded site • kitchens • women-owned/run • $95-115
Golden Gate Cottage B&B RT7 Box 182, 72631-9225 • 253-5291 • women only • on the lake • hot tub • swimming • kitchens • women-owned/run • $40-45
Greenwood Hollow Ridge B&B Rte 4, Box 155, 72632 • 253-5283 • exclusively gay • on 5 quiet acres • full brkfst • near outdoor recreation • shared/private baths • kitchens • RV hookups • $45-65
Heart of the Hills B&B 5 Summit • 253-7468/(800) 253-7468 • gay-friendly • full brkfst • evening desserts • patio
Maple Leaf Inn 6 Kings Hwy. • 253-6876/(800) 372-6542 • gay-friendly • restored Victorian • full brkfst • hot tub • kids ok • gay-owned/run • $85-105

Morningstar Retreat Rte. 1 Box 653, 72632 • 253-5995/(800) 298-5995 • gay-friendly • cabins • $95/double • $10/each add'l person

Palace Hotel & Bath House 135 Spring St. • 253-7474 • gay-friendly • bath house open to all • wheelchair access

Pond Mountain Lodge & Resort Rte. 1, Box 50, 72632 • 253-5877/(800) 583-8043 • gay-friendly • mountain-top inn on 159 acres • cabins • full brkfst • swimming • smokefree • kids ok • wheelchair access • lesbian-owned/run • $68-140

Rock Cottage Gardens 10 Eugenia St. • 253-8659/(800) 624-6646 • gay-friendly • cottages • full brkfst • hot tub • gay-owned/run • $95-110

Singleton House B&B 11 Singleton • 253-9111/(800) 833-3394 • gay-friendly • full brkfst • kids ok • restored 1890s country Victorian home • near shops • women-owned/run • $65-95

The Woods 50 Wall St. • 253-8281 • gay-friendly • cottages • jacuzzis • kitchens • wheelchair access • $99-139

BARS

Celebrity Club 75 Prospect (Crescent Hotel) • 253-9766 • gay-friendly • 6pm-1am Fri-Sat • grill • under $5 • also sports bar • karaoke on wknds

Center Street Bar & Grille 10 Center St. • 253-8102 • 6pm-2am, kitchen open til 10pm Th-Mon, clsd Sun • gay-friendly • dancing/DJ • live shows • also a restaurant • Mexican • plenty veggie • $4-12

Chelsea's Corner Cafe 10 Mountain St. • 253-6723 • 11am-2am, clsd Sun • gay-friendly • patio • also a restaurant • plenty veggie • women-owned/run • $5-8

RESTAURANTS & CAFES

Ermilio's 26 White • 253-8806 • 5pm-8:30pm, clsd Th • Italian • plenty veggie • $8-17

The Plaza 55 S. Main • 253-8866 • lunch & dinner • French cuisine • $9-19

BOOKSTORES & RETAIL SHOPS

The Emerald Rainbow 45-1/2 Spring St. • 253-5445

SPIRITUAL GROUPS

MCC of the Living Spring 17 Elk St. (Unitarian Church) • 253-9337 • 7pm Sun

Fayetteville   (501)

INFO LINES & SERVICES

AA Live & Let Live Group 756-8367 • 7pm Tue

BGLAD PO Box 2897, 72702

Gay/Lesbian Student Association University of Arkansas, AU517, 72701 • hours vary

Spinsterhaven PO Box 718, 72702 • search committee planning women's retirement community in NW Arkansas

BOOKSTORES & RETAIL SHOPS

Passages 200 W. Dickson • 442-5845 • 10am-6pm, til 8pm Fri, 1pm-6pm Sun • new age/metaphysical

SPIRITUAL GROUPS

MCC of the Living Word 10571 N. Hwy. 265 • 443-4278 • 11am Sun

PUBLICATIONS

Ozark Feminist Review PO Box 1662, 72701

Fort Smith   (501)

INFO LINES & SERVICES

WAGLTF (Western Arkansas Gay/Lesbian Task Force) PO Box 5824, 72913

BOOKSTORES & RETAIL SHOPS

Talisman 4119 Grand Ave. • 782-7522 • 11am-6pm

Helena   (501)

ACCOMMODATIONS

Foxglove B&B 229 Beech • 338-9391/863-1926 • gay-friendly • $59-70

Hot Springs   (501)

BARS

Our House Lounge & Restaurant 660 E. Grand Ave. • 624-6868 • 7pm-3am • popular • lesbians/gay men • dancing/DJ • shows monthly • wheelchair access

Little Rock   (501)

INFO LINES & SERVICES

AA Gay/Lesbian 3rd & Pulaski (Capitol View Methodist) • 664-7303 • 8pm Wed, 6pm Sun

Gay/Lesbian Task Force Switchboard PO Box 45053, 72214 • 375-5504/(800) 448-8305 (in AR) • 6:30pm-10:30pm • info • statewide crisis line • referrals

Women's Project 2224 Main St. • 372-5113 • 10am-5pm Mon-Fri • library open Sat • educational group • lesbian support group 7pm 2nd & 4th Tue • bookstore

ACCOMMODATIONS

Little Rock Inn 601 Center St. • 376-8301 • gay-friendly • swimming • kids/pets ok • full bar • wheelchair access • $30

BARS

Backstreet 1021 Jessie Rd. #Q • 664-2744 • 9pm-? • lesbians/gay men • dancing/DJ • live shows • private club • wheelchair access

Discovery III 1021 Jessie Rd. • 664-4784 • from 9pm, clsd Sun-Wed • popular • gay-friendly • dancing/DJ • transgender-friendly • live shows • private club • wheelchair access

Michael's 601 Center St. (at Little Rock Inn) • 376-8301 • 9pm-2am, 4pm-10pm Sun • lesbians/gay men • dancing/DJ • live shows • wheelchair access

Silver Dollar 2710 Asher Ave. • 663-9886 • 4pm-1am, til midnight Sat, clsd Sun • mostly women • dancing/DJ • beer/wine • women-owned/run

RESTAURANTS & CAFES

Vino's Pizza 923 W. 7th St. • 375-8466 • beer/wine • inquire about monthly women's coffeehouse

BOOKSTORES & RETAIL SHOPS

Twisted Entertainment 7201 Asher Ave. • 568-4262 • 11am-10pm, clsd Tue • gift shop

Wild Card 400 N. Bowman • 223-9071 • 10am-8pm, 1pm-5pm Sun • novelties & gifts

TRAVEL & TOUR OPERATORS

Arkansas Department of Tourism One Capitol Mall, 72201 • (800) 628-8725

Travel by Philip PO Box 250119, 72225-5119 • 227-7690 • IGTA • specializes in gay motorcoach tours

SPIRITUAL GROUPS

MCC of the Rock 2017 Chandler, North Little Rock • 753-7075 • 11am Sun, 7pm Wed

Unitarian Universalist Church 1818 Reservoir Rd. • 255-1503 • 11am Sun • child care avail. • wheelchair access

Little Rock   (501)

WHERE THE GIRLS ARE: Scattered. Popular hangouts are the Women's Project, local bookstores, and Vino's Pizza - women's coffeehouse.

LESBIGAY PRIDE: June.

CITY INFO: Arkansas Dept. of Tourism: (800) 628-8725.

ATTRACTIONS: Hot Springs National Park.

BEST VIEW: Quapaw Quarter (in the heart of the city)

WEATHER: When it comes to natural precipitation, Arkansas is far from being a dry state. Be prepared for the occasional severe thunderstorm or ice storm. Summers are hot and humid (mid 90°s). Winters can be cold (upper 30°s) with some snow and ice. Spring and fall are the best times to come and be awed by the colorful beauty of Mother Nature.

TRANSIT: Black & White Cab: 374-0333.

PUBLICATIONS

Lesbian/Gay News Telegraph PO Box 14229-A, St. Louis MO, 63108 • (314) 664-6411/(800) 301-5468 • covers AR,IL,KS,MO,TN

Triangle Journal News Box 11485, Memphis TN, 38111 • (901) 454-1411 • covers TN & sometimes AR

Triangle Rising PO Box 45053, 72214 • 374-2681

Texarkana (501)

BARS

The Gig 201 East St. (Hwy. 71 S.) TX • 773-6900 • 8pm-5am, clsd Mon • mostly gay men • dancing/DJ • live shows • private club

Little Rock

*I*f you want a city with a pace of life all its own, a city whose history reflects the dramatic changes within the South, and a city surrounded by natural beauty, you've made the right choice to visit Little Rock.

Here you can enjoy the summer days in the shade beside the slow-moving Arkansas River that winds through town. Or you can take off to the nearby lakes and national forests to camp, rock climb or water-ski. Stay in town and you can spend your days exploring the State Capitol, touring the historic homes of the Quapaw Quarter district or browsing in Little Rock's many shops. Rumor has it that Bill Clinton's boyhood home is owned by a friendly lesbian couple.

At night, you can make an evening of it with dinner, a program at the Arkansas Arts Center and a visit to Little Rock's two lesbian bars, **Backstreet** and **Silver Dollar**. If you're in town at the right time of the month, cruise by the monthly women's coffeehouse at **Vino's Pizza**—call the **Women's Project** to find out when.

Of course, if that isn't enough excitement, you can always head out for the northwest corner of the state. We've heard there are many lesbian landowners, living alone and in groups, throughout this region. And while you're out there, be sure to visit the funky Ozark Mountain resort town of Eureka Springs. There are loads of gay-friendly B&B's in this quaint town of old-fashioned arts, as well as a popular Passion Play. We hear that **Crescent Dragonwagon's Dairy Hollow House** is a must for unique, quirky accommodations (ask about their occasional dinners), **Golden Gate Cottage** is the women-only B&B, while **Center St. Bar** is the casual place to dance.

CALIFORNIA

Anaheim (714)

INFO LINES & SERVICES

Gay/Lesbian Community Services Center 12832 Garden Grove Blvd. Ste. A • 534-0862 • 10am-10pm

ACCOMMODATIONS

Country Comfort B&B 5104 E. Valencia Dr., Orange • 532-2802 • lesbians/gay men • full brkfst • hot tub • swimming • inquire about kids & pets • 7 mi. from Disneyland • wheelchair access • women-owned/run • $65

Bakersfield (805)

INFO LINES & SERVICES

Friends PO Box 304, 93302 • 323-7311 • 6:30pm-11pm • info • support groups & community outreach

BARS

Casablanca Club 1030 20th St. • 324-1384 • 7pm-2am • lesbians/gay men • neighborhood bar • dancing/DJ

The Cellar 1927 'K' St. • 324-7711 • 5pm-midnight Mon-Th, til-2am Fri-Sun • lesbians/gay men • dancing/DJ • call for events • non-smoking bar upstairs • espresso bar

The Mint 1207 19th St. • 325-4048 • 6pm-2am • gay-friendly • neighborhood bar

The Place 3500 Wilson Rd. • 835-0494 • 11am-2am, from 6pm wknds • lesbians/gay men • dancing/DJ • country/western • wheelchair access

Town Casino Lounge 1813 'H' St. (Padre Hotel) • 324-2594 • 10am-2am • gay-friendly • live piano Th-Sun

SPIRITUAL GROUPS

MCC of the Harvest 2421 Alta Vista Dr. • 327-3724 • 7pm Sun

EROTICA

Deja Vu 1524 Golden State Hwy. • 322-7300

Wildcat Books 2620 Chester Ave. • 324-4243

Benicia (707)

ACCOMMODATIONS

Captain Walsh House 235 E. 'L' St. • 747-5653 • gay-friendly • gracious gothic charm • full brkfst • wheelchair access

BOOKSTORES & RETAIL SHOPS

Lielin West Jewelers PO Box 733, 94510 • 745-9000 • women's imagery in precious metals • studio hours by appt. • catalog

Berkeley (See **East Bay**)

Big Bear Lake (909)

ACCOMMODATIONS

Eagles' Nest B&B 41675 Big Bear Rd. • 866-6465 • gay-friendly • 7 cottages • spa • wheelchair access

Grey Squirrel Resort PO Box 1711-39372, 92315 • 866-4335 • gay-friendly • 18 private cabins • hot tub • swimming • kids/pets ok • lesbian-owned/run • $75-400

Hillcrest Lodge 40241 Big Bear Blvd. • 866-6040/(800) 843-4449 • gay-friendly • motel • cabins • hot tub • kitchens • fireplaces • non-smoking rms. avail. • kids ok • gay-owned/run • $35-169

▲ **Smoke Tree Resort** 40210 Big Bear Blvd. • 866-2415/(800) 352-8581 • gay-friendly • B&B • cabins • near outdoor recreation • hot tub • fireplaces • kids/pets ok • gay-owned/operated • $59-180

RESTAURANTS & CAFES

Ché Faccia 607 Pine Knot Ave. • 878-3222 • 11am-10pm (seasonal) • Italian • plenty veggie • full bar • $10-15

Big Sur (408)

ACCOMMODATIONS

Lucia Lodge Hwy. 1 • 667-2269/667-0161 • gay-friendly • cabins • kids ok • store • ocean view • also a restaurant • American/seafood • full bar • $8-24 • IGTA

Bishop (619)

INFO LINES & SERVICES

Wild Iris Women's Services PO Box 57, 93515 • 873-6601/873-7384 (24hrs) • counseling • shelter from domestic violence

ACCOMMODATIONS

Starlite Motel 192 Short St. • 873-4912 • gay-friendly • swimming • kids ok • 1 rm. avail. for pets

BOOKSTORES & RETAIL SHOPS

Spellbinder Books 124 N. Main • 873-4511 • 9:30am-5:30pm, clsd Sun • small women's section • wheelchair access

Buena Park (714)

BARS

Ozz Supper Club 6231 Manchester Blvd. • 522-1542 • 6pm-2am, clsd Mon • popular • lesbians/gay men • dancing/DJ • live shows • cabaret • women's country/western dancing Sun • also a restaurant • some veggie • $9-25

Cambria (805)

ACCOMMODATIONS

The J. Patrick House B&B 2990 Burton Dr. • 927-3812/(800) 341-5258 • gay-friendly • authentic log cabin • fireplaces • smoke-free • kids ok

Carmel (408)

ACCOMMODATIONS

Happy Landing Inn PO Box 2619, 93921 • 624-7917 • gay-friendly • Hansel & Gretel 1925 inn • full brkfst • smokefree • kids 12+ okay • gay-owned/run • $90-155

Chico (916)

INFO LINES & SERVICES

Gay Hotline 893-3336/893-3338 • hours vary

Stonewall Alliance Center 820 W. 7th St. • 893-3338/893-3336 • social 6pm-10pm Fri • Gay AA 7pm Tue • hotline

BARS

Rascal's 900 Cherry St. • 893-0900 • 6pm-2am • lesbians/gay men • dancing/DJ

BOOKSTORES & RETAIL SHOPS

Travellin' Pages 1174 East Ave. • 342-6931 • hours vary • lesbigay section

Chula Vista (619)

EROTICA

▲ **F St. Bookstore** 1141 3rd Ave. • 585-3314 • 24hrs

Clearlake (707)

ACCOMMODATIONS

Blue Fish Cove Resort 10573 E. Hwy 20, Clearlake Oaks • 998-1769 • gay-friendly • lakeside resort cottages • kitchens • kids ok • pets ok by arr. • boat facilities • $45-95

Edgewater Resort 6420 Soda Bay Rd., Kelseyville • 279-0208 • gay-friendly • cabin • $25-65

Lake Vacations Reservations 1855 S. Main St. • 263-7188 • vacation-home rental service

Sea Breeze Resort 9595 Harbor Dr., Glenhaven • 998-3327 • gay-friendly • cottages • RV hookups • swimming • kids ok • gay-owned/operated • $55-85

Cloverdale (707)

ACCOMMODATIONS

Vintage Towers B&B 302 N. Main St. • 894-4535 • gay-friendly • Queen Anne mansion • full brkfst • smokefree • kids 10+ ok

Corona del Mar (714)

TRAVEL & TOUR OPERATORS

New Directions Travel Company 2435 E. Coast Hwy. • 675-5000/(800) 222-5531

Costa Mesa (714)

BARS

Lion's Den 719 W. 19th St. • 645-3830 • 8pm-2am, from 6pm Sat • lesbians/gay men • dancing/DJ • women's night Sat • monthly live band

Metropolis 4255 Campus Dr., Irvine • 725-0300 • 7pm-2am, from 8pm Tue • gay-friendly • lesbians/gay men Sun • dancing/DJ • 18+ Fri & Sun • call for events • live bands • also a restaurant • Californian & sushi • dress code on wknds

Newport Station 1945 Placentia • 631-0031 • 9pm-2am Th-Sat • dancing/DJ • live shows • videos • more women Th • wheelchair access

Tin Lizzie Saloon 752 St. Clair • 966-2029 • noon-2am, from 2pm wknds • mostly gay men • neighborhood bar • more women Sun • wheelchair access

SPIRITUAL GROUPS

First MCC of Orange County 1259 Victoria St. (Unitarian Church) • 548-2955 • 7pm Sun

Cupertino (408)

BARS

Silver Fox 10095 Saich Wy. • 255-3673 • 2pm-2am • mostly gay men • neighborhood bar • live shows • wheelchair access

Davis (916)

RESTAURANTS & CAFES

Cafe Roma 231 'E' St. • 756-1615 • 7:30am-11pm • coffee & pastries • student hangout • wheelchair access

East Bay (510)

INFO LINES & SERVICES

Berkeley Women's Health Center 2908 Ellsworth St., Berkeley • 843-6194 • 9am-6pm Tue-Th, 8am-5pm Mon & Fri, clsd wknds

▲ **Dyke TV** Channel 8 • 7:30pm Wed • 'weekly half-hour TV show produced by lesbians for lesbians'

Gay/Lesbian/Bisexual/Transgender Switchboard (at the Pacific Center), Berkeley • 841-6224 (also TDD) • 8pm-10pm Mon, Tue & Fri, 4pm-6pm Wed

Infoshop 3124 Shattuck Ave. (Long Haul Activist Space), Berkeley • 540-0751 • from 4pm • women's night Mon • workshops • readings

La Peña 3105 Shattuck Ave., Berkeley • 849-2568/849-2572 • 10am-5pm Mon-Fri • also cafe 6pm-10pm Wed • multicultural center • hosts meetings, dances, events • mostly Latino-American /African-American

Pacific Center 2712 Telegraph Ave., Berkeley • 548-8283 • 10am-10pm, from noon Sat, 6pm-9pm Sun • support groups & counseling

What's Up! Events Hotline for Sistahs 835-6126 • for lesbians of African descent

Womanlink 2124 Kittredge #257, Berkeley, 94704 • women's S/M penpals & contacts

Women's Cancer Resource Center 3023 Shattuck Ave., Berkeley • 548-9272 • support groups • networking & referral service • Spanish spoken

ACCOMMODATIONS

Elmwood House 2609 College Ave., Berkeley • 540-5123/(800) 540-3050 • gay-friendly • guesthouse • IGTA • gay-owned/run • $65-80 (double occupancy)

La Grande Maison B&B 1 Arlington Ct., Kensington • 526-0265 • women only • French chateau in the Berkeley Hills • full brkfst • hot tub • smokefree • patio • $75-90

BARS

Bench & Bar 120 11th St., Oakland • 444-2266 • 3pm-2am, from 5pm Sat • popular • mostly men • dancing/DJ • professional • live shows • Fri-Sun Latin nights • wheelchair access

Cabel's Reef 2272 Telegraph Ave., Oakland • 451-3777 • noon-2am • mostly gay men • women's night Wed • dancing/DJ • multi-racial

Country Nights 3903 Broadway (Masonic Hall), Oakland • 8:30pm-11:30pm Fri • women only • lessons at 7:30pm • smoke/alcohol/scent-free

Town & Country 2022 Telegraph Ave., Oakland • 444-4978 • 11am-2am • mostly gay men • neighborhood bar • wheelchair access

White Horse 6551 Telegraph Ave., Oakland • 652-3820 • 1pm-2am, from 3pm Mon-Tue • popular Fri night • lesbians/gay men • dancing/DJ • wheelchair access

RESTAURANTS & CAFES

Betty's To Go 1807 4th St., Berkeley • 548-9494 • 6:30am-5pm, 8am-4pm Sun • sandwiches • some veggie • $5

Bison Brewery 2598 Telegraph at Parker, Berkeley • 841-7734 • 11am-1am • live music • sandwiches • some veggie • beer/wine • wheelchair access • $5-10

Brick Hut 2512 San Pablo, Berkeley • 486-1124 • 7:30am-2pm, 8:30am-3pm wknds, dinner 5:30pm-10pm Wed-Sat • popular for breakfast • lesbians/gay men • some veggie • $5-10

Cafe Sorrento 2510 Channing, Berkeley • 548-8210 • 7am-7pm, 9am-4pm wknds • multi-racial • Italian • vegetarian • $5-10

Cafe Strada corner of College & Bancroft, Berkeley • 843-5282 • popular • students • great patio & bianca (white choc.) mochas

The Edible Complex 5600 College, Oakland • 658-2172 • 7am-midnight, til 1am Fri-Sat • popular • mostly students • some sandwiches & soups • cafe • $5-10

East Bay   (510)

WHERE THE GIRLS ARE: Though there's no lesbian ghetto, you'll find more of us in north Oakland and north Berkeley, Lake Merritt, around Grand Lake & Piedmont, the Solano/Albany area, or at a cafe along 4th St. Berkeley.

LESBIGAY PRIDE: June in Berkeley

ANNUAL EVENTS: June - Gay Prom/Project Eden: 247-8200. $15. For ages 16-25, preregistered. October - Halloween Spiral Dance: 893-3097. Annual rite celebrating the crone.

CITY INFO: Oakland Visitors Bureau: 839-9000

ATTRACTIONS: Berkeley: U.C. Berkeley, Telegraph Ave., The Claremont Hotel. Emeryville: Marina Public Market. Oakland: Jack London Square, The Paramount Theater.

BEST VIEW: Claremont Hotel, or various locations in Berkeley and Oakland Hills

WEATHER: While San Francisco is fogged in during the summers, the East Bay remains sunny and warm. Some areas even get hot (90°s-100°s). As for the winter, the temperature drops along with rain (upper 30°s-40°s in the winter). Spring is the time to come – the usually brown hills explode with the colors of green grass and wildflowers.

TRANSIT: Yellow Cab (Berkeley): 848-3333, Yellow Cab (Oakland): 836-1234.

East Bay

*S*o just what exactly is the East Bay? For most it's simply the string of cities and counties across the Bay Bridge from San Francisco—with weather that's consistently sunnier and 10-20° warmer than the Fog City. For this book, it is the cities of Berkeley and Oakland.

Berkeley—the city and the campus of the University of California—was immortalized in the '60s as a hotbed of student/counterculture activism. Today, most of the people taking to the streets, especially Telegraph and College Avenues, are tourists or kids from the suburbs in search of anything tie-dyed, a good book, exotic cuisine, or just a cup of coffee.

So what do you do there? Enjoy people-watching on Telegraph or University Avenues and later relax with a shopping/eating/coffee-sipping spree along College Ave. Or just take to the hills—Tilden Park offers incredible views and trails to hike and bike.

As for Oakland, Gertrude Stein once said, "There is no there there." Of course, a lot has happened since either Gertrude or her lover Alice—natives both—were last in Oakland.

Today Oakland is a city with an incredible diversity of races, cultures, and classes. The birthplace of the Black Panthers, this city has been especially influential in urban African-American music, fashion, and politics. Lately Oakland has also become an artists' enclave, as Bay Area artists flee high rent in San Francisco for spacious lofts downtown or in West Oakland.

And where are all the women? Well, many are in couples or covens, which can make them hard to find. But if you want to start a couple or a coven of your own, start searching at **Mama Bear's** or one of the other women's bookstores—they're also great informal resource centers, and often host popular performances and author signings. Better yet, try breakfast at the famous, cooperatively-run **Brick Hut**.

For info on groups and events, cruise by the **Pacific Center**, the Bay Area's only lesbian/gay center, located in Berkeley. The center hosts meetings for lesbian moms & kids, bisexuals, transgendered women, separatists, and more. Those interested in women's spirituality should drop by **Ancient Ways**.

If you're the outdoors type, consider an adventure in Northern California with **Mariah Wilderness Expedition**. Or make a day of it at one of the nearby state parks: Pt. Reyes is a beautiful destination with a hostel, and Pt. Isabel is rumored to be a good meeting place for lesbians with dogs. We've heard that Sister Boom, a multicultural women's drum corps, practices at Waterfront Park in Jack London Square (left onto 11th St. exit off I-80, then right on Broadway), and the Emeryville Marina Public Market off I-80 is popular with gastronomically inclined lesbians.

If you'd rather exercise indoors, make some moves on the dance-floor of the **White Horse** or at the Masonic Hall in downtown Oakland on **Country Dance Night**. For plays, performances and events, grab a copy of the **Bay Times** and check out the calendar section. Or pick up some entertainment of your own at the East Bay **Good Vibrations** or **Passion Flower**—both are friendly, clean sex toy stores.

There are also lots of resources for women of color in the East Bay. Start with **La Peña Cultural Center**, an active center with many events for Latino-Americans and African-Americans. Then there's **What's Up!**, an events hotline for lesbian sistahs of African descent. For anarchists and radicals of any color, the **Infoshop** at Longhaul Activist Space has weekly women's social nights.

Mama's Royale 4012 Broadway, Oakland • 547-7600 • 7am-3pm, from 8am wknds • popular • come early for excellent weekend brunch • $5-10

Mimosa Cafe 462 Santa Clara, Oakland • 465-2948 • 11am-9pm, clsd Mon • natural & healthy • plenty veggie • $7-12

Bookstores & Retail Shops

Ancient Ways 4075 Telegraph Ave., Oakland • 653-3244 • 11am-7pm • extensive occult supplies • classes • readings • woman-owned

Boadecia's Books 398 Colusa Ave., Kensington • 559-9184 • 11am-9pm, til 7pm Sun • women's • readings • wheelchair access • women-owned/run

Cody's 2454 Telegraph Ave., Berkeley • 845-7852 • 10am-10pm • general • lesbigay section • frequent readings & lectures

Easy Going 1385 Shattuck (at Rose), Berkeley • 843-3533 • 10am-7pm, til 6pm Sat, noon-6pm Sun • travel books & accessories • also 1617 Locust, Walnut Creek • 947-6660

Gaia Bookstore & Catalogue Co. 1400 Shattuck Ave., Berkeley • 548-4172 • 10am-7pm • feminist • eco-spiritual/goddess

Mama Bears Bookstore 6536 Telegraph Ave., Oakland • 10:30am-8pm • women's books • readings & performances • also 'Mama Bears News & Notes' book review • lesbian-owned/run

Shambhala Booksellers 2482 Telegraph Ave., Berkeley • 848-8443 • 10am-8pm • metaphysical feminist/goddess section • wheelchair access

West Berkeley Women's Books 2514 San Pablo Ave., Berkeley • 204-9399

Travel & Tour Operators

Call of the Wild Wilderness Trips 2519 Cedar St., Berkeley • 849-9292 • women only • hiking & wilderness trips for all levels

▲ **Mariah Wilderness Expeditions** PO Box 248, Point Richmond, 94807 • 233-2303 • white water rafting & other adventures for women • IGTA • women-owned/run (see ad in back Tour Operators section)

New Venture Travel 404 22nd St., Oakland • 835-3800 • women-owned/run • IGTA

Travel By Design 3832 Piedmont Ave., Oakland • 653-6668 • women-owned/run

Spiritual Groups

Albany Unified Methodist Church 980 Stannage Ave., Albany • 526-7346 • 10am Sun

MCC New Life 1823 9th St., Berkeley • 843-9355 • 12:30pm Sun • wheelchair access

Publications

San Francisco Bay Times 288 7th St., San Francisco, 94103 • (415) 626-8121 • popular • a 'must read' for Bay Area resources & personals

Erotica

▲ **Good Vibrations** 2504 San Pablo, Berkeley • 841-8987 • 11am-7pm • clean, well-lighted sex toy store • also mail order • wheelchair access

Hollywood Adult Books 5686 Telegraph Ave., Oakland • 654-1169

L'Amour Shoppe 1801 Telegraph Ave., Oakland • 835-0381

L'Amour Shoppe 1905 San Pablo Ave., Oakland • 465-4216

Passion Flower 4 Yosemite Ave., Oakland • 601-7750 • toys • lingerie • leather

El Cajon (619)

Erotica

▲ **F St. Bookstore** 158 E. Main • 447-0381 • 24hrs

El Monte (818)

Bars

Infinities 2253 Tyler Ave. • 575-9164 • 4pm-2am • mostly women • dancing/DJ • mostly Latina-American • wheelchair access

Escondido (619)

Erotica

▲ **F St. Bookstore** 237 E. Grand Ave. • 480-6031 • 24hrs

Video Specialties 2322 S. Escondido Blvd. • 745-6697 • 24hrs

Eureka (707)

Info Lines & Services

Gay/Lesbian Alliance of Humboldt County PO Box 2368, 95502 • 444-1061 • info • call for events

Accommodations

An Elegant Victorian Mansion 1406 'C' St. • 444-3144 • gay-friendly • $95-185

Carter House Victorians 301 'L' St. • 444-8062/(800) 404-1390 • gay-friendly • enclave of 4 unique inns • full brkfst • smokefree • kids ok • wheelchair access • $65-350

BARS

Club Triangle (Club West) 535 5th St. • 444-2582 • 9pm-2am • gay-friendly • dancing/DJ • alternative • 18+ • gay Sun • also 'Star's Hamburgers' • 8pm-11pm • wheelchair access

Lost Coast Brewery Pub 617 4th St. • 445-4480 • 11am-2am • gay-friendly • food served • beer/wine • wheelchair access • women-owned/run

BOOKSTORES & RETAIL SHOPS

Booklegger 402 2nd St. • 445-1344 • some lesbian titles • wheelchair access

PUBLICATIONS

The 'L' Word PO Box 272, Bayside, 95524 • lesbian newsletter for Humboldt • available at Booklegger

Fairfax   (415)

TRAVEL & TOUR OPERATORS

▲ **Common Earth Wilderness Trips** PO Box 1191, 94978 • 455-0646 • women only • backpacking & kayaking in CA, AK & Southwest • women-owned/run (see ad in back Tour Operators section)

Fairfield   (707)

INFO LINES & SERVICES

Solano County Gay/Lesbian Info Line PO Box 9, Vacaville, 95696 • 448-1010 • evenings call 449-0550 • ask for Kristin or Kathy

Ferndale   (707)

ACCOMMODATIONS

The Gingerbread Mansion Inn 400 Berding St. • 786-4000/(800) 952-4136 • popular • gay-friendly • a grand lady in the Victorian village of Ferndale w/ beautifully restored interior • full brkfst • afternoon tea • near outdoor recreation • smokefree • kids ok • $140-350

Fort Bragg   (707)

ACCOMMODATIONS

Aslan House 24600 N. Hwy. 1 • 964-2788/(800) 400-2189 • gay-friendly • cottages • ideal place for romance & privacy on the Mendocino Coast • partial ocean view • hot tub • kids 10+ ok • $130 + $10 extra person (4 max)

Cleone Lodge Inn 24600 N. Hwy. 1 • 964-2788/(800) 400-2189 • gay-friendly • cottages • country garden retreat on 9-1/2 acres • hot tub • $74-130 (2 persons)

Jug Handle Beach B&B 32980 Gibney Ln. • 964-1415 • gay-friendly • full brkfst • kids ok

BOOKSTORES & RETAIL SHOPS

Windsong Books & Records 324 N. Main • 964-2050 • 10am-5:30pm, til 4pm Sun • general • large selection of women's titles

Fremont   (510)

EROTICA

Cupid's Corner 34129 Fremont Blvd. • 796-8697 • boutique • lingerie • large sizes • videos

L'Amour Shoppe 40555 Grimmer Blvd. • 659-8161 • 24hrs

Fresno   (209)

INFO LINES & SERVICES

Bulletin Board at Valley Women's Books popular resource for community info

Community Link PO Box 4959, 93744 • 266-5465 • info • lesbigay support • also publishes Pink Pages

GUS Inc. (Gay United Service) 1999 Tuolumne Ste. 625 • 268-3541 • 8am-5pm Mon-Fri • counseling • referrals

Serenity Fellowship AA 925 N. Fulton • 221-6907 • various mtg. times • women's mtg. 7pm Mon

The Yosemite Chapter, Knights of Malta PO Box 4162, 93744 • 496-4144 • lesbigay leather group

BARS

The Express 708 N. Blackstone • 233-1791 • 5pm-2am, from 3pm Sun • lesbians/gay men • dancing/DJ • piano bar • cafe • videos • popular patio • wheelchair access

Palace 4030 E. Belmont Ave. • 264-8283 • 3pm-2am • mostly women • neighborhood bar • dancing/DJ • country/western • live shows • wheelchair access

Red Lantern 4618 E. Belmont Ave. • 251-5898 • 2pm-2am • mostly men • neighborhood bar • country/western • wheelchair access

RESTAURANTS & CAFES

Cafe Express 708 N. Blackstone • 233-1791 • 6pm-9pm, champagne brunch 10am-3pm Sun, clsd Mon • fine dining

Java Cafe 805 E. Olive • 237-5282 • 7am-11pm, til midnight Fri-Sat • popular • bohemian • plenty veggie • wheelchair access • women-owned/run • $8-12

BOOKSTORES & RETAIL SHOPS
Valley Women's Books 1118 N. Fulton St.
• 233-3600 • 10am-6pm, til 9pm Th-Fri •
women's • lesbigay section • wheelchair
access

TRAVEL & TOUR OPERATORS
The Travel Address 6465 N. Blackstone
Ave. • (800) 800-9095 • IGTA

SPIRITUAL GROUPS
Morrigan Tower Coven of Wyrd PO Box
7137, 93744-7137 • monthly • co-gender

EROTICA
Only For You 1468 N. Van Ness Ave. • 498-
0284 • noon-9pm, til 10pm Th-Sat • lesbigay

Wildcat Book Store 1535 Fresno St. • 237-
4525

Garberville   (707)
ACCOMMODATIONS
Giant Redwoods RV & Camp PO Box 222,
Myers Flat, 95554 • 943-3198 • gay-friendly
• campsites • RV • located off the Avenue
of the Giants on the Eel River • shared
baths • kids/pets ok • $16-22

Garden Grove   (714)
INFO LINES & SERVICES
AA Gay/Lesbian 9872 Chapman Ave. #15
(Ash Inc.) • 534-5820/537-9968 • 6pm-
10pm, clsd Fri, Sun

BARS
Frat House 8112 Garden Grove Blvd. • 897-
3431 • 9am-2am • popular • lesbians/gay
men •dancing/DJ • multi-racial • live
shows • theme nights • piano bar • wheelchair access

Happy Hour 12081 Garden Grove Blvd. •
537-9079 • 2pm-2am, from noon wknds •
mostly women • dancing/DJ • wheelchair
access • women-owned/run

Nick's 8284 Garden Grove Blvd. • 537-1361
• 9pm-2am, 24hrs wknds • mostly gay men
• neighborhood bar • dancing/DJ • wheelchair access

EROTICA
Hip Pocket 12686 Garden Grove Blvd. •
638-8595

Glendale   (818)
SPIRITUAL GROUPS
MCC Divine Redeemer 346 Riverdale Dr. •
500-7124 • 10:45am Sun, 7:30pm Wed

Grass Valley (916)

ACCOMMODATIONS

Murphy's Inn 318 Neal St. • 273-6873 • gay-friendly • full brkfst • smokefree • wheelchair access

Gualala (707)

ACCOMMODATIONS

Starboard House 140 Starboard • 884-4808 • gay-friendly • vacation house • ocean views • hot tub • smokefree • kids ok • wheelchair access • women-owned/run

Half Moon Bay (415)

ACCOMMODATIONS

Mill Rose Inn 615 Mill St. • 726-8750/(800) 900-7673 • gay-friendly • classic European elegance by the sea • full brkfst • hot tub • smokefree • kids 10+ ok • $165-265

Hawthorne (310)

BARS

El Capitan 13825 S. Hawthorne • 675-3436 • 4pm-2am, from noon Fri-Sun • lesbians/gay men • neighborhood bar • beer/wine • more women Tue

Hayward (510)

BARS

Driftwood Lounge 22170 Mission Blvd. • 581-2050 • 2pm-2am • mostly women • dancing/DJ • wheelchair access • women-owned/run

I.J.'s Getaway 21859 Mission Blvd. • 582-8078 • noon-2am, til 4am Fri-Sat • lesbians/gay men • dancing/DJ

Rumors 22554 Main St. • 733-2334 • 10am-2am • mostly men • neighborhood bar • wheelchair access

Turf Club 22517 Mission Blvd. • 881-9877 • 10am-2am • lesbians/gay men• dancing/DJ • country/western • live shows • patio bar in summer

EROTICA

L'Amour Shoppe 22553 Main St. • 886-7777

Healdsburg (707)

ACCOMMODATIONS

Camellia Inn 211 North St. • 433-8182/(800) 727-8182 • gay-friendly • full brkfst • wheelchair access • $70-135

Madrona Manor PO Box 818, 95448 • 433-4231 • gay-friendly • elegant Victorian country inn • full brkfst • swimming • smokefree • some rooms okay for kids • pets ok • wheelchair access

Twin Towers River Ranch 615 Bailhache • 433-4443 • gay-friendly • 1864 Victorian farmhouse located on 5 rolling acres • also vacation house • kids & pets by arr. • B&B:$105 Apt: $450-570/week

Hermosa Beach (310)

EROTICA

U.S.J. Video & Books 655 Pacific Coast Hwy. • 374-9207

Huntington Beach (714)

EROTICA

Paradise Specialties 7344 Center • 898-0400

Idyllwild (909)

ACCOMMODATIONS

The Pine Cove Inn 23481 Hwy. 243 • 659-5033 • gay-friendly • on 3 wooded acres • full brkfst • fireplaces • kids ok • $70-90

The Rainbow Inn PO Box 3384, 92549 • 659-0111 • gay-friendly • full brkfst • shared/private baths • kitchen • smokefree • patio • conference room avail. • gay-owned/run • $75-95

Wilkum Inn B&B PO Box 1115, 92549 • 659-8087/(800) 659-4086 • gay-friendly • 1938 shingle-style inn • cabin avail. • shared/private baths • fireplaces • smoke-free • kids ok • $75-100 (plus tax)

Inglewood (310)

BARS

Annex 835 S. La Brea • 671-7323 • noon-2am • mostly men • neighborhood bar

Caper Room 244 S. Market St. • 677-0403 • 11am-2am, from 4pm Sun • mostly gay men • dancing/DJ • mostly African-American

Lafayette (510)

RESTAURANTS & CAFES

Java Jones 100 Lafayette Cir. #101 • 284-5282 • 9am-3pm, til 10pm Th-Sat, clsd Mon • lesbians/gay men • brunch Sun • some veggie • wheelchair access • lesbian-owned/run • $6-13

Laguna Beach   (714)

INFO LINES & SERVICES

AA Gay/Lesbian 31872 Coast Hwy. (South Coast Medical Hospital) • 499-7150 • 8:30pm Fri

Laguna Outreach 497-4237 • educational/social group for Orange County • call for details

ACCOMMODATIONS

Best Western Laguna Brisas Spa Hotel 1600 S. Coast Hwy. • 497-7272/(800) 624-4442 • gay-friendly • resort • swimming • kids ok • whirlpool spas in rooms • non-smoking rms avail. • wheelchair access • $99-229

California Riviera 800 1400 S. Coast Hwy. Ste. 104 • (800) 621-0500 • extensive reservation & accommodation services • IGTA

▲ **Casa Laguna B&B Inn** 2510 S. Coast Hwy. • 494-2996/(800) 233-0449 • gay-friendly • romantic mission-style inn & cottages overlooking the Pacific • swimming • kids/pets ok • $89-249

The Coast Inn 1401 S. Coast Hwy. • 494-7588/(800) 653-2697 • lesbians/gay men • resort • swimming • kids ok • oceanside location w/ 2 bars & restaurant • $60-140

Holiday Inn Laguna Beach 696 S. Coast Hwy. • 494-1001 • gay-friendly • swimming • kids ok • food served • wheelchair access

Inn By The Sea 475 N. Coast Hwy. • 497-6645/(800) 297-0007 • gay-friendly • hot tub • swimming • kids ok • wheelchair access

BARS

Boom Boom Room (at the Coast Inn) • 494-7588 • 10am-2am • lesbians/gay men • dancing/DJ • live shows • videos • wheelchair access

Little Shrimp 1305 S. Coast Hwy. • 494-4111 • opens 1pm, from 11am wknds, brunch Sun • popular • lesbians/gay men • seafood • some veggie • patio • $8-30

Main St. 1460 S. Coast Hwy. • 494-0056 • noon-2am • mostly gay men • piano bar • women-owned/run

Casa Laguna INN

A Romantic - Intimate Setting - Spectacular Ocean Views
Tropical Gardens - Heated Pool - Continental Plus
Breakfast - Afternoon Tea & Wine

20 Lovely Rooms - Suites - Cottages

From $69 - Ocean Views $89

2510 S. Pacific Coast Hwy
Laguna Beach
800-233-0449

Laguna Beach

Newport Station (see Costa Mesa) • 631-0031 • 9pm-2am Th-Sat • more women Th • dancing/DJ • live shows • videos • wheelchair access

RESTAURANTS & CAFES

Cafe Zinc 350 Ocean Ave. • 494-6302 • 7am-5:30pm, til 5pm Sun • vegetarian • beer/wine • patio • also market • wheelchair access • $5-10

Cafe Zoolu 860 Glenneyre • 494-6825 • dinner • Californian • some veggie • wheelchair access • $10-20

The Cottage 308 N. Coast Hwy. • 494-3023 • 7am-9:30pm, til 10:30 Sat-Sun • home-style cooking • some veggie • $10-12

Dizz's As Is 2794 S. Coast Hwy. • 494-5250 • open 5:30pm, seating at 6pm, clsd Mon • cont'l • full bar • patio • $16-27

Leap of Faith 1440 Pacific Coast Hwy. • 494-8595 • 6:30am-11pm, til midnight Fri-Sat, from 7:30am wknds • lesbians/gay men • American/gourmet desserts • plenty veggie • patio • $10-20

BOOKSTORES & RETAIL SHOPS

A Different Drummer 1294-C S. Coast Hwy. • 497-6699 • 11am-8pm • women's lesbigay section • wheelchair access • women-owned/run

▲ **Jewelry by Ponce** 219 N. Broadway #331 • 494-1399 • 11am-7pm Wed-Sun, by appt. Mon-Tue • lesbigay jewelry

TRAVEL & TOUR OPERATORS

Festive Tours 1220 N. Coast Hwy. • 494-9966 • IGTA

SPIRITUAL GROUPS

Christ Chapel of Laguna 976 S. Coast Hwy. • 376-2099 • 10am Sun, 7pm Wed

Evangelicals Concerned Laguna 451-3777 • call for info • newsletter

Unitarian Universalist Fellowship 429 Cypress Dr. • 497-4568/645-8597 • 10:30am Sun

PUBLICATIONS

Orange County Blade PO Box 1538, 92652 • 494-4898

EROTICA

Video Horizons 31674 Coast Hwy • 499-4519

Laguna Niguel   (714)

SPIRITUAL GROUPS

S.D.A. Kinship PO Box 7320, 92677 • 248-1299

Lake Tahoe   (916)

(See also **Lake Tahoe, NV**)

ACCOMMODATIONS

Bavarian House B&B PO Box 624507 •
544-4411/(800) 431-4411 • exclusively
gay/lesbian • smokefree • $75-125

▲ **Holly's Place** PO Box 13197, S. Lake Tahoe,
96151 • 544-7040/(800) 745-7041 • women
only • guesthouse • cabin • kitchens •
nudity • kids/pets ok • 2 blks to the lake •
2 miles to casinos • 3 miles to gay bar •
$85-155

Inn Essence 865 Lake Tahoe Blvd., South
Lake Tahoe • 577-0339/(800) 578-2463 •
lesbians/gay men • $79-125

Ridgewood Inn 1341 Emerald Bay Rd. •
541-8589/(800) 800-4640 • gay-friendly •
hot tub • kids/pets ok • quiet wooded setting • $40-150

Secrets Honeymooners' Inn 924 Park Ave.,
South Lake Tahoe • 544-6767/(800) 441-
6610 • gay-friendly • quiet, romantic adult-
only inn • spas

Sierrawood Guest House PO Box 11194,
96155-0194 • 577-6073/700-3802 • les-
bians/gay men • kids ok by arr. • romantic,
cozy chalet • $110-150

Silver Shadows Lodge 1251 Emerald Bay
Rd., South Lake Tahoe • 541-3575/(800)
406-6478 • gay-friendly • motel • swimming • kids/pets ok • $35 & up

Tradewinds Motel 944 Friday (at Cedar),
South Lake Tahoe • 544-6459/(800) 628-
1829 • gay-friendly • swimming • suite w/
spas & fireplace avail.

BARS

Faces 270 Kingsbury Grade, Stateline, NV •
588-2333 • 4pm-4am • lesbians/gay men •
dancing/DJ

RESTAURANTS & CAFES

Driftwood Cafe 4119 Laurel Ave. • 544-
6545 • 7:30am-2pm • homecooking • some
veggie • $4-8

Syd's Bagelry 550 North Lake Rd., Tahoe
City • 583-2666 • 6:30am-7:30pm daily •
bagel sandwiches • plenty veggie • cafe

BOOKSTORES & RETAIL SHOPS

The Funkyard 265-A North Lake Blvd.,
Tahoe City • 581-3483 • 11am-7pm daily •
eccentric consignment/thrift store •
women-owned/run

Lancaster   (805)

INFO LINES & SERVICES

Antelope Valley Gay/Lesbian Alliance PO
Box 2013, 93539 • 942-2812 • call for
events

BARS

Back Door 1255 W. Ave. 'I' • 945-2566 •
6pm-2am • lesbians/gay men • dancing/DJ

SPIRITUAL GROUPS

**Antelope Valley Unitarian Universalist
Fellowship** 43843 N. Division St. • 272-
0530 • 11am Sun

Sunrise MCC of the High Desert 45303
23rd St. W. • 942-7076 • 11am Sun

Long Beach   (310)

INFO LINES & SERVICES

AA Gay/Lesbian (Atlantic Alano Club) 441
E. 1st St. • 432-7476 • hours vary

Lesbian/Gay Center & Switchboard 2017
E. 4th St. • 434-4455 • 9am-10pm, til-6pm
Sat, clsd Sun

**South Bay Lesbian/Gay Community
Organization** PO Box 2777, Redondo
Beach, 90278 • 379-2850 • support/educa-
tion for Manhattan, Hermosa & Redondo
Beaches, Torrance, Palos Verdes, El
Segundo

ACCOMMODATIONS

Bed & Breakfast of California 3924 E.
14th St., 90804 • (800) 383-3513 • B&B
reservation service of California

BARS

The Brit 1744 E. Broadway • 432-9742 •
10am-2am • mostly gay men • neighborhood bar

The Broadway 1100 E. Broadway • 432-
3646 • 10am-2am • mostly gay men •
neighborhood bar

The Bulldogs (The Crest) 5935 Cherry Ave.
• 423-6650 • 2pm-2am • lesbians/gay men

Club 5211 5211 N. Atlantic St. • 428-5545
• 6am-2am • mostly gay men • neighborhood bar • karaoke Wed • wheelchair
access

The Club 740 740 E. Broadway • 437-7705
• 6pm-2am • popular • mostly gay men •
dancing/DJ • mostly Latino-American

Club Broadway 3348 E. Broadway • 438-
7700 • 11am-2am • mostly women • neighborhood bar • wheelchair access • women-
owned/run

Have You Been Yet?

<u>Only 2-Blocks From The Lake!</u>
Hiking, Bicycling, BBQ's, Boating,
Fishing, Casinos, Great Restaurants,
and Entertainment.

Business calls   Reservations
916-544-7040   800-745-7041

Holly's
A SPECIAL PLACE FOR WOMEN
LAKE TAHOE, CALIFORNIA

De De's (on the Queen Mary) • 433-1470 • mostly women • dancing/DJ • call for events

Executive Suite 3428 E. Pacific Coast Hwy. • 597-3884 • 8pm-2am, clsd Tue • popular • lesbians/gay men • more women wknds • dancing/DJ • wheelchair access

Floyd's 2913 E. Anaheim St. (entrance on Gladys St.) • 433-9251 • 6pm-2am, from 2pm Sun, clsd Mon • lesbians/gay men • more women Fri • dancing/DJ • country/western • dance lessons Tue-Th • wheelchair access

Pistons 2020 E. Artesia • 422-1928 • 6pm-2am, til 4am Fri-Sat • mostly gay men • leather • patio

Que Sera 1923 E. 7th St. • 599-6170 • 3pm-2am, from 2pm wknds • mostly women • dancing/DJ • live shows • wheelchair access • women-owned/run

Ripples 5101 E. Ocean • 433-0357 • noon-2am • popular • mostly gay men • dancing/DJ • piano bar • videos • food served • patio

Silver Fox 411 Redondo • 439-6343 • noon-2am, from 8am Sun • popular happy hour • mostly gay men • karaoke 9pm Wed & Sun • videos

Sweetwater Saloon 1201 E. Broadway • 432-7044 • 6am-2am • mostly gay men • neighborhood bar • popular days

Whistle Stop 5873 Atlantic • 422-7927 • 11am-2am, from 8am wknds • mostly gay men • neighborhood bar

RESTAURANTS & CAFES

Birds of Paradise 1800 E. Broadway • 590-8773 • 10am-1am • lesbians/gay men • Sun brunch • cocktails • live piano Wed-Sun • some veggie • $10

Cha Cha Cha 762 8th • 436-3900 • lunch & dinner • Caribbean • plenty veggie • wheelchair access • $20-30

Long Beach

*T*hough it's often overshadowed by Los Angeles, Long Beach is a large harbor city with plenty of bars, shopping, and of course, lesbians.

According to local rumor, Long Beach is second only to San Francisco in lesbian/gay population, at approximately 45,000 – though many of these gay residents are "married," making this a bedroom community of professional couples.

The city itself is melded from overlapping suburbs and industrial areas. The cleaner air, mild weather, and reasonable traffic make it an obvious choice for those looking for a livable refuge from L.A. Of course the nightlife is milder as well, but nobody's complaining about the women's bars – **Club Broadway** for casual hanging out, and **Que Será** for dancing and shows. Though it's a mixed club, we hear the **Executive Suite** is packed with lesbians on weekends. For other events, check with **Pearls Book-sellers**, the women's bookstore, or the **Lesbian/Gay Center**.

Egg Heaven 4358 E. 4th St. • 433-9277 • 7am-2pm, til 3pm wknds • some veggie • $4-7

Madame JoJo 2941 Broadway • 439-3672 • 5pm-10pm • popular • lesbians/gay men • Mediterranean • some veggie • beer/wine • wheelchair access • $12-20

Original Pack Pantry 2104 E. Broadway • 434-0451 • lunch & dinner • Mexican/American/Asian • some veggie • $8-12

BOOKSTORES & RETAIL SHOPS

By The Book 2501 E. Broadway • 930-0088 • 10am-8pm, til 6pm Sun • large lesbigay section • wheelchair access

Dodd's Bookstore 4818 E. 2nd St. • 438-9948 • 10am-10pm, noon-6pm Sun • strong lesbigay section • wheelchair access

Hot Stuff 2121 E. Broadway • 433-0692 • 11am-7pm, til 5pm wknds • cards • gifts • toys

Out & About On Broadway 1724 E. Broadway • 436-9930 • 12:30pm-10pm, noon-8pm Sun • clothing • videos • books

Pearls Booksellers 224 Redondo Ave. • 438-8875 • 11am-7pm, noon-5pm wknds • women's • wheelchair access • women-owned/run

TRAVEL & TOUR OPERATORS

Touch of Travel 3918 Altantic Ave. • 427-2144/(800) 833-3387 • IGTA

SPIRITUAL GROUPS

Christ Chapel 3935 E. 10th St. • 438-5303 • 10am & 6pm Sun, 7pm Wed • non-denominational • wheelchair access

Dignity PO Box 15037, 90815 • 984-8400 • call for service times & locations

First United Methodist Church 507 Pacific Ave. • 437-1289 • 9am & 11am Sun • wheelchair access

Trinity Lutheran Church 759 Linden Ave. • 437-4002 • 10 am Sun • wheelchair access

Universal Mind Science Church 3212 E. 8th St. • 434-3453 • 11:30am Sun & 8pm Th

PUBLICATIONS

Directory - Long Beach 4102 E. 7th St. #621 • 434-7129 • directory of gay & gay-supportive businesses • also publishes Orange County directory

EROTICA

The Crypt on Broadway 1712 E. Broadway • 983-6560 • leather • toys

---

Long Beach (310)

WHERE THE GIRLS ARE:
Schmoozing with the boys on Broadway between Atlantic and Cherry Avenues, or elsewhere between Pacific Coast Hwy. and the beach. Or at home snuggling.

LESBIGAY PRIDE: 987-9191.

ANNUAL EVENTS:
AIDSWalk in April. Pride Celebration in June. Pride Picnic in Sept. The Gatsby in Nov. at the Sheraton, benefitting the Center.

CITY INFO: 436-3645.

ATTRACTIONS: The Queen Mary.

BEST VIEW:
On the deck of the Queen Mary, docked overlooking most of Long Beach. Or Signal Hill, off 405 - take the Cherry exit.

WEATHER:
Quite temperate: highs in the mid-80°s July through September, and cooling down at night. In the "winter," January to March, highs are in the upper 60°s, and lows in the upper 40°s.

TRANSIT:
Long Beach Yellow Cab: 435-6111. Super Shuttle: 782-6600. Long Beach Transit & Runabout (free downtown shuttle): 591-2301.

Los Angeles

WHERE THE GIRLS ARE: Hip dykes hang out in West Hollywood, with the boys along Santa Monica Blvd., or cruising funky Venice Beach and Santa Monica. The S&M ("Stand & Model") glamour-dykes pose in chichi clubs and posh eateries in West LA and Beverly Hills. There's a scattered community of women in Silverlake. And more suburban lesbians frequent the women's bars in Studio City and North Hollywood. If you're used to makeup-free lesbians, you may be surprised that coiffed and lipsticked lesbian style is the norm in LA.

ENTERTAINMENT: Celebration Theatre: (213) 957-1884. 7051-B Santa Monica Blvd. Highways: (310) 453-1755. 1651 18th Santa Monica. Theatre Geo: (213) 466-1767. 1229 N. Highland Ave. Gay Men's Chorus: (213) 650-0756.

LESBIGAY PRIDE: June: (213) 656-6553 (Christopher St. West).

ANNUAL EVENTS: April - AIDS Dance-a-thon: (213) 466-9255. Lesbians Rights Award Banquet: (213) 654-7298. TBA. May - California AIDS Ride: (213) 874-7474 / (800) 474-3395. AIDS benefit bike ride from San Francisco to L.A. June - One Mighty Party (OMP): (310) 659-3555 June 20. July - Outfest: (213) 951-1247. Los Angeles' lesbian & gay film and video festival. August - Sunset Junction Fair: (213) 661-7771. Carnival, arts & information fair on Sunset Blvd. in Silverlake benefits Sunset Junction Youth Center. August - Labor Day L.A.: (800) 522-7329. Weekend-long AIDS fundraising celebration with many events. September - AIDS Walk LA: (213) 466-9255. AIDS benefit. September - Gay Night at Knotts Berry Farm: (818) 893-2777. Gay Cruise Catalina: (818) 893-2777. November - Gay Night at Disneyland: (818) 893-2777. December - New Years Cruise in Long Beach Harbor: (818) 893-2777.

CITY INFO: (213) 624-7300.

ATTRACTIONS: Melrose Ave., W. Hollywood. City Walk in Universal Studios. Venice Beach. Sunset Blvd. in Hollywood. Westwood Village. Chinatown. Theme Parks: Disneyland, Knotts Berry Farm or Magic Mountain.

BEST VIEW: Drive up Mulholland Drive, in the hills between Hollywood and the Valley, for a panoramic view of the city, and the Hollywood sign.

WEATHER: Summers are hot, dry and smoggy with temperatures in the 90°s -100°s. LA's weather is at its finest — sunny, blue skies and moderate temperatures (mid 70°s) — during the months of March, April and May.

TRANSIT: Yellow Cab: (213) 870-4664. United Yellow: (310) 855-7070. LA Express: (800) 427-7483 ext. 2. Super Shuttle: (310) 782-6600. Metro Transit Authority: (213) 626-4455.

Los Angeles

*T*here is no city more truly American than the city that is known simply as L.A. Here fantasy and reality have become inseparable. The mere mention of the 'City of Angels' conjures up images of palm-lined streets, sun-drenched beaches, and wealth beyond imagination, along with smog, over-crowded freeways, searing poverty, and urban violence.

Most travellers come only for the fantasy. They come to 'stargaze' at Mann's Chinese Theatre in Hollywood, at movie and television studios (Fox, Universal) in Burbank, at famous restaurants (Spago, The City, Chasen's, Citrus, Ivy's, Chaya Brasserie, Morton's, etc.) and, of course, all along Rodeo Drive. (Our favorite stargazing location is **Canter's Deli** after 2am.)

But if you take a moment to focus your gaze past the usual tourist traps, you'll see the unique – and often tense – diversity that L.A. offers as a city on the borders of Latin America, the Pacific Rim, Suburbia USA, and the rest of the world. You'll find museums, centers and theatres celebrating the cultures of the many peoples who live in this valley. An excellent example is West Hollywood's **June L. Mazer Lesbian Collection**. Other cultural epicenters include Olvera Street, Korea Town, China Town and the historically Jewish Fairfax District. Call the L.A. Visitor's Bureau for directions and advice.

L.A.'s art scene rivals New York's, so if you're an art-lover be sure to check out the galleries and museums, as well as the performance art scene (check a recent LA Weekly). Our favorite gallery, reknowned for its trashy kitsch art, is La Luz de Jesus Gallery (on Melrose above the famous neon "Wacko" sign, 213/651-4875).

Other kitsch fans should explore cult store **Archaic Idiot/Mondo Video** or video theater EZTV (on Melrose, 310/657-1532) while trash or kink fans should schedule time at Trashy Lingerie (on LaCienega, 310/652-4543) and the **Pleasure Chest**, or pick up some new body ornaments at the **Gauntlet**.

L.A. is a car-driven city — remember the song, "Nobody Walks in L.A.?" Nobody takes the bus, either, if they can avoid it. So plan on spending a day just driving; don't miss Mulholland Drive at night.

As for lesbian nightlife in L.A., there are 5 full-time women's bars (3 of them in the Valley), and 5 or 6 women's nights. L.A. is where the one-night-a-week women's dance bar revolution began, so make sure to double-check the papers before you go out.

But the big new deal for women in L.A. is the retro-chic supperclub—a perfect combo of dinner, schmooze and entertainment. Call to find out about the latest **Klub Banshee** supperclub. For coffee and girls with British accents, stop by **Van Go's Ear** in Venice. Also, check out Madonna's new neighborhood, **Los Feliz**.

You'll really find out the buzz at **Sisterhood Bookstore**, another great spot to get caught up or checked out. While you're there pick up a copy of **Female FYI** party guide, **Girl Guide** nightclub guide, or the more topical **Lesbian News**. And you can always check out the local lesbians at **The Palms**.

LOS ANGELES

Los Angeles is divided into 7 geographical regions:

L.A. - Overview

INFO LINES & SERVICES

AA Gay/Lesbian (213) 936-4343 (AA#)/(213) 993-7400 • call for meeting times & locations

Alcoholics Together Center 1773 Griffith Park Blvd. • (213) 663-8882 • call for mtg. times • 12-step groups

Asian/Pacific Lesbians/Gays West Hollywood PO Box 433 Ste. 109, 90096 • (213) 980-7874 • call for events • Asian/Pacific Islanders & friends

Bi-Social (Pansocial) Center & Bi-Line 7136 Matilija Ave., Van Nuys • (213) 873-3700/(818) 989-3700 • 24hr hotline for bi, transgender & gay info/referrals

Black Gay/Lesbian Leadership Forum 1219 S. La Brea, 90019 • (213) 964-7820 • nat'l group • sponsors annual conference

The Celebration Theatre 7051-B Santa Monica Blvd. • (213) 957-1884 • lesbigay theater • call for more info

Gay/Lesbian Youth Talk Line (213) 993-7475 • 7pm-10pm, clsd Sun • referrals & support for those 23 & under • women's night Mon

IMRU Gay Radio KPFK LA 90.7 FM • (818) 985-2711 • 10pm Sun • also 'This Way Out' 4:30pm Tue

International Gay/Lesbian Archives USC • (310) 854-0271 • by appt.

June Mazer Collection 626 N. Robertson, West Hollywood • (310) 659-2478 • 11am-3pm Tue, 6pm-9pm Wed, noon-4pm Sun and by appt. • lesbian archives

Los Angeles Gay/Lesbian Community Center 1625 N. Shrader • (213) 993-7400 • 9am-10pm, til 6pm Sun • wide variety of services

South Bay Lesbian/Gay Community Organization PO Box 2777, Redondo Beach, 90278 • (310) 379-2850 • support/education for Manhattan, Hermosa & Redondo Beaches, Torrance, Palos Verdes, El Segundo

Southern CA Women for Understanding (SCWU) 7985 Santa Monica #207, 90046 • (213) 654-7298 • call for events • professional group working to challenge lesbian stereotypes

Uptown Gay/Lesbian Alliance PO Box 65111, 90065 • (213) 258-8842 • monthly social 2pm-5pm 2nd Sun • also publishes newsletter

Women's Business Network (818) 995-6646 • 9am-5pm • parent group of Women's Yellow Pages & Women's Referral Service

ACCOMMODATIONS

Bed & Breakfast of California 3924 E. 14th St., Long Beach, 90804 • (310) 498-0552/(800) 383-3513 • B&B reservation service for California

TRAVEL & TOUR OPERATORS

Damron Atlas World Travel 8923 S. Sepulveda Blvd. • (310) 670-6991 • (888) 907-9777 • IGTA

SPIRITUAL GROUPS

Beth Chayim Chadashim 6000 W. Pico Blvd. • (213) 931-7023 • 8pm Fri

PUBLICATIONS

Community Yellow Pages 2305 Canyon Dr., 90068 • (213) 469-4454/(800) 745-5669 • annual survival guide to lesbigay southern CA

The Edge 6434 Santa Monica Blvd., Hollywood, 90038 • (213) 962-6994

Female FYI 8033 Sunset Blvd. Ste. 2013, 90046 • (310) 657-5592 • monthly • lesbian lifestyle/entertainment magazine

L.A. Girl Guide (310) 391-8877

Leather Journal 7985 Santa Monica Blvd. #109-368, 90046 • (213) 656-5073

Lesbian News 2953 Lincoln Blvd., Santa Monica, 90405 • (310) 392-8224/(800) 458-9888

Nightlife 6363 Santa Monica Blvd., 90038 • (213) 462-5400

Pink Pages (714) 241-7465/(800) 844-6574 • semi-annual directory for southern CA

The Women's Yellow Pages 13601 Ventura Blvd. #374, Sherman Oaks, 91423 • (818) 995-6646

L.A. - West Hollywood   (310)

ACCOMMODATIONS

The Grove Guesthouse 1325 N. Orange Grove Ave. • (213) 876-7778 • lesbians/gay men • 1-bdrm cottage in a quiet & historic neighborhood • hot tub • designated smoking areas • kitchens • pets ok by arr. • $125-150

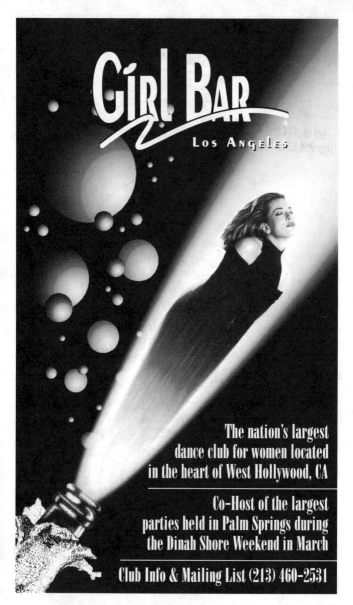

Girl Bar
LOS ANGELES

The nation's largest
dance club for women located
in the heart of West Hollywood, CA

Co-Host of the largest
parties held in Palm Springs during
the Dinah Shore Weekend in March

Club Info & Mailing List (213) 460-2531

Holloway Motel 8465 Santa Monica Blvd. • (213) 654-2454 • mostly gay men • kitchens • kids ok • centrally located to the gay community • IGTA • $55-85

▲ **Le Montrose Suite Hotel** 900 Hammond St. • 855-1115/(800) 776-0666 • gay-friendly • hot tub • swimming • kitchens • fireplaces • smokefree • gym • kids/pets ok • also full restaurant • rooftop patio • IGTA • wheelchair access • $150-475

Le Parc Hotel de Luxe 733 N. West Knoll Dr. • 855-8888/578-4837 • popular • gay-friendly • swimming • tennis courts • kids/pets ok • also a restaurant • IGTA • wheelchair access • $165-265

Le Reve 8822 Cynthia St. • 854-1114/(800) 835-7997 • gay-friendly • swimming • kids ok • IGTA • wheelchair access

Ma Maison Sofitel 8555 Beverly Blvd. • 278-5444/(800) 521-7772 • gay-friendly • swimming • food served • wheelchair access

Ramada West Hollywood 8585 Santa Monica Blvd. • 652-6400/(800) 845-8585 • gay-friendly • modern art deco hotel & suites • swimming • kids ok • IGTA • wheelchair access • $79-250

San Vincente B&B Resort 845 San Vincente Blvd. • 854-6915 • mostly gay men • swimming • hot tub • nudity • $59-129

BARS

7702 SM Club 7702 Santa Monica Blvd. • (213) 654-3336 • 6am-2am, 24hrs wknds • lesbians/gay men • neighborhood bar • dancing/DJ • wheelchair access

7969 7969 Santa Monica Blvd. • (213) 654-0280 • 9pm-2am • gay-friendly • live shows • transgender- & leather-friendly • theme nights

Axis 652 N. La Peer • 659-0471 • 9pm-2am Tue-Sun • mostly gay men • dancing/DJ • alternative • live shows • videos • 'Girl Bar' Fri (women only)

Checca Bar & Cafe 7323 Santa Monica Blvd. • (213) 850-7471 • 11:30am-2am • popular • lesbians/gay men • dancing/DJ • live shows • theme nights • also a restaurant (dinner only) • French/Italian • some veggie • patio

Comedy Store 8433 Sunset Blvd. • (213) 656-6225 • 8pm-1am • gay-friendly • stand-up club • lesbigay comedy Sat in 'Belly Room'

Fuel 626-5659 • women's nightclub Sun • call for events

D I N A H
S H O R E
WEEKEND
MARCH 27-30, 1997
PALM SPRINGS

▲ **Girl Bar at Axis** 652 N. La Peer Dr. • (213) 460-2531 • 9pm-2am Fri • popular • women only • dancing/DJ • call hotline for events

Improvisation 8162 Melrose Ave. • (213) 651-2583 • gay-friendly • stand-up comedy • also a restaurant

Klub Banshee Hotline 8512 Santa Monica (Benvenuto Cafe) • 288-1601 • 8pm-2am Mon • popular • mostly women • call for events • dance parties in the LA area

Libido (213) 960-4329 • mostly gay men • after hours club • call for events

Love Lounge 657 N. Robertson Blvd. • 659-0471 • 9pm-2am • lesbians/gay men • dancing/DJ • alternative • live shows • theme nights • women only Sat

Maverick Productions (714) 854-4337 • special events for women including 'Singlefest' & 'County Fever'

▲ **The Palms** 8572 Santa Monica Blvd. • 652-6188 • noon-2am • popular • mostly women • neighborhood bar • dancing/DJ • wheelchair access

Rage 8911 Santa Monica Blvd. • 652-7055 • 1pm-2am • popular • mostly gay men • dancing/DJ • live shows • videos • T-dance 5pm Sun • lunch daily • wheelchair access

Revolver 8851 Santa Monica Blvd. • 659-8851 • 4pm-2am, til 4am Fri-Sat, from 2pm Sun • popular • mostly gay men • alternative • videos

Union 8210 Sunset Blvd. • gay-friendly• (213) 654-1001 • 8pm-2am

Viper Room 8852 Sunset Blvd. • gay-friendly • 358-1880 • 9pm-2am

RESTAURANTS & CAFES

The 442 Restaurant 442 N. Fairfax • (213) 651-4421 • 6pm-10:30pm, clsd Sun • fresh healthy cuisine • plenty veggie • full bar • wheelchair access • $20-30

The Abbey 692 N. Robertson • 289-8410 • 7am-3am • lesbians/gay men • patio • wheelchair access

Amigos 7953 Santa Monica Blvd. • (213) 650-8517 • lunch & dinner • popular • Mexican • some veggie • $10-15 • wheelchair access

THE • PALMS

C O C K T A I L   L O U N G E

PARKING AVAILABLE — CALL FOR INFO
8572 SANTA MONICA BOULEVARD • (310) 652-6188

Baja Bud's 8575 Santa Monica Blvd. • 659-1911 • 7am-10pm, til 11pm Fri-Sat • healthy Mexican • under $10

Benvenuto 8512 Santa Monica Blvd. • 659-8635 • lunch Mon-Fri, dinner 5:30-10:30pm, til 11pm Fri-Sat • Italian • $8-16

Bossa Nova 685 N. Robertson Blvd. • 657-5070 • 11am-11pm • Brazilian • patio • $7 & up

Caffe Luna 7463 Melrose Ave. • (213) 655-9177 • 8am-3am, til 4am wknds • popular afterhours • Italian country food • some veggie • wheelchair access • $15-25

Canter's Deli 419 N. Fairfax • (213) 651-2030 • 24hrs • hip afterhours • Jewish/American • some veggie • wheelchair access

Club Cafe 8560 Santa Monica Blvd (in World's Gym) • 659-6630 • 7am-9pm, til 6pm Sat, til 5pm Sun • salads & sandwiches • $5-10

Crostini 846 N. La Cienega Blvd. • 652-8254 • lunch & dinner, clsd Sun • Italian bistro • $7-16

Daily Grind 8861 Santa Monica Blvd. • 652-6040 • 8am-3am, from 10am wknds • lesbians/gay men • coffeehouse • live shows

Figs 7929 Santa Monica Blvd. • (213) 654-0780 • dinner, Sun brunch • Californian • some veggie • $8-15

French Quarter Market Place 7985 Santa Monica Blvd. • (213) 654-0898 • 7am-midnight, til 3:30am Fri-Sat • popular • lesbians/gay men • some veggie • $5-12

The Greenery 8945 Santa Monica Blvd. • 275-9518 • 8am-1am, til 3am Fri-Sat • Californian • some veggie • wheelchair access • $7-12

The Heights Cafe 1118 N. Crescent Heights Blvd. • (213) 650-9688 • 7am-11pm, 8pm-midnight Fri-Sat, til 9pm Sun • lesbians/gay men • bistro • plenty veggie • BYOB

Hoy's Wok 8163 Santa Monica Blvd. • (213) 656-9002 • noon-11pm, from 4pm Sun • Mandarin • plenty veggie • wheelchair access • $8-12

L'Orangerie 903 N. La Cienega Blvd. • 652-9770 • lunch & dinner, clsd Mon • haute French • patio • $28-38

La Masía 9077 Santa Monica Blvd. • 273-7066 • Spanish/cont'l • $14-24

Little Frida's Coffee House 8730 Santa Monica Blvd. • 854-5421 • 8am-midnight, til 1am Fri-Sat, clsd Mon

Luna Park 655 N. Robertson • 652-0611 • dinner • eclectic European/Mediterranean • some veggie • cabaret • wheelchair access • $10-15

Mani's Bakery 519 S. Fairfax Ave. • (213) 938-8800 • 6:30am-11:45pm, 7:30am-1am wknds • coffee & dessert bar • wheelchair access

Marix Tex Mex 1108 N. Flores • (213) 656-8800 • 11am-midnight • lesbians/gay men • TexMex • some veggie • great margaritas • $10-15

Mark's Restaurant 861 N. La Cienega Blvd. • 652-5252 • 6pm-10pm • Californian • plenty veggie • $7-16

Melrose Place 650 N. La Cienega Blvd. • 657-2227 • 5pm-11pm • cont'l/Californian • some veggie • full bar • $8-15

Nature Club Cafe 7174 Melrose Ave. (at Formosa) • (213) 931-8994 • noon-10pm • vegetarian • also elixir bar • yoga & massage • $8-12

Paradise Grill 8745 Santa Monica Blvd. • 659-6785 • dinner • also lunch & brunch wknds • lesbians/gay men • Californian • plenty veggie • beer/wine • patio • wheelchair access • $10-15

The Shed 8474 Melrose Ave. • (213) 655-6277 • dinner • cont'l • $12-17

Skewers 8939 Santa Monica Blvd. • 271-0555 • 11am-2am • grill, salads, dips • beer/wine • under $10

Tango Grill 8807 Santa Monica Blvd. • 659-3663 • noon-11pm • lesbians/gay men • some veggie • beer/wine • wheelchair access • $6-12

Tommy Tang's 7313 Melrose Ave. • 937-5733 • noon-11pm • popular Tue nights w/ 'Club Glenda' • beer/wine

Trocadero 8280 Sunset Blvd. • (213) 656-7161 • 6pm-3am • pastas & salads • full bar • patio • $6-14

Who's On Third Cafe 8369 W. 3rd St. • (213) 651-2928 • 8am-6pm, til 3pm Sun • $8-12

Yukon Mining Co. 7328 Santa Monica Blvd. • 851-8833 • 24hrs • popular • champagne Sun brunch • beer/wine • $6-11

GYMS & HEALTH CLUBS

Easton's Gym 8053 Beverly Blvd. • (213) 651-3636 • gay-friendly

World Gym-West Hollywood 8560 Santa Monica Blvd. • 659-6630 • also 'Club Cafe'

BOOKSTORES & RETAIL SHOPS

A Different Light 8853 Santa Monica Blvd. • 854-6601 • 10am-11pm, til midnight Fri-Sat • popular • lesbigay

Dorothy's Surrender 7985 Santa Monica Blvd. #111 • (213) 650-4111 • 10am-11:30pm • cards • magazines • gifts

TRAVEL & TOUR OPERATORS

Cruise Holidays of Beverly Hills 224 S. Robertson • 652-8521

Embassy Travel 906 N. Harper Ave. Ste. B • (213) 656-0743/(800) 227-6668 • IGTA

Friends Travel 322 Huntley Dr. Ste. 100 • 652-9600/(800) GAY-0069

Gunderson Travel, Inc. 8543 Santa Monica Blvd. #8 • 657-3944/(800) 872-8457 • IGTA

Magnum Select Travel Service 8500 Wilshire Blvd. Ste. 900 • 652-7900/(800) 782-9429 • IGTA

SPIRITUAL GROUPS

West Hollywood Presbyterian Church 7350 Sunset Blvd. • (213) 874-6646 • 11am Sun • wheelchair access

EROTICA

Circus of Books 8230 Santa Monica Blvd. • (213) 656-6533 • videos • erotica • toys

Drake's 8932 Santa Monica Blvd. • 289-8932 • gifts • toys • videos • also at 7566 Melrose Ave. • (213) 651-5600

Gauntlet 8720-1/2 Santa Monica Blvd. • 657-6677 • noon-7pm, til 5pm Sun • body piercings

Pleasure Chest 7733 Santa Monica Blvd. • (213) 650-1022

Skin Graffiti Tattoo 8722 Santa Monica Blvd. (upstairs) • 358-0349 • noon-7pm, til 4pm Sun, clsd Mon

L.A. - Hollywood   (213)

ACCOMMODATIONS

Hollywood Celebrity Hotel 1775 Orchid Ave. • 850-6464/(800) 222-7017 • gay-friendly • 1930s Art Deco hotel • IGTA • $55-115

Hollywood Metropolitan Hotel 5825 Sunset Blvd. • 962-5800/(800) 962-5800 • gay-friendly • kids ok • also a restaurant • $49-129

BARS

Blacklite 1159 N. Western • 469-0211 • 6am-2am • lesbians/gay men • neighborhood bar

Faultline 4216 Melrose • 660-0889 • 3pm-2am • beer/soda bust 3pm-7pm Sun • popular • mostly gay men • leather • occasional leatherwomen's events • videos • food served • patio • also Faultline Store • 660-2952

Temple (call for location) • 243-5221 • mostly gay men • dancing/DJ • alternative • underground house Sat • call for events

Tempo 5520 Santa Monica Blvd. • 466-1094 • from 8pm, from 6pm Sun, til 4am wknds • mostly gay men • dancing/DJ • mostly Latino-American • live shows

RESTAURANTS & CAFES

Hollywood Canteen 1006 Seward St. • 465-0961 • 11:30am-10pm • popular • classic

Il Piccolino Trattoria 641 N. Highland Ave. • 936-2996 • lunch, dinner til midnight, clsd Mon • Italian/cont'l • $6-17

La Poubelle 5907 Franklin Ave. • 465-0807 • 6pm-midnight • French/Italian • some veggie • wheelchair access • $20-25

Prado 244 N. Larchmont Blvd. • 467-3871 • lunch & dinner • Caribbean • some veggie • wheelchair access • $20-30

Quality 8030 W. 3rd St. (at Laurel) • 658-5959 • 8am-4pm • homestyle brkfst • some veggie • wheelchair accessible • $8-12

GYMS & HEALTH CLUBS

Gold's Gym 1016 N. Cole Ave. • 462-7012

BOOKSTORES & RETAIL SHOPS

Archaic Idiot/Mondo Video 1724 N. Vermont • 953-8896 • noon-10pm • vintage clothes • cult & lesbigay videos

Videoactive 2522 Hyperion Ave. • 669-8544 • 10am-11pm Sun-Th, 10am-midnight Fri-Sat • lesbigay section • adult videos

TRAVEL & TOUR OPERATORS

Jacqleen's Travel Service 6222 Fountain Ave. #314 • 463-7404 • IGTA

SPIRITUAL GROUPS

Dignity-LA PO Box 42040, 90042 • 344-8064 • 5:30pm Sun • Spanish Mass 3rd Sat

L.A. - West L.A. & Santa Monica (310)

INFO LINES & SERVICES

Women Motorcyclists of Southern California (213) 664-3964 • monthly Sun brunch • also publishes newsletter

ACCOMMODATIONS

Malibu Beach Inn 22878 Pacific Coast Hwy. • 456-5428/(800) 462-6444 • gay-friendly • on the ocean • kids ok • wheelchair access

Rose Avenue Beach House 55 Rose Ave., Venice • 396-2803 • gay-friendly • Victorian beach house • 1 blk. from ocean & boardwalk

BARS

Connection 4363 Sepulveda Blvd., Culver City • 2pm-2am, from noon wknds • popular • mostly women • neighborhood bar • dancing/DJ • women-owned/run

J.J.'s Pub 2692 S. La Cienega • 837-7443 • 11am-2am • neighborhood bar • wheelchair access

Trilogy 2214 Stoner Ave., West Los Angeles • 477-2844 • opens 6pm • transgender-friendly • full bar • dinner theater w/drag waitresses/performers

RESTAURANTS & CAFES

Golden Bull 170 W. Channel Rd., Santa Monica • 230-0402 • full bar

The Local Yolk 3414 Highlands Ave., Manhattan Beach • 546-4407 • 6:30am-2:30pm

Siamese Princess 8048 W. 3rd St. • (213) 653-2643 • 5:30pm-11pm, clsd Mon & Th • lunch weekdays • Thai • beer/wine • $6-10

Van Go's Ear 796 Main St., Venice • 314-0022 • 24hrs • $2-9

BOOKSTORES & RETAIL SHOPS

Her Body Books 8721 Beverly Blvd., Beverly Hills • 553-5821 • 9am-6pm • women's health books • gifts & supplies • women-owned/run

NaNa 1228 3rd St., Santa Monica • 394-9690 • 11am-9pm, til 11pm Fri-Sat • hip shoes & clothes • also Nana outlet at 8727 W. 3rd St. • (213) 653-1252

Sisterhood Bookstore 1351 Westwood Blvd., Westwood • 477-7300 • 10am-8pm • women's • periodicals • music & more • women-owned/run

TRAVEL & TOUR OPERATORS

Atlas Travel Service 8923 S. Sepulveda Blvd. • 670-3574/(800) 952-0120 (outside L.A.) • IGTA

Firstworld Travel Express 1990 S. Bundy Dr. Ste. 175 • 820-6868/(800) 366-0815 • IGTA

SPIRITUAL GROUPS

MCC LA PO Box 46609, 90046 • (213) 460-2911 • 9am & 11:15am Sun • Spanish service 10am Sun

L.A. - Silverlake   (213)

BARS

Drag Strip 66 2500 Riverside Dr. (Rudolpho's) • 969-2596 • popular • queer dance club • call for events

RESTAURANTS & CAFES

Casita Del Campo 1920 Hyperion Ave. • 662-4255 • 11am-10pm • popular • Mexican • patio • also 'Plush Cabaret' Wed • call 969-2596 for details

Cha Cha Cha 656 N. Virgil (at Melrose) • 664-7723 • 8am-10pm, til 11pm Fri-Sat • lesbians/gay men • Caribbean • plenty veggie • wheelchair access • $20-30

The Cobalt Cantina 4326 Sunset Blvd. • 953-9991 • 11am-11pm • lesbians/gay men • Cal-Mex • some veggie • full bar • patio • $10-15

The Crest Restaurant 3725 Sunset Blvd. • 660-3645 • 6am-11pm • diner/Greek • $5-10

Da Giannino 2630 Hyperion Ave. • 664-7979 • lunch (Tue-Fri) & dinner, clsd Mon

El Conquistador 3701 Sunset Blvd. • 666-5136 • 5pm-11pm, from 11am wknds • Mexican • $5-10

Rudolpho's 2500 Riverside Dr. • 669-1226 • 8pm-2am • lesbians/gay men • salsa music & dancing lessons • patio

Zen Restaurant 2609 Hyperion Ave. • 665-2929/665-2930 • 11:30am-2am • Japanese • some veggie • $9-12

GYMS & HEALTH CLUBS

Body Builders 2516 Hyperion Ave. • 668-0802 • gay-friendly

TRAVEL & TOUR OPERATORS

Burgan Travel 428 N. Azusa Ave., West Covina • (818) 915-8617

SPIRITUAL GROUPS

Holy Trinity Community Church 4209 Santa Monica Blvd. • 662-9118 • 10am Sun

MCC Silverlake 3621 Brunswick Ave. • 665-8818 • 1:30pm Sun

EROTICA

Circus of Books 4001 Santa Monica Blvd. • (213) 666-1304 • 24hrs Fri-Sat

L.A. - Midtown   (213)

BARS

Jewel's Catch One Disco 4067 W. Pico Blvd. • 734-8849 • noon-2am, til 5am Fri-Sat • upstairs opens 9pm Th-Sun for dancing • popular • lesbians/gay men • multi-racial • wheelchair access • women-owned/run

The Red Head 2218 E. 1st St. • 263-2995 • 2pm-midnight, til 2am wknds • lesbians/gay men • neighborhood bar • beer only • women's night Fri

RESTAURANTS & CAFES

Atlas 3760 Wilshire Blvd. • 380-8400 • lunch & dinner except Sun • global cuisine • some veggie • also bar • $8-19

L.A. - Valley   (818)

BARS

Apache Territory 11608 Ventura Blvd., Studio City • 506-0404 • 8pm-2am, til 4am Fri-Sat • popular • lesbians/gay men • dancing/DJ • live shows

Escapades 10437 Burbank Blvd., North Hollywood • 508-7008 • 1pm-2am • popular • lesbians/gay men • neighborhood bar • live shows • wheelchair access

Gold 9 13625 Moorpark St., Sherman Oaks • 986-0285 • 11am-2am, from 7am wknds • mostly gay men • neighborhood bar

Incognito Valley 7026 Reseda Blvd., Reseda • 996-2976 • noon-2am • popular • mostly gay men • dancing/DJ • wheelchair access

Mag Lounge 5248 N. Van Nuys Blvd., Van Nuys • 981-6693 • 11am-2am • popular • mostly gay men • wheelchair access

Oasis 11916 Ventura Blvd., Studio City • 980-4811 • 3pm-2am • lesbians/gay men • piano bar

Oxwood Inn 13713 Oxnard, Van Nuys • 997-9666 (pay phone) • 3pm-2am, from noon Fri & Sun • mostly women • neighborhood bar • one of the oldest bars in the country • women-owned/run

Queen Mary 12449 Ventura Blvd., Studio City • 506-5619 • 11am-2am, clsd Mon-Tue • popular • gay-friendly • shows wknds

Rawhide 10937 Burbank Blvd., North Hollywood • 760-9798 • 7pm-2am, from 2pm Sun, clsd Mon-Wed • popular • mostly gay men • dancing/DJ • country/western

Rumors 10622 Magnolia Blvd. • 506-9651 • 6pm-2am, from 3pm Fri-Sun • mostly women • neighborhood bar • women-owned/run

RESTAURANTS & CAFES

Venture Inn 11938 Ventura Blvd., Studio City • 769-5400 • lunch & dinner, champagne brunch Sun • popular • lesbians/gay men • full bar • $10-15

Wellington's 4354 Lankershim Blvd., North Hollywood • 980-1430 • 11am-11pm • lesbians/gay men • live shows • $15-20

GYMS & HEALTH CLUBS

Gold's Gym 6233 N. Laurel Canyon Blvd., North Hollywood • 506-4600

SPIRITUAL GROUPS

Christ Chapel of the Valley 5006 Vineland Ave., North Hollywood • 985-8977 • 10am Sun, 7:30pm Wed • full gospel fellowship

MCC in the Valley 5730 Cahuenga Blvd., North Hollywood • 762-1133 • 10am Sun

EROTICA

Le Sex Shoppe 4539 Van Nuys Blvd., Sherman Oaks • 501-9609 • 24hrs

Stan's Video 7505 Foothill Blvd., Tujunga • 352-8735

Manhattan Beach (310)

ACCOMMODATIONS

▲ **Seaview Inn at the Beach** 3400 Highland Ave. • 545-1504 • gay-friendly • ocean views • pool • courtyard

Marina del Rey (310)

ACCOMMODATIONS

▲ **The Mansion Inn** 327 Washington Blvd., Venice • 821-2557/(800) 828-0688 • gay-friendly • 43- room European-style inn • kids ok • wheelchair access • $69-125

Mendocino (707)

ACCOMMODATIONS

Agate Cove Inn 11201 N. Lansing • 937-0551/(800) 527-3111 • full brkfst • fireplaces • smokefree • kids 12+ ok • $99-250

Bellflower Box 867, 95460 • 937-0783 • lesbians only • secluded cabin with kitchen • near outdoor recreation • hot tub • fireplaces • smokefree • pets ok • 2-night min. • $55-80

Glendeven 8221 N. Hwy. 1, Little River • 937-0083 • gay-friendly • charming farmhouse on the coast • full brkfst • smokefree • kids ok

McElroy's Inn 998 Main St. • 937-1734/937-3105 • gay-friendly • pleasant rooms & stes. • located in the Village • smokefree • kids ok

Mendocino Coastal Reservations PO Box 1143, 95460 • (800) 262-7801 • 9am-6pm • gay-friendly • call for available rentals

Sallie & Eileen's Place PO Box 409, 95460 • 937-2028 • women only • cabins • hot tub • kitchens • fireplaces • kids/pets ok • 2 night min. • A-frame: $65; Cabin: $80; $15 each additional person

Seagull Inn 44594 Albion St. • 937-5204 • gay-friendly • 9 units in the heart of historic Mendocino • smokefree • kids ok • wheelchair access

Stanford Inn by the Sea Coast Hwy. 1 & Comptche-Ukiah Rd. • 937-5615 • gay-friendly • full brkfst • near outdoor recreation • kitchens • fireplaces • smokefree • kids/pets ok • wheelchair access • $175-275

Wildflower Ridge PO Box 2132, San Ramon, 94583 • (510) 735-2079 • women only • secluded cabin in Medocino • kids/pets ok ($5/night for dogs) • women-owned/run

Restaurants & Cafes

Cafe Beaujolais 961 Ukiah • 937-5614 • dinner • California country food • some veggie • wheelchair access • women-owned/run • $20-30

Bookstores & Retail Shops

Book Loft 45050 Main • 937-0890 • 10am-6pm • wheelchair access

Publications

Visible Box 1494, 95460 • 964-2756 • March, July, Nov • ageful lesbian (50+) publication • essays • letters • drawings • women-owned/run

Menlo Park   (See **Palo Alto**)

Midway City   (714)

Bars

The Huntress 8122 Belsa Ave. • 892-0048 • 2pm-2am, from noon Sat-Sun • mostly women • dancing/DJ • wheelchair access

Mission Viejo   (714)

Travel & Tour Operators

Sunrise Travel 23891 Via Fabricante #603 • 837-0620

Modesto   (209)

Info Lines & Services

AA Gay/Lesbian 1203 Tully Rd. Ste. B • 572-2970/531-2040 • 8pm daily, 7pm Sun

Bars

Brave Bull 701 S. 9th • 529-6712 • 7pm-2am, from 4pm Sun • mostly men • leather

The Mustang Club 413 N. 7th St. • 577-9694 • 4pm-2am, from 2pm Fri-Sun • open 30 years! • lesbians/gay men • dancing/DJ • live shows • women-owned/run

Restaurants & Cafes

Espresso Caffe 3025 Mettenig Ave. • 571-3337 • 7am-11pm, til midnight Fri-Sat • $4-7

Bookstores & Retail Shops

Bookstore 2400 Coffee Rd. • 521-0535 • 10am-6pm, til 8:30pm Fri, til 5pm Sat, noon-5pm Sun • wheelchair access

Erotica

Liberty Adult Book Store 1030 Kansas Ave. • 524-7603 • 24hrs

Monterey   (408)

Info Lines & Services

AA Gay/Lesbian at the Little House in the Park, at Central & Forest • 373-3713 • 8pm Th • also 10:30am Sat at Unitarian Church, Hwy. 1 @ Aguajito

Accommodations

Gosby House Inn 643 Lighthouse Ave., Pacific Grove • 375-1287 • gay-friendly • full brkfst • smokefree • kids ok • wheelchair access

Misty Tiger 9422 Acorn Circle, Salinas • 633-8808 • women only • hot tub • video library • smokefree • women-owned/run

Monterey Fireside Lodge 1131 10th St. • 373-4172/(800) 722-2624 • gay-friendly • hot tub • fireplaces • kids ok • $79-250

Sapaque Valley Ranch Inn 48491 Sapaque Valley Rd., Bradley • (805) 472-2750 • gay-friendly • near Big Sur & San Simeon • food served

Bars

After Dark 214 Lighthouse Ave. • 373-7828 • 8pm-2am • lesbians/gay men • dancing/DJ • videos • patio

Title IX 281 Lighthouse Ave., New Monterey • 373-4488 • 3pm-2am • lesbians/gay men

RESTAURANTS & CAFES
The Clock Garden Restaurant 565 Abrego • 375-6100 • 11am-midnight • American/cont'l • some veggie • patio • wheelchair access • $10-20

Moraga (510)

BOOKSTORES & RETAIL SHOPS
Lonesome Traveller 450 Center St. • 376-2057 • 10am-7pm, til 5pm wknds • wheelchair access

Mountain View (415)

BARS
Daybreak 1711 W. El Camino Real • 940-9778 • 3pm-2am, from 4pm wknds • mostly women • dancing/DJ • karaoke Th & Sun • wheelchair access

Napa (707)

ACCOMMODATIONS
Bed & Breakfast Inns of Napa (Napa County Visitors Bureau) 1310 Napa Town Center • 226-7459 • 9am-5pm • gay-friendly • call for extensive brochure

The Ink House B&B 1575 St. Helena Hwy., St. Helena • 963-3890 • gay-friendly • historic & grand 1884 Italianate Victorian among the vineyards • full brkfst • smokefree • kids okay • sunset wine • $110-155

Willow Retreat 6517 Dry Creek Rd. • 944-8173 • gay-friendly • hot tub • swimming • day use avail. • wheelchair access • $55-110

BOOKSTORES & RETAIL SHOPS
Ariadne Books 3780 Bel Aire Plaza • 253-9402 • 10am-6pm, til 5pm Sat, clsd Sun • spiritual • lesbigay section • also espresso bar • women-owned/run

Nevada City (916)

RESTAURANTS & CAFES
Friar Tucks 111 N. Pine St. • 265-9093 • dinner nightly • American/fondue • full bar • wheelchair access • $15-20

BOOKSTORES & RETAIL SHOPS
Nevada City Postal Company 228 Commercial St. • 265-0576 • 9am-6pm, til 5pm Sat, clsd Sun • community bulletin board avail.

Novato (415)

TRAVEL & TOUR OPERATORS
Dimensions in Travel, Inc. 2 Commercial Blvd. • 883-3245x202/(800) 828-2962

Oakland (See **East Bay**)

Oceanside (619)

BARS
Capri Lounge 207 N. Tremont • 722-7284 • 10am-2am • mostly gay men • neighborhood bar • wheelchair access

RESTAURANTS & CAFES
Greystokes 1903 S. Coast Hwy. • 757-2955 • lesbians/gay men • live shows • $8-14

Orange (714)

SPIRITUAL GROUPS
Calvary Open Door Tabernacle 608 W. Katella (Phil's Ballroom) • 284-5775 • 10:30am & 6:30pm Sun

Palm Springs (619)

Note: In March, 1997, the area code for
Palm Springs will change to 760.

Info Lines & Services

AA Gay/Lesbian 324-4880 • call for mtg
schedule

Desert Business Association PO Box 773,
92263 • 324-0178 • lesbigay business association • IGTA

Palm Springs Lesbian/Gay Pride PO Box
861, Cathedral City, 92235 • 322-8769 •
24hr helpline

SCWU Desert Women PO Box 1335,
Morongo Valley, 92256-9751 • 363-7565 •
social/support group

Accommodations

The Abbey West 772 Prescott Cir. • 320-
4333/(800) 223-4073 • mostly gay men •
hot tub • swimming • gym • kitchens • private patios • wheelchair access • IGTA •
$135-250

Aruba Hotel Suites 671 S. Riverside Dr. •
325-8440/(800) 842-7822 • lesbians/gay
men • gorgeous apartments on 2 levels •
hot tub • swimming • kitchens • nudity •
IGTA • $109-169

▲ **Bee Charmer Inn** 1600 E. Palm Canyon Dr.
• 778-5883 • women only • swimming •
smokefree • lesbian-owned/run • $77-97

Casa Rosa 589 Grenfall Rd. • 322-
4143/(800) 322-4151 • mostly gay men •
B&B service in a private resort • full brkfst
• hot tub • swimming • mist system •
kitchens • nudity • private patios • wheelchair access • $65-120

Delilah's Enclave 641 San Lorenzo Rd. •
621-6973/(800) 621-6973 • mostly women •
hotel • hot tub • swimming • nudity • pets
ok • private patios • wheelchair access

Desert Palms Inn 67-580 Hwy. 111,
Cathedral City • 324-3000/(800) 801-8696 •
lesbians/gay men • hot tub • swimming •
also a restaurant • some veggie • full bar
$8-12 • huge courtyard • wheelchair access

Desert Shadows 260 Chuckwalla • 325-
6410/(800) 292-9298 • gay-friendly • natur-
ist hotel • hot tub • swimming • nudity •
kids ok • also a restaurant • $5-20

El Mirasol Villas 67-580 Warm Sands Dr. •
327-5913/(800) 327-2985 • lesbians/gay
men • hot tub • swimming • kitchens •
nudity • food served • $95-180

Ingleside Inn 200 W. Ramon Rd. • 325-0046 • gay-friendly • hot tub • swimming • also a restaurant • French con'tl • $25 • wheelchair access

Le Garbo Inn 287 W. Racquet Club Rd. • 325-6737 • mostly women • hot tub • swimming • private baths • fireplaces • nudity • lesbian-owned/run • $55-120

Mira Loma Hotel 1420 N. Indian Canyon Dr. • 320-1178 • lesbians/gay men • swimming • smokefree • kids ok

Smoke Tree Inn 1800 Smoke Tree Ln. • 327-8355 • gay-friendly • secluded on 4-1/2 acres • hot tub • swimming • wheelchair access

The Villa Hotel 67-670 Carey Rd., Cathedral City • 328-7211/(800) 845-5265 • mostly men • individual bungalows • hot tub • swimming • sauna • massage • kitchens • IGTA • $45-120

Palm Springs

*P*alm Springs has a well-deserved reputation as one of the top resort destinations for lesbian and gay travelers. However, it's a man's world—except during **Dinah Shore Weekend** in late March. The same is true for this desert resort's bumper crop of gay inns and guesthouses. Most are men-only, either in practice or policy. However, there are three women's inns: **Delilah's Enclave**, **Le Garbo Inn**, and **The Bee Charmer Inn**. Wherever you're staying, make sure they have a misting machine to take the edge off the dry desert summers. For nightlife, you have **Choices** for dancing with the boys, and **Backstreet Pub** or **Streetbar** for more casual pursuits. To find out about special events for women, call the **Desert Women's Association**.

For a little danger and an amazing view, catch a ride on the Aerial Tram that goes from the desert floor to the top of Mount San Jacinto. When you come back to earth, it's time to lay back and treat yourself to some sun and outdoor fun.

The most popular event for women—a sort of informal Lesbian Festival, attracting thousands of lesbians from all over the western United States—is the **Nabisco Dinah Shore Golf Tournament** (call 619-324-4546 for details) in late March. The local lesbian and gay paper, **The Bottom Line**, and L.A.'s **Lesbian News**, publish special editions in March just to keep up with all the parties, contests and jubilation.

BARS

Backstreet Pub 72-695 Hwy. 111 #A-7, Palm Desert • 341-7966 • 2pm-2am • lesbians/gay men • neighborhood bar • wheelchair access • women-owned/run

Choices 68-352 Perez Rd., Cathedral City • 321-1145 • 7pm-2am • dancing/DJ • live shows • videos • patio • wheelchair access

Delilah's 68-657 Hwy. 111, Cathedral City • 324-3268 • 5pm-2am, clsd Mon-Tue • mostly women • dancing/DJ • live shows • country/western & karaoke Sun

Iron Horse Saloon 36-650 Sun Air Plaza, Cathedral City • 770-7007 • 4pm-2am • lesbians/gay men • country/western • patio

Richard's 68-599 E. Palm Canyon Dr., Cathedral City • 321-2841 • 10am-2am • lesbians/gay men • piano bar • also a restaurant • lunch & dinner • $8-29 • wheelchair access

Streetbar 224 E. Arenas • 320-1266 • 2pm-2am • lesbians/gay men • popular • neighborhood bar • live shows • wheelchair access

Two Gloria's 2400 N. Palm Canyon Dr. • 322-3224 • 4pm-2am • mostly gay men • piano bar • also a restaurant (lesbians/gay men) • wheelchair access • women-owned/run

RESTAURANTS & CAFES

Bangkok 5 69-930 Hwy. 111, Rancho Mirage • 770-9508 • lunch & dinner, seasonal • Thai • $8-15

Billy Reed's 1800 N. Palm Canyon Rd. • 325-1946 • some veggie • full bar • also bakery • $7-13

Bistro 111 70-065 Hwy. 111, Rancho Mirage • 328-5650 • clsd Sun-Tue, seasonal • some veggie

Palm Springs (619)

(As of March, 1997, the area code for Palm Springs will be 760.)

WHERE THE GIRLS ARE: Socializing with friends at private parties—you can meet them by getting in touch with a women's social organization like the SCWU Desert Women. Vacationers will be staying on E. Palm Canyon near Sunrise Way. Women do hang out at the boys' bars too; try the popular disco Choices, the bar at The Desert Palms Inn, or just about anywhere on Perez Rd.

LESBIGAY PRIDE: November: 322-8769.

ANNUAL EVENTS: March 27-30, 1997 - Nabisco Dinah Shore Golf Tournament: 324-4546, one of the biggest gatherings of lesbians on the continent. Lesbo Expo: 363-7565. April, White Party: (310) 659-3555/(213) 874-4007, buffed, tan & beautiful party circuit gay boys.

CITY INFO: Palm Springs Visitors Bureau: 778-8418.

ATTRACTIONS: Palm Springs Aerial Tramway to the top of Mt. San Jacinto, on Tramway Rd.

BEST VIEW: Top of Mount San Jacinto. Driving through the surrounding desert, you can see great views of the mountains. But be careful in the summer. Always carry water in your vehicle, be sure to check all fluids in your car before you leave and frequently during your trip.

TRANSIT: Airport Taxi: 321-4470. Desert City Shuttle: 329-3334. Sun Line Transit Agency: 343-3451.

Donatello Ristorante Italiano 196 S. Indian Canyon • 778-5200 • dinner • Italian • beer/wine • some veggie • $9-17

El Gallito Mexican Restaurant 68820 Grove St., Cathedral City • 328-7794 • Mexican • beer/wine • $3-8

Elan Brasserie 415 N. Palm Canyon Dr. • 323-5554 • lunch & dinner • Provençal/Mediterranean • full bar • live shows

Maria's Italian Cuisine 67-778 Hwy. 111, Cathedral City • 328-4378 • 5:30pm-9:30pm dinner only, clsd Mon • Italian • plenty veggie • beer/wine • $8-15

Mortimer's 2095 N. Indian Canyon • 320-4333 • lunch & dinner • California/French • full bar • live shows • $15-30

Rainbow Cactus Cafe 212 S. Indian Canyon • 325-3868 • 11am-2am • Mexican • full bar

Red Tomato 68-784 Grove St. at Hwy. 111, Cathedral City • 328-7518 • pizza & pasta • beer/wine • plenty veggie • wheelchair access • $45

Robí 78-085 Avenida La Fonda, La Quinta • 564-0544 • dinner only, clsd Mon (seasonal April-Oct) • cont'l • some veggie • wheelchair access • $45

Shame on the Moon 69-950 Frank Sinatra Dr., Rancho Mirage • 324-5515 • 6pm-10:30pm, clsd Mon (summer only) • cont'l • plenty veggie • full bar • patio • wheelchair access • $10-20

Silas' on Palm Canyon 664 N. Palm Canyon Dr. • 325-4776 • clsd Sun • intimate dining • cont'l • full bar • patio • $11-19

The Wilde Goose 67-938 Hwy. 111, Cathedral City • 328-5775 • from 5:30pm • cont'l/wild game • plenty veggie • full bar • live shows • $20-40

GYMS & HEALTH CLUBS

Gold's Gym 40-70 Airport Center Dr. • 322-4653 • 6am-10pm, 8am-8pm Sat, 9am-5pm Sun • gay-friendly

Palm Springs Athletic Club 543 S. Palm Canyon • 323-7722 • 6am-11pm, til midnight Fri-Sat, til 9pm Sun • gay-friendly

BOOKSTORES & RETAIL SHOPS

Between the Pages 214 E. Arenas Rd., Cathedral City • 320-7158 • 11am-9pm • lesbigay • also espresso bar

Bloomsbury Books 555 S. Sunrise Way • 325-3862 • 11am-9pm, clsd Sun • lesbigay • gay-owned/run

Moonlighting 307 E. Arena • 323-8830 • 6pm-2am, til 6am Th-Sun

TRAVEL & TOUR OPERATORS

Journey's Travel 42462 Bob Hope Dr. at Hwy. 111, Rancho Mirage • 340-4545/(800) 733-3646

Las Palmas Travel 403 N. Palm Canyon Dr. • 325-6311/(800) 776-6888 • IGTA

Rancho Mirage Travel 71-428 Hwy. 111, Rancho Mirage • 341-7888/(800) 369-1073 • IGTA

SPIRITUAL GROUPS

Christ Chapel of the Desert 4707 E. Sunny Dunes • 327-2795 • 10am Sun

Integrity of the Desert 125 W. El Alameda • 322-2150 • 4th Fri, call for location • lesbigay Episcopalians

Unity Church of Palm Springs 815 S. Camino Real • 11am Sun, 7:30pm Tue • also bookstore & classes

PUBLICATIONS

The Bottom Line 1243 N. Gene Autry Tr. Ste. 121-122, 92262 • 323-0552

Directory-Palm Springs 4102 E. 7th St. #621, Long Beach, 90804 • (310) 434-7129 • annual directory of gay & gay-supportive businesses

Hijinx 15-685 Palm Dr. #36, Desert Hot Springs • 329-2421 • free lesbigay guide to Palm Springs & desert resorts

Lifestyle Magazine PO Box 2803, Rancho Mirage, 92270 • 321-2685

EROTICA

Black Moon Leather 68-449 Perez Rd. #7, Cathedral City • 770-2925/(800) 945-3284 • 3pm-midnight, til 2am wknds

Palmdale   (805)

EROTICA

Sunshine Gifts 38519 Sierra Hwy. • 265-0652 • 24hrs

Palo Alto   (415)

INFO LINES & SERVICES

Palo Alto Lesbian Rap 4161 Alma (YMCA) • 583-1649 • 7:30pm Th

Peninsula Women's Group (at Two Sisters Bookstore), Menlo Park • 7:30pm Wed

BOOKSTORES & RETAIL SHOPS

Books Inc. 157 Stanford Shopping Center • 321-0600 • 9:30am-9pm, 10am-8pm Sat, til 6pm Sun • general w/ lesbigay section

Stacey's Bookstore 219 University Ave. • 326-0681 • 9am-9pm, til 10pm Fri-Sat, 11am-6pm Sun • general w/ lesbigay section

▲ Two Sisters 605 Cambridge Ave., Menlo Park • 323-4778 • 11am-9pm, 10am-5pm Sat, from noon Sun, clsd Mon • women's • wheelchair access • women-owned/run

Pasadena (818)

INFO LINES & SERVICES
Hugo Au Go-Go's Video Lending Library 126 W. Del Mar Blvd. • (800) 543-8272 • free video lending library for people w/ HIV/AIDS

BARS
Boulevard 3199 E. Foothill Blvd. • 356-9304 • 1pm-2am • mostly gay men • neighborhood bar • piano bar Sun

Club Three-Seven-Seven-Two 3772 E. Foothill Blvd. • 578-9359 • 4pm-2am, from noon Fri, clsd Sun-Mon • mostly women • dancing/DJ • live bands Fri-Sat • country/western dance lessons Tue • wheelchair access

Encounters 203 N. Sierra Madre Blvd. • 792-3735 • 2pm-2am • mostly gay men • dancing/DJ

Nardi's 665 E. Colorado Blvd. • 449-3152 • 1pm-2am • mostly gay men • neighborhood bar • wheelchair access

RESTAURANTS & CAFES
La Risata 60 N. Raymond (at Union) • 793-9000 • lunch & dinner • Northern Italian • patio • wheelchair access • $10-25

Little Richy's 39 S. Fair Oaks Ave. • 440-0306 • 11am-10pm, clsd Mon • Latin American • some veggie • wheelchair access • $7-14

BOOKSTORES & RETAIL SHOPS
Page One Books 1200 E. Walnut • 796-8418 • 11am-6:30pm, noon-5pm Sun, clsd Mon • women's • wheelchair access • women-owned/run

SPIRITUAL GROUPS
First Congregational United Church of Christ 464 E. Walnut • 795-0696 • 10am Sun

Pescadero (415)

ACCOMMODATIONS
Oceanview Farms PO Box 538, 94060 • 879-0698/(800) 642-9438 • lesbians/gay men • on working horse breeding farm • full brkfst • nudity • smokefree • $75

Petaluma (707)

TRAVEL & TOUR OPERATORS

Sunquest Travel Co. 789 Hudis St., Rohnert Park • 588-8747 • also business language school

Pismo Beach (805)

ACCOMMODATIONS

The Palomar Inn 1601 Shell Beach Rd., Shell Beach • 773-4207 • lesbian/gay men • close to nude beach • gay-owned/run

Placerville (209)

ACCOMMODATIONS

Rancho Cicada Retreat PO Box 225, Plymouth, 95669 • 245-4841 • lesbians/gay men • secluded riverside retreat in the Sierra foothills w/ two-person tents & cabin • swimming • nudity • $100-200, lower during wk

Pleasant Hill (510)

EROTICA

Pleasant Hill Books 2298 Monument Blvd. • 676-2962

Pomona (909)

INFO LINES & SERVICES

Gay/Lesbian Community Center Hotline 884-5447 • 6:30pm-10pm

BARS

Alibi East 225 E. San Antonio Ave. • 623-9422 • 10am-2am, til 4am Fri-Sat • mostly gay men • dancing/DJ • live shows Wed

BVD's/Dynasty Club 732 W. Holt Ave. • 622-7502/622-1403 • 2pm-2am • mostly gay men • dancing/DJ • piano bar • call for events

Mary's 1047 E. 2nd St. • 622-1971 • 2pm-2am • lesbians/gay men • dancing/DJ • also a restaurant • wheelchair access

Robbie's 390 E. 2nd St. (at College Plaza) • 620-4371 • 6pm-2am, clsd Tue-Wed • lesbians/gay men • ladies night Th • dancing/DJ • live shows • call for events

RESTAURANTS & CAFES

Haven Coffeehouse & Gallery 296 W. 2nd St. • 623-0538 • 11am-11pm • sandwiches & salads • live shows

EROTICA

Mustang Books 961 N. Central, Upland • 981-0227

Redding (916)

BARS

Club 501 1244 California St. (enter rear) • 243-7869 • 6pm-2am, from 4pm Sun • lesbians/gay men • dancing/DJ • food served

Redondo Beach (310)

INFO LINES & SERVICES

South Bay Lesbian/Gay Community Organization PO Box 2777, 90278 • (310) 379-2850 • support/education for Manhattan, Hermosa & Redondo Beaches, Torrance, Palos Verdes, El Segundo

BARS

Dolphin 1995 Artesia Blvd. • 318-3339 • 1pm-2am • mostly gay men • neighborhood bar • wheelchair access

Redwood City (415)

BARS

Shouts 2034 Broadway • 369-9651 • 11am-2am • lesbians/gay men • neighborhood bar • dancing/DJ • wheelchair access

SPIRITUAL GROUPS

MCC of the Peninsula 2124 Brewster Ave. (Unitarian Church) • 368-0188 • 5pm Sun

Riverside (909)

(See also **San Bernardino**)

BARS

Menagerie 3581 University Ave. • 788-8000 • 4pm-2am • mostly gay men • women's night Mon • dancing/DJ • wheelchair access • women-owned/run

VIP Club 3673 Merrill Ave. • 784-2370 • 4pm-2am, til 3am Fri-Sat • lesbians/gay men • dancing/DJ • food served • wheelchair access

SPIRITUAL GROUPS

St. Bride's PO Box 1132, 92501 • 369-0992 • 11am Sun • Celtic Catholic service

Russian River (707)

INFO LINES & SERVICES

Country Inns of the Russian River PO Box 2416, Guerneville, 95446 • (800) 927-4667 • info & referrals for 6 inns

GLBA (Gay/Lesbian Business Association) 869-9000

Russian River Tourist Bureau (800) 253-8800 • info

Fern Falls

Romance & Redwoods
A spirtual habitat
in a hillside canyon,

with natural waterfall,
swimming hole,
creeks,
gardens,
gazebo,
jacuzzi....

private cabins:
w/fireplaces
elegant furn.
kitchens
decks
pets ok.

Close to Guerneville,
Coast & Russian River
Darrel / Peter PO 228
Cazadero Ca. 95421
PH:　707/ 632- 6108
FAX: 707/ 632- 6216

ACCOMMODATIONS

Applewood- An Estate Inn 13555 Hwy. 116, Guerneville • 869-9093 • gay-friendly • 21+ • full brkfst • swimming • smokefree • food served • wheelchair access • $125-250

Avalon 4th & Mill St., Guerneville • 869-9566 • gay-friendly • swimming

The Chalet 864-4061 • rental home on 1/4 acre sleeps 6 • 4 min. to downtown Guerneville

Faerie Ring Campground 16747 Armstrong Woods Rd., Guerneville • 869-2746/869-4122 • gay-friendly • on 14 acres • RV spaces • near outdoor recreation • pets ok • $20-25

▲ **Fern Falls** PO Box 228, Cazadero, 95421 • 632-6108 • lesbians/gay men • main house w/deck overlooking creek • also cabin • hot tub • waterfall • smokefree • kids ok by arr. • pets ok • $85-135

Fern Grove Inn 16650 River Rd., Guerneville • 869-9083/(800) 347-9083 • gay-friendly • California craftsman cottages circa 1926 • swimming • kids ok • $79-199

Fife's Resort PO Box 45, Guerneville, 95446 • 869-0656/(800) 734-3371 • lesbians/gay men • cabins • campsites • also a restaurant • some veggie • full bar • $10-20 • IGTA • $50-215

Golden Apple Ranch 17575 Fitzpatrick Ln., Occidental • 874-3756 • gay-friendly • wheelchair access

▲ **Highland Dell Inn** 21050 River Blvd., Monte Rio • 865-1759/(800) 767-1759 • gay-friendly • serene retreat on the river • full brkfst • swimming • wheelchair access • $85-250

▲ **Highlands Resort** 14000 Woodland Dr., Guerneville • 869-0333 • lesbians/gay men • country retreat on 4 wooded acres • hot tub • swimming • nudity • pets ok • $45-105

House of a Thousand Flowers 11 Mosswood Cir., Cazadero • 632-5571 • gay-friendly • country B&B overlooking the Russian River • full brkfst • kids ok • pets ok by arr. • $80-85

Huckleberry Springs Country Inn 8105 Old Beedle, Monte Rio • 865-2683/(800) 822-2683 • gay-friendly • private cottages • swimming • Japanese spa • massage cottage • smokefree • dinner served • $25 • IGTA • women-owned/run • $145

Jacques' Cottage at Russian River 6471 Old Trenton Rd., Guerneville • 575-1033 • lesbians/gay men • hot tub • swimming • nudity • pets ok

Mountain Lodge 16350 First St., Guerneville • 869-3722 • lesbians/gay men • condo-style 1-bdrm apartments on the river • hot tub • swimming • kids ok • wheelchair access • $50-125

Paradise Cove Resort 14711 Armstrong Woods Rd., Guerneville • 869-2706 • lesbians/gay men • studio units • hot tub • fireplaces • decks

Redwood Grove RV Park & Campground 16140 Neely Rd., Guerneville • 869-3670 • gay-friendly

Rio Villa Beach Resort 20292 Hwy. 116, Monte Rio • 865-1143 • gay-friendly • on the river • cabins • kids ok • $68-150

Riverbend Campground & RV Park 11820 River Rd., Forestville • 887-7662 • gay-friendly • kids ok • wheelchair access

Russian River Resort/Triple 'R' Resort 16390 4th St., Guerneville • 869-0691/(800) 417-3767 • lesbians/gay men • hot tub • swimming • also a restaurant • some veggie • full bar • $5-10 • wheelchair access • $40-90

Schoolhouse Canyon Park 12600 River Rd. • 869-2311 • gay-friendly • campsites • RV • private beach • kids/pets ok

Villa Messina 316 Burgundy Rd., Healdsburg • 433-6655 • lesbians/gay men • in-room hot tubs • full brkfst • $115-225

Wildwood Resort Retreat Old Cazadero Rd., Guerneville • 632-5321 • gay-friendly • facilities are for groups of 20 or more • swimming • smokefree • kids ok • wheelchair access

The Willows 15905 River Rd., Guerneville • 869-2824/(800) 953-2828 • lesbians/gay men • old-fashioned country lodge & campgound • smokefree • $49-119

Russian River (707)

WHERE THE GIRLS ARE: Guerneville is a small town, so you won't miss the scantily-clad, vacationing women walking toward the bars downtown or the beach.

ANNUAL EVENTS: May & Sept- Women's Weekend: 869-9000 ext. 8, ext. 3.

CITY INFO: Russian River Visitors Info: (800) 253-8800.

ATTRACTIONS: Armstrong Redwood State Park. Bodega Bay. Mudbaths of Calistoga.

Wineries of Napa and Sonoma counties.

BEST VIEW: Anywhere in Armstrong Woods, the Napa Wine Country and on the ride along the coast on Highway 101.

WEATHER: Summer days are sunny and warm (80°s - 90°s) but usually begin with a dense fog. Winter days have the same pattern but are a lot cooler. Winter nights can be very damp and chilly (low 40°s).

TRANSIT: Bill's Taxi Service: 869-2177

Russian River

*T*he Russian River resort area is nestled in the redwood forests of northern California, an hour and a half north of the San Francisco Bay Area. The warm summer days and cool starlit nights have made it a favorite secret getaway for many of San Francisco's lesbians and gays—especially when they can't stand another foggy, cold day in the City.

Life at 'the River' is laid back. You can take a canoe ride, hike under the redwoods, or just lie on the river bank and soak up the sun. There's plenty of camping and RV parking, including the lesbian/gay **Redwood Grove**, **The Willows** (camping) and **Fifes' Resort** (camping & RV). Country/western lovers have **Fife's Resort** on Fridays and Saturdays, and **Molly's Country Club** all week.

If you're in the mood for other soothing and sensual delights, you're in luck. 'The River' is in the heart of the famous California Wine Country. Plan a tour to the many wineries—don't forget to designate a sober driver, so you can taste the world-class wines as you go. Or see some of the world's most beautiful coastline as you cruise the car along the Pacific Coast Highway—only fifteen minutes away!

'The River' becomes a lesbian garden of earthly delights several times a year. **Women's Weekend** happens in May and late September, with shuttles taking women from resort to resort as they enjoy the many entertainers, dances, barbecues, etc.

The Woods Resort 16881 Armstrong Woods Rd., Guerneville • 869-0111/(800) 479-6637 • lesbians/gay men • cabin • swimming • nudity • cafe • full bar • $50-110

BARS

Molly's Country Club 14120 Old Cazadero Rd., Guerneville • 869-0511 • 4pm-2am, from noon wknds, til midnight Sun-Th • lesbians/gay men • dancing/DJ • country/western • food served

Mr. T's Bullpen 16246 1st St., Guerneville • 869-3377 • mostly gay men • neighborhood bar

Rainbow Cattle Co. 16220 River Rd., Guerneville • 869-0206 • 6am-2am • mostly gay men • neighborhood bar

RESTAURANTS & CAFES

Big Bertha's Burgers 16357 Main St., Guerneville • 869-2239 • 11am-8pm • beer/wine

Breeze-Inn Barb-Q 15640 River Rd., Guerneville • 869-9208/869-9209 • popular • take-out & delivery • some veggie • women-owned/run • $5-10

Burdon's 15405 River Rd., Guerneville • 869-2615 • call for hours • lesbians/gay men • cont'l/pasta • plenty veggie • wheelchair access • $10-15

Coffee Bazaar 14045 Armstrong Woods Rd., Guerneville • 869-9706 • 7am-8pm • cafe • soups/salads/pastries

Flavors Unlimited 16450 Main St. (River Rd.), Guerneville • 869-0425 • hours vary • custom-blended ice cream • women-owned/run

Hiding Place 9605 Old River Rd., Forestville • 887-9506 • 8am-9pm • home-cooking • some veggie • $5-12

International Cafe 10940 River Rd., Forestville • 887-4644 • 6am-8pm, 8am-10pm wknds • cybercafe • wheelchair access

Lalita's 16225 Main St., Guerneville • 869-3238 • 11am-midnight • mostly women • Mexican • some veggie • full bar • live shows • $5-9

Mill St. Grill (at Triple 'R' Resort), Guerneville • 869-0691 • lesbians/gay men • some veggie • full bar • patio • wheelchair access • $5-10

River Inn Restaurant 16141 Main St., Guerneville • 869-0481 • seasonal • local favorite • wheelchair access • $10-15

Sweet's River Grill 16251 Main St., Guerneville • 869-3383 • noon-9pm • popular • beer/wine

BOOKSTORES & RETAIL SHOPS

Up the River 16212 Main St., Guerneville • 869-3167 • cards • gifts • T-shirts

SPIRITUAL GROUPS

MCC of the Redwood Empire 14520 Armstrong Woods Rd. (Guerneville Community Church), Guerneville • 869-0552 • noon Sun

Sacramento (916)

INFO LINES & SERVICES

Lambda Community Center 1931 'L' St. • 442-0185/442-7960 • 10am-7pm • youth groups & more

Northall Gay AA 2015 'J' St. #32 • 454-1100 • 8pm Wed

Sacramento Area Career Women's Network 3031 'F' St. #201 • 451-8034 • networking • monthly socials • newsletter

Sacramento Women's Center 1924 'T' St. • 736-6942 • 9am-5pm • employment services & resources

ACCOMMODATIONS

Hartley House B&B Inn 700 22nd St. • 447-7829/(800) 831-5806 • gay-friendly • full brkfst • smokefree • older kids ok • turn-of-the-century mansion • conference facilities • $85-145

BARS

Buffalo Club 1831 'S' St. • 442-1087 • 3pm-2am • mostly women • dancing/DJ • also dinner nightly • some veggie • wheelchair access • women-owned/run • $5-10

Faces 2000 'K' St. • 448-7798 • 5pm-2am, from 1pm wknds • mostly gay men • dancing/DJ • country/western • videos • live bands • wheelchair access

Joseph's Town & Country Bar 3514 Marconi • 483-1220 • 4pm-2am • lesbians/gay men • dancing/DJ • live shows • also a restaurant • Italian • some veggie • $7-12

Mirage 601 15th St. • 444-3238 • 6pm-2am • lesbians/gay men • neighborhood bar • wheelchair access • women-owned/run

The Townhouse 1517 21st St. • 441-5122 • 3pm-2am, from 10am wknds • also dinner Fri-Sat, Sun brunch • mostly gay men • neighborhood bar • wheelchair access

RESTAURANTS & CAFES

Cafe Lambda (at the Lambda Center) • 442-0185 • 8pm-midnight Fri • lesbians/gay men • live shows

Constant Cravings 6494 Broadway • 457-2233 • 6am-8pm, clsd Sun

Ernesto's 1901 16th St. • 441-5850 • 11am-10pm, from 9am wknds • Mexican • full bar

Hamburger Mary's 1630 'J' St. • 441-4340

Rick's Dessert Diner 2322 'K' St. • 444-0969 • 10am-11pm Sun-Mon, til midnight Tue-Th, til 1am Fri-Sat • coffee & dessert

GYMS & HEALTH CLUBS

Valentis 921 11th St. • 863-9629 • gay-friendly • swimming • also juice bar

BOOKSTORES & RETAIL SHOPS

Films for Days 2300 '0' St. • 448-3456 • noon-10pm, til 11pm Fri-Sun • lesbigay titles

Lioness Book Store 2224 'J' St. • 442-4657 • 11am-7pm, noon-6pm Sat, til 5pm Sun • women's • wheelchair access • women-owned/run

The Open Book 910 21st St. • 498-1004 • 9am-midnight • lesbigay bookstore & coffeehouse

TRAVEL & TOUR OPERATORS

Aladdin Travel 818 'K' St. Mall • 446-0633/(800) 655-0633 (in CA) • IGTA

Mad About Travel 930 Bell Ave. • 567-1958/(800) 856-0441

Sports Leisure Travel 9527-A Folsom Blvd. • 361-2051/(800) 951-5556 • IGTA

SPIRITUAL GROUPS

Integrity Northern California 2620 Capital Ave. • 394-1715 • lesbigay Episcopalians • group meets at Trinity Cathedral

PUBLICATIONS

MGW (Mom Guess What) 1725 'L' St. • 441-6397 • bi-monthly • women-owned/run

Outword 709 28th St. • 329-9280 • monthly

EROTICA

Adult Discount Center 1800 Del Paso Blvd. • 920-8659

Goldies I 201 N. 12th St. • 447-5860 • 24hrs • also 2138 Del Paso Blvd. location • 922-0103

L'Amour Shoppe 2531 Broadway • 736-3467

Salinas (408)

EROTICA

L'Amour Shoppe 325 E. Alisal St. • 758-9600

San Bernardino (909)

(See also **Riverside**)

INFO LINES & SERVICES

AA Gay/Lesbian 825-4700 • numerous mtgs for Inland Empire • call for times

Gay/Lesbian Community Center 1580 N. 'D' St. Ste. 7 • 884-5447 • 6:30pm-10pm • raps • counseling • library

Great Outdoors Inland Empire Chapter PO Box 56586, 92517 • 627-3442 • outdoor social group • 3rd Th

Inland Empire Couples PO Box 3023, Rancho Cucamonga, 91729 • 864-7883 • call for mtg. times & location

Project Teen 335-2005 • 7:30pm Tue • support group for lesbigay teens

RESTAURANTS & CAFES

Green Carnation Coffeehouse 1580 N. 'D' St. Ste. 7 • 384-1940 • 7pm-midnight, clsd Sun • lesbians/gay men

SPIRITUAL GROUPS

St. Aelred's Parish 1580 N. 'D' St. Ste. 5 • 384-1940 • 11am Sun, 7pm Wed

EROTICA

Bearfacts Book Store 1434 E. Baseline • 885-9176 • 24hrs

San Diego (619)

INFO LINES & SERVICES

AA Gay/Lesbian 1730 Monroe St. • 298-8008 • 10:30am-10pm • 'Live & Let Live Alano' • also contact for 'Sober Sisters'

Center for Community Solutions 2467 'E' St. • 233-8984/272-1767 • 24hrs • crisis & workshop center • counseling • shelter

Gay/Lesbian Association of North County PO Box 2866, Vista, 92085 • 945-2478 • social/support group

Gay/Lesbian Info Line 294-4636 • 24hrs

Lesbian/Gay Men's Community Center 3916 Normal St. • 692-4297 • 9am-10pm • resource information line

Lesbians in North County 744-0780 • Fri night • social group

SAGE of California 282-1395 • seniors' social group • 1st Wed

San Diego

*S*an Diego is a west coast paradise. This city sprawls from the bays and beaches of the Pacific to the foothills of the desert mountains. The days are always warm and the nights can be refreshingly cool. There are even palm trees and, better yet, lesbians. Lots of them!

If there is a drawback with San Diego, it's that the overall social and political climate has been chilled by the constant conservative cold front blowing out of Orange County. But, if you're a lesbian traveller 'just passing through,' you'll find San Diego to be near-perfect.

Stay at one of the city's quaint lesbian-friendly inns. During the days, follow the tourist circuit which includes the world-famous San Diego Zoo and Sea World. Call the Visitor's Center for a brochure on all the sites.

Once the sun sets, you're ready to tour the lesbian circuit. Where to begin? Check out **Club Bombay** and **The Flame**, San Diego's two lesbian dance bars. If you're a country/western gal, **Kicker's** is a popular place to two-step. In the mood for theater? Look up Labris Productions (297-0220 8am-5pm), the city's own lesbian theater group, or check out Diversionary Theatre (574-1060) for gay & lesbian theater.

If you'll be in town in early December, don't miss the annual **Lesbian Community Cultural Arts** fest, with multicultural performances, workshops, and more. Call 281-0406 or 464-3831 for info. In mid-August, there's the Hillcrest Street Fair, popular with the many lesbian and gay residents of Hillcrest. If you're staying in North County, try the **Lesbians in North County** for casual fun.

When you're feeling adventurous, cruise by the **Crypt** for some sex toys or a piercing, and pick up your safer sex supplies at **Condoms Plus**. If you just want to network, stop in at the **Community Center** or pick up one of the lesbigay papers to find out all the latest information about San Diego's lesbian community.

Womancare Clinic 2850 6th Ave. Ste. 311 • 298-9352 • 8:30am-5pm • feminist healthcare clinic • also mental health referrals

ACCOMMODATIONS

Balboa Park Inn 3402 Park Blvd. • 298-0823/(800) 938-8181 • gay-friendly • charming guest house in the heart of San Diego • wheelchair access • IGTA • $80-190

Banker's Hill B&B 3315 2nd Ave. • 260-0673/(800) 338-3748 • gay-friendly • $85-125

The Beach Place 2158 Sunset Cliffs Blvd. • 225-0746 • lesbians/gay men • hot tub • nudity • kids ok • pets by arr. • 4 blks from beach • $50-60 (nightly); $300-350 (weekly)

The Blom House B&B 1372 Minden Dr. • 467-0890 • gay-friendly • charming 1948 cottage style home w/ a magnificent view • smokefree • $55-85

Carole's B&B Inn 3227 Grim Ave. • 280-5258 • gay-friendly • full brkfst • swimming • smokefree • kids ok • comfy early California bungalow • $65-85

Clarke's Flamingo Lodge 1765 Union • 234-6787

Dmitri's B&B 931 21st St. • 238-5547 • lesbians/gay men • swimming • hot tub • smokefree • overlooks downtown • wheelchair access • $45-75

Embassy Hotel 3645 Park Blvd. • 269-3141

Friendship Hotel 3942 8th Ave. • 298-9898 • gay-friendly • kids/pets ok • $18-27

Heritage Park B&B 2470 Heritage Park Row • 239-4738 • gay-friendly • full brkfst • smokefree • kids ok • wheelchair access

Hill House B&B 2504 'A' St. • 239-4738

▲ **Hillcrest Inn Hotel** 3754 5th Ave. • 293-7078/(800) 258-2280 • lesbians/gay men • int'l hotel in the heart of Hillcrest • wheelchair access • IGTA • $49-55

Kasa Korbett 1526 Van Buren Ave. • 291-3962 • lesbians/gay men • comfortable craftsman-designed B&B in Hillcrest • wheelchair access • spa • smokefree • kids ok

Keating House 2331 2nd Ave. • 239-8585/(800) 995-8644 • gay-friendly • graceful 150-yr-old Victorian on Bankers Hill • full brkfst • smokefree • kids ok • $60-85

Park Manor Suites 525 Spruce St. • 291-0999/(800) 874-2649 • gay-friendly • 1926 hotel • kids/pets ok • $69-169

San Diego   (619)

WHERE THE GIRLS ARE: Lesbians tend to live near Normal Heights, in the northwest part of the city. But for partying, women go to the bars near I-5, or to Hillcrest to hang out with the boys.

ENTERTAINMENT: Diversionary Theatre. 574-1060. gay & lesbian theater. Labrys Productions, lesbian theater company. 297-0220 (M-F, 8am-5pm). Aztec Bowl, 4356 30th St., North Park, 283-3135.

LESBIGAY PRIDE: July: 297-7683.

CITY INFO: San Diego Visitors Bureau: 232-3101

ATTRACTIONS: Balboa Park. Cabrillo National Monument. La Jolla. Sea World. Torrey Pines State Park.

BEST VIEW: Cabrillo National Monument on Point Loma or from a harbor cruise.

TRANSIT: Yellow Cab: 234-6161. Radio Cab: 232-6566. Cloud Nine Shuttle: (800) 974-8885. Super Shuttle: 278-8877. San Diego Transit System: 233-3004. San Diego Trolley (through downtown or to Tijuana).

Quince St. Trolley B&B PO Box 7654, 92167 • 226-8454

Travelodge 2223 El Cajon Blvd. • 296-2101 • gay-friendly • swimming • kids ok • also a restaurant • wheelchair access

Welcome Inn 1550 E. Washington St. • 298-8251 • gay-friendly • kids ok • wheelchair access • $30-50

BARS

Club Bombay 3175 India St. (enter from Spruce St.) • 296-6789 • 4pm-2am, from 2pm wknds • Sun BBQ • popular • mostly women • dancing/DJ • live shows • patio • wheelchair access • women-owned/run

Club Montage 2028 Hancock St. • 294-9590 • 8pm-2am Wed, Fri-Sat • mostly gay men • dancing/DJ • patio • wheelchair access

David's Place 3766 5th Ave. • 294-8908 • 7am-midnight, til 3am wknds • lesbians/gay men • non-profit coffeehouse for positive people & their friends • live shows • wheelchair access

Eagle 3040 North Park Wy. • 295-8072 • 4pm-2am • mostly gay men • leather • wheelchair access

The Flame 3780 Park Blvd. • 295-4163 • 5pm-2am, from 4pm Fri • popular • mostly women • dancing/DJ • women-owned/run

Kickers 308 University Ave. • 491-0400 • 7pm-2am • mostly gay men • dancing/DJ • country/western • wheelchair access

The No. 1 Fifth Ave. (no sign) 3845 5th Ave. • 299-1911 • noon-2am • mostly gay men • professional • videos • patio

North Park Country Club 4046 30th St. • 563-9051 • 1pm-2am • lesbians/gay men • neighborhood bar • beer/wine • wheelchair access

Redwing Bar & Grill 4012 30th St. • 281-8700 • 10am-2am • mostly gay men • neighborhood bar • food served • wheelchair access • $5-10

RESTAURANTS & CAFES

Bayou Bar & Grill 329 Market St. • 696-8747 • lunch & dinner, Sun champagne brunch • Creole/Cajun • full bar • $12-16

Big Kitchen 3003 Grape St. • 234-5789 • 7am-2pm • some veggie • wheelchair access • women-owned/run • $5-10

Cafe Eleven 1440 University Ave. • 260-8023 • dinner, clsd Mon • country French • some veggie • wheelchair access • $15-20

Cafe Roma UCSD Price Carter #76, La Jolla • 450-2141 • 7am-midnight

California Cuisine 1027 University Ave. • 543-0790 • 11am-10pm, 5pm-10:30pm wknds, clsd Mon • French/Italian • some veggie • wheelchair access • $15-20

City Deli 535 University Ave. • 295-2747 • 7am-midnight, til 2am Fri-Sat • NY deli • plenty veggie • beer/wine • $5-10

Crest Cafe 425 Robinson • 295-2510 • 7am-midnight • some veggie • wheelchair access • $5-10

Grill 2201 & Desserts 2201 Adams Ave. • 298-8440 • 11am-10pm, from 10am Sun • bistro • plenty veggie • gay owned/run

Hamburger Mary's 308 University Ave. • 491-0400 • 11am-10pm, from 8am wknds • some veggie • full bar • wheelchair access • $5-10

Liaison 2202 4th Ave. • 234-5540 • dinner & Sun brunch • French country • wheelchair access • $18-24 (prix fixe)

Pannikin 523 University Ave. • 295-1600 • 6am-11pm, til midnight wknds • cafe

GYMS & HEALTH CLUBS

Hillcrest Gym 142 University Ave. • 299-7867 • lesbians/gay men

BOOKSTORES & RETAIL SHOPS

Auntie Helen's 4028 30th St. • 584-8438 • 10am-5pm, clsd Sun-Mon • thrift shop benefits PWAs

Blue Door Bookstore 3823 5th Ave. • 298-8610 • 9am-9pm • large lesbigay section

Eclectic Pleasures 3825 5th Ave. • 298-2260 • 11am-9:30pm, til 8pm Sun • gifts • candles • incense

Groundworks Books UCSD Student Center 0323, La Jolla • 452-9625 • 9am-7pm, 10am-6pm Fri-Sat, clsd Sun • alternative • lesbigay section • wheelchair access

Moose Leather 2923 Upas St. • 297-6935 • noon-9pm, clsd Sun-Mon

Obelisk the Bookstore 1029 University Ave. • 297-4171 • 11am-10pm, noon-8pm Sun • lesbigay • cafe • wheelchair access

TRAVEL & TOUR OPERATORS

Firstworld Travel of Mission Gorge 7443 Mission Gorge Rd. • 265-1916 • contact Dennis • IGTA

Hillcrest Travel 431 Robinson Ave. • 291-0758/(800) 748-5502 • IGTA

Midas Travel 525 University Ave. • 298-1160 • IGTA

Sports Travel International Ltd. 4869 Santa Monica Ave. Ste. B • 225-9555/(800) 466-6004 • IGTA

Undersea Expeditions PO Box 9455, Pacific Beach, 92169 • 270-2900/(800) 669-0310 • scuba trips worldwide • IGTA

SPIRITUAL GROUPS

Anchor Ministries 3441 University Ave. • 284-8654 • 10am & 6pm Sun • non-denominational

Dignity 4190 Front St. (First Unitarian Universalist Church), Hillcrest • 645-8240 • 6pm Sun

First Unitarian Universalist Church 4190 Front St. • 298-9978 • 10am (July-Aug); 9am & 11am (Sept-June)

Integrity/San Diego PO Box 34253, 92163-0801 • 236-8176 • lesbigay Episcopalians • call for mtg. times

MCC 4333 30th St. • 280-4333 • 9am & 11am Sun

Spirit Eagle MCC 2770 Glebe Rd., Lemon Grove • 447-4660 • 6pm Sun

Yachad PO Box 3457, 92163 • 492-8616 • Jewish lesbian/gay/bisexual social group

PUBLICATIONS

Gay/Lesbian Times 3636 5th Ave. Ste. 101 • 299-6397

San Diego Dyke/Dyke Review 1010 University Ave. #183, 92103

Update 2801 4th Ave. • 299-4104

EROTICA

▲ **Condoms Plus** 1220 University Ave. • 291-7400 • 11am-midnight, til 2am Fri-Sat, 1pm-9pm Sun • safer sex gifts for women & men

The Crypt 1515 Washington • 692-9499 • 11am-9:45pm, 2pm-10pm wknds • also 30th St. location • 284-4724

▲ **F St. Bookstore** 2004 University Ave. • 298-2644 • 24hrs

▲ **F St. Bookstore** 3112 Midway Dr. • 221-0075 • 24hrs

▲ **F St. Bookstore** 4626 Albuquerque • 581-0400 • 24hrs

▲ **F St. Bookstore** 751 4th Ave. • 236-0841 • 24hrs

▲ **F St. Bookstore** 7865 Balboa Ave., Kearney Mesa • 292-8083 • 24hrs

▲ **F St. Bookstore** 7998 Miramar Rd. • 549-8014 • 24hrs

SAN FRANCISCO

San Francisco is divided into 7 geographical regions:

S.F. - Overview   (415)

INFO LINES & SERVICES

18th St. Services/Operation Concern 861-4898 • 9am-7pm Mon-Fri • lesbigay AA mtgs. at 15th & Market • offices at 217 Church St.

AA Gay/Lesbian 621-1326

APSLBN (Asian Pacific Sisters Lesbian/Bisexual Network) PO Box 170596, 94117-0596 • (510) 814-2422 • social/support group for lesbian/bi women of Asian/Pacific Islander descent • special events • newsletter

BACW (Bay Area Career Women) 55 New Montgomery St. Ste. 606, 94105 • 495-5393 • 9am-5pm • lesbian professional group

The Bay Area Bisexual Resource Line 703-7977 • info & referrals

Brothers Network 973 Market St. #650 • 356-8140 • 1:30pm-3:30pm Tue • transgender support group

▲ **Dyke TV** Channel 53 • 6pm Sun • 'weekly half hour TV show produced by lesbians for lesbians'

ETVC PO Box 426486, 94142 • (510) 549-2665 • 8pm last Th • transgender group

▲ **Frameline** 346 9th St. • 703-8650/(800) 869-1996 (outside CA) • lesbigay media arts foundation • sponsors annual SF Int'l Lesbian/Gay Film Festival in June (see ad in front color section)

FTM International 5337 College Ave. #142, Oakland, 94618 • (510) 287-2646 • 2pm-5pm 2nd Sun • info & support for female-to-male transgendered people • newsletter • resource guide

Gay/Lesbian Historical Society of Northern California PO Box 424280, 94142 • 777-5455

Gay/Lesbian Sierrans 281-5666 • outdoor group

San Francisco

(415)

WHERE THE GIRLS ARE: Younger, radical dykes call the Mission or the lower Haight home, while upwardly-mobile couples stake out Bernal Heights and Noe Valley. Hip, moneyed dykes live in the Castro. The East Bay is home to lots of lesbian feminists, older lesbians and lesbian moms (see East Bay listing).

ENTERTAINMENT: Theatre Rhinoceros: 861-5079, 2926 16th St.

LESBIGAY PRIDE: June. 864-3733.

ANNUAL EVENTS: March - AIDS Dance-a-thon: 392-9255. AIDS benefit dance at the Moscone Center. April - Readers/Writers Conference: 431-0891, 3rd annual weekend of workshops at Women's Building. May - California AIDS Ride: (800) 474-3395. AIDS benefit bike ride from San Francisco to L.A. June - San Francisco Int'l Lesbian/Gay Film Festival: 703-8650. Get your tickets early for a slew of films about us. Physique'96: 978-9495, national gay/lesbian body building championships. July - Up Your Alley Fair: 861-3247. Local SM/leather street fair held in Dore Alley, South-of-Market. September - Folsom St. Fair, 861-3247. Huge SM/leather street fair, topping a week of kinky events. Mr. Drummer Contest: 252-1195. International leather title contest & vendors. Festival of Babes: (510) 452 392-9255, annual women's soccer tournament. October - Castro St. Fair: 467-3354, arts and community groups street fair.

CITY INFO: San Francisco Convention & Visitors Bureau: 391-2000.

ATTRACTIONS: Alcatraz. Chinatown. Coit Tower. Fisherman's Warf. Exploratorium. Golden Gate Park. Haight & Ashbury Sts. North Beach. Mission San Francisco de Assisi. Twin Peaks.

BEST VIEW: After a great Italian meal in North Beach, go to the top floor of the North Beach parking garage on Vallejo near Stockton, next to a police station. If you're in the Castro or the Mission, head for Dolores Park, at Dolores and 18th St. Other good views: Golden Gate Bridge, Kirby Cove (a park area to the left just past Golden Gate Bridge in Marin), Coit Tower, Twin Peaks, and anywhere along the beach at sunset.

WEATHER: A beautiful summer comes at the end of September through October. Much of the city is cold and fogged-in June through September, though the Castro and Mission are usually sunny. The cold in winter is damp, so bring lots of layers. When there isn't a drought, it also rains in the winter months of November through February.

TRANSIT: Yellow Cab: 626-2345. Luxor Cab: 282-4141. Quake City Shuttle: 255-4899. Muni: 673-6864. Bay Area Rapid Transit (BART): 673-6864, subway.

San Francisco

*S*an Francisco may be a top tourist destination because of its cable cars, beatniks, quaint beauty, and the Haight-Ashbury district, but we know what really makes it shine: its legendary population of lesbians and gays. So unless kitsch is your thing, skip Fisherman's Wharf, Pier 39, and the cable cars, and head for the Mission, the Castro, Noe Valley, or South of Market (SoMa).

Any lesbian walking along Valencia between Market St. and 24th St. will spot hot women of all sizes and colors. Valencia St. borders the gay-boy Castro area and the Mission, one of San Francisco's Latino neighborhoods. This intersection of cultures results in a truly San Franciscan mix of punk dykes, dykes of color, lesbian-feminists, working class straights and funky artists.

Your first stop in the Mission should be either punk dyke hangout **Red Dora's Bearded Lady Café & Gallery** (don't miss their gingerbread!) or the more traditional resource center **The Women's Building**. After that, rush to **Good Vibrations** women's sex toy store before they close at 7pm. Pick up a famous "San Francisco Mission-Style Burrito" (as they're advertised in New York these days) at one of the many cheap and delicious taquerias. Definitely avoid the icky, wannabehip-fratboy bars like The Elbo Room (which used to be famous women's bar Amelia's). Another must-see for lesbians along Valencia is **Osento**, the women's bathhouse. Just off Valencia on 16th is The Roxie (957-1212), a dyke-friendly repertory cinema.

For nightlife, you'll have to head to SoMa for dancing, but the Mission has lots of fun queer performance at places like **Build** and **Brava!** and **Luna Sea**—check the bi-weekly Bay Times calendar. If you're into artsy or radical video, get a calendar from Artists' Television Access (824-3890).

You'll also find lots of lesbians in nearby Noe Valley, though this area tends to be a 'couples heaven' for professional women. If that's your dream, call **Bay Area Career Women** about their upcoming social events, or drop in on their TGIF social, down-

town. And enjoy an afternoon in one or all of the many quirky shops and cafés along 24th St.

If you cruise the Castro, you'll be surprised how many sisters—ranging from executives to queer chicks—you'll see walking the streets of what was the 'Boys' Town' of the 1970s. Drop in at **A Different Light**, the lesbigay bookstore, or **The Café** for a game of pool or girl-watching from the balcony. The Castro also hosts three great 24-hour diners—**Bagdad Café, Sparky's,** and **Orphan Andy's**—as well as **Josie's Cabaret & Juice Joint**, great for vegetarian brunch, comedy and performance. For lesbian/gay-centric films, don't miss an evening at **The Castro Theater** (621-6120).

You might also want to check out the women's S/M scene in this kinky city: **Stormy Leather** is one women-owned/run fetish store. You might also want to finally get that piercing you've been thinking about at one of the queer-friendly piercing parlors—our favorite is **Body Manipulations,** right between the Mission and the Castro on 16th St. at Guerrero.

SoMa also contains lots of art, poetry and kink for the daring. For the less daring, there's the ever-popular, more mainstream **Box** on Thursday nights and **G-Spot (Girl-Spot)** on Saturday nights. For a truly hot dance party, call the **ABLUNT** hotline to find out when their latest dance for Asian, Black and Latina women (and their friends) will be. Also check the calendar of **ICON**, the city's lesbian newspaper, or **Odyssey**, the queer party paper of choice.

Finally, if you're a fan of Diane Di Prima, Anne Waldman, Allen Ginsberg, or other beatniks, **City Lights Bookstore** in North Beach is a required pilgrimage. Afterward, have a drink or an espresso at beatnik hangout **Café Vesuvius**, just across Jack Kerouac Alley from City Lights.

Sound like a lot? They don't call it Mecca for nothing.

You could still explore the many other women's events and groups throughout the rest of 'The City' and the East Bay, like the critically acclaimed **Women's Philharmonic** (543-2297).

Intersex Society PO Box 31791, 94131 • support for physically intersexed (hermaphroditic) people

Lesbian/Gay Switchboard (510) 841-6224 • 10am-10pm Mon-Fri • info • referrals • rap line

LGBA (Lesbian/Gay/Bisexual Alliance) SFSU Student Center #M-100-A, 1650 Holloway Ave., 94132 • 338-1952

LINKS PO Box 420989, 94142 • 703-7159 • S/M play parties & calendar • transgender-friendly

Lyon-Martin Women's Health Services 1748 Market St. Ste. 201 • 565-7667 • sliding scale medical services for women • also support groups & other services • transgender-friendly

LYRIC (Lavender Youth Recreation/ Information Cntr) 127 Collingwood • 703-6150/(800) 246-7743 (outside Bay Area) • support & social groups • also crisis counseling for lesbigay & transgendered youth under 24 at 863-3636 (hotline #)

San Francisco Gender Information 3637 Grand Ave. #C, Oakland, 94610 • send $3 & SASE for listings of transgender resources in northern CA

TARC Transgender Support Group 187 Golden Gate Ave. • 431-7476 • 1pm-3pm Wed & Fri

Transgender Support Groups 50 Lech Walesa (Tom Waddell Clinic) • 554-2940 • 6pm-7:30 pm Tue • support groups & counseling for MTF & FTM transsexuals • low-cost TG health clinic

ACCOMMODATIONS

American Property Exchange 170 Page St. • 863-8484/(800) 747-7784 • daily, weekly & monthly furnished rentals in San Francisco • women-owned/run

Mi Casa Su Casa (510) 268-8534/(800) 215-2272 • lesbians/gay men • int'l home exchange network

BARS

Club Q 647-8258 • women only • popular • roving dance party DJ'd by mixtress Page Hodel

Just-Us 139 8th St (CoCo Club) • 703-0862 • 1st & 3rd Wed • popular • multi-racial • roving dance parties

▲ **MT Productions** 337-4962 • women only • women's dance parties including 'Girl Spot' & 'Club Skirts' (see ad in front color section)

TRAVEL & TOUR OPERATORS

▲ **Bob Leach Auto Rental** (800) 325-1240 • see ad this section

My Favorite City 273-5812/(800) 605-1357

SPIRITUAL GROUPS

Bay Area Pagan Assemblies (408) 559-4242

Dharma Sisters 255-0798 • events & weekly meditations for lesbians & bi women interested in practicing Buddhism

Dignity/San Francisco 1329 7th Ave., 94122 • 681-2491 • 5:30pm Sun • lesbigay Roman Catholic services

Evangelicals Concerned 621-3297 • also in East Bay & San Jose • sponsors annual women's retreat

Hartford Street Zen Center 57 Hartford St. • 863-2507

Lutherans Concerned 566 Vallejo St. #25, 94133-4033 • 956-2069

Native American Two-Spirit Talking Circle 217 Church St. (18th St. Services office) • 6:30pm Wed

Oasis/California 110 Julian Ave. • 522-0222/(800) 419-0222 • lesbian/gay ministry of the Episcopal Diocese of California

Reclaiming PO Box 14404, 94110 • 929-9249 • pagan infoline & network • classes • newsletter

PUBLICATIONS

BAR (Bay Area Reporter) 395 9th St., 94103 • 861-5019

Cuir Underground 3288 21st St. #19, 94110 • 487-7622 • bi-monthly • S/M newsmagazine w/ calendar of events • e-mail: cuirpaper@aol.com

▲ **Curve (formerly Deneuve)** 2336 Market St #15, 94114 • 863-6538 • popular • lesbian magazine (see ad front color section)

Fat Girl 2215-R Market St. #197, 94114 • 552-8733 • fat dyke 'zine

FBN (Feminist Bookstore News) PO Box 882554, 94188 • 626-1556 • nat'l journal about feminist bookstores & publications

▲ **Girlfriends** 3415 Cesar Chavez Ste. 101, 94110 • 648-9464 • lesbian lifestyle magazine (see front color section)

▲ **GirlJock** PO Box 882723, 94188-2723 • 282-6833 • pan-athletic magazine for lesbians (see ad in front color section)

▲ **ICON: The Thinking Lesbian's Newspaper (formerly Dykespeak)** 4104 24th St. #181, 94114 • 282-0942

Oblivion 519 Castro St. #24 • 487-5498

Odyssey Magazine 584 Castro St. #302, 94114 • 621-6514 • all the dish on SF's club scene

San Francisco Bay Times 288 7th St., 94103 • 626-8121 • bi-weekly • popular • a 'must read' for Bay Area resources & personals

San Francisco Frontiers 2370 Market St. 2nd. flr, 94114 • 487-6000

Women's Sports Connection PO Box 31580, 94131-0580 • 241-8879 • general women's quaterly newsletter • provides game schedules & ticket info

S.F. - Castro & Noe Valley (415)

INFO LINES & SERVICES

Castro Country Club 4058 18th St. • 552-6102 • 11am-midnight, til 11am Fri-Sat, from 10am Sun • alcohol & drug-free club

Gay/Lesbian Outreach to Elders 1853 Market St. • 626-7000 • 10am-2pm

Harvey Milk Public Library 3555 16th St. • 554-9445 • call for hours

ACCOMMODATIONS

24 Henry 24 Henry St. • 864-5686/(800) 900-5686 • mostly gay men • smokefree • one-bdrm apt. also available 1 blk from guesthouse • IGTA • $55-120

▲ **Albion House Inn** 135 Gough St. • 621-0896/(800) 625-2466 • gay-friendly • smokefree • kids ok • also a restaurant • $85-195

Anna's Three Bears 114 Divisadero St. • 255-3167/(800) 428-8559 • gay-friendly • rental apt. B&B • IGTA • $225-295

Beck's Motor Lodge 2222 Market St. • 621-8212 • gay-friendly

Castro Victorian Guest House 604 Castro St. • (888) 413-4333 • gay-friendly • in the heart of the Castro

The Cumberland 255-3086/(800) 605-1357 • gay-friendly • guesthouse above the Castro • full brkfst • $100-175

Dolores Park Inn 3641 17th St. • 621-0482 • gay-friendly • historic two-story Italianate Victorian mansion • hot tub • private/shared baths • kitchens • fireplaces • smokefree • kids ok • $60-200

Ethel's Garden in the Castro 864-6171 • women only • B&B • hot tub • near everything • $40-75

▲ **House O' Chicks Guesthouse** 861-9849 • women only • $50-100

Inn on Castro 321 Castro St. • 861-0321 • lesbians/gay men • B&B known for its hospitality & friendly atmosphere • full brkfst • smokefree • $80-150

Le Grenier 347 Noe St. • 864-4748 • lesbians/gay men • suite • kitchen • $60-90

Nancy's Bed 239-5692 • women only • private home • kitchen • smokefree • kids ok

Noe's Nest B&B 3973 23rd St. • 821-0751 • gay-friendly • kitchens • fireplace • smokefree • kids ok • dogs ok (no cats) • IGTA • $75-125

▲ **Pension SF** 1668 Market St. • 864-1271 • private/shared baths • also a restaurant

Ruth's House 641-8898 • women only • shared bath • smokefree • small kids ok • lesbian owned/run • $35-45

▲ **San Francisco Cottage** 224 Douglass St. • 861-3220 • lesbians/gay men • self-catering cottage & studio apt • smokefree • $105

▲ **San Francisco Views — The Villa** 379 Collingwood St. • 282-1367/(800) 358-0123 • lesbians/gay men • swimming • kids ok • wheelchair access • $90-150

Terrace Place 584 Castro St. Ste. 112, 94114 • 241-0425 • lesbians/gay men • guest suite • $75-175

Travelodge Central 1707 Market St. • 621-6775/(800) 578-7878 • gay-friendly • non-smoking rms. avail. • $59-159

The Willows B&B Inn 710 14th St. • 431-4770 • mostly gay men • in the true European country tradition • non-smoking rms avail. • IGTA • $70-125

BARS

▲ **The Cafe** 2367 Market St. • 861-3846 • noon-2am • lesbians/gay men • dancing/DJ • deck overlooking Castro & Market Sts. • more women Fri night

Cafe du Nord 2170 Market St. • 861-5016 • 4pm-2am • gay-friendly • supper club • some veggie • theme nights • live jazz • $5-10

Castro Country Club 4058 18th St. • 552-6102 • 11am-midnight, til 11am Fri-Sat, from 10am Sun • mostly gay men • alcohol & drug-free club

Daddy's 440 Castro St. • 621-8732 • 9am-2am, from 6am wknds • popular • mostly gay men • neighborhood bar • leather • women genuinely welcome

Harvey's 500 Castro St. • 431-4278 • lesbians/gay men • neighborhood bar • live shows • also a restaurant • wheelchair access • under $10

Josie's Cabaret & Juice Joint 3583 16th St. • 861-7933 • lesbians/gay men • cabaret • live comedy • call for events • food served • healthy American • plenty veggie • $8-12

Martuni's 4 Valencia St. • 241-0205 • mostly gay men • neighborhood bar • professional • piano bar

The Metro 3600 16th St. • 703-9750 • 2:30pm-2am • mostly gay men • karaoke Tue • also a restaurant • Chinese

The Mint 1942 Market St. • 626-4726 • 11am-2am • lesbians/gay men • karaoke • videos • also a restaurant

Moby Dick's 4049 18th St. • mostly gay men • neighborhood bar • videos

Phoenix 482 Castro St. • 552-6827 • 1pm-2am • mostly gay men • dancing/DJ • some Latinas

Pilsner Inn 225 Church St. • 621-7058 • mostly gay men • 6am-2am • patio

Uncle Bert's Place 4086 18th St. • 431-8616 • 6am-2am • mostly gay men • neighborhood bar • patio

RESTAURANTS & CAFES

2223 Market 2223 Market St. • 431-0692 • popular • contemporary American • full bar • wheelchair access • $13-16

Amazing Grace 216 Church St. • 626-6411 • 11am-10pm • vegetarian • wheelchair access • $5-10

Anchor Oyster Bar 579 Castro St. • 431-3990 • lesbians/gay men • seafood • some veggie • beer/wine • women-owned/run • $10-20

Bad Man Jose's 4077 18th St. • 861-1706 • 11am-11pm • healthy Mexican • some veggie • $5-7

Bagdad Cafe 2295 Market St. • 621-4434 • 24hrs • lesbians/gay men • diner • some veggie • $5-10

▲ **Cafe Cuvee** 2073 Market St. • 621-7488 • breakfast & lunch, call for dinner hours, clsd wknds • lesbian owned/run

Cafe Flore 2298 Market St. • 621-8579 • 7:30am-11:30pm, til midnight Fri-Sat • popular • lesbians/gay men • some veggie • great patio • $5-8

Caffe Luna Piena 558 Castro St. • 621-2566 • lunch & dinner • lesbians/gay men • Californian • patio

---

China Court 599 Castro • 626-5358 • 5pm-11pm • Chinese • some veggie • beer/wine • $5-10

Chloe's Cafe 1399 Church St., Noe Valley • 648-4116 • 8am-3:30pm, til 4pm wknds • popular • come early for the excellent weekend brunch

Counter Culture 2073 Market St. • 621-7488 • gourmet take-out • some veggie • $5-10

Cove Cafe 434 Castro St. • 626-0462 • 7am-10pm • lesbians/gay men • plenty veggie • wheelchair access • $8-12

Eric's Chinese Restaurant 1500 Church St., Noe Valley • 282-0919 • 11am-9pm • popular • some veggie • $7-12

Hot 'N Hunky 4039 18th St. • 621-6365 • 11am-11pm • lesbians/gay men • hamburgers • some veggie • $5-10

It's Tops 1801 Market St. • 431-6395 • 7am-3pm, 8pm-3am • diner • $5-7

Jumpin' Java 139 Noe St. • 431-5282 • 7am-10pm

Just Desserts 248 Church St. • 626-5774 • 7am-11pm • lesbians/gay men • cafe • great patio

Little Italy 4109 24th St. • 821-1515 • dinner only • plenty veggie • beer/wine • $15-20

M&L Market (May's) 691 14th St. • 431-7044 • great huge sandwiches • some veggie

Ma Tante Sumi 4243 18th St. • 552-6663 • cont'l cuisine w/ a Japanese accent

Mecca 2029 Market St. • 621-7000 • popular • full bar • Mediterranean • $13-19 • wheelchair access

Orbit Room Cafe 1900 Market St. • 252-9525 • 7am-midnight, til 2am Fri-Sat • beer/wine • great view of Market St. & street cars

Patio Cafe 531 Castro St. • 621-4140 • lesbians/gay men • enclosed patio dining • $10-20

Pozole 2337 Market St. • 626-2666 • Mexican specialties • some veggie • beer/wine • $5-10

The Quarterdeck 718 14th St. • 431-0253 • 3pm-midnight • mostly gay men • piano bar

The Sausage Factory 517 Castro St. • 626-1250 • noon-1am • lesbians/gay men • pizza & pasta • some veggie • beer/wine • $8-15

Sparky's 242 Church St. • 626-8666 • 24hrs • diner • some veggie • $8-12

▲ **Valentine's Cafe** 1793 Church St., Noe Valley • 285-2257 • clsd Mon, call for hours • lunch, dinner, wknd brunch • plenty veggie

Welcome Home 464 Castro St. • 626-3600 • 8am-11pm • popular • lesbians/gay men • homestyle • some veggie • beer/wine • JJ's favorite • $7-12

Without Reservations 460 Castro St. • 861-9510 • 7am-2am • lesbians/gay men • diner • some veggie • wheelchair access • $7-12

Zuni Cafe 1658 Market St. • 552-2522 • clsd Mon • popular • upscale cont'l/Mediterranean • full bar • $30-40

GYMS & HEALTH CLUBS

Market Street Gym 2301 Market St. • 626-4488 • lesbians/gay men • day passes avail.

Women's Training Center 2164 Market St. • 864-6835 • popular • women only • day passes avail.

BOOKSTORES & RETAIL SHOPS

A Different Light 489 Castro St. • 431-0891 • 10am-11pm, til midnight Fri-Sat • lesbigay • bookstore & queer info clearinghouse

Books Etc. 538 Castro St. • 621-8631 • 11am-10pm, til midnight Fri-Sat

Books Inc. 2275 Market St. • 864-6777 • 10am-11pm, til 10pm Sun • wheelchair access • also located at San Francisco Int'l Airport, North Terminal • 3315 California St., 221-3666

Botanica 1478 Church St. at 27th, Noe Valley • 285-0612 • 11am-7pm • Afro-Caribbean religious articles

CD Record Rack 3897 18th St. • 552-4990 • best selection of local DJ's mixes

Does Your Mother Know? 4079 18th St. • 864-3160 • 10am-8pm • cards • T-shirts

Don't Panic 541 Castro St. • 553-8989 • 10am-10pm • T-shirts • gifts

The Gauntlet 2377 Market St. • 431-3133 • noon-7pm • piercing parlor • jewelry

Headlines 557 Castro • 626-8061 • 10am-9pm • clothes • cards • novelties

Headlines for Women 549 Castro St. • 252-1280 • 10am-9pm • clothing • jewelry

Image Leather 2199 Market St. • 621-7551 • 9am-10pm, 11am-7pm Sun • custom leather clothing • accessories • toys

Just for Fun 3982 24th St., Noe Valley • 285-4068 • 9am-9pm, til 7pm Sun • gift shop

Leather Zone 2352 Market St. • 255-8585 • 11am-7pm • new & used fetishwear

Rolo 2351 Market St. • 431-4545 • designer labels • also 450 Castro location • 626-7171

Under One Roof 2362 Market St. • 252-9430 • 11am-7pm • 100% of sales are donated for AIDS relief

TRAVEL & TOUR OPERATORS

Ascento Travel Services 864-1630 • English & Spanish

Cruisin' the Castro 550-8110 • guided walking tour of the Castro • IGTA

Now, Voyager 4406 18th St. • 626-1169/(800) 255-6951 • IGTA

Passport to Leisure 2265 Market St. • 621-8300/(800) 322-1204 (outside CA) • IGTA

Scandia Travel 76 Gough St. • 552-5300/(800) 536-4359

Victorian Home Walks 2226 15th St., 94114 • 252-9485 • custom-tailored walking tours w/ San Francisco resident • IGTA

Winship Travel 2321 Market St. • 863-2555/(800) 545-2557 • ask for Susan • IGTA

SPIRITUAL GROUPS

Congregation Sha'ar Zahav 220 Danvers St. • 861-6932 • 8:15pm Fri • lesbian/gay synagogue

MCC of San Francisco 150 Eureka St. • 863-4434 • 9am, 11am & 7pm Sun

Most Holy Redeemer Church 100 Diamond St. • 863-6259 • 7:30am & 10am Sun, 5pm Sat (vigil mass) • mostly gay/lesbian Roman Catholic parish

SEX CLUBS

Club Ecstasy 985-5252 • call for times & locations • lesbian sex club

EROTICA

Jaguar 4057 18th St. • 863-4777

Le Salon 4126 18th St. • 552-4213

The MMO (Mercury Mail Order) 4084 18th St. • 621-1188 • leather • toys

Rob Gallery 1925 Market St. • 252-1198 • 11am-7pm • leather • latex • artwork

S.F. - South of Market (415)

ACCOMMODATIONS

Victorian Hotel 54 4th St. • 986-4400/(800) 227-3804 • gay-friendly • 1913 landmark hotel • private/shared baths • also a restaurant • SF cuisine • full bar • $49-89

BARS

The Box 715 Harrison St. • 647-8258 • Th only • popular • lesbians/gay men • dancing/DJ • multi-racial

Brain Wash 1122 Folsom St. • 431-9274 • 7:30am-midnight, til 1am Fri-Sat • gay-friendly • popular • live shows • beer/wine • laundromat & cafe

C.W. Saloon 917 Folsom St. • 974-1585 • 10am-2am • gay-friendly • Wed 'Faster Pussycat' women's night

Cat's Alley Club 1190 Folsom • 431-3332 • Tue 8pm 'Women w/ Balls' stand-up comedy • Fri 'Litterbox' (back alley entrance)

Club Universe 177 Townsend • 985-5241 • 9:30pm-7am Sat • popular • lesbians/gay men • dancing/DJ • alternative

The CoCo Club 139 8th St. (entrance on Minna) • 626-2337 • mostly women • multi-racial • live shows • call for events

Diva 487-6305 • monthly • lesbian dance parties • call for events

Endup 401 6th St. • 495-9550 • mostly gay men • dancing/DJ • multi-racial • many different theme nights • esp. popular Sun mornings

Girl Spot (G-Spot) 401 6th St. • 337-4962 • 9pm Sat only • popular • mostly women • dancing/DJ • go-go dancers

Jaded 165 10th St. (at Club Rococo) • 697-0375x3 • monthly alternative club • lesbians/gay men • dancing/DJ • multi-racial • transgender-friendly

Pleasuredome 177 Townsend (at 3rd St.) • 255-6434x69 • Sun night dance club • mostly gay men • dancing/DJ • call hotline for details

Rawhide II 280 7th St. • 621-1197 • noon-2am • mostly gay men • dancing/DJ • country/western

San Francisco Eagle 398 12th St. • 626-0880 • 4pm-2am, from 2pm Sat, from noon Sun • mostly gay men • leather • occasional women's leather events • patio

The Stud 399 9th St. • 863-6623 • 5pm-2am • lesbians/gay men • dancing/DJ • theme nights • mostly men Wed

Twenty Tank Brewery 316 11th St. • 255-9455 • gay-friendly • microbrewery • food served • some veggie

San Francisco's small hotels,

UNION SQUARE . . . .

THE ANDREWS HOTEL
from $92 *"One of SF's Top Ten for value."* —NY Times •Down comforters & floral decor •FREE gourmet breakfast •Italian restaurant •Walk to Cable Cars & Chinatown
624 POST   1-800-926-3739

THE NOB HILL LAMBOURNE
from $165 *"A holistic approach to hospitality."* —USA Today   •SF's ultra-pampering spa hotel •In-room business center & kitchenettes •FREE gourmet breakfast & wine hour •Massage & Aromatherapy   725 PINE   1-800-274-8466

THE COMMODORE
from $79   This is..."where to stay in San Francisco!" —NY Times •Stylish & contemporary •Unusually spacious & comfortable rooms •Sophisticated cocktail lounge: The Red Room •Charming diner-style cafe: Titanic •Walk to Cable Cars & Chinatown
825 SUTTER   1-800-338-6848

HOTEL REX
from $125   *"New SF hotel goes big on the ambiance."* —SF Chronicle •1920's club-like atmosphere inspired by SF arts & literary spirit •Antiquarian bookstore •Restaurant & stylish lounge •Walk to Cable Cars & Chinatown
562 SUTTER   1-800-433-4434

. . . . PACIFIC HEIGHTS

THE HOLIDAY LODGE
from $99   *"A refreshing oasis edged by palm trees."* —NY Times •Secluded atmosphere •Heated pool & lush gardens •Free parking •AAA approved •Near Fisherman's Wharf & Marina
1901 VAN NESS   1-800-367-8504

most unique
inns and B&Bs.

CIVIC CENTER
. . . .& HISTORIC DISTRICT

THE ABIGAIL

from **$79**   *"Absolutely perfect for travelers who like charm, great food and international company." —Frommer's Guide*   •Antiques & down comforters •FREE continental breakfast •Vegetarian restaurant •Steps from Symphony Hall & new Main Library •Near Castro, SOMA and The Mission   246 McALLISTER   1-800-243-6510

THE PHOENIX

from **$99**   *"Ambiance is pure Fantasy Island" —People Magazine* •Tropical, fun, hip & artistic •Pool •Miss Pearl's Jam House Restaurant •Bungalow-style rooms •FREE breakfast & parking •Near Castro, SOMA and Mission   562 SUTTER   1-800-433-4434

THE ARCHBISHOP'S MANSION

from **$149**   *"Most elegant small hotel on the West Coast." —USA Today* •Historic chateau •15 romantic rooms •Jacuzzi tubs & fireplaces •FREE breakfast-in-bed & parking •Walk to Castro   1000 FULTON   1-800-543-5820

Visit all these hotels on the Internet:
www.sftrips.com   Or call JOIE DE VIVRE:
1-800-SF-TRIPS for centralized
info & reservations at all these fine hotels.

RESTAURANTS & CAFES

Bistro Roti 155 Steuart • 495-6500 • lunch & dinner • country French • full bar • $15-20

Caribbean Zone 55 Natoma St. • 541-9465 • lunch & dinner • some veggie • cocktails • festive decor • $7-15

Fringale 570 4th St. • 543-0573 • lunch & dinner • Mediterranean • wheelchair access • $11-16

Half Shell 64 Rausch Alley • 552-7677 • lunch & dinner • lesbians/gay men • seafood • some veggie • $8-15

Hamburger Mary's 1582 Folsom St. • 626-5767/626-1985 • 10am-2am, clsd Mon • some veggie • wheelchair access • $7-15

Line Up 398 7th St. • 861-2887 • 11am-10pm • lesbians/gay men • Mexican • some veggie • $8-15

Lulu 816 Folsom St. • 495-5775 • lunch & dinner • upscale Mediterrranean • some veggie • full bar • $12-20

Slow Club 2501 Mariposa • 241-9390 • 7am-2am, clsd Sun • full bar • wheelchair access

Wa-Ha-Ka! 1489 Folsom • 861-1410 • Mexican • plenty veggie • $5-10

BOOKSTORES & RETAIL SHOPS

Leather Etc. 1201 Folsom St. • 864-7558 • 10:30am-7pm, from 11am Sat

Stompers 323 10th St. • 255-6422 • noon-8pm, clsd Mon • boots, cigars & gloves

TRAVEL & TOUR OPERATORS

Above & Beyond Travel 330 Townsend • 284-1666/(800) 397-2681 • IGTA

Castro Travel Company 435 Brannan Ste. 214 • 357-0957/(800) 861-0957 • IGTA

China Basin Travel Center 185 Berry St. • 777-4747

EROTICA

A Taste of Leather 317-A 10th St. • 252-9166/(800) 367-0786 • noon-8pm

City Entertainment 960 Folsom St. • 543-2124 • 24hrs wknds

Mr. S Leather 310 7th St. • 863-7764 • 11am-7pm, noon-6pm Sun • erotic goods • leather • latex

▲ **Stormy Leather** 1158 Howard St. • 626-1672 • noon-6pm • leather • latex • toys • magazines • women-owned/run

S.F. - Polk Street Area (415)

ACCOMMODATIONS

Atherton Hotel 685 Ellis St. • 474-5720/(800) 474-5720 • gay-friendly • non-smoking rms. avail. • also a restaurant • full bar • IGTA • $59-89

▲ **Essex Hotel** 684 Ellis St. • 474-4664/(800) 443-7739 • gay-friendly • boutique hotel w/ European-style hospitality • wheelchair access • $59-89

Hotel Richelieu 1050 Van Ness Ave. • 673-4711/(800) 227-3608 • lesbians/gay men • gym • full bar • wheelchair access • $99-169

The Lombard Hotel 1015 Geary St. • 673-5232/(800) 777-3210 • gay-friendly • swimming • kids ok • non-smoking rms. avail. • wheelchair access • up to $100

Pensione International Hotel 875 Post St. • 775-3344/(800) 358-8123 • gay-friendly • Victorian-styled hotel built in early 1900s • shared/private baths • $30-65

▲ **The Phoenix Hotel** 601 Eddy St. • 776-1380/(800) 248-9466 • gay-friendly • 1950s-style motor lodge • popular • swimming • kids ok • also a restaurant • Caribbean • some veggie • full bar • IGTA • $89-150

BARS

Mother Lode 1002 Post St. • 928-6006 • 6am-2am • mostly gay men • neighborhood bar • dancing/DJ • multi-racial • TS/TVs & their admirers • live shows

RESTAURANTS & CAFES

Grubstake II 1525 Pine St. • 673-8268 • 5pm-4am, 10am-4am wknds • lesbians/gay men • beer/wine

Rendezvous Cafe 1760 Polk St. • 292-4033 • 7am-10pm • some veggie • $6-10

Spuntino 524 Van Ness Ave. • 861-7772 • 7am-8pm • cont'l • also cafe & desserts • beer/wine • $8-12

Stars Cafe 500 Van Ness Ave. • 861-4344 • lunch & dinner • beer/wine • $15-25

BOOKSTORES & RETAIL SHOPS

A Clean Well Lighted Place For Books 601 Van Ness Ave. • 441-6670 • 10am-11pm • general • lesbigay section

Hog On Ice 1630 Polk St. • 771-7909 • 10am-10pm, til 6pm Sat • novelties • books • CDs

▲ **My Boyfriend's Closet** 1350 Larkin St. • 563-5999 • clothing, fashions, jewelry & art for women

TRAVEL & TOUR OPERATORS

Beyond the Bay 726 Polk St. • 421-7721/(800) 542-1991 • women-owned/run • IGTA

Jackson Travel 1829 Polk St. • 928-2500 •

S.F. - Downtown & North Beach (415)

ACCOMMODATIONS

▲ **The Abigail Hotel** 246 McAllister St. • 861-9728/(800) 243-6510 • gay-friendly • also 'Millennium' restaurant • vegetarian • IGTA • $79-129

Amsterdam Hotel 749 Taylor St., Nob Hill • 673-3277/(800) 637-3444 • gay-friendly • charming European-style hotel • shared/private baths • $69-89

▲ **The Andrews** 624 Post St. • 563-6877/(800) 926-3739 • gay-friendly • also a restaurant • Italian • $10-15

▲ **The Commodore International Hotel** 825 Sutter St. • 923-6800/(800) 338-6848 • gay-friendly • $69-109

Dakota Hotel 606 Post St. • 931-7475 • gay-friendly • near Union Square • $60-90

Dockside Boat & Bed 77 Jack London Sq., Oakland, 94607 • 444-5858/436-2574 • gay-friendly • private houseboats with kitchen • smokefree • kids ok • $95-275

Hotel Griffon 155 Steuart St. • 495-2100/(800) 321-2201 • kitchens • fitness center • non-smoking rms. avail. • kids ok • also a restaurant • bistro/cont'l • wheelchair access • $155-250

▲ **The Hotel Rex** 562 Sutter St. • 433-4434/(800) 433-4434 • gay-friendly • full brkfst • full bar • non-smoking rms. avail.

Hotel Triton 342 Grant Ave. • 394-0500/(800) 433-6611 • gay-friendly • wheelchair access • IGTA • $99-149

Hotel Vintage Court 650 Bush St. • 392-4666/(800) 654-1100 • gay-friendly • fireplaces • also world-famous 5-star Masa's restaurant • French • $75 prix fixe • wheelchair access • $129-169

Howard Johnson Pickwick Hotel 85 5th St. • 421-7500/(800) 227-3282 • gay-friendly • kids ok • $99+

Hyde Park Suites 2655 Hyde St. (at North Point) • 771-0200/(800) 227-3608 • gay-friendly • Mediterranean-inspired 1- & 2-bdrm suites • gym • sundeck • kitchens • IGTA • $165-220

King George Hotel 334 Mason St. • 781-5050/(800) 288-6005 • gay-friendly • European-style boutique hotel • non-smoking rms. avail. • kids ok • also 'The Bread & Honey Tearoom' w/ morning & afternoon teas • $115-125

▲ **Nob Hill Lambourne** 725 Pine St., Nob Hill • 433-2287/(800) 274-8466 • gay-friendly • luxurious 'business accommodation' • kitchens • kids ok • $99-199

Nob Hill Pensione 835 Hyde St. • 885-2987 • gay-friendly • European-style hotel • shared/private baths • smokefree • kids ok • also a restaurant • $30-50

The Pacific Bay Inn 520 Jones St. • 673-0234/(800) 445-2631 • gay-friendly • also 'Dottie's True Blue Cafe' • $199-299 (weekly)

Ramada Market St. 1231 Market St. • 626-8000/(800) 227-4747 • gay-friendly • full brkfst • wheelchair access

Ramada Union Square 345 Taylor St. • 673-2332/(800) 228-2828 • gay-friendly • full breakfast • wheelchair access

Savoy Hotel 580 Geary St. • 441-2700/(800) 227-4223 • gay-friendly • non-smoking rms. avail. • $105-195

The York Hotel 940 Sutter St. • 885-6800/(800) 808-9675 • gay-friendly • boutique hotel • IGTA • $99-200

BARS

The Gate 1093 Pine St. • 885-9871 • 4pm-2am, 11am-2am wknds, Sun brunch • mostly gay men • neighborhood bar

RESTAURANTS & CAFES

Akimbo 116 Maiden Ln. • 433-2288 • lunch & dinner, clsd Sun • lesbians/gay men

Basque Hotel & Restaurant uphill alley off Broadway between Columbus & Kearny • 788-9404 • beer/wine

Cafe Claude 7 Claude • 392-3505 • 8am-10pm • live jazz • as close to Paris as you can get in SF

Campo Santo 240 Columbus Ave., North Beach • 433-9623 • lunch & dinner, from 5:30pm wknds • Mexican • some veggie • beer/wine • hip decor • $8-15

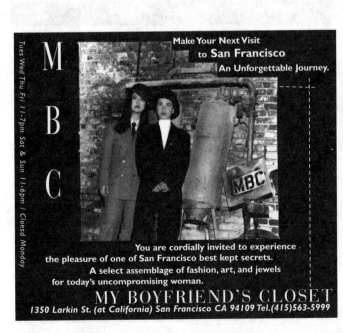

China Moon Cafe 639 Post St. • 775-4789 • lunch & dinner • California nouvelle w/ Chinese accent • some veggie • $15-25

Millennium 246 McAllister St. (at Abigail Hotel) • 487-9800 • 11:30am-2:30pm Tue-Fri, 5pm-9:30pm Tue-Sun, clsd Mon • Euro-Mediterranean • upscale vegetarian

US Restaurant 431 Columbus Ave., North Beach • 362-6251 • 7am-9pm, clsd Sun-Mon • Italian food just like home • beer/wine

BOOKSTORES & RETAIL SHOPS

Billy Blue 54 Geary (at Grant) • 781-2111/(800) 772-BLUE • men's clothing

City Lights Bookstore 261 Columbus Ave., North Beach • 362-8193 • 10am-midnight • historic beatnik bookstore • many progressive titles

TRAVEL & TOUR OPERATORS

Doin' It Right Tours & Travel 1 St. Francis Pl. Ste. 2106 • 621-3576/(800) 936-3646 • Gay Travel Club meets 1st Wed • IGTA • women-owned/run

S.F. - Mission District   (415)

INFO LINES & SERVICES

Brava! 2180 Bryant St. #208 (at 20th) • 641-7657 • culturally diverse performances by women • theater at 2789 24th St. (formerly York Theater) • wheelchair access

Luna Sea 2940 16th St. Rm. 216-C • 863-2989 • lesbian performances

The Marsh 1062 Valencia (at 22nd St.) • 641-0235 • queer-positive theater

Theatre Rhinoceros 2926 16th St. (at So.Van Ness) • 861-5079 • lesbigay theater

Women's Building 3543 18th St. • 431-1180 • hours vary • space for many women's organizations • social/support groups • housing & job listings • beautiful murals

ACCOMMODATIONS

▲ **Andora Inn** 2434 Mission • 282-0337/(800) 967-9219 • lesbians/gay men • guesthouse • near Castro & public transportation • smokefree • also a restaurant • full bar • IGTA • $79-185

▲ **The Inn San Francisco** 943 S. Van Ness Ave. • 641-0188/(800) 359-0913 • gay-friendly • Victorian mansion • full brkfst • hot tub • shared/private baths • kitchens • fireplaces • patio • IGTA • $75-195

Nancy's Bed 134 Del Vale Ave., Glen Park • 239-5692 • women only • B&B-private home • shared bath • lesbian-owned/run • $25

BARS

Baby Judy's 527 Valencia (at the Casanova) • 863-9328 • 9pm-2am Wed • mostly gay men • dancing/DJ

El Rio 3158-A Mission St. • 282-3325 • 3pm-2am, til midnight Mon • gay-friendly • neighborhood bar • mostly Latino-American • live bands • patio • popular Sun afternoons

Esta Noche 3079 16th St. • 861-5757 • 2pm-2am • mostly men • dancing/DJ • mostly Latino-American • live shows • salsa & disco

Phone Booth 1398 S. Van Ness Ave. • 648-4683 • 10am-2am • lesbians/gay men • neighborhood bar

Red 540 Valencia (at Blondies') • 864-2419 • 9pm-2am Sun • women only • dancing/DJ

Wild Side West 424 Cortland • 647-3099 • 1pm-2am • mostly women • neighborhood bar • patio • magic garden

RESTAURANTS & CAFES

Cafe Commons 3161 Mission St. • 282-2928 • 7am-7pm • sandwiches • plenty veggie • patio • wheelchair access • women-owned/run • $4-7

Cafe Istanbul 525 Valencia St. • 863-8854 • 11am-midnight • Mediterranean • some veggie • authentic Turkish coffee • belly-dancers Sat

Farleys 1315 18th St., Potrero Hill • 648-1545 • 7am-10pm, from 8am wknds • coffeehouse

Just For You 1453 18th St., Potrero Hill • 647-3033 • 7am-3pm • popular • lesbians/gay men • American/Cajun • some veggie • women-owned/run • $4-7

Klein's Delicatessen 501 Connecticut St., Potrero Hill • 821-9149 • 7am-7pm • patio • sandwiches & salads • some veggie • beer/wine • women-owned/run • $4-10

New Dawn Cafe 3174 16th St. • 553-8888 • 8am-3pm • hearty breakfasts • some veggie • $4-7

Pancho Villa 3071 16th St. • 864-8840 • 11am-10pm • best 'Mission-style' burritos in city • some veggie • $4-8 • wheelchair access • also 'El Toro' at 18th & Valencia

Pauline's Pizza Pie 260 Valencia St. • 552-2050 • dinner only, clsd Sun-Mon • popular • lesbians/gay men • beer/wine

Picaro 3120 16th St. • 431-4089 • Spanish tapas bar

Radio Valencia 1199 Valencia St. • 826-1199 • 5pm-midnight, from noon Sat-Sun • sandwiches & dessert • artsy cafe

Red Dora's Bearded Lady (Dyke Cafe & Gallery) 485 14th St. (at Guerrero) • 626-2805 • 7am-7pm • mostly women • funky brunch & sandwiches • plenty veggie • performances Fri-Sat nights (call for events) • patio • women-owned/run • $4-7

Ti-Couz 3108 16th St. • 252-7373 • 11am-11pm • Breton dinner & dessert crepes • plenty veggie • beer/wine • wheelchair access • $5-10

Val 21 995 Valencia St. • 821-6622 • dinner, Sat-Sun brunch • eclectic Californian • some veggie • $7-15

GYMS & HEALTH CLUBS
Osento 955 Valencia St. • 282-6333 • 1pm-midnight • women only • baths • hot tub • massage

BOOKSTORES & RETAIL SHOPS
381 381 Guerrero St. • 621-3830 • 11am-6pm, til 7pm wknds • great kitsch & candles

Bernal Books 401 Cortland Ave., Bernal Hts. • 550-0293 • 10am-7pm, til 4pm Sun, clsd Mon • lesbigay section

Body Manipulations 3234 16th St. • 621-0408 • noon-6:30pm, til 7:30pm Fri-Sat • piercing (walk-in basis) • jewelry

Leather Tongue Video 714 Valencia St. • 552-2900 • noon-11pm • great collection of camp, cult & obscure video

Modern Times Bookstore 888 Valencia St. • 282-9246 • 11am-9pm, til 6pm Sun • alternative • lesbigay section • wheelchair access

SPIRITUAL GROUPS
The Episcopal Church of St. John the Evangelist 1661 15th St. • 861-1436 • mostly gay/lesbian parish • open to all

EROTICA
▲ **Good Vibrations** 1210 Valencia St. • 550-7399 • 11am-7pm • mostly women • clean, well-lighted sex toy store • also mail order • women-owned/run

S.F. - Haight, Fillmore & West   (415)

ACCOMMODATIONS
Alamo Square Inn 719 Scott St. • 922-2055/(800) 345-9888 • gay-friendly • 1895 Queen Anne & 1896 Tudor Revival Victorian mansions • full brkfst • smokefree • kids ok • $85-275

▲ **The Archbishops Mansion** 1000 Fulton St. • 563-7872/(800) 543-5820 • gay-friendly • one of SF's grandest homes • $149-385

Auberge des Artistes 829 Fillmore • 776-2530 • gay-friendly • full brkfst • hot tub • shared/private baths • kids ok • computer access • $55-100

Bock's B&B 1448 Willard St. • 664-6842 • gay-friendly • restored 1906 Edwardian residence • shared/private baths • IGTA • women-owned/run • $40-75

Carl Street Unicorn House 156 Carl St. • 753-5194 • gay-friendly • 1895 Victorian house • shared baths • smokefree • kids 6+ ok • women-owned/run • $40-55

Casa Loma Hotel 610 Fillmore St. • 552-7100 • gay-friendly • shared bath • kids ok

▲ **The Chateau Tivoli** 1057 Steiner St. • 776-5462/(800) 228-1647 • gay-friendly • historic San Francisco B&B

Gough Hayes Hotel 417 Gough St. • 431-9131 • lesbians/gay men

▲ **Holiday Lodge** 1901 Van Ness Ave., Pacific Heights • 776-4469/(800) 367-8504 • gay-friendly • tropical resort & pool oasis in the heart of San Francisco • motel • kitchens • IGTA • $59-99

Hotel Majestic 1500 Sutter St., Pacific Heights • 441-1100/869-8966 • gay-friendly • one of SF's earliest grand hotels • also a restaurant • Mediterranean • wheelchair access • $125-250

Inn at the Opera 333 Fulton St. • 863-8400/(800) 325-2708 • gay-friendly • also a restaurant • Mediterranean

Lombard Plaza Motel 2026 Lombard St. • 921-2444 • gay-friendly • $59-150

The Mansions 2220 Sacramento St., Pacific Heights • 929-9444/(800) 826-9398 • gay-friendly • full brkfst • $129-350

Metro Hotel 319 Divisadero St. • 861-5364 • gay-friendly • food served

The Queen Anne Hotel 1590 Sutter St., Pacific Heights • 441-2828/(800) 227-3970 • gay-friendly • beautifully restored 1890 landmark • popular • fireplaces • non-smoking rms. avail. • kids ok • IGTA • $99-275

Chateau Tivoli B&B

San Francisco's
opulent landmark mansion
800-228-1647
415-776-5462

Radisson Miyako Hotel 1625 Post St., Japantown • 922-3200/(800) 333-3333 • gay-friendly • located in the heart of Japantown • non-smoking rms. avail. • wheelchair access • IGTA • $119-299

Stanyan Park Hotel 750 Stanyan St. • 751-1000 • gay-friendly • fireplaces • kids ok

BARS

Alta Plaza 2301 Fillmore • 922-1444 • 4pm-2am • mostly gay men • professional • also a restaurant • cont'l • some veggie • $10-15

Hayes & Vine 377 Hayes St. • 626-5301 • 5pm-midnight, til 1am Fri-Sat • lesbians/gay men • wine bar

The Lion Pub 2062 Divisadero St. • 567-6565 • 3pm-2am • mostly gay men • professional • theme nights

Marlena's 488 Hayes St. • 864-6672 • 10am-2am • lesbians/gay men • neighborhood bar • drag shows Fri-Sat nights

Noc Noc 557 Haight St. • 861-5811 • 5pm-2am • gay-friendly • beer/wine

The Top 424 Haight St. • 864-7386 • gay-friendly • dancing/DJ • alternative • theme nights • call for events

Traxx 1437 Haight St. • 864-4213 • noon-2am • mostly gay men • neighborhood bar • wheelchair access

RESTAURANTS & CAFES

Blue Muse 409 Gough St. • 626-7505 • 7:30am-11pm • some veggie • $10-15

Cha Cha Cha's 1801 Haight St. • 386-7670 • 11:30am-11pm • Cuban/Cajun • excellent sangria • worth the long wait!

Charpe's Grill 131 Gough St. • 621-6766 • dinner nightly • some veggie • full bar • wheelchair access • $10-15

Geva's Caribbean 482 Hayes St. • 863-1220 • dinner • lesbians/gay men • wheelchair access

Greens Fort Mason • 771-6222 • dinners, Sun brunch, clsd Mon • gourmet prix fixe vegetarian • $20-40

Ivy's 398 Hayes St. • 626-3930 • lunch & dinner • vegetarian • $15-25

Kan Zaman 1793 Haight • 751-9656 • noon-11:30pm, til 1:30am Fri-Sat • Mediterranean • some veggie • beer/wine • hookahs & tobacco avail.

Mad Magda's Russian Tearoom & Cafe
579 Hayes St. • 864-7654 • popular • lesbians/gay men • eclectic crowd • magic garden • tarot & palm readers daily

Ya Halla 494 Haight St. • 522-1509 • lunch & dinner • Middle Eastern • plenty veggie • $4-9

BOOKSTORES & RETAIL SHOPS

La Riga 1391 Haight St. • 552-1525 • leather

Mainline Gifts 1928 Fillmore St. • 563-4438 • 10am-6pm, til 8pm Fri, from 11am Sun

Nomad 1881 Hayes St. • 563-7771 • noon-7pm • piercing (walk-in) • jewelry

TRAVEL & TOUR OPERATORS

Damron Atlas World Travel 1801 Bush St., Ste. 106 • 440-1601 • (888) 907-9777 • IGTA

EROTICA

▲ **Romantasy** 199 Moulton St. • 673-3137 • noon-7pm • books • videos • toys • clothing • women-owned/run

San Jose   (408)

INFO LINES & SERVICES

AA Gay/Lesbian 297-3555 • lesbian mtg 7:30pm Fri • call for more info

Billy DeFrank Lesbian/Gay Community Center 175 Stockton Ave. • 293-2429 • 3pm-9pm, from noon Sat, 9am-6pm Sun

Leather W.I.S.D.O.M. PO Box 2519, Santa Clara, 95055 • leatherwomen's group

Rainbow Gender Association PO Box 700730, 95170-0730 • 984-4044 • transgender group • recorded info

BARS

641 Club 641 Stockton • 998-1144 • 2pm-2am, from 11am wknds • lesbians/gay men • dancing/DJ • multi-racial

Buck's 301 W. Stockton Ave. • 286-1176 • noon-2am, from noon Fri til 2am Sun • lesbians/gay men • neighborhood bar • dancing/DJ

Greg's Ballroom 551 W. Julian • 286-4388 • noon-2am • lesbians/gay men • dancing/DJ • live shows • leather night Th

RESTAURANTS & CAFES

Cafe Leviticus 1445 The Alameda • 279-8877 • 7am-midnight • lesbians/gay men

El Faro 610 Coleman Ave. • 294-1846 • lunch & dinner, Sun champagne brunch 10am-3pm • Mexican • some veggie • $10-20

Hamburger Mary's 170 W. St. John St. • 947-1667 • 11:30am-2am, from 9am wknds • some veggie • full bar

BOOKSTORES & RETAIL SHOPS

Sisterspirit 175 Stockton Ave. • 293-9372 • 6:30pm-9pm, 4pm-9pm Wed, noon-6pm Sat, 1pm-4pm Sun • women's • periodic coffeehouse

TRAVEL & TOUR OPERATORS

Damron Atlas World Travel 776-1660 • (888) 907-9777 • IGTA

Yankee Clipper Travel 260 Saratoga Ave., Los Gatos • 354-6400/(800) 624-2664 • contact Jim • IGTA

SPIRITUAL GROUPS

Hosanna Church of Praise 24 N. 5th St. • 293-0708 • 2pm Sun • charismatic pentecostal • wheelchair access

Integrity El Camino 81 N. Second St. • 377-4411 • 2nd Tue • lesbigay Episcopalians

MCC of San Jose 65 S. 7th St. • 279-2711 • 10:30am Sun

PUBLICATIONS

Entre Nous PO Box 412, Santa Clara, 95052 • 378-7787 • monthly • lesbian newsmagazine & calendar for South Bay

Out Now! 45 N. 1st St. #124 • 991-1873

EROTICA

Leather Masters 969 Park Ave. • 293-7660 • leather & fetish • clothes • toys • publications

San Leandro   (510)

BARS

Bill's Eagle 14572 E. 14th • 357-7343 • noon-2am • lesbians/gay men • neighborhood bar • dancing/DJ • live shows • patio • women-owned/run

San Lorenzo   (510)

SPIRITUAL GROUPS

MCC of Greater Hayward 100 Hacienda (Christ Lutheran Church) • 481-9720 • 12:30pm Sun

San Luis Obispo   (805)

INFO LINES & SERVICES

GALA (Gay/Lesbian Alliance of the Central Coast) PO Box 3558, 93403 • 541-4252 • info & referrals • newsletter

Lesbian Rap Groups in Santa Maria • social/support groups • lesbians of color meet 3rd Sat • 534-0808

CHAMELEON
Restaurant & Bar · Santa Barbara

Lunch / Dinner / Weekend Brunch / Cocktail Bar
Game Room / Banquet Facilities / Outdoor Patio

Atmosphere Provided by
World Of Magic
Santa Barbara's Queerest Store

421 East Cota Street, Santa Barbara, CA 93101
(805) 965-9536 / chamel421@aol.com

Women's Resource Center 1009 Morro St. #201 • 544-9313 • counseling • support • referrals

ACCOMMODATIONS

Adobe Inn 1473 Monterey St. • 549-0321 • gay-friendly • cozy, comfortable & congenial inn • full brkfst • kitchens • smoking rm. avail. • $49-95

Amber Hills B&B 239-2073 • gay-friendly • rural setting • kids/pets ok ($5 extra per) • women-owned/run • $65 ($5 /extra person)

Casa De Amigas B&B 1202 8th St., Los Osos • 528-3701 • lesbians/gay men • smokefree • women-owned/run

Palomar Inn 1601 Shell Beach Rd., Shell Beach • 773-4207 • lesbians/gay men • close to nude beach • gay-owned/run

BARS

Breezes Pub & Grill 11560 Los Osos Valley Rd., Laguna Village #160 • 544-8010 • 8pm-2am Wed-Sat • lesbians/gay men • dancing/DJ • beer/wine • also a restaurant • Caribbean • some veggie • $5-10

RESTAURANTS & CAFES

Linnea's Cafe 1110 Garden • 541-5888 • til midnight, til 1am wknds • healthy American • plenty veggie • $5

BOOKSTORES & RETAIL SHOPS

Coalesce Bookstore & Garden Wedding Chapel 845 Main St., Morro Bay • 772-2880 • 10am-5:30pm, 11am-4pm Sun • lesbigay section • women-owned/run

Volumes of Pleasure 1016 Los Osos Valley Rd., Los Osos • 528-5565 • 10am-6pm, clsd Sun • general • lesbigay section • lesbian-owned/run

SPIRITUAL GROUPS

MCC of the Central Coast 2333 Meadow Ln. • 481-9376 • 10:30am Sun

San Mateo (415)

BARS

'B' Street 236 S. 'B' St. • 348-4045 • hours vary • lesbians/gay men • more women Fri • dancing/DJ • live shows • theme nights • live bands • patio • wheelchair access

San Rafael (415)

BARS

Aunt Ruby's 815 W. Francisco Blvd. • 459-6079 • 4pm-11pm, 2pm-2am Fri-Sat, from noon Sun • lesbians/gay men • dancing/DJ • wheelchair access

San Ysidro (619)

EROTICA

▲ **F St. Bookstore** 4650 Border Village • 497-6042

Santa Ana (714)

SPIRITUAL GROUPS

Christ Chapel MCC 720 N. Spurgeon • 835-0722 • 10am Sun

Santa Barbara (805)

INFO LINES & SERVICES

Gay/Lesbian Resource Center 126 E. Haley St. Ste. A-17 • 963-3636 • 10am-5pm Mon-Fri • social/educational & support services • youth groups

ACCOMMODATIONS

Glenborough Inn 1327 Bath St. • 966-0589/(800) 962-0589 • lesbians/gay men • 3 different homes w/ 3 different personalities • full brkfst • private/shared baths • fireplaces • smokefree • kids ok • $90-225

Ivanhoe Inn 1406 Castillo St. • 963-8832/(800) 428-1787 • gay-friendly • lovely old Victorian house • private/shared baths • kitchens • smokefree • kids/pets ok • $95-195

BARS

▲ **Chameleon Restaurant & Bar** 421 E. Cota • 965-9536 • 11am-2am • lesbians/gay men • Californian • plenty veggie • patio • wheelchair access

Fathom 423 State St. • 730-0022 • lesbians/gay men • call infoline for events • 882-2082

Gold Coast 30 W. Cota • 965-6701 • 4pm-2am • mostly gay men • dancing/DJ • wheelchair access

Zelo's 630 State • 966-5792 • 10pm-2am • popular • gay-friendly • dancing/DJ • also a restaurant

RESTAURANTS & CAFES

Acacia 1212 Coast Village Rd. • 969-8500 • dinner, lunch wknds • modern American • full bar • wheelchair access • $15-20

Hot Spot Espresso Bar & Reservation Service 564-1637 • 24hrs

Mousse Odile 18 E. Cota St. • 962-5393 • French • patio

Sojourner 134 E. Canon Perdido • 965-7922 • 11am-11pm • veggie • beer/wine • wheelchair access

BOOKSTORES & RETAIL SHOPS

Chaucer's Books 3321 State St. • 682-6787 • 9am-9pm, til 10pm Fri-Sat, 10am-5pm Sun • general • lesbigay section

Earthling Books & Cafe 1137 State St. • 965-0926 • 9am-11pm, til midnight Fri-Sat • lesbigay

TRAVEL & TOUR OPERATORS

Cloud Canyon Backpacking 411 Lemon Grove Ln. • 969-0982 • women only • hiking in southern Utah

SPIRITUAL GROUPS

Integrity El Norte 1500 State St. • 965-7419 • 4th Sun • meets at Trinity Episcopal Church • lesbigay Episcopalians

PUBLICATIONS

The Bulletin 126 E. Haley St. #A-17 • 963-3636

Santa Clara (408)

BARS

Savoy 3546 Flora Vista • 247-7109 • 3pm-2am • popular • mostly women • dancing/DJ • live shows • wheelchair access • women-owned/run

Tynker's Damn 46 N. Saratoga • 243-4595 • 3pm-2am, 1pm-2am wknds • mostly gay men • dancing/DJ

EROTICA

Borderline 36 N. Saratoga Ave. • 241-2177 • toys • videos

Santa Cruz (408)

INFO LINES & SERVICES

AA Gay/Lesbian 457-2559 • call for mtgs

Lesbian/Gay/Bisexual/Transgender Community Center 1328 Commerce Ln. • 425-5422 • noon-8pm • info • referrals • social/support groups • call for events

ACCOMMODATIONS

Battle Mountain B&B 105 Country Estates Ter. • 429-8687 • lesbians/gay men • $90/room, $25/camping

Chateau Victorian B&B Inn 118 1st St. • 458-9458 • gay-friendly • 1885 Victorian inn w/ a warm friendly atmosphere • fireplaces • smokefree • $110-140

El Mar Vista 5115 Ironwood Dr., Soquel • 476-5742 • women only • full brkfst • shared baths

BARS

Blue Lagoon 923 Pacific Ave. • 423-7117 • 4pm-2am • lesbians/gay men • dancing/DJ • alternative • transgender-friendly • live shows • videos • wheelchair access

RESTAURANTS & CAFES

Costa Brava Taco Stand 505 Seabright • 423-8190 • 11am-11pm • Mexican • some veggie • $4-8

Crêpe Place 1134 Soquel Ave. • 429-6994 • 11am-midnight, 10am-1am wknds • plenty veggie • beer/wine • garden patio • wheelchair access • $5-11

Herland Book Cafe 902 Center St. • 429-6641(cafe)/429-6636 (bookstore) • 8am-6pm, bookstore from 10am • vegetarian & vegan • wheelchair access • $3-6

Saturn Cafe 1230 Mission • 429-8505 • noon-midnight • sandwiches/salads/soups • plenty veggie • $4-7

GYMS & HEALTH CLUBS

Heartwood Spa Hot Tub & Sauna Garden 3150-A Mission Dr. • 462-2192 • noon-11pm • women only 6:30pm-11pm Sun

Kiva Retreat House Spa 702 Water St. • 429-1142 • noon-11pm, til midnight Fri-Sat • women-only 9am-noon Sun

BOOKSTORES & RETAIL SHOPS

Book Loft 1207 Soquel Ave. • 429-1812 • 10am-10pm, noon-6pm Sun, 10am-6pm Mon • mostly used books

Bookshop Santa Cruz 1520 Pacific Garden Mall • 423-0900 • 9am-11pm • general • lesbigay section • cafe • wheelchair access

Chimney Sweep Books 419 Cedar St. • 458-1044 • hours vary • lesbigay section • mostly used books

TRAVEL & TOUR OPERATORS

Eco-Explorations PO Box 7944, 95061 • 662-0652 • lesbigay & women's scuba & sea kayaking trips • IGTA • women-owned/run

Pacific Harbor Travel 519 Seabright Ave. • 427-5000/(800) 435-9463 • women-owned/run • IGTA

Santa Cruz Tours 95 Country Estates Ter. • 429-8687/(800) 757-3891x7928 • sightseeing • winetasting • artist studio tours

Santa Maria (805)

INFO LINES & SERVICES
Gay/Lesbian Resource Center 2255 S. Broadway #4 • 349-9947 • info • referrals • counseling

RESTAURANTS & CAFES
Cafe Monet 1555 S. Broadway • 928-1912 • 7am-7pm, til 10pm Wed & Fri, 9am-5pm Sun • wheelchair access

EROTICA
Book Adventure 306 S. Blosser Blvd. • 928-7094

Santa Rosa (707)

BARS
Club Heaven 120 5th St. • 544-6653 • 9pm-4am Sun only • lesbians/gay men • dancing/DJ

Santa Rosa Inn 4302 Santa Rosa Ave. • 584-0345 • noon-2am • lesbians/gay men • dancing/DJ

RESTAURANTS & CAFES
Aroma Roasters 95 5th St. (Railroad Square) • 576-7765 • 7am-midnight, til 11pm wknds • lesbians/gay men • wheelchair access • lesbian-owned/run

BOOKSTORES & RETAIL SHOPS
North Light Books 95 5th St. (Historic Railroad Square) • 579-9000 • 9am-9pm, til 10pm Fri-Sat, 10am-8pm Sun • anti-establishment • strong lesbigay emphasis • also coffeehouse • lesbian-owned/run

Sawyer's News 733 4th St. • 542-1311 • 7am-9pm, til 10pm Fri-Sat • general news & bookstand

TRAVEL & TOUR OPERATORS
Santa Rosa Travel 542 Farmers Ln. • 542-0943/(800) 227-1445

Sun Quest 1208 4th St. • 573-8300/(800) 444-8300 • IGTA

SPIRITUAL GROUPS
1st Congregational United Church of Christ 2000 Humboldt St. • 546-0998 • 10:30am Sun

Chapel of the Saints Sergius & Bacchus 200 5th St. • 573-9463 • 10am Sun

New Hope MCC 3632 Airway Dr. • 526-4673 • 12:15pm Sun

PUBLICATIONS
We the People PO Box 8218, 95407 • 573-8896

EROTICA
Santa Rosa Adult Books 3301 Santa Rosa Ave. • 542-8248

Sebastopol (707)

BOOKSTORES & RETAIL SHOPS
Milk & Honey 137 N. Main St. • 824-1155 • 10am-6pm, til 5pm Sun • woman crafts • goddess crafts

Stinson Beach (415)

ACCOMMODATIONS
A Place to Heal B&B 868-1965/(800) 861-7326 • a getaway for all people in relationship with HIV/AIDS

Stockton (209)

BARS
Paradise 10100 N. Lower Sacramento Rd. • 477-4724 • 6pm-2am, from 4pm wknds • lesbians/gay men • dancing/DJ • live shows • live bands

Tustin (714)

BOOKSTORES & RETAIL SHOPS
A Different Drummer II 14131 Yorba St. Ste. 102 • 731-0224/3632 • opens 11am, clsd wknds • lesbigay • self-help titles

Ukiah (707)

BARS
Sunset Grill 228 E. Perkins St. • 463-0740 • lunch & dinner, clsd Mon • gay-friendly • dancing/DJ • also a restaurant • Californian • $10-15

Upland (909)

EROTICA
Mustang Books 961 N. Central • 981-0227

Vacaville (707)

INFO LINES & SERVICES
Solano County Gay/Lesbian Infoline PO Box 9, 95696 • 448-1010/449-0550

BOOKSTORES & RETAIL SHOPS
Vacaville Book Co. & Coffeehouse 315 Main St. • 449-0550 • 9am-6pm, til 9pm Fri, from 8am Sat, clsd Sun • women-owned/run

SPIRITUAL GROUPS
St. Paul's United Methodist Church 101 West St. • 448-5154 • 10:30am Sun

Vallejo (707)

BARS

Nobody's Place 437 Virginia St. • 645-7298 • 10am-2am • mostly gay men • dancing/DJ • live shows • patio • wheelchair access

The Q 412 Georgia St. • 644-4584 • noon-2am, from 4pm Mon-Wed • mostly gay men • dancing/DJ • wheelchair access

Venice (310)

ACCOMMODATIONS

▲ **The Mansion Inn** 327 Washington Blvd. • 821-2557/(800) 828-0688 • gay-friendly • European-style inn

Rose Avenue Beach House 55 Rose Ave. • 396-2803 • gay-friendly • Victorian beach house 1 blk. from ocean & boardwalk

Ventura (805)

INFO LINES & SERVICES

AA Gay/Lesbian 739 E. Main • 389-1444 • women's mtg 6:30pm Wed at G/L Comm. Ctr.

Gay/Lesbian Community Center 1995 E. Main • 653-1979 • 10am-4pm & 6:30pm-9pm Mon-Th, clsd wknds

BARS

Club Alternative 1644 E. Thompson Blvd. • 653-6511 • 2pm-2am • lesbians/gay men • dancing/DJ • live shows • patio

Paddy McDermott's 577 E. Main St. • 652-1071 • 2pm-2am • lesbians/gay men • dancing/DJ • live shows • karaoke

SPIRITUAL GROUPS

MCC Ventura 1848 Poli (Church of Latter Day Saints) • 643-0502 • 6:30pm Sun

EROTICA

Three Star Adult News 359 E. Main St. • 653-9068 • 24hrs

Victorville (619)

BARS

West Side 15 16868 Stoddard Wells Rd. • 243-9600 • 2pm-2am • lesbians/gay men • beer/wine

Walnut Creek (510)

INFO LINES & SERVICES

AA Gay/Lesbian 1924 Trinity Ave. (St. Paul's Episc. Church) • 939-4155 • 8:30pm Fri • 5:30pm Sat at 193 Mayhew Wy.

BARS

D.J.'s 1535 Olympic Blvd. • 930-0300 • 4pm-2am • lesbians/gay men • piano bar • also a restaurant • some veggie • wheelchair access • $8-12

J.R.'s 2520 Camino Diablo • 256-1200 • 5pm-2am, til 4am Fri-Sat • lesbians/gay men • more women Sat • dancing/DJ • country/western • wheelchair access

Twelve Twenty 1220 Pine St. • 938-4550 • 4pm-2am, from 3pm wknds • mostly gay men • dancing/DJ • wheelchair access

SPIRITUAL GROUPS

MCC Diablo Valley 1543 Sunnyvale (United Methodist Church) • 283-2238 • 1pm Sun

Whittier (310)

ACCOMMODATIONS

Whittier House 12133 S. Colima Blvd. • (310) 941-7222 • mostly women • full brkfst • hot tub • smokefree • kids/pets ok • IGTA

SPIRITUAL GROUPS

MCC Good Samaritan 11931 E. Washington Blvd. • 696-6213 • 10am Sun, 7:30pm Wed

Willits (707)

RESTAURANTS & CAFES

Tsunami 50 S. Main St. • 459-4750 • 9:30am-8pm • Japanese/Int'l • $8-13

BOOKSTORES & RETAIL SHOPS

Leaves of Grass 630 S. Main St. • 459-3744 • 10am-5:30pm, noon-5pm Sun • alternative

TRAVEL & TOUR OPERATORS

Skunk Train California Western 299 E. Commercial St. • 459-5248 • scenic train trips

Yosemite Nat'l Park (209)

ACCOMMODATIONS

The Ahwahnee Hotel Yosemite Valley Floor • 252-4848 • gay-friendly • incredibly dramatic & expensive grand fortress • swimming • also a restaurant

▲ **The Homestead** 41110 Rd. 600, Ahwahnee • 683-0495 • gay-friendly • cottages • full brkfst • kitchens • fireplaces • smokefree • $125-175

RECIPE FOR THE PERFECT GETAWAY

START with two people who want to be alone.

BLEND with a cozy four cottage getaway on 160 wooded acres at the gateway to YOSEMITE National Park.

SIMMER a few days or a week for romance, relaxation, and pampering.

THE HOMESTEAD is a great place to do nothing, or take advantage of the nearby sight-seeing, golf, horseback riding, hiking, antique shops & restaurants. **Call** proprietors Cindy & Larry for planning that well-deserved getaway! **(209) 683-0495**
 41110 Road 600   Ahwahnee, CA   93601
or www.sierranet.net/~homestead

COLORADO

Alamosa (719)

ACCOMMODATIONS

Cottonwood Inn 123 San Juan Ave. • 589-3882/(800) 955-2623 • gay-friendly • $64-85

Aspen (970)

INFO LINES & SERVICES

Aspen Gay/Lesbian Community PO Box 3143, 81612 • 925-9249 • info/resources • outdoor activities • monthly events

ACCOMMODATIONS

Aspen B&B Lodge 311 W. Main • 925-7650/(800) 362-7736 • gay-friendly • hot tub • swimming

Hotel Aspen 110 W. Main St. • 925-3441/(800) 527-7369 • gay-friendly • mountain brkfst • hot tub • swimming • wheelchair access

Hotel Lenado 200 S. Aspen St. • 925-6246/(800) 321-3457 • gay-friendly • full brkfst • hot tub • full bar

Rising Star Guest Ranch (888) 429-7624 • lesbians/gay men • call for location • swimming • IGTA

Sardy House 128 E. Main St. • 920-2525/(800) 321-3457 • gay-friendly • hot tub • swimming • also a restaurant

BARS

Double Diamond 450 S. Galena • 920-6905 • seasonal • gay-friendly • live shows

Silver Nugget Hyman Ave. Mall • 925-8154 • 10pm-2am • gay-friendly • dancing/DJ • live shows • wheelchair access

The Tippler 535 E. Dean • 925-4977 • 11:30am-2am (seasonal) • gay-friendly • dancing/DJ • live entertainment • also a restaurant • Italian • wheelchair access

RESTAURANTS & CAFES

Syzygy 520 E. Hyman • 925-3700 • 5pm-10pm, bar til 2am • live shows • some veggie • wheelchair access

BOOKSTORES & RETAIL SHOPS

Explore Booksellers & Bistro 221 E. Main • 925-5336 • 10am-11pm • vegetarian • wheelchair access

Boulder (303)

INFO LINES & SERVICES

LBGT (Lesbian/Bisexual/Gay/Transgendered) Alliance University Memorial Center Rm. 28, Colo. Univ., 80309 • 492-8567 • events schedule & resource info

TLC (The Lesbian Connection) 2525 Arapahoe Ave. • 443-1105 • social/cultural/business group • newsletter • info & referrals

ACCOMMODATIONS

Boulder Guesthouse 1331 Marshall St. • 938-8908 • mostly women • private home • kitchen privileges • smokefree • kids/pets ok

Boulder Victorian Historic B&B 1305 Pine St. • 938-1300 • gay-friendly • patio

The Briar Rose B&B 2151 Arapahoe Ave. • 442-3007 • gay-friendly

BARS

Boulder Blue Steel Aspen Plaza • 786-8860 • 7pm-2am, clsd Mon • popular • gay-friendly • dancing/DJ • wheelchair access

Marquee 1109 Walnut • 447-1803 • 7pm-2am • gay-friendly • dancing/DJ • live shows • wheelchair access

The Yard 2690 28th St. #C • 443-1987 • 4pm-2am, from 2pm wknds • lesbians/gay men • dancing/DJ • wheelchair access • women-owned/run

RESTAURANTS & CAFES

Walnut Cafe 3073 Walnut • 447-2315 • 7am-11pm, til 3pm Sun-Mon • popular • plenty veggie • patio • wheelchair access • women-owned/run • $5-9

BOOKSTORES & RETAIL SHOPS

Aria 2043 Broadway • 442-5694 • 10am-6pm, noon-5pm Sun • cards • T-shirts • gifts • wheelchair access

Left Hand Books 1825 Pearl St., 2nd flr. • 443-8252 • noon-9pm, 1pm-4pm Sun

Word Is Out 1731 15th St. • 449-1415 • 10am-6pm, noon-5pm Sun, clsd Mon • women's • lesbigay section • wheelchair access

TRAVEL & TOUR OPERATORS

Adventure Bound Expeditions 711 Walnut St. • 449-0990 • mountain tours & hiking excursions

SPIRITUAL GROUPS
Gay/Lesbian Concerned Catholics 904 14th St. • 443-8383 • monthly events

PUBLICATIONS
Colorado Community Directories PO Drawer 2270, 80306 • 443-7768 • extensive statewide resources

EROTICA
The News Stand 1720 15th St. • 442-9515

Breckenridge (303)

ACCOMMODATIONS
Allaire Timbers Inn 9511 Hwy. 9, S. Main St. • 453-7530/(800) 624-4904 • gay-friendly • full brkfst • hot tub • wheelchair access

Mountain Lodge 453-6475 • rental home

Colorado Springs (719)

INFO LINES & SERVICES
Pikes Peak Gay/Lesbian Community Center Helpline PO Box 574, 80901 • 471-4429 • 6pm-9pm Mon-Fri • call for events

ACCOMMODATIONS
Amara's Guesthouse 9425 Mohawk Tr., Chipita Park • 684-9169 • gay-friendly • full brkfst • private entrance • smokefree • $73

Pikes Peak Paradise PO Box 5760, Woodland Park, 80866 • 687-7112/(800) 354-0989 • gay-friendly • mansion w/ view of Pikes Peak • full brkfst • hot tub • fireplaces • smokefree • kids 12+ ok • $95-165

BARS
Hide & Seek Complex 512 W. Colorado • 634-9303 • 10:30am-2am, til 4am Fri-Sat • popular • lesbians/gay men • dancing/DJ • country/western • live shows • also a restaurant • some veggie • wheelchair access • $5-12

Hour Glass Lounge 2748 Airport Rd. • 471-2104 • 10am-2am • gay-friendly • neighborhood bar

The Penthouse 1715 N. Academy • 597-3314 • 3pm-2am, til 4am Fri-Sat • mostly men • neighborhood bar • dancing/DJ • wheelchair access

True Colors 1865 N. Academy Blvd. • 637-0773 • 3pm-2am, clsd Sun-Tue • mostly women • dancing/DJ • multi-racial • wheelchair access • women-owned/run

RESTAURANTS & CAFES
Art of Espresso 2021 W. Colorado Ave. • 632-9306 • 8am-10pm, til midnight Fri-Sat, til 6pm Sun • art gallery

Dale Street Cafe 115 E. Dale • 578-9898 • 11am-9pm, clsd Sun • vegetarian • full bar • $6-11

SPIRITUAL GROUPS
Pikes Peak MCC 730 N. Tejon (Unitarian Church) • 634-3771 • 5pm Sun

PUBLICATIONS
New Phazes PO Box 6485, 80934 • 634-0236 • monthly • women's newsletter

EROTICA
First Amendment Adult Bookstore 220 E. Fillmore • 630-7676

Crested Butte (303)

ACCOMMODATIONS
The Crested Beauty PO Box 1204, 81224 • 349-1201

Denver (303)

INFO LINES & SERVICES
AA Gay/Lesbian 322-4440 • many meetings

▲ **Dyke TV** Channel 12 • call (212) 343-9335 for more information

Gay/Lesbian/Bisexual Community Center 1245 E. Colfax Ave. Ste. 125 • 831-6268/837-1598 • 10am-6pm Mon-Fri • extensive resources & support groups • wheelchair access

Gender Identity Center of Colorado (GIC) 1455 Ammons St., Lakewood, 80215-4993 • 202-6466 • transgender resources & support

Rocky Mountain Career Women PO Box 18156, 80218 • 889-1001 • 6:30pm 3rd Fri • newsletter • social/networking group for professional women

Sister II Sister Black lesbian support group • contact Community Center

Women's Outdoor Club PO Box 300085, 80203

Young Alive Group 860-1819 • social/support group for ages 18-29 • sponsored by MCC

ACCOMMODATIONS
Elyria's Western Guest House 1655 E. 47th Ave. • 291-0915 • lesbians/gay men • Western ambiance in historic Denver neighborhood • hot tub • shared baths • smokefree • $30-40

Lumber Baron Inn 2555 W. 37th Ave. • 477-8205/(800) 697-6552 • gay-friendly • furnished w/ antiques • full brkfst • hot tub • $125-185

P.T. Barnum Estate 360 King St. • 830-6758 • popular • gay-friendly • B&B on turn-of-the-century estate • shared/private baths

The Queen Anne Inn 2147 Tremont Pl. • 296-6666 • gay-friendly • full brkfst

The Spectacular View B&B Capital Hill • 830-6758 • gay-friendly• high-rise apartment • swimming • smokefree • wheelchair access

Stapleton Plaza Hotel 3333 Quebec St. • 321-3500/(800) 950-6070 • gay-friendly • swimming • also a restaurant • wheelchair access

Victoria Oaks Inn 1575 Race St. • 355-1818/662-6257 • gay-friendly • fireplaces • $50-85

BARS

Adonis (Club America) NW corner of the Tivoli • 534-1777 • 9pm-2am Sun only • mostly men • dancing/DJ • alternative

B.J.'s Carousel 1380 S. Broadway • 777-9880 • 10am-2am • popular • mostly men • neighborhood bar • live shows • volleyball court • patio • also a restaurant • wheelchair access

Brick's 1600 E. 17th Ave. • 377-5400 • 11am-2am • lunch daily • mostly men • neighborhood bar • wheelchair access

Club 22 22 Broadway • 733-2175 • lesbians/gay men • dancing/DJ

Club Proteus 1669 Clarkson • 869-4637 • 9pm-2am, from 5pm Fri & Sun • lesbians/gay men • dancing/DJ • videos • patio • wheelchair access

Club Synergy 3240 Larimer • 575-5680 • 11pm-5am Th-Sat, til 3am Sun • popular • mostly women • dancing/DJ • alternative

Colfax Mining Co. 3014 E. Colfax Ave. • 321-6627 • 10am-2am • lesbians/gay men • neighborhood bar • dancing/DJ • wheelchair access

The Compound 145 Broadway • 722-7977 • 7am-2am, from 8am Sun • mostly gay men • neighborhood bar • also 'Basix' • mostly gay men • dancing/DJ • alternative • 9pm-2am

Den 5110 W. Colfax Ave. • 534-9526 • 10am-2am • lesbians/gay men • neighborhood bar • food served

Denver Detour 551 E. Colfax Ave. • 861-1497 • 11am-2am • popular • lesbians/gay men • dancing/DJ • live shows • lunch & dinner daily • some veggie • $5-9 • wheelchair access

The Elle 716 W. Colfax • 572-1710 • 6pm-2am, 2pm-midnight Sun, clsd Mon-Tue • mostly women • dancing/DJ • patio • wheelchair access

Denver   (303)

WHERE THE GIRLS ARE: Many lesbians reside in the Capitol Hill area, near the gay and mixed bars, but hang out in cafés and women's bars scattered around the city.

LESBIGAY PRIDE: July: 831-6268 ext. 26.

ANNUAL EVENTS: Denver Women's Chorus: 274-4177.

CITY INFO: 892-1112.

ATTRACTIONS: Black American West Museum and Heritage Center. Denver Art Museum. Larimer Square. Mile Hight Flea Market.

BEST VIEW: Lookout Mountain (at night especially) or the top of the Capitol rotunda.

WEATHER: Summer temperatures average about 90° and winter ones about 40°s. The sun shines an average of 300 days a year.

TRANSIT: Yellow Cab: 777-7777. Metro Taxi: 333-3333. Denver Airport Shuttle: 342-5450. RTD: 628-9000 / 299-6000 (infoline).

Flavors 1700 Logan • 830-0535 • 10am-2am • lesbians/gay men • dancing/DJ • live shows • wheelchair access

The Grand Bar 538 E. 17th Ave. • 839-5390 • 3pm-2am • lesbians/gay men • upscale piano bar • patio • wheelchair access

Highland Bar 2532 15th St. • 455-9978 • 2pm-2am • mostly women • neighborhood bar • wheelchair access

Industry 1222 Glenarm Pl. • 620-9554 • mostly gay men • dancing/DJ • call for events

Maximilian's 2151 Lawrence St. • 297-0015 • 9pm-2am Fri & Sat • gay-friendly • dancing/DJ • multi-racial

Metro Express 314 E. 13th Ave. • 894-0668 • 4pm-2am, from 2pm Sun • popular • lesbians/gay men • dancing/DJ • live shows • videos • patio • wheelchair access

Mike's 60 S. Broadway • 777-0193 • 2pm-2am • lesbians/gay men • dancing/DJ • wheelchair access • women-owned/run

Ms C's 7900 E. Colfax Ave. • 322-4436 • 5pm-midnight, til 2am Fri-Sat, from 2pm Sun • mostly women • dancing/DJ • multi-racial • wheelchair access

Denver

*F*or many of us, Denver immediately brings to mind Amendment 2, the hateful denial of civil rights that was overturned by Colorado's Supreme Court. For the less politically inclined, it evokes images of the Rocky Mountains and snow. But to those who live here, Denver is a big city with a friendly small town feel, where the sun always shines.

First off, hit the women's **Book Garden** or the **Gay/Lesbian/Bisexual Center**. Here you'll get the inside scoop on where to go and what to do in Denver. If you ask, you'll even pick up some hints on how to 'have a gay old time' in Cheesman Park or at touristy sites like the 16th St. Mall. Next, pick up a copy of **Lesbians in Colorado (LIC)**, sip coffee at the **Blue Note Cafe**, and peruse the books at the lesbigay **Category Six**. For night-time fun, taste the local cuisine at the women-owned **Basil Cafe**, have a cocktail at **The Elle** women's bar, dance at the **Denver Detour**, a popular gay nightclub, or hoof it up at **Ms. C's** country/western bar.

Outside the 'Mile High City', be sure to take advantage of the Rocky Mountain snows with a ski trip to one of the many nearby resorts: Aspen, Telluride or Rocky Mountain National Park.

Rock Island 1614 15th St. • 572-7625 • gay-friendly • dancing/DJ • alternative • call for events • wheelchair access

Snake Pit 608 E. 13th Ave • 831-1234 • 5pm-2am • popular • mostly gay men • dancing/DJ • alternative • wheelchair access

Three Sisters 3358 Mariposa St. • 458-8926 • 12:30pm-2am • mostly women • neighborhood bar • dancing/DJ

Ye 'O Matchmaker Pub 1480 Humboldt • 839-9388 • 10am-2am • lesbians/gay men • dancing/DJ • multi-racial • live shows • also a restaurant • Mexican/American

RESTAURANTS & CAFES

Alfresco's 100 E. 9th (at Lincoln) • 894-0600 • lunch & dinner, Sun brunch, full bar from 11am • Italian • great patio

Basil's Cafe 30 S. Broadway • 698-1413 • lunch & dinner, clsd Sun • beer/wine • nouvelle veggie • plenty veggie • wheelchair access • women-owned/run • $5-10

Blue Note Cafe 70 S. Broadway • 744-6774 • 8am-10pm, til midnight Fri-Sat, clsd Mon • lesbians/gay men • live shows

City Spirit 1434 Blake • 575-0022 • 11am-midnight • live shows • full bar

Daily Planet Cafe 1560 Broadway • 894-8308 • clsd wknds • full bar • wheelchair access

Denver Sandwich Co. 1217 E. 9th Ave. • 861-9762 • 10:30am-9pm, noon-8pm Sun • wheelchair access

Diced Onions 609 Corona St. • 831-8353 • 7am-3pm, 5pm-8pm Fri & Sat, clsd Mon • diner/deli • under $10

Footloose Cafe 104 S. Broadway • 722-3430 • 9am-10pm, til 5pm Sun • lesbians/gay men • some veggie • full bar • wheelchair access • women-owned/run • $8-12

Java Creek 287 Columbine St. • 377-8902 • 7am-10pm, til 5pm Sun • coffeehouse • live shows • sandwiches & desserts • wheelchair access

Las Margaritas 1066 Old S. Gaylord St. • 777-0194 • from 11am, bar til 2am • Mexican • some veggie • wheelchair access • $6-14

DINAH SHORE
PALM SPRINGS WEEKEND
MARCH 27-30, 1997

The Ultimate Hotel & Entertainment Package at the All Inclusive

DOUBLE TREE RESORT

Book today to ensure availability.
For hotel and party ticket Info Call

310.281.7358

For Airline reservations call
1•800•433•1790 • Star#: S0237LG

Produced by JOANI WEIR PRODUCTIONS • POM POM PRODUCTIONS • KLUB BANSHEE

Michael's Supper Club & Lounge 1509 Marion • 863-8433 • 5pm-10pm, clsd Sun, lounge til 2am Fri-Sat • piano bar • patio

GYMS & HEALTH CLUBS

Broadway Bodyworks 160 S. Broadway • 722-4342 • 6am-9pm, 7am-6pm Sat, 10am-4pm Sun • gay-friendly • wheelchair access

BOOKSTORES & RETAIL SHOPS

Book Garden 2625 E. 12th Ave. • 399-2004/(800) 279-2426 • 10am-6pm, til 8pm Th • women's bookstore • also jewelry • posters • spiritual items • wheelchair access • women-owned/run

Category Six 42 S. Broadway • 777-0766 • 10am-6pm, 11am-5pm wknds • lesbigay

Isis Bookstore 5701 E. Colfax Ave. • 321-0867 • 10am-7pm, til 6pm Fri-Sat, noon-5pm Sun • new age • metaphysical • wheelchair access

Magazine City 200 E. 13th Ave. • 861-8249 • 8am-7pm, 10am-6pm wknds

Newsstand Cafe 630 E. 6th Ave. • 777-6060 • 7am-10pm, til 4pm Sun • popular • wheelchair access • women-owned/run

Tattered Cover Book Store 2955 E. 1st Ave. • 322-7727/(800) 833-9327 • 9:30am-9pm, 10am-6pm Sun • 4 flrs. • wheelchair access

Thomas Floral & Adult Gifts 1 Broadway Ste. 108 (at Ellsworth) • 744-6400 • 8:30am-6pm, til 5pm Sat, clsd Sun • wheelchair access

Unique of Denver 2626 E. 12th • 355-0689 • 10am-6pm, til 7pm in summer • lesbigay gift shop

TRAVEL & TOUR OPERATORS

B.T.C. World Travel 2120 S. Holly Ste. 100 • 691-9200 • women-owned/run

Colorado Tourism Board PO Box 38700, 80238 • (800) 265-6723

Compass Travel 1001 16th St. Ste. A-150 • 534-1292/(800) 747-1292 • women-owned/run • IGTA

Let's Talk Travel/Carlson Travel Network 1485 S. Colorado Blvd. #260 • 759-1318/(800) 934-2506 • IGTA

Lizard Head Expeditions 1280 Humboldt St #32 • 820-2066/(800) 444-5238 • women-only tours avail. • mountaineering, canyoneering & other wilderness skills • tours in central Rocky Mountains & Utah canyon country

Metro Travel 90 Madison Ste. 101 • 333-6777 • women-owned/run • IGTA

Travel 16th St. 535 16th St. #250 • 595-0007/(800) 222-9229 • IGTA

Travel Junction 5455 W. 38th Ave. Ste. C • 420-4646/(800) 444-8980 • women-owned/run • IGTA

SPIRITUAL GROUPS

Congregation Tikvat Shalom Box 6694, 80206 • 331-2706 • lesbigay Jewish fellowship

Dignity-Denver 1100 Fillmore (Capitol Hts. Presb. Church) • 322-8485 • 5pm Sun

Integrity 1280 Vine St. (St. Barnabas) • 388-6469 • 7pm Sun • lesbigay Episcopalians

MCC of the Rockies 980 Church St. • 860-1819 • 9am & 11am Sun • wheelchair access

Pagan Rainbow Network PO Drawer E , 80218 • 377-6283 • 11am 3rd Sun • at Community Center • wheelchair access

St. Paul's Church (Methodist) 1615 Ogden • 832-4929 • 11am Sun

PUBLICATIONS

Colorado Woman News PO Box 22274, 80222 • 355-9229 • professional/feminist newspaper

Lesbians in Colorado PO Box 12259 , 80212 • 482-4393 • statewide • calendar w/ political, social & arts coverage

Out Front 244 Washington, 80203 • 778-7900 • bi-weekly

Quest/H. Magazine 430 S. Broadway • 722-5965 • newspaper • bar guide

EROTICA

The Crypt 131 Broadway • 733-3112 • 10am-10pm, noon-8pm Sun • erotica • leather

Durango (970)

ACCOMMODATIONS

The Guest House 477 E. 4th Ave. • 382-8161 • women only • historic Victorian • smokefree • women-owned/run

Leland House 721 2nd Ave. • 385-1920/(800) 664-1920 • popular • gay-friendly • full brkfst

Estes Park (970)

ACCOMMODATIONS

Distinctive Inns of Colorado PO Box 2061, 80517 • 866-0621 • great brochure

Sundance Cottages PO Box 4830, 80517 • 586-3922 • gay-friendly • women-owned/run • wheelchair access

Fort Collins (970)

INFO LINES & SERVICES

Gay/Lesbian/Bisexual Alliance Lory Student Ctr., LSU Box 206, 80523 • 491-7232 • call for info

BARS

Nightingales 1437 E. Mulberry St. • 493-0251 • 4pm-2am, clsd Mon • lesbians/gay men • dancing/DJ • country/western Th •18+ Fri • call for events • patio • wheelchair access

TRAVEL & TOUR OPERATORS

Fort Collins Travel 333 W. Mountain Ave. • 482-5555/(800) 288-7402

Never Summer Nordic PO Box 1983, 80522 • 482-9411 • lesbians/gay men • yurts (tipi-like shelters) sleep 8-12 in Colorado Rockies • mountain-biking & skiing

Grand Junction (303)

BARS

Quincy's 609 Main St. • 242-9633 • gay-friendly • neighborhood bar • gay after 8pm • wheelchair access

Grand Lake (970)

ACCOMMODATIONS

Grandview Lodge 12429 Hwy. 34 • 627-3914 • gay-friendly • popular • hot tub • sundeck • women-owned/run

Greeley (970)

INFO LINES & SERVICES

Greeley Gay/Lesbian Alliance at U. of Northern Colorado • 351-2065 • hours vary • call for events • leave message for referrals

BARS

C Double R Bar 1822 9th St. Plaza • 353-0900 • 4pm-2am, from 2pm Sun • lesbians/gay men • dancing/DJ • alternative • country/western • wheelchair access

Idaho Springs (303)

ACCOMMODATIONS

Glacier House B&B 603 Lake Rd. • 567-0536 • lesbians/gay men • home-style B&B in a modern mountain chalet • full brkfst • hot tub • $75-85

Keystone (970)

ACCOMMODATIONS

Tanrydoon 463 Vail Circle • 468-1956 • lesbians/gay men • full brkfst • magnificent mountain home amidst the world-class resorts of Keystone, Breckenridge, Copper Mtn. • $50-95

Pueblo (719)

INFO LINES & SERVICES

Pueblo After 2 PO Box 1602, 81002 • 564-4004 • social/educational network • newsletter

BARS

Pirate's Cove 409 N. Union • 542-9624 • 2pm-2am, from 4pm Sun, clsd Mon • lesbians/gay men • neighborhood bar • wheelchair access

SPIRITUAL GROUPS

MCC Pueblo Bonforte & Liberty (Christ Cong. Church) • 543-6460 • 12:30pm Sun

Steamboat Springs (970)

ACCOMMODATIONS

Elk River Estates PO Box 5032, 80477-5032 • 879-7556 • gay-friendly • suburban townhouse B&B near hiking, skiing & natural hot springs • full brkfst • $35-40

Vail (970)

ACCOMMODATIONS

Antlers at Vail 680 W. Lionshead Pl. • 476-2471/(800) 843-8245 • gay-friendly • apts. • hot tub • swimming • fireplace • balcony • kids ok • $205-755

RESTAURANTS & CAFES

Sweet Basil 193 E. Gore Creek Dr. • 476-0125 • lunch & dinner • some veggie • full bar • wheelchair access

Winter Park (970)

ACCOMMODATIONS

Silverado II 490 Kings Crossing Rd. • 726-5753 • gay-friendly • condo ski resort

RESTAURANTS & CAFES

Silver Zephyr (at Silverado II) • 726-8732 • 5pm-10pm • full bar • wheelchair access

CONNECTICUT

Bethel (203)

RESTAURANTS & CAFES
Emerald City Cafe 269 Greenwood Ave. •
778-4100 • lunch, dinner & Sun brunch,
clsd Mon

Bridgeport (203)

RESTAURANTS & CAFES
Bloodroot Restaurant 85 Ferris St. • 576-
9168 • clsd Mon • women's night Wed •
vegetarian • call for events • patio •
wheelchair access • women-owned/run •
$8-12

BOOKSTORES & RETAIL SHOPS
Bloodroot 85 Ferris St • 576-9168 • clsd
Mon • wheelchair access

SPIRITUAL GROUPS
Church of the Celestial Ministries 384-
1660 • call for events

Bristol (860)

BARS
The Stadium 107 South St. • 583-3225 •
mostly gay men • dancing/DJ • live shows

Collinsville (860)

BOOKSTORES & RETAIL SHOPS
Gertrude & Alice's 2 Front St. • 693-3816 •
10am-9pm, til 11pm wknds • live shows •
cafe • patio • wheelchair access

Danbury (203)

INFO LINES & SERVICES
Lesbian Support Group at Women's
Center • 7:30pm Wed
Women's Center of Danbury 256 Main St •
731-5200 • 9am-2:30pm Mon-Fri • exten-
sive info & referrals • support groups

BARS
The Hangar Restaurant & Club 1 Wibling
Rd. (at the Danbury Airport) • 744-4471 •
11:30am-11:30pm, til 2am Fri-Sat • les-
bians/gay men • dancing/DJ
Triangles Cafe 66 Sugar Hollow Rd. Rte. 7
• 798-6996 • 5pm-2am, clsd Mon • popular
• lesbians/gay men • dancing/DJ • live
shows • patio

TRAVEL & TOUR OPERATORS
Aldis The Travel Planner 46 Mill Plain Rd.
• 778-9399/(800) 442-9386 • IGTA

East Windsor (203)

RESTAURANTS & CAFES
The Eatery 297 S. Main St. • 627-7094 •
lunch Mon-Fri, dinner nightly • full bar •
wheelchair access • $6-12

Enfield (203)

EROTICA
Bookends 44 Enfield St. (Rte. 5) • 745-
3988

Hamden (203)

TRAVEL & TOUR OPERATORS
Adler Travel 2323 Whitney Ave. • 288-
8100/(800) 598-2648 • IGTA

Hartford (860)

INFO LINES & SERVICES
AA Gay/Lesbian (see listing in 'Metroline'
magazine) • daily at Gay/Lesbian Comm.
Ctr.
Gay/Lesbian Community Center 1841
Broad St. • 724-5542 • 10am-10pm, wknd
hours vary • also coffeehouse • wheelchair
access
Gay/Lesbian Guide Line 366-3734 • 7pm-
10pm Tue-Th • statewide info
Lesbian Rap Group 135 Broad St. (YWCA)
• 525-1163 • 7:30pm Tue
XX Club PO Box 387, 06141-0387 • trans-
sexual support group

ACCOMMODATIONS
The 1895 House B&B 97 Girard Ave. •
232-0014 • gay-friendly • Victorian home
designed by woman architect, Genevra
Whittemore Buckland • $60-75

BARS
A Bar With No Name 115 Asylum St. •
522-4646 • 4pm-2am, clsd Mon-Wed • gay-
friendly • dancing/DJ • Sun gay night •
wheelchair access
Chez Est 458 Wethersfield Ave. • 525-3243
• 3pm-2am, from noon wknds • popular •
mostly gay men • dancing/DJ
Metro Club & Cafe 22 Union Pl. • 549-
8023 • 4pm-1am, til 2am Fri-Sat, from 3pm
Sun • lesbians/gay men • dancing/DJ • live
shows • food served • patio
Nick's Cafe House 1943 Broad St. • 956-
1573 • 4pm-1am, til 2am Fri-Sat • les-
bians/gay men • quiet front cafe • disco in
back • dancing/DJ

OUT (412) 243-4067/(800) 876-1199 • women only • roving parties • also newsletter • see 'Metroline' for time & place

The Sanctuary 2880 Main St. • 724-1277 • 8pm-2am, from 6pm Sun, clsd Mon-Tue • mostly gay men • dancing/DJ • videos • wheelchair access

Starlight Playhouse & Cabaret 1022 Main St., East Hartford • (860) 289-0789 • 4:30pm-1am Th (club), Fri-Sat (shows) • lesbians/gay men • food served • deli menu • wheelchair access

BOOKSTORES & RETAIL SHOPS

MetroStore 493 Farmington Ave. • 231-8845 • 8am-8pm, til 5:30pm Tue, Wed, Sat, clsd Sun • books • leather • more

Reader's Feast Bookstore Cafe 529 Farmington Ave. • 232-3710 • 10am-9pm, til 10pm Fri-Sat, til 2:30pm Sun • feminist progressive bookstore & cafe • some veggie • live shows

Water Hole Custom Leather 982 Main St., East Hartford • 528-6195 • clsd Mon

TRAVEL & TOUR OPERATORS

Damron Atlas World Travel 653-2492/(888) 907-9777

SPIRITUAL GROUPS

Congregation Am Segulah (800) 734-8524 in CT only • lesbigay Shabbat services

Dignity-Hartford 144 S. Quaker Ln. (Quaker Mtg. House) • 522-7334 • 6pm Sun

MCC 50 Bloomfield Ave. (meeting house) • 724-4605 • 7pm Sun

PUBLICATIONS

Metroline 846 Farmington Ave. Ste. 6, W. Hartford, 06119 • 570-0823 • regional newspaper & entertainment guide

Manchester (860)

INFO LINES & SERVICES

Women's Center at Manchester Community College 60 Bidwell • 647-6056 • 8:30am-4:30pm, til 7pm Tue & Th, clsd wknds

BARS

Encounters 47 Purnell Pl. • 645-6688 • 8pm-1am, til 2am wknds • lesbians/gay men • dancing/DJ • wheelchair access • ladies night Sun

Middletown (203)

INFO LINES & SERVICES

Wesleyan Women's Resource Center 287 High St. • 347-9411 • library

New Britain (860)

TRAVEL & TOUR OPERATORS

Weber's Travel Services 24 Cedar St. • 229-4846 • IGTA

New Haven (203)

INFO LINES & SERVICES

Yale Women's Services 198 Elm St. • 432-0388 • resources • support groups • library • wheelchair access

BARS

168 York St. Cafe 168 York St. • 789-1915 • 2pm-1am • lesbians/gay men • also a restaurant • some veggie • patio • wheelchair access • $6-14

The Bar 254 Crown St. • 495-8924 • 4pm-1am • gay-friendly • more gay Tue • dancing/DJ • wheelchair access

DV8 148 York St. • 865-6206 • 4pm-1am • lesbians/gay men • neighborhood bar • dancing/DJ • wheelchair access

RESTAURANTS & CAFES

Elm City Roasters 59 Elm St. • 776-2555 • 7am-6pm, 9am-1pm Sat, clsd Sun

TRAVEL & TOUR OPERATORS

Plaza Travel Center 208 College St. • 777-7334/(800) 887-7334 • IGTA

SPIRITUAL GROUPS

Dignity PO Box 9362, 06533 • 6:30pm Sun

MCC 34 Harrison St. (United Church) • 389-6750 • 11:30am & 4pm Sun

PUBLICATIONS

The Newsletter: A Lesbian Position PO Box 9205, 06533-0205

New London (203)

INFO LINES & SERVICES

New London People's Forum Affirming Lesbian/Gay Identity 76 Federal (St. James) • 443-8855 • 7:30pm Wed • educational/support group

BARS

Frank's Place 9 Tilley St. • 443-8883 • 4pm-1am, til 2am Fri-Sat • lesbians/gay men • dancing/DJ • live shows • patio • wheelchair access

Heroes 33 Golden St. • 442-4376 • 4pm-1am • lesbians/gay men • more women Th • neighborhood bar • dancing/DJ

BOOKSTORES & RETAIL SHOPS

Greene's Books & Beans 140 Bank St. • 443-3312 • 7am-5:30pm, til 9pm Fri & Sat, from 9am Sat, clsd Sun • wheelchair access

Norfolk (860)

ACCOMMODATIONS

Loon Meadow Farm 41 Loon Meadow Dr. • 542-1776 • gay-friendly • full brkfst • near outdoor recreation • women-owned/run • $65-95

Manor House B&B 69 Maple Ave. • 542-5690 • gay-friendly • elegant & romantic 1898 Victorian Tudor estate • full brkfst • fireplaces • smokefree • kids 12+ ok • $95-190

Norwalk (203)

INFO LINES & SERVICES

Triangle Community Center 25 Van Zant St. • 853-0600 • 7:30pm-9:30pm Mon-Fri • activities • newsletter

ACCOMMODATIONS

Silk Orchid 847-2561 • women only • 1 suite • full brkfst • swimming • $95

TRAVEL & TOUR OPERATORS

B.W. Travel 852-0200 • IGTA

Norwich (203)

INFO LINES & SERVICES

Info Line for Southeastern Connecticut 74 W. Main St. • 886-0516 • 8am-8pm Mon-Fri • crisis counseling

Portland (203)

TRAVEL & TOUR OPERATORS

Brownstone Travel Agency 278 Main St. • 342-3450/(800) 888-4169

Stamford (203)

INFO LINES & SERVICES

Gay/Lesbian Guide Line PO Box 8185, 06905 • 366-3734 • 7pm-10pm Tue-Th • statewide

Thompson Realty 1845 Summer St. • 324-1012 • ask for Debbie

BARS

Art Bar 84 W. Park Pl. • 973-0300 • 9pm-1am • gay-friendly • gay night Sun from 8pm • dancing/DJ • alternative

Storrs (203)

INFO LINES & SERVICES

Bisexual/Gay/Lesbian Association Box U-8, 2110 Hillside Rd., Univ. of CT, 06268 • 486-3679 • 7:30pm Th

Women's Center 417 Whitney Rd. Box U-118 • 486-4738 • wheelchair access

Stratford (203)

BARS

Stephanie's Living Room 377-2119 • popular • mostly women • 'quality social events for women' • dances • concerts • bus trips • multi-racial • wheelchair access • discounts for physically challenged

Wallingford (203)

BARS

Choices 8 North Turnpike Rd. • 949-9380 • 7pm-1am • mostly gay men • 'Girl Twirl' Fri • dancing/DJ • live shows

Waterbury (203)

BARS

The Brownstone 29 Leavenworth St. • 597-1838 • 5pm-1am, clsd Mon • lesbians/gay men • women's night Th • live shows • wheelchair access

Maxie's Cafe 2627 Waterbury Rd. • 574-1629 • 6pm-1am, til 2am Fri-Sat, clsd Mon • lesbians/gay men • dancing/DJ • live shows • women-owned/run

SPIRITUAL GROUPS

Integrity/Waterbury Area 16 Church St. (St. John's) • 754-3116 • call for mtg times

West Haven (203)

ACCOMMODATIONS

Beach Club 295 Beach St. • 937-8100 • lesbians/gay men • swimming • also bar • opens 4pm • dancing/DJ • food served • wheelchair access

Westport (203)

BARS

The Brook Cafe 919 Post Rd. E. • 222-2233 • 5pm-1am, til 2am Fri-Sat, 4pm-11pm Sun • popular • mostly gay men • dancing/DJ • patio • wheelchair access downstairs

Willimantic (302)

EROTICA

Thread City Book & Novelty 503 Main St. • 456-8131

DELAWARE

Bethany Village (302)

BARS

Nomad Village Rte. 1 (3 mi. N. in Tower Shores) • 539-7581 • 10am-1am (seasonal) • lesbians/gay men • also 'Oasis' • dancing/DJ

Claymont (302)

RESTAURANTS & CAFES

Queen Bean Cafe 8 Commonwealth Ave. • 792-5995

Dover (302)

BARS

Rumors 2206 N. DuPont Hwy. • 678-8805 • 11am-2am, from 5pm Sun • popular • lesbians/gay men • ladies night Wed • dancing/DJ • live shows • also a restaurant • wheelchair access • $10-15

TRAVEL & TOUR OPERATORS

Delaware Tourism Office PO Box 1401, 19903 • (800) 441-8846 (outside DE)/(800) 282-8667 (in-state only) • info

Milton (302)

ACCOMMODATIONS

▲ **Honeysuckle** 330 Union St. • (302) 684-3284 • women only • full brkfst • swimming • nudity • women-owned/run • $80-95 • rental houses $125-150

Rehoboth Beach (302)

INFO LINES & SERVICES

Camp Rehoboth 39-B Baltimore Ave. • 227-5620 • 10am-5pm, clsd wknds • info service for lesbigay businesses • newsletter

ACCOMMODATIONS

At Melissa's B&B 36 Delaware Ave. • 227-7054/(800) 396-8090 • gay-friendly • women-owned/run

Beach House B&B 15 Hickman St. • 227-7074/(800) 283-4667 • gay-friendly • swimming • women-owned/run

Mallard Guest House 67 Lake Ave. • 226-3448 • lesbians/gay men • also 60 Baltimore Ave.

Rehoboth Guest House 40 Maryland Ave. • 227-4117 • lesbians/gay men • Victorian beach house • near boardwalk & beach

Honeysuckle

A Women's Victorian Inn & Adjoining Houses near the Delaware beaches

by day
- Inn guests will enjoy a great breakfast
- Go to the women's beach
- Swim nude in our pool
- Schedule a massage
- Use our hot tubs & sauna
- Enjoy our women-only space

by night
- Go out to a marvelous restaurant
—Well, use your imagination!

Reservations required • Mary Ann & Julie   (302) 684-3284

Renegade Restaurant & Lounge/Motel
4274 Hwy. 1 • 227-4713 • lesbians/gay men• 10-acre resort • swimming • full bar • dancing/DJ • also a restaurant (dinner only) • some veggie • wheelchair access • $7-14

Sand in My Shoes Canal & 6th St. • 226-2006/(800) 231-5856 • lesbians/gay men • full brkfst • hot tub • sundeck • kitchens • pets ok

Shore Inn at Rehoboth 703 Rehoboth Ave. • 227-8487/(800) 597-8899 • mostly gay men • hot tub • swimming

▲ **Silverlake** 133 Silver Lake Dr., Rehoboth • 226-2115/(800) 842-2115 • lesbians/gay men • near Poodle Beach • IGTA

Summer Place Hotel 30 Olive Ave. • 226-0766/(800) 815-3925 • gay-friendly • also apts.

BARS

Blue Moon 35 Baltimore Ave. • 227-6515 • 4pm-2am, clsd Jan • gay-friendly • popular happy hour • T-dance • also a restaurant • Sun brunch • plenty veggie • $12-26

RESTAURANTS & CAFES

Back Porch Cafe 59 Rehoboth Ave. • 227-3674 • lunch & dinner • Sun brunch • seasonal • some veggie • full bar • wheelchair access • $9-20

Celsius 50-C Wilmington Ave. • 227-5767 • 5:30pm-11pm • Italian/French • some veggie • wheelchair access • $15-20

Iguana Grill 52 Baltimore Ave. • 227-0948 • 11am-1am • Southwestern • full bar • patio • $7-12

Java Beach 59 Baltimore Ave. • 227-8418 • 7am-6pm • cafe • patio

La La Land 22 Wilmington Ave. • 227-3887 • 6pm-1am (seasonal) • full bar • patio • $18-24

Mano's Restaurant & Bar 10 Wilmington Ave. • 227-6707 • 5pm-10pm

Square One 37 Wilmington Ave. • 227-1994 • 5pm-1am (seasonal) • lesbians/gay men • full bar • $14-22

Sydney's Side Street Restaurant & Blues Place 25 Christian St. • 227-1339 • 5pm-1am, from 11am Sun, clsd Mon-Tue • healthy entrees • full bar • live shows • patio • $12-20

Tijuana Taxi 207 Rehoboth Ave. • 227-1986 • 5pm-10pm, from noon wknds • full bar • wheelchair access • $5-11

GYMS & HEALTH CLUBS

Body Shop 401 N. Boardwalk • 226-0920 • 8am-7pm • lesbians/gay men

BOOKSTORES & RETAIL SHOPS

Lambda Rising 39 Baltimore Ave. • 227-6969 • 10am-midnight (seasonal) • lesbigay • wheelchair access

Wilmington (302)

INFO LINES & SERVICES

Gay AA at the Gay/Lesbian Alliance • 8pm Tue & Th

Gay/Lesbian Alliance of Delaware 601 Delaware Ave. • 652-6776/(800) 292-0429 • 10am-9pm, til 7pm Sat, clsd Sun

Women's Support Group call Gay/Lesbian Alliance • (800) 292-0429

BARS

814 Club 814 Shipley St. • 657-5730 • 5pm-1am • lesbians/gay men • dancing/DJ • also a restaurant • $8-15

Renaissance 107 W. 6th St. • 652-9435 • 10am-2am • popular • lesbians/gay men • dancing/DJ • live shows • sandwiches served

Roam 913 Shipley St. (upstairs) • 658-7626 • 5pm-1am • popular • lesbians/gay men • dancing/DJ • multi-racial

RESTAURANTS & CAFES

The Shipley Grill 913 Shipley St. • 652-7797 • lunch & dinner • fine dining • full bar • live shows • $13-22

SPIRITUAL GROUPS

More Light Hanover Presb. Church (18th & Baynard) • 764-1594 • 1st & 3rd Sun • dinner 5:30pm & worship 6:45pm

Rehoboth Beach (302)

CITY INFO: Rehoboth Beach-Dewey Beach Chamber of Commerce: 227-2233/ (800) 441-1329.

ATTRACTIONS: Anna Hazzard Museum. Cape Henlopen State Park. Poodle Beach. Zwaanendael Museum.

TRANSIT: Seaport Taxi: 645-8100. Shore Leave: (202) 986-6888 (weekend shuttle from Washington D.C. during the season). Jolly Trolley: 227-1197 (seasonal tour & shuttle).

DISTRICT OF COLUMBIA

Washington (202)

INFO LINES & SERVICES

Adventuring PO Box 18118, 20036 • lesbi-gay outdoors group

Asians & Friends 387-2742 • weekly happy hour 5:30pm-7:30pm at Trumpets, call for more info

BiCentrist Alliance PO Box 2254, 20013-2254 • 828-3065 • national bisexual organization with mtgs. & newsletter • taped info

Black Lesbian Support Group 1736 14th St. NW • 797-3593 • 3pm 2nd & 4th Sat

▲ **Bon Vivant** PO Box 576, Derwood MD, 20855 • (301) 907-7920 • social club for lesbian professionals • call for details

Coalition of Gay Sisters (301) 868-8225 • social group for DC area

▲ **Dyke TV** Channel 25 • 9pm Wed • weekly half-hour TV show produced by lesbians for lesbians

Feminist Walking Tours of Capitol Hill PO Box 30563, Bethesda MD, 20824 • (301) 805-5611 • April-Oct

Gay/Lesbian Hotline (Whitman-Walker Clinic) • 833-3234 • 7pm-11pm • resources • crisis counseling

Gay/Lesbian Switchboard 628-4667/628-4669 • 7:30pm-10:30pm • peer counseling & referrals • also 'Lesbian Line' • 628-4666

Hola Gay 332-2192 • 7pm-11pm Th • hot-line en español

Latino/a Lesbian/Gay Organization (LLEGO) 703 'G' St. SE • 466-8240 • 9am-6pm Mon-Fri • also produces bi-monthly newsletter 'Noticias de LLEGO'

Lesbian Resources & Counseling 1407 'S' St. NW (Whitman-Walker Clinic) • 332-5935 • 7pm-9pm Mon w/ rap group 7:30pm-9pm

Lesbian/Gay Youth Helpline (at Sexual Minority Youth Assistance League) • 546-5911 • 7pm-10pm Mon-Fri • for youth under 21

Nubian Womyn Box 65274, 20035-5274 • group for black lesbians over 35

OWLS (Older, Wiser Lesbians) 11212 Lombard Rd., Silver Spring MD, 20901 • (301) 593-6371 • women 39 & better

Roadwork (Sisterfire) 1475 Harvard St. NW • 234-9308 • clsd Mon • organization of women artists

S&Mazons PO Box 53394, 20009 • 722-0056 • women's S/M group

Washington, D.C.

*E*ven though Washington D.C. is known worldwide as a show-case of American culture and a command center of global politics, many people overlook this international 'hot spot' when travelling in the United States. Instead, they're off to exciting cities like New York, LA or Miami. But D.C. is not all boring museums and egocentric bureaucrats.

For instance, begin your stay in D.C. at one of the quaint lesbian/gay B&Bs not far from the city. **Creekside B&B** in Maryland is for women only.

Of course, you could tour the usual sites—starting with the heart of D.C., the 'Mall', a two-mile-long grass strip bordered by many museums and monuments: the Smithsonian, the National Air and Space Museum, the National Gallery of Art, the Museum of Natural History, the Museum of American History, the Washington Monument, the Lincoln Memorial and the Vietnam Veterans Memorial.

But for real fun and infotainment, check out these less touristy attractions: the outstanding National Museum of Women in the Arts, a **Feminist Walking Tour of Capitol Hill**, the hip shops and exotic eateries along Massachusetts Ave., and of course, DuPont Circle, the pulsing heart of lesbigay D.C. The Circle is also home to the lesbian/feminist **Lammas Women's Books & More**, lesbigay bookstore **Lambda Rising** and the kinky **Pleasure Place**.

For nightlife, don't miss the **Hung Jury**, D.C.'s hippest dyke dancespot. **Phase One** is a more casual bar for lesbians, and there are several women's nights at the mixed bars.

Still can't find your crowd? Try **Hola Gay** the lesbian/gay hot-line in Spanish and English, or the **Black Lesbian Support Group**. For the more serious minded, D.C. is home to plenty of political and social women's groups—just call the **Lesbian/Gay Switchboard** or the **Lesbian Resources** line for info.

Transgender Education Association PO Box 16036, Arlington VA, 22215 • (301) 949-3822 • social/support group for cross-dressers & transsexuals

Triangle Club 2030 'P' St. NW • 659-8641 • site for various 12-step groups • see listings in 'The Washington Blade'

ACCOMMODATIONS

1836 California 1836 California St. NW • 462-6502 • gay-friendly • 1900s house w/ period furnishings & sundeck • $60-115

The Brenton B&B 1708 16th St. NW • 332-5550/(800) 673-9042 • mostly gay men • IGTA • $69-79

Capitol Hill Guest House 101 5th St. NE • 547-1050 • gay-friendly • Victorian row-house in historic Capitol Hill district • gay-owned/run • $50-120

The Carlyle Suites 1731 New Hampshire Ave. NW • 234-3200/(800) 964-5377 • gay-friendly • art deco hotel • 'Neon Cafe' on premises • wheelchair access

Creekside B&B south of Annapolis, MD • (301) 261-9438 • women only • private home • 45 min. from DC • swimming

The Embassy Inn 1627 16th St. NW • 234-7800/(800) 423-9111 • gay-friendly • small hotel w/ B&B atmosphere • $69-125

▲ **Kalorama Guest House at Kalorama Park** 1854 Mintwood Pl. NW • 667-6369 • gay-friendly • IGTA • $50-95

▲ **Kalorama Guest House at Woodley Park** 2700 Cathedral Ave. NW • 328-0860 • gay-friendly • IGTA • $45-95

Maison Orleans 414 5th St. SE • 544-3694 • gay-friendly • smokefree • shared/private baths • $65-85

The River Inn 924 25th St. NW (at 'K' St.) • 337-7600/(800) 424-2741 • gay-friendly • also 'Foggy Bottom Cafe' • wheelchair access

Savoy Suites Hotel 2505 Wisconsin Ave. NW, Georgetown • 337-9700/(800) 944-5377 • gay-friendly • also a restaurant • Italian • wheelchair access

The William Lewis House B&B 1309 'R' St. NW • 462-7574 • turn-of-the-century building near Logan & Dupont Circles • $65-75

The Windsor Inn 1842 16th St. NW • 667-0300/(800) 423-9111 • gay-friendly • small hotel w/ B&B atmosphere • $69-150

BARS

Bachelors Mill (downstairs in Back Door Pub) • 544-1931 • 8pm-2am, til 5am Fri-Sat, clsd Mon • lesbians/gay men • more women • dancing/DJ • multi-racial • live shows • wheelchair access

Back Door Pub 1104 8th St. SE • 546-5979 • 5pm-2am, til 3am Fri-Sat • mostly gay men • mostly African-American

Bent 1344 'U' St. NW • 986-6364 • 9pm-3am Fri-Sat • gay-friendly • dancing/DJ • videos

Cafe Escandalo 2122 'P' St. • 822-8909 • 4pm-2am, til 5am Fri-Sat • lesbians/gay men • women's night Th • dancing/DJ • mostly Latino-American • also a restaurant • tapas • some veggie • $5-13

Chief Ike's Mambo Room 1725 Columbia Rd. NW • 332-2211 • 4pm-2am • gay-friendly • dancing/DJ

The Circle 1629 Connecticut Ave. NW • 462-5575 • 11am-2am • popular • mostly gay men • women's night Wed • dancing/DJ • live shows

D.C. Eagle 639 New York Ave. NW • 347-6025 • 6pm-2am, from noon Fri-Sun, til 3am Fri-Sat • popular • mostly gay men • leather • wheelchair access

Diversité 1526 14th St. NW • 234-5740 • Fri & Sun only • gay-friendly • dancing/DJ

El Faro 2411 18th St. NW • 387-6554 • noon-2am • lesbians/gay men • mostly Latino-American • live shows • also a restaurant • Mexican/El Salvadoran • some veggie • $9-14

Fireplace 2161 'P' St. NW • 293-1293 • 1pm-2am • mostly gay men • neighborhood bar • videos

Hung Jury 1819 'H' St. NW, 20006 • 785-8181 • open Fri-Sat only • mostly women • dancing/DJ • call for events • wheelchair access

J.R.'s Bar & Grill 1519 17th St. NW • 328-0090 • 11am-2am, til 3am Fri-Sat • popular • mostly gay men • videos

Larry's Lounge 1836 18th St. (at 'T' St. NW) • 483-1483 • 5pm-midnight, til 2am Fri-Sat • mostly gay men • neighborhood bar • food served • Malaysian • wheelchair access

Mr. Henry's Capitol Hill 601 Pennsylvania Ave. SE • 546-8412 • 11am-1am • popular • gay-friendly • also a restaurant • lunch & dinner • wheelchair access

Washington   (202)

WHERE THE GIRLS ARE: Strolling around DuPont Circle or cruising a bar in the lesbigay bar ghetto southeast of The Mall.

ENTERTAINMENT: Gay Men's Chorus: 338-3464.

LESBIGAY PRIDE: June: 298-0970.

ANNUAL EVENTS: October - Reel Affirmations Film Festival: 986-1119. PFLAG Convention: (415) 328-0852. Annual convention of Parents, Friends and Family of Lesbians and Gays.

CITY INFO: D.C. Visitors Assoc.: 789-7000.

ATTRACTIONS: Ford's Theatre. Jefferson Memorial. JFK Center for the Performing Arts. National Museum of Women in the Arts. Smithsonian. Vietnam Veteran's Memorial.

BEST VIEW: From the top of the Washington Monument.

WEATHER: Summers are hot (90°s) and MUGGY (The city was built on marshes). In the winter, temperatures drop to the low 30°s and some rain. Spring is the time of cherry blossoms.

TRANSIT: Yellow Cab: 544-1212. Washington Flier: (703) 685-1400 (from Dulles or National). Metro Transit Authority: 637-7000.

Nob Hill 1101 Kenyon NW • 797-1101 • 5pm-2am, from 6pm wknds • mostly gay men • dancing/DJ • mostly African-American • live shows • food served

Ozone 1214 18th St. NW • 293-0303 • 9pm-4am, 4pm-9pm Sun, clsd Mon-Wed • mostly gay men • Sun women's night • dancing/DJ

Phase One 525 8th St. SE • 544-6831 • 7pm-2am, til 3am Fri-Sat • mostly women • dancing/DJ • neighborhood bar • wheelchair access

Remington's 639 Pennsylvania Ave. SE • 543-3113 • 4pm-2am • popular • mostly gay men • dancing/DJ • country/western • videos • wheelchair access

Tavern Terrace 1629 Connecticut Ave. NW (at the Circle Bar) • 462-5575 • 2pm-2am, til 3am Fri-Sat • popular • lesbians/gay men • karaoke • videos • popular happy hour

Tracks 1111 First St. SE • 488-3320 • 9pm-4am • popular • lesbians/gay men • women's T-dance last Tue • dancing/DJ • live shows • food served • call for events • wheelchair access

Trumpets 1603 17th St. NW • 232-4141 • 4pm-2am, from 11am Sun (brunch) • popular • lesbians/gay men • ladies night Wed • also a restaurant • New American • some veggie • wheelchair access • $10-18

The Underground 1629 Connecticut Ave. NW (at the Circle bar) • 462-5575 • 9pm-2am • popular • lesbians/gay men • women's night Wed • dancing/DJ • live shows

Ziegfields 1345 Half St. SE • 554-5141 • 8pm-3am Th-Sun • lesbians/gay men • dancing/DJ • alternative • live shows • wheelchair access

Restaurants & Cafes

Annie's Paramount Steak House 1609 17th St. NW • 232-0395 • opens 11am, 24hrs Fri-Sat • popular • full bar

Arizona 1211 Connecticut Ave. NW • 785-1211 • 11:30am-9:30pm, clsd Sun • Southwestern • plenty veggie • dance club Th-Sat til 2am • $6-11

Armand's Chicago Pizza 4231 Wisconsin Ave. NW • 686-9450 • 10am-11pm, til 1am Fri-Sat • full bar • also 226 Massachusetts Ave. NE, Capitol Hill • 547-6600

The Belmont Kitchen 2400 18th St. NW • 667-1200 • clsd Mon • popular brunch • plenty veggie • full bar • patio • wheelchair access • women-owned/run • $12-18

Cafe Berlin 322 Massachusetts Ave. NE • 543-7656 • lunch & dinner, dinner only Sun • German • some veggie • $7-20

Cafe Japoné 2032 'P' St. NW • 223-1573 • 5:30pm-2am • mostly Asian-American • Japanese food • full bar • live shows • karaoke • $10-15

Cafe Luna 1633 'P' St. • 387-4005 • 11am-11pm • popular • lesbians/gay men • multi-racial • healthy • plenty veggie

Cafe Parma 1724 Connecticut Ave NW • 462-8771 • lunch & dinner • full bar

Cusano's Meet Market 1613 17th St. NW • 319-8757 • 8am-11pm, til midnight wknds • lesbians/gay men • cafe • newspapers & magazines • wheelchair access

Gabriel 2121 'P' St. NW • 956-6690 • 10:30am-midnight • Southwestern • some veggie • full bar • live shows • wheelchair access • $13-18

Greenwood 1990 'K' St. NW • 833-6572 • lunch & dinner, clsd Sun • vegetarian/seafood • full bar • wheelchair access

Guapo's 4515 Wisconsin Ave. NW • 686-3588 • lunch & dinner • Mexican • some veggie • full bar • wheelchair access • $5-11

Hannibal's Connecticut Ave. at 'Q' St. NW • 232-5100 • 7am-10pm, til 11pm Fri-Sat • coffee/desserts • wheelchair access

HIV+ Coffeehouse 2111 Florida Ave. NW (Friends Meeting House) • 483-3310 • 7:30pm-10:30pm Sat • HIV+ & friends

Howard's Grill 613 Pennsylvania Ave. SE • 543-2850 • 11am-2am • lesbians/gay men • some veggie • full bar • wheelchair access

The Islander 1762 Columbia Rd. NW • 234-4955 • noon-10pm, from 5pm Mon, clsd Sun • Caribbean • some veggie • BYOB

Lauriol Plaza 1801 18th St. NW • 387-0035 • noon-midnight • Latin American

Pepper's 1527 17th St. NW • 328-8193 • global American • full bar • wheelchair access • $7-14

Randy's Cafe 1517 17th St. NW • 387-5399 • noon-11:30pm, til 2am wknds • lesbians/gay men • Italian/American • inexpensive

Roxanne 2319 18th St. NW • 462-8330 • 5pm-11pm, bar til 2am wknds • also 'Peyote Cafe' • Tex/Mex • some veggie • $8-18

Sala Thai 2016 'P' St. NW • 872-1144 • lunch & dinner • some veggie

Skewers 1633 'P' St. NW • 387-7400 • noon-11pm • Middle-Eastern • full bar • $7-13

Stage Door 1433 'P' St. NW • 234-4050 • open 5pm for cocktails, 6pm for dinner • full bar • transgender-friendly

Straits of Malaya 1836 18th St. NW • 483-1483 • lunch & dinner • Singaporean/Malaysian • full bar • rooftop patio

Trio 1537 17th St. NW • 232-6305 • 7:30am-midnight • some veggie • full bar • wheelchair access • $6-10

Trocadero Cafe 1914 Connecticut Ave. (Hotel Pullman) • 797-2000 • French • intimate setting • wheelchair access • $25-35

Two Quail 320 Massachusetts Ave. NE • 543-8030 • lunch Mon-Fri & dinner nightly • popular • New American • some veggie • full bar • $10-18

GYMS & HEALTH CLUBS

Washington Sports Club 1835 Connecticut Ave. NW • 332-0100 • gay-friendly

BOOKSTORES & RETAIL SHOPS

Earth Star Connection 1218 31st St. NW • 965-2989 • 10am-7pm • rock shop • crystals • Native American handcrafts

Kramer Books & Afterwords 1517 Connecticut Ave. NW • 387-1400 • opens 7:30am, 24hrs wknds • general • cafe • wheelchair access

Lambda Rising 1625 Connecticut Ave. • 462-6969 • 10am-midnight • lesbigay • wheelchair access

▲ **Lammas Women's Books & More** 1426 21st St. NW • 775-8218 • 10am-10pm, 11am-8pm Sun • lesbian/feminist • readings • gifts • music • wheelchair access • women-owned/run

The Map Store, Inc. 1636 'I' St. NW • 628-2608/(800) 544-2659 • extensive maps & travel guides

Outlook 1706 Connecticut Ave. NW • 745-1469 • 10am-10pm, til midnight Fri-Sat • cards • gifts

Vertigo Books 1337 Connecticut Ave. NW • 429-9272 • 10am-7pm, noon-5pm Sun • global politics • literature • African-American emphasis • wheelchair access

TRAVEL & TOUR OPERATORS

Kasper's Livery Service 201 'I' St. Ste. 512 • 554-2471/(800) 455-2471 • limousine service serving DC, MD & VA • gay-owned/run

Passport Executive Travel 1025 Thomas Jefferson St. NW • 337-7718/(800) 222-9800 • IGTA

Travel Escape 1725 'K' St. NW • 223-9354/(800) 223-4163 • IGTA

Washington, DC Convention & Visitors Association 1212 New York Ave. NW • 789-7000

SPIRITUAL GROUPS

Bet Mishpachah 5 Thomas Cir. NW • 833-1638 • 8:30pm Fri • lesbigay synagogue

Dignity Washington 1820 Connecticut Ave. NW (St. Margaret's Church) • 387-4516 • 4:30pm & 7:30pm Sun

Faith Temple (Evangelical) 1313 New York Ave. NW • 232-4911 • 1pm Sun

Friends (Quaker) 2111 Florida Ave. NW (enter on Decatur) • 483-3310 • 9am, 10am, 11am Sun, 7pm Wed

Integrity/Washington 1772 Church St. NW (St. Thomas' Parish) • (301) 953-9421 • 7:30pm 2nd & 4th Fri

Lambda Light-DC PO Box 7355, Silver Springs MD, 20907 • (301) 961-1001 • new age meditation group

Lesbian/Gay Zen Meditation Box 21022, Kalorama Station, 20009-0522 • mail-access only • include your phone number

MCC Washington 474 Ridge St. NW • 638-7373 • 9am, 11am & 7pm Sun

More Light Presbyterians 400 'I' St. SW (Westminister Church) • 484-7700 • 7pm, 11am Sun

PUBLICATIONS

Ibelle 1429 'Q' St. NW • 667-6498

LLEGO Informacion 300 'I'St. NE, 4th flr. • 544-0092 • Latina newsletter

MW/Metro Arts & Entertainment 1649 Hobart St. NW, 20010 • 588-5220

Off Our Backs 2337-B 18th St. NW • 234-8072 • international feminist newspaper

Washington Blade 1408 'U' St. NW, 2nd flr. • 797-7000

Women's Monthly 1001 N. Highland St., Arlington VA, 22201 • (703) 527-4881 • covers DC & VA community events

EROTICA

Leather Rack 1723 Connecticut Ave. NW • 797-7401

▲ **Pleasure Place** 1710 Connecticut Ave. NW • 483-3297 • leather • body jewelry • wheelchair access

▲ **Pleasure Place** 1063 Wisconsin Ave. NW, Georgetown • 333-8570 • leather • body jewelry • wheelchair access

FLORIDA

Amelia Island (904)

ACCOMMODATIONS

The Amelia Island Williams House 103 S. 9th St. • 277-2328 • gay-friendly • magnificent 1856 antebellum mansion • $135-165

Boca Grande (941)

TRAVEL & TOUR OPERATORS

Whelk Women PO Box 10067, 33921 • 964-2027 • boat tours for women • dolphin watching • outfitted camping offered • women-owned/run

Boca Raton (561)

INFO LINES & SERVICES

Boca Lesbian Rap Group PO Box 485, Deerfield Beach, 33443 • 368-6051 • 7:30pm Tue

ACCOMMODATIONS

Floresta Historic B&B 755 Alamanda St. • 391-1451 • lesbians/gay men • swimming

BARS

Choices 21073 Powerline Rd. 2nd flr. • 482-2195 • 3pm-2am, til 3am Fri-Sat • mostly gay men • dancing/DJ • live shows • videos • wheelchair access

SPIRITUAL GROUPS

Church of Our Savior MCC 4770 Boca Raton Blvd. Ste. C • 998-0454 • 10:30am & 7pm Sun • wheelchair access

Bonita Springs (941)

TRAVEL & TOUR OPERATORS

Bonita Beach Travel 4365 Bonita Beach Rd. #124 • 498-0877/(800) 856-4575 • IGTA

Bradenton Beach (941)

ACCOMMODATIONS

Bungalow Beach Resort 2000 Gulf Dr. N. • 778-3600 • gay-friendly • hot tub • kitchens • grills avail. • non-smoking rms. avail. • private beach on Gulf of Mexico

Cape Coral (941)

RESTAURANTS & CAFES

Palate Pleasers 3512 Del Prado S. • 945-6333 • women only Sat night • inquire locally

Clearwater (813)

INFO LINES & SERVICES

Gay/Lesbian Referral Service of Pinellas County 586-4297 • 7pm-11pm • also touch-tone service 24hrs

BARS

Lost & Found 5858 Roosevelt Blvd. (State Rd. 686) • 539-8903 • 4pm-2am, clsd Mon • mostly gay men • live shows • karaoke • patio • wheelchair access

Pro Shop Pub 840 Cleveland • 447-4259 • 11:30am-2am, from 1pm Sun • mostly gay men • neighborhood bar

Cocoa Beach (407)

BARS

Blondies 5450 N. Atlantic Ave. • 783-5339 • 2pm-2am • lesbians/gay men • dancing/DJ • live shows • wheelchair access

RESTAURANTS & CAFES

Mango Tree 118 N. Atlantic Ave. • 799-0513 • opens 6pm, clsd Mon • fine dining • full bar • wheelchair access • $12-17

SPIRITUAL GROUPS

Breaking the Silence MCC 1261 Range Rd., Cocoa • 631-4524 • 7pm Sun

Crescent City (904)

ACCOMMODATIONS

Crescent City Campground Rte. 2 Box 25, 32112 • 698-2020/(800) 634-3968 • gay-friendly • tenting sites • RV hookups • swimming • laundry • showers • $15 day, $90 week, $200 month

Daytona Beach (904)

INFO LINES & SERVICES

Lambda Center 320 Harvey Ave. • 255-0280 • support groups

Live & Let Live AA 1130-B Ridgewood Ave. (Easy Does It Club) • 258-9407 • wheelchair access

RESPECT, Inc. PO Box 5218, 32118 • 257-7071 • gay youth educational group • also referrals

ACCOMMODATIONS

Buccaneer Motel 2301 N. Atlantic Ave. • 253-9678/(800) 972-6056 • gay-friendly • swimming • $55-65

Coquina Inn 544 S. Palmetto Ave. • 254-4969/(800) 805-7533 • gay-friendly • swimming • fireplaces • wheelchair access • IGTA

The Villa 801 N. Peninsula Dr. • 248-2020 • gay-friendly • historic Spanish mansion • swimming • nudity • IGTA • $65-185

BARS

7-69 Restaurant & Lounge 769 Alabama • 253-4361 • 5pm-3am • lesbians/gay men • neighborhood bar • food served • wheelchair access • $3-4

Barndoor 615 Main St. • 252-3776 • 11am-3am • lesbians/gay men • neighborhood bar • also a restaurant • $3-7 • also 'Hollywood Complex' • mostly gay men • dancing/DJ

The Barracks 952 Orange Ave. • 254-3464 • 5pm-3am, from 4pm Sun (BBQ) • popular • mostly gay men • dancing/DJ • live shows • theme nights • wheelchair access

Beach Side Club 415 Main St. • 252-5465 • 2pm-3am, from noon wknds • popular • mostly gay men • dancing/DJ • live shows

RESTAURANTS & CAFES

Cafe Frappes 174 Beach St. • 254-7999 • lunch & dinner • some veggie • patio

TRAVEL & TOUR OPERATORS

Monahan Travel Services 485 S. Nova Rd., Daytona • 677-4495/(800) 476-5876 • IGTA

SPIRITUAL GROUPS

Hope MCC 56 N. Halifax (Unitarian Church) • 254-0993 • 7pm Sun

Dunedin   (813)

BARS

1470 West 325 Main St. • 736-5483 • 4pm-2am, from 8pm Mon • lesbians/gay men • dancing/DJ • live shows • patio • wheelchair access

Fort Lauderdale   (954)

INFO LINES & SERVICES

Broward Women in Network PO Box 9744, 33310 • 564-4946 • professional women's organization

Gay/Lesbian Community Center 1164 E. Oakland Park Blvd. • 563-9500 • 10am-10pm • wheelchair access

Lambda South 1231 E. Las Olas Blvd. • 761-9072 • 12-step clubhouse • wheelchair access

ACCOMMODATIONS

Admiral's Court 21 Hendricks Isle • 462-5072/(800) 248-6669 • lesbians/gay men • motel • swimming • IGTA

Fort Lauderdale   (954)

WHERE THE GIRLS ARE: On the beach near the lesbigay accommodations, just south of Birch State Recreation Area. Or at one of the cafes or bars in Wilton Manors or Oakland Park.

LESBIGAY PRIDE: June: 771-1653.

CITY INFO: 765-4466.

ATTRACTIONS: Antique Row in Dania. Butterfly World. Flamingo Gardens. Museum of Archaeology. Ocean World. Sawgrass Mills, world's largest outlet mall. Six Flags Atlantis:The Water Kingdom.

WEATHER: The average year-round temperature in this sub-tropical climate is 75-90°.

TRANSIT: Yellow Cab: 565-5400. Super Shuttle: 764-1700. Broward County Transit: 357-8400.

Fort Lauderdale

*F*ort Lauderdale, one of Florida's most popular cities and resort areas, has everything that makes the state a natural paradise—sunny skies, balmy nights, hot sands and a clear blue sea.

Honeycombed by the Intercoastal Waterway of rivers, bays, canals and inlets, Fort Lauderdale is an American Venice, where boats are used for transportation!

Land-lubbers can go to the Seminole Indian Reservation, the Everglades, shopping at Sawgrass Mills outlet mega-mall, or to a *jai-alai* game.

For more breathtaking attractions, however, check out Fort Lauderdale's growing lesbian community.

First, you'll find a number of lesbian-friendly accommodations, including the **La Casa del Mar**. Spend the day on a chartered **Rainbow Adventure** cruise. Then replenish your erotica collection from **Fallen Angel**'s supply of fetish and sex toys.

As for lesbian bars, Fort Lauderdale has two: **Otherside** and **Our Playhouse**. Of course, there are several lesbian-friendly bars like **The Copa**, a complete bar complex, where women can mix it up with the gay boys. Or check out Gay Skate Night on Tuesdays at **Gold Coast Roller Rink**.

Tom Rosenblatt Travel 927-8697/(800) 877-8389 • IGTA

Up, Up & Away 701 E. Broward Blvd. • 523-4944/(800) 234-0841 • IGTA

Spiritual Groups

Congregation Etz Chaim 3970 NW 21st. Ave. • 714-9232 • 8:30pm Fri • lesbigay synagogue

Dignity Fort Lauderdale 330 SW 27th St. (at MCC location) • 463-4528 • 2nd & 4th Sun

Sunshine Cathedral MCC 330 SW 27th St. • 462-2004 • 8:30am, 10am, 11:30am, 7pm Sun • wheelchair access

Publications

The Fountain 2221 Wilton Dr., 33305 • 565-7479 • statewide lesbian magazine

Hot Spots 5100 NE 12th Ave., 33334 • 928-1862 • weekly bar guide

Scoop Magazine 2219 Wilton Dr., 33305 • 561-9707

Erotica

Fetish Factory 821 N. Federal Hwy. • 462-0032 • 11am-7pm, noon-6pm Sun

Fort Myers (941)

Info Lines & Services

Gay Switchboard PO Box 546, 33902 • 332-2272 • 8am-11pm • also publishes 'Support-line' newsletter

Accommodations

▲ **Carefree Resort** 3000 Carefree Blvd. • (800) 326-0364 • women's community development on 50 acres • homes to buy or rent • recreation • nature trails

Bars

Attitudes 1605 Hendry St. • 332-3504 • 3pm-2am • mostly gay men • dancing/DJ • wheelchair access

Bottom Line 3090 Evans Ave. • 337-7292 • 3pm-2am • lesbians/gay men • dancing/DJ • live shows • wheelchair access

Office Pub 3704 Grove • 936-3212 • noon-2am • mostly men • neighborhood bar • beer/wine

Restaurants & Cafes

Black Coffee Cafe 2236 First St. • 332-3779 • 10:30am-11pm, 11am-1am Fri, noon-midnight Sat, clsd Sun-Mon • coffeehouse • deli • wheelchair access

Oasis 2222 McGregor Blvd. • 334-1566 • beer/wine • wheelchair access • women-owned/run • $4-6

The Velvet Turtle 1404 Cape Coral Pkwy. • 549-9000 • 5am-9pm, clsd Sun • nouvelle • plenty veggie • full bar • wheelchair access • $10-16

Spiritual Groups

St. John the Apostle MCC 2209 Unity • 278-5181 • 10am & 7pm Sun, 7pm Wed • wheelchair access

Fort Walton Beach (904)

Bars

Frankly Scarlett 223 Hwy. 98 E. • 664-2966 • 8pm-2am, til 4am wknds • lesbians/gay men • dancing/DJ • live shows • patio • wheelchair access

Gainesville (352)

Info Lines & Services

Gay Switchboard 332-0700 • volunteers 6pm-11pm, 24hr touchtone service • extensive info on Gainesville area • AA info

Lesbian/Gay/Bisexual Student Union (U of FL) PO Box 118505, 32611-8505 • 392-1665 x310 • several mtgs. weekly

Bars

Ambush Room (at Melody Club) • 376-3772 • 4pm-2am • popular • mostly gay men • country/western

Melody Club 4130 NW 6th St. • 376-3772 • 8pm-2am, clsd Sun-Mon • popular • lesbians/gay men • dancing/DJ • live shows • patio • wheelchair access • also 'Fishbowl Bar' from 1pm daily

The Oz 7118 W. University Ave. • 332-2553 • 5pm-2am, 11am-11pm Sun • lesbians/gay men • dancing/DJ • patio • wheelchair access

The University Club 18 E. University Ave. • 378-6814 • 5pm-2am, til 4am Fri-Sat, til 11pm Sun • lesbians/gay men • more women Fri • dancing/DJ • live shows • patio • wheelchair access

Bookstores & Retail Shops

Wild Iris Books 802 W. University Ave. • 375-7477 • 10am-6pm, 11am-4pm Sun • feminist bookstore • lesbigay

Travel & Tour Operators

Destinations PO Box 15321, 32604 • 373-3233 • IGTA • also publishes resource directory for Gainesville area

Spiritual Groups

Trinity MCC 11604 SW Archer Rd. • 495-3378 • 10:15am Sun • wheelchair access

Hallandale (305)

ACCOMMODATIONS

Club Atlantic Resort 2080 S. Ocean Dr. • 458-6666/(800) 645-8666 • gay-friendly • rooms & suites on the beach • swimming • also a restaurant • wheelchair access

Holiday (813)

SPIRITUAL GROUPS

Spirit of Life MCC 4810 Mile Stretch Dr. • 942-8616 • 10:30am Sun, 7:30pm Wed • wheelchair access

Hollywood (305)

ACCOMMODATIONS

Maison Harrison Guesthouse 1504 Harrison • 922-7319 • gay-friendly • spa

BARS

Zachary's 2217 N. Federal Hwy. • 920-5479 • 4pm-2am, from 11am wknds • mostly women • neighborhood bar • beer/wine • wheelchair access • women-owned/run

EROTICA

Hollywood Book & Video 1235 S. State Rd. 7 • 981-2164 • 24hrs

Jacksonville (904)

INFO LINES & SERVICES

Gay/Lesbian Information & Referral System 396-8044 • touchtone database for NE Florida

BARS

Boot Rack Saloon 4751 Lenox Ave. • 384-7090 • 2pm-2am • mostly gay men • country/western • patio

Eagle 1402-6 San Marco Blvd. • 396-8551 • 10am-2am • mostly gay men • leather • food served • patio • wheelchair access

Edgewater Junction 1261 King St. • 388-3434 • 2pm-2am • mostly gay men • neighborhood bar • beer/wine

Exile 616 Park St. • 354-2025 • 3pm-2am, from 5pm wknds • mostly gay men • neighborhood bar • live shows • beer/wine • patio

HMS 1702 E. 8th St. • 353-9200 • 2pm-2am • mostly gay men • neighborhood bar • beer/wine • patio

In Touch Tavern 10957 Atlantic Blvd. • 642-7506 • noon-2am, from 3pm Sun • lesbians/gay men • neighborhood bar • beer/wine • wheelchair access

The Metro 2929 Plum St. • 388-8719 • 4pm-2am, clsd Mon • lesbians/gay men • dancing/DJ • neighborhood bar • patio

My Little Dude/Jo's Place 2952 Roosevelt Blvd. • 388-9503 • 4pm-2am • mostly women • dancing/DJ • live shows • wheelchair access

Park Place Lounge 2712 Park St. • 389-6616 • noon-2am • mostly gay men • neighborhood bar • wheelchair access

Tackee's 1746 Talleyrand • 355-1700 • 3pm-2am • mostly gay men • patio

Third Dimension 711 Edison Ave. • 353-6316 • 3pm-2am, from 5pm wknds • mostly gay men • dancing/DJ • alternative • live shows • wheelchair access

BOOKSTORES & RETAIL SHOPS

Otherside of the Rainbow 2709 Park St. • 389-5515/(800) 429-7723 • 11am-7pm, clsd Sun • lesbigay books • also pride gift store • t-shirts • flags • cards • wheelchair access

SPIRITUAL GROUPS

St. Luke's MCC 1140 S. McDuff Ave. • 389-7726 • 10am & 6pm Sun

PUBLICATIONS

The Last Word PO Box 60582, 32236 • 384-6514/(800) 677-0772

Jacksonville Beach (904)

BARS

Bo's Coral Reef 201 5th Ave. N. • 246-9874 • 2pm-2am • lesbians/gay men • dancing/DJ • live shows

Jasper (904)

ACCOMMODATIONS

The Swan Lake B&B 238 Rte. 129 • 792-2771 • lesbians/gay men • full brkfst • hot tub • swimming • nudity

Key West (305)

INFO LINES & SERVICES

Gay AA 296-8654 • call for times & locations

Helpline 296-4357 • gay-friendly referrals & assistance

Key West Business Guild PO Box 1208, 33041 • 294-4603/(800) 535-7797 • IGTA

ACCOMMODATIONS

1004 Eaton 1004 Eaton St. • 296-8132/(800) 352-4414 • lesbians/gay men • restored 1880s conch house • swimming • nudity • $99-149

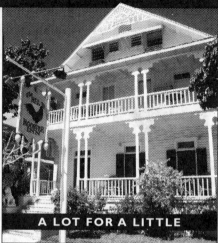

Alexander Palms Court 715 South St. • 296-6413/(800) 858-1943 • gay-friendly • swimming • $125-295

▲ **Alexander's Guest House** 1118 Fleming St. • 294-9919/(800) 654-9919 • mostly gay men • swimming • nudity • IGTA • $120-214

Andrew's Inn Zero Whalton Ln. • 294-7730 • popular • lesbians/gay men • elegantly restored rooms & garden cottages • swimming • wheelchair access • $148-378

The Artist House 534 Eaton St. • 296-3977/(800) 593-7898 • gay-friendly • Victorian guesthouse • hot tub

Atlantic Shores Resort 510 South St. • 296-2491/(800) 526-3559 • gay-friendly • swimming • also a restaurant • 3 bars • IGTA • $105-135

Author's of Key West 725 White St. • 294-7381/(800) 898-6909 • gay-friendly • swimming

Banana's Foster Bed 537 Caroline St. • 294-9061/(800) 653-4888 • gay-friendly • historic Conch house B&B • swimming • wheelchair access • $160-180

Big Ruby's Guesthouse 409 Appelrouth Ln. • 296-2323/(800) 477-7829 • mostly gay men • full brkfst • swimming • nudity • evening wine service • wheelchair access • IGTA

Blue Parrot Inn 916 Elizabeth St. • 296-0033/(800) 231-2473 • gay-friendly • swimming • nudity

The Brass Key Guesthouse 412 Frances St. • 296-4719/(800) 932-9119 • mostly gay men • popular • luxury guesthouse • full brkfst • swimming • spa • IGTA • wheelchair access • $130-215

▲ **Chelsea House** 707 Truman Ave. • 296-2211/(800) 845-8859 • gay-friendly • swimming • nudity • wheelchair access • IGTA • $75-260

Coconut Grove Guesthouse 817 Flemming St • 296-5107/(800) 262-6055 • mostly gay men • 2 Victorian mansions set in lush tropical gardens • swimming • nudity • IGTA • $85-220

Colours - The Guest Mansion 410 Fleming St. • 294-6977/(800) 277-4825 • popular • lesbians/gay men • swimming • complimentary sunset cocktails • IGTA

Cuban Club Suites 1102-A Duval St. • 296-0465/(800) 432-4849 • gay-friendly • award-winning historic hotel overlooking Duval St. • IGTA • $200-300

Key West

This tiny 'Caribbean' island at the very tip of Florida, closer to Cuba than to Miami, is a lesbian and gay tropical paradise. Key West is a way of life, not just an exotic resort. Locals have perfected a laissez-faire attitude and visitors quickly fall into the rhythm.

The famous Old Town area is dotted with Victorian homes and mansions. Many of them are now fully renovated as accommodations, such as the women-only **Rainbow House**.

Perhaps because the Key West life is so relaxed, there's only one mixed bar, **Club International**, and a few boys' bars. But you'll be thoroughly entertained spending your days lounging poolside with warm tropical breezes in your hair and a cool drink in your hand.

Or get out of that lounge chair and sail the emerald waters around Key West with **Women on the Water**. The ocean is home to the hemisphere's largest living coral reef, accessible by snorkeling and scuba vessels. Rent a moped from one of the many bike rental shops to cruise the island—an inexpensive and fun way to get around.

Don't miss **Women Fest** in July, the annual women's week in Key West—the ideal time and place to experience women entertainers, sailing, boating, snorkeling, a street fair, dances, and more. **Fantasy Fest** in October is seven days of Halloween in tropical heaven: costumes, contests, parades, and parties galore. The **Key West Gay Arts Festival** features a week-long cultural celebration. Contact the **Key West Business Guild** for further information.

For other fun events, pick up a **Southern Exposure** paper.

Key West (305)

WHERE THE GIRLS ARE: You can't miss 'em during Women Fest in July, but other times they're just off Duval St. somewhere between Eaton and South Streets. Or on the beach. Or in the water.

ANNUAL EVENTS: July- Women Fest: 296-4238 / (800) 535-7797. October- Fantasy Fest: (800) 535-7797, week-long Halloween celebration with parties, masquerade balls and parades. December (1997, usually held in June)- International Gay Arts Fest: (800) 535-7797, cultural festival of film, theatre, art, concerts, seminars, parties and a parade.

CITY INFO: Key West Chamber of Commerce: 294-2587.

ATTRACTIONS: Audobon House and Gardens. Dolphin Research Center. Glass-bottom boats. Mallory Market. Red Barn Theatre. Southernmost Point U.S.A.

BEST VIEW: Old Town Trolley Tour (1/2 hour).

WEATHER: The average temperature year-round is 78°, and the sun shines nearly everyday—any time is the right time for a visit.

TRANSIT: Yellow Cab: 294-2227.

▲ **Deja Vu Resort** 611 Truman Ave. • 292-1424/(800) 724-5351 • lesbians/gay men • hot tub • swimming

Duval House 815 Duval St. • 294-1666/(800) 223-8825 • popular • gay-friendly • swimming • IGTA • $75-250

Duval Suites 724 Duval St. • 293-6600/(800) 648-3780 • lesbians/gay men • nudity

Early House 507 Simonton St. • 296-0214

Eaton Lodge 511 Eaton St. • 292-2170/(800) 294-2170 • gay-friendly • 1886 mansion & conch house adjacent to Duval St. • hot tub • swimming • $125-175

Garden House 329 Elizabeth St. • 296-5368/(800) 695-6453

Incentra Carriage House Inn 729 Whitehead St. • 296-5565/(800) 636-7432 • gay-friendly • 3 houses surrounding lush garden • swimming • $79-365

▲ **The Island Key Courts** 910 Simonton St. • 296-1148/(800) 296-1148 • gay-friendly • inquire for packages for women

Key Lodge Motel 1004 Duval St. • 296-9750/(800) 458-1296 • popular • gay-friendly • swimming

La Casa de Luces 422 Amelia St. • 296-3993/(800) 432-4849 • gay-friendly • early 1900s conch house • wheelchair access • $70-120

La Terraza/La Te Da 1125 Duval St. • 296-6706/(800) 528-3320 • popular • lesbians/gay men • tropical setting • swimming • gourmet restaurant • 2 bars • Sun T-dance • IGTA

Marquesa Hotel 600 Fleming St. • 292-1919/(800) 869-4631 • gay-friendly • swimming • also a restaurant • some veggie • full bar • $17-26 • wheelchair access

Merlin Guesthouse 811 Simonton St. • 296-3336/(800) 642-4753 • gay-friendly • full brkfst • swimming • wheelchair access • $90-150

The Mermaid and the Alligator 729 Truman Ave. • 294-1894/(800) 773-1894 • gay-friendly • full brkfst • swimming • nudity

Pegasus International 501 Southard • 294-9323/(800) 397-8148 • gay-friendly • swimming • also a restaurant

Pier House Resort & Caribbean Spa | Duval St. • 296-4600/(800) 327-8340 • gay-friendly • private beach • swimming • restaurants • bars • spa • fitness center • IGTA

Pilot House Guest House 414 Simonton St. • 294-8719/(800) 648-3780 • lesbians/gay men • 19th century Victorian in Old Town • hot tub • swimming • nudity

▲ **The Rainbow House** 525 United St. • 292-1450/(800) 749-6696 • women only • hot tub • swimming • nudity • smokefree • wheelchair access • lesbian-owned/run • $99-169

▲ **Red Rooster Inn** 709 Truman Ave. • 296-6558/(800) 845-0825 • gay-friendly • 19th century wooden 3-story inn • swimming

Sea Isle Resort 915 Windsor Ln. • 294-5188/(800) 995-4786 • mostly gay men • hot tub • swimming • nudity • large private courtyard • gym • sundeck • IGTA • $75-250

Seascape Guest House 420 Olivia • 296-7776/(800) 765-6438 • gay-friendly • recently restored inn circa 1889 located in the heart of Old Town • swimming • $94-109

▲ **Simonton Court Historic Inn & Cottages** 320 Simonton St. • 294-6386/(800) 944-2687 • popular • lesbians/gay men • 23-unit compound built in 1880s • hot tub • 3 pools • IGTA • $150-350

Watson House 525 Simonton St. • 294-6712/(800) 621-9405 • gay-friendly • swimming

William Anthony House 613 Caroline St. • 294-2887/(800) 613-2276 • gay-friendly • award-winning historic inn • swimming • social hour • wheelchair access

The William House 1317 Duval St. • 294-8233/(800) 848-1317 • gay-friendly • turn-of-the-century guesthouse • spa • $115-170

BARS

801 Bar 801 Duval St. • 294-4737 • 11am-4am • mostly gay men • neighborhood bar • live shows • also 'Dan's Bar' from 9pm • mostly gay men • leather

Bourbon Street Pub 730 Duval St. • 296-1992 • noon-4am • lesbians/gay men • live shows • videos • wheelchair access

Club International 900 Simonton St. • 296-9230 • 1pm-4am • mostly women • neighborhood bar • videos

Copa 623 Duval St. • 296-8522 • mostly gay men • dancing/DJ • live shows • videos • patio

Donnie's 618 Duval St. (rear) • 294-5620 • 24hrs • gay-friendly • neighborhood bar • wheelchair access

One Saloon 524 Duval St. (enter on Appelrouth Ln.) • 296-8118 • 10pm-4am • mostly gay men • 3 bars • dancing/DJ • patio • wheelchair access

RESTAURANTS & CAFES

Antonia's 615 Duval St. • 294-6565 • 6pm-11pm • popular • Northern Italian • beer/wine • some veggie • $16-22

B.O.'s Fish Wagon corner of Duval & Fleming • 294-9272 • popular • lunch • 'seafood & eat it' • $3-8

Cafe des Artistes 1007 Simonton St. • 294-7100 • 6pm-11pm • tropical French • full bar • $22-30

Croissants de France 816 Duval St. • 294-2624 • 7:30am-4pm • lesbians/gay men • French pastries/crepes/gallettes • some veggie • beer/wine • patio • $5-7

Dim Sum 613-1/2 Duval St. • 294-6230 • clsd Tue • Pan-Asian • plenty veggie • beer/wine • sake cocktails • $13-17

Duffy's Steak & Lobster House 600 Truman Ave. • 296-4900 • 11am-11pm • full bar • $15-30

Dynasty 918 Duval St. • 294-2943 • 5:30pm-10pm • Chinese • beer/wine • $7-16

La Trattoria Venezia 524 Duval St. • 296-1075 • lesbians/gay men • Italian • full bar • $12-22

Lobos 611 1/2 Duval St. • 296-5303 • 11am-6pm, clsd wknds • plenty veggie • lesbian-owned/run • $4-7

Louie's Backyard 700 Waddell Ave. • 294-1061 • lunch & dinner, bar 11:30am-2am • popular • fine cont'l dining • $22-30

Mango's 700 Duval St. • 292-4606 • 11am-2am • int'l • plenty veggie • full bar • wheelchair access • $10-22

Palm Grill 1029 Southard St. • 296-1744 • some veggie • $16-20

Pancho & Lefty's Southwestern Cafe 632 Olivia St. • 294-8212 • 5pm-10:30pm, clsd Tue • Mexican • beer/wine • $5-10

The Quay 10 Duval St. • 294-4446 • gourmet • some veggie • $13-18

Rooftop Cafe 310 Front St. • 294-2042 • American/Caribbean • some veggie • live shows • $10-22

Savannah 915 Duval St. • 296-6700 • dinner nightly • popular • lesbians/gay men • Southern homecooking • garden bar • beer/wine • $11-16

South Beach Seafood & Raw Bar 1405 Duval St. • 294-2727 • 7am-10pm • around $15 for dinner

Square One 1075 Duval St. • 296-4300 • 6:30pm-10:30pm, Sun brunch • full bar • wheelchair access • $14-22

The Twisted Noodle 628 Duval St. • 296-6670 • 5pm-10:30pm • Italian • $7-15

Yo Sake 722 Duval St. • 294-2288 • 6pm-11pm • Japanese/sushi bar • beer/wine • $10-18

GYMS & HEALTH CLUBS

Club Body Tech 1075 Duval St. • 292-9683 • 6am-11pm, 9am-10pm wknds • lesbians/gay men • full gym • sauna • massage therapy avail.

Pro Fitness 1111 12th St. • 294-1865 • 6am-9pm, from 9am-7pm Sat & 11am-5pm Sun • women-owned/run

BOOKSTORES & RETAIL SHOPS

Aloegenetic 524 Front St. • (800) 445-2563 • mail order avail.

Blue Heron Books 538 Truman Ave. • 296-3508 • 10am-10pm, til 9pm Sun • general w/ lesbigay section

Caroline St. Books & Cafe 800 Caroline St. • 294-3931 • 10am-10pm • alternative • also coffee bar • wheelchair access

Fast Buck Freddie's 500 Duval St. • 294-2007 • 11am-7pm • clothing • gifts

Key West Island Books 513 Fleming St. • 294-2904 • 10am-6pm • new & used rare books

Lido 532 Duval St. • 294-5300 • 10am-7pm, til 10pm Th-Sat, 11am-7pm Sun • clothing • gifts • gay-owned/run

Star Gazers 425-A Front St. • 296-1186/(800) 291-1186 • 10am-10pm • new age • metaphysical

TRAVEL & TOUR OPERATORS

Escape Cruises Key West Bight marina • 296-4608 • 3-hr reef trip & sunset cruise on 'SS Sunshine'

Hans Ebensten Travel 513 Fleming St. • 294-8174

IGTA (International Gay Travel Association) PO Box 4974, 33041 • 296-6673/(800) 448-8550 • active organization for lesbian/gay travel industry

Regency Travel 1075 Duval St. #19 • 294-0175/(800) 374-2784 • IGTA

▲ **Women on the Water** PO Box 502, 33041 • 294-0662 • day & evening sails • snorkel trips • lesbian-owned/run

SPIRITUAL GROUPS

MCC Key West 1215 Petronia St. • 294-8912 • 9:30am & 11am Sun • wheelchair access

PUBLICATIONS

Southern Exposure 819 Peacock Plaza Ste. 575, 33041 • 294-6303

EROTICA

Leather Masters 418-A Appelrouth Ln. • 292-5051 • custom leather

Lake Worth (407)

BARS

Club 502 502 Lucerne Ave. • 540-8881 • 4pm-2am, 11am-midnight Sun, clsd Mon • lesbians/gay men • dancing/DJ • piano bar • T-dance Sun • also a restaurant • some veggie • wheelchair access

Inn Exile 6 S. 'J' St. • 582-4144 • 3pm-2am, til midnight Sun • mostly gay men • live shows • videos

K & E's 29 S. Dixie Hwy. • 533-6020 • 11am-2am, from 2pm wknds • lesbians/gay men • karaoke • food served

Lakeland (941)

INFO LINES & SERVICES

PGLA (Polk Gay/Lesbian Alliance) PO Box 8221, 33802-8221 • 644-0085

ACCOMMODATIONS

Sunset Motel & RV Resort 2301 New Tampa Hwy. • 683-6464 • gay-friendly • motels, apts, RV hookups & private home on 3 acres • swimming • wheelchair access

BARS

Dockside 3770 Hwy. 92 E. • 665-2590 • 4pm-2am • lesbians/gay men • dancing/DJ • live shows • gay owned/run

Roy's Green Parrot 1030 E. Main St. • 683-6021 • 4pm-2am, til midnight Sun • popular • mostly gay men • dancing/DJ • live shows • beer/wine

Largo (813)

BARS

Sports Page Pub 13344 66th St. N. • 538-2430 • noon-2am, from 1pm Sun • lesbians/gay men • sports bar • food served • wheelchair access

Madeira Beach (813)

BARS

Surf & Sand Lounge/Back Room Bar 14601 Gulf Blvd. • 391-2680 • 8am-2am • mostly gay men • neighborhood bar • beach access • wheelchair access

Melbourne (407)

BARS

Loading Zone 4910 Stack Blvd. • 727-3383 • 8pm-2am, clsd Mon • popular • lesbians/gay men • dancing/DJ • videos • wheelchair access

Saturday's Lounge 4060 W. New Haven Ave. • 724-1510 • 2pm-2am • popular • lesbians/gay men • dancing/DJ • live shows

Miami (305)

INFO LINES & SERVICES

Gay/Lesbian/Bisexual Hotline of Greater Miami 759-3661

Lambda Dade AA 573-9608 • 8:30pm daily • call for other mtg. times • wheelchair access

Lesbian/Gay/Bisexual Community Center 1335 Alton Rd. • 531-3666 • 6pm-9pm, clsd Sun-Mon

PALS-Lesbian Social 759-6423 • 2nd Fri • call for location

Switchboard of Miami 358-4357 • 24hrs • gay-friendly info & referrals for Dade County

BARS

Cheers 2490 SW 17th Ave., Coconut Grove • 857-0041 • 9pm-3am, clsd Mon-Tue • mostly women • dancing/DJ • live shows • wheelchair access

On the Waterfront 3615 NW South River Dr. • 635-5500 • popular • lesbians/gay men • dancing/DJ • multi-racial • live shows • call for events

Splash 5922 S. Dixie Hwy. • 662-8779 • 4pm-2am, clsd Mon • mostly gay men • dancing/DJ • live shows • 'Bliss' Fri only • mostly women

Sugar's 17060 W. Dixie • 940-9887 • 3pm-6am • mostly gay men • more women Fri • neighborhood bar • dancing/DJ • videos • wheelchair access

RESTAURANTS & CAFES

Oak Feed 2911 Grand Ave. , Coconut Grove • 446-9036 • 11am-10pm • sushi/vegetarian

Something Special 7762 NW 14th Ct. (private home) • 696-8826 • noon-9pm, 2pm-7pm Sun • women only • vegetarian • plenty veggie • also tent space

The Strand 671 Washington Ave. • 532-2340 • 6pm-2am • some veggie • full bar • wheelchair access • $7-12

BOOKSTORES & RETAIL SHOPS

Lambda Passages Bookstore 7545 Biscayne Blvd. • 754-6900 • 11am-9pm, noon-6pm Sun • lesbigay/ feminist bookstore

WOW Boutique 3415 Main Hwy., Coconut Grove • 443-6824 • club clothes

TRAVEL & TOUR OPERATORS

Professional Travel Management 195 SW 15th Rd. Ste. 403 • 858-5522/(800) 568-4064 • IGTA

Vision Travel: Carlson Travel Network 2222 Ponce de Leon Blvd. • 444-8484/(800) 654-4544

SPIRITUAL GROUPS

Christ MCC 7701 SW 76th Ave. • 284-1040 • 9:30am & 7pm Sun • wheelchair access

Grace MCC 10390 NE 2nd Ave., Miami Shores • 758-6822 • 11:30am Sun

PUBLICATIONS

The Fountain 2221 Wilton Dr., Fort Lauderdale • (954) 565-7479 • statewide lesbian magazine

TWN (The Weekly News) 901 NE 79th St. • 757-6333

EROTICA

Le Jeune Road Books 928 SW 42nd Ave. • 443-1913 • 24hrs

Pleasure Emporium 1019 5th St. • 673-3311 • large section for women only

Miami Beach/South Beach (305)

INFO LINES & SERVICES

South Beach Business Guild 234-7224 • maps & info

ACCOMMODATIONS

Abbey Hotel 300 21st St. • 531-0031 • gay-friendly • studios • kitchens

Miami (305)

WHERE THE GIRLS ARE: In Miami proper, Coral Gables and the University district, as well as Biscayne Blvd. along the coast, are the lesbian hangouts of choice. You'll see women everywhere in South Beach, but especially along Ocean Dr., Washington, Collins and Lincoln Roads.

ENTERTAINMENT: Bridge Theater Play Readings at the Community Center, Wednesdays.

LESBIGAY PRIDE: June: 771-1653.

ANNUAL EVENTS: March - Winter Party: (305) 593-6666. AIDS benefit dance on the beach. November - White Party Vizcaya: (305) 757-4444. AIDS benefit.

CITY INFO: Greater Miami Convention and Visitors Bureau: 539-3000.

ATTRACTIONS: Bass Museum of Art. Bayside Market Place. Miami Beach Art Deco District. Miami Museum of Science & Space Transit Planetarium. Orchid Jungle. Parrot Jungle and Gardens.

BEST VIEW: If you've got money to burn, a helicopter flight over Miami Beach is a great way to see the city. Otherwise, hit the beach.

WEATHER: Warm all year. Temperatures stay in the 90's during the summer and drop into the mid-60's in the winter. Be prepared for sunshine!

TRANSIT: Yellow Cab: 444-4444. Metro Taxi: 888-8888.

Miami & South Beach

*A*s a key center of business and politics in the Americas, Miami has an incredibly multicultural look and feel. You'll discover a diversity of people, from a growing population of transplanted senior citizens to large communities of Cubans, Latin-Americans, and Americans of African descent.

Miami is also a tourist's 'winter wonderland' of sun, sand and sea. Make the most of it with trips to Miami Beach, Seaquarium, Key Biscayne or the nearby Everglades. As for Miami's 'women wonderland', check out **Cheers** or try one of the multi-racial, mixed lesbian/gay bars. For a more low-key evening, try the 3rd Friday Night Womyn's Group at the **Lesbian/Gay/Bisexual Community Center** or the **Women's Film Series** on the 4th Friday at the New Alliance Theater (600 Lincoln Rd. #219 at Penn Ave.).

Or make reservations to dine at **Something Special**, a women-only restaurant in a private home. Get the latest dirt from **Lips**, South Florida's 'newspaper for the contemporary woman,' or **The Fountain** women's magazine, both available at **Lambda Passages**, the lesbigay bookstore.

But if you're really hungry for loads of lesbigay culture, head directly for South Beach. This section of Miami Beach has been given an incredible makeover by gays and lesbians.

Much of the scene there is gay boys and drag queens, but svelte, hot-blooded women are in abundance too. During the day, 12th St. beach is the place to be seen. Try the **Palace Grill** for a queer mid-afternoon munch and great people-watching across from the 12th St. gay beach. **821** attracts professional women on their women's nights hosted by Mary D, and on Saturdays Latinas exercise social graces at the Miami Racquet & Fitness Club on Bird Rd. at 93rd Ave. Saturday afternoons **The Penguin's** ladies happy hour is the place for lesbian lounge lizards. Serious dance-aholics cruise the **Kremlin** on Saturday nights. Later, head to **Wolfie's** or the **News Cafe** for an after-dancing meal.

If you're dazzled by South Beach's historic Art Deco architecture, take the walking tour that leaves from the Miami Welcome Center at 1224 Ocean Dr. (672-2014) for under $10.

The Bayliss 504 14th St. • 534-0010 • lesbians/gay men • art deco hotel

Bohemia Gardens 825 Michigan Ave. • 758-3902/(800) 472-4102 • gay-friendly • hot tub • $75-150

Chelsea Hotel 944 Washington Ave. • 534-4069 • gay-friendly

Collins Plaza 318 20th St. • 532-0849 • gay-friendly • hotel

The Colours - The Mantell Guest Inn 255 W. 24th St. • 538-1821/(800) 277-4825 • lesbians/gay men • several art deco hotels & apts avail. • swimming • IGTA • $79-159

European Guesthouse 721 Michigan Ave. • 673-6665 • lesbians/gay men • full brkfst • hot tub • IGTA • $69-89

Fountainbleu Hilton Resort & Spa 4441 Collins Ave. • 538-2000/(800) 445-8667 • gay-friendly • swimming • wheelchair access

Hotel Impala 1228 Collins Ave. • 673-2021/(800) 646-7252 • gay-friendly • luxury hotel near beach • wheelchair access

Jefferson House B&B 1018 Jefferson • 534-5247 • gay-friendly • tropical garden • IGTA • $80-130

Kenmore Hotel 1050 Washington Ave. • 531-4199 • gay-friendly • swimming • $69-89

Lily Guesthouse 835 Collins Ave. • 535-9900 • popular • gay-friendly • studios • suites • sundeck

Lord Balfour 350 Ocean Dr. • 673-0401/(800) 501-0401 • gay-friendly

Marlin Hotel 1200 Collins Ave. • 673-8770/(800) 688-7678 • gay-friendly • upscale • wheelchair access

Moline Garden Guesthouse 825 Michigan Ave. • 556-9997 • gay-friendly

Park Washington 1020 Washington • 532-1930 • gay-friendly • hotel • swimming

Penguin Hotel & Bar 1418 Ocean Dr. • 534-9334/(800) 235-3296 • lesbians/gay men • also a restaurant • plenty veggie • full bar • cafe/juice bar

The Shelborne Beach Resort 1801 Collins Ave. • 531-1271/(800) 327-8757 • gay-friendly • poolside bar • terrace cafe

Shore Club Resort 1901 Collins Ave. • 534-3443/(800) 327-8330

South Beach Destinations 666-0163/(800) 443-8224 • reservation service

South Florida Hotel Network 538-3616/(800) 538-3616 • gay-friendly • hotel reservations • vacation rentals • IGTA • gay-owned/run

Villa Paradiso Guesthouse 1415 Collins Ave. • 532-0616 • gay-friendly • studios • $75-115

The Winterhaven 1400 Ocean Dr. • 531-5571/(800) 395-2322 • gay-friendly • classic example of deco architecture • also a restaurant • full bar • cafe • IGTA • $45-125

BARS

821 821 Lincoln Rd. • 534-0887 • 3pm-4am • gay-friendly • women's night Th from 6pm • neighborhood bar • dancing/DJ • live shows

Bash 655 Washington Ave. • 538-2274 • 10pm-5am, clsd Mon • gay-friendly • dancing/DJ • patio

Comedy Zone 1121 Washington Ave. • 672-4788 • gay-friendly • gay night Tue • call for events

Kremlin 727 Lincoln Rd. • 673-3150 • 10am-4am, clsd Sun-Wed • lesbians/gay men • more women Sat • dancing/DJ

Salvation 1771 West Ave. • 673-6508 • lesbians/gay men • dancing/DJ • alternative • call for events

Swirl 1049 Washington Ave. • 534-2060 • lesbians/gay men • dancing/DJ • call for events

Twist 1057 Washington Ave. • 538-9478 • 1pm-5am • popular • mostly gay men • neighborhood bar • dancing/DJ • wheelchair access

The Warsaw 1450 Collins Ave. • 531-4555 • 9:30pm-5am Wed-Sun, clsd Mon-Tue & Th • popular • mostly gay men • dancing/DJ • live shows • alternative

Westend 942 Lincoln Rd. • 538-9378 • noon-5am • mostly gay men • neighborhood bar

RESTAURANTS & CAFES

11th Street Diner 11th & Washington • 534-6373 • til midnight, 24hrs on wknds • some veggie • full bar • $6-14

A Fish Called Avalon 700 Ocean Dr. • 532-1727 • 6pm-11pm • popular • some veggie • full bar • patio • wheelchair access • $12-22

Bang 1516 Washington • 531-2361 • popular • int'l • full bar • $17-28

Beehive 630 Lincoln Rd. • 538-7484 • noon-midnight • pizza/pasta • patio

Cafe Atlantico 429 Espanola Wy. • 672-1168 • 6pm-midnight, bar til 3am • New World tapas • some veggie • wheelchair access • $15-25

El Rancho Grande 1626 Pennsylvania Ave. • 673-0480 • Mexican

The Front Porch 1420 Ocean Dr. • 531-8300 • 8am-midnight • healthy homecooking • some veggie • full bar • $6-10

Jams Tavern & Grill 1331 Washington • 532-6700 • 11am-5am • full bar

Jeffrey's 1629 Michigan Ave. • 673-0690 • 6pm-11pm, from 5pm Sun, clsd Mon • bistro

Larios on the Beach 820 Ocean Dr. • 532-9577 • 11am-midnight, til 2am Fri-Sat • Cuban • $5-12

Lucky Cheng's 1412 Ocean Dr. • 672-1505 • 6pm-midnight • popular • live shows • full bar

Lulu's 1053 Washington • 532-6147 • 11am-2am • popular • Southern homecooking • full bar • wheelchair access • $5-11

News Cafe 800 Ocean Dr. • 538-6397 • 24hrs • popular • healthy sandwiches • some veggie • $4-6

Norma's on the Beach 646 Lincoln Ave. • 532-2809 • opens 4pm, clsd Mon • popular • New World Caribbean • full bar • $11-19

Pacific Time 915 Lincoln Rd. • 534-5979 • lunch & dinner weekdays • Pan-Pacific • some veggie • beer/wine • $10-30

Palace Bar & Grill 1200 Ocean Dr. • 531-9077 • 8am-2am • full bar • $10-15

Piola 637 Washington Ave. • 531-7787 • 6pm-2am • pasta & thin crust pizza • some veggie • full bar • $5-13

Sushi Rock Cafe 1351 Collins Ave. • 532-2133 • sushi • full bar

Wolfie's Jewish Deli 2038 Collins Ave. (at 21st) • 538-6626 • 24hrs • gourmet deli • $6-8

GYMS & HEALTH CLUBS

Club Body Tech 1253 Washington Ave. • 674-8222 • popular • gay-friendly

BOOKSTORES & RETAIL SHOPS

The 9th Chakra 817 Lincoln Rd. • 538-0671 • clsd Mon • metaphysical books • supplies • gifts

GW's 720 Lincoln Rd. Mall • 534-4763 • 11am-10pm, til 8pm Sun • lesbigay emporium

Whittal & Schön 1319 Washington • 538-2606 • 11am-9pm, til midnight Fri-Sat • funky clothes

TRAVEL & TOUR OPERATORS
Amazon Tours & Cruises 8700 W. Flagler Ste. 190 • (800) 423-2791 • IGTA

Colours Destinations 255 W. 24th St. • 532-9341/(800) 277-4825 • gay owned/run

Connections Tours 169 Lincoln Rd. #302 • 673-3153/(800) 688-8463

SPIRITUAL GROUPS
MCC 2100 Washington Ave. • 759-1015 • 11am Sun

PUBLICATIONS
Lips 2699 Collins Ave. #121 • 534-4830 • 'Florida's #1 newspaper for the contemporary woman'

Wire 1638 Euclid Ave., 33139 • 538-3111 • weekly guide to South Beach

Naples (941)

INFO LINES & SERVICES
Lesbian/Gay AA 262-6535

ACCOMMODATIONS
Festive Flamingo B&B 455-8833 • lesbians/gay men • swimming

BARS
The Galley 509 3rd St. S. • 262-2808 • 4pm-2am, from 1pm Sun • lesbians/gay men • more women Fri • neighborhood bar • food served

RESTAURANTS & CAFES
Cafe Flamingo 536 9th St. N. • 262-8181 • 8am-2pm • some veggie • women-owned/run • $3-5

BOOKSTORES & RETAIL SHOPS
Book Nook 824 5th Ave. S. • 262-4740 • 8am-7pm • general • wheelchair access

Lavender's 5600 Trail Blvd. #4 • 594-9499 • 11am-7pm, til 4pm Sat, clsd Sun-Mon • lesbigay bookstore & pride shop

Ocala (352)

BARS
Connection 3331 S. Pine Ave. (US 441) • 620-2511 • 3pm-2am • lesbians/gay men • neighborhood bar • wheelchair access

BOOKSTORES & RETAIL SHOPS

Barnes & Noble 3500 SW College Rd. • 620-9195 • lesbigay section

EROTICA

Secrets of Ocala 815 N. Magnolia Ave. • 622-3858

Orlando   (407)

INFO LINES & SERVICES

Family Values WPRK 91.5 FM • 7pm Wed • lesbigay radio from Rollins College

Gay/Lesbian Community Center 714 E. Colonial Dr. • 425-4527 • 11am-9pm, noon-5pm Sat, clsd Sun • also lesbigay library

Gay/Lesbian Community Services of Central Florida 843-4297 • 24hr touchtone helpline • extensive referrals

LCN (Loving Committed Network) PO Box 149512, 32814-9512 • 332-2311 • lesbian community social/support group • monthly events • 'LCN Express' newsletter

Metropolitan Business Association PO Box 568041, 32856 • 420-2182 • 6:30pm 1st Th at the Radisson Hotel

ACCOMMODATIONS

A Veranda B&B 115 N. Summerlin Ave. • 849-0321/(800) 420-6822 • gay-friendly • located in downtown Orlando • hot tub • wheelchair access • $99-189

▲ **The Garden Cottage B&B** 1309 E. Washington Ave. • 894-5395 • popular • lesbians/gay men • quaint & romantic 1920s private cottage in gay downtown area • women-owned/run • $70-95

Leora's B&B PO Box 6094, 32853 • 649-0009 • women only • $45-75

Parliament House Motor Inn 410 N. Orange Blossom Trail • 425-5571 • popular • mostly gay men • swimming • live shows • food served • full bar from 8pm • $44

Rick's B&B PO Box 22318, Lake Buena Vista, 32830 • 396-7751 • lesbians/gay men • full brkfst • swimming • patio

Things Worth Remembering B&B 7338 Cabor Ct. • 291-2127/(800) 484-3585x6908 • gay-friendly • collection of memorabilia from TV, movies, Broadway • kitchen use • smokefree • $65-70

Garden Cottage

Antiques
TV-Films
Stereo
Kitchen
Private
Garden
Courtyard
Close to
Disney
Hosts Lisa
& Sherry

in historic
downtown
orlando

4 0 7 8 9 4 5 3 9 5

Bed & Breakfast

BARS

The Cactus Club 1300 N. Mills Ave. • 894-3041 • 3pm-2am • mostly gay men • professional • patio

City Lights Cabaret (at The Complex) • 422-6826 • noon-2am • popular • lesbians/gay men • dancing • live shows

The Club 578 N. Orange Ave. • 426-0005 • popular • lesbians/gay men • dancing/DJ • 18+ • live shows • videos • call for events

The Complex 3400 S. Orange Blossom Tr. • 422-6826 • noon-2am • lesbians/gay men • various bars • gym • video store • dancing/DJ • live shows • wheelchair access

Copper Rocket 106 Lake Ave., Maitland • 645-0069 • 11:30am-2am, from 4pm wknds • lesbians/gay men • also a restaurant • micro brews • internet access • wheelchair access

The Edge 100 W. Livingston St. • 839-4331 • gay-friendly • dancing/DJ • call for events

Faces 4910 Edgewater Dr. • 291-7571 • 4pm-2am • popular • mostly women • dancing/DJ • live shows • wheelchair access

Full Moon Saloon 500 N. Orange Blossom Tr. • 648-8725 • noon-2am • mostly gay men • leather • country/western • patio

Hank's 5026 Edgewater Dr. • 291-2399 • noon-2am • mostly gay men • neighborhood bar • patio • wheelchair access

Ladies 7124 Aloma Ave., Winter Park • 678-3043 • 8pm Mon-Th & Sat • women only • dancing/DJ • live shows • private club

Mannequins Paradise Island at Disney World • popular on Th (Employee Night) • otherwise very straight • dancing/DJ

Phoenix 7124 Aloma Ave., Winter Park • 678-9220 • 4pm-2am • lesbians/gay men • live shows • wheelchair access

Renaissance 22 S. Magnolia • 422-3595 • gay-friendly • dancing/DJ • gay night Th • rooftop patio

Southern Nights 375 S. Bumby Ave. • 898-0424 • 4pm-2am • lesbians/gay men • more women Sat • dancing/DJ • live shows • wheelchair access

Stable (at Parliament House) • 425-7571 • 8pm-2am • mostly gay men • country/western

Uncle Walt's Backstage 5454 International Dr. • 351-4866 • 4pm-2am • gay-friendly • appetizers • piano bar & cabaret • wheelchair access

Orlando   (407)

WHERE THE GIRLS ARE: Women who live here hang out at Will's Pub or Moorefield's restaurant. Tourists are—where else?—at the tourist attractions, including the Mannequins bar in Disney World.

ENTERTAINMENT: Orlando Gay Chorus: 645-5866.

LESBIGAY PRIDE: June.

CITY INFO: 363-5871.

ATTRACTIONS: Walt Disney World: 824-4321. Universal Studios. Wet & Wild Waterpark. Sea World.

WEATHER: Mild winters, hot summers.

TRANSIT: Yellow Cab: 699-9999. Gray Line: 422-0744. Rabbit: 291-2424. Lynx: 841-8240.

Will's Pub 1820-50 N. Mills Ave. • 898-5070 • 4pm-2am • gay-friendly • many lesbians • neighborhood bar • food served • beer/wine • wheelchair access • also 'Loch Haven Motor Inn' • 896-3611

RESTAURANTS & CAFES

Dug Out Diner (at Parliament House) • 425-7571x711 • 24hrs • lesbians/gay men

Moorefields 123 S. Orange Ave. • 872-6960 • lunch & dinner, clsd Sun-Mon • popular • lesbians/gay men • healthy cont'l • some veggie • beer/wine • $13-20

Thorton Park Cafe 900 E. Washington • 425-0033 • 11am-10pm • seafood/Italian • some veggie • beer/wine • patio • wheelchair access • $9-17

Orlando

*O*rlando is a city exploding with growth—just trying to keep up with the Walt Disney World amusement complex, home to the enormous Epcot Center, the Magic Kingdom, MGM Studios, shopping and much more. You'll need at least three days to traverse the 27,000 acres of this entertainment mecca. Of course Pride month—June—is when Disney World hosts an unofficial Gay/Lesbian day. Call Disney World for info; if they claim ignorance, try the **Gay/Lesbian Community Services (GLCS)** touchtone info line (press "o" to talk to a live person).

And if you still crave infotainment, visit Universal Studios, Wet 'n' Wild, Sea World, the Tupperware Museum (yes, Tupperware), Busch Gardens, or Cypress Gardens, a natural wonderland of lagoons, moss-draped trees and exotic plants from around the world. Call the GLCS to find out when the next Gay Day in the Busch (Gardens, that is) will be—the last one was in September. If you like fairs, be sure to stop by the Central Florida Fair in February for Gay/Lesbian day at the fair.

Faces is the neighborhood dyke bar, while **Southern Nights** and **The Club (aka Firestone)** are the places to dance. For education, stop by the local lesbigay store, **Out & About Books**, or the Gay/Lesbian Community Center, and pick up a copy of **The Triangle** or **Watermark**. And for fun, go rollerskating at the bimonthly **GaySkate** in nearby Castleberry, or watch a lesbian/gay-themed movie at The Club on Monday nights. Lesbian social group **LCN** sponsors plenty of other events, including picnics at Wekiva Falls in the spring and around Halloween, and a dance in mid-January.

White Wolf Cafe & Antique Shop 1829 N. Orange Ave. • 895-5590 • 10am-midnight, clsd Sun • salads/sandwiches • plenty veggie • beer/wine • live shows • wheelchair access • $5-12

BOOKSTORES & RETAIL SHOPS

Alobar 709 W. Smith St. • 841-3050 • 10am-9pm, noon-5pm Sun • books • music • wheelchair access

Out & About Books 930 N. Mills Ave. • 896-0204 • 10am-8pm, noon-6pm Sun • lesbigay

Rainbow City 934 N. Mills Ave. • 898-6096 • lesbigay giftshop

TRAVEL & TOUR OPERATORS

'Alley-Gator' Houseboat 2161 Saragossa Ave., Deland • 775-7423 • houseboat tour on St. Johns River • gay-owned/operated

Odyssey 334 E. Michigan St. • 841-8686/(800) 327-4441 • IGTA

SPIRITUAL GROUPS

Integrity/Central Florida PO Box 530031, 32853 • 332-2743

Joy MCC 2351 S. Ferncreek Ave • 894-1081 • 9:15am & 11am, 7:30pm Wed • wheelchair access

PUBLICATIONS

The Triangle PO Box 533446, 32853 • 425-4527

Watermark PO Box 533655, 32853-3655 • 481-2243

Women's Network Yellow Pages 4524 Curry Dr., 32812 • 896-4444

EROTICA

Absolute Leather 3400 S. Orange Blossom Tr. • 843-8168/(800) 447-4820 • noon-9pm, til midnight Th-Sat • wheelchair access

Fairvilla Video 1740 N. Orange Blossom Tr. • 425-5352

The Leather Closet 498 N. Orange Blossom Tr. • 649-2011 • noon-2am • wheelchair access

Palm Beach (561)

ACCOMMODATIONS

Heart of Palm Beach 160 Royal Palm Wy. • 655-5600 • gay-friendly • charming, friendly European-style hotel • swimming • kids ok • also a restaurant • full bar • $69-199

Palm Beach Gardens (407)

TRAVEL & TOUR OPERATORS

Vagabond Travels 601 Northlake Blvd. • 848-0648/(800) 226-3830 • IGTA

Panama City (904)

BARS

Bottoms Up 14896 Front Beach Rd. • 233-7151 • 10am-4am • gay-friendly • neighborhood bar • food served

Fiesta Room 110 Harrison Ave. • 784-9285 • 8pm-3am • popular • lesbians/gay men • dancing/DJ • live shows • wheelchair access

La Royale Lounge & Liquor Store 100 Harrison • 784-9311 • 3pm-3am • lesbians/gay men • neighborhood bar • courtyard • wheelchair access

Pembroke Pines (305)

RESTAURANTS & CAFES

Blue Goose Cafe 1491 N. Palm Ave. • 436-8677 • from 5:30pm, clsd Mon • pasta/steak/seafood • some veggie • beer/wine • $7-15

Pensacola (904)

INFO LINES & SERVICES

AA Gay/Lesbian 415 N. Alcaniz (MCC location) • 433-8528 • 8pm Fri

ACCOMMODATIONS

Noble Manor B&B 110 W. Strong St. • 434-9544 • gay-friendly • hot tub

BARS

Numbers Pub 200 S. Alcaniz • 438-9004 • 3pm-3am • mostly men • dancing/DJ

The Office 406 E. Wright St. • 433-7278 • mostly women

Red Carpet 937 Warrington Rd. • 453-9918 • 3pm-3am • mostly women • dancing/DJ • live shows • patio • wheelchair access

Red Garter 1 W. Main St. • 433-9292 • 5pm-3am, from 3pm wknds • lesbians/gay men • dancing/DJ • live shows • wheelchair access

Round-up 706 E. Gregory • 433-8482 • 2pm-3am • popular • mostly gay men • videos • wheelchair access

RESTAURANTS & CAFES

The Secret Cafe 23 S. Palafox Pl. • 444-9020 • 10am-6pm, noon-midnight Fri-Sat, clsd Sun-Mon • coffeehouse & gallery • women-owned/run

BOOKSTORES & RETAIL SHOPS

Silver Chord Bookstore 10901 Lillian Hwy. • 453-6652 • 10am-6pm, clsd Mon • metaphysical • lesbigay section • wheelchair access

SPIRITUAL GROUPS

Holy Cross MCC 415 N. Alcaniz • 433-8528 • 11am Sun, 7pm Wed

PUBLICATIONS

Christopher St. South PO Box 2752, 32513 • 433-0353

Pompano Beach (954)

INFO LINES & SERVICES

The Eden Society PO Box 1692, 33061-1692 • 316-8470 • transgender social/support group • excellent newsletter

Port Richey (813)

BARS

BT's 7737 Grand Blvd. • 841-7900 • 6pm-2am • lesbians/gay men • dancing/DJ • live shows • wheelchair access

Port St. Lucie (407)

BARS

Bourbon St. Cabaret & Cafe 2727 SE Morningside Blvd. • 335-8608 • 4pm-2am • popular • lesbians/gay men • more women 1st & 3rd Sun • live shows • food served • steak & seafood • some veggie • patio • wheelchair access • $6-14

Sarasota (941)

INFO LINES & SERVICES

Friends Group (Gay AA) 2080 Ringling Blvd. #302 • 951-6810 • 8pm Mon & Wed • also 8pm Fri at 538 Payne Pkwy.

ACCOMMODATIONS

Normandy Inn 400 N. Tamiami Tr. • 366-8979/(800) 282-8050 • gay-friendly

Siesta Holiday House 1011-1015 Crescent St., Siesta Key • 488-6809/(800) 720-6885 • gay-friendly • fully furnished apts • complimentary bikes • kitchens • BBQ • gay-owned/run

BARS

Bumpers (Club X) 1927 Ringling Blvd. • 951-0335 • 9pm-2:30am • gay-friendly • more gay Th-Sun • dancing/DJ

Christopher Street 6543 Gateway Ave. (behind Gulf Gate Mall) • 927-8766 • 4pm-2am • mostly gay men • dancing/DJ • live shows • call for events

HG Rooster's 1256 Old Stickney Pt. Rd. • 346-3000 • 3pm-2am • mostly gay men • neighborhood bar • live shows

Ricky J's 1330 Martin Luther King Jr. Wy. • 953-5945 • 4pm-2am • popular • mostly gay men • dancing/DJ • live shows • patio • wheelchair access

BOOKSTORES & RETAIL SHOPS

Charlie's 1341 Main St. • 953-4688 • 9am-10pm, til 5pm Sun • books & magazines • cards

TRAVEL & TOUR OPERATORS

Galaxsea Cruises 6584 Superior • 921-3456/(800) 633-5159 • IGTA

Sarasota Bay Watcher 377-0799 • fishing from the shore • everything provided • woman-owned/run

SPIRITUAL GROUPS

Church of the Trinity MCC 7225 N. Lockwood Ridge Rd. • 355-0847 • 10am Sun • wheelchair access

Suncoast Cathedral MCC 3276 Venice Ave. • 484-7068 • last Sat of month women's 45+ group

PUBLICATIONS

Rainbow Pages Magazine PO Box 448, Nokomis, 34274 • 488-4496 • quarterly local lesbigay magazine

Satellite Beach (407)

BOOKSTORES & RETAIL SHOPS

Sissy's Inc. 1670 Hwy. A1A • 779-0086 • 11am-9pm daily • pride gifts • books • local artwork • wheelchair access • women-owned/run

EROTICA

Space Age Books & Temptations 63 Ocean Blvd. • 773-7660

Sebastian (407)

ACCOMMODATIONS

The Pink Lady Inn 1309 Louisiana Ave. • 589-1345 • mostly women • swimming • kitchens • women-owned/run

St. Augustine (904)

ACCOMMODATIONS

Pagoda 2854 Coastal Hwy. • 824-2970 • women only • guesthouse • near beach • swimming • kitchen privileges • wheelchair access • women-owned/run • $15

St. Petersburg (813)

INFO LINES & SERVICES

Gay Information Line (The Line) 586-4297 • volunteers 7pm-11pm • touchtone 24hrs

WEB (Women's Energy Bank) 823-5353 • many services & activities for lesbians

ACCOMMODATIONS

The Barge House PO Box 46526, St. Petersburg Beach, 33706 • 360-0729 • women only • cabana & cottages avail. • 1/2 blk to the beach • hot tub • women-owned/run • $74-85

Bay Gables B&B and Garden 136 4th Ave. NE • 822-8855/(800) 822-8803 • gay-friendly • smokefree • kids ok

Boca Ciega 3526 Boca Ciega Dr. N. • 381-2755 • women only • swimming • lesbian-owned/run

Feathers B&B 2107 Burlington Ave. N., 33713 • 321-1766 • women only • full brkfst

Frog Pond Guesthouse 145 29th Ave. N. • 823-7407 • gay-friendly • $65

Pass-A-Grille Beach Motel 709 Gulfway Blvd., St. Petersburg Beach • 367-4726 • gay-friendly • apartment avail. • swimming

Sea Oats & Dunes 12625 Sunshine Lane, Treasure Island • 367-7568 • gay-friendly • motel & apts on the Gulf of Mexico • $295-595/week

BARS

Bedrox 8000 W. Gulf Blvd., Treasure Island • 367-1724 • 10am-2am • lesbians/gay men • dancing/DJ • 4 bars • on the beach • live shows • also a restaurant • wheelchair access • $5-15

D.T.'s 2612 Central Ave. • 327-8204 • 2pm-2am • mostly gay men • neighborhood bar • wheelchair access

The Hideaway 8302 4th St. N. • 570-9025 • 2pm-2am • mostly women • neighborhood bar • wheelchair access

The New Connection 3100 3rd Ave. N. • 321-2112 • 11am-2am • lesbians/gay men • separate lesbian bar next door from 7pm Th-Sat • neighborhood bar • dancing/DJ

Sharp A's 4918 22nd Ave. S., Gulfport • 327-4897 • 3pm-2am • popular • lesbians/gay men • dancing/DJ • wheelchair access

RESTAURANTS & CAFES

Beaux Arts 7711 60th St. N. • 328-0702 • noon-5pm • historic gallery w/coffeehouse • sponsors events • call for info

BOOKSTORES & RETAIL SHOPS

Affinity Books 2435 9th St. N. • 823-3662 • 10am-6pm, til 8pm Th, noon-5pm Sun • lesbigay • wheelchair access

Brigit Books 3434 4th St. N. • 522-5775 • 10am-8pm, til 6pm Fri-Sat, 1pm-5pm Sun • women's/feminist

P.S. 111 2nd Ave. NE • 823-2937 • 10am-6pm • cards • gifts

St. Petersburg (813)

ENTERTAINMENT: Women's Chorus: 932-7329.

LESBIGAY PRIDE: June.

ANNUAL EVENTS: October - Film Festival & Gay Men's Chorus: (800) 729-2787.

CITY INFO: Chamber of Commerce: 821-4715, 9am-5pm.

ATTRACTIONS: The Dali Museum, Great Explorations (interactive kids museum).

BEST VIEW: Pass-A-Grille beach in Tampa.

WEATHER: Some say it's the Garden of Eden—winters sometimes get as cold as 40°, but mostly temperatures are in the 70-80°s.

SPIRITUAL GROUPS

King of Peace MCC 3150 5th Ave. N. • 323-5857 • 10am • wheelchair access

PUBLICATIONS

Womyn's Words PO Box 15548, 33733 • 823-5353

Tallahassee   (904)

BARS

Brothers Bar 926 W. Tharpe St. • 386-2399 • 4pm-2am • lesbians/gay men • dancing/DJ • 18+ • live shows • videos • wheelchair access

Club Park Ave. 115 E. Park Ave. • 599-9143 • 10pm-2am • popular • gay-friendly • more gay wknds • mostly African-American Sun • dancing/DJ • live shows

RESTAURANTS & CAFES

The Village Inn 2690 N. Monroe St. • 385-2903 • dinner • 24hrs wknds • popular

BOOKSTORES & RETAIL SHOPS

Rubyfruit Books 666 W. Tennessee St. #4 • 222-2627 • 10:30am-6:30pm, til 8pm Th, clsd Sun • alternative bookstore • gay titles • wheelchair access

TRAVEL & TOUR OPERATORS

Florida Division of Tourism 487-1462

SPIRITUAL GROUPS

Integrity Big Bend PO Box 10731, 32302 • 224-4661 • 7:30pm Wed • call for location

Tampa   (813)

INFO LINES & SERVICES

Gay Information Line (The Line) 586-4297 • volunteers 7pm-11pm

Tampa Bay Business Guild 1222 S. Dale Mabry #656, 33629

University of South Florida Gay/Lesbian/Bisexual CTR 2466, 4202 E. Fowler Ave. • 974-4297

Women's Center 677-8136 • women's helpline • info & referrals

The Women's Show WMNF 88.5 FM • 238-8001 • 10am-noon Sat

ACCOMMODATIONS

Gram's Place B&B & Artist Retreat 3109 N. Ola Ave. • 221-0596 • lesbians/gay men • nudity • hot tub • BYOB • $45-100

Ruskin House B&B 120 Dickman Dr. SW, Ruskin • 645-3842 • gay-friendly • 1910 multi-story home • 30 min. S. of Tampa & 30 min. N. of Sarasota • full brkfst • $45-65

BARS

2606 2606 N. Armenia Ave. • 875-6993 • 3pm-3am • popular • mostly gay men • also leather shop opens after 9pm • wheelchair access

Cherokee Club 1320 9th Ave., 2nd flr., Ybor City • 247-9966 • 9pm-3am, Fri-Sat only • mostly women • dancing/DJ • live shows • call for events

City Side 3810 Neptune St. • 254-6466 • noon-3am • lesbians/gay men • neighborhood bar • professional • patio

Eden 913 Franklin • gay-friendly • dancing/DJ • late night rave crowd

Howard Avenue Station 3003 N. Howard Ave. • 254-7194 • 8pm-3am • popular • mostly gay men • dancing/DJ

Impulse Channelside Village 302 S. Nebraska Ave. • 223-2780 • 3pm-3am • Sunday T-dance • mostly gay men • dancing/DJ • videos • patio • wheelchair access

Metropolis 3447 W. Kennedy Blvd. • 871-2410 • noon-3am, 1pm-3am Sun • mostly gay men • neighborhood bar • live shows Fri • wheelchair access

Northside Lounge 9002 N. Florida Ave. • 931-3396 • noon-3am • mostly gay men • neighborhood bar

Rascal's 105 W. Martin Luther King Blvd. • 237-8883 • 4pm-3am, from noon Sun • lesbians/gay men • also a restaurant • cont'l/American • some veggie • $4-13

Sahara's 4643 W. Kennedy Blvd. • 282-0183 • noon-3am • mostly women • neighborhood bar

Solar 911 Franklin St. • 226-9227 • gay-friendly • downtown

Tracks Tampa 1430 E. 7th Ave. • 247-2711 • 9pm-3am, clsd Wed & Sun • popular • mostly gay men • dancing/DJ • live shows • videos • wheelchair access

Tremors 15212 N. Nebraska Ave. • 977-3433 • 9pm-3am • gay-friendly • dancing/DJ • alternative • live shows

GYMS & HEALTH CLUBS

Metro Flex Fitness 2511 Swann Ave. • 876-3539

BOOKSTORES & RETAIL SHOPS

Tomes & Treasures 202 S. Howard Ave. • 251-9368 • 11am-8pm, 1pm-6pm Sun • lesbigay bookstore

SPIRITUAL GROUPS

MCC 408 Cayuga St. • 239-1951 • 10:30am Sun

PUBLICATIONS

Encounter 1222 S. Dale Mabry Hwy. #913 • 877-7913

Gazette PO Box 2650, Brandon, 33509-2650 • 689-7566

Southern Exposure PO Box 8092, 33674

Stonewall 3225 S. Madill #220 • 832-2878

Venice (941)

RESTAURANTS & CAFES

Maggie May's 1550 US 41 Bypass South • 497-1077 • 8:30am-5pm Mon-Fri, til 4pm Sat, til 2pm Sun • home cooking • some veggie • beer/wine • women-owned/run

West Palm Beach (407)

INFO LINES & SERVICES

The Whimsey 686-1354 • resources & archives • also camping/RV space

ACCOMMODATIONS

Hibiscus House B&B 501 30th St. • 863-5633/(800) 203-4927 • lesbians/gay men • full brkfst • swimming • complimentary sunset cocktails • IGTA • $75-160

West Palm Beach B&B 419 32nd St. Old Northwood • 848-4064/(800) 736-4064 • mostly gay men • swimming • IGTA • $65-115

BARS

5101 Bar 5101 S. Dixie Hwy. • 585-2379 • 7am-3am, til 4am Fri-Sat, from noon Sun • mostly gay men • neighborhood bar

B.G.'s Bar 5700 S. Dixie Hwy. • 533-3800 • 7am-3am, from noon Sun • mostly gay men • ladies night Th • neighborhood bar • karaoke • live shows

Enigma 109 N. Olive Ave. • 832-5040 • 9pm-3am, clsd Mon-Tue • lesbians/gay men • dancing/DJ • alternative • 18+

H.G. Rooster's 823 Belvedere Rd. • 832-9119 • 3pm-3am, til 4am Fri-Sat • popular • mostly gay men • neighborhood bar • wheelchair access

Heartbreaker 2677 Forrest Hill Blvd. • 966-1590 • 10pm-5am Wed-Sun • popular • lesbians/gay men • more women Fri • 'Chatters Lounge' open 5pm daily • dancing/DJ • live shows • karaoke • videos

Kozlow's 6205 Georgia Ave. • 533-5355 • noon-2am • popular • mostly gay men • neighborhood bar • country/western • private club • patio • wheelchair access

Leather & Spurs WPB 5004 S. Dixie Hwy. • 547-1020 • 4pm-3am, clsd Mon-Wed • mostly gay men • leather • food served

RESTAURANTS & CAFES

Antonio's South 3001 S. Congress Ave., Palm Springs • 965-0707 • dinner • popular • southern Italian • beer/wine • $9-18

Down Dixie Grill 3815 S. Dixie Hwy. • 832-4959 • lunch & dinner Mon-Fri

Respectable Street Cafe 518 Clematis St. • 832-9999 • lunch & dinner • live shows

Rhythm Cafe 3238 S. Dixie Hwy. • 833-3406 • from 6pm Tue-Sat (seasonal) • some veggie • beer/wine • $12-19

BOOKSTORES & RETAIL SHOPS

Changing Times Bookstore 911 Village Blvd. Ste. 806 • 640-0496 • 10am-7pm, noon-5pm Sun • spiritual • lesbigay section • community bulletin board • wheelchair access

Eurotique 3109 45th St. #300 • 684-2302 • 11am-7pm Mon-Fri, noon-6pm Sat • leather • books • videos

SPIRITUAL GROUPS

MCC 3500 W. 45th St. Ste. 2-A • 687-3943 • 11am Sun

PUBLICATIONS

Community Voice PO Box 17975, 33416 • 471-152

GEORGIA

Athens   (706)

INFO LINES & SERVICES
Lesbian Support Group PO Box 7864, 30604 • 546-4611

LGBSU (Lesbian/Gay/Bisexual Student Union) Memorial Hall Rm. 213 • 549-9368 • 7pm Mon

BARS
Boneshakers 433 E. Hancock Ave. • 543-1555 • 7pm-2am, clsd Sun • lesbians/gay men • dancing/DJ • country/western Th • 18+ • wheelchair access

Forty Watt Club 285 W. Washington St. • 549-7871 • gay-friendly • alternative • theme nights • wheelchair access

Georgia Bar 159 W. Clayton • 546-9884 • 4pm-2am, clsd Sun • gay-friendly • wheelchair access

The Globe 199 N. Lumpkin • 353-4721 • 4pm-2am, clsd Sun • gay-friendly • 30 single-malt scotches

RESTAURANTS & CAFES
The Athens Coffeehouse 105 College Ave. • 369-8802 • 9am-midnight, til 2am Th-Sat • some veggie • full bar • wheelchair access • $6-11

The Bluebird 493 E. Clayton • 549-3663 • 8am-9pm • popular Sun brunch • plenty veggie • $5-10 • wheelchair access

Espresso Royale Cafe 297 E. Broad St. • 613-7449 • 7am-midnight, from 8am wknds • best coffee in Athens

The Grit 199 Prince Ave. • 543-6592 • 10am-11pm • ethnic vegetarian • great Sun brunch • wheelchair access • $5-10

BOOKSTORES & RETAIL SHOPS
Barnett's Newsstand 147 College Ave. • 353-0530 • 8am-10pm

Atlanta   (404)

INFO LINES & SERVICES
AALGA (African-American Lesbian/Gay Alliance) PO Box 50374, 30302 • 239-8184 • 4pm 1st Sun • social/political group

AEGIS (American Educational Gender Information Service) PO Box 33724, Decatur, 33003-0724 • 939-0224 • transgender info • helpline

Atlanta Gay Center 71 12th St. NE • 876-5372 • 1pm-5pm Mon-Fri • social services center

Atlanta Gender Exploration PO Box 77562, 30357 • transgender group

Chrysalis Women's Center 320-3355 • social, educational & informational programs

▲ **Dyke TV** Channel 12 • 'weekly, half hour TV show produced by lesbians for lesbians' • call (212) 343-9335 for more info

Fourth Tuesday PO Box 7817, 30309 • 662-4353 • networking & social group for professional women

Friday Night Lesbian Support Group 627-7387 • call for times & locations

Galano AA 585 Dutch Valley • 881-9188 • lesbigay club

Gay Graffiti WRFG 89.3 FM • 523-8989 • 7pm Th • lesbigay radio program

Gay Helpline 892-0661 • 6pm-11pm • info & counseling

Greater Atlanta Business Coalition 377-4258

WINK (Women in Kahoots) 1003 Hicksmil Ct. SW, Marietta, 30060 • (770) 438-1421 • lesbian social group • monthly parties • newsletter

ACCOMMODATIONS

Alternative Accommodations (800) 209-9408 • IGTA

The Bonaventure 650 Bonaventure Ave. • 817-7024 • gay-friendly • graciously restored Victorian • private/shared baths • French spoken • $100-150

Colony Square Hotel 118 14th St. • 892-6000

Hello B&B 892-8111 • mostly gay men • private home

Kirkwood Inn 1702 Bridgeport Dr. NE, 30329 • 982-0012 • women only • hot tub

Magnolia Station B&B 1020 Edgewood Ave. NE • 523-3923 • mostly gay men • swimming • $50-80

▲ **Midtown Manor** 811 Piedmont Ave. NE • 872-5846/(800) 724-4381 • lesbians/gay men • charming Victorian guesthouse • $65+

Our Place 297-9825 • fully furnished vacation home in N. Georgia Mtns. • lesbian-owned/run

Sheraton Colony Square Hotel 188 14th St. • 892-6000 • gay-friendly • gym • food served • full bar

Upper Echelons 1845 Branch Valley Dr., Roswell, 30076 • (770) 642-1313 • luxury penthouse in downtown Atlanta • swimming • women-owned/run

BARS

Armory 836 Juniper St. NE • 881-9280 • 4pm-4am • popular • mostly gay men • dancing/DJ • videos • 3 bars

Backstreet 845 Peachtree St. NE • 873-1986 • 24hrs • popular • mostly gay men • dancing/DJ • live shows • videos • 3 flrs

Burkhart's Pub 1492-F Piedmont Rd. (Ansley Sq. Shopping Center) • 872-4403 • 4pm-4am, from 2pm wknds • lesbians/gay men • neighborhood bar • wheelchair access

E.S.S.O. 489 Courtland St. • 872-3776 • noon-? • gay-friendly • dancing/DJ • also a restaurant • nouvelle • some veggie • rooftop deck • wheelchair access • $10-16

Guys & Dolls 2788 E. Ponce de Leon Ave., Decatur • (770) 377-2956 • 11:30am-4am, from 7pm Sat, from 4pm Sun • gay-friendly • more gay Tue & Sun • live shows • stripper bar • food served • wheelchair access

Hoedowns 1890 Cheshire Bridge Rd. • 874-0980 • 5pm-3am, from 2pm wknds • popular • mostly gay men • dancing/DJ • country/western • live shows • wheelchair access

Karats 511 Peachtree St. • 872-9777 • 7pm-3am, clsd Mon-Tue

Kaya 1068 Peachtree St. • 874-4460 • 6pm-midnight, til 4am Fri • lesbians/gay men • dancing/DJ • mostly African-American • also a restaurant • some veggie • live shows • patio • $6-12

Le Buzz 585 Franklin Rd., Marietta • (770) 424-1337 • noon-2am • lesbians/gay men • neighborhood bar

The Limit 735 Ralph McGill • 523-1535 • 5pm-4am, from 2pm wknds • lesbians/gay men • dancing/DJ • live shows • wheelchair access

Loretta's 708 Spring St. NW • 874-8125 • 6pm-4am • gay-friendly • neighborhood bar • dancing/DJ • mostly African-American • live shows • wheelchair access

Model T 699 Ponce de Leon • 872-2209 • noon-4am • lesbians/gay men • neighborhood bar • live shows • wheelchair access

Atlanta

*I*f you watched the Olympic Games last year, you saw how proud the residents of Atlanta are of their city. Southerners are working hard to move beyond stereotypes of the Old South. Of course, Atlanta's large population of lesbians and gay men is an integral part of that work.

But the South's checkered past is a powerful agent for future understanding. Atlanta houses the must-see **Martin Luther King Jr. Center** and the **Carter Presidential Center**—tributes to icons of peace and positive change—as well as the nationally known **Black Arts Festival** (730-7315).

Lesbian culture in Atlanta is spread out (a car is a must) between **Charis** women's bookstore in L'il Five Points (cruise their Thursday night readings), the **Atlanta Gay Center** in posh Midtown, and in between, along Piedmont and Cheshire Bridge roads. Midway between the gay **Ansley Square** area (Piedmont at Monroe) and downtown, stop by **Outwrite**, Atlanta's lesbian/gay bookstore. Pick up a copy of **Southern Voice** to scope out the political scene or **Etc.** to dish the bar scene.

For more shopping, **Brushstrokes** is Atlanta's only lesbigay goodies store. While strolling around quaint, queer Virginia Highlands, stop to smell the flowers at **Maddix**.

Just a couple miles south on Highland, you'll run smack into funky shopping, dining, and live music in the punk capital of Atlanta: **L'il Five Points** (not to be confused with "Five Points" downtown). Unless you're a serious mall-crawler, skip the overly commercial (but much hyped) Underground Atlanta, and head for **Lenox Mall** instead—you'll see more stylish queers and fewer hetero-tourists.

Some of the women's accommodations listed in Atlanta are actually an hour north in lush, wooded Dahlonega. So if you need to stay in the city, try **Kirkwood Inn** or one of the mixed hotels or B&Bs.

If you're a fan of R.E.M., head northeast on Hwys. 306 or 78 about an hour-and-a-half to Athens, Georgia. Avoid going on weekends during footbal season, though, since traffic is hellish. Pick up a **Flagpole** magazine to find out what's going on, and stop by **Boneshakers**, Athens' lesbian/gay dancebar.

Atlanta

WHERE THE GIRLS ARE: Many lesbians live in DeKalb county, in the northeast part of the city Decatur. For fun, women head for Midtown or Buckhead if they're professionals, Virginia-Highlands if they're funky or 30ish, and Little Five Points if they're young and wild.

ENTERTAINMENT: Atlanta Feminist Women's Chorus: (770) 438-5823. Lefont Screening Room: (404) 231-1924, gay film.

LESBIGAY PRIDE: June. (404) 662-4533.

ANNUAL EVENTS: April- Lesbian/Gay Arts Fest: (404) 874-8710, gallery, performances. Gay/Lesbian Film Festival: (404) 733-6112. May- Wigswood: (404) 874-6782, annual festival of peace, love and wigs, street party Act Up fundraiser, wig watchers welcome. May - Armory Sports Classic: (404) 874-2710, softball & many other sports competitions. August - Hotlanta: (404) 874-3976, a weekend of river rafting, pageants & parties for boys. December - Women's Christmas Ball/Good Friends for Good Causes: (404) 939-6527.

CITY INFO: (404) 521-6600.

ATTRACTIONS: Martin Luther King Memorial Center. Atlanta Botanical Gardens. Piedmont Park. CNN Center. Coca-Cola Museum. Underground Atlanta.

BEST VIEW: 70th floor of the Peachtree Plaza, in the Sun Dial restaurant. Also from the top of Stone Mountain.

WEATHER: Summers are warm and humid (upper 80ºs to low 90ºs) with occasional thunderstorms. Winters are icy with occasional snows. Temperatures can drop into the low 30ºs. Spring and fall are temperate—spring brings blossoming dogwoods and magnolias, while fall festoons the trees with Northeast Georgia's awesome fall foliage.

TRANSIT: (404) 521-0200. Atlanta Airport Shuttle: (404) 524-3400. Marta: (404) 848-4711.

(404/770)

Live Female Impersonation

12 Big Screen TVs

Billiard areas

Starlit Weatherized Patio

9200 Sq Ft
High Energy Dance

Martini Room

Live DJs and VJs

OTHERSIDE

Live Bands

Valet Parking

THE OTHERSIDE
CONTINUOUS ENTERTAINMENT COMPLEX
1924 PIEDMONT RD NE ATLANTA 404. 875. 5238

Moreland Tavern 1196 Moreland Ave. SE • 622-4650 • 11am-4am • lesbians/gay men • neighborhood bar • food served • patio • wheelchair access

My Sister's Room 931 Monroe Dr. • 875-6699 • 5pm-2am • mostly women • food served • some veggie • wheelchair access

Opus I 1086 Alco St. NE • 634-6478 • 9pm-4am • mostly gay men • neighborhood bar • wheelchair access

▲ **The Otherside of Atlanta** 1924 Piedmont Rd. • 875-5238 • 6pm-4am • popular • lesbians/gay men • dancing/DJ • country/western • live shows • food served • videos • patio • women-owned/run

Revolution-Midtown 1492 Piedmont (Ansley Sq. Shopping Cntr.) • 874-8455 • 11am-2am, from 4pm Tue & Sat, from noon Sun, clsd Mon • mostly women • dancing/DJ • live shows • deck • wheelchair access

Scandals 1510-G Piedmont Rd. NE (Ansley Sq. Shopping Ctr.) • 875-5957 • noon-4am • popular • mostly gay men • neighborhood bar • wheelchair access

Sol 917 Peachtree St. • 815-8070 • gay-friendly • dancing/DJ • live shows • call for events

Transfer 931 Monroe Dr. • 872-5200 • 4pm-4am • popular • mostly gay men • dancing/DJ • wheelchair access

RESTAURANTS & CAFES

Bridgetown Grill 689 Peachtree (across from Fox Theater) • 873-5361 • noon-11pm • popular • funky Caribbean • some veggie • $5-10 • also Li'l 5 Points location • 653-0110

Chow 1026-1/2 N. Highland Ave. • 872-0869 • lunch & dinner • popular Sun brunch • some veggie • $8-15

Cowtippers 1600 Piedmont Ave. NE • 874-3469 • 11:30am-11pm • transgender-friendly

Dunk N' Dine (aka Drunk N' Dyke) 2276 Cheshire Bridge Rd. • 636-0197 • 24hrs • popular • lesbians/gay men • downscale diner • some veggie • $4-10

Eat Your Vegetables 438 Moreland Ave. • 523-2671 • lunch & dinner, Sun brunch • mostly veggie • wheelchair access • $5-10

Einstein's 1077 Juniper • 876-7925 • noon-1am • American • some veggie • full bar • $8-12

The Flying Biscuit Cafe 1655 McLendon Ave. • 687-8888 • 8:30am-10pm, clsd Mon • healthy brkfst all day • plenty veggie • beer/wine • wheelchair access • lesbian-owned/run • $6-12

Intermezzo 1845 Peachtree Rd. NE • 355-0411 • 8am-2am, 9am-3am Fri-Sat • classy cafe • plenty veggie • full bar • $7-10

Little 5 Points, Moreland & Euclid Ave. S. of Ponce de Leon Ave. • hip & funky area w/ too many restaurants & shops to list

Majestic Diner 1031 Ponce de Leon (near N. Highland) • 875-0276 • 24hrs • popular diner right from the '50s • cantankerous waitresses included • some veggie • $3-8

Murphy's 997 Virginia Ave. • 872-0904 • 7am-10pm, til midnight Fri-Sat • popular • cont'l • plenty veggie • great brunch • wheelchair access • $5-15

R. Thomas 1812 Peachtree Rd. NE • 872-2942 • 24hrs • popular • beer/wine • healthy Californian/juice bar • plenty veggie • $5-10

Veni Vidi Vici 41 14th St. • 875-8424 • lunch & dinner • upscale Italian • some veggie • $14-25

GYMS & HEALTH CLUBS

Boot Camp 1544 Piedmont Ave. #105 • 876-8686 • gay-friendly • full gym

The Fitness Factory 500 Amsterdam • 815-7900 • popular • gay-friendly • full gym

Mid-City Fitness Center 2201 Faulkner Rd. • 321-6507 • lesbians/gay men

BOOKSTORES & RETAIL SHOPS

Bill Hallman's 1054 N. Highland Ave. • 876-6055 • noon-1pm, til 6pm Sun-Tue • hip designer fashions

The Boy Next Door 1447 Piedmont Ave. NE • 873-2664 • 11am-7pm • clothing

▲ **Brushstrokes** 1510-J Piedmont Ave. NE • 876-6567 • 10am-10pm, noon-9pm Sun • lesbigay variety store

Charis Books & More 1189 Euclid St. • 524-0304 • 10:30am-6:30pm, til 8pm Wed, til 10pm Fri-Sat, noon-6pm Sun • lesbigay/feminist • wheelchair access

Condomart 632 N. Highland Ave. NE • 875-5665 • 11am-11pm, noon-7pm Sun • wheelchair access

The Junkman's Daughter 464 Moreland Ave. • 577-3188 • 11am-7pm • hip stuff

Maddix 1034 N. Highland • 892-9337 • 11am-10pm, til 7pm Sun • flowers • chocolates • artful gifts • wheelchair access

▲ **Outwrite Books** 991 Piedmont Ave. • 607-0082 • 8am-10pm, til midnight Fri-Sat • lesbigay • cafe • wheelchair access

Oxford Books 2345 Peachtree • 364-2700 • 9am-midnight, til 2am Fri-Sat • many lesbigay books & magazines • also at 360 Pharr Rd. • 262-3333 • 'Cup & Chaucer' cafe at both locations

TRAVEL & TOUR OPERATORS

Conventional Travel 1658 Lavista Rd. NE • 315-0107/(800) 747-7107 • IGTA

Esquire Travel Service 3433 Havalyn Ln. • 457-6696/(800) 786-6402

Midtown Travel Consultants 1830 Monroe Dr. Ste. F • 872-8308/(800) 548-8904 • IGTA

Real Travel NE Plaza #1030, 3375 Buford Hwy • 872-8308/(800) 551-4202 • IGTA

Travel Affair 1205 Johnson Ferry Rd. #116, Marietta • (770) 977-6824/(800) 332-3417 • IGTA

Trips Unlimited 1004 Virginia Ave. NE • 872-8747/(800) 275-8747

SPIRITUAL GROUPS

All Saints MCC 575 Boulevard SE • 622-1154 • 7pm Sun • wheelchair access

Congregation Bet Haverim 701 W. Howard Ave., Decatur • (770) 642-3467 • call for hours • lesbigay synagogue

First MCC of Atlanta 1379 Tullie Rd. NE • 325-4143 • 9am,11am & 7:30pm Sun, 7:30pm Wed • wheelchair access

Integrity Atlanta 2089 Ponce de Leon (church) • (770) 642-3183 • 6:30pm 2nd & 4th Sun

Presbyterians for Lesbian/Gay Concerns PO Box 8362, 30306 • 373-5830 • social group

PUBLICATIONS

Atlanta Community Yellow Pages 1888 Emery St. Ste. 220, 30318 • 350-6720/(800) 849-0406

ETC Magazine PO Box 8916, 30306 • 525-3821 • bar & restaurant guide

Southern Voice 1095 Zenolite Rd., 30306 • 876-1819

Venus Magazine PO Box 89238, 30312 • 622-8069

Women's Yellow Pages of Greater Atlanta 180 Allen Rd. N. Bldg. #303 • 255-4144

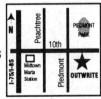

EROTICA
The Poster Hut 2175 Cheshire Bridge Rd. • 633-7491

Starship 2275 Cheshire Bridge Rd. • 320-9101 • leather • novelties • 5 locations in Atlanta

Augusta (706)

BARS
Walton Way Station 1632 Walton Wy. • 733-2603 • 9pm-3am, clsd Sun • lesbians/gay men • dancing/DJ • live shows

SPIRITUAL GROUPS
MCC 609 Charton Dr. • 722-6454 • 7pm Sun • wheelchair access

Bowden (706)

BARS
Rainbow Pub 1174 Hwy 166 • 258-7766 • 8:30pm til ?, clsd Mon-Wed • lesbians/gay men

RESTAURANTS & CAFES
Scandals 110 City Hall Ave. • 258-7771 • 11am-10pm, from 5pm Fri-Sat, clsd Sun • pizza

Carrollton (770)

BOOKSTORES & RETAIL SHOPS
Blue Moon Gifts 113 Newnan St. • 836-0014 • 11am-6:30pm, clsd Sun

Dahlonega (706)

ACCOMMODATIONS
Above the Clouds Rte. 4 Box 250 , 30533 • 864-5211 • women only • mountainside B&B • full breakfast • 1 ste. w/ hot tub • 1 bdrm w/ private bath • lesbian-owned/run

Swiftwaters Rte. 3 Box 379, 30533 • (706) 864-3229 • seasonal • women only • on scenic river • hot tub • deck • women-owned/run • $60-75 (B&B) • $40 (cabins) • $10 (camping)

Triangle Pointe Rte. 4 Box 242, 30533 • (706) 867-6029 • lesbians/gay men • full brkfst • hot tub

Macon (912)

BARS
Cherry St. Pub 425 Cherry St. • 755-1400 • mostly gay men • live shows

Topaz 695 Riverside Dr. • 750-7669 • 5pm-2am, clsd Sun • lesbians/gay men • dancing/DJ • live shows • wheelchair access

Mountain City (706)

ACCOMMODATIONS
The York House York House Rd. • 746-2068 • gay-friendly • 1896 historic country inn

Savannah (912)

INFO LINES & SERVICES
First City Network, Inc. 335 Tatnall St. • 236-2489 • complete info & events line • social group

ACCOMMODATIONS
912 Barnard Victorian B&B 912 Barnard • 234-9121 • lesbians/gay men • hot tub • nudity • shared baths • fireplaces • smoke-free • balcony

BARS
Club One 1 Jefferson St. • 232-0200 • 5pm-3am • lesbians/gay men • dancing/DJ • food served • live shows Wed, Fri-Sun

Faces II 17 Lincoln St. • 233-3520 • 11am-3am • mostly gay men • neighborhood bar • also a restaurant • patio • $8-10

Valdosta (912)

BARS
Club Paradise 2100 W. Hill Ave. (exit 4 I-95) • 242-9609 • 9pm-2am, clsd Sun-Mon • lesbians/gay men • dancing/DJ • live shows • patio

HAWAII

HAWAII (BIG ISLAND)

Captain Cook   (808)

ACCOMMODATIONS

Hale Aloha Guest Ranch 84-4780 Mamalahoa Hwy., Captain Cook • 328-8955/(800) 897-3188 • gay-friendly • hot tub • nudity • workout equipment • $65-120

▲ **RBR Farms** PO Box 930, Captain Cook, 96704 • 328-9212/(800) 328-9212 • popular • lesbians/gay men • swimming • nudity • on working macadamia nut & coffee plantation • IGTA • $60-150

Samurai House RR1 Box 359, Captain Cook, 96704 • 328-9210 • popular • gay-friendly • traditional house brought from Japan • hot tub • wheelchair access

Honokaa   (808)

ACCOMMODATIONS

Paauhau Plantation Inn PO Box 1375, Honokaa, 96727 • 775-7222/(800) 789-7614 • gay-friendly • B&B w/ cottages built on ocean point

Kailua-Kona   (808)

ACCOMMODATIONS

Dolores B&B 77-6704 Kilohana, Kailua-Kona • 329-8778 • gay-friendly • ocean views • full gourmet brkfst

Hale Kipa 'O Pele PO Box 5252, Kailua-Kona, 96745 • 329-8676/(800) 528-2456 • lesbians/gay men • plantation-style B&B • hot tub • IGTA • $65-135

▲ **Royal Kona Resort** 75-5852 Alii Dr., Kailua-Kona • 329-3111/(800) 774-5662 • gay-friendly • set atop dramatic lava out-croppings, overlooking Kailua Bay • swimming • private beach • $155-390 (see ad in front color section)

Tropical Tune-ups PO Box 390847, Kailua-Kona, 96739 • (800) 587-0405 • women only • small group retreats for women • B&B avail. on off-weeks • full brkfst • jacuzzi • sweat lodge • kids ok • lesbian-owned/run • $350-1495/week

BARS

Mask Bar & Grill 75-5660 Kopiko St., Kailua-Kona • 329-8558 • 6pm-2am • popular • lesbians/gay men • neighborhood bar • dancing/DJ • live shows • karaoke • only lesbian/gay bar on the island

TRAVEL & TOUR OPERATORS

Ecoscapes 75-5626 Kuakini Hwy. Ste.1, Kailua-Kona • 329-7116/(800) 949-3483 • IGTA

Rainbow Tours 87-3203 Road Guava, Captain Cook • 328-8406

Kamuela (808)

ACCOMMODATIONS

Ho'onanea PO Box 6450, Kamuela, 96743 • 882-1177 • women only • hot tub • near beaches • tennis • golf • horseback riding • women-owned/run

Kurtistown (808)

ACCOMMODATIONS

▲ **The Butterfly Inn** PO Box 6010, Kurtistown, 96760 • 966-7936/(800) 546-2442 • women only • tropical brkfst • hot tub • kitchens • women-owned/run • $55-65

PUBLICATIONS

The Jungle Vine PO Box 325, Kurtistown, 96760 • 966-8584 • lesbian newsletter

Na'alehu (808)

ACCOMMODATIONS

▲ **Earthsong** PO Box 916, 96772 • 929-8043 • women only • retreat center w/ cottages on 3 acres • Hawaiian massage • Goddess temple • substance-free • lesbian-owned/run

Pahala (808)

ACCOMMODATIONS

Wood Valley B&B Inn PO Box 37, Pahala, 96777 • 928-8212 • mostly women • plantation home B&B • tent sites • veggie brkfst • sauna • nudity • women-owned/run • $35-55

Pahoa (808)

ACCOMMODATIONS

Huliaule'a B&B PO Box 1030, Pahoa, 96778 • 965-9175 • lesbians/gay men • $45-80

Kalani Honua Seaside Retreat RR2 Box 4500, Beach Rd., Pahoa, 96778 • 965-7828/(800) 800-6886 • gay-friendly • coastal retreat • conference center & campground w/in Hawaii's largest conservation area • swimming • food served • IGTA

Lava Tree Guest Farm PO Box 881, Pahoa, 96778-0881 • 965-7325 • renovated plantation home on working Macadamia farm

Pamalu RR 2 Box 4023, Pahoa, 96778 • 965-0830 • gay-friendly • swimming • country retreat on 5 secluded acres • near hiking • snorkeling • warm ponds

PUBLICATIONS

Outspoken PO Box 601, Pahoa, 96778 • 982-7617 • newsletter

Volcano Village (808)

ACCOMMODATIONS

Hale Ohia Cottages PO Box 758, Volcano Village, 96785 • (808) 967-7986/(800) 455-3803 • gay-friendly • wheelchair access • IGTA • $75-95

KAUAI

Anahola (808)

ACCOMMODATIONS

Mahina Kai B&B PO Box 699, Anahola, 96703 • 822-9451/(800) 337-1134 • popular • lesbians/gay men • Asian-Pacific country villa overlooking Anahola Bay • swimming • hot tub • $95-175

Hanalei (808)

ACCOMMODATIONS

Hale Maha PO Box 1438, Hanalei, 96714 • 826-4447

BARS

Tahiti Nui Kuhio Hwy., Hanalei • 826-6277 • gay-friendly • more gay Fri-Sat • luau Fri • country/western Mon • live bands wknds • food served • wheelchair access • $12-18

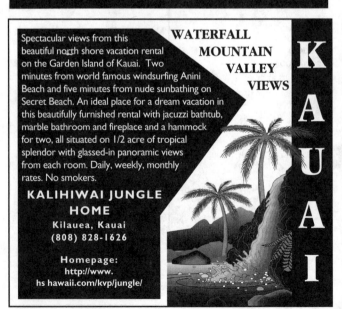

Kalaheo (808)

ACCOMMODATIONS

Black Bamboo Guest House 3829 Waha Rd., Kalaheo • 332-7518/(800) 527-7789 • popular • lesbians/gay men • plantation-style house • swimming • IGTA • wheelchair access

Kapaa (808)

ACCOMMODATIONS

Aloha Kauai B&B 156 Lihau St., Kapaa • 822-6966/(800) 262-4652 • lesbians/gay men • full brkfst • swimming • wheelchair access • $60-95

Hale Kahawai 185 Kahawai Pl., Wailua • 822-1031 • lesbians/gay men • hot tub • mountain views • $60-90

▲ **Kauai Coconut Beach Resort** PO Box 830, Kapaa, 96746 • 822-3455/(800) 222-5642 • gay-friendly • newly redecorated oceanfront resort • swimming • tennis • nightly torchlighting ceremony & luau • $125-500 (see ad in front color section)

Mala Lani 5711 Lokelani Blvd., Kapaa • 823-0422 • lesbians/gay men • suites • lush gardens • mountain views • hot tub • IGTA • $85-195 dbl occupancy

Mohala Ke Ola B&B Retreat 5663 Ohelo Rd., Kapaa • 823-6398 • gay-friendly • swimming • $70-85

Ola Hou Guest Retreat 332 Aina Loli Pl., Kapa'a • 822-3052/(800) 772-4567 • lesbians/gay men • swimming • vacation rental • $95-125

Royal Drive Cottages 147 Royal Dr., Wailua • 822-2321 • lesbians/gay men • private garden cottages w/ kitchenettes • $50-90

BARS

Sideout 4-1330 Kuhio Hwy. • 822-0082 • noon-1:30am • popular • gay-friendly • live bands Tue, Th & wknds • wheelchair access

Kilauea (808)

ACCOMMODATIONS

Kai Mana PO Box 612, Kilauea, 96754 • 828-1280/(800) 837-1782 • gay-friendly • Shakti Gawain's paradise home • set on a cliff surrounded by ocean & mountains • cottages • kitchens • $75-150

▲ **Kalihiwai Jungle Home** PO Box 717, Kilauea, 96754 • 828-1626 • lesbians/gay men • clifftop hideaway overlooking jungle & waterfalls • near beaches • nudity • wheelchair access • $100-135

▲ **Pali Kai** PO Box 450, Kilauea, 96754 • 828-6691 • popular • lesbians/gay men • hilltop B&B w/ ocean view • cottages • hot tub • women-owned/run

MAUI

Haiku　　　　　　　　　　　(808)

ACCOMMODATIONS

Golden Bamboo Ranch 1205 Kaupakalua, Haiku • 572-7824/(800) 344-1238 • lesbians/gay men • 7-acre estate w/ panoramic ocean views • cottages • IGTA • $60-80

Halfway to Hana House PO Box 675, Haiku, Maui, 96708 • 572-1176 • gay-friendly • private studio w/ ocean view

Kailua Maui Gardens SR Box 9, Haiku • 572-9726/(800) 258-8588 • gay-friendly • also suites • hot tub • swimming • nudity • wheelchair access • IGTA • $70-200

Hana　　　　　　　　　　　(808)

ACCOMMODATIONS

Hana Alii Holidays Hana • 248-7742/(800) 548-0478 • accommodations reservations service

Napualani O'Hana PO Box 118, Hana, 96713 • 248-8935 • gay-friendly • 2 full units • lanai • ocean & mtn views • wheelchair access

Kahului　　　　　　　　　　(808)

TRAVEL & TOUR OPERATORS

Fodor's Island Travel 415 Dairy Rd. #E-201, Kahului • 875-7000 • IGTA

Kihei　　　　　　　　　　　(808)

ACCOMMODATIONS

▲ **Andrea & Janet's Maui Vacation Rentals** (800) 289-1522 • 1- & 2-bdrm oceanfront/beachfront condos • swimming • close to snorkeling, golf, fine dining • IGTA • lesbian-owned/run

▲ **Anfora's Dreams** Box 74030, Los Angeles CA, 90004 • (213) 737-0731 • mostly gay men • rental condo near ocean • hot tub • swimming • $60-135

Hale Makaleka 879-2971 • women only • full brkfst • women-owned/run • $60

Hale O'Wahine 2777 S. Kihei Rd. #B-105, Kihei • 874-5148 • women only • swimming • women-owned/run • $75-95

Jack & Tom's Maui Condos PO Box 365, Kihei, 96753 • 874-1048/(800) 800-8608

Ko'a Kai Rentals Box 1969, Kihei, 96753 • 879-6058 • gay-friendly • inexpensive rentals • swimming • $38 day/$225 weekly

Koa Lagoon 800 S. Kihei Rd., Kihei • 879-3002/(800) 367-8030 • gay-friendly • oceanfront suites • 5 night min. • swimming • wheelchair access

Royal Hawaiian Accommodations PO Box 424, Puunene, 96784 • (800) 285-1522 • deluxe oceanfront accommodations • women-owned/run

Triple Lei B&B PO Box 593, Kihei, 96753 • 874-8645/(800) 871-8645 • mostly gay men • full brkfst • hot tub • swimming • nudity • near nude beach

Kula (808)

ACCOMMODATIONS

Camp Kula - Maui B&B PO Box 111, Kula, 96790 • 878-2528 • popular • lesbians/gay men • on the slopes of Mt. Haleakala • HIV+ welcome • wheelchair access • $35-78

Lahaina (808)

INFO LINES & SERVICES

AA Gay/Lesbian Lahaina • 244-9673 • 8pm Wed, 7:30am Sun

▲ **Maui Dreamtime Weddings** (800) 779-1320 • traditional & non-traditional commitment ceremonies in secluded Maui locations

▲ **Royal Hawaiian Weddings** PO Box 424, Puunene, 96784 • 875-0625/(800) 659-1866 • specializes in scenic gay weddings • IGTA • women-owned/run

ACCOMMODATIONS

▲ **Kahana Beach Condominium Hotel** 4221 Lower Honoapiilani Rd., Lahaina • 669-8611/(800) 222-5642 • gay-friendly • oceanfront studios & 1-bdrm suites • kitchenettes • private lanai • $110-210 (see ad in front color section)

▲ **The Royal Lahaina Resort** 2780 Kekaa Dr., Lahaina • 661-3611/(800) 447-6925 • gay-friendly • full service resort on 27 tropical acres of Ka'anapali • world-class tennis courts & golf courses • swimming • wheelchair access • $195-1,500 (see ad in front color section)

Skin Deep
TATTOO HAWAII
626 FRONT ST.
LAHAINA, HI. 96761

BOOKSTORES & RETAIL SHOPS

▲ **Skin Deep Tattoo** 626 Front St. • 661-8531 • 10am-10pm • traditional, custom, fine line & Hawaiian tattoos • 20 yrs in Lahaina

TRAVEL & TOUR OPERATORS

▲ **Maui Surfing School** PO Box 424, Puunene, 96784 • 875-0625/(800) 851-0543 • lessons for beginners, cowards & non-swimmers • 'surf-aris' for advanced • women-owned/run

Makawao (808)

ACCOMMODATIONS

Maui Network 572-9555/(800) 367-5221 • condo reservation service

TRAVEL & TOUR OPERATORS

Personal Maui 572-1589/(800) 326-5336 • guide & driver for tours of the hidden Maui

Paia (808)

INFO LINES & SERVICES

Women's Event Hotline 573-3077 • covers entire island

ACCOMMODATIONS

Huelo Point Flower Farm PO Box 1195, Paia, 96779 • 572-1850 • gay-friendly • vacation rental • oceanfront estate & organic farm • swimming • kids 10+ ok • $110-300 + 10.17% state tax

PUBLICATIONS

Island Lesbian Connection Box 356 Ste. 171, Paia, 96779 • 575-2681 • newsletter • covers all islands

Wailea

ACCOMMODATIONS

Coconuts Wailea • (800) 289-1522 • lesbians/gay men • swimming • hot tub • kitchens • wheelchair access

Wailuku (808)

BARS

Hamburger Mary's 2010 Main St., Wailuku • 244-7776 • 10am-2am • popular • lesbians/gay men • food served til 10pm • plenty veggie • $7-15

RESTAURANTS & CAFES

Cafe Kup A Kuppa 79 Church St., Wailuku • 244-0500 • 7am-4pm, 8am-1pm Sat, clsd Sun • some veggie • wheelchair access

MOLOKAI

Kaunakakai (808)

ACCOMMODATIONS

Kainehe HC-01 Box 751-Pukoo, Kaunakakai, 96748 • 558-8207 • gay-friendly • fruit brkfst • kitchen • kids ok • on the water • lesbian-owned/run

Molokai Beachfront Escapes PO Box 248, Hana, 96713 • 248-7868/(800) 228-4262 • gay-friendly • beachfront units on the exotic island of Molokai • IGTA • $89-109

OAHU

Honolulu (808)

INFO LINES & SERVICES

▲ **Always Yours by The Wedding Connection** Honolulu • 537-9427/(800) 388-6933 • lesbigay commitment ceremonies

Gay/Lesbian AA 277 Ohua (Waikiki Health Ctr.) • 946-1438 • 8pm daily

Gay/Lesbian Community Center 1566 Wilder Ave. (YWCA) • 951-7000 • 9am-5pm Mon-Fri • info & referrals

Leis of Hawaii (888) 534-7644 • personalized Hawaiian greeting service, complete w/ fresh flower leis

ACCOMMODATIONS

Bed & Breakfast Honolulu (Statewide) 3242 Kaohinani Dr. • 595-7533/(800) 288-4666 • clientele & ownership vary (most gay-friendly) • represents 350 locations on all islands • $40-175

Bed & Breakfast in Manoa Valley 2651 Terrace Dr. • 988-6333 • gay-friendly • spectacular views • women-owned/run

Blair's Original Hana Plantation Houses 2957 Kala Kaua Ave., 96713 • 248-7868/(800) 228-4262 • popular • mostly gay men • tropical cottages & houses in exotic gardens • swimming • IGTA • $60-200

The Coconut Plaza 450 Lewers St. • 923-8828/(800) 882-9696 • gay-friendly • swimming • near beach • wheelchair access • $87-150

Hotel Honolulu 376 Kaiolu St. • 926-2766/(800) 426-2766 • popular • mostly gay men • IGTA • $79-115

Honolulu (808)

WHERE THE GIRLS ARE: Where else? On the beach. Or cruising Kuhio Ave.

LESBIGAY PRIDE: June: 951-7000.

ANNUAL EVENTS: February - Hawaii Women's Festival: (904) 826-0410.

CITY INFO: 923-1811.

ATTRACTIONS: Bishop Museum. Foster Botanical Gardens. Hanauma Bay. Honolulu Academy of Arts. Polynesian Cultural Center. Waimea Falls Park.

BEST VIEW: Helicopter tour.

WEATHER: Usually paradise perfect, but humid. It rarely gets hotter than the upper 80°s.

TRANSIT: Charley's: 955-2211.

Honolulu

*T*he city of Honolulu suffers from a bad case of mistaken identity. The tourist brochure version of high-rise hotels clustered along the bay with the Diamond Head crater in the background is actually Waikiki, 6 miles south of the city. The virtually unknown downtown area of Honolulu is the center of the state government, and teeming with a vibrant culture all its own. **Chinatown**, a designated National Historic Landmark, offers a living history of Asian immigration to Hawaii, with street vendors, grocers, herbalists, acupuncture clinics and authentic Chinese, Vietnamese and Filipino restaurants crammed into the area north of downtown, off of North King Street.

On the other side of the downtown, on South King St., sits **'Iolani Palace**, the heart and soul of modern Hawaiian history. The graceful structure served as a prison for Queen Lili'uokalani, Hawaii's last reigning monarch, when she was placed under house arrest by armed US forces intent on her signing over the nation's sovereignty. The newly refurbished **Aloha Tower Marketplace**, one of the busiest ports in the Pacific, is drawing a fair share of visitors to the waterfront. Don't miss the unforgettable **Hawaii Maritime Center** next door for a glance back at the history of the islands and the often injurious effects Western culture has had on this most isolated of island chains. If you're staying in Waikiki, you can catch a trolley downtown from any of the main streets, saving yourself a mountain of parking headaches.

Waikiki sits on the Southwest corner of Oahu and offers a mind boggling number of hotels, restaurants and shops that are just waiting to consume your tourist dollars. Campy though it is, enjoying a mai tai on the patio of the magnificently restored Sheraton Moana Surfrider (the 1st hotel built in Honolulu) while the sun sets over the Pacific is one of life's greatest pleasures. Old Waikiki, situated along **Kuhio Avenue**, is where you'll find a small collection of men's bars, a couple of shops, one restaurant, **Hamburger Mary's**, and a hotel, **Hotel Honolulu**, that cater to the gay and lesbian community. **Hula's**, a neighborhood bar with a homey feel to it, located just behind Hamburger Mary's, is the most welcoming of the bunch. Down the street you can dance

the night away at **Fusion** or drop in at **Melia's** on Lewers St., for drinks, dancing and occasional live entertainment. **Island Lifestyle**, the lesbigay monthly, runs a complete calendar, and offers a better bet for locating local 'sistahs,' their organizations and events.

There's much more to Oahu than Waikiki, and if you've come this far you owe it to yourself to investigate the rest of the island. Between downtown and the airport is the **Bishop Museum**, repository of Hawaiian culture and guardian of its heritage. If you're at all interested in Hawaii's story, the Bishop Museum offers a crash course in its history, art, traditions and culture. Take the H1 freeway north past the airport and you'll see the exit for one of Hawaii's most famous landmarks, **Pearl Harbor**, and the **Arizona Memorial**. Further north, the road splits, and the H2 to the East takes you through the pineapple fields of Wahiawa and onto the **North Shore**. This world famous surfer's paradise is a bounty of tiny hamlets, unspoiled shoreline and very laid back attitudes. If you're game to grab a board and hang ten, do so with extreme caution and by all means talk with the local surfers and lifeguards before catching a wave.

Oahu's Windward (East) Side offers calmer, safer swimming, boogie boarding and wind surfing. This is also where you'll find Sea Life Park, a combination theme park and marine mammal research facility. Southeastern Oahu's **Hanauma Bay**, an underwater marine preserve, offers the best snorkeling on Oahu. It's operated by the Department of Parks and Recreation and sea life experts are on-hand to offer tours, snorkeling recommendations and Bay folklore. Get there early (before 8am) because once the park reaches capacity for the day, they close it to additional visitors.

—By Deirdre S. Green

(See back section on how to submit an essay about your favorite city.)

▲ **Mango Cottage** 2087-A Iholena St. • 595-6682/(800) 776-2646 • vacation rental (sleeps 4) • kids ok • ocean/park views • IGTA • women-owned/run

▲ **The Mango House** 2087 Iholena St. • 595-6682 (also fax)/(800) 776-2646 • popular • women only • kids 10+yrs ok • ocean view • IGTA • women-owned/run • $60-85 + tax

▲ **Pleasant Holiday Isle Hotel** 270 Lewers St. • 923-0777/(800) 222-5642 • gay-friendly • swimming • private lanai • 1 blk from Waikiki beach • also a full restaurant & lounge (see ad in front color section)

Waikiki Vacation Condos 1860 Ala Moana Blvd. #108 • 946-9371/(800) 543-5663 • furnished 1- & 2-bdrm units • reservation service • $75-175

BARS

Club Michaelangelo 444 Hobron Ln. #P-8 • 951-0008 • 4pm-2am • lesbians/gay men • dancing/DJ • karaoke

Fusion Waikiki 2260 Kuhio Ave., 3rd flr. • 924-2422 • 10pm-4am, from 8pm wknds • popular • mostly gay men • dancing/DJ • transgender-friendly • live shows

Hula's Bar & Lei Stand 2103 Kuhio Ave. • 923-0669 • 10am-2am • popular • lesbians/gay men • dancing/DJ • live shows • videos • patio

Trixx 2109 Kuhio Ave. • 923-0669 • 5pm-2am, from 3pm Sun (barbecue) • lesbians/gay men • dancing/DJ • also 'Treats' deli & the 'Fruit Bar' from 10am • wheelchair access

Windows 444 Hobron Ln., Waikiki • 946-4442 • 11am-2am • lesbians/gay men • lunch & Sun brunch • live shows • wheelchair access

RESTAURANTS & CAFES

Banana's 2139 Kuhio Ave. #125, Waikiki • 922-6262 • 5pm-2am, clsd Mon • lesbians/gay men • Thai • full bar • wheelchair access

Cafe Sistina 1314 S. King St. • 596-0061 • lunch Mon-Fri, dinner nightly • northern Italian • some veggie • full bar • wheelchair access • $9-16

Caffe Aczione 1684 Kalakaua Ave. • 941-9552 • 9am-midnight, til 2am Fri-Sat, til 10pm Sun • Italian • some veggie • BYOB

Caffe Guccinni 2139 Kuhio Ave., Waikiki • 922-5287 • 4pm-10:30pm • Italian • some veggie • full bar • women-owned/run

Crepe Fever/Mocha Java Ward Center • 591-9023 • 8am-9pm, til 4pm Sun • plenty veggie

The Jungle 311 Lewers St. • 922-7808 • pasta plus • some veggie • full bar • dancing/DJ • live shows • wheelchair access

Keo's Thai 1200 Ala Moana Blvd. • 533-0533 • dinner • popular • also 1486 S. King St. • 947-9988

La Provence 2139 Kuhio Ave. • 924-6696 • 4:30pm-10:30pm, clsd Mon • country French

Pieces of Eight 250 Lewers St., Waikiki • 923-6646 • 5pm-11pm • steak & seafood • full bar • wheelchair access • $8-15

Singha Thai 1910 Ala Moana • 941-2898 • 11am-11pm • live shows

Bookstores & Retail Shops

Eighty Percent Straight 2139 Kuhio Ave., 2nd flr., Waikiki • 923-9996 • 10am-midnight • lesbigay clothing • books • cards

Travel & Tour Operators

Bird of Paradise Travel PO Box 4157, 96812-4157 • 735-9103 • IGTA

Hawaii Visitors Bureau 2270 Kalakaua Ave. #801 • 923-1811

Island Pride Taxi & Tour 3151 Monsarrat Ave. #402 • 732-6518 • IGTA

Pacific Ocean Holidays PO Box 88245, 96830 • 923-2400/(800) 735-6600 • IGTA • also publishes semi-annual 'Pocket Guide to Hawaii'

Travel Travel 320 Ward Ave. Ste. 204 • 596-0336 • IGTA

Spiritual Groups

Dignity Honolulu 539 Kapahulu Ave. (St. Mark's Church) • 536-5536 • 7:30pm Sun

Ke Annenue O Ke Aloha MCC 1212 University Ave. (Church of the Crossroads) • 942-1027 • 7pm Sun • also 11am at Cafe Valentino • 2139 Kuhio Ave.

Unitarian Universalists for Lesbian/Gay Concerns (Interweave) 2500 Pali Hwy. • 595-4047 • 10:15am Sun • wheelchair access

Unity Church of Hawaii 3608 Diamond Head Cir. • 735-4436 • 7:30pm, 9am & 11am Sun • wheelchair access

Publications

Island Lifestyle Magazine PO Box 11840, 96828 • 737-6400 • monthly • inquire about resource/travel guide • women-owned/run

Erotica

Diamond Head Video 870 Kapahulu Ave. • 735-6066 • also 25 Kaneohe Bay Dr., Kailau • 254-6066

Kaneohe (808)

Accommodations

Windward Oahu B&B 46-251 Ikiiki, Kaneohe • 235-1124/(800) 235-1151 • lesbians/gay men • swimming • overlooks the bay • IGTA

IDAHO

Boise (208)

INFO LINES & SERVICES
AA Gay/Lesbian 23rd & Woodlawn (First Cong. Church) • 344-6611 • 8pm Sun & Tue

Community Center PO Box 323, 83701 • 336-3870 • 7pm-10pm • info • referrals

Womyn's Night 336-8471

BARS
8th Street Balcony Pub 150 N. 8th St. • 336-1313 • 2pm-midnight, til 2am Th-Sat • gay-friendly • live shows • also a restaurant for lunch • gay-owned/run

Emerald City Club 415 S. 9th • 342-5446 • 10am-2:30am • lesbians/gay men • dancing/DJ • live shows • women-owned/run

Papa's Club 96 1108 Front St. • 333-0074 • 2pm-2am • mostly gay men • neighborhood bar • patio

Partners 2210 Main St. • 331-3551 • 2pm-2am • lesbians/gay men • dancing/DJ • live shows • wheelchair access

RESTAURANTS & CAFES
Flicks & Rick's Cafe American 646 Fulton St. • 342-4288 • opens 4:30pm, from noon wknds • multi-racial • live shows • beer/wine • 2 movie theaters • patio • women-owned/run

BOOKSTORES & RETAIL SHOPS
Blue Unicorn 1809 W. State St. • 345-9390 • 10am-9pm, 11am-5pm Sun • self-help • women's • lesbigay section • wheelchair access

Retrospect 111 N. 11th St. • 336-5034 • 11am-6pm, til 9pm Fri, noon-5pm Sun • sassy stuff

TRAVEL & TOUR OPERATORS
Idaho Travel Council 700 W. State St. • (800) 635-7820

SPIRITUAL GROUPS
MCC 408 N. Garden St. • 342-6764 • 5:45pm Sun

PUBLICATIONS
Diversity PO Box 323, 83701 • 323-0805

Coeur D'Alene (208)

ACCOMMODATIONS
The Clark House on Hayden Lake 4550 S. Hayden Lake Rd. • 772-3470/(800) 765-4593 • popular • gay-friendly • mansion on a wooded 12-acre estate • full brkfst • wheelchair access • $125-165

Lava Hot Springs (208)

ACCOMMODATIONS
Lava Hot Springs Inn 5 Portneuf Ave. • 776-5830 • gay-friendly • full brkfst • hot tub • mineral pool • wheelchair access

Lewiston

INFO LINES & SERVICES
Lewiston Lesbian/Gay Society PO Box 2054, 83501 • meets 1st & 3rd Tue

Moscow (208)

INFO LINES & SERVICES
Inland Northwest PO Box 8135, 83843 • 882-8034 • 1st Mon

University of Idaho Gay/Lesbian/Bisexual Group 885-2691

Women's Center (Univ. of Idaho) corner of Idaho & Line Sts. • 885-6616 • library & resources • support • limited outreach • call first

BOOKSTORES & RETAIL SHOPS
Bookpeople 512 S. Main • 882-7957 • 9am-8pm • general

Pocatello (208)

BARS
Continental Bistro 140 S. Main St. • 233-4433 • 11am-1am, clsd Sun • gay-friendly • also a restaurant • northern Italian • plenty veggie • patio • $10-20

BOOKSTORES & RETAIL SHOPS
The Silver Fox 143 S. 2nd St. • 234-2477 • 11am-10pm, clsd Sun

Stanley (208)

ACCOMMODATIONS
Las Tejanas B&B 3610 Rampart St., Boise, 83704 • 376-6077/774-3301 • May-Sept • lesbians/gay men • full brkfst • natural hot tub • between 2 wilderness areas in the Sawtooth Mtns • near outdoor recreation

ILLINOIS

Alton (314)

ACCOMMODATIONS
River Spirit Retreat B&B 187 W. 19th St. • (314) 569-5795 • St. Louis & Alton locations

BARS
Alton Metro 602 Belle • 465-8687 • 4pm-1:30am, from 2pm wknds • mostly gay men • dancing/DJ • live shows • wheelchair access

Arlington Heights (708)

BOOKSTORES & RETAIL SHOPS
Prairie Moon 8 N. Dunton Ave. • 342-9608 • 11am-6pm, til 8pm Th, clsd Mon • feminist • special events • wheelchair access • women-owned/run

Aurora (284)

EROTICA
Denmark Book Store 1300 US Hwy. 30 • 898-9838 • 24hrs

Bloomington (309)

BARS
Bistro 316 N. Main St. • 829-2278 • 4pm-1am, from 8pm Sat, from 6pm Sun • lesbians/gay men • dancing/DJ • wheelchair access

BOOKSTORES & RETAIL SHOPS
Once Upon a Time (O.U.T.) 311 N. Main • 828-3998 • 1pm-8pm,10am-8pm Sat, noon-5pm Sun, clsd Mon • lesbigay

EROTICA
Risques 1506 N. Main • 827-9279 • 24hrs

Blue Island (708)

BARS
Clubhouse Players 13126 S. Western • 389-6688 • 8pm-2am, til 3am Fri-Sat • lesbians/gay men • dancing/DJ • wheelchair access

Calumet City (708)

BARS
Are You Crazy 48 154th Pl. • 862-4605 • 7pm-2am • mostly gay men

Intrigue 582 State Line Rd. • 868-5240 • 6pm-2am, 7pm-3am Sat, 2pm-2am Sun • mostly women • dancing/DJ • women-owned/run

Mr. B's 606 State Line Rd. • 862-1221 • 2pm-2am, til 3am Wed, Fri-Sat • popular • mostly gay men • dancing/DJ

Patch 201 155th St. • 891-9854 • 3pm-2am, til 3am Sat, 6pm-2am Sun, clsd Mon • mostly women • neighborhood bar • women-owned/run

Pour House 103 155th Pl. • 891-3980 • 8pm-2am, til 3am Wed, Fri-Sat • mostly gay men • dancing/DJ

Carbondale (618)

INFO LINES & SERVICES
AA Lesbian/Gay 549-4633

Gay/Lesbian/Bisexuals & Friends at Southern Illinois University • 453-5151

Women's Services 453-3655 • 8am-4:30pm

Champaign/Urbana (217)

INFO LINES & SERVICES
People for Lesbian/Gay/Bisexual Concerns of Illinois (at University of Illinois) • 333-1187 • 6pm Tue

BARS
Chester Street 63 Chester St. • 356-5607 • 5pm-1am • gay-friendly • dancing/DJ • 'Trash Disco' Tue • wheelchair access

BOOKSTORES & RETAIL SHOPS
Horizon Book Store 1115-1/2 W. Oregon • 328-2988 • 10am-6pm, clsd Sun

Jane Addams Book Shop 208 N. Neil • 356-2555 • 10am-5pm, noon-4pm Sun • full service antiquarian bookstore w/children's room • lesbigay & women's sections

CHICAGO

Chicago is divided into 4 geographical regions:

Chicago - Overview (312)

INFO LINES & SERVICES

AA Gay/Lesbian-Newtown Al-Anon Club 4407 N. Clark • 271-6822 • 3pm-11pm, from 8:30am wknds • wheelchair access

Gay/Lesbian South Asians (SANGAT) PO Box 268463, 60626

Gerber/Hart Library & Archives 3352 N. Paulina St. • 883-3003 • 6pm-9pm Mon & Th, noon-4pm wknds • lesbigay resource center

Horizons Community Services 961 W. Montana • 472-6469 • 9am-10pm Mon-Th, til 5pm Fri

Leather Archives & Musuem 5007 N. Clark St. • 275-1570 • 4pm-midnight Sat or by appt.

Lesbian/Gay Helpline 929-4357 • 6pm-10pm

Lesbigay Radio WCBR 92.7 FM • 506-1521 • 8am-noon Sun

BOOKSTORES & RETAIL SHOPS

Barbara's Bookstore 1350 N. Wells St. • 642-5044 • 9am-10pm, 10am-9pm Sun • women's/lesbigay • also 3130 N. Broadway: 477-0411 • also Oak Park (708) 848-9140

TRAVEL & TOUR OPERATORS

The Concierge Exclusif 75 E. Wacker Dr. Ste. 3600 • 849-3604 • personalized assistance for visitors

Illinois Tourist Information Center 310 S. Michigan Ste. 108 • (800) 822-0292

SPIRITUAL GROUPS

Congregation or Chadash 656 W. Barry (2nd Unitarian Church) • 248-9456 • 8pm Fri

Dignity Chicago 3344 N. Broadway • 296-0780 • 7pm Sun

Chicago (312)

WHERE THE GIRLS ARE: In the Belmont area—on Halstead or Clark streets—with the boys, or hanging out elsewhere in New Town. Upwardly-mobile lesbians live in Lincoln Park or Wrigleyville, while their working-class sisters live in Andersonville (way north).

LESBIGAY PRIDE: June: 348-8243.

ANNUAL EVENTS: February- Hearts Party: 404-8726 AIDS benefit. May- International Mr. Leather: (800) 545-6753. Weekend of events and contest on Sunday. Lambda Literary Awards: (202) 462-7924, the 'Lammies' are the Oscars of lesbigay writing and publishing. August- Halstead St. Fair. October- Chicago Gay/Lesbian Film Festival: 384-5533.

CITY INFO: Chicago Office of Tourism: 744-2400/(800) 487-2446.

ATTRACTIONS: 900 North Michigan Shops. Historic Water Tower. Museum of Science and Industry. Sears Tower Skydeck Observatory. Second City and the Improv Comedy Clubs. The Art Institute of Chicago.

BEST VIEW: Skydeck of the 110-story Sears Tower.

WEATHER: 'The Windy City' earned its name. Winter temperatures have been known to be as low as -46°. Summers are humid, normally in the 80°s.

TRANSIT: Yellow & Checker Cabs: 829-4222. Chicago Airport Shuttle Service: 247-7678. Chicago Transit Authority: 836-7000.

Chicago

*K*nown for its frigid winters and legendary political corruption, Chicago is also home to strong communities of political radicals, African-Americans, artists and performers, and of course, lesbians and gays.

If you remember the Chicago 7, you might want to stop by the **Heartland Cafe** (465-8005) in Rogers Park for a drink, some food, or a T-shirt from their radical variety store! Or check in with **Horizons Community Services** to find out about local lesbian/gay political (and social) groups.

The African-American communities in Chicago are large and influential, making up about 40% of Chicago's population. In fact, Chicago was settled by an African-French man, whose name graces the Du Sable Museum of African-American History (947-0600). The South Side is the cultural center for Chicagoans of African descent, and houses the South Side Community Art Center (373-1026), and the Olivet Baptist Church (842-1081), a station on the Underground Railroad and site of Mahalia Jackson's 1928 debut. We've heard the home cooking at Army & Lou's Restaurant (483-3100) will put a smile in your stomach.

Many of Chicago's other immigrant neighborhoods also house the museums, centers and restaurants the city is famous for— call the **Chicago Office of Tourism** for details. However, if you love Indian food, don't miss the many delicious and cheap Indian buffets on Devon, just west of Sheridan.

What else is there to do? For starters, take a cruise on Lake Michigan. You have your choice of wine-tasting cruises, narrated history cruises, brunch, dinner or cocktail cruises. On land, you'll find superb shopping, real Chicago-style pizza, a great arts and theater scene, and clubs where jazz and blues thrive, like the Green Mill (878-5552), known for originating 'poetry slams', and for its house big band.

And you'll never have a dull moment in Chicago's women's scene. For a good book or a good time, find **People Like Us**, the city's lesbigay bookstore, or **Women & Children First** bookstore. Pick up a copy of **Outlines** or **Nightlines** for the dish on what's hot. And while you're in New Town, cruise by **Girlbar**, or check out **Vortex** for one of their monthly women's parties.

On the Northside, treat yourself to the art at **Womanwild** women's gallery, grab a cup of java at the truly **Mountain Moving Coffeehouse** on Saturday, then boogie down at **Paris Dance** disco, or two-step Tuesdays at **Lost & Found**.

Integrity/Chicago PO Box 2516, 60690 • 348-6362 • call for mtg time & location

MCC Good Shepherd 615 W. Wellington Ave. • 262-0099 • 7pm Sun

PUBLICATIONS

The Alternative Phone Book 425 W. Surf St. #114 • 472-6319 • directory of local businesses

Gab 3223 N. Sheffield, 60657 • 248-4542

Gay Chicago 3121 N. Broadway • 327-7271

▲ **Outlines/Nightlines** 1115 W. Belmont Ave. #2-D • 871-7610

Windy City Times 325 W. Huron Ste. 510 • 397-0020

Women in Business Yellow Pages 7358 N. Lincoln St. #150 • (708) 679-7800

Chicago - Near North (312)

ACCOMMODATIONS

Gold Coast Guesthouse 113 W. Elm St. • 337-0361 • gay-friendly • women-owned/run • $105-150

Old Town B&B 440-9268 • lesbians/gay men • patio • $75

BARS

Artful Dodger 1734 W. Wabansia • 227-6859 • 5pm-2am, from 8pm Sat, clsd Sun • gay-friendly • dancing/DJ

Baton Show Lounge 436 N. Clark St. • 644-5269 • 8pm-4am Wed-Sun • lesbians/gay men • live shows • wheelchair access

Cairo 720 N. Wells • 266-6620 • 8pm-4am, 9am-5am Sat, clsd Sun-Mon • gay-friendly • more gay Sat • dancing/DJ • videos • wheelchair access

The Crowbar 1543 N. Kingsbury • 243-4800 • 10pm-4am, clsd Mon-Tue • popular • gay-friendly • more gay Sun • dancing/DJ

The Generator 306 N. Halsted • 243-8889 • 9pm-4am, clsd Mon-Tue • lesbians/gay men • dancing/DJ • alternative • mostly African-American • wheelchair access

Gentry 712 N. Rush St. • 664-1033 • 1pm-2am • popular • mostly gay men • live shows • videos

Icon 710 N. Clark • 649-1192 • 5pm-2am, from 8pm Sat, clsd Sun-Tue • mostly women

Ka-Boom 747 N. Green, River North • 243-4800 • from 9pm, clsd Sun-Wed • gay-friendly • dancing/DJ

Vinyl 1615 N. Clybourn • 587-8469 • opens 5:30pm daily • gay-friendly • live shows • food served

RESTAURANTS & CAFES

Fireplace Inn 1448 N. Wells St. • 664-5264 • 4:30pm-midnight, from 11am wknds (summer) • lesbians/gay men • BBQ/American • full bar • $10-20

Iggy's 700 N. Milwaukee, River North • 829-4449 • dinner nightly, til 4am Th-Sat • Italian • some veggie • full bar • $8-12

Urbis Orbis Coffeehouse 1934 W. North Ave. • 252-4446 • 9am-midnight • lesbigay periodicals

GYMS & HEALTH CLUBS

Thousand Waves 1212 W. Belmont Ave. • 549-0700 • 5pm-10pm, 10am-3pm Sat, clsd Sun • women only • martial arts & self-defense for women & children • health spa • women-owned/run

TRAVEL & TOUR OPERATORS

C.R.C. Travel 2121 N. Clybourn • 525-3800/(800) 874-7701 • IGTA

Envoy Travel 740 N. Rush St. • 787-2400/(800) 443-6869 • IGTA

River North Travel 432 N. Clark St. • 527-2269 • IGTA

Travel With Us, Ltd. 919 N. Michigan Ave. #3102 • 944-2244/(800) 775-0919 • IGTA

SPIRITUAL GROUPS

Presbyterians for Lesbian/Gay Concerns 600 W. Fullerton Pkwy. (Lincoln Park Preb.) • 784-2635 • 11am Sun (10am summers) • 'More Light' congregation

Chicago - North Side (312)

ACCOMMODATIONS

A Sister's Place 3712 N. Broadway #918 • 275-1319 • women only • guestrooms in artist's flat • women-owned/run • $25-45

BARS

Big Chicks 5024 N. Sheridan • 728-5511 • noon-2am • lesbians/gay men • neighborhood bar • wheelchair access

DINAH SHORE
PALM SPRINGS WEEKEND
MARCH 27-30, 1997

Chicago Eagle 5015 N. Clark St. • 728-0050 • 8pm-4am • lesbians/gay men • women's night Th • leather • wheelchair access

Clark's on Clark 5001 N. Clark St. • 728-2373 • 4pm-4am • popular • mostly gay men • neighborhood bar

Different Strokes 4923 N. Clark St. • 989-1958 • noon-2am, til 3am Sat • mostly gay men • neighborhood bar

El Gato Negro 1461 W. Irving Park • 472-9353 • gay-friendly • mostly Latino-American • transgender-friendly • live shows

Lost & Found 3058 W. Irving Park Rd. • 463-9617 • 7pm-2am, from 4pm wknds, clsd Mon • mostly women • neighborhood bar

Madrigal's 5316 N. Clark St. • 334-3033 • 5pm-2am • lesbians/gay men • food served • live shows

Off the Line 1829 W. Montrose • 528-3253 • 5pm-2am, from 3pm wknds • mostly women • neighborhood bar • women-owned/run

Paris Dance 1122 W. Montrose • 769-0602 • 5pm-2am, 2pm-3am Sat, noon-2am Sun • popular • mostly women • dancing/DJ • also cafe • clsd Mon-Tue • wheelchair access

Touché 6412 N. Clark St. • 465-7400 • 5pm-4am, from 3pm wknds • mostly gay men • leather

RESTAURANTS & CAFES

Fireside 5739 N. Ravenswood • 878-5942 • 11am-4am • plenty veggie • full bar • patio • wheelchair access • $6-15

Mountain Moving Coffeehouse 1545 W. Morse • 477-8362 • Sat only • women & girls only • non-alcoholic beverages • live shows • collectively run

Tendino's 5335 N. Sheridan • 275-8100 • 11am-11pm • pizzeria • full bar • wheelchair access

BOOKSTORES & RETAIL SHOPS

Gay Mart 3457 N. Halsted St. • 929-4272 • open 11am daily

KOPI: A Traveler's Cafe 5317 N. Clark St. • 989-5674 • 8am-11pm • live shows • also boutique & gallery

WomanWild/Treasures by Women 5237 N. Clark St. • 878-0300 • 11am-7pm, til 8pm Fri, til 6pm wknds • art & gift gallery • commitment rings & gift registry • wheelchair access • lesbian-owned/run

Women & Children First 5233 N. Clark St. • 769-9299 • 11am-7pm, til 9pm Wed-Fri, from 10am Sat, til 6pm Sun • women's bookstore • also videos & music • wheelchair access • women-owned/run

Chicago - New Town (312)

INFO LINES & SERVICES

Chicago 35 (at Ann Sather's Restaurant) • 271-5909 • 3:30pm-6pm, 3rd Sun of month • group for women over 35

ACCOMMODATIONS

City Suites Hotel 933 W. Belmont • 404-3400/(800) 248-9108 • gay-friendly • accommodations w/ a touch of European style • IGTA • $79-89

Park Brompton Inn 528 W. Brompton Pl. • 404-3499/(800) 727-5108 • gay-friendly • romantic 19th century atmosphere • $75-89

Surf Hotel 555 W. Surf St. • 528-8400/(800) 787-3108 • gay-friendly • 1920s hotel in Lincoln Park

Villa Toscana Guesthouse 3447 N. Halstead St. • 404-2643/(800) 684-5755 • lesbians/gay men • full brkfst

BARS

Annex 3 3160 N. Clark St. • 327-5969 • noon-2am, til 3am Sat • lesbians/gay men • videos • wheelchair access

Beat Kitchen 2100 W. Belmont • 281-4444 • noon-2am • gay-friendly • live shows • also grill • some veggie • wheelchair access

Berlin 954 W. Belmont • 348-4975 • opening time varies, closes 4am • popular • lesbians/gay men • women's night w/ dancers 1st & 3rd Wed • dancing/DJ • live shows • videos • wheelchair access

Buddies Restaurant & Bar 3301 N. Clark St. • 477-4066 • 7am-2am, from 9am Sun • lesbians/gay men • some veggie • $8-12

The Closet 3325 N. Broadway St. • 477-8533 • 2pm-4am, from noon wknds • popular • lesbians/gay men • videos • Clem's favorite

Cocktail 3359 Halsted St. • 477-1420 • 4pm-2am, from 2pm wknds • lesbians/gay men • wheelchair access

Dandy's Piano Bar 3729 N. Halsted St. • 525-1200 • noon-2am • lesbians/gay men • neighborhood bar • piano bar • wheelchair access

Gentry 3320 N. Halsted • 348-1053 • 4pm-2am • lesbians/gay men • live shows

Girlbar 2625 N. Halsted St. • 871-4210 • 6pm-2am, from 3pm Fri & Sun • mostly women • dancing/DJ • 'Boybar' Wed

Roscoe's 3354-3356 N. Halsted St. • 281-3355 • 2pm-2am, noon-3am Sat • popular • lesbians/gay men • neighborhood bar • dancing/DJ • videos • food served • patio

Smart Bar/Cabaret Metro 3730 N. Clark St. • 549-4140 • 9:30pm-4am • gay-friendly • dancing/DJ • live shows

Spin 3200 N. Halsted • 327-7711 • 4pm-2am • mostly gay men • 2nd & 4th Tue women's night • dancing/DJ • videos

Vortex 3631 N. Halsted • 975-6622 • 9pm-4am, clsd Sun-Mon • lesbians/gay men • monthly women's parties • dancing/DJ • alternative • live shows • videos • wheelchair access

RESTAURANTS & CAFES

Angelina Ristorante 3561 Broadway • 935-5933 • 5:30pm-11pm, Sun brunch • Italian • $10-20

Ann Sather's 929 W. Belmont Ave. • 348-2378 • 7am-10pm, til midnight Fri-Sat • popular • some veggie • $5-10

Cornelia's 750 Cornelia Ave. • 248-8333 • dinner, clsd Mon • some veggie • full bar • wheelchair access • $10-20

Mike's Broadway Cafe 3805 N. Broadway • 404-2205 • 7am-10pm, 24hrs Fri-Sat • lesbians/gay men • some veggie • wheelchair access • $5-10

The Pepper 3441 N. Sheffield • 665-7377 • 6pm-2am, clsd Mon • lesbians/gay men • supper club • gourmet Italian • plenty veggie • full bar • $12-20

Perk 3322 N. Halsted • 549-9900 • noon-1am • lesbians/gay men

The Raw Bar & Grill 3720 N. Clark St. • 348-7291 • 5pm-2am • seafood • $8-12

Scenes Coffee House & Dramatist Bookstore 3168 N. Clark St. • 525-1007 • 9:30am-midnight • soups/salads

GYMS & HEALTH CLUBS

Chicago Sweat Shop 3215 N. Broadway • 871-2789 • gay-owned/run

BOOKSTORES & RETAIL SHOPS

▲ **People Like Us** 1115 W. Belmont • 248-6363 • 10am-9pm • Chicago's only exclusively lesbigay bookstore

PEOPLE LIKE US

The exclusively gay and lesbian bookstore for Chicago

New Location!

1115 W. Belmont Ave.
Chicago, IL 60657

and introducing

The Espress Yourself Cybercafe

Open daily.
phone 312.248.6363 fax 312.248.1550
e-mail plubooks@aol.com

Unabridged Books 3251 N. Broadway St. • 883-9119 • 10am-10pm, til 8pm wknds • wheelchair access

We're Everywhere 3434 N. Halsted St. • 404-0590 • noon-7pm • also mail order catalog

EROTICA

Male Hide Leathers 2816 N. Lincoln Ave. • 929-0069 • noon-8pm, til midnight Fri-Sat, clsd Mon

Chicago - South Side (312)

BARS

Escapades 6301 S. Harlem • 229-0886 • 10pm-4am, til 5am Sat • mostly gay men • dancing/DJ • videos

Inn Exile 5758 W. 65th St. • 582-3510 • 6pm-2am, from noon Sun • mostly gay men • dancing/DJ • wheelchair access

Jeffery Pub/Disco 7041 S. Jeffery • 363-8555 • 11am-4am • mostly gay men • dancing/DJ • multi-racial clientele • wheelchair access

Elgin (847)

INFO LINES & SERVICES

Fox Valley Gay Association PO Box 393, 60120 • 392-6882 • 7pm-10pm Mon-Fri

Elk Grove Village (847)

BARS

Hunters 1932 E. Higgins • 439-8840 • 4pm-4am • popular • mostly gay men • dancing/DJ • videos

Evanston (847)

INFO LINES & SERVICES

Kinheart Women's Center 2214 Ridge Ave. • 604-0913 • lesbian-only programs 8pm 2nd, 3rd & 4th Fri

Forest Park (708)

BARS

Nut Bush 7201 Franklin • 366-5117 • 3pm-2am, til 3am Fri-Sat • mostly gay men • dancing/DJ • videos

Franklin Park (708)

BARS

Temptations 10235 W. Grand Ave. • 455-0008 • 4pm-4am, 3pm-2am Sun • popular • mostly women • dancing/DJ • transgender-friendly • live entertainment • videos

Granite City (618)

BARS

Club Zips 3145 W. Chain of Rocks Rd. • 797-0070 • 6pm-2am • popular • lesbians/gay men • live entertainment • videos • outdoor complex

Hinsdale (708)

SPIRITUAL GROUPS

MCC Holy Covenant 17 W. Maple (Unitarian Church) • 325-8488 • 6pm Sun • wheelchair access

Joliet (815)

BARS

Maneuvers 118 E. Jefferson • 727-7069 • 8pm-2am, til 3am Fri-Sat • lesbians/gay men • dancing/DJ • patio

Lansing (708)

RESTAURANTS & CAFES

Outriggers 2352 172nd St. • 418-0202 • 11am-11pm • popular • seafood • some veggie • full bar • live shows • wheelchair access • $11-18

Lincolnwood (708)

TRAVEL & TOUR OPERATORS

Edward's Travel Advisors 7301 N. Lincoln Ave. #215 • 677-4420/(800) 541-5158 • IGTA

Naperville (708)

TRAVEL & TOUR OPERATORS

Classic Travel 1271 E. Ogden Ave. #123 • 963-3030/(800) 932-5789 • IGTA

Nauvoo (217)

ACCOMMODATIONS

Ed-Harri-Mere B&B 290 N. Page St. • 453-2796 • gay-friendly • quiet Victorian bungalow • close to historic sites • $30-35

Oak Park (708)

BOOKSTORES & RETAIL SHOPS

The Left Bank Bookstall 104 S. Oak Park Ave. • 383-4700 • 10am-8pm Mon-Th, til 9pm Fri-Sat, noon-5pm Sun

The Pride Agenda 1109 Westgate • 524-8429 • 11am-7pm, til 8pm Th-Fri, 11am-5pm wknds • lesbigay • wheelchair access

Peoria (309)

BARS

D.J.'s Timeout 703 SW Adams • 674-5902 • 1pm-1am • lesbians/gay men • dancing/DJ • wheelchair access

Quench Room 631 W. Main • 676-1079 • 5pm-1am, from 1pm wknds • lesbians/gay men • neighborhood bar • wheelchair access

Red Fox Den 800 N. Knoxville Ave. • 674-8013 • 9pm-4am • lesbians/gay men • dancing/DJ • food served • live shows

PUBLICATIONS

The Alternative Times PO Box 5661, 61601 • 688-1930

Quincy (217)

INFO LINES & SERVICES

AA Gay/Lesbian 124-1/2 N. 5th (MCC) • 224-2800

BARS

Irene's Cabaret 124 N. 5th St. • 222-6292 • 9pm-1am, from 7pm Fri-Sat, clsd Mon • lesbians/gay men • dancing/DJ • live shows • wheelchair access

SPIRITUAL GROUPS

MCC 124-1/2 N. 5th • 224-2800 • 6pm Sun

Rock Island (309)

BARS

Augie's 313 20th St. • 788-7389 • 6am-3am, from 10am Sun • mostly women • neighborhood bar

J.R.'s 325 20th St. • 786-9411 • 3pm-3am, from noon Sun • lesbians/gay men • dancing/DJ • live shows • wheelchair access

Madison Square 319 20th St. • 786-9400 • 4pm-3am • lesbians/gay men • dancing/DJ • live shows • wheelchair access

BOOKSTORES & RETAIL SHOPS

All Kinds of People 1806 2nd Ave. • 788-2567 • 10am-11pm • alternative • also bistro • some veggie • wheelchair access • $5-12

Rockford (815)

BARS

Office 513 E. State St. • 965-0344 • 5pm-2am, noon-midnight Sun • popular • lesbians/gay men • dancing/DJ • videos • beer only

RESTAURANTS & CAFES

Cafe Esperanto 107 N. Main • 968-0123 • noon-1am, 7pm-midnight Sun • full bar • also gallery

Lucernes 845 N. Church St. • 968-2665 • 5pm-11pm, clsd Mon • fondue • full bar • wheelchair access

Maria's 828 Cunningham • 968-6781 • 5pm-9pm, clsd Sun-Mon • Italian • full bar • Denise's favorite • $6-12

Springfield (217)

BARS

New Dimensions 3036 Peoria Rd. • 753-9268 • 8pm-3am Th-Sat • mostly gay men • dancing/DJ • beer only

Smokey's Den 411 E. Washington • 522-0301 • 6pm-1am, til 3am Fri-Sat • lesbians/gay men • dancing/DJ • wheelchair access

The Station House 306 E. Washington • 525-0438 • 7am-1am, from noon Sun • gay-friendly • neighborhood bar • wheelchair access

SPIRITUAL GROUPS

MCC Faith Eternal 304 W. Allen • 525-9597 • 10am & 6pm Sun

Sterling

INFO LINES & SERVICES

IAWIA (I Am What I Am) PO Box 1314, 61081 • support group for northwest IL • meetings & newsletter

Waukegan (708)

TRAVEL & TOUR OPERATORS

Carlson Travel Network/Cray's Travel 410 S. Greenbay Rd. • 623-4722 • IGTA

INDIANA

Bloomington (812)

INFO LINES & SERVICES
Bloomington Gay/Lesbian/Bisexual Switchboard 855-5688 • irregular volunteer hours • recorded info 24hrs

Indiana Youth Group (800) 347-8336 • 7pm-midnight Th-Fri • lesbigay youth hotline

Outreach Memorial Hall East #127 • 855-3849 • 6:30pm 2nd & 4th Tue • support/discussion groups • call for info

ACCOMMODATIONS
Burr House 210 E. Chestnut St. • 828-7686 • gay-friendly • full brkfst

Enchanted Otter PO Box 5217, 47407 • 323-9800 • women only • lake retreat for all seasons • full brkfst • hot tub • kitchen • fireplace • smokefree • women-owned/run • $60-85

BARS
Bullwinkle's 201 S. College St. • 334-3232 • 7pm-3am, clsd Sun • lesbians/gay men • more women Th • dancing/DJ • live shows

The Other Bar 414 S. Walnut • 332-0033 • 4pm-3am, clsd Sun • lesbians/gay men • more women Tue & Th • neighborhood bar • patio • wheelchair access

RESTAURANTS & CAFES
Village Deli 409 E. Kirkwood • 336-2303 • 7am-9pm • some veggie

BOOKSTORES & RETAIL SHOPS
Athena Gallery 108 E. Kirkwood • 339-0734 • 11am-6pm, til 8pm Fri-Sat, til 4pm Sun • wheelchair access

SPIRITUAL GROUPS
Integrity Bloomington 400 E. Kirkwood Ave. (Trinity Episcopal Church) • 336-4466 • 7:30pm 2nd Wed • wheelchair access

Elkhart (219)

INFO LINES & SERVICES
Switchboard Concern 293-8671 (crisis only) • 24hrs

SPIRITUAL GROUPS
Unitarian Universalist Fellowship 1732 Garden • 264-6525 • 10:30am Sun • wheelchair access

Evansville (812)

INFO LINES & SERVICES
Tri-State Alliance PO Box 2901, 47728 • 474-4853 • info • monthly social group • newsletter

BARS
Someplace Else 930 Main St. • 424-3202 • 4pm-3am, clsd Sun • lesbians/gay men • dancing/DJ

Uptown Bar 201 W. Illinois St. • 423-4861 • 1pm-1am, til 3am Fri-Sat, clsd Sun • lesbians/gay men • dancing/DJ • videos • food served • pizza • patio • wheelchair access

BOOKSTORES & RETAIL SHOPS
A.A. Michael Books 1541 S. Green River Rd. • 479-8979 • noon-6pm, til 8pm Fri, 10am-5pm Sat • spiritual • wheelchair access

Fort Wayne (219)

INFO LINES & SERVICES
Gay/Lesbian AA (at Up the Stairs Community Center) • 744-1199 • 7:30pm Tue & Sat, 4:30pm Sun

Up the Stairs Community Center 3426 Broadway • 744-1199 • helpline 7pm-10pm, til midnight Fri-Sat, 6:30pm-9pm Sun • space for various groups

BARS
After Dark 231 Pearl St. • 424-6130 • 6pm-3:30am, clsd Sun • lesbians/gay men • dancing/DJ • live shows • wheelchair access

Downtown On The Landing 110 W. Columbia St. • 420-1615 • 7pm-3am, clsd Sun-Tue • lesbians/gay men • dancing/DJ

Riff Raff's 2809 W. Main St. • 436-4166 • 4pm-3am, clsd Sun • mostly gay men • neighborhood bar • food served • wheelchair access

SPIRITUAL GROUPS
New World Church & Outreach Center 222 E. Leigh • 456-6570 • 11am Sun • wheelchair access

Open Door Chapel (at Up the Stairs Community Center) • 744-1199 • 7pm Sun

Hammond (219)

RESTAURANTS & CAFES
Phil Smidt & Son 1205 N. Calumet Ave. • 659-0025 • lunch & dinner • full bar

Indianapolis (317)

INFO LINES & SERVICES

AA Gay/Lesbian 632-7864

Coming Out Positively (at Dreams & Swords) • 7:30pm 1st & 3rd Tue • lesbian coming out group

Fellowship Indianapolis PO Box 2331, 46206-2331 • 326-4614 • social & support groups for lesbians/gay men

Gay/Lesbian Hotline PO Box 2152, 46206 • 630-4297 • 7pm-11pm daily • resources • crisis counseling

Lesbians Over 40 Group (at Dreams & Swords) • 7:30pm 1st & 3rd Th

Sweet Misery PO Box 11690, 46201-0690 • S/M support group primarily for lesbians

Thursday Night Lesbian Discussion Group (at Dreams & Swords) • 7:30pm 2nd & 4th Th

BARS

501 Tavern 501 N. College Ave. • 632-2100 • 3pm-3am, clsd Sun • popular • mostly gay men • country/western Tue • dancing/DJ Fri-Sat • also leather shop

Betty Boop's Lounge 637 Massachusetts Ave. • 637-2310 • 10am-midnight, til 3am wknds, clsd Sun • gay-friendly • neighborhood bar • food served

Brothers Bar & Grill Inc. 822 N. Illinois St. • 636-1020 • 11am-midnight, 4pm-1am wknds • lesbians/gay men • live shows • also a restaurant • some veggie • wheelchair access • $7-14

Club Cabaret 151 E. 14th St. • 767-1707 • 8pm-3am, clsd Sun & Tue • lesbians/gay men • dancing/DJ • patio • call for events • wheelchair access

Illusions 1456 E. Washington • 266-0535 • 7am-3am, clsd Sun • lesbians/gay men • dancing/DJ • live shows

Jimmy's Bar & Restaurant 924 N. Pennsylvania St. • 638-9039 • 5pm-3am • popular • mostly gay men • neighborhood bar • live shows • food served • cont'l • $9-15

The Metro 707 Massachusetts • 639-6022 • 4pm-3am, noon-12:30am Sun • lesbians/gay men • dancing/DJ • also a restaurant • some veggie • patio • wheelchair access • $5-11

Indianapolis

*I*ndianapolis, the capital of the 'Hoosier' state, looks like your typical midwestern industrial city. But you'll find a few surprises under the surface.

You probably won't find lesbians dancing in the streets (unless it's Pride Day). But they're there. Start at the women's bookstore, **Dreams & Swords**. While you're in the neighborhood, check out some of the fun boutiques and restaurants in the Broad Ripple district. Later fuel up on caffeine at **Coffee Zone** and dance with the girls at **The Ten**.

If you're into women's music, or plan on being in Indiana during the first weekend in June, drive down to Bloomington for the **National Women's Music Festival** (call Dreams & Swords for info). If fast cars are more your style, be in Indianapolis for the Indy 500 on Memorial Day weekend.

The Ten 1218 N. Pennsylvania St. (entrance in rear) • 638-5802 • 6pm-3am, clsd Sun • popular • mostly women • country/western Mon • dancing/DJ • live shows • wheelchair access

Tomorrow's 2301 N. Meridian • 925-1710 • 5pm-3am, til 12:30am Sun • lesbians/gay men • more women Tue & Th • dancing/DJ • live shows • also a restaurant • Chinese/American • wheelchair access • $7-10

The Varsity 1517 N. Pennsylvania St. • 635-9998 • 10am-3am, noon-midnight Sun • mostly gay men • neighborhood bar • food served • $4-10

The Vogue 6259 N. College Ave. • 259-7029 • 9pm-1am • gay-friendly • more gay Sun • dancing/DJ • alternative • live shows

RESTAURANTS & CAFES

Aesop's Tables 631-0055 • 11am-9pm, til 10pm Fri-Sat • beer/wine • authentic Mediterranean • some veggie • wheelchair access • $9-12

Coffee Zone 137 E. Ohio St. • 684-0432 • 6:30am-6pm, clsd wknds • lesbians/gay men • cafe • some veggie • $4-6

The Iron Skillet 2489 W. 30th St. • 923-6353

BOOKSTORES & RETAIL SHOPS

Borders Book Shop 5612 Castleton Corner Ln. • 849-8660 • 9am-10pm, 11am-6pm Sun • general

▲ **Dreams & Swords** 6503 Ferguson St. • 253-9966/(800) 937-2706 • 10am-6pm, 10:30am-5pm Sat, noon-5pm Sun • feminist bookstore

Indy News 121 S. Pennsylvania • 632-7680 • 6am-7pm, til 6pm wknds

Just Cards 145 E. Ohio St. • 638-1170 • 9am-5:30pm, clsd Sun • wheelchair access

Southside News 8063 Madison Ave. • 887-1020 • 6am-8pm, til 6pm Sun

TRAVEL & TOUR OPERATORS

Ross & Babcock Travel 832 Broad Ripple Ave. • 259-4194/(800) 229-4194 • IGTA

UniWorld Travel 1010 E. 86th St. #65E • 573-4919/(800) 573-4919

SPIRITUAL GROUPS

Jesus MCC 3620 N. Franklin Rd. (church) • 895-4934 • 6pm Sun • wheelchair access

PUBLICATIONS

▲ **The Indiana Word** 225 E. North St. Tower 1 Ste. 2800 • 579-3075 • monthly

Indianapolis   (317)

WHERE THE GIRLS ARE: Spread throughout the city, but Broad Ripple serves as a friendly meeting point.

ENTERTAINMENT: Women's Chorus: 638-9039. Men's Chorus at the Crossroads Performing Arts: 931-9464. The Irving (film): 357-3792.

LESBIGAY PRIDE: June: 634-9212, Justice Inc.

ANNUAL EVENTS: May- National Women's Music Festival: (317) 927-9355/253-9966 in Bloomington.

CITY INFO: Indianapolis Visitor's Bureau: 639-4282.

ATTRACTIONS: Union Station, Art Museum, Zoo, Speedway 500.

WEATHER: The spring weather is moderate (50°s-60°s) with occasional storms. The summers are typically midwestern: hot (mid-90°s) and humid. The autumns are mild and colorful in southeastern Indiana. As for winter, it's the wind chill that'll get to you.

TRANSIT: Yellow Cab: 487-7777. Metro Transit: 635-3344.

Out & About Indiana 133 W. Market St. #105 • 923-5550

Swagger & Sway PO Box 11690, 46201-0690 • quarterly • nat'l newsletter for butch/femme

Lafayette (317)

BARS

The Sportsman 644 Main St. • 742-6321 • 9am-3am, from 5pm Sat, clsd Sun • lesbians/gay men • neighborhood bar • dancing/DJ

SPIRITUAL GROUPS

Dignity-Lafayette PO Box 4665, 47903 • 742-1926 • 7:30pm Wed • at Morton Community Center

EROTICA

The Fantasy 119 N. River Rd., W. Lafayette • 743-5042 • noon-4am, 4pm-1am Sun • bookstore • videos

Fantasy East 2320 Concord Rd. • 474-2417 • books & videos

Monroe City (812)

TRAVEL & TOUR OPERATORS

The Travel Club City Centre, Box 128, 47557 • 743-2919 • international membership-only non-profit travel club

Muncie (317)

INFO LINES & SERVICES

Live & Let Live AA 300 S. Madison (at Grace Church) • 284-3331 • 7:30pm Mon

BARS

Carriage House 1100 Kilgore • 282-7411 • gay-friendly • neighborhood bar • also a restaurant • steak/seafood • wheelchair access • gay owned/run • $9-12

Mark III Tap Room 107 E. Main St. • 282-8273 • 11am-3am, clsd Sun • lesbians/gay men • dancing/DJ

Richmond (317)

INFO LINES & SERVICES

Earlham Lesbian/Bisexual/Gay Peoples Union Box E-565 Earlham College, 47373

BARS

Coachman 911 E. Main St. • 966-2835 • 6pm-3am, clsd Sun • lesbians/gay men • more women Sat • dancing/DJ • alternative • wheelchair access

South Bend (219)

INFO LINES & SERVICES

Community Resource Center Helpline 232-2522 • 8am-5pm • limited gay/lesbian info • also 24hr crisis hotline

IUSB Women's Resource Center Northside IUSB Rm. #203 • 237-4491 • 8am-5pm Mon-Fri

ACCOMMODATIONS

Kamm's Island Inn 700 Lincoln Wy. W., Mishawaka • 256-1501/(800) 955-5266 • gay-friendly • swimming • wheelchair access

BARS

Sea Horse II Cabaret 1902 Western Ave. • 237-9139 • 8pm-3am, clsd Sun • lesbians/gay men • dancing/DJ • live shows • wheelchair access

Starz Bar & Restaurant 1505 S. Kendall St. • 288-7827 • 9pm-3am, clsd Sun • mostly gay men • dancing/DJ • live shows • wheelchair access

Truman's The 100 Center, Mishawaka • 259-2282 • 5pm-3am, til midnight Sun • popular • lesbians/gay men • dancing/DJ • piano bar Fri-Sat • large outdoor area • swimming • also cafe • plenty veggie

BOOKSTORES & RETAIL SHOPS

Little Professor Book Center Martins Ironwood Plaza North • 277-4488 • 9am-9pm, 10am-5pm wknds

Terre Haute (812)

INFO LINES & SERVICES

Gay/Lesbian/Bisexual Terre Haute Info Line 237-6916 • extensive touchtone directory of resources, bars & more

Heartland Care Center 237-7886

IYG-Terre Haute 231-6829 • local chapter of statewide youth group • 21 years & under

BARS

Hightowers 13th at Chestnut • 232-3443 • 8pm-3am • gay-friendly • dancing/DJ • alternative • multi-racial

R-Place 684 Lafayette Ave. • 232-9119 • 8pm-3am, clsd Sun-Mon • lesbians/gay men • dancing/DJ • alternative

Whiting (219)

RESTAURANTS & CAFES

Vogel's 1250 Indianapolis Blvd. • 659-1250

IOWA

Ames   (515)

INFO LINES & SERVICES

Gay/Lesbian Alliance Iowa State University, 39 Memorial Union, 50011 • 294-2104 • 10am-4pm • meets 7:30pm Wed in rm. 245

Help Central 232-0000 • 9am-5pm • community info service • some lesbigay referrals

Margaret Sloss Women's Center Sloss House (ISU) • 294-4154 • call for programs

RESTAURANTS & CAFES

Lucallen's 400 Main St. • 232-8484 • 11am-11pm • Italian • some veggie • full bar • $6-12

Pizza Kitchen 120 Hayward • 292-1710 • 11am-10pm • gay-friendly • beer/wine

Burlington   (319)

ACCOMMODATIONS

Arrowhead Motel 2520 Mt. Pleasant St. • 752-6353/(800) 341-8000 • gay-friendly • suites avail. • kitchenettes

BARS

Steve's Place 852 Washington • 752-9109 • 9am-2am • gay-friendly • neighborhood bar • wheelchair access

Cedar Rapids   (319)

INFO LINES & SERVICES

Gay/Lesbian Resource Center PO Box 1643, 52406 • 366-2055 • 6pm-9pm Mon • support group 1st & 3rd Wed

BARS

Rockafellas 2739 6th St SW • 399-1623 • 3pm-2am, from 5pm wknds • lesbians/gay men • dancing/DJ

Side Saddle Saloon 525 'H' St. SW • 362-2226 • 5pm-2am • lesbians/gay men • 2 bars (one smokefree) • dancing/DJ • dance lessons Mon & Th 8:30pm • country/western • live shows • wheelchair access

Davenport   (319)

BOOKSTORES & RETAIL SHOPS

Crystal Rainbow 1615 Washington St. • 323-1050 • 10am-5pm, clsd Sun • feminist bookstore • will order gay titles

SPIRITUAL GROUPS

MCC Quad Cities 3707 Eastern Ave. • 2:30pm Sun

Decorah

BOOKSTORES & RETAIL SHOPS

Phil's Fun Stuff PO Box 431, 52101-0431 • rainbow & AIDS awareness flags

Des Moines   (515)

INFO LINES & SERVICES

GLRC (Gay/Lesbian Resource Center) 522 11th St. • 281-0634 (24hr info) • youth groups • many other meetings

Out-Reach PO Box 70044, 50311 • social/support group

Women's Cultural Collective PO Box 22063, 50322 • newsletter • monthly coffeehouses • social events • support groups

Women's Rap Group 7pm 1st & 3rd Th • contact GLRC for info

Young Women's Resource Center 1909 Ingersoll Ave • 244-4901 • 8:30am-5pm Mon-Fri

ACCOMMODATIONS

Kingman House 2920 Kingman Blvd. • 279-7312 • lesbians/gay men • turn-of-the-century B&B • full brkfst • wheelchair access

Racoon River Resort 2920 Kingman Blvd. • 279-7312 • lesbians/gay men • on the river • available for large groups • full brkfst • hot tub • nudity • food served • wheelchair access

BARS

Blazing Saddles 416 E. 5th St. • 246-1299 • 2pm-2am, from noon wknds • popular • mostly gay men • leather • wheelchair access

Garden 112 SE 4th St. • 243-3965 • 5pm-2am, from 7pm Mon-Wed • popular • lesbians/gay men • dancing/DJ • live shows • patio

Our Place Lounge 424 E. Locust • 243-9626 • 5pm-2am • lesbians/gay men • dancing/DJ • live shows • wheelchair access

Shooters Lounge 515 E. 6th • 245-9126 • noon-2am • lesbians/gay men • neighborhood bar • wheelchair access

RESTAURANTS & CAFES

Chat Noir Cafe 644 18th St. • 244-1353 • 10am-11pm, clsd Sun-Mon • some veggie • beer/wine • wheelchair access • $6-12

BOOKSTORES & RETAIL SHOPS

Borders Bookshop 1821 22nd St., West Des Moines • 223-1620 • 9am-9pm, 11am-6pm Sun • wheelchair access

TRAVEL & TOUR OPERATORS
Iowa Division of Tourism 200 E. Grand Ave. • (800) 345-4692

PUBLICATIONS
Outword PO Box 7008, 50309 • 281-0634

EROTICA
Axiom 412-1/2 E. 5th St. • 246-0414 • tattoos • piercings

Grinnell (515)

INFO LINES & SERVICES
Stonewall Resource Center Grinnell College Box U-5, 50112 • 269-3327 • also quarterly newsletter

Iowa City (319)

INFO LINES & SERVICES
AA Gay/Lesbian 338-9111
Gay/Lesbian/Bisexual People's Union c/o SAC/IMU University of Iowa, 52242 • 335-3251 • also publishes 'Gay Hawkeye' newsletter
Women's Resource/Action Center 130 N. Madison • 335-1486 • community center & lesbian support group • wheelchair access

BARS
6:20 Club 620 S. Madison St. • 354-2494 • 9pm-2am, clsd Sun-Tue • popular • lesbians/gay men • dancing/DJ • wheelchair access

BOOKSTORES & RETAIL SHOPS
Alternatives 323 E. Market St. • 337-4124 • 10am-6pm, clsd Sun • wheelchair access
Prairie Lights Bookstore 15 S. Dubuque St. • 337-2681 • 9am-9pm, til 5pm wknds • wheelchair access

Mason City

INFO LINES & SERVICES
GLNCI (Gays/Lesbians of North Central Iowa) Box 51, 50401

Newton (515)

ACCOMMODATIONS
La Corsette Maison Inn 629 1st Ave. E. • 792-6833 • gay-friendly • 3-course brkfst • antique jacuzzi • 4-star restaurant

Sioux City (712)

BARS
3 Cheers 414 20th St. • 255-8005 • lesbians/gay men • neighborhood bar • dancing/DJ • live shows • wheelchair access
Kings & Queens 417 Nebraska St. • 252-4167 • 7pm-2am • lesbians/gay men • dancing/DJ

Waterloo (319)

INFO LINES & SERVICES
Access PO Box 1682, 50704 • 232-6805 • weekly info & support • monthly newsletter
Lesbian/Bisexual Support Group PO Box 2241, 50704 • 233-7519 • 7:30pm 4th Mon

BARS
The Bar Ltd. 903 Sycamore • 232-0543 • 7pm-2am • lesbians/gay men • dancing/DJ • live shows • wheelchair access

RESTAURANTS & CAFES
Joe's Country Grill 4117 University, Cedar Falls • 277-8785 • 11am-11pm, 24hrs wknds

KANSAS

Hays (913)

INFO LINES & SERVICES
Western Kansas Gay/Lesbian Services Ft. Hays Univ., 600 Park St., 67701 • 628-5514

Kansas City (See Kansas City, MO)

Lawrence (913)

INFO LINES & SERVICES
Decca Center AA Support & Counseling 841-4138 • info on Gay/Lesbian AA

GLOSK (Gay/Lesbian Services of Kansas) University of Kansas Box 13 KS Union, 66045 • 864-3091

BARS
Club Hideaway 106 N. Park • 841-4966

Jazzhaus 926-1/2 Massachusetts • 749-3320 • 4pm-2am • gay-friendly • live shows

Teller's Restaurant & Bar 746 Massachusetts Ave. • 843-4111 • 11am-2am • gay-friendly • 'Gay Family Night' Tue • live shows • also a restaurant • southern Italian/pizza • some veggie • $9-15

BOOKSTORES & RETAIL SHOPS
Terra Nova Books & Cafe 920 Massachusetts St. • 832-8300 • 10am-9pm, til 10pm Fri-Sat, noon-6pm Sun • progressive • lesbigay section • wheelchair access

Matfield Green (316)

ACCOMMODATIONS
Prairie Women Retreat PO Box 2, 66862 • 753-3465 • women only • working cattle ranch • full brkfst & dinner avail. • women-owned/run

Topeka (913)

INFO LINES & SERVICES
AA Gay/Lesbian 2425 SE Indiana Ave. (MCC) • 8pm Tue & Fri • call Gay Rap Telephone for info

Gay Rap Telephone PO Box 223, 66601 • 233-6558 • 8pm-midnight Wed-Sun

LIFT (Lesbians in Fellowship Together) (at MCC) • 232-6196 • 6pm 3rd Th • call for details

BARS
Classics 110 SW 8th • 233-5153 • 4pm-2am, from noon Sun • lesbians/gay men • dancing/DJ • live shows

BOOKSTORES & RETAIL SHOPS
Town Crier Books 1301 SW Gage Blvd. Ste. 120 • 272-5060 • 9am-9pm, noon-6pm Sun

TRAVEL & TOUR OPERATORS
Kansas Travel & Tourism Department (800) 252-6727

SPIRITUAL GROUPS
MCC Topeka 2425 SE Indiana Ave. • 232-6196 • 10am & 6pm Sun

Wichita (316)

INFO LINES & SERVICES
Gay/Lesbian Outreach 267-1852

Transitions 265-6657 • monthly parties for lesbigay youth 18-21 yrs.

Wichita Gay Info Line PO Box 16782, 67216 • 269-0913 • 6pm-10pm

Wichita Gay/Lesbian Community Center
111 N. Spruce • 262-3991 • call for hours

ACCOMMODATIONS

Apartments by Appointments 1257 N.
Broadway • 265-4323 • gay-friendly •
unique apt. rentals • day, week, or month

BARS

Dreamers 3210 E. Osie • 682-4461 • 4pm-
2am, from 3pm Sun • mostly women •
neighborhood bar • karaoke

Kirby's Beer Store 3227 E. 17th • 685-7013
• 2pm-2am • lesbians/gay men • live
bands • food served

Our Fantasy 3201 S. Hillside • 682-5494 •
8pm-2am Wed-Sun • lesbians/gay men •
dancing/DJ • live shows • swimming • also
'South Forty' • from 4pm • country/western
• wheelchair access

Sidestreet Saloon 1106 S. Pattie • 267-
0324 • 2pm-2am • lesbians/gay men •
neighborhood bar

The T-Room 1507 E. Pawnee • 262-9327 •
3pm-2am, from noon wknds • lesbians/gay
men • neighborhood bar

RESTAURANTS & CAFES

The Harbor (at Our Fantasy bar) • 682-
5494 • 8pm-4am, clsd Mon-Tue • les-
bians/gay men • full bar • $4-7

The Lassen 155 N. Market St. • 263-2777 •
lunch & dinner, clsd Sun • some veggie •
$9-12

The Upper Crust 7038 E. Lincoln • 683-
8088 • lunch only, clsd wknds • homestyle
• some veggie • $4-7

BOOKSTORES & RETAIL SHOPS

Mother's 3100 E. 31st St.S. • 686-8116 •
noon-10pm, til 1am Fri-Sat • lesbigay

SPIRITUAL GROUPS

1st Metropolitan Community Church 156
S. Kansas Ave. • 267-1852 • 10:30am &
6:30pm Sun

Wichita Praise & Worship Center 754 S.
Pattie • 267-6270 • 11am Sun

PUBLICATIONS

▲ **The Liberty Press** PO Box 16315, 67216-
0315 • 262-8289

KENTUCKY

Covington (606)

(See also **Cincinnati, OH**)

BARS

Rosie's Tavern 643 Bakewell St. • 291-9707
• 3pm-1am, from1pm wknds • gay-friendly
• gay-owned/run

Lexington (606)

INFO LINES & SERVICES

Gay/Lesbian AA 224-4067

BARS

The Bar Complex 224 E. Main St. • 255-
1551 • 4pm-1am, til 3:30am Fri-Sat, clsd
Sun • popular • lesbians/gay men • danc-
ing/DJ • live shows • wheelchair access

Club 141 141 W. Vine St. • 233-4262 •
8:30am-1am, til 3am Sat, clsd Sun-Mon •
lesbians/gay men • dancing/DJ • live shows
• wheelchair access

Joe's Bar & Cafe 120 S. Upper St. • 252-
7946 • lunch & dinner • lesbians/gay men •
neighborhood bar • also a restaurant •
French eclectic menu • $5-10

RESTAURANTS & CAFES

Alfalfa 557 S. Limestone • 253-0014 •
11am-9pm, til 5pm Mon, 10am-2pm Sun •
live folk music Fri-Sat • healthy multi-ethnic • plenty veggie • $6-12

BOOKSTORES & RETAIL SHOPS

Imperial Flowers 393 Waller Ave.
(Shopping Ctr.) • 233-7486/(800) 888-7486 •
women-owned/run

Joseph-Beth 3199 Nicholasville Rd. • 271-
5330 • 9am-10pm, 11am-6pm Sun

TRAVEL & TOUR OPERATORS

Pegasus Travel Inc. 245 Lexington Ave •
253-1644 • IGTA • women-owned/run

SPIRITUAL GROUPS

Lexington MCC 134 Church St. • 271-1407
• 11:30am Sun • wheelchair access

Pagan Forum PO Box 24203, 40524 • 268-
1640 • 7:30pm every other Fri

PUBLICATIONS

GLSO (Gay/Lesbian) News PO Box 11471,
40575 • calendar

Louisville (502)

INFO LINES & SERVICES

Gay/Lesbian Hotline PO Box 2796, 40202 • 897-2475/454-7613 • 6pm-10pm • also info for lesbigay AA

Louisville Gender Society PO Box 5458, 40255-0458 • 966-8701 • TS/TV group • contact Michelle • 222-3182

Louisville Youth Group (800) 347-8336 • 24hrs recorded info • live 7pm-10pm Th-Sun

The Williams-Nichols Institute PO Box 4264, 40204 • 636-0935 • 6pm-9pm • lesbigay archives • library • referrals

BARS

Connection Complex 120 S. Floyd St. • 585-5752 • 8pm-4am, clsd Mon • popular • lesbians/gay men • dancing/DJ • live shows • also a restaurant • from 6pm Wed-Sun • some veggie • $5-15

Magnolia's 1398 S. 2nd St. • 637-9052 • 11am-4am • gay-friendly • neighborhood bar

Main Exchange 117 W. Main St. • 584-8230 • 5pm-2am, 7pm-4am Fri-Sat, clsd Mon • mostly women • dancing/DJ • country/western • live shows

Murphy's Place 306 E. Main St. • 587-8717 • 11am-4am • mostly gay men • neighborhood • wheelchair access

Sparks 104 W. Main St. • 587-8566 • 10pm-4am • lesbians/gay men • dancing/DJ • alternative • live shows • wheelchair access

Tryangles 209 S. Preston St. • 583-6395 • 4pm-4am, from 1pm Sun • mostly gay men • dancing/DJ • wheelchair access

The Upstairs 306 E. Main St. (Murphy's Place) • 587-1432 • 9pm-4am, clsd Mon • lesbians/gay men • dancing/DJ

BOOKSTORES & RETAIL SHOPS

Carmichael's 1295 Bardstown Rd. • 456-6950 • 10am-10pm, 11am-6pm Sun • lesbigay section • women-owned/run

Hawley Cooke Books 3042 Bardstown Rd. • 456-6660 • 9am-9:30pm, 11am-6pm Sun • also 27 Shelbyville Rd. Plaza • 893-0133

Louisville (502)

WHERE THE GIRLS ARE: On Main or Market Streets near 1st, and generally in the north-central part of town, just west of I-65.

ENTERTAINMENT: Bowling League: 456-5780, Monday nights. Community Chorus: 584-1627. The Vogue: 893-3646.

LESBIGAY PRIDE: June.

ANNUAL EVENTS: Halloween Cruise on the Ohio River.

CITY INFO: Louisville Tourist Commission: (800) 626-5646.

ATTRACTIONS: Kentucky Derby. The Waterfront. Belle Of Louisville. Churchill Downs. Farmington. Hadley Pottery. Locust Grove. St. James Court. West Main Street Historic District.

BEST VIEW: The Spire Restaurant and Cocktail Lounge on the 19th floor of the Hyatt Regency Louisville.

WEATHER: Mild winters and long, hot summers!

TRANSIT: Yellow Taxi: 636-5511.

SPIRITUAL GROUPS

Dignity 1432 Highland Ave. (Trinity Church) • 473-1408 • 7pm 2nd & 4th Sun

MCC Louisville 4222 Bank St. • 775-6636 • 11am Sun • wheelchair access

Phoenix Rising PO Box 2093, 40259 • 636-2161 • lesbigay pagans

PUBLICATIONS

The Kentucky Word 225 E. N. St. Tower 1 Ste 2800, Indianapolis IN, 46204 • (317) 579-3075

The Letter PO Box 3882, 40201 • 772-7570

Rainbow Pages 899-3551 • lesbigay resource guide

Owensboro   (502)

INFO LINES & SERVICES

Owensboro Gay Alliance 685-5246

BARS

Mixer's Night Club 2123 Triplett St. • 691-2611 • 8pm-2am, clsd Sun-Mon • lesbians/gay men • dancing/DJ • call for events • wheelchair access

Paducah   (502)

BARS

Club DV8 1200 N. 8th St. • 443-2545 • 8pm-3am, clsd Sun • lesbians/gay men • dancing/DJ • live shows • beer garden • gift shop

Moby Dick 500 Broadway • 442-9076 • 5pm-3am, from 7pm Sat, clsd Sun • lesbians/gay men • dancing/DJ • live shows • wheelchair access

SPIRITUAL GROUPS

MCC of Paducah Ritz Hotel, 6th flr. (22nd & Broadway) • 898-2581 • 11am & 7pm Sun • wheelchair access

Somerset   (606)

INFO LINES & SERVICES

Cumberland Cares 678-5814 • 4pm 1st Sat • lesbigay social & support for southcentral & southeastern KY

Louisville

*B*eautiful Louisville sits on the banks of the Ohio River and is home to the world famous **Kentucky Derby**. This spectacular race occurs during the first week of May at Churchill Downs.

Louisville is also home to many whiskey distilleries. If neither watching horses run in circles, nor swilling home-grown booze excites you, you'll enjoy this city's slower pace of life and Southern charm—Louisville is known as the 'northern border for southern hospitality.'

Before you leave, check out the whiskey and the hospitality at the **Main Exchange** women's bar.

And only a few hours to the east, stop by for a spell in Lexington, Kentucky.

LOUISIANA

Alexandria (318)

BARS
Unique Bar 3117 Masonic Dr. • 448-0555 • 7pm-2am, clsd Sun-Mon • popular • mostly gay men • dancing/DJ

TRAVEL & TOUR OPERATORS
Over the Rainbeaux Travel 1706 Pierce Rd. • 442-0540

Baton Rouge (504)

INFO LINES & SERVICES
AA Gay/Lesbian 924-0030 • 7pm Mon, 8pm Th, 9pm Sat

ACCOMMODATIONS
Brentwood House PO Box 40872, 70835-0872 • 924-4989 • mostly gay men • 100+ yr old B&B on beautifully landscaped acre of land • hot tub • $60-75

BARS
Argon 2160 Highland Rd. • 336-4900 • 9pm-2am Wed-Sat • popular • lesbians/gay men • dancing/DJ • alternative

The Blue Parrot 450 Oklahoma St. • 267-4211 • 2pm-2am • mostly gay men

George's Place 860 St. Louis • 387-9798 • 3pm-2am, clsd Sun • popular • mostly gay men • neighborhood bar • wheelchair access

Hideaway 7367 Exchange Pl. • 923-3632 • 8pm-2am Wed-Sat • mostly women • neighborhood bar • dancing/DJ • wheelchair access • women-owned/run

Mirror Lounge 111 3rd St. • 387-9797 • 3pm-2am, from 6pm Sat, clsd Sun • lesbians/gay men • dancing/DJ • live shows • wheelchair access

Traditions 2183 Highland Rd. • 344-9291 • 9pm-2am, clsd Sun-Tue • lesbians/gay men • dancing/DJ • alternative • 18+ • wheelchair access

RESTAURANTS & CAFES
Third Street Tavern & Deli 140 N. 3rd St. • 336-4281 • 5pm-midnight, clsd Mon • lesbians/gay men • full bar • $5-15

BOOKSTORES & RETAIL SHOPS
Hibiscus Book Store 635 Main St. • 387-4264 • 11am-6pm • lesbigay

TRAVEL & TOUR OPERATORS
Out & About Travel 11528 Old Hammond Hwy. Ste. 610 • 272-7448 • IGTA

Trips Unlimited 10249 Cashel Ave. • 927-7191/(800) 256-9661 • gay-owned/run

SPIRITUAL GROUPS
Church of Mercavah PO Box 66703, 70896 • 665-7815 • 3pm Sun • interfaith • call for locations

Dignity PO Box 4181, 70821 • 383-6010

Joie de Vivre MCC 333 E. Chimes St. • 383-0450 • 11am Sun

PUBLICATIONS
Voices Magazine Licorice Unicorn Press, PO Box 66703, 70896 • 665-7815 • off-beat articles on everything • original artwork & writings

Gretna (504)

BARS
Cheers 1711 Hancock • 367-0149 • 10am-3am • gay-friendly • neighborhood bar

Houma (504)

BARS
The Cha Cha Palace 1709 Havers • 868-0007 • opens 9pm • gay-friendly • dancing/DJ • live entertainment • call for events

Kixx 112 N. Hollywood • 876-9587 • 6pm-2am, clsd Sun-Mon • lesbians/gay men • dancing/DJ • live shows • wheelchair access

Lafayette (318)

INFO LINES & SERVICES
AA Gay/Lesbian 234-7814 • call for locations

BARS
Frank's Bar 1807 Jefferson • 235-9217 • 2pm-2am, noon-midnight Sun • mostly gay men • neighborhood bar • wheelchair access

The Girl's Gym 408 Maurice St. • 234-6688 • 8pm-2am, from 5pm-midnight Sun, clsd Mon • mostly women • dancing/DJ • patio • wheelchair access

Images 524 W. Jefferson • 233-0070 • 9pm-2am, clsd Mon-Tue • lesbians/gay men • dancing/DJ • food served • live shows • wheelchair access

Lake Charles (318)

BARS
Crystal's 112 W. Broad St. • 433-5457 • 9pm-2am, clsd Sun-Tue • lesbians/gay men • dancing/DJ • country/western • live shows • food served • wheelchair access

SPIRITUAL GROUPS

MCC Lake Charles 510 Broad St. • 436-0921 • 11am Sun

Monroe (318)

BARS

Hot Shotz 110 Catalpa St. • 388-3262 • from 9pm, clsd Sun-Mon • mostly gay men • dancing/DJ

New Orleans (504)

INFO LINES & SERVICES

AA Lambda Center 2106 Decatur • 947-0548 • noon daily • call for info

Gay/Lesbian Business Association 940 Royal #350 • 271-0631 • mtg. 2nd Tue • call for further details

Gulf Area Gender Alliance PO Box 56836, 70156 • 833-3046 • 2nd Sat

Lesbian/Gay Community Center 816 N. Rampart • 522-1103 • noon-6pm Mon-Fri • wheelchair access

ACCOMMODATIONS

A Private Garden 1718 Philip St. • 523-1776 • lesbians/gay men • B&B-private home • hot tub • 2 private apts • enclosed garden • $50-75 (special holiday rates)

Alternative Accommodations / Tande Reservations 828 Royal St. #233 • 529-2915/(800) 209-9408

Andrew Jackson Hotel 919 Royal St. • 561-5881/(800) 654-0224 • gay-friendly • historic inn

The B&W Courtyards B&B 2425 Chartres St. • 949-5313/(800) 585-5731 • gay-friendly • hot tub • gay-owned/run

Big D's B&B 704 Franklin Ave. • 945-8049 • lesbians/gay men • women-owned/run

New Orleans (504)

WHERE THE GIRLS ARE: Wandering the Quarter, or in the small artsy area known as mid-city, north of the Quarter up Esplanade St., and spread out elsewhere.

LESBIGAY PRIDE: June. 897-3939.

ANNUAL EVENTS: February- Pantheon of Leather: (213) 656-5073, annual SM community service awards at the Radisson Hotel: (800) 824-3359. Mardi Gras: 566-5011, North America's rowdiest block party. April- Gulf Coast Womyn's Festival at Camp SisterSpirit: (601) 344-1411, they won their lawsuit against the homophobes, now go support a celebration of womyn's land in the South! September - Southern Decadence: 529-2860, gay mini-Mardi Gras.

CITY INFO: 522-3500.

ATTRACTIONS: Bourbon St. in the French Quarter. Cafe du Monde for beignets. Pat O'Brien's for a hurricane. Preservation Hall. Moon Walk. Top of the Market.

BEST VIEW: Top of the Mart Lounge (522-9795) on the 33rd floor of the World Trade Center of New Orleans.

WEATHER: Summer temperatures hover in the 90°s with subtropical humidity. Winters can be rainy and chilly. The average temperature in February (Mardi Gras month) is 58° while the average precipitation is 5.23".

TRANSIT: United Cab: 522-9771. Airport Shuttle: 522-3500. Regional Transit Authority: 569-2700.

New Orleans

*Y*ou haven't been to New Orleans for **Mardi Gras**?! Then you've missed the party of the year. But there's still time to plan next year's visit to the French Quarter's blowout of a block party with elaborate balls, parades and dancing in the streets. It all starts the day before Ash Wednesday (usually February).

Of course, there is more to New Orleans than Mardi Gras, especially if you like life hot, humid and spiced with steamy jazz and hot pepper. Start by staying in one of the ten lesbian/gay inns in the area. Then venture into the **French Quarter**, where you'll find the infamous Bourbon Street with people walking from jazz club to jazz club, bar to bar, restaurants to shops, twenty-four hours a day. Non-recovering alcoholics and kitsch-lovers won't want to miss Pat O'Brien's, home of the Hurricane and the #1 bar in the country for alcohol volume sold —a campy photo in front of the fountain is a must. Jazz lovers, don't forget Preservation Hall.

If you love to shop, check out the French Market, the Jackson Brewery and Riverwalk. Antique hunting is best on Rue Royal or Decatur St. And you can't leave New Orleans without a trip through the Garden District to see the incredible antebellum and revival homes—a trip best made on the St. Charles Trolley.

Gourmands must try real Cajun and Creole food in its natural environment—though if you're vegetarian, the **Old Dog New Trick Cafe** is your best bet. For melt-in-your-mouth, hot, sugar-powdered beignets, Cafe du Monde (525-4544) is the place.

New Orleans is a town that knows how to party, and the lesbians are no different. Try **Charlene's** for drinks and tall tales, or get wild in the French Quarter with the boys (try **Rubyfruit Jungle**)—Gay Central in New Orleans is also party central for everyone. And during **Southern Decadence**, the gay mardi gras on Labor Day weekend, the quarter becomes a little queerer.

To find out the current women's nights at the guys' bars, stop by **Faubourg Marigny Bookstore**—the lesbian/gay bookstore—and pick up an **Impact** or an **AMbush** newspaper. Or drop by the **Lesbian/Gay Community Center** on North Rampart.

Of course, the morbidly inclined among us will see shadows of vampires and other creatures of the night in this town of mysticism and the occult. With residents like Anne Rice, Poppy Z. Brite, and the deceased Marie LaVeau stirring up the spirits, perhaps a protective amulet from Marie LaVeau's House of Voodoo (581-3751; 739 Bourbon St.) would be a good idea. For a peek at traditional voodoo—the creative spirituality, not the spooky movie gore—take the swamp tour that ends at a cottage in the bayou, with gumbo dinner and a performance by the Mask Dance Voodoo Theater (522-2904) for $75. Or sate that urge for blood with a body piercing at **Rings of Desire** or some fresh fetish wear from **Second Skin Leather**.

Go for a splash in our refreshing heated pool. Enjoy beautiful cottages and rooms with color cable TV, phone, private baths, gym and continental breakfast. Just 5 minutes from the French Quarter.

MACARTY PARK GUEST HOUSE

3820 Burgundy Street
New Orleans, LA 70117
504-943-4994 • 800-521-2790

The Big Easy Guest House 2633 Dauphine St. • 943-3717 • gay-friendly • 8 blocks from French Quarter

The Biscuit Palace 730 Dumaine • 525-9949 • gay-friendly • B&B & apts • in the French Quarter

Bon Maison Guest House 835 Bourbon St. • 561-8498 • popular • gay-friendly • 3 studio apts • 2 suites • $65-115

Bourbon Orleans Hotel Bourbon & Orleans • 523-2222/(800) 521-5338 • popular • gay-friendly

Bourgoyne Guest House 839 Bourbon St. • 524-3621/525-3983 • popular • lesbians/gay men • 1830s Creole mansion • courtyard • $60-150

Bywater B&B 1026 Clouet St. • 899-6167 • gay-friendly • kitchen • fireplace • kids/pets ok • women-owned/run • $60/shared bath • $75/private bath

Casa de Marigny Creole Guest Cottages 818 Frenchmen St. • 948-3875 • lesbians/gay men • swimming

Chartres St. House 2517 Chartres • 945-2339 • lesbians/gay men • handsome 1850s home • swimming • patio • $65-125 (higher special events)

The Chimes B&B Constantinople at Coliseum • 488-4640/(800) 729-4640 • gay-friendly • 5 guest suites & rms in an 1876 home • $51-161

Deja Vu Guest House 1835 N. Rampart St. • 945-5912/(800) 238-1577 • mostly gay men • individual Creole cottages

Faubourg Guest House 1703 Second St. • 895-2004 • lesbians/gay men • 1860s Greek Revival • $40-125

Fourteen Twelve Thalia - A B&B 1412 Thalia • 522-0453 • gay-friendly • 1-bdrm apt in the Lower Garden District • $75-150

French Quarter B&B 1132 Ursuline • 525-3390 • lesbians/gay men • apt • full brkfst • swimming • $65-125

▲ **French Quarter Reservation Service** 940 Royal St. Ste. 263 • 523-1246/(800) 523-9091 • IGTA

The Frenchmen Hotel 417 Frenchmen St. • 948-2166/(800) 831-1781 • popular • lesbians/gay men • 1860s Creole townhouses • spa • swimming • wheelchair access

▲ **The Greenhouse** 1212 Magazine St. • 561-8400/(800) 966-1303 • lesbians/gay men • swimming • $65-125

Hotel de la Monnaie 405 Esplanade Ave. • 947-0009 • gay-friendly • wheelchair accesss • IGTA • $140-190

▲ **La Residence** 1300 Marais St. • 522-4828/(800) 826-9718 • lesbians/gay men • 1- & 2-bdrm apts • kitchens

Lafitte Guest House 1003 Bourbon St. • 581-2678/(800) 331-7971 • popular • gay-friendly • elegant French manor house • full bar • $85-165

▲ **Macarty Park Guesthouse** 3820 Burgundy St. • 943-4994/(800) 521-2790 • lesbians/gay men • swimming • rooms & cottages • 5 minutes from the French Quarter • IGTA

Maison Burgundy 1860 Rue Burgundy • 948-2355/(800) 863-8813 • gay-friendly • swimming • hot tub

Maison Dauphine 2460 Dauphine St. • 943-0861 • mostly gay men • near French Quarter • gay-owned/run

Marigny Guest House 621 Esplanade • (800) 367-5858

Mazant St. Guest House 906 Mazant • 944-2662 • gay-friendly • $21-48 (higher Mardi Gras & other events)

The McKendrick-Breaux House 1474 Magazine St. • 586-1700 • gay-friendly

Mentone B&B 1437 Pauger St. • 943-3019 • gay-friendly • suite in a Victorian home in the Faubourg Marigny district • $100-150

New Orleans Guest House 1118 Ursulines St. • 566-1177/(800) 562-1177 • gay-friendly • Creole cottage dated back to 1848 • courtyard • $69-99

Parkview Guest House 726 Frenchmen St. • 945-7875/(800) 749-4640 • lesbians/gay men • apartment • $82-150

Pauger Guest Suites 1750 N. Rampart St. • 944-2601/(800) 484-8334x9834 • gay-owned/run • near French Quarter

Rainbow House 2311-15 N. Rampart St. • 943-5805 • lesbians/gay men • walking distance to French Quarter • also apts

Rathbone Inn 1227 Esplanande Ave. • 947-2100/(800) 947-2101 • 1850s Greek Revival mansion • 2 blks from the French Quarter • IGTA • $75-125

Renaissance Realty (800) 238-1577 • fully equipped rental properties

Rober House Condos 822 Ursuline St. • 529-4663 • lesbians/gay men • apt • courtyard • swimming • IGTA • $110-150

The Robert Gordy House 2630 Bell St. • 486-9424/(800) 889-7359

Royal Barracks Guest House 717 Barracks St. • 529-7269 • lesbians/gay men • hot tub • private patios

▲ **Rue Royal Inn** 1006 Royal St. • 524-3900/(800) 776-3901 • gay-friendly • historic 1830s Creole townhouse in the heart of the French Quarter • IGTA • $60-130

St. Charles Guest House 1748 Prytania St. • 523-6556 • gay-friendly • pensione-style guest house • swimming • patio • $30-85 (higher special events)

St. Peter Guest House 1005 St. Peter • 524-9232/(800) 535-7815 • gay-friendly • historic location • authentically appointed

Sun Oak B&B 2020 Burgundy St. • 945-0322 • lesbians/gay men • Greek Revival Creole cottage circa 1836 • gardens • $75-125

Ursuline Guest House 708 Ursuline St • 525-8509/(800) 654-2351 • popular • mostly gay men • hot tub • evening socials w/wine • IGTA

Vieux Carre Rentals 841 Bourbon • 525-3983 • gay-friendly • 1- & 2-bdrm apts

BARS

Angles 2301 N. Causeway, Metairie • 834-7979 • 4pm-4am • lesbians/gay men • neighborhood bar • dancing/DJ • wheelchair access

Another Corner 2601 Royal St. • 945-7006 • 11am-? • mostly gay men • neighborhood bar

Big Daddy's 2513 Royal • 948-6288 • 24hrs • lesbians/gay men • neighborhood bar • wheelchair access

Bourbon Pub 801 Bourbon St. • 529-2107 • 24hrs • popular • lesbians/gay men • videos • also 'The Parade' • dancing/DJ

Buffa's 1001 Esplanade • 945-9373 • 11am-3am • gay-friendly • neighborhood bar • food served

Cafe Lafitte in Exile/The Corral 901 Bourbon St. • 522-8397 • 24hrs • popular • mostly gay men • videos

Charlene's 940 Elysian Fields • 945-9328 • 5pm-?, from 2pm Fri-Sun, clsd Mon • mostly women • neighborhood bar • dancing/DJ • B&B accommodations avail.

Copper Top 706 Franklin Ave. • 948-2300 • 24hrs • lesbians/gay men • neighborhood bar • dancing/DJ • Cajun & country/western • wheelchair access

Country Club 634 Lousia St. • 945-0742 • 10am-11pm • lesbians/gay men • swimming • live shows

The Double Play 439 Dauphine • 523-4517 • 24hrs • gay-friendly • neighborhood bar

Footloose 700 N. Rampart • 524-7654 • 24hrs • lesbians/gay men • dancing/DJ • transgender-friendly • shows on wknds

The Four Seasons 3229 N. Causeway, Metairie • 832-0659 • 3pm-4am • lesbians/gay men • neighborhood bar • dancing/DJ

The Friendly Bar 2801 Chartres St. • 943-8929 • 11am-3am • lesbians/gay men • neighborhood bar • wheelchair access • women-owned/run

Good Friends Bar 740 Dauphine • 566-7191 • 24hrs • popular • gay-friendly • professional • good cocktails • wheelchair access • also 'Queens Head Pub' • 6pm-3am Wed-Sun • mostly gay men • neighborhood bar

M.R.B./Mr. B's on the Patio 515 St. Philip • 586-0644 • 24hrs • lesbians/gay men • neighborhood bar • live shows

The Mint 504 Esplanade • 525-2000 • noon-3am • popular • lesbians/gay men • professional • live shows • wheelchair access

Oz 800 Bourbon St. • 593-9491 • 24hrs • lesbians/gay men • dancing/DJ • wheelchair access

Parade (above Bourbon Pub) • 529-2107 • popular • mostly gay men • dancing/DJ

Rawhide 2010 740 Burgundy • 525-8106 • 24hrs • popular • mostly gay men • neighborhood bar • country/western • leather/fetish

▲ **Rubyfruit Jungle** 640 Frenchmen • 947-4000 • 4pm-?, from 1pm wknds • popular • lesbians/gay men • dancing/DJ • alternative • live shows • wheelchair access

Xis 1302 Allo St., Marerro • 340-0049 • 5pm-? • lesbians/gay men • neighborhood bar • dancing/DJ • wheelchair access

RESTAURANTS & CAFES

Cafe Istanbul 534 Frenchmen (upstairs) • 944-4180 • clsd Tue • Turkish • live shows

Cafe Sbisa 1011 Decatur • 522-5565 • dinner & Sun brunch • French Creole • patio

Clover Grill 900 Bourbon St. • 523-0904 • 24hrs • popular • diner fare • $5-10

Feelings Cafe 2600 Chartres St. • 945-2222 • dinner nightly, Fri lunch, Sun brunch • Creole • piano bar wknds • $10-20

Fiorella's Cafe 45 French Market Pl. • 528-9566 • dinner, Sun brunch • homecooking

Gram's Cafe Creole 533 Toulouse • 524-1479 • 11:30am-? • wheelchair access

Jack Sprat 3240 S. Carrollton • 486-2200 • 11am-10pm, noon-5pm Sun • healthy vegetarian • $6-12

La Peniche 1940 Dauphine St. • 943-1460 • 24hrs • diner • some veggie • $5-10

Lucky Cheng's 720 St. Louis • 529-2045

Mama Rosa 616 N. Rampart • 523-5546 • 11am-10pm, clsd Mon • Italian • $5-10

Mona Lisa 1212 Royal St. • 522-6746 • 11am-11pm • Italian • some veggie • $8-15

Old Dog New Trick Cafe 307 Exchange Alley • 522-4569 • 11am-9pm • vegetarian • wheelchair access • $5-10

Olivier's 911 Decatur St. • 525-7734 • 10am-10pm • Creole • wheelchair access • $10-15

Petunia's 817 St. Louis • 522-6440 • 8am-midnight • popular • Cajun/Creole • $10-20

PJ's 634 Frenchmen St. • 949-2292 • 7pm-midnight • popular • wheelchair access

Poppy's Grill 717 St. Peter • 524-3287 • 24hrs • diner • wheelchair access

Quarter Scene 900 Dumaine • 522-6533 • 24hrs, clsd Tue • homecooking • some veggie • $8-15

Sammy's Seafood 627 Bourbon St. • 525-8442 • 11am-midnight • Creole/Cajun • $9-28

Sebastian's 538 St. Philip • 524-2041

St. Ann's Cafe & Deli 800 Dauphine • 529-4421 • 24hrs • popular • American • some veggie • wheelchair access • $5-10

Vera Cruz 1141 Decatur St. • 561-8081 • noon-11pm, clsd Mon-Tue • Mexican • wheelchair access • $8-20

Whole Foods 3135 Esplanade Ave. • 943-1626 • 9am-9pm • healthy deli • plenty veggie • $5-10

BOOKSTORES & RETAIL SHOPS

Alternatives 907 Bourbon St. • 524-5222 • 11am-9pm , til 11pm Fri & Sat, clsd Tue-Wed • lesbigay

Bookstar 414 N. Peters • 10am-11pm, til 8pm Sun • wheelchair access

Faubourg Marigny Bookstore 600 Frenchmen St. • 943-9875 • 10am-8pm, til 6pm wknds • lesbigay • wheelchair access

Gay Mart 808 Rampart St. • 523-6005 • noon-7pm

Postmark New Orleans 631 Toulouse St. • 529-2052/(800) 285-4247

Rings of Desire 1128 Decatur St., 2nd flr. • 524-6147 • 11am-7pm • piercing studio

Sidney's News Stand 917 Decatur • 524-6872 • 8am-9pm • general magazine store w/ lesbigay titles

TRAVEL & TOUR OPERATORS

Alternative Tours & Travel 3003 Chartres • 949-5917/(800) 576-0238 • IGTA

Avalon Travel Advisors 1206 Magazine, 70151 • 561-8400/(800) 966-1303 • IGTA

Community Travel 612 N. Rampart • 552-2913/(800) 811-5028 • IGTA

Louisiana Office of Tourism (800) 334-8626

Old Quarter Livery 3328 Marigny • 945-3796 • limousine & tour service

Uptown Travel & Tours 4001 Toulouse St. Ste. 101 • 488-9993/(800) 566-9312 • IGTA

SPIRITUAL GROUPS

Integrity 1339 Jackson Ave. (Trinity Episcopal Church) • 944-5346 • 3rd Tue

Vieux Carre MCC 1128 St. Roch • 945-5390 • 11am Sun

PUBLICATIONS

Ambush PO Box 71291, 70171-1291 • 522-8049

Impact PO Box 52079, 70152 • 944-6722

▲ **The Pink Pages** 928 Port St., 70117 • 947-3969

The Second Stone PO Box 8340, 70182 • 891-7555 • nat'l paper for lesbigay Christians

EROTICA

Gargoyle's 1205 Decatur St. • 529-4387 • 11am-7pm, til 10pm Fri-Sat • leather/fetish store

Second Skin Leather 521 St. Philip St. • 561-8167 • noon-10pm, til 6pm Sun • also 'Above & Below' piercing studio upstairs

Shreveport (318)

BARS

Central Station 1025 Marshall • 222-2216 • 4pm-4am, til midnight Sun • popular • lesbians/gay men • dancing/DJ • country/western • wheelchair access

Korner Lounge 800 Lousiana • 222-9796 • 5pm-2am, clsd Sun • mostly gay men • neighborhood bar

Outrageous 1309 Centenary Blvd. • 221-7596 • 2pm-2am, clsd Sun • lesbians/gay men • ladies night Tue • food served • videos • patio

EROTICA

Fun Shop 1601 Marshall • 226-1308

Slidell (504)

BARS

Billy's 2600 Hwy. 190 W. • 847-1921 • 5pm-2am • mostly gay men • neighborhood bar

MAINE

Augusta (207)

BARS

P.J.'s 80 Water St. • 623-4041 • 7pm-1am Tue-Sat • popular • lesbians/gay men • dancing/DJ

Bangor (207)

INFO LINES & SERVICES

AA Gay/Lesbian 126 Union (Unitarian Church)

TRAVEL & TOUR OPERATORS

Dignity Bangor 300 Union St. • 6pm 2nd & 4th Sun

Bar Harbor (207)

ACCOMMODATIONS

Manor House Inn 106 West St. • 288-3759 • open May-Nov • gay-friendly • full brkfst

Bath (207)

ACCOMMODATIONS

The Galen C. Moses House 1009 Washington St. • 442-8771 • gay-friendly • 1874 Victorian • full brkfst • gay-owned/run

Belfast (207)

INFO LINES & SERVICES

Women's Center 9-A Main St., 2nd flr. (above Jaret & Cohn) • 338-5702 • weekly meetings

BOOKSTORES & RETAIL SHOPS

Womankind Gifts 10 Beaver St. • 338-2913 • lesbian fiction • women's music • jewelry • pride gifts • woman-owned/run

Bethel (207)

ACCOMMODATIONS

Speckled Mountain Ranch RR 2, Box 717 • 836-2908 • gay-friendly • on a horse farm • full brkfst • lesbian-owned • $45-55

Biddeford

INFO LINES & SERVICES

Out for Good PO Box 727, 04005

Brunswick (207)

INFO LINES & SERVICES

College Gay/Lesbian/Straight Alliance Hubbard Hall 2nd flr., Bowdoin College, 04011 • 725-3620 • 9pm Wed

ACCOMMODATIONS

The Vicarage by the Sea B&B Rte. 1 Box 368-B, S. Harpswell, 04079 • 833-5480 • gay-friendly • full brkfst • wheelchair access • women-owned/run • $55-80

BOOKSTORES & RETAIL SHOPS

Gulf of Maine Books 134 Maine St. • 729-5083 • 9:30am-5pm, clsd Sun • alternative

Camden (207)

ACCOMMODATIONS

The Old Massachusetts Homestead Campground PO Box 5 Rte. 1, Lincolnville Beach • 789-5135 • open May-Nov • gay-friendly • cabins, tentsites & RV hookups • swimming

Caribou (207)

INFO LINES & SERVICES

Gay/Lesbian Phoneline 398 S. Main St. • 498-2088 • hours vary

Northern Lambda Nord PO Box 990, 04736 • social & networking for northern ME & western Brunswick

ACCOMMODATIONS

The Westman House B&B PO Box 1231, 04736 • 896-5726 • lesbians/gay men • great view

Corea Harbor (207)

ACCOMMODATIONS

The Black Duck Inn on Corea Harbor PO Box 39, 04624 • 963-2689 • gay-friendly • full brkfst • $60-125

Dexter (207)

ACCOMMODATIONS

Brewster Inn 37 Zions Hill • 924-3130 • gay-friendly • historic mansion • women-owned/run

Freeport (207)

ACCOMMODATIONS

Country at Heart B&B 37 Bow St. • 865-0512 • gay-friendly • located in Maine's outlet shopping mecca

Kennebunk (207)

ACCOMMODATIONS

Arundel Meadows Inn Rte. 1, Arundel • 985-3770 • gay-friendly • full brkfst • $85-125

Kennebunkport   (207)

ACCOMMODATIONS

The Colony Hotel Ocean Ave. & Kings Hwy.
• 967-3331/(800) 552-2363 • gay-friendly
• 1914 grand oceanfront property

White Barn Inn 37 Beach St. • 967-2321 •
gay-friendly • food served

RESTAURANTS & CAFES

Bartley's Dockside by the bridge • 967-
5050 • 11am-10pm • seafood • some veggie • full bar • wheelchair access

Lewiston   (207)

INFO LINES & SERVICES

Bates Gay/Lesbian/Straight Alliance
Hirasawa Lounge, Chase Hall, Bates
College • 786-6255 • 8:30pm Sun

BARS

The Sportsman's Club 2 Bates St. • 784-
2251 • 8pm-1am, from 7pm Sun • popular
• lesbians/gay men • dancing/DJ

EROTICA

Paris Book Store 297 Lisbon St. • 783-
6677

Lincolnville Beach   (207)

ACCOMMODATIONS

Sign of the Owl B&B RR 2 Box 85 • 338-
4669 • lesbians/gay men • full brkfst

Lovell   (207)

ACCOMMODATIONS

The Stone Wall B&B RR1, Box 26, 04051 •
925-1080/(800) 413-1080 • lesbians/gay
men • full brkfst • IGTA • $80-105

Mt. Desert Island   (207)

ACCOMMODATIONS

Duck Cove Retreat 244-9079/(617) 864-
2372 • women only • swimming • seasonal
• wheelchair access • $10-15

Naples   (207)

ACCOMMODATIONS

▲ **Lambs Mill Inn** Box 676 Lamb's Mill Rd. •
693-6253 • mostly women • full brkfst •
hot tub • swimming • IGTA • women
owned/run • $75-105

TRAVEL & TOUR OPERATORS

Maine Mountain Bike Adventures RR2
Box 550-F, 04055 • 787-2379

THE HERITAGE OF OGUNQUIT

"Beautiful Place by the Sea"

5 min walk to Beach
Non-Smoking
private & shared baths
lesbian owned
hot tub & deck

'year around'

PO BOX 1295
MARGINAL AVE.
OGUNQUIT, MAINE
03907

(207) 646-7787
e-mail: Heritage O
@cyberTours.com

Ogunquit (207)

ACCOMMODATIONS

Admiral's Inn 70 S. Main St. • 646-7093 • gay-friendly • swimming

The Clipper Ship B&B Box 236, 03907 • 646-9735 • gay-friendly

The Gazebo B&B Rte. 1 • 646-3733 • gay-friendly • 165-yr-old Greek Revival farmhouse • full brkfst • swimming • $95-105

▲ **The Heritage of Ogunquit** 14 Marginal Ave. • 646-7787 • mostly women • lesbian owned/run • $70-80

The Inn at Tall Chimney 94 Main St. • 646-8974 • open April-Nov • lesbians/gay men

The Inn at Two Village Square 135 Main St. • 646-5779 • seasonal • mostly gay men • oceanside Victorian • $50-120

Leisure Inn 6 School St. • 646-2737 • seasonal • gay-friendly • B&B & apts • $60-95

▲ **Moon Over Maine** Berwick Rd. • 646-6666/(800) 851-6837 • gay-friendly

The Ogunquit House 7 Kings Hwy. • 646-2967 • popular • lesbians/gay men • Victorian B&B w/ beautiful gardens • $59-130

Old Village Inn 30 Main St. • 646-7088 • gay-friendly • food served

Rockmere Lodge B&B 40 Stearns Rd. • 646-2985 • gay-friendly

The Seasons Hotel 178 US Rte. 1 • 646-6041/(800) 639-8508 • seasonal • gay-friendly

Yellow Monkey Guest Houses/Hotel 168 Main St. • 646-9056 • seasonal • lesbians/gay men

BARS

The Black Swan Tavern Rte. 1 N. • 646-9934 • 5pm-1am, clsd Sun (seasonal) • gay-friendly • piano bar • upscale menu • plenty veggie • $14-25

The Club 13 Main St. • 646-6655 • open April-Oct, 9pm-1am, from 4pm Sun • popular • mostly gay men • dancing/DJ • food served

Maxwell's Pub 27 Main St. • 646-2345 • noon-1am • gay-friendly • live shows • sports bar • food served • patio

RESTAURANTS & CAFES

Arrows Berrick Rd. (1.8 mi. W. of Center) • 361-1100 • 6pm-9pm Tue-Sun, clsd Dec-May • popular • cont'l • some veggie • $20-27

Cafe Amoré 37 Shore Rd. • 646-6661 • open daily 7:30am

Clay Hill Farm Agamenticus Rd. (2 mile W. of Rte. 1) • 646-2272 • some veggie • also piano bar • $13-24

Front Porch Cafe Ogunquit Sq. • 646-3976 • Mexican/American • full bar • $6-12

Grey Gull Inn 321 Webhannet Dr., Wells • 646-7501 • dinner • New England fine dining • $10-22

Johnathan's Bourne Ln. • 646-4777 • 5pm-9pm • cont'l • full bar • wheelchair access • $13-25

Poor Richard's Tavern Perkins Cove at Shore Rd. & Pine Hill • 646-4722 • 5:30pm-9:30pm • New England fare • some veggie • full bar • $10-18

TRAVEL & TOUR OPERATORS
Beyond Ogunquit PO Box 1424, 03907 • 879-7323

Old Orchard Beach (207)

ACCOMMODATIONS
Sea View Motel 65 W. Grand Ave. • 934-4180 • gay-friendly

Orono (207)

INFO LINES & SERVICES
Wilde-Stein Club Sutton Lounge, Memorial Union, Univ. of Maine • 581-1731 • 6pm Th (Sept-May)

ACCOMMODATIONS
Maine Wilderness Lake Island 866-4547 • lesbians/gay men • rental cabins in the forest

Pembroke (207)

ACCOMMODATIONS
Yellow Birch Farm RR 1 Box 248A • 726-5807 • mostly women • B&B on working farm • daily & weekly rates • also cottage • lesbian-owned/run • $45 night • $250 wk

Portland (207)

INFO LINES & SERVICES
Gays in Sobriety 32 Thomas St. (Williston W. Church) • 774-4060 • 6:30pm Sun, 8pm Th

Out Among Friends 87 Spring St. (YWCA) • 879-1037 • 7pm-8:30pm 1st & 3rd Th (downstairs club room) • lesbian social/discussion group

Outright 155 Brackett St • 774-4357 • Fri 7:30pm • youth support group

Queer Alliance Univ. of Maine, The Power's House • 874-6596

The Rainbow Business & Professional Association PO Box 6627, Scarborough, 04070-6627 • 775-0015 • mtgs. 2nd Mon

W.O.W. (Wild Outdoor Women) 787-2379/773-5083 • monthly mtg. • recreational group

ACCOMMODATIONS

Andrews Lodging B&B 417 Auburn St. • 797-9157 • gay-friendly • full brkfst • near outdoor recreation • shared bath • kitchens • pets ok • patio

The Danforth 163 Danforth St. • 879-8755 • gay-friendly • 1823 mansion • 3 blks to Old Port • conference/reception facilities • woman-owned

▲ **The Inn at St. John** 939 Congress St. • 773-6481/(800) 636-9127 • gay-friendly • unique historic inn

The Inn By The Sea 40 Bowery Beach Rd., Cape Elizabeth • 799-3134 • gay-friendly • condo-style suites w/ ocean views • 7 miles to Portland • woman-owned

The Pomegranate Inn 49 Neal St. • 772-1066/(800) 356-0408 • gay-friendly • upscale B&B

West End Inn 146 Pine St. • 772-1377 • gay-friendly • 1870 townhouse in West End (Portland's lesbigay district)

BARS

The Blackstones 6 Pine St. • 775-2885 • 4pm-1am • mostly gay men • neighborhood bar

Raoul's Roadside Attraction 865 Forest Ave. • 773-6886 • 11:30am-1am • gay-friendly • live shows • also a restaurant • Mexican/American • $5-7

Sisters 45 Danforth St. • 774-1505 • 4pm-1am, from 6pm Sat, clsd Mon-Tue • mostly women • dancing/DJ • call for events

Underground 3 Spring St. • 773-3315 • 4pm-1am • popular • lesbians/gay men • dancing/DJ • live shows

Zootz 31 Forest Ave. • 773-8187 • 9pm-1am • gay-friendly • dancing/DJ • alternative music • live shows

RESTAURANTS & CAFES

Cafe Always 47 Middle St. • 774-9399 • dinner Tue-Sat • some veggie • full bar • $10-20

Katahdin 106 Spring St. • 774-1740 • 5pm-10pm, clsd Sun • full bar

Street & Co. 33 Wharf St. • 775-0887 • 5:30pm-9:30pm, til 10pm Fri-Sat • seafood • $12-18 • Nancy's favorite

Tabitha Jean's Restaurant 94 Free St. • 780-8966 • lunch & dinner • casually elegant dining • some veggie • woman-owned

Walter's Cafe 15 Exchange St. • 871-9258 • 11am-9pm • some veggie • $10-14

Westside 58 Pine St. • 773-8223 • lunch & dinner, clsd Mon • Maine game & seafood • some veggie • wheelchair access • $14-20

Woodford's Cafe 129 Spring St. • 772-1374 • 11am-10pm, til 1pm Fri-Sat, clsd Mon • full bar • wheelchair access • $5-9

BOOKSTORES & RETAIL SHOPS

Communiques 3 Moulton St. • 773-5181 • 10am-7pm, til 9pm (summer) • cards • gifts • clothing

Condom Sense, Inc. 424 Fore St. • 871-0356 • hours vary • condoms • cards • gifts

Drop Me A Line 611 Congress St. • 773-5547 • 10am-6pm, til 7pm Th-Fri, noon-5pm Sun

TRAVEL & TOUR OPERATORS

Adventure Travel 2 Elsie Wy., Scarborough • 885-5060 • IGTA

Bob's Airport Livery 25 Alton St. • 773-5135 • shuttle & tour service • also covers Ogunquit

Maine Publicity Bureau (800) 533-9595

SPIRITUAL GROUPS

Am Chofshi 874-2970 • montly mtg. • contact Rheatha

Circle of Hope MCC 156 High St. • 773-0119 • 4pm Sat

Congregaton Bet Ha'am 879-0028 • gay-friendly synagogue

Dignity/Maine PO Box 8113, 04104 • 646-2820/878-0546 • 6pm 3rd Sun at St. Luke's Cathedral, side chapel (143 State St.) • lesbigay Catholics

Feminist Spiritual Community 797-9217 • 7pm Mon • call for info

Integrity 143 State St. (Church Chapel) • 646-2820 • 6pm 3rd Sun

PUBLICATIONS

Community Pride Reporter PO Box 178, Saco, 04101 • 282-4311 • extensive resource listings for ME & NH

EROTICA

Video Expo 666 Congress St. • 774-1377

Rockport (207)

ACCOMMODATIONS

White Cedar Accommodations 378 Commercial St. • 236-9069 • lesbians/gay men • weekly apt. rental • seasonal • lesbian-owned

Saco Bay (207)

ACCOMMODATIONS

Sea Forest Women's Retreat 282-1352 • women only • full brkfst • lesbian-owned/run • $50-up

Sebago Lake (207)

ACCOMMODATIONS

Maine-ly For You RR2 Box 745, Harrison • 583-6980 • gay-friendly • cottages • campsites

Stonington (207)

ACCOMMODATIONS

Sea Gnomes Home PO Box 33, 04681 • 367-5076 • clsd Oct-May • women only • lesbian-owned/run • $40

Tennants Harbor (207)

ACCOMMODATIONS

Eastwind Inn PO Box 149, 04860 • 372-6366 • gay-friendly • full brkfst • also restaurant • old fashioned New England fare • $14-18

Waterville (207)

INFO LINES & SERVICES

Colby College Bi/Lesbian/Gay Community Bridge Room • 872-4149 • 7:30pm Mon

EROTICA

Priscilla's Book Store 18 Water St. • 873-2774 • clsd Sun

York Harbor (207)

ACCOMMODATIONS

Canterbury House 432 York St. • 363-3505 • gay-friendly • spacious Victorian home • $69-110

MARYLAND

Annapolis (410)

ACCOMMODATIONS
Bed & Breakfast of Maryland 269-6232/(800) 736-4667 • gay-friendly • accommodations service

William Page Inn 8 Martin St. • 626-1506/(800) 364-4160 • gay-friendly • elegantly renovated 1908 home • full brkfst

RESTAURANTS & CAFES
Grattis Cafe 47 State Circle • 267-0902 • 9am-8pm, from 11am Sat, clsd Sun

PUBLICATIONS
Women's Yellow Pages of Maryland 114 West St. • 267-0886

EROTICA
20/20 Books 2020 West St. • 266-0514

Baltimore (410)

INFO LINES & SERVICES
AA Gay/Lesbian 433-4843

FIST (Females Investigating Sexual Terrain) PO Box 41032, 21203-6032 • 675-0856 • leather-S/M group

Gay/Lesbian Community Center 241 W. Chase St. • 837-5445 • 10am-4pm, clsd wknds • inquire about 'Womanspace'

Gay/Lesbian Switchboard 837-8888/837-8529 (TDD) • 7pm-10pm

PACT (People of all Colors Together) PO Box 33186, 21218 • 323-4720

Transgender Support Group at the Center

ACCOMMODATIONS
Abacrombie Badger B&B 58 W. Biddle St. • 244-7227 • gay-friendly

Alternative Accommodations (800) 209-9408

Biltmore Suites 205 W. Madison St. • 728-6550/(800) 868-5064 • gay-friendly

Chez Claire B&B 17 W. Chase St. • 685-4666 • lesbians/gay men • 4-story townhouse in historic area

Mr. Mole B&B 1601 Bolton St. • 728-1179 • popular • gay-friendly • splendid suites on historic Bolton Hill • $97-155

BARS
Allegro 1101 Cathedral St. • 837-3906 • 6pm-2am, from 4pm Sun • mostly gay men • women's night Th • dancing/DJ

Baltimore Eagle 2022 N. Charles St. (enter on 21st) • 823-2453 • 6pm-2am • popular • mostly gay men • leather • wheelchair access

Central Station 1001 N. Charles St. • 752-7133 • 11:30am-2am • popular • lesbians/gay men • neighborhood bar • videos • also a restaurant • some veggie • $7-15

Club Atlantis 615 Fallsway • 727-9099 • 9pm-2am, from 4pm Sun, clsd Mon • mostly gay men • dancing/DJ • live shows

Club Bunns 608 W. Lexington St. • 234-2866 • 5pm-2am • lesbians/gay men • women's night Tue • dancing/DJ • mostly African-American

Club Mardi Gras 228 Park Ave. • 625-9818 • 4pm-2am, from noon Th-Fri • mostly gay men • neighborhood bar • wheelchair access

Club Seventeen Twenty-Two 1722 N. Charles St. • 727-7431 • 1:30am-5am Th-Sun • mostly gay men • dancing/DJ • BYOB

Coconuts Cafe 311 W. Madison • 383-6064 • 11am-2am, from 4pm wknds, clsd Mon • mostly women • dancing/DJ • food served • light fare • wheelchair access • $5-7

The Drinkery 203 W. Read St. • 669-9820 • 11am-2am • lesbians/gay men • neighborhood bar

The Gallery Studio Restaurant 1735 Maryland Ave. • 539-6965 • 1pm-2am • lesbians/gay men • dinner nightly • $10-12

Hepburn's 504 S. Haven St. • 276-9310 • 7pm-2am, from 4pm wknds, clsd Mon-Tue • lesbians/gay men • dancing/DJ

Hippo 1 W. Eager St. • 547-0069 • 3pm-2am • popular • lesbians/gay men • more women Fri & Sun T-dance • dancing/DJ • transgender-friendly • karaoke • videos • wheelchair access

Lynn's of Baltimore 774 Washington Blvd. • 727-8924 • 6pm-1am, from 11am Sat, clsd Sun • mostly gay men • neighborhood bar

Orpheus 1001 E. Pratt St. • 276-5599 • gay-friendly • dancing/DJ • 18+ • call for events

Port in a Storm 4330 E. Lombard St. • 732-5608 • 10am-2am • mostly women • neighborhood bar • dancing/DJ • wheelchair access • women-owned/run

Randy's Sportsman's Bar 412 Park Ave. • 727-8935 • 6am-2am • mostly gay men • neighborhood bar

Stagecoach 1003 N. Charles St. • 547-0107 • 4pm-2am • lesbians/gay men • dancing/DJ • country/western • piano bar • also a restaurant • Tex/Mex • some veggie • rooftop cafe • $5-18

Unicorn 2218 Boston St. • 342-8344 • 4pm-2am, from 2pm wknds • popular • mostly gay men • neighborhood bar • live shows

RESTAURANTS & CAFES

Cafe Hon 1009 W. 36th St. • 243-1230 • 8am-10pm, clsd Sun • some veggie • $6-11

City Diner 911 Charles St. • 547-2489 • 24hrs • full bar

Donna's Coffee Bar 2 W. Madison • 385-0180 • beer/wine

Great American Melting Pot (GAMPY's) 904 N. Charles St. • 837-9797 • 11:30am-2am, til 3am Fri-Sat • lesbians/gay men • plenty veggie • wheelchair access • $5-12

Guiseppe's 3215 N. Charles • 467-1177 • pizza & pasta • full bar

Gypsy Cafe 1103 Hollins St. • 625-9310 • 11am-1am, til 3pm Sun

Loco Hombre 413 W. Cold Spring Ln. • 889-2233 • Mexican

Louie's The Bookstore Cafe 518 N. Charles • 962-1224 • live shows • plenty veggie • full bar • wheelchair access • $4-12

M. Gettier 505 S. Broadway • 732-1151 • dinner nightly, clsd Sun • modern French • full bar • wheelchair access • $16-23

Mencken's Cultured Pearl Cafe 1114 Hollins St. • 837-1947 • Mexican • full bar • wheelchair access • $6-12

Metropol Cafe & Art Gallery 1713 N. Charles St. • 385-3018 • 6pm-11pm, 10am-pm Sun, clsd Mon

Michael's Rivera Grill 120 E. Lombard St. (The Brookshire Hotel) • 547-8986 • 5pm-10pm, til 11pm Fri-Sat • popular • upscale cont'l • some veggie • rooftop dining • $19-25

Mount Vernon Stable & Saloon 909 N. Charles St. • 685-7427 • bar 11:30am-2am • lunch & dinner • some veggie • $8-12

Baltimore (410)

LESBIGAY INFO: Gay/Lesbian Community Center: 837-5445, 241 W. Chase St., 10am-4pm Gay/Lesbian Switchboard: 837-8888/837-8529 (TDD).

LESBIGAY PAPER: Baltimore Gay Paper: 837-7748. Baltimore Alternative: 235-3401.

WHERE THE GIRLS ARE: The women's bars are in southeast Baltimore, near the intersection of Haven and Lombard. Of course, the boy's playground, downtown around Chase St. and Park Ave. is also a popular hang-out.

ENTERTAINMENT: Home and movie-set of John Waters, tasteless queer moviemaker extraordinaire. Finally you too can follow the immortal footsteps of Divine, the biggest transvestite movie star we know. This city is also home to Thirty-First St. Book Store for women, and lesbian/gay bookstore Lambda Rising. The Gay/Lesbian Community Center sponsors Womonspace.

LESBIGAY AA: AA Gay/Lesbian: 433-4843.

LESBIGAY PRIDE: June: 837-5445.

CITY INFO: Baltimore Tourism Office: 659-7300.

ATTRACTIONS: Baltimore, one of the 'hub' cities of the Chesapeake Bay, is a quaint, working-class city by the sea, with a friendly and diverse population. It's not far from Washington, D.C., and likewise is packed with museums and history. But the more twisted among us know Baltimore as the site of Edgar Allen Poe's home and grave. Baltimore Art Museum. Harbor Place. National Aquarium.

BEST VIEW: Top of the World Trade City at the Inner Harbor.

WEATHER: Unpredictable rains and heavy winds. In summer, the weather can be hot (90°s) and sticky.

TRANSIT: Yellow Cab: 685-1212. 859-0800. Bus: MASS Transit 539-5000. Train: Metro Rail System: 333-2700.

Spike & Charlie's Restaurant & Wine Bar
1225 Cathedral St. • 752-8144 • lunch, dinner & Sun brunch, clsd Mon • live shows

BOOKSTORES & RETAIL SHOPS

Adrian's Book Cafe 714 S. Broadway, Fells Point • 732-1048 • 8am-8pm, til 11pm Fri-Sat, from 11am wknds • new & used • some gay titles

Lambda Rising 241 Chase St. • 234-0069 • 10am-10pm • lesbigay • wheelchair access

TRAVEL & TOUR OPERATORS

Maryland Office of Tourism (800) 543-1036

Mt. Royal Travel Inc. 1303 N. Charles St. • 685-6633/(800) 767-6925 • IGTA

Safe Harbors Travel 25 South St. • 547-6565/(800) 344-5656 • IGTA

SPIRITUAL GROUPS

MCC 3401 Old York Rd. • 889-6363 • 10:30am Sun

PUBLICATIONS

The Baltimore Alternative PO Box 2351, 21203 • 235-3401

The Baltimore Gay Paper PO Box 22575, 21203 • 837-7748

Gay Community Yellow Pages-Baltimore 547-0380

EROTICA

Leather Underground 136 W. Read St. • 528-0991 • 11am-7pm, til 8pm Fri, 10am-6am Sat, clsd Sun

Beltsville (301)

TRAVEL & TOUR OPERATORS

Your Travel Agent in Beltsville 10440 Baltimore Blvd. • 937-0966/(800) 872-8537 • IGTA

Columbia

INFO LINES & SERVICES

Gay/Lesbian Community of Howard County PO Box 2115, 21045

Cumberland (301)

ACCOMMODATIONS

Red Lamp Post 849 Braddock Rd. • 777-3262 • lesbians/gay men • dinner optional • hot tub • $55-65

Frederick (301)

INFO LINES & SERVICES

Lesbian Info Line 620-7595

RESTAURANTS & CAFES

The Frederick Coffee Co. & Cafe 100 East St. • 698-0039 • 8am-7pm, til 9pm Fri-Sat, 9am-6pm Sun • women-owned/run

Gaithersburg (301)

TRAVEL & TOUR OPERATORS

Monarch Travel Center 9047 Gaither Rd. • 258-0989/(800) 800-4669 • IGTA • gay-owned/run

Laurel

INFO LINES & SERVICES

Gay People Of Laurel PO Box 25, 20725

Parkton (410)

ACCOMMODATIONS

Hidden Valley Farm B&B 1419 Mt. Carmel Rd. (30 min. N. of Baltimore) • 329-8084 • lesbians/gay men • hot tub

Rockville (888)

TRAVEL & TOUR OPERATORS

Damron Atlas World Travel (888) 907-9777

SPIRITUAL GROUPS

MCC of Rockville 15817 Barnesville Rd., 20849 • 601-9112 • 9am & 10:30am Sun

Silver Spring (301)

INFO LINES & SERVICES

GLASS (Gay/Lesbian Assoc. of Silver Spring) PO Box 8518, 20907 • 588-7330

TRAVEL & TOUR OPERATORS

Central Travel of Silver Spring 8609 2nd Ave. • 589-9440 • IGTA

Travel Central 8209 Fenton St. • 587-4000/(800) 783-4000

EROTICA

Max Wonder 9421 Georgia Ave. • 942-4196 • 8am-11pm

Smith Island

ACCOMMODATIONS

Smith Island Get-A-Way PO Box 187, Westport, 21824 • (203) 579-9400 • gay-friendly • apt • secluded community accessible only by boat • $150 wknd/ $350 wk

St. Michaels (410)

ACCOMMODATIONS

The Rainbow House 745-3422 • mostly women • full brkfst • swimming

MASSACHUSETTS

Amherst   (413)

INFO LINES & SERVICES

Everywomen's Center Wilder Hall, UMass • 545-0883 • call for office hours

Women's Media Project WMUA 91.1 FM • 545-2876 • radio shows • 'Girl Talk' 6pm-9pm Tue • 'Oblivion Express' 6am-9am Tue • 'Now's Time' 6pm-9pm Wed

ACCOMMODATIONS

Ivy House B&B 1 Sunset Ct. • 549-7554 • gay-friendly • restored Colonial Cape

BOOKSTORES & RETAIL SHOPS

Food For Thought 106 N. Pleasant St. • 253-5432 • 10am-6pm, til 8pm Wed-Fri, noon-5pm Sun • progressive bookstore • wheelchair access • collectively run

TRAVEL & TOUR OPERATORS

Adventura Travel 233 N. Pleasant St. • 549-1256

SPIRITUAL GROUPS

Integrity/Western MA Grace Church Chapel, Boltwood Ave. • 532-5060 • 7pm last Sun

PUBLICATIONS

Valley Women's Voice UMass • 545-2436

Barre   (508)

ACCOMMODATIONS

Jenkins House B&B Inn Scenic Rte.122 at Barre Common • 355-6444/(800) 378-7373 • gay-friendly • wrap-around porch • English garden

Boston   (617)

INFO LINES & SERVICES

BAGLY (Boston Alliance of Gay/Lesbian Youth) PO Box 814, 02103 • (800) 422-2459/(800) 399-7337 • extensive services for lesbigay youth 22 & under • women's mtg 6:45pm Wed

Bisexual Resource Center 29 Stanhope St. 3rd flr. • 424-9595 • also Women's Bi-Network • PO Box 639, 02140

Cambridge Women's Center 46 Pleasant St., Cambridge • 354-8807

Daughters of Bilitis 1151 Massachusetts Ave. (Harvard Sq.), Cambridge • 661-3633 • women's social & support networks • call for schedule

Boston   (617)

WHERE THE GIRLS ARE: Sipping coffee and reading somewhere in Cambridge or Harvard Square, strolling the South End near Columbus & Mass. Avenues, or hanging out in the Fenway or Jamaica Plain.

ENTERTAINMENT: Gay Men's Chorus: 247-BGMC. Triangle Theatre Co.: 426-3550. United Fruit Company & The Theatre Offensive: 547-7728.

LESBIGAY PRIDE: June. 1-976-PRIDE, $1.50 per call.

ANNUAL EVENTS: February - Outwrite: (617) 426-4469. Annual national lesbian/gay writers & publishers conference at the Boston Park Plaza Hotel.

CITY INFO: Boston Visitor's Bureau: (800) 374-7400 (touchtone).

ATTRACTIONS: Back Bay. Beacon Hill. Black Heritage Trail. Boston Common. Faneuil Hall. Freedom Trail. Harvard University. Museum of Afro-American Artists. Old North Church. Thoreau Lyceum.

WEATHER: Extreme. From freezing winters to boiling summers with a beautiful spring and fall.

TRANSIT: Boston Cab: 536-5010. MBTA: Blue Line, 5:30am-1am, 85¢. MBTA: (800) 392-6100. From the Airport: (800) 235-6486.

▲ **Dyke TV** Cambridge Channel 66, Cambridge • 9pm Th • 'weekly half-hour TV show produced by lesbians, for lesbians'

Entre Nous, Inc. PO Box 984, 02103 • men's & women's leather group

Gay/ Lesbian Helpline 267-9001 • 4:30pm-10pm, from 6pm wknds

International Foundation for Gender Education PO Box 367, Wayland, 01778 • 894-8340 • transgender info & support

Lesbian Al-Anon (at the Women's Center) • 354-8807 • 6:30pm Wed

Musically Speaking Women's Radio WMBR 88.1 FM • 253-8810 • 6:30pm Mon • also 'Say It Sister' 7:30pm Wed • women-owned/run

Boston

*H*ome to 65 colleges and universities, Boston has been an intellectual center for the continent. Since that famed tea party, it's also been home to some of New England's most rebellious radicals. The result is a city whose character is both traditonal and free-thinking, high-brow and free-wheeling*, stuffy and energetic.

Not only is this city complex, it's cluttered—with plenty of historic and mind-sparking sites to visit. Start with **Globe Corner Bookstore** for tourist maps and info—but if you're easily bored, check out the high/low culture in Harvard Square, the shopping along Newbury Street in the Back Bay, and the touristy vendors in Faneuil Hall.

Boston's women's community is, not surprisingly, strong and politically diverse. To find out what the latest hotspots are, pick up a copy of **Bay Windows** or **IN** at well-stocked women's bookstore **New Words Books** or lesbigay **Glad Day Books**. While you're there, check out the many national lesbian magazines published in Boston, from feminist newsjournal **Sojourner**, to **Bad Attitude**, an erotic 'zine for S/M dykes.

Tired of reading? Restore your body with some boogy at **Quest** on Wednesday, or **Avalon** on Sunday. Like San Francisco, Boston has no full-time women's bar, so you'll have to seek out the latest one-nighter at the mixed bars, like **Jungle** or **Icon**.

* About driving in Boston: its drivers are notoriously the most 'freeform' in the country. The streets of Boston can be confusing—often streets of the same name intersect, and six-way intersections are the rule.

OLE (Older Lesbian Energy) PO Box 1214, E. Arlington, 02174 • social group for lesbians 40 & better

Tiffany Club of New England PO Box 2283, Woburn, 01888 • 891-9325 • transgender hotline Tue night

Women's Health Group 720 Harrison Ave. #404 • 638-7428 • medical & mental health services

ACCOMMODATIONS

463 Beacon St. Guest House 463 Beacon St. • 536-1302 • popular • gay-friendly • residential area, minutes from Boston's heart • IGTA

Amsterdammertje PO Box 865, 02103 • 471-8454 • lesbians/gay men • Euro-American B&B • full brkfst

▲ **Chandler Inn** 26 Chandler St. • 482-3450/(800) 842-3450 • popular • gay-friendly • centrally located • IGTA

Citywide Reservation Service, Inc. 25 Huntington Ave. Ste. 500 • 267-7424/(800) 468-3593 • covers most of New England

Clarendon Square B&B 81 Warren Ave. • 536-2229 • lesbians/gay men • restored Victorian townhouse • fireplaces • gay-owned/run • $110-130

Holworthy Place 102 Holworthy St., Cambridge • 864-7042 • gay-friendly • full brkfst • near Harvard Square

Iris B&B PO Box 4188, Dedham, 02026 • 329-3514 • women only • private home • shared baths • $60

▲ **Oasis Guest House** 22 Edgerly Rd. • 267-2262 • popular • mostly gay men • Back Bay location • IGTA • $55-87

Thoreau's Walden B&B 2 Concord Rd. • 259-1899 • gay-friendly • near historic Walden Pond • full brkfst • $75

Victorian B&B 156 Warren Ave. • 536-3285 • women only • full brkfst • smokefree • women-owned/run • $50-85 (1-4 guests)

BARS

The Avalon 15 Lansdowne St. • 262-2424 • 9pm-2am Sun only • popular • mostly gay men • dancing/DJ

The Bar 99 St. Botolph St. • 266-3030 • 5pm-1am, from noon Sun • lesbians/gay men • neighborhood bar • food served

The Bolt 174 Lincoln • 695-1475 • 11am-2am • lunch daily • lesbians/gay men • neighborhood bar • dancing/DJ • live shows • wheelchair access

Buzz 67 Stuart St. • 267-8969 • 10pm Sat only • popular • lesbians/gay men • dancing/DJ

Campus/Man-Ray 21 Brookline, Cambridge • 864-0400 • 9pm-1am, clsd Mon-Tue • gay-friendly • gay night Th • more women Sun • dancing/DJ • alternative

Chaps 27 Huntington Ave. • 266-7778 • noon-2am • popular • mostly gay men • more women Wed • Latin night Wed • dancing/DJ • videos • wheelchair acces

Club Cafe 209 Columbus • 536-0966 • 2pm-2am, from 11:30am Sun • popular • lesbians/gay men • more women Wed • 3 bars • live shows • videos • also a restaurant • some veggie • wheelchair access • $10-20

Excaliber Rte. 1 South, Peabody • 535-3545 • 9pm-2am, clsd Mon-Wed • lesbians/gay men • dancing/DJ • wheelchair access

Heaven/Hombre 7 Lansdowne St. • 421-9595 • 10pm-2am Wed & Sun • lesbians/gay men • dancing/DJ

Icon @ Europa 67 Stuart St. • 267-8969 • 8pm-2am Sun • mostly women • dancing/DJ

The Jungle @ Coco's 965 Massachusetts Ave. • 427-7807 • 9pm-2am Fri-Sat • lesbians/gay men • dancing/DJ • 'Girl Bar' Fri • popular

Luxor 69 Church • 423-6969 • 4pm-1am • mostly gay men • videos • also Mario's restaurant • Italian • $9-13

Paradise 180 Massachusetts Ave., Cambridge • 864-4130 • 4pm-2am • popular • mostly gay men • dancing/DJ • live shows • videos • wheelchair access

Quest 1270 Boylston St. • 424-7747 • 9pm-2am, clsd Sun • popular • lesbians/gay men • dancing/DJ • videos • roof deck

Upstairs at the Hideaway 20 Concord Ln. • 661-8828 • Th & Sun only • mostly women • free pool bar for women

RESTAURANTS & CAFES

Art Zone Cafe 150 Kneeland St. • 695-0087 • 11am-4pm, til 4am Th, 24hrs Fri-Sat • lesbians/gay men • Southern BBQ • plenty veggie • full bar • $7-15

The Blue Wave 142 Berkeley St. • 424-6711/424-6664 • noon-11pm, til 5pm Sun • lesbians/gay men • plenty veggie • $7-10

The Casa Romero 30 Gloucester St. • 536-4341 • 5pm-10pm, til 11pm wknds • Mexican • $10-20

Cedar's 253 Shawmut Ave. (Milford) • 338-7528 • 5pm-11pm, clsd Sun • Lebanese

Icarus 3 Appleton St. • 426-1790 • dinner & Sun brunch • New American • $30-40

Rabia's 73 Salem St. • 227-6637 • lunch & dinner • fine Italian • some veggie • wheelchair access • $10-25

Regalia Restaurant & Wine Bar 480 Columbus Ave. • 236-5252 • dinner nightly, Sun brunch • inventive American & tapas • some veggie • $10-20

Ristorante Lucia 415 Hanover St. • 367-2353 • great North End pasta • some veggie • $8-15

Roberto's at Cafe Amalfi 8 Westland Ave. • 536-6396 • dinner & Sun brunch • full bar

GYMS & HEALTH CLUBS

Metropolitan Health Club 209 Columbus • 536-3006 • 6pm-11pm, 9am-9pm wknds • gay-friendly

Mike's Gym 560 Harrison Ave. • 338-6210 • popular • gay-owned/run

BOOKSTORES & RETAIL SHOPS

Designs for Living 52 Queensberry St. • 536-6150 • 7am-9pm • cafe

Glad Day Books 673 Boylston St. • 267-3010 • 9:30am-10pm, til 11pm Fri-Sat, noon-9pm Sun • lesbigay

Globe Corner 1 School St. • (800) 358-6013 • also 49 Palmer St., Cambridge

New Words Bookstore 186 Hampshire St., Cambridge • 876-5310 • 10am-8pm, til 6pm Sat, noon-6pm Sun • women's

Trident Booksellers & Cafe 338 Newbury St. • 267-8688 • 9am-midnight • beer/wine • wheelchair access

Unicorn Books 1210 Massachusetts Ave., Arlington • 646-3680 • 10am-9pm, til 5pm wknds • spiritual titles • women-owned/run

Waterstone's Booksellers 26 Exeter • 859-7300 • 9am-11pm • huge general bookstore • wheelchair access

We Think The World of You 540 Tremont St. • 423-1965 • open daily • popular • lesbigay

Wordsworth 30 Brattle St., Cambridge • 354-5201 • 9am-11pm, 10am-10pm Sun • general • lesbigay titles

TRAVEL & TOUR OPERATORS

5 Star Travel 164 Newbury St. • 536-1999/(800) 359-1999 • IGTA

Alyson Adventures PO Box 181223, 02118 • 353-0595/(800) 825-9766 • IGTA

Friend in Travel 5230 Washington St., W. Roxbury • 327-8600/(800) 597-8267 • IGTA

Gibb Travel 673 Boylston St. • 353-0595/(800) 541-9949 • IGTA

Just Right Reservations 18 Piedmont St. • 423-3550 • covers Boston, NYC & Provincetown

Massachusetts Office of Travel & Tourism 100 Cambridge St., 13th flr. • (800) 447-6277

Omega International Travel 99 Summer St. • 737-8511/(800) 727-0599 • IGTA

Travel Management 160 Commonwealth Ave. • 424-1908/(800) 532-0055

SPIRITUAL GROUPS

Am Tikva PO Box 11, Cambridge, 02238 • 926-2536 • lesbigay Jewish group

Dignity Beacon Hill (St. John's Evangelist Church) • 421-1915 • 5:30pm Sun

Ecumenical Catholic Church 35 Bowdin St. • 227-5794 • 5:30pm Sun

Integrity 12 Quincy Ave. (Christ Church), Quincy • 773-0310 • last Fri

MCC 131 Cambridge St. (Old West Church) • 288-8029 • 7pm Sun

PUBLICATIONS

Bad Attitude, Inc. PO Box 390110, Cambridge, 02139 • magazine of lesbian erotica • women-owned/run

Bay Windows 1523 Washington St. • 266-6670

Gay Community News 29 Stanhope St • 262-6969

In 544 Tremont • 426-8246 • newsmagazine

Let's Go Harvard Student Agencies, Cambridge • info for travelling lesbigay youths

Sojourner-The Women's Forum 42 Seaverns Ave. • 524-0415 • monthly

EROTICA

Innovations in Leather 1254 Boylston St. (at Ramrod Bar) • 536-1546 • 10pm-1am, clsd Mon-Wed • leather • piercings • body jewelry

Marquis de Sade 73 Berkeley St. • 426-2120

Charlemont (413)

ACCOMMODATIONS

The Inn at Charlemont Rt. 2, Mohawk Trail • 339-5796 • gay-friendly • also a restaurant • some veggie • full bar • women-owned/run • $10-20

Chelsea (617)

BARS
Club 9-11 9-11 Williams St. • 884-9533 •
4pm-1am • lesbians/gay men • dancing/DJ
• live shows • wheelchair access

Chicopee (413)

BARS
Eclipse 13 View St. • 534-3065 • 7pm-2am,
clsd Mon-Wed • lesbians/gay men • neighborhood bar • dancing/DJ

Our Hide-away 16 Bolduc Ln. • 534-6426 •
6pm-2am, clsd Mon • mostly women •
neighborhood bar • dancing/DJ • outdoor
volleyball • women-owned/run

Cochituate

PUBLICATIONS
Women's Investment Newsletter PO Box
5015, 01778 • 'advice on stocks, bonds, etc.
without macho mystification'

Fitchburg (508)

BARS
The Country Lounge 860 Ashby State Rd.
• 345-6703 • 7pm-1am • lesbians/gay men
• dancing/DJ

Gloucester (508)

BOOKSTORES
The Bookstore 61 Main St. • 281-1548 •
9am-6pm

Great Barrington

PUBLICATIONS
Hikane: The Capable Woman PO Box 841,
01230-0841 • 'disabled wimmin's magazine
for lesbians & our wimmin friends'

Greenfield (413)

BOOKSTORES & RETAIL SHOPS
World Eye Bookshop 60 Federal St. • 772-
2186 • open 9am, from noon Sun • general
• community bulletin board • women-
owned/run

Haverhill (508)

BOOKSTORES & RETAIL SHOPS
Radzukina's 714 N. Broadway • 521-1333 •
call for hours • books • jewelry • music •
women-owned/run

Hyannis (508)

INFO LINES & SERVICES
Gay/Lesbian AA 775-7060 • 6pm Sun

ACCOMMODATIONS
Gull Cottage 10 Old Church St., Yarmouth
Port • 362-8747 • lesbians/gay men • near
beach • wheelchair access • $50

BARS
Duval Street Station 477 Yarmouth Rd. •
775-9835 • 6pm-1am • popular •
lesbians/gay men • Cape Cod's largest gay
complex • dancing/DJ • live shows • food
served

Lenox (413)

ACCOMMODATIONS
Summer Hill Farm 830 East St. • 442-2057
• gay-friendly • colonial guesthouse & cottage • full brkfst • wheelchair access

Walker House 64 Walker St. • 637-
1271/(800) 235-3098 • gay-friendly • wheelchair access

Lowell (508)

INFO LINES & SERVICES
Shared Times PO Box 8822, 01853-8822 •
441-9081 • social/support group for women
• newsletter • dances

Lynn (617)

BARS
Fran's Place 776 Washington • 598-5618 •
1pm-2am • lesbians/gay men • neighborhood bar • dancing/DJ • wheelchair access

Joseph's 191 Oxford St. • 599-9483 • 5pm-
2am • lesbians/gay men • dancing/DJ •
videos • wheelchair access

Manchester (603)

INFO LINES & SERVICES
**LINC (Lesbians Inviting New
Connections)** PO Box 10033 , Bedford NH,
03110 • (603) 668-9245 • network for
women in rural areas in southern New
England

Marblehead (508)

INFO LINES & SERVICES
North Shore Gay/Lesbian Alliance Box
806, 01945 • 745-3848 • event line

TRAVEL & TOUR OPERATORS
Around the World Travel Townhouse
Square • 631-8620/(800) 733-4337

Martha's Vineyard (508)

INFO LINES & SERVICES
ILGA (Island Lesbian/Gay Association)
PO Box 1809, Vineyard Haven, 02568 •
social group • also publishes newsletter

ACCOMMODATIONS
Captain Dexter House of Edgartown 35
Pease's Point Way, Box 2798 • 627-7289 •
gay-friendly • country inn circa 1840 •
$110-180

▲ **Martha's Place Inn** 114 Main St., PO Box
1182, Vineyard Haven, 02568 • 693-0253 •
lesbians/gay men • harbor views • brkfst in
bed • jacuzzi • fireplaces • wheelchair
access • $175-275

Webb's Camping Area RFD 3 Box 100,
02568 • 693-0233 • open May-Sept • gay-
friendly • women-owned/run

RESTAURANTS & CAFES
Black Dog Bakery 157 State Rd., Vineyard
Haven • 693-8190

Louis' Cafe State Rd., Vineyard Haven •
693-325

Oyster Bar 162 Circuit Ave., Oak Bluffs •
693-3300

Wintertide Coffee House 5 Corners,
Vineyard Haven • 693-8830 • also live jazz

BOOKSTORES & RETAIL SHOPS
Bunch of Grapes Main St., Vineyard Haven
• 693-2291 • general • some lesbian/gay
titles & magazines

TRAVEL & TOUR OPERATORS
Martha's Vineyard Steamship Authority
540-2022 • call for info & schedule of fer-
ries from Boston

Methuen (508)

BARS
Xposure 280 Merrimack St. • 685-9911 •
9pm-2am Fri, til 1am Sat only • gay-friendly • dancing/DJ

Nantucket (508)

ACCOMMODATIONS
House of Orange 25 Orange St. • 228-9287
• May-Oct • old captain's home

New Bedford (508)

BARS

Le Place 20 Kenyon St. • 992-8156 • 2pm-2am, from noon-1am Sat • popular • lesbians/gay men • dancing/DJ • women-owned/run

Puzzles 428 N. Front St. • 991-2306 • 4pm-2am • lesbians/gay men • dancing/DJ • live shows • food served • local fish menu & Sun brunch from 11am • wheelchair access

Newbury (508)

ACCOMMODATIONS

46 High Road B&B 46 High Rd. • 462-4664 • gay-friendly

Newton

INFO LINES & SERVICES

▲ **Dyke TV** Channel 13 • 10pm Tue • 'weekly half-hour TV show produced by lesbians, for lesbians'

Northampton (413)

INFO LINES & SERVICES

Community Pride Line 585-0683 • recorded info

▲ **Dyke TV** Channel 2 • 10:30pm Mon • 'weekly half-hour TV show produced by lesbians, for lesbians'

East Coast FTM Group PO Box 60585 Florence Stn., 01060 • 584-7616 • support group for FTM transgendered people & their partners only • contact Bet Power

Lesbian/Gay Business Guild PO Box 593, 01061 • 585-8839

New Alexandria Lesbian Library PO Box 402, 01060 • 584-7616 • archives • library • call for appt.

Out & About Cable TV Channel 2 • 9pm Mon

Shelix PO Box 416 Florence Stn., 01060 • 584-7616 • New England S/M support group for lesbian/bi & transgendered women • write for info

ACCOMMODATIONS

Corner Porches Baptist Corner Rd., Ashfield • 628-4592 • gay-friendly • full brkfst

The Inn at Northampton 1 Atwood Dr. • 586-1211/(800) 582-2929 • gay-friendly • swimming • restaurant & bar

Innamorata B&B PO Box 113, Goshen, 01032 • 268-0300 • mostly women • full brkfst • near outdoor recreation • women-owned/run • $70-99

Little River Farm B&B 967 Huntington Rd., Worthington • 238-4261 • seasonal • women only • full brkfst • women-owned/run • $75

Old Red Schoolhouse 67 Park St., 01060 • 584-1228 • apts • studios • also 'Lesbian Towers' in East Hampton • gay-owned/run • $40-200

▲ **Tin Roof B&B** PO Box 296, Hadley, 01035 • 586-8665 • mostly women • 1909 farmhouse w/ spectacular view of the Berkshires • women-owned/run • $60

Northampton (413)

WHERE THE GIRLS ARE: Just off Main St., browsing in the small shops, strolling down an avenue, or sipping a beverage at one of the cafes.

BEST VIEW: At the top of Skinner Mountain, up Route 47 by bus, car or bike.

WEATHER: Late summer/early fall is the best season, with warm, sunny days. Mid-summer gets to the low 90°s, while winter brings snow from November to March, with temperatures in the 20°s and 30°s.

TRANSIT: Mystery Taxi: 584-0055. Peter Pan Shuttle: 586-1030. Pioneer Valley Transit Authority (PVTA): 586-5806.

BARS

Club Metro 492 Pleasant St. • 582-9898 • gay-friendly • gay night Wed • dancing/DJ • alternative • live shows

The Grotto 25 West St. • 586-6900 • 5pm-1am • lesbians/gay men • dancing/DJ • live shows • food served

The Iron Horse 20 Center St. • 584-0610 • 8:30pm-? • gay-friendly • live shows • food served • Fresh American • some veggie • $5-15

Pearl Street Cafe 10 Pearl St. • 584-7810 • 9pm-1am Wed & Sat • lesbians/gay men • dancing/DJ • women-owned/run

RESTAURANTS & CAFES

Bela 68 Masonic St. • 586-8011 • noon-8pm, til 10pm Th-Sat, clsd Sun-Mon • vegetarian • women-owned/run • $5-10

Curtis & Schwartz 116 Main St. • 586-3278 • 7:30am-3pm • neo-Eurpoean • some veggie • $8-15

Green Street Cafe 64 Green St. • 586-5650 • lunch & dinner • plenty veggie • beer/wine • $11-17

Haymarket Cafe 15 Amber Ln. • 586-9969 • 9am-midnight, clsd Mon • fresh pastries

Paul & Elizabeth's 150 Main St. • 584-4832 • seafood • plenty veggie • beer/wine • wheelchair access • $7-12

Squire's Smoke & Game Club Rte. 9, Williamsburg • 268-7222 • from 5pm Wed-Sun • popular • some veggie • full bar • live shows • Ali & Bear's favorite • $12-17

BOOKSTORES & RETAIL SHOPS

Pride & Joy 20 Crafts Ave. • 585-0683 • 11am-6pm, til 8pm Th, from noon-5pm Sun • lesbigay books & gifts

Third Wave Feminist Booksellers 90 King St. • 586-7851 • 10am-6pm, til 8pm Th, til 5pm Sun, clsd Mon • wheelchair access • lesbian-owned/run

PUBLICATIONS

Lesbian Calendar 351 Pleasant St. #132 • 586-5514

Metroline 846 Farmington Ave. Ste. 6, W. Hartford CT, 06119 • (860) 570-0823 • regional newspaper & entertainment guide

TRAVEL AGENTS

Adventura Travel 122 Main St. • 584-9441

Provincetown (508)

INFO LINES & SERVICES

▲ **Dyke TV** Channel 8 • 11pm Fri • 'weekly half-hour TV show produced by lesbians, for lesbians'

▲ **Provincetown Business Guild** 115 Bradford St., 02657 • 487-2313/(800) 637-8696 • IGTA

ACCOMMODATIONS

A Tall Ship 452 Commercial St. • 487-2247 • gay-friendly • beach house

Admiral's Landing Guest House 158 Bradford St. • 487-9665 • seasonal • mostly gay men • 1840s captain's home & cottages • IGTA

Ampersand Guesthouse 6 Cottage St. • 487-0959 • lesbians/gay men • mid-19th century Greek Revival architecture

▲ **Anchor Inn Guest House** 175 Commercial St. • 487-0432/(800) 858-2657 • popular • lesbians/gay men • central location • private beach • harbor view

Angel's Landing 353-355 Commercial St. • 487-1600 • seasonal • lesbians/gay men • efficiency units on waterfront

Asheton House 3 Cook St. • 487-9966 • gay-friendly • restored 1840s captain's house • $80-105

Beachfront Realty 145 Commercial St. • 487-1397 • vacation rentals & housing/condo sales

Beaconlite Inn 12 Winthrop St. • 487-9603 • popular • lesbians/gay men

▲ **Benchmark Inn & Annex** 6-8 Dyer St. • 487-7440/(888) 487-7440 • lesbians/gay men • moderate & luxurious • in heart of Provincetown • swimming • IGTA

The Blue Beacon 8 Bradford St. • 487-0516 • gay-friendly

Boatslip Beach Club 161 Commercial St. • 487-1669/(800) 451-7547 • seasonal • popular • lesbians/gay men • resort • swimming • also a restaurant • cont'l/seafood • some veggie • several bars • popular T-dance • $110-150

▲ **Bradford Gardens Inn** 178 Bradford St. • 487-1616/(800) 432-2334 • popular • mostly women • 1820s colonial • full brkfst • gardens • women-owned/run • $65-225

Bradford House & Motel 41 Bradford St. • 487-0173 • lesbians/gay men

The Brass Key Guesthouse 9 Court St. • 487-9005/(800) 842-9858 • popular • mostly gay men • full brkfst • heated spa • swimming • wheelchair access • IGTA • $155-220

The Buoy 97 Bradford St. • 487-3082 • lesbians/gay men • $50-115

Provincetown (508)

WHERE THE GIRLS ARE: In this small resort town, you can't miss 'em!

LESBIGAY PRIDE: June: 521-0811.

ANNUAL EVENTS: August - Provincetown Carnival, (800) 637-8696. October - Women's Week: (800) 637-8696, very popular - make your reservations early!

CITY INFO: Chamber of Commerce: 487-3424.

ATTRACTIONS: The beach. Commercial St. Herring Cove Beach. Whale Watching.

BEST VIEW: Girl-watching at an outdoor cafe or on the beach.

WEATHER: New England weather is unpredictable. Be prepared for rain, snow or extreme heat! Otherwise, the weather during the season consists of warm days and cooler nights.

Provincetown

*T*he country's largest lesbian and gay resort—with 17 women's guesthouses, and more than 65 gay-friendly B&B's—is a quintessential New England whaling village on the very tip of Cape Cod.

Provincetown has been popular for summers ever since Native American tribes came here to fish. The Vikings also stopped in for quick repairs, and the Pilgrims even made their first landing here. Over the centuries, Provincetown has shifted from a whaling village to a haven for whale-watching. Before you leave, treat yourself to the excitement of a whale-watching cruise. There are several cruise lines, and **Portuguese Princess Whale Watch** is women-owned.

Provincetown is also a haven for lesbians—the majority of the guest inns are lesbian-run. According to one regular, the typical lesbian itinerary goes as follows:

Arrival: Rent a bike and explore the town's lesbigay shops and bookstores. Nobody drives in Provincetown. Pick up lunch at a deli on the way to Herring Cove. At the beach, head left to find the women.

At the Beach: Go ahead, take off your top. Nudity is desirable here, but watch for the cops—they'll give you a ticket for bare breasts. Tip: if you're heading toward the sand dunes for a tryst (like everyone else), don't forget your socks. The hot, white sand can burn your feet.

3pm: Bike back to your room for a shower, then head to the afternoon T-dance at **Boatslip Beach Club** on Commercial St. Drink and dance til dinnertime, then take a relaxing few hours for dinner.

After Dinner: Check out the bars; **The Pied Piper** is the pick for women. If your energy's too low for the bar scene, most

stores are open til 11pm during the summer. When the bars close, grab a slice of pizza and an espresso milkshake at **Spiritus**, and cruise the streets until they're empty—sometimes not til 4 or 5 am.

If you like your women packed together like sardines, pencil in Provincetown's **Women's Weekend**, the third weekend in October. The **Women Innkeepers of Provincetown** will be sponsoring games, barbecues, live shows, dances, cruises, and more. Don't forget to call your favorite guesthouse early to make your reservations!

Just one last bit of advice: you may have heard others refer to Provincetown as 'P-town' but nothing rankles a native faster.

Bradford Gardens Inn

Bradford Gardens Inn, woman-owned and featured in most national and international B & B guides, offers you charming, spacious rooms with fireplaces, private baths, cable TV and ceiling fans.

Included are full gourmet breakfasts, such as shirred eggs with tarragon mornay sauce, Portuguese flippers, homemade cinnamon-walnut pancakes with blueberry maple syrup...You can also choose fire-placed cottages situated in our beautiful gardens surrounding the inn.

Just park your car in our lot, and you are 5 minutes from the center of town for fine dining, nightclubs, whalewatching, beaches, galleries and shopping.

Built in 1820, this historic inn offers you New England charm combined with a natural informality. Rates: $69-$145. One block from the beach.

Bradford Gardens Inn
178 Bradford St.
Provincetown, MA 02657
(508) 487-1616

(800) 432-2334

GABRIEL'S

Come close to heaven

APARTMENTS & GUEST ROOMS

SIRENS WORKSHOP CENTER

Conference Center & Holistic Workshops
Sauna & Hot Tubs & Steam Room
Massage & Exercise Room & Bicycles
Gardens & Sundecks & Barbeque
Fireplaces & Breakfast
Air Conditioning & Cable TV & Phones
Internet Access & Computer Facilities
Always Open & In the Heart of Town

Find us on the World Wide Web:
www.provincetown.com/gabriels

(800) 9MY-ANGEL

104 Bradford Street
Provincetown, MA
02657-1440

(508) 487•3232
FAX (508) 487•1605
gabriels@provincetown.com

Having a wonderful time... Wish you were here!

☆ *Centrally located in the heart of Provincetown*
☆ *Expanded continental breakfast*
☆ *Parking and airport pickup available*
☆ *Open year round*

7 Center Street, Provincetown, MA 02657
(508) 487-3692

Escape to

Quiet West End

APARTMENTS & COTTAGE
14 WEST VINE • PROVINCETOWN, MA 02657
RESERVATIONS: (508) 487-6310

Lady Jane's Inn

- Lovely, spacious rooms
- Color remote televisions
- Continental breakfast
- Hospitality room
- Full private baths
- On site parking
- Individually heated / AC
- Open all year

Lady Jane's Inn is a woman owned and operated guest house in the heart of Provincetown, on a quiet side street, just steps away from shops, restaurants and beaches. The Inn has been carefully and tastefully designed to meet the vacationers' need for comfort and privacy. Each spacious room is scrupulously clean and beautifully appointed with turn-of-century furnishings and ceiling fans. Whatever the season, guests will delight in a lovingly prepared continental breakfast served in the cozy common room or in the sunny, flower filled patio. Provincetown, and Lady Jane's Inn, have much to offer the vacationer.

Your Innkeepers,
Jane Antolini & Sharlene Marchette

7 Central Street, Provincetown, MA 02657
(508) 487-3387   Email: ladyjanes@wn.net

BENCHMARK INN, debuting April 1997, promises top-notch comfort and style. Six brand new bedrooms and penthouse suite offer a variety of luxuries including fireplaces, whirlpool baths, queen-sized beds, wet bars, private balconied entrances, stunning harborviews and a long list of deluxe amenities. **Benchmark Inn–The Best Is For You.**

BENCHMARK ANNEX is a cozy, quiet gem. Many thoughtful features, a beautiful flowering garden, splash pool, large sundeck and moderate tariffs make Benchmark Annex an attractive choice for your Provincetown getaway.

PROVINCETOWN • 6 & 8 DYER STREET • 508 487-7440

TOLL FREE 1•888•487•7440

www.CapeCodAccess.com/benchmark/

Monument House

Charming, newly remodeled 1840's home.
Nice amenities plus free parking. **Freshly baked pastries,
good coffee and warm hospitality
are offered daily.**

PROVINCETOWN • 129 BRADFORD STREET • 508 487-9664

TOLL FREE 1•888•487•9664

www.CapeCodAccess.com/monument/

More Reservation Services
- Condos, Guest Houses, Motels, Cottages.
- Shows, Plays, Concerts, Theatre.
- Airlines, Cruises, Cars, Rail – Worldwide.
- 24-Hour-A-Day Internet Reservations.

More You Can Count On
- More experience than anyone in P'town
- More hours of operation – Open 7 Days.
- More Provincetown information on the web

and coming soon, More than just Provincetown...

PROVINCETOWN
RESERVATIONS
SYSTEM®

1-800 648-0364

www.ptownres.com

293 COMMERCIAL ST. PROVINCETOWN MA 02657 FAX 508 487-6517

Plums
Bed & Breakfast Inn

Drive past the tumble of Cape Cod houses to Plums Bed & Breakfast, an 1860s Dutch Gambrel. Inside the white picket fence, a garden of lilies, irises and dahlias beckon you across the wisteria-draped porch. Your key unlocks the quiet elegance of the Victorian whaling captain's house. Inside, wide pine floors shine beneath Eastlake and Renaissance Revival antiques that grace Plums' large rooms. Fresh flowers add to the romance! And white lace curtains adorn windows that reach to high ceilings. Sit at a table of women for breakfast amid sterling silver, brass and period curios. Under a crystal chandelier, enjoy conversation, fresh fruit, baked goods, and gourmet entrees like cheese souffle or French toast stuffed with cream cheese and strawberries. Innkeepers to pamper you, parking and private baths for your comfort.

Come, experience the magic of Plums!
160 Bradford Street • Provincetown, MA 02657
(508) 487-2283 • Brochure available

Burch House 116 Bradford St. • 487-9170 • seasonal • mostly gay men • studios

The Captain & His Ship 164 Commercial St. • 487-1850/(800) 400-2278 • seasonal • popular • mostly gay men • 19th century sea captain's home • $75-140

Captain Lysander's Inn 96 Commercial St. • 487-2253 • gay-friendly

▲ **Captain's House B&B** 350-A Commercial St. • 487-9353/(800) 458-8885 • lesbians/gay men

Chancellor Inn 17 Center St. • 487-9423 • mostly gay men

▲ **Check'er Inn** 25 Winthrop St. • 487-9029/(800) 894-9029 • women only • $85-125, $775-1200 apts weekly

Chicago House 6 Winslow St. • 487-0537 • mostly gay men

The Claredon House 118 Bradford St. • 487-1645 • gay-friendly

Coat of Arms 7 Johnson St. • 487-0816 • seasonal • popular • mostly gay men • Victorian • in the heart of Provincetown

Commons Guesthouse & Bistro 386 Commercial St. • 487-7800/(800) 487-0784 • gay-friendly

Crown & Anchor 247 Commercial St. • 487-1430 • mostly gay men • swimming • also a restaurant • full bar • cafe • $10-20

▲ **Dexter's Inn** 6 Conwell St. • 487-1911 • mostly women • smokefree • women-owned/run • $50-90

The Dunes Motel & Apartments PO Box 361, 02657 • 487-1956 • seasonal • lesbians/gay men • $65-145

▲ **Dusty Miller Inn** 82 Bradford St. • 487-2213 • mostly women • women-owned/run • $45-115

▲ **Elephant Walk Inn** 156 Bradford St. • 487-2543/(800) 889-9255 • popular • lesbians/gay men • in the heart of Provincetown

Elliot House 6 Gosnold St. • 487-4029 • lesbians/gay men • full brkfst • central location • private gardens

▲ **Fairbanks Inn** 90 Bradford St. • 487-0386/(800) 324-7265 • popular • lesbians/gay men • IGTA • $75-150

Four Bays 166 Commercial St. • 487-0859/(800) 414-2297 • lesbians/gay men • Victorian • near Cape Cod Bay

▲ **Gabriel's Guestrooms & Apartments** 104 Bradford St. • 487-3232/(800) 969-2643 • popular • mostly women • hot tub • workshop center • IGTA • $50-150

Grand View Inn 4 Conant St. • 487-9193 • lesbians/gay men

▲ **The Gull Walk Inn** 300-A Commercial St. • 487-9027 • women only • sundeck • women-owned/run • $45-90

▲ **Halle's** 14 W. Vine St. • 487-6310 • mostly women • apt • women-owned/run • $65-95

▲ **Hargood House at Bayshore** 493 Commercial St. • 487-9133 • gay-friendly • apts • private beach • women-owned/run • $72-142

Haven House 12 Carver St. • 487-3031 • mostly gay men • swimming

▲ **Heritage House** 7 Center St. • 487-3692 • popular • lesbians/gay men • lesbian-owned/run • $49-85

Holiday Inn of Provincetown Rte. 6-A Box 392, 02657 • 487-1711/(800) 422-4224 • gay-friendly • swimming • also a restaurant • full bar • wheelchair access • IGTA

The Inn at Cook Street 7 Cook St. • 487-3894/(888) 266-5655 • gay-friendly • intimate & quiet

The Inn at the Egg 1944 Rte. 6-A, Brewster • 896-3123/(800) 259-8235 • gay-friendly • 20 min. from Provincetown • women-owned/run

Ireland House 18 Pearl St. • 487-7132/(800) 474-7434 • lesbians/gay men • in the heart of Provincetown • $62-70

John Randall House 140 Bradford St. • 487-3533 • lesbians/gay men

▲ **Lady Jane's Inn** 7 Central St. • 487-3387/(800) 523-9526 • mostly women • women-owned/run • IGTA • $80

Lamplighter Inn 26 Bradford St. • 487-2529 • lesbians/gay men • wonderful views • $40-135

Land's End Inn 22 Commercial St. • 487-0706 • lesbians/gay men

▲ **The Lavender Rose Guest House** 186 Commercial St. • 487-6648 • seasonal • mostly women • patio • women-owned/run

The Little Inn 31 Pearl St. • 487-2407 • women only • women-owned/run • $45-75

Lotus Guest House 296 Commercial St. • 487-4644 • seasonal • lesbians/gay men • decks • gardens

Marigolds B&B PO Box 39, 02652 • 487-9160 • May-Oct • women only • smokefree • women-owned/run • $40-85

Mayflower Apartments 6 Bangs St. • 487-1916 • gay-friendly • kitchens

▲ **Monument House** 129 Bradford St. • 487-9664 • seasonal • lesbians/gay men • 1840s banker's home • very central • deck • IGTA • $60-95

Normandy House 184 Bradford St. • 487-1197 • lesbians/gay men • intimate guest house on the tip of Cape Cod • hot tub • $65-125

Pilgrim House 336 Commercial St. • 487-6424 • mostly women • also a restaurant • full bar

▲ **Plums B&B** 160 Bradford St. • 487-2283 • March-Nov • women only • full brkfst • also condos & apts • $70-95

Provincetown Inn 1 Commercial St. • 487-9500 • gay-friendly • swimming • harbor view restaurant • wheelchair access

▲ **Provincetown Reservations System** 293 Commercial St. #5 • 487-2400/(800) 648-0364 • IGTA

▲ **Ravenwood Guest House** 462 Commercial St. • 487-3203 • mostly women • 1830 Greek Revival • also apts & cottages • $75-145

Red Inn 15 Commercial St. • 487-0050 • lesbians/gay men • elegant waterfront dinner & lodging

Renaissance Apartments 48 Commercial St. • 487-4600 • seasonal • lesbians/gay men • decks

Revere Guesthouse 14 Court St. • 487-2292 • lesbians/gay men • restored 1820s captain's home

Roomers 8 Carver St. • 487-3532 • seasonal • mostly gay men

▲ **Rose Acre** Center St. • 487-2347 • women only • shuttle to beach avail. • $65-145

Rose & Crown Guest House 158 Commercial St. • 487-3332 • lesbians/gay men • Victorian antiques

Sandbars 570 Shore Rd., 02657 • 487-1290 • lesbians/gay men • oceanfront rooms • kitchens • private beach • women-owned/run

Sandpiper Beach House 165 Commerical St. • 487-1928/(800) 354-8628 • popular • lesbians/gay men • Victorian • IGTA • gay-owned/run • $80-135

Seventy Bradford Street 70 Bradford St. • 487-4966 • women only • women-owned/run • $68-80

Shamrock Motel, Cottages & Apartments 49 Bradford St. • 487-1133 • seasonal • gay-friendly • swimming

WINDAMAR HOUSE

Guests

This stately, historic home is located in the quiet, residential East End of town directly across from picturesque Cape Cod Bay. We offer guest rooms and apartments distinctively decorated with antiques and original artwork. The front rooms have water views while rooms on the side and back of the house offer views of English flower gardens and manicured lawns. The common room, a central mingling space, is equipped with sink, refrigerator and cable TV with VCR. Homebaked continental breakfast is provided complimentary every morning for our guest rooms. Guests are encouraged to barbeque, picnic or sunbathe on our beautiful, spacious grounds. Ample on-site parking is provided for all our accommodations.

568 Commercial Street
Provincetown, Massachusetts 02657

508-487-0599

"It's all you'd imagine a grand ole Cape Cod home to be."

Bette Adams, Innkeeper

▲ **Six Webster Place** 6 Webster Pl. • 487-2266/(800) 693-2783 • popular • lesbians/gay men • 1750s B&B • wheelchair access • $50-95

Somerset House 378 Commercial St. • 487-0383 • seasonal • popular • gay-friendly • $60-95

South Hollow Vineyards Rte. 6-A, North Truro • 487-6200 • gay-friendly • women-owned/run

Sunset Inn 142 Bradford St. • 487-9810 • seasonal • lesbians/gay men

Swanberry Inn 8 Johnson St. • 487-4242/(800) 847-7926 • lesbians/gay men • $49-110

Three Peaks 210 Bradford St. • 487-1717/(800) 286-1715 • lesbians/gay men • 1870s Victorian • IGTA • $50-115

Trade Winds 12 Johnson St. • 487-0138 • mostly gay men

▲ **Tucker Inn** 12 Center St. • 487-0381 • seasonal • gay-friendly

Victoria House 5 Standish St. • 487-4455 • lesbians/gay men

Watermark Inn Guest House 603 Commercial St. • 487-2506 • gay-friendly • kitchens • beachside

Watership Inn 7 Winthrop • 487-0094/(800) 330-9413 • popular • lesbians/gay men • $64-95

Westwinds Guest House 28 Commercial St. • 487-1841 • seasonal • lesbians/gay men • swimming

▲ **White Wind Inn** 174 Commercial St. • 487-1526 • lesbians/gay men • 1800s Victorian • women-owned/run • $85-160 (stay 2 nights & get 3rd free)

▲ **Windamar House** 568 Commercial St. • 487-0599 • mostly women • 1840s sea captain's home • women-owned/run • $60-125

Windsor Court 15 Cottage St. • 487-2620 • lesbians/gay men • hot tub • swimming • kitchens

BARS

Back Room (at Crown & Anchor accommodations) • 487-1430 • 10:30pm-1am, seasonal • popular • lesbians/gay men • check locally for women's night • dancing/DJ • live shows

The Boatslip Beach Club (at Boatslip accommodations) • 487-1669 • seasonal • popular • lesbians/gay men • resort • T-dance every day during season • swimming • also a restaurant • cont'l/seafood • some veggie • $10-25

Governor Bradford 312 Commercial St. • 487-9618 • 11am-1am • gay-friendly • food served • check schedule for 'Space Pussy' performance times

The Iguana Grill 135 Bradford St. • 487-8800 • 9am-1am, restaurant from 5pm • mostly gay men • live shows • also a restaurant • Mexican • some veggie

Pied Piper 193-A Commercial St. • 487-1527 • noon-1am • popular • mostly women • dancing/DJ • women-owned/run

Rooster Bar (at the Crown & Anchor accommodations) • 487-1430 • 6pm-1am • lesbians/gay men • more women off-season • neighborhood bar • videos • food served

Town House 291 Commercial St. • 487-0292 • 11am-1am • popular • lesbians/gay men • live shows • food served

Vixen 336 Commercial St. • 487-6424 • 11am-1am • mostly women • dancing/DJ • live shows

Zax 67 Shank Painter Rd. • 487-3122 • food served

RESTAURANTS & CAFES

▲ **Cactus Garden** 186 Commercial St. • 487-6661 • clsd Tue-Wed • Southwestern • plenty veggie • live shows • women-owned/run

Cafe Express 214 Commercial St. • 487-3382 • 9am-2am • lesbians/gay men • vegetarian • wheelchair access • $5-10

Dodie's Diner 401-1/2 Commercial St. • 487-3868 • 8am-10pm • some veggie • women-owned/run • $5-10

Dodie's Pizza 333 Commercial St. • 487-3388 • 9am-2am • popular • women-owned/run

The Flagship 463 Commercial St. • 487-4200 • live shows • women-owned/run

Franco's 133 Bradford St. • 487-3178 • lunch & dinner • popular • lesbians/gay men • some veggie • $15-35 • 'Luigi's' upstairs • Italian

Front Street Restaurant 230 Commercial St. • 487-9715 • 6pm-10:30pm, bar til 1am, April-Oct • lesbians/gay men • full bar • $15-25

Gallerani's 133 Commercial St. • 487-4433 • 8am-2pm, 6am-10:30pm Th-Mon • popular • lesbians/gay men • some veggie • beer/wine • $20-30

Grand Central 5 Masonic St. • 487-7599 • dinner • $15-20

Landmark Inn Restaurant 404 Commercial St. • 487-9319 • dinner nightly 5:30pm-10pm April-Oct • lesbians/gay men • New England fare • $15-25

Lobster Pot 321 Commercial St. • 487-0842 • noon-10pm • seafood • some veggie • wheelchair access • $15-20

Mews 429 Commercial St. • 487-1500 • lunch & dinner, seasonal • popular • cont'l/cafe • some veggie • wheelchair access • $15-30

Napi's 7 Freeman St. • 487-1145 • int'l/seafood • plenty veggie • wheelchair access • $15-25

Post Office Cafe Cabaret 303 Commercial St. (upstairs) • 487-3892 • 8am-midnight (brkfst til 3pm) • lesbians/gay men • live shows • some veggie • $8-15

Pucci's Harborside 539 Commercial St. • 487-1964 • seasonal • popular • some veggie • full bar • wheelchair access • $10-20

Sal's Place 99 Commercial St. • 487-1279 • popular • publisher's choice: cheese & butter pasta

Sebastian's Long & Narrow 177 Commercial St. • 487-3286 • 11am-10pm • wheelchair access • $10-15

Spiritus 190 Commercial St. • 487-2808 • 11am-2am • popular • great espresso shakes & late-night hang out

GYMS & HEALTH CLUBS

The Mussel Beach 33 Bradford St. • 487-0001 • 6am-9pm • lesbians/gay men

The Provincetown Gym Inc. 170 Commercial St. • 487-2776 • lesbians/gay men

BOOKSTORES & RETAIL SHOPS

Don't Panic 192 Commercial St. • 487-1280 • lesbigay gifts • t-shirts

Far Side of the Wind 389 Commercial St. • 487-3963 • 11am-11pm, til 5pm off-season • New Age books & gifts • Native American artifacts • wheelchair access

Now, Voyager 357 Commercial St. • 487-0848 • 11am-11pm, til 5pm off season • lesbigay bookstore

Pride's 182 Commercial St. • 487-1127 • 10am-11pm (in-season) • lesbigay gifts • t-shirts • books

Provincetown Bookshop 246 Commercial St. • 487-0964 • 10am-11pm, til 5pm off-season

Recovering Hearts 2-4 Standish St. • 487-4875 • 10am-11pm (in-season) • recovery • lesbigay & New Age books • wheelchair access

▲ **Womencrafts** 376 Commercial St. • 487-2501 • 10am-11pm

TRAVEL & TOUR OPERATORS

All Provincetown 487-9000/(800) 786-9699 • rental hotline

Cape Air Barnstable Municipal Airport • 771-6944/(800) 352-0714 • IGTA

Portuguese Princess Whale Watch Shank Painter Rd., McMillan Wharf • 487-2651 • day & evening cruises • women's event cruises • wheelchair access • women-owned/run

▲ **RSVP-Town Reservations** PO Box 614, 02657 • 487-1883/(800) 677-8696 • IGTA

Your Way Travel 145 Commercial St. • 487-2992 • IGTA

SPIRITUAL GROUPS

Dignity 1 Commercial St. (Provincetown Inn) • 487-9500 • 10:30am Sun (May-Oct)

PUBLICATIONS

In 398 Columbus Ave., Boston • (617) 426-8246

Provincetown Banner PO Box 1978, 02657 • 487-7400

Provincetown Magazine 14 Center St., 02657 • 487-1000

EROTICA

Wild Hearts 244 Commercial St. • 487-8933 • noon-5pm, til 11pm wknds (seasonal) • toys for women

Randolph   (508)

BARS

Randolph Country Club 44 Mazeo Dr. (Rte. 139) • 961-2414 • 2pm-2am, (10am summer) • popular • lesbians/gay men • dancing/DJ • live shows • volleyball court • swimming • wheelchair access

Springfield   (413)

INFO LINES & SERVICES

Gay/Lesbian Info Service PO Box 80891, 01138 • 731-5403

BARS

David's 397 Dwight St. • 734-0566 • 8pm-2am, clsd Sun-Tue • lesbians/gay men • dancing/DJ • wheelchair access

Just Friends 23 Hampden St. • 781-5878 • 11am-2am • lesbians/gay men • dancing/DJ • videos • wheelchair access

Pub 382 Dwight • 734-8123 • 11am-2am, dinner Fri-Sun & Sun brunch • mostly gay men • neighborhood bar • dancing/DJ • live shows • wheelchair access

TRAVEL & TOUR OPERATORS

A&D Travel 30 Main St., West Springfield • 737-5706/(800) 737-5712 • IGTA

SPIRITUAL GROUPS

Integrity/Western MA Grace Church Chapel, Boltwood Ave., Amherst • 532-5060 • 7pm last Sun

EROTICA

Video Expo 486 Bridge St. • 747-9812

Sturbridge (508)

RESTAURANTS & CAFES

The Casual Cafe 538 Main St. • 347-2281 • 5pm-10pm, clsd Sun-Mon • Italian/Japanese • plenty veggie • BYOB • wheelchair access • lesbian-owned/run • $7-14

Vineyard Haven (508)

ACCOMMODATIONS

Captain Dexter House of Vineyard Haven 100 Main St., Box 2457, 02568 • 693-6564 • gay-friendly • 1840s sea captain's home • $100-165

Waltham (617)

BOOKSTORES & RETAIL SHOPS

Synchronicity Transgender Bookstore 123 Moody St. • 899-2212 • over 100 TG titles

Ware (413)

ACCOMMODATIONS

The Wildwood Inn 121 Church St. • 967-7798 • gay-friendly • full brkfst • wheelchair access • $50-80

Williamstown (413)

ACCOMMODATIONS

River Bend Farm B&B 643 Simonds Rd. • 458-3121 • seasonal • gay-friendly

Worcester (508)

INFO LINES & SERVICES

AA Gay/Lesbian 752-9000

Face the Music WCUM 91.3 FM • 8pm Th • women's radio show

Floating Dance Floor 791-1327 • produces women's dances • call for info

Gay/Lesbian Youth Group PO Box 592, Westside Stn., 01602 • 755-0005 • 24hrs

WOBBLES (West of Boston Lesbians) 478-0242 • 3rd Sun • social group • covers eastern MA

BARS

A-MEN 21-23 Foster St. • 754-7742 • clsd Mon-Tue • lesbians/gay men • dancing/DJ • alternative

Club 241 241 Southbridge • 755-9311 • 6pm-2am, from 2pm wknds, clsd Mon-Wed • popular • lesbians/gay men • dancing/DJ • live shows • rooftop deck • wheelchair access

GYMS & HEALTH CLUBS

Midtown Athletic Club 22 Front St. 2nd flr. • 798-9703 • 8am-8pm • gay-friendly

SPIRITUAL GROUPS

Morning Star MCC 231 Main St. • 892-4320 • 11:15am Sun • wheelchair access

MICHIGAN

Ann Arbor (313)

INFO LINES & SERVICES
Gay/Lesbian Open House 518 E. Washington St. • 665-0606 • 8:45pm Mon

Lesbian/Gay AA 482-5700

Lesbian/Gay Male/Bisexual Programs Office 3116 Michigan Union, 530 S. State St. • 763-4186 • 9am-5pm

Ozone House 608 N. Main St. • 662-2222 • 6:30pm Tue • lesbigay youth support group for ages 12-20

ACCOMMODATIONS
Judy's Place 906 Edgewood Pl. • 662-4812 • gay-friendly • full brkfst • lesbian-owned/run

BARS
The Ark 637-1/2 S. Main St. • 761-1451 • gay-friendly • concert house • women's music shows

\'aut\ Bar 315 Braun Ct. • 994-3677 • 4pm-2am, from 11am Sun(brunch) • lesbians/gay men • American/Mexican • some veggie • patio • wheelchair access • $5-8

Blind Pig 208 S. 1st St. • 996-8555 • 3pm-2am • gay-friendly • neighborhood bar • live bands • wheelchair access

Club Fabulous 763-4186 • lesbians/gay men • monthly chem-free dances during school

Flame Bar 115 W. Washington St. • 662-9680 • 7:30pm-2am • popular • mostly gay men • neighborhood bar

LesBiGay Happy Hour/Social At Dominick's 812 Monroe St. (at Tappan Ave.) • 662-5414 • 7pm-9pm Fri

The Nectarine 516 E. Liberty • 994-5835 • 9pm-2am Tue & Fri only • lesbians/gay men • dancing/DJ • videos

RESTAURANTS & CAFES
The Earle 121 W. Washington • 994-0211 • 6pm-10pm, til midnight Fri-Sat, clsd Sun (summer) • French/Italian • some veggie • beer/wine • wheelchair access • $15-25

Sweet Lorraines 303 Detroit St. • 665-0700 • 11am-10pm, til midnight Fri-Sat • plenty veggie • full bar • patio • wheelchair access • $10-15

BOOKSTORES & RETAIL SHOPS
Borders Book Shop 303 S. State St. • 668-7652 • 9am-9pm, 11am-6pm Sun

Common Language 215 S. 4th Ave. • 663-0036 • open daily • lesbigay • wheelchair access

Crazy Wisdom Books 206 N. 4th Ave. • 665-2757 • 10am-6pm, from noon Sun • holistic/metaphysical

Webster's 2607 Plymouth Rd. • 662-6150 • 8am-11pm • lesbigay section

TRAVEL & TOUR OPERATORS
Horizons Travel 475 Market Pl. • 663-3434/(800) 878-7477 • IGTA

SPIRITUAL GROUPS
Huron Valley MCC 1001 Green Rd. • 434-1452 • 2pm Sun

Atwood (616)

ACCOMMODATIONS
Stelle Wunderschönes 12410 Entrim Dr. • 599-2847 • lesbians/gay men • red cedar log home • full brkfst

Battle Creek (616)

BARS
Partners 910 North Ave. • 964-7276 • 6pm-2am • lesbians/gay men • more women Fri • dancing/DJ • wheelchair access

Belleville (313)

BARS
Granny's Place 9800 Haggerty Rd. • 699-8862 • 11am-2am, from 4pm wknds • live shows • food served • wheelchair access

Detroit (313)

INFO LINES & SERVICES
Affirmations Lesbian/Gay Community Center 195 W. 9-Mile Rd. Ste. 106, Ferndale • (810) 398-7105 • 1pm-6pm, 9am-2pm Sat

Lesbian/Gay Switchboard (810) 398-4297 • 4:30pm-11pm, clsd Sat

Motor City Business Forum (810) 546-9347 • business/social group • call for info

BARS
Backstage/Footlights 214 W. 6th St., Royal Oak • (810) 546-0526 • 4pm-2am, from 11am wknds • lesbians/gay men • live shows • patio • also restaurant • plenty veggie • wheelchair access • $5-15

Backstreet 15606 Joy • 272-8959 • 8pm-2am Wed & Sat • popular • mostly gay men • dancing/DJ • wheelchair access

The Body Shop 22061 Woodward Ave., Ferndale • (810) 398-1940 • 4pm-2am, from 5pm Sat, from 2pm Sun • lesbians/gay men • dancing/DJ • food served • wheelchair access • $5-10

Club Gold Coast 2971 E. 7-Mile Rd. • 366-6135 • popular • mostly gay men • dancing/DJ • live shows • wheelchair access

The Edge 12322 Conant • 891-3343 • 4pm-2am, fropm 2pm wknds • mostly gay men • more women Fri • dancing/DJ • live shows • patio • wheelchair access

Gigi's 16920 W. Warren (rear entrance) • 584-6525 • noon-2am, from 2pm wknds • mostly gay men • dancing/DJ • transgender-friendly • karaoke • live shows

Off Broadway East 12215 Harper St. • 521-0920 • 9pm-2am • mostly gay men • more women Sat • dancing/DJ

Pronto 608 S. Washington, Royal Oak • (810) 544-7900 • 11am-midnight, til 2am Fri & Sat, from 9am wknds • gay-friendly • video bar • food served • wheelchair access

The Rainbow Room 6640 E. 8-Mile Rd. • 891-1020 • 7pm-2am, from noon Sun • lesbians/gay men • dancing/DJ • live shows

Silent Legacy 1641 Middlebelt Rd., Inkster • 729-8980 • 7pm-2am • lesbians/gay men • dancing/DJ • live shows

Stingers Lounge 19404 Sherwood • 892-1765 • 4pm-2am • lesbians/gay men • neighborhood bar • grill menu

Sugarbakers 3800 E. 8-Mile Rd. • 892-5203 • 6pm-2am • mostly women • sports bar & grill

Detroit

*K*nown for its cars and stars, 'Motown' is the home of General Motors and living legends like Aretha Franklin, Diana Ross & the Supremes, the Temptations, Michael Jackson, Stevie Wonder, Anita Baker, and Madonna.

Detroit is also rich in African-American culture. Be sure to check out the Museum of African-American History, multicultural gallery Your Heritage House, the Motown Museum, and lesbian/gay bar **Zippers**. And just under the river—via the Detroit/Windsor Tunnel—is the North American Black Historical Museum in Windsor, Canada.

Downtown, discover the impressive Renaissance Center. This office and retail complex that dominates the city skyline houses shopping, restaurants, a 73-story hotel, and an indoor lake! Before moving on to explore the districts of Greektown, Bricktown, or Rivertown, take a spin around the Civic Center district on the Detroit People Mover, an elevated transit system that carries travellers in automated, weatherproof cars.

You might want to start your stay with a visit to the **Affirmation Lesbian/Gay Community Center** or **A Women's Prerogative**, the women's bookstore, then check out **Sugarbakers**, a women's sports bar.

Zippers 6221 E. Davison • 892-8120 • opens 9pm, from 8pm Sun • popular • lesbians/gay men • dancing/DJ • mostly African-American • live shows • wheelchair access

Restaurants & Cafes

Como's 22812 Woodward, Ferndale • (810) 548-5005 • 11am-2am, til 4am Fri-Sat, from 2pm wknds • American/Italian • some veggie • full bar • wheelchair access • $5-15

Golden Star 22828 Woodward Ave., Ferndale • (810) 545-0994 • open til 1am wknds • Chinese

La Dolce Vita 17546 Woodward Ave. • 865-0331 • 4pm-2am, 11am-midnight Sun, clsd Mon-Tue • lesbians/gay men • Italian • plenty veggie • patio • wheelchair access • $7-16

Lavender Moon Cafe 205 W. 9-Mile Rd., Ferndale • (810) 398-6666 • 11am-11pm, til 2am Fri-Sat, from noon Sun, clsd Mon • live shows • wheelchair access • queer-owned/run

Rhinoceros 265 Riopelle • 259-2208 • 11:30am-2am •jazz club • $15-25

Sweet Lorraines 29101 Greenfield Rd., Southfield • (810) 559-5985 • 11am-10pm, til midnight Fri & Sat • plenty veggie • full bar • $10-15

Vivio's 2460 Market St. • 393-1711 • 7am-9pm, clsd Sun • American/Italian • full bar • $6-11

Bookstores & Retail Shops

A Women's Prerogative Bookstore 175 W. 9-Mile Rd. • (810) 545-5703 • noon-7pm, til 9pm Th, til 5pm Sun, clsd Mon • feminist • wheelchair access

Chosen Books 120 W. 4th St., Royal Oak • (810) 543-5758 • noon-10pm • lesbigay bookstore • wheelchair access

The Dressing Room 42371 Garfield Rd., Clinton Township • (810) 286-0412 • noon-9pm, 10am-5pm Sat, clsd Sun • cross-dressing boutique • larger sizes

Travel & Tour Operators

Royal International Travel Services, Inc. 31455 South Field Rd., Birmingham, 48025 • 644-1600/(800) 521-1600 • IGTA

Spiritual Groups

Dignity-Detroit 6th & Porter St. (Most Holy Trinity) • 961-4818 • 6pm Sun

Divine Peace MCC 23839 John R, Hazel Park • (810) 544-8335 • 10am Sun & 7pm (1st & 3rd Sun only)

Integrity 960 E. Jefferson Ave. (Christ Church) • 259-6688 • 7:30pm 3rd Fri

MCC of Detroit Pinecrest & Dreyton (Christ Church), Ferndale • (810) 399-7741 • 10am & 7pm Sun

Detroit (313)

Where the Girls Are: At the bars on 8-Mile Road between I-75 and Van Dyke Ave., with the boys in Highland Park or Dearborn, or shopping in Royal Oak.

Lesbigay Pride: May: (810) 825-6651.

Annual Events: August - Michigan Womyn's Music Festival: (616) 757-4766. One of the biggest annual gatherings of lesbians in the continent, in Walhalla.

City Info: 259-2680. Directory of Events Hotline: 567-1170 (touchtone).

Attractions: Belle Isle Park. Detroit Institute of Arts. Greektown. Montreux Detroit Jazz Festival. Motown Museum. Museum of African-American History. Renaissance Center.

Best View: From the top of the 73-story Westin Hotel at the Renaissance Center.

Transit: Checker Cab: 963-7000. Radio Cab: (810) 933-1111/283-4800. DOT (bus service): 933-1300.

PUBLICATIONS

Between the Lines 33523 8-Mile Rd. Ste. 185-A3, Livonia, 48152 • (810) 615-7003 • covers southeastern MI

Cruise Magazine 660 Livernois, Ferndale, 48220 • (810) 545-9040

Metra PO Box 71844, Madison Heights, 48071 • (810) 543-3500

EROTICA

Noir Leather 415 S. Main, Royal Oak • (810) 541-3979 • 11am-8pm, 1pm-5pm Sun • also toys & piercing • wheelchair access

Escanaba (906)

BARS

Club Xpress 904 Ludington St. • 789-0140 • 8pm-2am, from 6pm Fri-Sat, clsd Sun-Tue • lesbians/gay men • dancing/DJ • wheelchair access

Flint (810)

BARS

Club Triangle 2101 S. Dort • 767-7552 • 4pm-2am • lesbians/gay men • dancing/DJ • 18+

Merry Inn 2402 N. Franklin St. • 234-9481 • 1pm-2am • popular • lesbians/gay men • neighborhood bar • multi-racial clientele • 18+

State Bar 2512 S. Dort Hwy. • 767-7050 • 4pm-2am, from 1pm wknds • popular • lesbians/gay men • dancing/DJ • karaoke • wheelchair access

SPIRITUAL GROUPS

Redeemer MCC of Flint 1665 N. Chevrolet Ave. • 238-6700 • 11am Sun • wheelchair access

Gaylord (517)

ACCOMMODATIONS

Heritage House B&B 521 E. Main St. • 732-1199 • gay-friendly • full brkfst • $45-75

Glen Arbor (616)

ACCOMMODATIONS

Duneswood Retreat (at Sleeping Bear Dunes Nat'l Lakeshore) • 334-3346 • women only • also 'Marge & Joanne's B&B' • $45-85

Grand Rapids (616)

INFO LINES & SERVICES

Lesbian/Gay Network 909 Cherry SE • 458-3511 • 6pm-10pm, clsd wknds • AA meetings • lounge • library

BARS

The Apartment 33 Sheldon • 451-0815 • 11am-2am, from 1pm Sun • mostly gay men • neighborhood bar • sandwiches served • wheelchair access

The Cell 76 S. Division St. • 454-4499 • 7am-2am, from noon wknds • mostly gay men • dancing/DJ • leather • wheelchair access

The Club 67 67 S. Division Ave. • 454-8003 • 4pm-2am • popular • lesbians/gay men • dancing/DJ • live shows

Diversions 10 Fountain St. NW • 451-3800 • 11am-2am, from 8pm wknds • lesbians/gay men • dancing/DJ • live shows • food served • plenty veggie • wheelchair access • $5-10

Reptile House 242-9955 • gay-friendly • alternative • live shows • 18+ • call for events

Taylors 8 Ionia SW • 454-4422 • 11am-2am, til 4am Fri-Sat, from 6pm Sun • lesbians/gay men • burgers & soup served

RESTAURANTS & CAFES

Cherie Inn 969 Cherry St. • 458-0588 • 8am-3pm, clsd Mon • some veggie • wheelchair access • $4-6

BOOKSTORES & RETAIL SHOPS

Earth & Sky 6 Jefferson SE • 458-3520 • 11am-7pm, clsd Sun • feminist • wheelchair access

Sons & Daughters 962 Cherry SE • 459-8877 • noon-midnight, from 10am wknds • lesbigay bookstore • coffeehouse

TRAVEL & TOUR OPERATORS

Vacation Depot 907 Cherry SE • 454-4339 • ask for Karen • IGTA

SPIRITUAL GROUPS

Dignity 1850 Hall St. • 454-9779 • 7:30pm Wed

Reconciliation MCC 300 Graceland NE • 364-7633 • 10am Sun

Honor (616)

ACCOMMODATIONS

Labrys Wilderness Resort Rte. 1, Box 257 • 882-5994 • women only • $35-55

Kalamazoo (616)

INFO LINES & SERVICES

AA Gay/Lesbian 247 W. Level St. • 343-2711 • 8pm Tue

Alliance for Lesbian/Gay Support PO Box 226, Student Service Bldg., 49008 • 387-2123 • 2pm Sun (Kiba Room)

Kalamazoo Lesbian/Gay Resource Line 345-7878 • 7pm-10pm

Lavender Morning PO Box 729, 49005 • 388-5656 • sponsors women's dances & concerts • newsletter

BARS

Brother's Bar 209 Stockbridge • 345-1960 • 4pm-2am • lesbians/gay men • more women Sat • dancing/DJ • live shows • private club • patio • wheelchair access

Zoo 906 Portage St. • 342-8888 • 4pm-2am • mostly gay men • dancing/DJ • 18+ Sun-Tue

BOOKSTORES & RETAIL SHOPS

Pandora's Books for Open Minds 226 W. Lovell St. • 388-5656 • 11am-7pm, til 6pm Fri-Sat, clsd Sun-Mon • feminist/lesbigay

Triangle World 551 Portage St. • 373-4005 • noon-10pm, clsd Mon • lesbigay books • leather • gifts

SPIRITUAL GROUPS

Phoenix Community Church 1758 N. 10th St. (Peoples Church) • 381-3222 • 6pm Sun • wheelchair access

Lansing   (517)

INFO LINES & SERVICES

AA Gay/Lesbian 1118 S. Harrison St. (United Ministries), E. Lansing • 321-8781

Lansing Lesbian/Gay Hotline 332-3200 • 7pm-10pm Mon-Fri, 2pm-5pm Sun

Michigan Alliance for Lesbian/Gay Youth Service 484-0946 • statewide network for sexual minority youth

Our Living Room Concert Series 303 S. Holmes • 487-6495 • 7:30pm 1st Sat • women's music for women only & boys up to 6 yrs.

BARS

Club 505 505 Shiawassee • 374-6312 • 6pm-2am, til 3am wknds • mostly women • neighborhood bar • dancing/DJ

Esquire 1250 Turner • 487-5338 • noon-2am • mostly older gay men • neighborhood bar • wheelchair access

Paradise 224 S. Washington Square • 484-2399 • 9pm-2am • popular • mostly gay men • dancing/DJ • live shows

BOOKSTORES & RETAIL SHOPS

Community News Center 418 Frandor Shopping Center • 351-7562 • 9am-9pm, til 7pm Sun • wheelchair access

Real World Emporium 1214-16 Turner St. • 485-2665 • noon-8pm, clsd Mon • lesbigay books • cafe • wheelchair access

SPIRITUAL GROUPS

Dignity 327 M.A.C. (St. John's Parish), E. Lansing • 8pm Tue

Ecclesia 3020 S. Washington Ave. (church) • 7pm Sun

PUBLICATIONS

Lesbian Connection PO Box 811, E. Lansing, 48826 • 371-5257 • nationwide grassroots forum for all lesbians

Marquette   (906)

BOOKSTORES & RETAIL SHOPS

Sweet Violets 413 N. 3rd St. • 228-3307 • 10am-6pm, clsd Sun • feminist bookstore

Midland   (517)

ACCOMMODATIONS

Jay's B&B 4429 Bay City Rd. • 496-2498 • gay-friendly • deck • $50

TRAVEL & TOUR OPERATORS

Travel Together PO Box 1453, 48641 • 835-3452/(800) 433-5442

Mount Clemens   (810)

BARS

Mirage 27 N. Walnut • 954-1919 • 4pm-2am, from 2pm wknds • lesbians/gay men • dancing/DJ

Muskegon   (616)

SPIRITUAL GROUPS

Muskegon MCC Christ Community Church, Spring Lake • 861-5275 • 6pm Sun

New Buffalo   (708)

ACCOMMODATIONS

A Women's Place 17 W. Mechanic St. • 446-7638 • women only • rental home • also retreat w/ workshops & seminars • swimming • food served

Niles

INFO LINES & SERVICES

LSG PO Box 1281, 49120 • lesbian support/social group • newsletter

Owendale   (517)

ACCOMMODATIONS

Windover Resort 3596 Blakely Rd. • 375-2586 • women only • campsites • swimming • $20

Pontiac (810)

BARS

Club Flamingo 352 Oakland Ave. • 253-0430 • 2pm-2am • lesbians/gay men • dancing/DJ • live shows • wheelchair access

Port Huron (810)

BARS

Seekers 3301 24th St. • 985-9349 • 4pm-2am, from 2pm Th-Sun • lesbians/gay men • dancing/DJ

Saginaw (517)

BARS

Bambi's 1742 E. Genessee • 752-9179 • 7pm-2am • lesbians/gay men • dancing/DJ • live shows

Heidelberg 411 S. Franklin • 771-9508 • 4pm-2am, from noon wknds • mostly older gay men • neighborhood bar • wheelchair access

Saugatuck (616)

ACCOMMODATIONS

Camp It Rte. 6635 118th Ave., Fennville • 543-4335 • seasonal • lesbians/gay men • campsites & RV hookups

Deerpath Lodge 857-3337 • women only • on 45 secluded acres near beach • $80-90

Douglas Dunes Resort PO Box 369, Douglas, 49406 • 857-1401 • mostly gay men • swimming • food served • women's wknds: 1st week in April & Oct • $42-125

Drift-Woods 2731 Lakeshore Dr., Fennville • 857-2586 • mostly women • retreat w/ cottages • swimming • kitchens • $65

Grandma's House B&B 2135 Blue Star Hwy. • 543-4706 • lesbians/gay men • Victorian country estate • full brkfst • hot tub • $70-80

Hillby Thatch Cottages 1438 & 1440 71st, Glenn • 864-3553 • gay-friendly • cottages • kitchens • fireplaces • women-owned/run

Kirby House PO Box 1174, 49406 • 857-2904 • gay-friendly • Queen Anne Victorian • full brkfst • swimming • $75-115

▲ **The Lighthouse Motel** 130th Ave & Blue Star Hwy., 49406 • 857-2271 • seasonal • gay-friendly • swimming • wheelchair access • $65-110

Moore's Creek Inn 820 Holland St. • 857-2411/(800) 838-5864 • gay-friendly • old-fashioned farmhouse • full brkfst • $75-85

The New Richmond Guest House 3037 57th St. • 561-2591 • lesbians/gay men • full brkfst

The Newnham SunCatcher Inn 131 Griffith • 857-4249 • gay-friendly • full brkfst • hot tub • swimming • $75-120

BARS

Douglas Disco (at Douglas Dunes resort) • 857-1401 • mostly gay men • dancing/DJ • live shows

RESTAURANTS & CAFES

Cafe Sir Douglas (at Douglas Dunes resort) • 857-1401 • 5pm-10pm, til 11pm Fri-Sat, clsd Tue-Wed • cont'l • some veggie • $10-20

Loaf & Mug 236 Culver St. • 857-2974 • 8am-3pm, til 8pm Fri-Sat • some veggie • $5-10

Pumpernickel's 202 Butler St. • 857-1196 • 8am-4pm • sandwiches/fresh breads • some veggie • $5-10

Restaurant Toulouse 248 Culver St. • 857-1561 • lunch & dinner • country French • some veggie • full bar • wheelchair access • $10-20

Uncommon Grounds 123 Hoffman • 857-3333 • coffee & juice bar

BOOKSTORES & RETAIL SHOPS

Hoopdee Scootee 133 Mason • 857-4141 • 10am-9pm, til 6pm Sun, til 5pm winter • clothing • gifts

Sault Ste. Marie   (906)

BOOKSTORES & RETAIL SHOPS

Open Mind Books 223 Ashmun St. • 635-9008 • 10am-5pm (9am-7:30pm summer), clsd Sun • progressive • wheelchair access

St. Clair   (810)

ACCOMMODATIONS

William Hopkins Manor 613 N. Riverside Ave. • 329-0188 • gay-friendly • full brkfst

Traverse City   (616)

INFO LINES & SERVICES

Friends North 946-1804 • networking & social group • newsletter

ACCOMMODATIONS

The Interlochen 2275 M-137, Interlochen • 276-9291 • seasonal • gay-friendly • also coffeehouse 5pm-1am • wheelchair access

Neahtawanta Inn 1308 Neathawanta Rd. • 223-7315 • gay-friendly • swimming • sauna

BARS

Side Traxx Nite Club 520 Franklin • 935-1666 • 6pm-2am, from 2pm wknds • lesbians/gay men • dancing/DJ • live shows • wheelchair access

BOOKSTORES & RETAIL SHOPS

The Bookie Joint 120 S. Union St. • 946-8862 • 10am-6pm, clsd Sun • used books

Ypsilanti   (313)

SPIRITUAL GROUPS

Tree of Life MCC 218 N. Adams St. (1st Congregational Church) • 485-3922 • 6pm Sun & Wed

EROTICA

The Magazine Rack 515 West Cross • 482-6944

Saugatuck   (616)

CITY INFO: Saugatuck-Douglas convention & Visitors Bureau: 857-1701.

ATTRACTIONS: Saugatuck is a quaint resort town on the shores of Lake Michigan. The main tourists sites are its beaches, dunes and orchards. (If you've never been to one of the Great Lakes you'll think you made a wrong turn in Albuquerque and ended up on the shore of an ocean.) The historic city of Holland, home of the Wooden Shoe Factory, is also nearby.

MINNESOTA

Bemidji (218)

ACCOMMODATIONS
Meadowgrove Inn 13661 Powerdam Rd. NE • 751-9654 • gay-friendly • rural hideaway on 130 acres • full brkfst • lunch & dinner avail.

Duluth (218)

INFO LINES & SERVICES
Aurora: A Northern Lesbian Center 32 E. 1st St. #104 • 722-4903 • discussion groups & socials

ACCOMMODATIONS
Stanford Inn B&B 1415 E. Superior St. • 724-3044 • gay-friendly

BOOKSTORES & RETAIL SHOPS
At Sara's Table 728 E. Superior St. • 723-8569 • 8am-6pm • also cafe • wheelchair access • women-owned/run

Ely (218)

TRAVEL & TOUR OPERATORS
The Northern Alternative 36 N. 2nd Ave. W. • 365-2894/(800) 774-7520 • canoe outfitting & trips • also B&B avail. • mostly women • lesbian-owned/run • $35-40

Hastings (612)

ACCOMMODATIONS
Thorwood & Rosewood Inns 315 Pine St. • 437-3297 • gay-friendly • circa 1880 mansion • full brkfst

Hill City (218)

ACCOMMODATIONS
Northwoods Retreat 5749 Mt. Ash Dr. • 697-8119 • lesbians/gay men • 2 cabins w/700 ft. of lakeshore • all meals included • wheelchair access

Hinckley (612)

ACCOMMODATIONS
Dakota Lodge B&B Rte. 3, Box 178 • 384-6052 • gay-friendly • lodge on 9 acres • full brkfst • hot tub • wheelchair access

Kenyon (507)

ACCOMMODATIONS
Dancing Winds Farm 6863 Country 12 Blvd. • 789-6606 • lesbians/gay men • B&B on working dairy farm • tentsites • full brkfst • work exchange avail. • women-owned/run

Mankato (507)

INFO LINES & SERVICES
Mankato State U. Lesbigay Center 389-5131

RESTAURANTS & CAFES
The Coffee Hag 329 N. Riverfront • 387-5533 • 9am-11pm, 11am-6pm Sun, clsd Mon • veggie menu • live shows • wheelchair access • women-owned/run • $3-7

Minneapolis/St. Paul (612)

INFO LINES & SERVICES
Chrysalis Women's Center 2650 Nicollett Ave., St. Paul • 871-0118 • 8:30am-8pm Mon-Th, til 5pm Fri • many women's groups

District 202 2524 Nicollet Ave. S., St. Paul • 871-5559 • 3pm-11pm, 3pm-1am Fri, noon-1am Sat, clsd Sun & Tue • resource center for lesbigay youth

▲ **Dyke TV** Channel 33, Minneapolis • 10:30pm Mon • 'weekly half hour TV show produced by lesbians, for lesbians'

Fresh Fruit KFAI 90.3 FM, Minneapolis • 341-0980 • 7pm-8pm Th, gay radio program • 3-3:30pm Th, 'WINGS' (Women's Int'l News Gathering Svc) • 1pm-3pm Sat, 'Womenfolk' • 9pm-10:30pm Sun, 'Lesbian Power Authority'

Gay/Lesbian Community Action Council 310 E. 38th St., Minneapolis • 822-0127/(800) 800-0350 • 9am-5pm Mon-Fri • support groups

Gay/Lesbian Helpline 822-8661/(800) 800-0907(in-state) • noon-midnight, from 4pm Sat, clsd Sun & holidays • covers IA, MN, NE, ND, SD, WI

GLEAM (Gay/Lesbian Elders Active in MN) 1505 Park Ave., Minneapolis • 721-8913 • 1pm 2nd Sun

Green & Yellow TV Cable Channel 6, St. Paul • 11pm Th • gay news hour

Lambda AA 874-7430

Quatrefoil Library 1619 Dayton Ave., St. Paul • 641-0969 • 7pm-9pm Mon-Th, 1pm-4pm wknds • lesbigay library & resource center

U of MN Gay/Lesbian/Bi/Transsexual Groups 230 Coffman Memorial Library, Minneapolis • 626-2344 • 4:30pm Wed

WomenWorks PO Box 300106, Minneapolis, 55403 • 377-9114 • professional women's events

Womyn's Braille Press PO Box 8475, Minneapolis, 55408 • 872-4352 • quarterly newsletter • resource & info exchange

ACCOMMODATIONS

Abbotts Como Villa B&B 1371 W. Nebraska Ave., St. Paul • 647-0471 • lesbians/gay men • centrally located • full brkfst wknds

Eagle Cove B&B W 4387 120th Ave., Maiden Rock WI • (715) 448-4302/(800) 467-0279 • lesbians/gay men • hot tub • wheelchair access

Garden Gate B&B 925 Goodrich Ave., St. Paul • 227-8430/(800) 967-2703 • gay-friendly • massage avail.

Hotel Amsterdam 828 Hennepin Ave., Minneapolis • 288-0459/(800) 649-9500 • lesbians/gay men • European-style lodging

Nan's B&B 2304 Freemont Ave. S., Minneapolis • 377-5118/(800) 214-5118 • gay-friendly • 1895 Victorian family home

BARS

19 Bar 19 W. 15th St., Minneapolis • 871-5553 • 3pm-1am, from 1pm wknds • mostly gay men • neighborhood bar • beer/wine • wheelchair access

Brass Rail 422 Hennepin Ave., Minneapolis • 333-3016 • noon-1am • popular • mostly gay men • karaoke • videos • wheelchair access

Bryant Lake Bowl 1810 W. Lake Bowl, Minneapolis • 825-3737 • 8am-2am • gay-friendly • also theater • restaurant • bowling alley • wheelchair access

Checkers 1066 E. 7th St., St. Paul • 776-7915 • 6pm-1am • mostly gay men • dancing/DJ • live shows • wheelchair access

Club Metro 733 Pierce Butler Rte., St. Paul • 489-0002 • 3pm-1am • popular • mostly women • dancing/DJ • transgender-friendly • live shows • food served • $5-15 • women-owned/run

Gay 90s 408 Hennepin Ave., Minneapolis • 333-7755 • 8am-1am (dinner nightly 5pm-9pm) • lesbians/gay men • 5 bar complex • dancing/DJ • live shows • also erotica store • wheelchair access

Minneapolis (612)

LESBIGAY PRIDE: July: 339-8203.

ANNUAL EVENTS: September - Northern Lights Womyn's Music Festival (218) 722-4903.

CITY INFO: 348-4313 St. Paul Visitors' Bureau: 297-6985.

ATTRACTIONS: Minneapolis Institue of Arts. Minneapolis Sculpture Garden & Walker Art Center. Minnesota Zoo. St. Anthony Main Historic Waterfront Shopping & Entertainment Center.

BEST VIEW: Observation deck of the 32nd story of Foshay Tower (closed in winter).

WEATHER: Winters are harsh. If driving, carry extra blankets and supplies. The average temperature is 19°, and it can easily drop well below 0°, and then there's the wind chill! Summer temperatures are usually in the upper 80°s to mid-90°s.

TRANSIT: Town Taxi - Minn. : 331-8294. Yellow Cab - St. Paul: 222-4433. Airport Express: 827-7777. MTC: 349-7000.

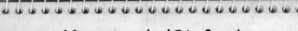

Minneapolis/St. Paul

*I*f you're searching for a liberal oasis in the heartland of America, if you love Siberian winters or if you crave a diverse, intensely political lesbian community, you'll fit right into the 'Twin Cities' of Minneapolis and St. Paul.

Located on the banks of the Mississippi River, the cities share the Minnesota Twins, 936 lakes & 513 parks, and a history of Native American and Northern European settlements. If you want more than glimpses into the various cultures of Minnesota, visit the Minneapolis American Indian Center or the American Swedish Institute.

Of course, you'll probably have more fun checking out the lesbian cultural scene. The place to go to find out about the latest poetry reading, play, or concert is **Amazon Bookstore** in Minneapolis. To find social groups for women of color, call the **Gay/Lesbian Community Action Council**.

Or stop by **Minnesota Women's Press** bookstore and library in St. Paul. Then go cafe-hopping in Minneapolis at the women-owned **Cafe Wyrd** or **Ruby's Cafe**. For a night on the town, you won't find any women's bars, but **Club Metro** is popular on weekends.

Whatever you do, don't stay indoors the whole time. In the summer, boating, fishing, sunbathing, water-skiing, walking, jogging, and bicycling are all popular. With winter, you can enjoy snowmobiling, ice hockey, cross-country skiing or snuggling by a fire. For women's outdoor adventures, try **Women in the Wilderness** in St. Paul or **Woodswomen** in Minneapolis.

Innuendo 510 N. Robert St., St. Paul • 224-8996 • 4pm-1am, clsd Sun • lesbians/gay men • neighborhood bar • wheelchair access

Over the Rainbow 249 W. 7th St., St. Paul • 228-7180 • 3pm-1am, from noon wknds • lesbians/gay men • dancing/DJ • karaoke • live shows

Rumours 490 N. Robert St., St. Paul • 224-0703 • 4pm-1am, from noon wknds • lesbians/gay men • dancing/DJ • also a restaurant • live shows • wheelchair access

The Saloon 830 Hennepin Ave., Minneapolis • 332-0835 • 9am-1am, til 3am Fri-Sun • mostly gay men • dancing/DJ • grill menu • $3-6 • wheelchair access

The Times Bar & Cafe 1036 Nicollet Ave., Minneapolis • 333-2762 • 11am-1am • lesbians/gay men • live shows • 'comfort food' • some veggie • $5-19 • wheelchair access

Town House 1415 University Ave., St. Paul • 646-7087 • 2pm-1am, from noon wknds • popular • lesbians/gay men • dancing/DJ • country/western

RESTAURANTS & CAFES

Cafe Wyrd 1600 W. Lake St., Minneapolis • 827-5710 • 7am-midnight • lesbians/gay men • plenty veggie • women-owned/run • $3-6

Cafe Zev 1362 LaSalle Ave., Minneapolis • 874-8477 • live shows

La Covina 1570 Selby Ave., St. Paul • 645-5288 • Mexican • wheelchair access • $6-10

Ole & Lena's 33rd & Bryant Ave. S., Minneapolis • 824-6611 • coffeeshop

Ruby's Cafe 1614 Harmon Pl., Minneapolis • 338-2089 • 7am-2pm, from 8am Sun • popular • lesbians/gay men • outdoor seating • women-owned/run • $5

Rudolph's Bar-B-Que 1933 Lyndale, Minneapolis • 871-8969 • 11am-midnight • wheelchair access

Safari 1424 Nicollet Ave., Minneapolis • 872-6375 • 7am-10pm, from 8am Sat, from 9am Sun • Egyptian • plenty veggie

Susan's Coffeehouse & Deli 2399 University Ave., Minneapolis • 644-7906 • 7am-5:30pm, 9am-4pm Sat, clsd Sun

Vintage Joe's 1008 Marquette Ave., Minneapolis • 371-9882 • 6am-midnight, 8am-2am Sat • wheelchair access

GYMS & HEALTH CLUBS

Body Quest 245 N. Aldrich Ave. N., Minneapolis • 377-7222 • gay-friendly

BOOKSTORES & RETAIL SHOPS

A Brother's Touch 2327 Hennepin Ave., Minneapolis • 377-6279 • 11am-9pm, til 5pm wknds, til 7pm Mon-Tue • lesbigay bookstore • wheelchair access

Amazon Bookstore 1612 Harmon Pl., Minneapolis • 338-6560 • 10am-9pm, til 7pm Fri, til 6pm Sat, til 5pm Sun • women's • wheelchair access

Borders Bookshop 3001 Hennepin S. (Calhoun Square), Minneapolis • 825-0336

Magus Books 1316 SE 4th St., Minneapolis • 379-7669 • noon-8pm, til 5pm wknds • alternative spirituality books & supplies • also mail order

The Rainbow Road 109 W. Grant, Minneapolis • 872-8448 • 10am-10pm • lesbigay retail & video • wheelchair access

TRAVEL & TOUR OPERATORS

All Airlines Travel 111 E. Kellogg Blvd. #225, St. Paul • 222-2210/(800) 832-0304 • IGTA

Partners In Travel, Ltd. 825 Nicollet Mall, Minneapolis • 338-0004/(800) 333-3177 • IGTA

The Travel Company 2800 University Ave. SE, Minneapolis • 379-9000/(800) 328-9131 • IGTA

Travel Quest 245 Aldrich Ave. N., Minneapolis • 377-7700/(800) 373-7244 • IGTA

Women in the Wilderness 566 Ottawa Ave., St. Paul • 227-2284 • outdoor adventure trips: canoeing, rafting, dogsledding, skiing, etc. • women-owned/run

Woodswomen 25 W. Diamond Lake Rd., Minneapolis • 822-3809/(800) 279-0555 • outdoor adventures • 1 day to 3 wks • domestic & int'l • also newsletter • women-owned/run

SPIRITUAL GROUPS

Dignity Twin Cities Prospect Park Unitarian Methodist (Malcom & Orwin), Minneapolis • 827-3103 • 7:30pm 2nd & 4th Fri

Integrity/Twin Cities 317 17th Ave. SE (Univ. Episcopal Ctr.), Minneapolis • 331-3552 • 7pm 1st Fri

Lutherans Concerned 100 N. Oxford, Minneapolis • 224-3371 • 7:30pm 3rd Fri • wheelchair access

MCC All God's Children 3100 Park Ave., Minneapolis • 824-2673 • 10am & 7pm Sun, 7pm Wed • wheelchair access

Shir Tikvah 5000 Girard Ave., Minneapolis • 822-1440 • 10am 1st Sat, then 8pm every Fri • lesbigay Jewish congregation

PUBLICATIONS

Focus Point 401 N. 3rd St. # 480, Minneapolis, 55401 • 288-9000

Lavender Lifestyles 2344 Nicollet Ave. Ste. 130, Minneapolis, 55404 • 871-2237

Maize PO Box 8742, Minneapolis, 55408 • lesbian country magazine

Matrices Women Studies Dept. U of MN, Minneapolis, 55455 • newsletter • also lesbian feminist resource network

Minnesota Women's Press 771 Raymond Ave., St. Paul • 646-3968 • newpaper • also bookshop & library • 9am-6pm, til 3pm Sat, clsd Sun

Q Monthly 10 S. 5th St. #200, Minneapolis, 55402 • 321-7300

EROTICA

Broadway Bookstore 901 Hennepin Ave., Minneapolis • 338-7303 • 24hrs

Rochester (507)

INFO LINES & SERVICES

Gay/Lesbian Community Service PO Box 454, 55903 • 281-3265 • 5pm-7pm Mon & Wed

Rushford (507)

ACCOMMODATIONS

Windswept Inn 2070 N. Mill St. • 864-2545 • gay-friendly

St. Peter (507)

ACCOMMODATIONS

Park Row B&B 525 W. Park Row • 931-2495 • gay-friendly • full brkfst

Two Harbors (218)

ACCOMMODATIONS

Star Harbor Resort 1098 Hwy. 61 E. • 834-3796 • gay-friendly • log cabins on the N. shore of Lake Superior • wheelchair ramps avail.

Wolverton (218)

RESTAURANTS & CAFES

District 31 Victoria's 995-2000 • 5:30pm-9:30pm, clsd Sun • cont'l • beer/wine • reservations required • $15-25

MISSISSIPPI

Biloxi (601)

INFO LINES & SERVICES

Gay/Lesbian Community Center 308 Caillavet St. • 396-3333 • 1pm-9pm, from 5pm Sun-Wed

BARS

Joey's 1708 Beach Blvd. (Hwy. 90) • 435-5639 • 9pm-2am, til 5am Fri-Sat, clsd Mon • lesbians/gay men • dancing/DJ • live shows

EROTICA

Satellite News 1632 Pass Rd. • 432-8229 • clsd Sun

Florence (601)

INFO LINES & SERVICES

Aurora Transgender Group PO Box 1306, 39073 • 373-8610x60/845-1328 • transgendered support in central MS

Hattiesburg (601)

BARS

The Courtyard 107 E. Front St. • 545-2714 • hours vary • lesbians/gay men • dancing/DJ • food served • live shows

Holly Springs (601)

ACCOMMODATIONS

Somerset Cottage 310 S. Cedar Hills Rd. • 252-4513 • gay-friendly • smokefree

Jackson (601)

INFO LINES & SERVICES

Gay/Lesbian Community Info-Line PO Box 4362, 39296-4362 • 346-4380/435-2398 • voicemail for many organizations • monthly publication

Lambda AA 4872 N. State St. (Unitarian Church) • 346-4379 • 6:30pm Mon & Wed, 8pm Sat

MGLTF (MS Gay/Lesbian Task Force) PO Box 4362, 39296-4362 • 346-4379 • also contact for AIDS project & MS monthly publications

BARS

Club City Lights 200 N. Mill St. • 353-0059 • 10pm-? Wed, Fri-Sun • lesbians/gay men • dancing/DJ • mostly African-American • live shows • beer/wine • BYOB

Jack's Construction Site (JC's) 425 N. Mart Plaza • 362-3108 • 5pm-?, from 2pm Sun • mostly gay men • more women Wed & Fri • neighborhood bar • beer/wine • BYOB

Spiritual Groups

Affirmation PO Box 4362, 39296 • 346-4379 • United Methodist gays & lesbians

Integrity Mississippi PO Box 68314, 39286 • 373-8610x47 • lesbigay Episcopalians

MCC of the Rainbow 5565 Robinson Rd. Ext. Ste. L • 992-6227/373-8610x45 • 11:30am Sun

Safe Harbor Family Church 2147 Henry Hill Dr. #203 • 373-8610x44 • 6pm Sun & 7pm Wed • non-denominational • social events • support groups

St. Stephen's Community Church 4872 N. State St. • 939-7181/373-8610x43 • 5pm 1st & 3rd Sun

Publications

Mississippi Voice PO Box 7737, 39284-7737 • 346-4378

Erotica

Terry Road Books 1449 Terry Rd. • 353-9156 • 24hrs

Meridian (601)

Bars

Crossroads Rte. 1, Box 170, Enterprise, 39330 • 655-8415 • 6pm-1am Fri, til 6am Sat • lesbians/gay men • dancing/DJ • live shows • call for directions • cabins avail. • wheelchair access

Olie Mae's at Crossroads, Enterprise • 655-8415 • 6pm-1am • gay-friendly • wheelchair access

Ovett (601)

Accommodations

Camp Sister Spirit PO Box 12, 39462 • 344-2005 • mostly women • 120 acres of camping & RV sites • $10-20

Starkville (601)

Info Lines & Services

Lesbigay Student Group PO Box 6220, MS State University, 39406 • 325-1321

MISSOURI

Branson (417)

Accommodations

Pine Wood B&B PO Box 572 • 779-5514 • gay-friendly • full brkfst • hot tub • smoke-free

Cape Girardeau (314)

Bars

Independence Place 5 S. Henderson St. • 334-2939 • 8:30pm-1:30am, from 7:30pm Fri-Sat, clsd Sun • lesbians/gay men • dancing/DJ • transgender-friendly • live shows Sat

Columbia (573)

Info Lines & Services

Gay/Lesbian Helpline 449-4477

Triangle Coalition A02 Brady Commons UMC, 65211 • 882-4427 • meets 7pm Th • also GLBGSA (Gay/Lesbian/Bisexual Graduate Student Association)

Women's Center 229 Brady Commons UMC • 882-6621

World Women KOPN 89.50 FM • 874-5676 • 10am-noon Tue

Bars

Contacts 514 E. Broadway • 443-0281 • 5pm-1:30am, from 8pm Sat, clsd Sun • lesbians/gay men • neighborhood bar • dancing/DJ • live shows

Styx Inc. 3111 Old 63 S. • 499-1828 • 3pm-1:30am, clsd Sun • lesbians/gay men • dancing/DJ • country/western Tue • patio

Restaurants & Cafes

Ernie's Cafe 1005 E. Walnut • 874-7804 • 6am-8pm • brkfst anytime • some veggie

Spiritual Groups

Christ the King Agape Church 515 Hickman Ave. • 443-5316 • 10:45am Sun & 6:30pm Wed

United Covenant Church PO Box 7152, 65205 • 449-7194 • 10am Sun • non-denominational • wheelchair access

Erotica

Eclectics 1122-A Wilkes Blvd. • 443-0873

Jefferson City (573)

Accommodations

Jefferson Victorian B&B 801 W. High St. • 635-7196 • gay-friendly

Joplin (417)

BARS

Partners 720 Main St. • 781-6453 • 3pm-1:30am, clsd Sun • lesbians/gay men • neighborhood bar • dancing/DJ • country/western

Kansas City (816)

INFO LINES & SERVICES

Gay Talk Crisis Line 931-4470 • 6pm-midnight

Live & Let Live AA 4243 Walnut St. • 531-9668 • many mtgs

Unicorn Theatre 3820 Main • 531-3033 • contemporary American theater

ACCOMMODATIONS

B&B in KC 9215 Slater, Overland Park • (913) 648-5457 • women only • full brkfst • smokefree

Doanleigh Wallagh Inn 217 E. 37th St. • 753-2667 • gay-friendly • full brkfst • smokefree • reservations required • lesbian-owned/run

Inn The Park 3610 Gillham Rd. • 931-0797/(800) 708-6748 • gay-friendly • full brkfst • swimming • smokefree

BARS

Cabaret 5024 Main St. • 753-6504 • 6pm-3am, from 3pm Sun, clsd Mon • popular • mostly gay men • dancing/DJ • food served • wheelchair access

Dixie Bell Saloon 1922 Main St. • 471-2424 • 11am-3am • popular • mostly gay men • leather • live shows • also leather shop • wheelchair access

The Edge 323 W. 8th (in the Lucas Place Bldg.) • 221-8900 • popular • lesbians/gay men • dancing/DJ • alternative • live shows • wheelchair access

The Fox 7520 Shawnee Mission Pkwy., Overland Park • 384-0369 • noon-2am, from 6pm Sat, clsd Sun • gay-friendly • neighborhood bar • more gay evenings

Jamie's 528 Walnut • 471-2080 • 10am-2am • mostly women • neighborhood bar • dancing/DJ • country/western • grill menu • wheelchair access

Mari's Saloon & Grill 1809 Grand Blvd. • 283-0511 • 5pm-10pm, from 11am Sun • lesbians/gay men • dancing/DJ • videos • food served • $5-12 • wheelchair access

Missie B's 805 W. 39th St. • 561-0625 • 11am-3am • mostly gay men • neighborhood bar • live shows

Other Side 3611 Broadway • 931-0501 • 3:30pm-1:30am, clsd Sun • mostly gay men • neighborhood bar • videos

Sidekicks 3707 Main St. • 931-1430 • 2pm-3am, clsd Sun • mostly gay men • dancing/DJ • country/western • wheelchair access

Soakie's 1308 Main St. • 221-6060 • 9am-1:30am, til 3am Fri-Sat, from 11am Sun • mostly gay men • dancing/DJ • mostly African-American • food served

Ted's Bar & Grill 529 Walnut • 472-0569 • 7am-1:30am, 11am-midnight Sun • gay-friendly • neighborhood bar • country/western • lunch served daily

Tootsie's 1822 Main • 471-7704 • 11:30am-1am • popular • mostly women • dancing/DJ • grill menu • some veggie • $3-6

View on the Hill 204 Orchard, Kansas City, KS • (913) 371-9370 • 4pm-2am, from noon wknds • mostly gay men • neighborhood bar

RESTAURANTS & CAFES

City Seen 1111 Main St. • 472-8833 • 11am-7pm, til 10pm Fri-Sat • some veggie • full bar • wheelchair access • $9-13

Classic Cup Cafe 301 W. 47th St. • 753-1840 • 7am-midnight, til 1am Fri-Sat • cont'l • some veggie • full bar • wheelchair access • $9-17

The Coffeehouse 1719 W. 39th St. • 756-1997 • 7am-midnight, from 8am wknds • also 318 E. 51st St. • 756-3121 • plenty veggie

The Corner Restaurant 4059 Broadway • 931-6630 • 7am-9pm, til 2am wknds • some veggie • beer/wine • wheelchair access • $5-7

Metropolis 303 Westport Rd. • 753-1550 • lunch & dinner, clsd Sun • popular • lesbians/gay men • wheelchair access • $9-17

Otto's Malt Shop 3903 Wyoming • 756-1010 • 11am-midnight, 24hrs wknds • burgers & malts

BOOKSTORES & RETAIL SHOPS

Larry's Gifts & Cards 205 Westport Rd. • 753-4757 • 10am-7pm, til 5pm Sun • lesbigay books

SPIRITUAL GROUPS

MCC of Johnson County 12510 W. 62nd Terrace #106, Shawnee KS, 66216 • (913) 631-1184 • 10:30am Sun & 7:30pm Wed

Spirit of Hope MCC 3801 Wyandotte • 931-0750 • 10:15 Sun & 7:15pm Wed

PUBLICATIONS

Current News 809 W. 39th St. Ste. 1 • 561-2679

News Telegraph PO Box 10085, 64171 • 561-6266/(800) 303-5468

Women's Yellow Pages of Greater Kansas City 10308 Metcalf #178, Overland Park KS • (913) 685-4940

EROTICA

Adrianne's Book Store 3314 Troust • 561-8996

Erotic City 8401 E. Truman Rd. • 252-3370 • 24hrs • boutique • books • lounge

Extremus 4037 Broadway • 756-1142 • noon-8pm, clsd Sun • body piercing

Hollywood at Home 9063 Metcalf, Overland Park • (913) 649-9666

Noel (417)

ACCOMMODATIONS

Sycamore Landing Drawer H, Hwy. 59 S., 64854 • 475-6460 • open May-Sept • campsites & canoe rental

Springfield (417)

INFO LINES & SERVICES

AA Gay/Lesbian SMS University at Ecumenical Ctr. (National off Cherry) • 862-9264 • 6pm Sat

BARS

The Gallery 424 N. Boonville • 865-1266 • 1pm-1:30am, clsd Sun • lesbians/gay men

Martha's Vineyard 219 W. Olive St. • 864-4572 • 4pm-1:30am, from 2pm Sat, clsd Sun • lesbians/gay men • neighborhood bar • 18+

RESTAURANTS & CAFES

Black Forest Inn 2185 S. Campbell • 882-6767 • 3pm-11pm • lesbians/gay men • full bar • live shows • $5-16

BOOKSTORES & RETAIL SHOPS

Renaissance Books & Gifts 1337 E. Montclair • 883-5161 • women's/alternative

EROTICA

Bolivar Road News 4030 N. Bolivar Rd. • 833-3354

St. Joseph (816)

BARS

Avis' Lounge 705 Esmond St. • 364-9748 • 5pm-1:30am, clsd Sun • lesbians/gay men • neighborhood bar • dancing/DJ • wheelchair access

St. Louis (314)

(See also **Alton, IL**)

INFO LINES & SERVICES

The Center 2256 S. Grand Ave. • 771-7995 • lesbigay/transgender community center

Gay/Lesbian Hotline PO Box 23227, 63156 • 367-0084 • 6pm-10pm

PACT (People of All Colors Together) PO Box 775402, 63177 • 995-4683/997-9897 • mtgs 2nd Th

St. Louis Gender Foundation 997-9897 • transgender info

Steps Alano Club 1935-A Park Ave. • 436-1858 • call for schedule

ACCOMMODATIONS

A St. Louis Guesthouse 1032-38 Allen Ave. • 773-1016 • lesbians/gay men • located in historic Soulard district

Brewers House B&B 1829 Lami St. • 771-1542 • lesbians/gay men • 1860s vintage house in South St. Louis

Lafayette House B&B 2156 Lafayette Ave. • 772-4429/(800) 641-8965 • gay-friendly • full brkfst • hot tub • kids/pets ok • women-owned/run

Napoleon's Retreat B&B 1815 Lafayette Ave. • 772-6979 • lesbians/gay men • restored 1880s townhouse

River Spirit Retreat B&B 187 W. 19th St., Alton IL • 569-5795/(618) 462-4051 • women only • reservation service

BARS

Alton Metro 602 Belle, Alton IL • (618) 465-8687 • 4pm-1:30am, from 2pm wknds • mostly gay men • dancing/DJ • live shows • wheelchair access

Atlantis 3954 Central • (618) 753-0112 • 9pm-3am Wed-Sat • popular • gay-friendly • ladies' night Wed • dancing/DJ • alternative

Attitudes 4100 Manchester • 534-3858 • 6pm-3am, clsd Sun-Mon • popular • mostly women • dancing/DJ

Bacchus 6 S. Sarah • 531-1109 • 5pm-1:30am, clsd Sun • mostly gay men • live shows • karaoke • wheelchair access

Char-Pei Lounge 400 Mascoutah Ave., Belleville IL • (618) 236-0810 • 6pm-2am • lesbians/gay men • dancing/DJ

Char-Pei's City Center Complex 657 E. Broadway, East St. Louis IL • (618f) 271-1755 • popular after hours• lesbians/gay men • dancing/DJ • food served • live entertainment

Clementine's 2001 Menard • 664-7869 • 10am-1:30am, from 11am wknds, til midnight Sun • popular • mostly gay men • leather • also a restaurant • dinners & wknd brunch • wheelchair access • $4-10

Club Zips 3145 W. Chain of Rocks Rd., Granite City IL • (618) 797-0700 • 6:30pm-1am • popular • lesbians/gay men • outdoor complex • live shows • videos

The Complex 3511 Chouteau • 772-2645 • 11am-3am, from 3pm Mon • popular • mostly gay men • multiple bars • patio • food served • $3-15 • wheelchair access

Drake Bar 3502 Papin St. • 865-1400 • 5pm-1:30am, clsd Sun • lesbians/gay men • live shows • wheelchair access

Ernie's Class Act Restaurant & Lounge 3756 S. Broadway • 664-6221 • 3pm-1:30am, from 11am Fri-Sat, clsd Sun • mostly women • dancing/DJ • transgender-friendly • food served • $5-7

Faces Complex 130 4th, E. St. Louis IL • (618) 271-7410 • 3pm-6am • mostly gay men • dancing/DJ • leather • live shows • 3 levels

St. Louis

Most visitors come to St. Louis to see the famous Gateway Arch, the tallest monument in the US at 630ft, designed by renowned architect Eero Saarinen.

After you've ridden the elevators in the Arch and seen the view, come down to earth and take a trip to historic Soulard, the 'French Quarter of St. Louis.' Established in 1779 by Madame and Monsieur Soulard as an open air market, it's now the place for great food and jazz. And the Market still attracts crowds—lesbigay and straight—on the weekends.

Laclede's Landing is also a popular attraction. While you're down by the Gateway Arch, treat yourself to riverfront dining aboard any of the several riverboat restaurants on the Mississippi. For accommodations, try **River Spirit Reservation Service**, a women's B&B reservations service in nearby Alton, Illinois. Dining and shopping is most fun on Euclid St. between Delmar and Forest Park Blvds. or on the University City Loop.

St. Louis has two bookstores of note: lesbigay **Our World Too** and **Left Bank Books**, which features extensive lesbian and gay sections. And check out the two women's bars: **Attitudes** is a loud-and-rowdy dance bar, and **Ernie's Class Act** is a mellower neighborhood place, perfect for drinks and conversation.

Flavour 1014 Locust • 567-8852 • 10pm-3am • gay-friendly • dancing/DJ • multiracial clientele • 18+ • no alcohol

Front Page 2330 Menard • 664-2939 • 8am-1:30am, clsd Sun • drag bar

The Green Room 1312 Washington Ave. • 421-4221 • til 3am, clsd Sun-Tue • gay-friendly • dancing/DJ • also 'Black List Lounge'

Hyperspace 1014 Locust • 421-0003 • 10pm-3am, clsd Th • lesbian/gay men • dancing/DJ • live shows • theme nights • 18+ Fri only

Loading Zone 16 S. Euclid • 361-4119 • 2pm-1:30am, clsd Sun • popular • lesbians/gay men • videos • wheelchair access

Magnolia's 5 S. Vandeventer • 652-6500 • 6pm-3am, dinner nightly • popular • mostly gay men • multi-racial clientele • live shows • wheelchair access

Tangerine 1405 Washington Ave. • 621-7335 • 11am-1am, clsd Sun • gay-friendly • lounge • dancing/DJ • 18+ Tue • ladies' night Wed • food served

Wired Women Productions 352-9473 • concerts & events

RESTAURANTS & CAFES

Cafe Balaban 405 N. Euclid Ave. • 361-8085 • popular • fine dining • some veggie • wonderful Sun brunch • full bar • wheelchair access • $10-16

Dressel's 419 N. Euclid • 361-1060 • excellent Welsh pub food • full bar

Duff's 392 N. Euclid Ave. • 361-0522 • clsd Mon • fine dining • some veggie • full bar • wheelchair access • $12-16

Einstein Bagels 2 N. Euclid Ave. • 361-2020

Majestic Bar & Restaurant 4900 Laclede • 361-2011 • 6am-1:30am • diner fare • $4-7

On Broadway Bistro 5300 N. Broadway • 421-0087 • 11am-3am • full bar • wheelchair access • $4-12

Redel's 310 Debaliviere • 367-7005 • hours vary • popular • some veggie • full bar • wheelchair access • $4-16

Sunshine Inn 8-1/2 S. Euclid Ave. • 367-1413 • 11:30am-9pm, from 10:30am Sun, clsd Mon • vegetarian • $5-8

BOOKSTORES & RETAIL SHOPS

Boxer's 310 N. Euclid Ave. • 454-0209 • 11am-6pm, 1pm-5pm Sun • boy underwear

St. Louis (314)

WHERE THE GIRLS ARE: Spread out, but somewhat concentrated in the Central West End near Forest Park. Younger, funkier crowds hang out in the Delmar Loop, west of the city limits, packed with ethnic restaurants.

LESBIGAY PRIDE: October: 772-8888/533-5322.

CITY INFO: 421-1023.

ATTRACTIONS: Forest Park. Gateway Arch. Laclede's Landing. Scott Joplin House. Six Flags Over Mid-America. St. Louis Cathedral.

BEST VIEW: Where else? Top of the Gateway Arch in the Observation Room.

WEATHER: 100% midwestern. Cold winters with little snow where temperatures can drop into the teens; hot summers that can go up into the 100°s. Spring and fall bring out the best in Mother Nature.

TRANSIT: County Cab: 991-5300. Airport Express: 429-4940. The Bi-State Bus System: 231-2345.

Cheap Trx 3211 S. Grand • 664-4011 • noon-8pm, til 6pm Sun • body piercing

Daily Planet News 243 N. Euclid Ave. • 367-1333 • 7am-8:30pm

Friends & Luvers 3550 Gravois • 771-9405 • 10am-10pm, noon-7pm Sun • novelties • videos • dating service

Heffalump's 387 N. Euclid Ave. • 361-0544 • 11am-8pm, til 10pm Fri-Sat, noon-5pm Sun • gifts

Left Bank Books 399 N. Euclid Ave. • 367-6731 • 10am-10pm, 11am-5pm Sun • lesbian, feminist & gay titles

Our World Too 11 S. Vandeventer • 533-5322 • 10am-9:30pm, noon-8pm Sun • lesbigay bookstore

Pages, Video & More 10 N. Euclid Ave. • 361-3420 • 9am-8pm, til 5pm Sun

TRAVEL & TOUR OPERATORS

Dynamic Travel 7750 Clayton Rd. Ste.105 • 781-8400/(800) 237-4083 • IGTA

Lafayette Square Travel Co. 1801 Lafayette Ave. • 776-8747/(800) 727-1480 • IGTA

Patrik Travel 22 N. Euclid Ave. Ste. 101 • 367-1468/(800) 678-8747 • IGTA

SPIRITUAL GROUPS

Agape Church 2026 Lafayette • 664-3588 • 10:45am Sun & 6:30pm Wed

Dignity St. Louis 6400 Minnesota Ave. • 997-9897x63 • 7:30pm Sun

MCC Living Faith 6501 Wydown, Clayton • 926-6387 • 5pm Sun

MCC of Greater St. Louis 1120 Dolman • 231-9100 • 9:30am & 11am Sun, 5:30 pm Sat

Trinity Episcopal Church 600 N. Euclid Ave. • 361-4655 • 8am & 10:30am Sun

PUBLICATIONS

The Lesbian/Gay News-Telegraph PO Box 14229-A, 63178 • 664-6411

SLAM! PO Box 63375, 63163 • 771-7739/752-3190 • alternative entertainment magazine

Women's Yellow Pages of Greater St. Louis 222 S. Maramac #203 • 725-1452

MONTANA

Billings   (406)

INFO LINES & SERVICES

AA Gay/Lesbian (at MCC location) • 245-7066 • 8pm Sat

BARS

Monte Carlo N.29th & 1st Ave. • 259-3393 • gay-friendly • neighborhood bar

RESTAURANTS & CAFES

Stella's Kitchen & Bakery 110 N. 29th St. • 248-3060 • 6am-3pm, bakery til 6pm, clsd Sun • some veggie

BOOKSTORES & RETAIL SHOPS

Barjon's 2718 3rd Ave. N. • 252-4398 • 9:30am-5:30pm, clsd Sun • alternative • women-owned/run

SPIRITUAL GROUPS

MCC Family of God 645 Howard St. • 245-7066 • 11am Sun & 7pm Wed • also 'Gospel Sing' 7pm 4th Sat

EROTICA

Big Sky Books 1203 1st Ave. N. • 259-0051

Boulder   (406)

ACCOMMODATIONS

Boulder Hot Springs Hotel & Retreat PO Box 930, 59632 • 225-4339 • gay-friendly • spiritual/recovery retreat • camping avail. • food served • smokefree • call for info

Bozeman   (406)

INFO LINES & SERVICES

Lambda Alliance of Gay Men/Lesbians/ Bisexuals PO Box 51, Strand Union Bldg., MSU, 59717 • 994-4551

Women's Center Hamilton Hall, MSU • 994-3836 • some lesbian referrals

ACCOMMODATIONS

Gallatin Gateway Inn 76405 Gallatin Rd. • 763-4672/(800) 676-3522 • gay-friendly • dinner nightly • Sun brunch • hot tub • swimming • non-smoking rms. avail. • wheelchair access

RESTAURANTS & CAFES

The Leaf & Bean 35 W. Main • 587-1580

Spanish Peaks Brewery 120 N. 19th St. • 585-2296 • 11am-2am • Italian • some veggie • $8-15

Butte (406)

BARS
M&M Bar & Cafe 9 N. Main St. • 723-7612
• 24hrs, bar til 2am • gay-friendly • some
veggie • $4-7

RESTAURANTS & CAFES
Matt's Place Montana & Rowe Rds. • 782-
8049 • 11:30am-7pm, clsd Sun-Mon • classic soda fountain diner

Pekin Noodle Parlor 117 S. Main, 2nd flr.
• 782-2217 • 5pm-9pm, clsd Tue • Chinese
• some veggie • $3-7

Pork Chop John's 8 W. Mercury • 782-0812
• 11am-9:30pm, clsd Sun • $3-5

Uptown Cafe 47 E. Broadway • 723-4735 •
lunch & dinner, clsd Sun • bistro •
beer/wine • $15-20

Corwin Springs (406)

RESTAURANTS & CAFES
The Ranch Kitchen Hwy. 89 • 848-7891 •
seasonal • lunch & dinner • some veggie •
$3-15

Great Falls (406)

SPIRITUAL GROUPS
MCC Shepherd of the Plains 1505 17th
Ave. SW • 771-1070 • 11am Sun, 7pm Wed

EROTICA
Studio 209 209 4th St. S. • 771-7266

Helena (406)

INFO LINES & SERVICES
PRIDE PO Box 775, 59624 • 442-9322/(800)
610-9322 (in MT) • social contacts &
newsletter

TRAVEL & TOUR OPERATORS
Travel Montana Dept. of Commerce •
(800) 541-1447

Livingston (406)

ACCOMMODATIONS
▲ **The River Inn** 4950 Hwy. 89 South • 222-
2429 • gay-friendly • full brkfst • kitchen
use • horse-boarding avail.

Missoula (406)

INFO LINES & SERVICES
AA Gay/Lesbian KC Hall 312 E. Pine • 523-
7799 • 9:30pm Wed

Lambda Alliance (U of MT) PO Box 7611,
59807 • 243-5922

Women's Resource Center (U of MT)
Campus Dr. University Ctr. #210 • 243-4153
• 2pm-5pm Mon, Wed-Fri

ACCOMMODATIONS
Foxglove Cottage B&B 2331 Gilbert Ave. •
543-2927 • gay-friendly • swimming

BARS
Amvets Club 225 Ryman • 543-9174 •
noon-2am, more gay after 8pm • gay-
friendly • dancing/DJ

RESTAURANTS & CAFES
Black Dog Cafe 138 W. Broadway • 542-
1138 • lunch & dinner, dinner only Sat, clsd
Sun • vegetarian • BYOB • wheelchair
access

Heidelhaus/Red Baron Casino 2620
Brooks • 543-3200 • 6am-11pm, til midnight wknds, casino 24hrs • full bar •
wheelchair access

BOOKSTORES & RETAIL SHOPS
Freddy's Feed & Read 1221 Helen Ave. •
549-2127 • 7:30am-8pm, 9am-7pm Sat,
10am-5pm Sun • alternative books • deli

Second Thought 529 S. Higgins • 549-2790
• 6:30am-10pm • bookstore • cafe & bakery
• wheelchair access

University Center Bookstore Campus
Drive (U of MT) • 243-4921 • 8am-6pm,
from 10am Sat, clsd Sun • gender studies
section

EROTICA
Fantasy for Adults Only 210 E. Main St. •
543-7760 • also 2611 Brooks Ave. • 543-
7510

Ovando   (406)
ACCOMMODATIONS
Lake Upsata Guest Ranch PO Box 6,
59854 • 793-5890 • gay-friendly • cabins •
wildlife programs & outings • meals provided

Ronan   (406)
ACCOMMODATIONS
North Crow Vacation Ranch 2360 North
Crow Rd. • 676-5169 • seasonal • les-
bians/gay men • cabins • tipis • 80 mi. S.
of Glacier Park • hot tub • nudity

NEBRASKA
Grand Island   (308)
INFO LINES & SERVICES
Helpline 234 East 3rd • 384-7474 • 24hrs •
some gay referrals • crisis calls

ACCOMMODATIONS
Midtown Holiday inn 2503 S. Locust •
384-1330 • gay-friendly • non-smoking rms.
avail. • kids/pets ok • also 'Images Pink
Cadillac Lounge' • wheelchair access

RESTAURANTS & CAFES
Tommy's 1325 S. Locust • 381-0440 • 24hrs

EROTICA
Exclusively Yours Shop 216 N. Locust •
381-6984 • adult toys

Sweet Dreams Shop 217 W. 3rd St. • 381-
6349 • 10am-6pm, til 5pm Sat, clsd Sun •
lingerie • adult toys

Kearney   (308)
INFO LINES & SERVICES
Gay & Lesbian Association of Greater NE
PO Box 2401, 68848 • 472-3249 • monthly
social • support • newsletter

Lincoln   (402)
INFO LINES & SERVICES
AA Gay/Lesbian 63rd & 'A' (Unitarian
Church) • 438-5214 • 7:30pm Th

Crisis Center 476-2110/475-7273 (24hrs)

Lambda Business Association PO Box
6341, 68506 • 483-6183 • 3pm 4th Sun

SAGE PO Box 22043, 68542-2043 •
social/support & info for older members of
the community (unverified for '97)

UNL Gay & Lesbian Student Assn.
Nebraska Student Union Rm. 234 • 472-
5644 • noon-6pm • meetings 7pm Tue during school year

Wimmin's Radio Show KZUM 89.3 FM •
474-5086 • noon-3pm Sun, 10am-noon Fri

Women's Resource Center Nebraska
Union Rm. 340, UNL • 472-2597 • lesbian
support services • wheelchair access

Youth Talkline 473-7932 • 7pm-midnight
Fri-Sat • lesbigay info & referrals for ages
23 & under

BARS
Panic 200 S. 18th St. • 435-8764 • 4pm-
1am, from 1pm wknds • lesbians/gay men •
dancing/DJ • live shows • videos • wheelchair access

The Q 226 S. 9th • 475-2269 • lesbian/gay men • dancing/DJ • 18+ Tue • country/western Wed

BOOKSTORES & RETAIL SHOPS
Avant Card 1323 'O' St. • 476-1918 • 10am-7pm

TRAVEL & TOUR OPERATORS
Good Life Tour & Travel 8200 Fletcher Ave. • 467-3900/(800) 233-0404

Nebraska Travel & Tourism PO Box 94666, 68509 • (800) 228-4307

Omaha   (402)

INFO LINES & SERVICES
AA Gay/Lesbian 345-9916 • call for times & location

Gay/Lesbian Information & Referral Line 558-5303

HGRA (Heartland Gay Rodeo Association) PO Box 3354, 68103 • 344-3103 • contact Dan

OPC (Omaha Players Club) PO Box 34463, 68134 • 451-7987 • S/M education & play group • pansexual mtgs. • 2nd Sat 2pm

River City Gender Alliance PO Box 3112, 68103-3112 • 398-1255 • 7pm 1st Sat (at Hawthorne Suites) • for CD, TS & inquiring • all orientations • newsletter

WomenSpace PO Box 24712, 68124 • annual women's music festival • newsletter

BARS
The Chesterfield 1901 Leavenworth St. • 345-6889 • 3pm-1am • mostly women • dancing/DJ • live shows • food served • gay owned/run • wheelchair access

CR Babe's 1951 St. Mary's Ave. • 344-2310 • lesbians/gay men • live shows • theme nights • karaoke

D.C.'s Saloon 610 S. 14th St. • 344-3103 • 3pm-1am, from 2pm wknds • mostly gay men • neighborhood bar • country/western • leather • live shows • wheelchair access

Diamond Bar 712 S. 16th St. • 342-9595 • 9am-1am, from noon Sun • mostly gay men • neighborhood bar • wheelchair access

Gilligan's Bar 1823 Leavenworth St. • 449-9147 • 2pm-1am, til 4am Fri-Sat • lesbians/gay men • neighborhood bar • karaoke • also a restaurant • burgers

The Infield 1401 Jackson • 346-3030 • 4pm-1am • lesbians/gay men • neighborhood bar • women-owned/run

The Max 1417 Jackson • 346-4110 • 4pm-1am • popular • mostly gay men • 4 bars • dancing/DJ • live shows • videos • wheelchair access

The New Run 1715 Leavenworth St. • 449-8703 • 2pm-1am, til 4am Fri-Sat • mostly gay men • dancing/DJ • live shows • volleyball court • wheelchair access

RESTAURANTS & CAFES
French Cafe 1017 Howard St. • 341-3547 • lunch & dinner, brunch Sun • $11-22

Neon Goose Cafe/Bar 1012 S. 10th • 341-2063 • lunch & dinner, clsd Mon • some veggie • wheelchair access • $7-14

BOOKSTORES & RETAIL SHOPS
New Realities 1026 Howard St. • 342-1863 • 11am-10pm, til 6pm Sun • progressive • wheelchair access

TRAVEL & TOUR OPERATORS
Regency Travel 10730 Pacific St. • 393-0585/(800) 393-5482

SPIRITUAL GROUPS
Lutherans Concerned 453-7137 • call for time & location

MCC of Omaha 819 S. 22nd St. • 345-2563 • 9am & 10:30am Sun • also support groups

PUBLICATIONS
New Voice PO Box 3512, 68103 • 556-9907

NEVADA

Carson City

INFO LINES & SERVICES
NV AIDS Hotline 505 E. King St. #304 •
(800) 842-2437 • 8am-10pm • community
info & resources • Spanish spoken

Lake Tahoe (916)

(See also **Lake Tahoe, CA**)

ACCOMMODATIONS
BeachSide Inn & Suites 930 Park Ave.,
South Lake Tahoe CA • 544-2400/(800) 884-
4920 • gay-friendly • walk to casinos & private beach access • outdoor spa & sauna

Haus Bavaria PO Box 3308, 89450 • 831-
6122/(800) 731-6222 • gay-friendly • mountain views • full brkfst

Lakeside B&B Box 1756, Crystal Bay,
89402 • 831-8281 • mostly gay men • full
brkfst • near great skiing • hot tub • sauna
• smokefree • kids/pets ok

Secret Honeymooners Inn 924 Park Ave.,
South Lake Tahoe CA • 544-6767/(800) 441-
6610 • gay-friendly • quiet, romantic adult-
only inn • spas

Tradewinds Motel 944 Friday (at Cedar),
South Lake Tahoe CA • 544-6459/(800) 628-
1829 • gay-friendly • swimming • suite w/
spa & fireplace avail.

BARS
Faces 270 Kingsbury Grade, Stateline •
588-2333 • 4pm-4am • lesbians/gay men •
dancing/DJ

Las Vegas (702)

INFO LINES & SERVICES
Alcoholics Together 953 E. Sahara Ste.
233 (entrance on State St.) • 737-0035 •
12:15pm & 8pm, noon wknds, 9pm Tue •
lesbigay club for 12-step recovery programs

Gay/Lesbian Community Ctr. 912 E.
Sahara Ln. • 733-9800 • 10am-8pm, til 5pm
wknds

Lesbigay Radio Cafe KLAV 1230 AM •
431-3309 • 10pm-midnight Mon • produced by women

ACCOMMODATIONS
Las Vegas Private B&B 384-1129 • mostly
gay men • swimming • hot tub • sauna •
nudity • smokefree • pets ok

Oasis Guest House 662 Rolling Green Dr. •
369-1396 • lesbians/gay men • swimming

Secret Garden B&B 3670 Happy Ln. •
451-3231 • lesbians/gay men • full brkfst •
swimming • nudity • smokefree

BARS
Angles 4633 Paradise Rd. • 791-0100/733-
9677 • 24hrs • mostly gay men • neighborhood bar • videos • wheelchair access

Las Vegas (702)

LESBIGAY PRIDE: June: 369-6260.

ANNUAL EVENTS: November -
Heart of The West: (800) GET-
PLUS (438-7587). Annual women's
extravaganza.

CITY INFO: Chamber of Commerce:
457-4664. Convention & Visitors
Authority: 892-0711.

ATTRACTIONS: Downtown Las
Vegas-"Glitter Gulch." Guiness
Book of World Records Museum.
Imperial Palace Auto Collection.
Liberace Museum. University of
Nevada-Las Vegas Museum of
Natural History.

TRANSIT: Western Cab: 382-7100.
Yellow Cab: 873-2000. Various
resorts have their own shuttle
service. Las Vegas Transit System:
384-3540.

Backdoor 1415 E. Charleston • 385-2018 • 24hrs • mostly gay men • neighborhood bar • dancing/DJ • wheelchair access

Backstreet 5012 S. Arville St. (Mosco Park) • 876-1844 • lesbians/gay men • dancing/DJ • country/western • wheelchair access

Badlands Saloon 953 E. Sahara Ste. 22-B • 792-9262 • 24hrs • mostly gay men • dancing/DJ • country/western • wheelchair access

Buffalo 4640 Paradise Rd. • 733-8355 • 24hrs • popular • mostly gay men • leather • videos • wheelchair access

Choices 1729 E. Charleston • 382-4791 • 24hrs • mostly gay men • neighborhood bar • live shows • wheelchair access

Faces Lounge 701 E. Stewart • 386-7971 • 24hrs • mostly women • dancing/DJ • live shows • wheelchair access

Gipsy 4605 Paradise Rd. • 731-1919/796-8793 • 24hrs • popular • mostly gay men • dancing/DJ • call for women's nights

Goodtimes 1775 E. Tropicana (Liberace Plaza) • 736-9494 • 24hrs • mostly gay men • more women Mon • neighborhood bar • dancing/DJ • piano bar

Lace 4633 Paradise Rd. (enter behind Angles) • 791-1947 • opens 6pm Th-Sat • popular • mostly women • dancing/DJ

The Las Vegas Eagle 3430 E. Tropicana • 458-8662 • 24hrs • mostly gay men • leather • DJ Wed & Fri

RESTAURANTS & CAFES

Coyote Cafe (at MGM Grand) • 891-7349 • 8:30am-11pm • the original Santa Fe chef • $8-13

Cyber City Cafe Flamingo & Maryland • 732-2001 • Internet cafe

Garlic Cafe 3650 S. Decatur Blvd. • 221-0266 • dinner, lunch Mon-Fri • int'l • full bar • $8 & up

New York, New York 6370 Windy St. • 896-1993 • 5pm-midnight • lesbians/gay men • live shows • some veggie • wheelchair access • $9-15

GYMS & HEALTH CLUBS

Great Shape 6020 W. Flamingo Rd. #8 • 221-0275

BOOKSTORES & RETAIL SHOPS

Alternatives 3507 S. Maryland Pkwy. #2 • 696-1885 • 11am-9pm • books • t-shirts • videos

Borders 2323 S. Decatur • 258-0999 • 9am-11pm Mon-Sat, 9am-9pm Sun • lesbigay section • cafe • call for gay events • wheelchair access

Cat O'Nine Tails Boutique 1717 S. Decatur Blvd. (at Fantastic Indoor Swap Meet) • 258-9754 • 10am-6pm Fri-Sun • contemporary evening wear • transgender-friendly

Get Booked 4643 S.Paradise • 737-7780 • 10am-midnight, til 2am Fri-Sat • lesbigay/feminist bookstore • videos

Lock, Stock & Leather 4640 Paradise Rd. #10 • 796-9801 • 3pm-10pm, noon-2am Fri-Sat, from 4pm Sun • bearwear & leather

TRAVEL & TOUR OPERATORS

Cruise One 5030 Paradise Dr. Ste. B-101 • 256-8082/(800) 200-3012 • IGTA

Dazey Travel Service 4511 W. Sahara Ave. • 876-8470

Gala Tours at A to Z Bargain Travel 3133 S. Industrial Rd. • 369-8671 • IGTA

Good Times Travel 624 N. Rainbow • 878-8900/(800) 638-1066 • IGTA

Players Express Vacations 2980 W. Meade Ave. Suite A • (800) 667-5607

SPIRITUAL GROUPS

Christ Church Episcopal 2000 Maryland Pkwy. • 735-7655 • 8am, 10am & 6pm Sun • 10am & 6pm Wed

Dignity/ Las Vegas 912 E. Sahara Ave. (G&L Comm.Ctr.) • 369-8127x344 • 6pm Sat

God's Word Fellowship 1121 Almond Tree Ln. (Comm. Counseling Ctr.) • 222-7814 (pager) • 7pm Th • Bible study • transgender-friendly

MCC of Las Vegas 2727 Civic Center Dr. • 369-4380 • 11:30am Sun

Unitarian Universalist Congregation 2200 W. Mesquite (Masonic Temple) • 894-8911 • 11am Sun

Valley Outreach Synagogue 436-4900 • 8pm 1st Fri • call for location & events

PUBLICATIONS

Las Vegas Bugle PO Box 14580, 89132 • 369-6260

Night Beat 3135 S. Industrial Rd. #204 • 734-7223 • lesbigay classified ads

Women's Yellow Pages of Southern Nevada 3021 Valley View #209 • 362-6507

EROTICA

Price Video 4640 Paradise Rd. Ste.11 • 734-1342

Pure Pleasure Book & Video 3177 S. Highland • 369-8044

Tattoos R Us 320 E. Charleston Ste. E • 387-6969 • piercing & tattoo studio

Video West 5785 W. Tropicana • 248-7055 • gay-owned/run

Reno (702)

BARS

1099 Club 1099 S. Virginia • 329-1099 • 24hrs wknds • popular • lesbians/gay men • neighborhood bar • live shows • wheelchair access

Bad Dolly's 535 E. 4th • 348-1983 • 3pm-3am, 24hrs Fri-Sun • popular • mostly women • dancing/DJ • live shows • wheelchair access

Five Star Saloon 132 West St. • 329-2878 • 24hrs • mostly gay men • dancing/DJ • wheelchair access

The Quest 210 Commercial Row • 333-2808 • noon-5am, 24hrs Fri-Sat • mostly gay men • dancing/DJ • live shows

Shouts 145 Hillcrest St. • 829-7667 • 10am-2am • gay-friendly • neighborhood bar • wheelchair access

Visions 340 Kietzke Ln. • 786-5455 • noon-4am, 24hrs Fri-Sun • popular • mostly gay men • dancing/DJ • theme nights • also 'Glitter Palace' gift shop wknds

BOOKSTORES & RETAIL SHOPS

Grapevine Books 1450 S. Wells Ave. • 786-4869 • 10am-6pm, til 8pm Fri-Sat, til 4pm Sun • lesbigay/feminist • wheelchair access

TRAVEL & TOUR OPERATORS

Deluxe Travel 102 California Ave. • 686-7000 • IGTA

SPIRITUAL GROUPS

MCC of the Sierras 3405 Gulling Rd. (Temple Sinai) • 829-8602 • 5pm Sun

EROTICA

The Chocolate Walrus Grove & Wrondell • 825-2267 • 10:30am-6:30pm Fri, til 5pm Sat, clsd Sun • videos • novelties

Fantasy Faire 1298 S. Virginia • 323-6969 • 11am-7pm, til 8pm Fri-Sat, noon- 4pm Sun • fetish • leather

Suzie's 195 Keitzke • 786-8557 • 24hrs

Sparks (702)

INFO LINES & SERVICES

Silver State Leather Association PO Box 50762, 89435 • 331-7059 • leather club

NEW HAMPSHIRE

Ashland (603)

ACCOMMODATIONS

▲ **Country Options** 27-29 N. Main St. • 968-7958 • full brkfst • lesbian following

Bethlehem (603)

ACCOMMODATIONS

▲ **Highlands Inn** PO Box 118 Valley View Ln., 03574 • 869-3978 • women-only • a lesbian paradise • full brkfst • hot tub • swimming • 15 miles of walking/ski trails • 20% off for 7 nights (except holidays) • wheelchair access • IGTA • $55-110

Bridgewater (603)

ACCOMMODATIONS

The Inn on Newfound Lake 1030 Mayhew Trpk. Rte. 3-A • 744-9111/(800) 745-7990 • gay-friendly • swimming • also a restaurant • 5pm-9pm • full bar • $65-185

Centre Harbor (603)

ACCOMMODATIONS

Red Hill Inn RFD #1, Box 99M, 03226 • 279-7001/(800) 573-3445 • gay-friendly • overlooking Squam Lake & White Mountains • also a restaurant • wheelchair access • IGTA

Chocorua (603)

ACCOMMODATIONS

Mount Chocorua View House Rte. 16 • 323-8350 • gay-friendly • smokefree • kids ok • 10 mi. S. of N. Conway

Concord (603)

INFO LINES & SERVICES

Gay Info Line 224-1686 • 6pm-8pm, clsd Tue & wknds • active social & support groups • also 'Citizens Alliance for Gay/Lesbian Rights'

New Hampshire Lambda PO Box 1043, 03302 • 627-8675 • 3rd Sat • statewide social group for lesbians

TRAVEL & TOUR OPERATORS

Travel & Tourism Office PO Box 1856, 03302-1856 • 271-2666

SPIRITUAL GROUPS

Spirit of the Mountain 177 N. Main (1st Cong. Church) • 225-5491 • 5pm 2nd & 4th Sun

PUBLICATIONS

Breathing Space PO Box 816, 03302

Bungay Jar Bed&Breakfast

Peaceful Privacy
in Franconia
New Hampshire

Splendid VIEWS
of the
White Mountains

70.-130. suites for 2
(603) 823-7775
fax: 603·444·0100

Kate
welcomes you!

smoke-free environment

WomenWise 38 S. Main St. • 225-2739 • published by NH Federation of Feminist Health Centers • also many support groups

Dover (603)

INFO LINES & SERVICES

Gay, Lesbian, Bisexual & Transgender Helpline 743-4292 • 6pm-10pm Mon-Fri, 9am-2pm wknds

ACCOMMODATIONS

Payne's Hill B&B 141 Henry Law Ave. • 742-4139 • mostly women • smokefree • $49-69

Durham (603)

INFO LINES & SERVICES

The UNH Alliance UNH, M.U.B., 03824 • 862-4522 • 7:30pm Mon

Exeter (603)

SPIRITUAL GROUPS

United Church of Christ 21 Front St., near Court St. (Exeter Cong.Church) • 772-6221 • 10am Sun

Franconia (603)

ACCOMMODATIONS

Blanche's B&B 351 Easton Valley Rd. • 823-7061 • gay-friendly • full brkfst • smokefree

▲ **Bungay Jar B&B** PO Box 15, Easton Valley Rd., 03580 • 823-7775 • gay-friendly • full brkfst • saunas • smokefree • kids ok • balconies • wheelchair access

Foxglove, A Country Inn Rte. 117 at Lovers Ln., Sugar Hill • 823-8840 • gay-friendly • food served

The Horse & Hound Inn 205 Wells Rd. • 823-5501 • clsd April & Nov • gay-friendly • full brkfst • kids/pets ok • restaurant open for dinner except Tue • $13-18

Raynor's Motor Lodge Main St. (Rtes. 142 & 18) • 823-9586 • gay-friendly • swimming • non-smoking rms. avail. • $45-65

Glen (603)

ACCOMMODATIONS

Will's Inn Rte. 302 • 383-6757 • gay-friendly • swimming • non-smoking rms avail. • kids ok • limited wheelchair access

Hart's Location (603)

ACCOMMODATIONS

The Notchland Inn Rte. 302 • 374-6131/(800) 866-6131 • gay-friendly • country inn on 400 acres • brkfst & dinner avail. • fireplaces • full bar

Jackson (603)

ACCOMMODATIONS

Wildcat Inn & Tavern Rte. 16A • 383-4245/383-6456 • gay-friendly • landscaped gardens • tavern 3pm-midnight wknds • restaurant 6pm-9pm • $14-23

Keene (603)

ACCOMMODATIONS

The Post and Beam B&B Center St., Sullivan • 847-3330 • gay friendly • full brkfst • wheelchair access • women owned/run • $50-90

BOOKSTORES

Oasis 45 Central Square • 352-5355 • 10am-9pm, 11am-6pm Sun • alternative spiritual books & supplies

Manchester (603)

BARS

Club Merri-Mac 201 Merrimack • 623-9362 • 2pm-1:30am • popular • lesbians/gay men • dancing/DJ • private club

Front Runner/Manchester Civic Club 22 Fir St. • 623-6477 • 3pm-1:30am • popular • lesbians/gay men • dancing/DJ • transgender-friendly • live shows • private club

Scandals Bar & Grill 333 Valley St. • 669-6383 • 11am-1am • lesbians/gay men • dancing/DJ • live shows • Mexican/American menu • wheelchair access • $5-11

Sporters 361 Pine St. • 668-9014 • 5pm-1am, from 3pm Sun • mostly gay men • neighborhood bar • dancing/DJ

Portsmouth (603)

INFO LINES & SERVICES

Out and About 129 Miller Ave. (United Methodist Church) • 772-8045 • 7pm 1st & 3rd Wed • lesbian support & education group

BARS

Desert Hearts 948 Rte. 1 Bypass • 431-5400 • from 8pm Wed-Sat, from 6pm Sun • mostly women • dancing/DJ • private club • wheelchair access

TRAVEL & TOUR OPERATORS

Worldwise Travel Co. Inc. 477 State St. • 430-9060/(800) 874-9473 • IGTA

NEW JERSEY

Asbury Park/Ocean Grove (908)

INFO LINES & SERVICES
Gay/Lesbian Community Center 515 Cookman Ave. • 774-1809/775-4429 • 2pm-7pm Sat & various evenings • call for events

BARS
Bond Street Bar 208 Bond St. • 776-9766 • 4pm-midnight, til ? Fri-Sat • mostly women • neighborhood bar

Down the Street 230 Cookman Ave., Asbury Park • 988-2163 • 2pm-2am (seasonal) • popular • mostly gay men • beach crowd • dancing/DJ • live shows • food served • videos • volleyball • wheelchair access

Key West 611 Heck St. • 988-7979 • 4pm-2am • mostly women • dancing/DJ • backyard

RESTAURANTS & CAFES
Raspberry Cafe 16 Main Ave. • 988-0833 • brkfst & lunch

The Talking Bird 224 Cookman • 775-9708 • lunch & dinner, til 4am Fri-Sat • $4-9

Atlantic City (609)

ACCOMMODATIONS
The Rose Cottage 161 S. Westminster Ave. • 345-8196 • lesbians/gay men • near bars & casinos

Surfside Hotel & Resort 18 S. Mt. Vernon Ave. • 347-0808 • lesbians/gay men • small, upscale straight-friendly hotel • sundeck • also restaurant in summer

BARS
Brass Rail Bar & Grill 12 S. Mt. Vernon Ave. • 348-0192 • 24hrs • popular • lesbians/gay men • women's night Fri • neighborhood bar • live shows • food served

Ladies 2000 PO Box 1, Oaklyn, 08107 • 784-8341 • scheduled parties for women by women • call for times & locations

Reflections 181 S. South Carolina Ave. • 348-1115 • 24hrs • lesbians/gay men • neighborhood bar • dancing/DJ • videos • wheelchair access

Studio Six Video Dance Club (upstairs at Brass Rail) • 348-3310 • 10pm-6am • popular • lesbians/gay men • dancing/DJ • live shows • videos

TRAVEL & TOUR OPERATORS
New Jersey Division of Travel & Tourism (800) 537-7397

Schreve Lazar Travel (at Bally's Park Place Casino Hotel, Boardwalk & Park Place) • 348-1189/(800) 322-8280 • IGTA

Bloomingdale (201)

INFO LINES & SERVICES
Gal-a-vanting Box 268, 07403 • 838-5318 • sponsors women's parties • call for details

Boonton (201)

BARS
Locomotion 202 Myrtle Ave. • 263-4000 • 8pm-? Wed-Sat • lesbians/gay men • ladies night Wed • dancing/DJ • food served

Brick (908)

TRAVEL & TOUR OPERATORS
Uniglobe Monarch Travel 291 Herbertsville Rd. • 840-2233 • IGTA

Cherry Hill (609)

SPIRITUAL GROUPS
Unitarian Universalist Church 401 N. Kings Hwy. • 667-3618 • 10:15am Sun

Denville (201)

BOOKSTORES & RETAIL SHOPS
Perrin & Treggett, Booksellers 3130 Rte. 10 W., Denville Commons • 328-8811/(800) 770-8811 • 10am-9pm, til 6pm Sat, noon-5pm • large lesbigay section

Florence (609)

EROTICA
Florence Book Store Rte. 103 S., 4 mi S. of Rte. 206 • 499-9853

Harrison (201)

PUBLICATIONS
The Lavender Express PO Box 514, 07029 • 235-0585

Hazlet (908)

TRAVEL & TOUR OPERATORS
Galaxy Travel 3048 Rte. 35 (K-Mart shopping ctr.) • 219-9600/(800) 331-7245 • IGTA

Highland Park (908)

BOOKSTORES & RETAIL SHOPS
All About Books 409 Raritan Ave. • 247-8744 • 9:30am-6pm, 11am-5pm Sun

Hoboken (201)

BARS

Excalibur 1000 Jefferson St. • 795-1023 • 9pm-3am, clsd Mon-Wed • popular • lesbians/gay men • dancing/DJ • live shows • wheelchair access

RESTAURANTS & CAFES

Maxwell's 1039 Washington St. • 656-9632 • 5pm-2am, til 3am Fri-Sat • mostly gay men • dancing/DJ • Italian/American • live shows • wheelchair access • $7-12

Jersey City (201)

BARS

Uncle Joe's 154 1st St. • 659-6999 • 8pm-2am • mostly gay men • dancing/DJ • neighborhood bar • Jersey girls night Sun

Lambertville (609)

EROTICA

Joy's Books 103 Springbrook Ave. • 397-2907

Lyndhurst (201)

BARS

Aldo's 749 Marin Ave. • 460-9824 • 9pm-2am • gay-friendly • dancing/DJ

Madison (201)

BOOKSTORES & RETAIL SHOPS

Pandora Book Peddlers 9 Waverly Pl. • 822-8388 • 10am-6pm, til 7:30pm Th, til 5pm Sat, clsd Sun-Mon • feminist bookstore & book club

Maplewood (201)

SPIRITUAL GROUPS

Dignity Metro New Jersey 550 Ridgewood Rd. (St. George's Episcopal Church) • 8pm 1st & 3rd Tue

Montclair (201)

INFO LINES & SERVICES

Crossroads Real Estate Referral Network PO Box 1708, 07042 • (800) 442-9735 • non-profit lesbigay realtor referrals

BOOKSTORES & RETAIL SHOPS

Cohen's 635 Bloomfield Ave. • 744-2399 • 6am-8pm, til 2pm Sun • magazines • cafe

Dressing for Pleasure 590 Valley Rd. • 746-5466 • noon-6pm, til 8pm Th-Fri, from 10am Sat, clsd Sun-Mon • lingerie • latex • leather

Morris Plains (201)

TRAVEL & TOUR OPERATORS

Frankel Travel 60 E. Hanover Ave. • 455-1111/(800) 445-6433 • IGTA

Morristown (201)

INFO LINES & SERVICES

GAAMC Gay/Lesbian Youth in NJ Helpline 21 Normandy Hgts. Rd. • 285-1595 • 7:30pm-10:30pm • mtgs 1:30pm-4:30pm Sat (call for location)

Gay Activist Alliance in Morris County 285-1595 • 7:30pm-10:30pm • meets 8:30pm Mon at 21 Normandy Hts. Rd. • also Women's Network

New Brunswick (908)

INFO LINES & SERVICES

Latinos Unidos (at Pride Center) • 846-2232

Lesbians/Gay Men of New Brunswick 109 Nichol Ave. (Quaker Meeting House) • 247-0515 • 8pm 2nd & 4th Tue

Pride Center of New Jersey 211 Livingston Ave. • 846-2232 • 7pm-10pm, 11am-1pm Tue, clsd wknds

Rutgers Univ. Lesbian/Gay/Bisexual Peer-Counseling 932-7886 • 7pm-11pm Tue & Fri • call for details

RESTAURANTS & CAFES

The Frog and the Peach 29 Dennis St. • 846-3216 • 11:30am-11pm, til 1am Th-Sat • full bar • $40-60

J. August Cafe 100 Jersey Ave. • 545-4646 • 9am-3pm Tue-Fri, 6pm-11pm Fri-Sat • lesbians/gay men

Stage Left 5 Livingston Ave. • 828-4444 • 5:30pm-2am, from 4:30pm Sun • popular • lesbians/gay men • some veggie • full bar • $10-12

SPIRITUAL GROUPS

Dignity/New Brunswick 109 Nichol Ave. (Friends Mtg. House) • 254-7942 • 7:30pm Fri

MCC Christ the Liberator 40 Davidson Rd. (St. Michael's Chapel), Piscataway • 846-8227 • 6:30pm Sun

Newark (201)

BARS

First Choice 533 Ferry St. • 465-1944 • 8pm-2am, til 3am Th-Sat • lesbians/gay men • more women Sat • dancing/DJ • mostly African-American • ladies night Th

Murphy's Tavern 59 Edison Pl. • 622-9176 • 11:30am-2am, lunch daily • lesbians/gay men • dancing/DJ • mostly African-American • wheelchair access

SPIRITUAL GROUPS

Oasis 621-8151 • Tue evenings • call for info • lesbigay ministry of the Episcopal Church

Oak Ridge (201)

BARS

Yacht Club 5190 Berkshire Valley Rd. (5 mi. off of Rte. 15) • 697-9780 • 7pm-3am, from 2pm Sun • popular • lesbians/gay men • dancing/DJ • Sun BBQ • wheelchair access

Oakland (201)

INFO LINES & SERVICES

Feminine Connection 337-6943 • social group for women over 25 • meets every other month • call for info

Orange (908)

INFO LINES & SERVICES

Intergroup AA 668-1882 • 24hrs info & referrals

Perth Amboy (908)

BARS

The Other Half Convery Blvd. (Rte. 35) & Kennedy • 826-8877 • 9pm-2am, til 3am Fri-Sat • popular • mostly gay men • dancing/DJ

Plainfield (908)

ACCOMMODATIONS

▲ **The Pillars** 922 Central Ave. • 753-0922/(800) 372-7378 • gay-friendly • Georgian/Victorian mansion • smokefree • infants & kids over 12 ok • dogs ok (call first)

Princeton (609)

TRAVEL & TOUR OPERATORS

Edwards Travel Service 8 S. Tulane St. • 924-4443/(800) 669-9692

Rahway (908)

BARS

Ms G's 1519 Main St. • 388-2465 • 9pm-? 2nd Sat • mostly women • dancing/DJ • hot tub • food served • BYOB

Red Bank (908)

INFO LINES & SERVICES
Monmouth Ocean Transgender Group
PO Box 8243, 07701 • 219-9094 • mtgs •
support

BOOKSTORES & RETAIL SHOPS
Earth Spirit 16 W. Front St. • 842-3855 •
10am-6pm, til 8pm Fri, noon-5pm Sun •
new age ctr. & bookstore w/ lesbigay sections

Ringwood (201)

ACCOMMODATIONS
Ensanmar 2 Ellen Dr. • 831-0898 • women
only • community retreat • support groups

River Edge (201)

BARS
Feathers 77 Kinder Kamack Rd. • 342-6410
• 9pm-2am, til 3am Sat • popular • mostly
gay men • dancing/DJ • live shows • theme
nights

Rocky Hill (609)

TRAVEL & TOUR OPERATORS
Travel Registry, Inc. 127 Washington St. •
921-6900/(800) 346-6901 • IGTA

Rosemont (609)

RESTAURANTS
The Cafe 88 Kingwood-Stockton Rd. • 397-
4097 • 8am-3pm, dinner from 5pm Wed-
Sat, clsd Mon • BYOB

Sayreville (908)

BARS
Colosseum Rte. 9 & Rte. 35 N. • 316-0670 •
9pm-3am, from 4pm Sun • lesbians/gay
men • ladies night Wed • dancing/DJ • live
shows

Sauvage 1 Victory Cir. • 727-6619 • 7pm-
3am, from 4pm Sun • popular • mostly
women • neighborhood bar • dancing/DJ •
food served

Somerset (908)

BARS
The Den 700 Hamilton St. • 545-7329 •
8pm-2am, from 7pm Sat, from 5pm Sun •
popular • lesbians/gay men • dancing/DJ •
live shows • 18+ • wheelchair access

South Plainfield (908)

TRAVEL & TOUR OPERATORS
Leisure Council PO Box 433, 07080 • 754-
1575

Teaneck (201)

INFO LINES & SERVICES
First Tuesday 61 Church St. (St. Paul's
Lutheran Church) • 779-1434 • 7:30pm 1st
Tue • lesbian social group

Trenton (609)

BARS
Buddies Pub 677 S. Broad St. • 989-8566 •
5pm-2am, from 6pm wknds • lesbians/gay
men • dancing/DJ

Center House Pub 499 Center St. • 599-
9558 • 4pm-2am, from 7pm wknds • les-
bians/gay men • neighborhood bar • quiet
conversation bar • garden patio

Union City (201)

BARS
Nite Lite 509 22nd St. • 863-9515 • 8pm-
3am Wed-Sun • lesbians/gay men • danc-
ing/DJ • live shows • gay-owned/run

Woodbury (609)

INFO LINES & SERVICES
Rainbow Place 1103 N. Broad • 848-2455
• info line & community center

NEW MEXICO

Albuquerque   (505)

INFO LINES & SERVICES

AA Gay/Lesbian 266-1900 • call for times/locations • smokefree mtgs

Alternative Erotic Lifestyles 345-6484 • pansexual S/M group

Bisexual Women's Social Network 836-5239 • meets twice a month

Common Bond Community Center 4013 Silver St. SE • 266-8041 • 6pm-9pm

New Mexico Outdoors PO Box 26836, 87125 • 822-1093 • active lesbigay outdoors group

Sirens PO Box 7726, 87194 • 877-7245 • women's motorcycle club • also sponsors Summer Solistice event

UNM Women's Resource Center 1160 Mesa Vista Hall NV • 277-3716 • 8am-5pm Mon-Fri • some lesbian outreach

Women in Movement 899-3627 • production company • Memorial Day festival

ACCOMMODATIONS

Dave's B&B PO Box 27214, 87125 • 247-8312 • mostly gay men • leatherfolk welcome • Southwestern home close to river • wheelchair access

Hacienda Antigua Retreat 6708 Tierra Dr. NW • 345-5399/(800) 484-2385x9954 • gay-friendly • full brkfst • hot tub • swimming • smokefree • kids 3+ yrs ok • gay-owned

▲ **Hateful Missy & Granny Butch's Boudoir & Manure Emporium** 29 Jara Millo Loop, Vequita • 243-7063/(800) 397-2482 • lesbians/gay men • full brkfst • hot tub • kitchen access

Mountain View PO Box 30123, 87190 • 296-7277 • mostly women • full brkfst wknds • smokefree • kids ok • wheelchair access • lesbian-owned/run

▲ **Nuevo Dia** 11110 San Rafael Ave. NE • 856-7910 • lesbians/gay men • hot tub • kids ok

The Rainbow Lodge 115 Frost Rd., Sandia Park • 281-7100 • lesbians/gay men • mtn retreat w/ panoramic views • full brkfst • smokefree • kids ok (call first) • pets ok

Rio Grande House 3100 Rio Grande Blvd. NW • 345-0120 • gay-friendly • landmark adobe residence close to Old Town • full brkfst • non-smoking rms avail. • older kids ok • pets ok (call first)

Tara Cotta 3118 Rio Grande Blvd. NW • 344-9443 • gay-friendly • nudity ok • smokefree • small dogs ok • priv. patio

W.E. Mauger Estate 701 Roma Ave. NW • 242-8755 • gay-friendly • intimate Queen Anne residence • full brkfst

W.J. Marsh House 301 Edith SE • 247-1001/(800) 956-2774 • gay-friendly • full • brkfst • shared bath • women-owned/run • $50-80

BARS

Albuquerque Mining Co. (AMC) 7209 Central Ave. NE • 255-4022 • noon-2am, til midnight Sun • popular • mostly gay men • dancing/DJ • women's night Mon

Albuquerque Social Club 4021 Central Ave. NE (rear alley) • 255-0887 • noon-2am, til midnight Sun • popular • lesbians/gay men • dancing/DJ • country/western • private club

Foxes Lounge 8521 Central Ave. NE • 255-3060 • 10am-2am, noon-midnight Sun • mostly gay men • dancing/DJ • live shows • wheelchair access

Kingsize at the Zone 2nd & Central • 343-5196 • 9pm Tue • gay-friendly • dancing/DJ • alternative

▲ **Legends West** 6132 4th St. NW • 343-9793 • 4pm-2am, from 6pm Sat, noon-midnight Sun, clsd Mon • lesbians/gay men • dancing/DJ

The Pulse 4100 Central SE • 255-3334 • 4pm-2am, til mid Sun • mostly gay men • dancing/DJ

The Ranch 8900 Central SE • 275-1616 • 11am-2am, til midnight Sun • mostly gay men • dancing/DJ • country/western • also 'Cuffs' leather bar inside • wheelchair access

RESTAURANTS & CAFES

Cafe Intermezzo 3513 Central NE • 265-2556 • 10am-11pm, til midnight Fri-Sat • sandwiches & salads • beer/wine

Chef du Jour 119 San Pasquale SW • 247-8998 • 11am-2pm, clsd wknds • plenty veggie • wheelchair access • $4-9

Chianti's 5210 San Mateo NE • 881-1967 • 11am-9pm, from noon wknds • Italian • some veggie • beer/wine • $5-11

Double Rainbow 3416 Central SE • 255-6633 • 6:30am-midnight • plenty veggie • wheelchair access • $4-8

BOOKSTORES & RETAIL SHOPS

Full Circle Books 2205 Silver SE • 266-0022/(800) 951-0053 • 10am-6pm, til 5pm wknds • feminist/lesbian

In Crowd 3106 Central SE • 268-3750 • 10am-6pm, noon-4pm Sun • lesbigay art • clothing • accessories

Newsland Books 2112 Central Ave. SE • 242-0694 • 8am-9pm

Page One 11018 Montgomery NE • 294-2026/(800) 521-4122 • 7am-11:30pm

Sisters and Brothers Bookstore 4011 Silver Ave. SE • 266-7317 • 9:30am-8pm • lesbigay

TRAVEL & TOUR OPERATORS

All World Travel 1930 Juan Tabo NE Ste. D • 294-5031/(800) 725-0695

North & South Travel & Tours 215 Central Ave. NW • 246-9100/(800) 585-8016 • IGTA

The Travel Scene 2424 Juan Tabo Blvd. NE • 292-4343/(800) 658-5779

SPIRITUAL GROUPS

Dignity New Mexico 1815 Los Lomas • 880-9031 • 7pm 1st Sun

Emmanuel MCC 341 Dallas NE • 268-0599 • 10am Sun

First Unitarian Church 3701 Carlisle NE • 884-1801 • 9:30am & 11am Sun

MCC 2404 San Mateo Pl. NE • 881-9088 • 10am Sun

PUBLICATIONS

Out! Magazine PO Box 27237, 87125 • 243-2540

Rainbow PO Box 4326, 87196-4326 • 255-1634

Women's Voices PO Box 40572, 87196 • 268-8623 • formerly 'Hembra' • feminist newspaper

EROTICA

The Leather Shoppe 4217 Central Ave. NE • 266-6690

Pussycat III 4012 Cental Ave. NE • 268-1631

Clovis (505)

INFO LINES & SERVICES

Clovis-Portales Common Bond PO Box 663, 88101 • 356-2656 • lesbigay social/support line

Galisteo   (505)

Accommodations

Galisteo Inn HC75 Box 4, 87540 • 466-4000 • clsd Jan • gay-friendly • 23 mi. SE of Santa Fe • swimming • smokefree • older kids ok • horse boarding avail. • also a restaurant • nouvelle Southwestern (Wed-Sun) • plenty veggie • wheelchair access

Las Cruces   (505)

Info Lines & Services

AA Gay/Lesbian 527-1803

Matrix PO Box 992, Mesilla, 88046 • local inquiries • newsletter

Bookstores & Retail Shops

Spirit Winds Gifts 2260 Locust St. • 521-0222 • 7:30am-8pm, til 10pm Fri-Sat, 8:30am-5pm Sun

Travel & Tour Operators

Uniglobe Above & Beyond Travel 2225 E. Lohman Ste. A • 527-0200/(800) 578-5888 • IGTA

Spiritual Groups

Holy Family Parish 1701 E. Missouri (church) • 522-7119 • 5:30pm Sat • inclusive Evangelical Anglican Church

Koinonia 521-1490 • 7:30pm Th • lesbigay group for people of all religious traditions

Madrid   (505)

Accommodations

Madrid Lodging 14 Opera House Rd. • 471-3450

Bars

Mineshaft Tavern 2846 State Hwy. 14 • 473-0743 • 11am-2am • gay-friendly • live shows • also a restaurant • some veggie

Restaurants & Cafes

Blondie's Coal Town Diner 2849 State Hwy. 14 • 8am-6pm • some veggie

Java Junction 2855 State Hwy. 14 • 438-2772 • 8am-7pm • coffee shop • also B&B

Bookstores & Retail Shops

▲ **Apache Kid & Standing Bear Gallery** 2874 State Hwy. 14 • 474-3945 • 10am-5pm • Native American artifacts & antiques

▲ **Diva Divine** 2850 State Hwy. 14 • 438-4360 • 11am-5pm • sensuality & spirituality boutique

▲ **Impatient Artifacts** 2875 State Hwy. 14 • 474-6878 • 10am-5pm, clsd Tue • folk art & rustic furniture

▲ **Jack of All Arts** 2870 State Hwy. 14 • 474-4044 • 11am-5pm • fun art gallery • monthly shows

▲ **Primitiva** 2860 State Hwy. 14 • 471-7904 • 10am-5:30pm • furniture • gifts • accessories

▲ **Woofy Bubbles Woowear** 2872 State Hwy. 14 • 471-1083 • 10am-5pm • clothing

Pecos   (505)

ACCOMMODATIONS

Wilderness Inn PO Box 1177, 87552 • 757-6694 • gay-friendly • adobe inn 20 mi. E. of Santa Fe • smokefree • wheelchair access

Ruidoso   (505)

ACCOMMODATIONS

Sierra Mesa Lodge PO Box 463, Alto, 88312 • 336-4515 • gay-friendly • full brkfst • smokefree

Santa Fe   (505)

INFO LINES & SERVICES

AA Gay/Lesbian 1915 Rosina St. (Friendship Circle) • 982-8932

Santa Fe Lesbian & Gay Hotline 982-3301 • recorded info

ACCOMMODATIONS

Arius Compound PO Box 1111, 1018-1/2 Canyon Rd., 87504 • 982-2621/(800) 735-8453 • gay-friendly • 3 adobe casitas • kitchens • hot tub • patio • gay-owned/run • $80-135

Casa Torreon 1613 Calle Torreon • 982-6815 • gay-friendly • adobe guesthouse w/ kitchen • smokefree • kids ok

Four Kachinas Inn 512 Webber St. • 982-2550/(800) 397-2564 • clsd Jan • gay-friendly • smokefree • kids 10+ ok • wheelchair access

Heart Seed B&B Retreat & Spa PO Box 6019, 87502 • 471-7026 • gay-friendly • located on Turquoise Trail 25 mi. S of Santa Fe • full brkfst • sundeck • hot tub • also day spa • $69-79

Hummingbird Ranch Rte. 10, Box 111, 87501 • 471-2921 • gay-friendly • 2-1/2 acre ranchette • women-owned/run • $75-125

Inn of the Turquoise Bear 342 E. Buena Vista St. • 983-0798/(800) 396-4104 • lesbians/gay men • hot tub

Marriott Residence Inn 1698 Galisteo St. • 988-7300/(800) 331-3131 • gay-friendly • swimming • non-smoking rms. avail. • wheelchair access

Open Sky B&B Rte.2, Box 918, 80575 • 471-3475/(800) 244-3475 • gay-friendly • smokefree • kids ok (call first) • wheelchair access

▲ **Triangle Inn** PO Box 3235, 87501-0235 • 455-3375 • lesbians/gay men • secluded rustic adobe compound • non-smoking casitas avail. • kids/pets ok • wheelchair access • lesbian-owned/run

RESTAURANTS & CAFES

Cafe Pasqual's 121 Don Gaspar • 983-9340 • 7am-10:30pm • popular • Southwestern • some veggie • beer/wine • wheelchair access • $12-18

Dave's Not Here 1115 Hickock St. • 983-7060 • 11am-10pm, clsd Sun • New Mexican • some veggie • beer/wine • women-owned/run

Paul's 72 Marcy St. • 982-8738 • dinner • modern int'l • some veggie • wheelchair access • $11-18

SantaCafe 231 Washington Ave. • 984-1788 • lunch & dinner • Southwestern/Asian • some veggie • full bar • $19-24

Tecolote Cafe 1203 Cerrillos Rd. • 988-1362 • 7am-2pm, clsd Mon • popular • great brkfst • some veggie • $5-8

Vanessie of Santa Fe 434 W. San Francisco • 982-9966 • 5:30pm-10:30pm (bar til 1am) • popular • lesbians/gay men • steak house • piano bar

BOOKSTORES & RETAIL SHOPS

The Ark 133 Romero St. • 988-3709 • 10am-8pm, til 5pm wknds • spiritual

Downtown Subscription 376 Garcia St. • 983-3085 • newsstand & coffee shop

Galisteo News 201 Galisteo St. • 984-1316 • 7am-7pm, til 9pm Fri-Sat • gay periodicals & coffee shop

TRAVEL & TOUR OPERATORS

Earth Walks 988-4157 • guided tours of American Southwest & Mexico

Hawk, I'm Your Sister PO Box 9109-WT, 87504 • 984-2268 • variety of women's wilderness trips & writers' retreats

Taos   (505)

ACCOMMODATIONS

▲ **The Ruby Slipper** PO Box 2069, 87571 • 758-0613 • lesbians/gay men • near Taos Plaza • full brkfst • smokefree • kids ok • wheelchair access • women-owned/run

RESTAURANTS & CAFES

Wild & Natural Cafe 812-B Paseo del Pueblo Norte • 751-0480 • 7am-9pm, clsd Sun • vegetarian • wheelchair access • women-owned/run • $2-9

TRAVEL & TOUR OPERATORS

Artemis Wilderness Tours PO Box 1574, El Prado, 87529 • 758-2203 • women's outdoor rafting trip May-Sept • cross-country skiing other months

Thoreau   (505)

ACCOMMODATIONS

White Eagle Retreat HC62 Box 5114, 87323-9515 • 862-7769 • gay-friendly • full brkfst • dinner • smokefree • wheelchair access

NEW YORK

Adirondack Mtns. (518)

INFO LINES & SERVICES

Adirondack GABLE 359-7358 • local contact for area

ACCOMMODATIONS

Amethyst B&B PO Box 522, Cranberry Lake, 12927 • 848-3529/(410) 252-5990 • summer only • women only • full brkfst • swimming

The Doctor's Inn Trudeau Rd., RR1, Box 375, Saranac Lake, 12983 • 891-3464/(800) 552-2627 • gay-friendly • IGTA

Stony Water B&B RR1 Box 69, Elizabethtown, 12932 • 873-9125/(800) 995-7295 • gay-friendly • full brkfst • swimming • wheelchair access • lesbian-owned/run

Albany (518)

INFO LINES & SERVICES

Face the Music WRPI 91.5 FM • 276-6248 • 4pm-6pm Sun • feminist radio

Gay AA (at Community Center) • 7:30pm Sun • lesbian AA at 7:30pm Tue

Homo Radio WRPI 91.5 FM • 276-6248 • noon-2:30pm Sun

KAT Productions 432-0818 • wknd multimedia events & dances for women

Lesbian/Gay Community Center 332 Hudson Ave. • 462-6138 • 7pm-10pm, til 11pm Fri-Sat, from 1pm Sun • 24hr directory

Lesbian/Gay/Bisexual Young People's Meeting (at the Community Center) • 7:30pm Th

TGIC (Transgenderists Independence Club) 436-4513 • volunteers 8pm-10pm Th • social group meets weekly

Two Rivers Outdoor Club 449-0758

Women's Building 79 Central Ave. • 465-1597 • community center

BARS

Cafe Hollywood 275 Lark St. • 472-9043 • 3pm-3am • gay-friendly • neighborhood bar • videos

JD's Playhouse 519 Central Ave. • 446-1407 • 4pm-4am, clsd Mon • lesbians/gay men • neighborhood bar • dancing/DJ

Longhorns 90 Central Ave. • 462-4862 • 4pm-4am • mostly gay men • country/western

Oh Bar 304 Lark St. • 463-9004 • 2pm-2am • mostly gay men • neighborhood bar • multi-racial • videos

Power Company 238 Washington Ave. • 465-2556 • 2pm-2am, til 4am wknds • mostly gay men • dancing/DJ • wheelchair access

Waterworks Pub 76 Central Ave. • 465-9079 • 4pm-4am • popular • mostly gay men • dancing/DJ • garden bar

RESTAURANTS & CAFES

Cafe Lulu 288 Lark St. • 436-5660 • 11am-midnight, til 1am Fri-Sat • beer/wine • Mediterranean • plenty veggie • $5-9

Debbie's Kitchen 290 Lark St. • 463-3829 • 10am-9pm, 11am-6pm Sat, clsd Sun • sandwiches & salads • $3-5

Donnie's Cafe 75 75 Central Ave. • 436-0378 • 7am-3pm, from 3am wknds • $4-7

El Loco Mexican Cafe 465 Madison Ave. • 436-1855 • clsd Mon • some veggie • full bar

Mother Earth 217 Western Ave. • 434-0944 • 11am-11pm • vegetarian • BYOB • 'Gay/Bi/Lesbian Club Night' 4th Mon • wheelchair access • $3-6

The Unlimited Feast 340 Hamilton St. • 463-6223 • lunch Mon-Fri, dinner Wed-Sat • some veggie • full bar • patio • wheelchair access • $14-20

Yono's 289 Hamilton St. • 436-7747 • 4:30pm-10pm, clsd Sun • Indonesian/cont'l • some veggie • full bar

BOOKSTORES & RETAIL SHOPS

Romeo's 299 Lark St. • 434-4014 • 11am-9pm, noon-5pm Sun

Video Central 37 Central Ave. • 463-4153 • 10am-10pm • lesbigay books & magazines

TRAVEL & TOUR OPERATORS

Atlas Travel Center Inc. 1545 Central Ave. • 464-0271 • IGTA

Freedom Travel 212 Clifton Country Mall • 371-3720

SPIRITUAL GROUPS

Integrity 498 Clinton Ave. at Robbins St. (Grace & Holy Innocents Church) • 465-1112 • 6pm Sun

MCC of the Hudson Valley 275 State St. (Emmanuel Baptist Church) • 785-7941 • 1pm Sun • wheelchair access

PUBLICATIONS

Community PO Box 131, 12201 • 462-6138

EROTICA

Savage Leather & Gifts 88 Central Ave. •
434-2324 • 11am-9pm, til midnight Fri-Sat,
clsd Sun-Mon

Annandale On Hudson   (914)

INFO LINES & SERVICES

Bard Bisexual/Lesbian/Gay Alliance Bard
College • 758-6822 (general switchboard)

Binghamton   (607)

INFO LINES & SERVICES

AA Gay/Lesbian 183 Riverside Dr.
(Unitarian Church) • 722-5983 • 7pm Wed
& Sat

Gay/Lesbian/Bi Resource Line 729-1921 •
7:30pm-9:30pm Wed

Lesbian/Gay/Bisexual Union 777-2202 •
mtgs 8pm Tue

Women's Center & Event Line 724-3462

BARS

Risky Business 201 State St. • 723-1507 •
9pm-1am, from 5pm Th-Fri, til 3am Fri-Sat
• popular • mostly gay men • dancing/DJ

Squiggy's 34 Chenango St. • 722-2299 •
5pm-1am, til 3am Fri-Sat, from 8pm Sun •
lesbians/gay men • dancing/DJ

RESTAURANTS & CAFES

Kara's Kafe 585 Main St., Johnson City •
797-8567 • clsd Sun • Californian • plenty
veggie • full bar • live shows • $10-15

Lost Dog Cafe 60 Main St. • 771-6063 •
11am-11pm, til 4am Fri-Sat • popular • les-
bians/gay men • some veggie • live shows

SPIRITUAL GROUPS

Affirmation (United Methodist) 83 Main
St. • 775-3986 • 7pm Sun

PUBLICATIONS

Amethyst PO Box 728 Westview Stn., 13905
• 723-5790

Hera c/o Women's Center PO Box 354,
13902 • 770-9011 • local feminist newspaper

Lavender Life PO Box 898, 13902 • 771-
1986

Buffalo   (716)

INFO LINES & SERVICES

▲ **Dyke TV** Channel 18 • 10:30pm Tue •
'weekly, half hour TV show produced by lesbians for lesbians'

Gay/Lesbian Community Network 239
Lexington Ave. • 883-4750 • 7pm-10pm Fri

Gay/Lesbian Youth Services 190 Franklin
St. • 855-0221 • 6:30pm-9pm Mon-Tue, Th-
Fri

Lesbian/Gay/Bisexual Alliance 362
Student Union SUNY-Buffalo, Amherst •
645-3063

BARS

Buddies 31 Johnson Park • 855-1313 •
1pm-4am • lesbian/gay men • dancing/DJ •
live shows • wheelchair access

Cathode Ray 26 Allen St. • 884-3615 •
1pm-4am • mostly gay men • neighborhood bar • videos • wheelchair access

Club Marcella 150 Theatre Pl. • 847-6850 •
10pm-4am, from 4pm Fri, clsd Mon • les-
bians/gay men • dancing/DJ • live shows •
wheelchair access

Compton's After Dark 1239 Niagara St. •
885-3275 • 4pm-4am • mostly women •
dancing/DJ • live shows • sandwiches •
some veggie • $4-7

Lavender Door 32 Tonawanda St. • 874-
1220 • 6pm-4am, from 4pm Fri, clsd Mon •
mostly women • neighborhood bar •
wheelchair access

Metroplex 729 Main St. • 856-5630 •
10pm-4am, clsd Mon • lesbians/gay men •
dancing/DJ • alternative • 18+

Mickey's 44 Allen St. • 886-9367 • 10am-
4am • gay-friendly • neighborhood bar

Stagedoor 20 Allen St. • 886-9323 • 5pm-
4am • mostly older gay men • neighborhood bar • karaoke • piano bar • patio

Tiffany's 490 Pearl St. • 854-4840 • 11am-
2am, til 6am Fri-Sat • lesbians/gay men •
dancing/DJ • food served • live shows •
patio

Underground 274 Delaware Ave. • 855-
1040 • 4pm-4am, from noon wknds • mostly gay men • more women Tue & Sun •
dancing/DJ

BOOKSTORES & RETAIL SHOPS

Talking Leaves 3158 Main St. • 837-8554 •
10am-6pm, til 8pm Wed-Th, clsd Sun

Village Green Bookstore 765-A Elmwood
Ave. • 884-1200 • 9am-11pm, til midnight
Fri-Sat • wheelchair access

TRAVEL & TOUR OPERATORS

Destinations Unlimited 130 Theater Pl. •
855-1955/(800) 528-8877 • IGTA

Earth Travelers, Inc. 683 Dick Rd. • 685-
2900/(800) 321-2901 • IGTA

SPIRITUAL GROUPS

Dignity PO Box 75, 14205 • 833-8995

Integrity 16 Linwood Ave. (Church of the Ascension) • 884-6362

PUBLICATIONS
Volumé PO Box 106 Westside Stn., 14213 • 885-4580

EROTICA
Village Books & News 3102 Delaware Ave., Kenmore • 877-5027 • 24hrs

Canaseraga (607)

ACCOMMODATIONS
Fairwise Llama Farm 1320 Rte.70 • 545-6247 • lesbians/gay men • full brkfst • located btwn. Letchworth & Stony Brook Parks

Catskill Mtns. (914)

ACCOMMODATIONS
Bradstan Country Hotel PO Box 312, White Lake, 12786 • 583-4114 • gay-friendly • also piano bar & cabaret • 9pm-1am Fri-Sun

Hasbrouck House B&B Rte. 209, Stone Ridge • 687-0736 • gay-friendly • full brkfst • also fine dining • full bar • $12-25 • patio • $95-145

Palenville House B&B (518) 678-5649 • gay-friendly • full brkfst

▲ **Point Lookout Mountain Inn** Rte. 23 Box 33, East Windham, 12439 • (518) 734-3381 • gay-friendly • close to Ski Windham & Hunter Mountain • also a restaurant • Mediterranean/classic American • $11-18 • women-owned/run • $60-125

River Run B&B Main St., Box D-4, Fleischmanns, 12430 • 254-4884 • gay-friendly • Queen Anne Victorian • full brkfst • IGTA

Stonewall Acres Box 556, Rock Hill • 791-9474/(800) 336-4208 • gay-friendly • guest farmhouse & cottages • full brkfst • swimming

RESTAURANTS & CAFES
Catskill Rose Rte. 212, Mt. Tremper • 688-7100 • from 5pm Wed-Sun • some veggie • full bar • patio • $13-19

Cooperstown (607)

ACCOMMODATIONS
Toad Hall B&B RD1 Box 120, Fly Creek, 13337 • 547-5774 • gay-friendly • full brkfst

Tryon Inn 124 Main St., Cherry Valley •
264-3790 • gay-friendly • also a restaurant
• French/American • some veggie • $12-16

Cuba (716)

ACCOMMODATIONS

Rocking Duck Inn 28 Genesee Pkwy. •
968-3335 • gay-friendly • full brkfst • also
'Aunt Minnie's Tavern'

Elmira (607)

ACCOMMODATIONS

Rufus Tanner House B&B 60 Sagetown
Rd., Pine City • 732-0213 • gay-friendly •
full brkfst • hot tub

BARS

Bodyshop 425-27 Railroad Ave. • 733-6609
• 4pm-1:30am, from 2pm Fri-Sat • lesbians/gay men • dancing/DJ • multi-racial •
live shows • patio

The David 511 Railroad Ave. • 733-2592 •
4pm-1am, from 7pm wknds • popular • lesbians/gay men • dancing/DJ

Fire Island (516)

INFO LINES & SERVICES

AA Gay/Lesbian (at the Fire House),
Cherry Grove • 654-1150

ACCOMMODATIONS

Boatel Pines/Dunes Yacht Club, Harbor
Walk • 597-6500 • lesbian/gay men • swimming

Cherry Grove Beach Hotel Main & Ocean,
Cherry Grove • 597-6600 • mostly gay men
• swimming • nudity • wheelchair access

Dune Point PO Box 78, Cherry Grove • 597-
6261 • lesbians/gay men • wheelchair
access

Holly House Holly Walk nr Bayview Walk,
Cherry Grove • 597-6911 • seasonal • lesbian/gay men

Island Properties 37 Fire Island Blvd. •
597-6900 • weekly, monthly, & seasonal
rentals • also properties for sale

Sea Crest Lewis Walk, Cherry Grove • 597-
6849 • seasonal • lesbians/gay men

BARS

Cherry's Cherry Grove • 597-6820 • noon-
4am • lesbians/gay men • piano bar

Ice Palace (at Cherry Grove Beach Hotel) •
597-6600 • hours vary • popular • lesbians/gay men • dancing/DJ • live shows

The Island Club & Bistro Fire Island Blvd.
• 597-6001 • 6pm-4am • mostly gay men •
dancing/DJ • live shows • food served •
$15-28

Pavillion Fire Island Blvd. • 597-6131 •
4pm-6am • lesbians/gay men • popular T-
dance & morning dancing • also 'Yacht
Club' restaurant • opens at noon

RESTAURANTS & CAFES

Michael's Dock Walk, Cherry Grove • 597-
6555 • 24hrs Sat

Top of the Bay Dock Walk at Bay Walk,
Cherry Grove • 597-6699 • 7pm-midnight •
popular • lesbians/gay men • $18-23

Glen Falls (518)

BARS

Club M 70 South St. • 798-9809 • noon-
4am • lesbians/gay men • dancing/DJ •
wheelchair access

Greenwood Lake (914)

BARS

The Quarter Deck Jersey Ave. (1/2 mile S.
of The Village Light) • 477-2070 • 6pm-2am
Th-Sun, from noon Sun • lesbians/gay men
• neighborhood bar

Highland (914)

BARS

Prime Time Rte. 9 W. • 691-8550 • 9pm-
4am, clsd Mon-Wed • mostly gay men •
dancing/DJ

Hudson Valley (914)
(See also Kingston, New Paltz, Poughkeepsie
& Stone Ridge)

RESTAURANTS & CAFES

Cafe Pongo 69 Broadway, Tivoli • 757-4403
• lunch, dinner & Sun brunch • gay night
Fri • call for details

Northern Spy Cafe Rte. 213, High Falls •
687-7298 • dinner nightly & Sun brunch,
clsd Tue • plenty veggie • full bar • wheelchair access • $11-18

PUBLICATIONS

▲ In The Life PO Box 921, Wappingers Falls,
12590 • 227-7456

Ithaca (607)

INFO LINES & SERVICES

AA Gay/Lesbian 201 E. Green St. (Mental
Health Serv. Bldg.) • 273-1541 • 5:30pm
Sun

Ithaca Gay/Lesbian Activities Board
(IGLAB) 273-1505 (Common Ground bar) •
3rd Tue • sponsors events including 'Finger
Lake Gay/Lesbian Picnic'

LesBiGay Info Line (Cornell University) •
255-6482 • noon-4pm Mon-Fri

Women's Community Building 100 W. Seneca • 272-1247 • 9am-5pm, evenings & wknds by appt.

ACCOMMODATIONS

Pleasant Grove B&B 168 Pleasant Grove Rd. • 387-5420/(800) 398-3963 • gay-friendly • above Cayuga Lake • full brkfst • sundeck

Sleeping Bear B&B 208 Nelson Rd. • 277-6220 • (formerly 'Cricket & Liz's Log Home') • women only • full brkfst • hot tub • swimming • lesbian-owned/run

BARS

Common Ground 1230 Danby Rd. • 273-1505 • 4pm-1:30am, clsd Mon • popular • lesbians/gay men • dancing/DJ • also a restaurant • some veggie • $5-8

RESTAURANTS & CAFES

ABC Cafe 308 Stewart Ave. • 277-4770 • lunch & dinner, wknd brunch, clsd Mon • beer/wine • vegetarian • $6-8

BOOKSTORES & RETAIL SHOPS

Borealis Bookstore, Inc. 111 N. Aurora St. • 272-7752 • 10am-9pm, noon-5pm Sun • independent alternative w/ lesbigay sections • wheelchair access

Jamestown (716)

INFO LINES & SERVICES

10% Network 1255 Pendergast Ave. (Unitarian Church) • 484-7285/664-5556 • 7pm 3rd Sat • lesbigay social group

BARS

Nite Spot 201 Windsor • 7pm-2am • lesbians/gay men • dancing/DJ • live shows

Sneakers 100 Harrison • 484-8816 • 2pm-2am • lesbians/gay men • dancing/DJ • wheelchair access

Kingston (914)

INFO LINES & SERVICES

Coalition for Lesbigay Youth 255-7123

Ulster County Gay/Lesbian Alliance 626-3203 • info & events line

RESTAURANTS & CAFES

Armadillo Bar & Grill 97 Abeel St. • 339-1550 • full bar • patio

Crossroads Food & Drink 33 Broadway • 330-0151 • clsd Mon • piano bar

Lake George (518)

ACCOMMODATIONS

King Hendrick Motel Lake George Rd. (Rte. 9) • 792-0418 • gay-friendly • swimming • also cabin avail.

Lake Placid (518)

RESTAURANTS & CAFES

Artists' Cafe 1 Main St. • 523-9493 • 8am-10pm • steak & seafood • full bar • $9-15

Dakota Cafe 124 Main St. • 523-2337 • steak & seafood

Long Island (516)

INFO LINES & SERVICES

EEGO (East End Gay Organization) PO Box 87, Southampton, 11968 • 324-3699

GLIB (Gay Men & Lesbians in Brookhaven) 286-6867 • women's support 8pm 1st & 3rd Th

Middle Earth Hotline 2740 Martin Ave., Bellmore • 679-1111 • 24hrs • crisis & referral counseling • especially for youth

Pride for Youth Coffeehouse 170 Fulton St., Farmingdale • 679-9000 • 7:30pm-11:30pm Fri

Women's Alternative Community Center 699 Woodfield Rd., West Hempstead • 483-2050 • call for events & info

ACCOMMODATIONS

132 North Main 132 N. Main, East Hampton • 324-2246 • seasonal • mostly gay men • mini-resort • swimming • wheelchair access

Centennial House 13 Woods Ln., East Hampton • 324-9414 • gay-friendly • full brkfst • swimming

Cozy Cabins Motel Box 848, Montauk Hwy., East Hampton, 11975 • 537-1160 • seasonal • lesbians/gay men

EconoLodge—MacArthur Airport 3055 Veterans Memorial Hwy., Ronkonkoma • 588-6000/(800) 553-2666 • gay-friendly

EconoLodge—Smithtown/Hauppauge 755 Rte. 347, Smithtown • 724-9000/(800) 553-2666 • gay-friendly

Gandalf House PO Box 385, Laurel, 11948 • 298-4769 • gay-friendly

Sag Harbor B&B 125 Mt. Misery Dr., Sag Harbor • 725-5945 • lesbians/gay men • wheelchair access

Summit Motor Inn 501 E. Main St., Bayshore • 666-6000/(800) 869-6363 • gay-friendly

BARS

Bedrock 121 Woodfield Rd., West Hempstead • 486-9516 • 8pm-3am, from 1pm Sun, clsd Mon • popular • mostly women • dancing/DJ • live shows

Blanche 47-2 Boundary Ave., South Farmingdale • 694-6906 • 4pm-4am • mostly gay men • neighborhood bar • live shows

Bunk House 192 N. Main St., Montauk Hwy., Sayville • 567-2865 • 8pm-4am, from 5pm Sun • popular • mostly gay men • dancing/DJ • live shows

Chameleon 40-20 Long Beach Rd., Long Beach • 889-4083 • 9pm-4am, clsd Mon-Wed • popular • lesbians/gay men • dancing/DJ • women's night Fri

Club Swamp Montauk Hwy. at E. Gate Rd., Wainscott • 537-3332 • 6pm-4am, daily during summer, clsd Tue-Wed • mostly gay men • dancing/DJ • also a restaurant • cont'l/seafood (clsd Sun) • $16-20

Forever Green 841 N. Broome Ave., Lindenhurst • 226-9357 • 8pm-4am, from 7pm Sun (DJ) • mostly women • neighborhood bar

Libations 3547 Merrick Rd., Seaford • 679-8820 • 3pm-4am • lesbians/gay men • neighborhood bar

Silver Lining 175 Cherry Ln., Floral Park • 354-9641 • 9pm-4am clsd Mon-Tue • lesbians/gay men • dancing/DJ • live shows • videos • wheelchair access

St. Mark's Place 65-50 Jericho Trnpk., Commack • 499-2244 • 4pm-4am • lesbians/gay men • dancing/DJ • also a restaurant • some veggie • wheelchair access • lesbian-owned • $4-14

Thunders 1017 E. Jericho Trnpk., Huntington Station • 423-5241 • 9pm-4am, clsd Mon • lesbians/gay men • dancing/DJ • piano bar

RESTAURANTS & CAFES

Bayman's Katch 220 Montauk Hwy., Sayville • 589-9744 • 4pm-2am, clsd Tue • full bar • $9-17

BOOKSTORES & RETAIL SHOPS

Womankind Books 5 Kivy St., Huntington Station, 11746 • 427-1289 • extensive women's mail order company • large selection of lesbian titles, music & jewelry

SPIRITUAL GROUPS

Dignity-Nassau County PO Box 48, East Meadow • 781-6225 • 8pm 2nd & 4th Sat

Dignity-Suffolk County Box 621-P, Bay Shore, 11706 • 654-5367 • 2nd & last Sun

Unitarian Universalist Fellowship 109 Brown Rd., Huntington • 427-9547 • 10:30am Sun

PUBLICATIONS

Sappho's Isle 960 Willis Ave., Albertson • 747-5417 • lesbian paper for NYC area & tri-state region

Nanuet (914)

TRAVEL & TOUR OPERATORS

Edlen Travel Inc. 161 S. Middletown Rd. • 624-2100/(800) 624-2315 • IGTA

Naples (716)

ACCOMMODATIONS

Landmark Retreat 6006 Rte. 21 • 396-2383 • gay-friendly • full brkfst • wheelchair access

New Paltz (914)

INFO LINES & SERVICES

Soujourner's Wimmin's Gathering Space PO Box 398, 12561 • sponsors variety of social/political events

ACCOMMODATIONS

▲ **Churchill Farm** 39 Canaan Rd. • 255-7291 • gay-friendly • full brkfst • hot tub • women-owned/run • $75-95

Ujjala B&B 2 Forest Glen • 255-6360 • gay-friendly • body therapy • sweat lodges

RESTAURANTS & CAFES

Locust Tree Inn 215 Hugenot St. • 255-7888 • lunch & dinner, clsd Mon • cont'l • full bar • patio • $14-20

BOOKSTORES & RETAIL SHOPS

The Painted Word 36 Main St. • 256-0825 • 10am-10pm, til 6pm Sun-Mon • lesbigay • cafe • wheelchair access

TRAVEL & TOUR OPERATORS

New Paltz Travel Center, Inc. 7 Cherry Hill Center • 255-7706 • IGTA

NEW YORK CITY

New York City is divided into 8 geographical regions:

N.Y.C. - Overview (212)

INFO LINES & SERVICES

AA Gay/Lesbian Intergroup 647-1680 • many mtgs. at Lesbian/Gay Community Ctr.

African Ancestral Lesbians United for Societal Change (at Lesbian/Gay Community Ctr.) • 8pm Th

Asians & Friends of NY (at Lesbian/Gay Community Ctr.) • 8pm 3rd Sat

Bisexual Gay/Lesbian Youth of NY (at Lesbian/Gay Community Ctr.) • 3:30pm Sat

Bisexual Network 459-4784 • info on variety of social & political groups

Bisexual Women of Color (at Lesbian/Gay Community Ctr.) • 6:30pm 1st & 3rd Fri

Bisexual Women's Group (at Lesbian/Gay Community Ctr.) • 6:30pm 2nd & 4th Wed

Butch/Femme Society (at Lesbian/Gay Community Ctr.) • 6:30pm 3rd Wed

▲ **Dyke TV** Manhattan Channel 34 • 8pm Tue • 'weekly half-hour TV show produced by lesbians, for lesbians'

EDGE (Education in a Disabled Gay Environment) 929-7178/749-9438(TTY) • wheelchair access

Eulenspiegel Society 388-7022 • 7:30pm Tue & Wed • pansexual S/M group • newsletter

FLAB (Fat is a Lesbian Issue) (at Lesbian/Gay Community Ctr.) • 5pm 2nd Sun • fat-positive discussion group • allies welcome

Gay Women's Alternative 160 Central Park W. (Unitarian Universalist Church) • 865-3979/595-1658(church) • 8pm 1st Th (Oct-June)

Gay/Lesbian National Hotline (888) 843-4564 • 6pm-11pm

GGALA (Greek Gay/Lesbian Association) (at Lesbian/Gay Community Ctr.) • 8pm 2nd & 4th Th

Hetrick-Martin Institute 2 Astor Pl. • 674-2400/674-8695(TTY) • extensive services for lesbigay youth • also publishes 'You Are Not Alone' resource directory

New York City

*I*n the film Mondo New York, demi-monde denizen Joey Arias put it best: "New York is the clit of the world!"

Get ready for the most stimulating trip of your life! You've come to the city of world-famous tourist attractions, from tall buildings, to the power centers of the hemisphere, to the theater and art pinnacles of the world.

In fact, do your homework before you come, and call or write the huge **Lesbian/Gay Community Services Center** which houses meeting spaces for every conceivable group of lesbigaytrans+ people.

Whether you pride yourself on your cultural sophistication, or lack thereof, you're going to find endless entertainment. For starters, there are plays, musicals, operas, museums, gallery shows, performance art, street theater and street life.

New York's performance art is a must-see for any student of modern culture. The best bets for intelligent, cutting edge shows by women and queers are **W.O.W. (Women's One World) Cafe** (460-8067, at 59 E. 4th St.), and **P.S. 122** on 1st Ave. at 9th St. Lesbian artist Holly Hughes got her start here, as have many other thorns in Jesse Helms' side.

For half-price tickets to Broadway and off-Broadway shows available the day of the show, stop by the TKTS booth on 47th St. at Broadway. For the latest reviews and hot off-off-Broadway theaters, check the **Village Voice** (extremely queer-friendly).

Of course, you can stimulate a lot more than your cultural sensibilities in New York. With endless time or credit, your palate could experience oral orgasms ranging from a delicate quiver to a blinding throb every day. And that's just your taste buds. For instance, before that Broadway show, head to one of the many restaurants along 46th St. at 9th Ave. When in Brooklyn, brunch along 7th Ave.; you'll find plenty of lesbigay company on a Sunday morning.

Shopping, too, affords shivers of delight. Check out the fabulous thrift shops and the designer boutiques (look up your favorite— we like classic Pucci, funky Anna Sui and clubby Patricia Fields). Cruise Midtown on Madison Ave., E. 57th St., or 5th Ave. in the 50's, at Trump Tower or another major shopping mall, and touch—actually touch—clothing more expensive than your last car.

Other recommended districts for blowing cash on the coolest/

funnest/ neatest stuff include St. Mark's Place in the Village (8th St. btwn. 1st and 2nd Avenues); Broadway from 8th to Canal St., and any major intersection in Soho and the East Village.

For a respite from overwhelming consumerism, peruse the shelves at the lesbigay **Oscar Wilde Memorial Bookshop**, or **Eve's Garden**, New York's women's erotic boutique, where men must be escorted in by a woman! Or stop by the **Lesbian Herstory Archives** in Brooklyn.

You could spend days at the big art museums in Uptown near Central Park, but budget some time for the galleries in SoHo (south of Houston, between Broadway and 6th Ave.). Pick up a gallery map in the area.

For musical entertainment, make your pilgrimage to **The Kitchen**, legendary site of experimental and freestyle jazz, or **CBGB**'s, legendary home of noisy music for the next decade (the Ramones started American punk here in 1974).

Nightlife... yeah, you've been holding your breath. Wait no more, go directly to the **Clit Club**, do not pass go. Friday nights on W. 14th St. are the sexiest, hottest dyke nights in, oh, the Northeast. **Crazy Nanny's** happens seven days a week, and several other women's bars are nearby like the ever-popular **Meow Mix**. Kinky dykes should also check out **Buster's**, an S/M bar in Midtown, and get the latest schedule for **The Vault** partyspace in the Village.

Pick up a copy of **Homo Xtra** for up-to-the-minute club happenings—even though it's boy-heavy, it's got the skinny on hip. If clubbing's not your thing, try **Sappho's Isle**, a monthly for lesbians in the tri-state area.

Although it's the hot and humid season, June is when New York hosts a plethora of Lesbian/Gay Pride-related cultural events, from their week-long Film Festival to the Pride March itself. Immerse yourself in queer culture in the San Francisco of the East Coast (no offense, New Yorkers!).

Nassau Countyites should stop by the **Women's Alternative Community Center** or **Bedrock** women's bar. In Suffolk County, **Forever Green** or **Thunders** are the bars of choice, while **Womankind Books** is the only one of its kind.

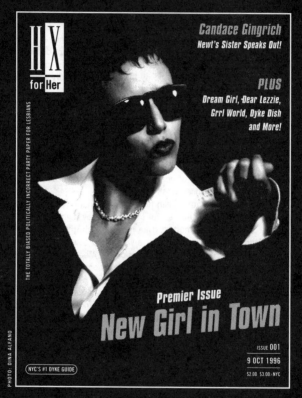

There's a New Girl in Town!

HX for Her

Candace Gingrich
Newt's Sister Speaks Out!

PLUS
Dream Girl, Dear Lezzie,
Grrl World, Dyke Dish
and More!

THE TOTALLY BIASED POLITICALLY INCORRECT PARTY PAPER FOR LESBIANS

PHOTO: DINA ALFANO

Premier Issue
New Girl in Town

ISSUE 001
9 OCT 1996
$2.00 $3.00 NYC

NYC'S #1 DYKE GUIDE

HX for Her, the totally biased politically incorrect party paper for lesbians, will change New York dyke-life as we know it. Offering complete listings on the who, what, where, when and how of the New York scene. Now available for FREE at over 100 locations in the New York City area.

FOR ADVERTISING INFORMATION, CALL 212-627-0747

New York City (212)

WHERE THE GIRLS ARE: Upwardly mobile literary types hang in the West Village, hipster dykes cruise the East Village, upper-crusty lesbians have cocktails in Midtown, and working class dykes live in Brooklyn.

LESBIGAY PRIDE: June: 626-6925.

ANNUAL EVENTS: February - Saint-at-Large White Party: 674-8541. March - Saint-at-Large Black Party: 674-8541. June- New York Int'l Gay/Lesbian Film Festival: 343-2707, week-long fest. September - Wigstock: 620-7310, outrageous wig/drag/performance festival in Tompkins Square Park in the East Village. October - All Saint's Party: 674-8541. November- AIDS Dance-a-thon: 807-9255, AIDS benefit. New York Lesbian/Gay Experimental Film/Video Fest: 501-2309, film, videos, installations & media performances. December 31- Saint-at-Large New Year's Party: 674-8541.

CITY INFO: 397-8222.

ATTRACTIONS: Broadway. Carnegie Hall. Central Park. Ellis Island. Empire State Building. Greenwich Village. Lincoln Center. Metropolitan Museum of Art. Radio City Music Hall. Rockefeller Center. Statue of Liberty. Times Square. United Nations. Wall Street. World Trade Center.

BEST VIEW: Coming over any of the bridges into New York, the Empire State Building or the World Trade Center.

WEATHER: A spectrum of extremes with pleasant moments thrown in.

TRANSIT: An experience you'll always remember. Just hail one, and find out for yourself. Carey Airport Shuttle: (718) 632-0500. (718) 330-1234.

YOUR HOME AWAY FROM HOME

The Lesbian and Gay Community Services Center/New York

▼ 400 lesbian and gay organizations hold their meetings at the Center.

▼ 5,000 people visit the Center each week.

Come and enjoy our dances, our sexuality and health workshops, 12 step meetings, our readings, exhibits, library and lectures, our garden to rest your feet after a day of sightseeing and more!

LESBIAN AND GAY COMMUNITY SERVICES CENTER

208 West 13th Street, Greenwich Village

(14th Street stop on the 1,2 and 3 subway lines)

(212) 620-7310

Visit the Center's Web site at
http://www.panix.com/~dhuppert/gay/center

- -

Please add my name to the Center mailing list.

Name: _____

Address: _____

_____

Telephone: _____

Mail to: The Center, 208 W. 13th Street, New York, NY 10011-7799

Just Couples (at Lesbian/Gay Community Ctr.) • 3:30pm 1st Sun

Kambal Sa Lusog (at Lesbian/Gay Community Ctr.) • Philippinas/os lesbigay group

Las Buenas Amigas (at Lesbian/Gay Community Ctr.) • 2pm 1st & 3rd Sun • Latina lesbian group

Legal Clinic (at Lesbian/Gay Community Ctr.) • 6:30pm Tue • free legal consultation

Lesbian Breast Cancer Support Group (at Lesbian/Gay Community Ctr.) • 6pm 2nd & 4th Tue

Lesbian Herstory Archives PO Box 1258, 10116 • (718) 768-3953 • exists to gather & preserve records of lesbian lives & activities • located in Park Slope, Brooklyn • wheelchair access

Lesbian Switchboard 741-2610 • 6pm-10pm Mon-Fri

▲ **Lesbian/Gay Community Services Center** 208 W. 13th St. • 620-7310 • 9am-11pm • wheelchair access

LSM (Lesbian Sex Mafia) PO Box 993, Murray Hill Stn., 10156 • women's S/M support group

Metropolitan Gender Network 561 Hudson St. #45, 10014 • (718) 461-9050 • call for free information

NY CyberQueers (at Lesbian/Gay Community Ctr.) • 7pm 3rd Th • lesbigay & transgender 'computer pros'

Party Talk Manhattan Cable Ch. 35 • 9pm Th & 11pm Sun • club reviews

SAGE: Senior Action in a Gay Environment (at Lesbian/Gay Community Ctr.) • 741-2247

SAL (Social Activities for Lesbians) PO Box 150118, 11215 • 630-9505 • 8pm 3rd Th

SALGA (South Asian Lesbian/Gay Association) (at Lesbian/Gay Community Ctr.) • 3:30pm 2nd Sat

Sirens Motorcycle Club (at Lesbian/Gay Community Ctr.) • 8pm 3rd Tue

Support Group for Single Lesbians (at Lesbian/Gay Community Ctr.) • 6:30pm Tue & Fri

Twenty Something (at Lesbian/Gay Community Ctr.) • 8pm 1st & 3rd Tue • social alternative to bars for lesbigays in late teens, 20s & early 30s

Village Playwrights (at the Center) • (718) 596-9905 • 6pm Tue

Women About: The Adventure Social Club for Lesbians PO Box 280 JAF Stn., 10116 • 947-7439 • indoor/outdoor activities for women in tri-state area • quarterly calendar

Women Playwrights Collective (at Lesbian/Gay Community Ctr.) • 6pm 1st, 3rd & 5th Wed

ACCOMMODATIONS

Aaah! Bed & Breakfast PO Box 2093, 10108 • 246-4000/(800) 362-8585 • gay-friendly • reservations agency

New York Reservation Center PO Box 2646, 11969 • 977-3512 • lesbians/gay men • IGTA

SPIRITUAL GROUPS

Axios (at Lesbian/Gay Community Center) • (718) 805-1952 • 8pm 2nd Fri • Eastern Orthodox Christians

Buddhist Lesbians/Gays: Maitri Dorje (at Lesbian/Gay Community Center) • 6pm 2nd Tue

Congregation Beth Simchat Torah 57 Bethune St. • 929-9498 • 8:30pm Fri (8pm summers) • lesbigay synagogue • wheelchair access

Dignity 110 Christopher St. • 627-6488

Evangelicals Concerned c/o Dr. Ralph Blair 311 E. 72nd St. #1G, 10021 • 517-3171

Gay/Lesbian Yeshiva Day School Alumni (at Lesbian/Gay Community Center) • 8:30pm 4th Th • social/support to integrate Jewish & lesbian/gay identities

Integrity NYC 691-7181

MCC of New York 446 W. 36th St. • 629-7440 • 10am & 7pm Sun

Meditation for Gays/Lesbians/Bisexuals (at Lesbian/Gay Community Center) • 8pm 1st & 3rd Wed

National Conference for Catholic Lesbians PO Box 436 Planetarium Stn., 10024 • (718) 680-6107 • national group • bi-annual conference • quarterly newsletter • for local NY chapter call (212) 663-2963

Society of Friends (Quakers) 15 Rutherford Pl. (Meeting House) • 777-8866 • 9:30am & 11am Sun

PUBLICATIONS

Colorlife 301 Cathedral Park Wy. Box 287, 10026 • 222-9794 • focuses on lesbians/gays of color

Feminist Caucus of NAAFA PO Box 1154, 10023 • 721-8259 • fat women's newsletter

Gayellow Pages Box 533 Village Stn., 10014-0533 • 674-0120 • annual guidebook • national & regional editions

Homo Xtra 19 W. 21st St., Ste 504 • 627-0747 • weekly complete party paper

Lesbian & Gay New York 225 Lafayette St. #1103 • 343-7200

Manhattan Spirit 242 W. 30th St. 5th flr. • 268-0454

New York Native/Stonewall News PO Box 1475 Church St. Stn. • 627-2120

Next 121 Varick St. 3rd flr. • 627-0165 • the scoop on New York's nightlife

N.Y.C. - Greenwich Village & Chelsea (212)

INFO LINES & SERVICES

WOW Cafe Cabaret 59 E. 4th St. • 460-8067 • Th-Sat • women's theater

ACCOMMODATIONS

Abingdon B&B 13 8th Ave. (at W. 12th) • 243-5384 • lesbians/gay men • smokefree

Chelsea Inn 46 W. 17th St. • 645-8989 • gay-friendly

Chelsea Mews Guest House 344 W. 15th St. • 255-9174 • mostly gay men

Chelsea Pines Inn 317 W. 14th St. • 929-1023 • lesbians/gay men • IGTA

▲ **Colonial House Inn** 318 W. 22nd St. • 243-9669/(800) 689-3779 • mostly gay men • IGTA

East Village B&B 260-1865 • women only • apt. rental

Holiday Inn 138 Lafayette St. • 966-8898 • gay-friendly

Incentra Village House 32 8th Ave. • 206-0007 • lesbians/gay men

BARS

The Bar 68 2nd Ave. (4th St.) • 674-9714 • 4pm-4am • mostly gay men • neighborhood bar • wheelchair access

Barracuda 275 W. 22nd St. (8th Ave) • 645-8613 • 4pm-4am • popular • mostly gay men • live shows

The Boiler Room 86 E. 4th St. • 254-7536 • 4pm-4am • popular • mostly gay men • neighborhood bar • 'Dyke Night' 10pm Sun

Boots & Saddle 76 Christopher St. • 929-9684 • 8am-4am, noon-4pm Sun • mostly gay men • neighborhood bar • leather

The Box 40 W.8th St. (40 Below) • 631-1000 • 9pm-3am Th • mostly women • dancing/DJ • multi-racial • live shows

The Break 232 8th Ave. (22nd St.) • 627-0072 • 2pm-4am • mostly gay men

Cake 99 Ave. 'B' (6th) • 388-2570/505-2226 • 10:30pm Sun 'Club Casanova' • a drag king/queen event • 9pm Tue 'Cup Cakes' • mostly women • lounge affair

Clit Club 432 W. 14th St. (Bar Room) • 366-5680 • 10pm Fri only • popular • mostly women • dancing/DJ • multi-racial • live shows • wheelchair access

Crazy Nanny's 21 7th Ave. S. • 929-8356 • 4pm-4am • mostly women • dancing/DJ after 10pm Th-Sat • live shows

Crow Bar 339 E. 10th St. • 420-0670 • 9pm-4am • lesbians/gay men • live shows

Cubbyhole 281 W. 12th St. • 243-9041 • 3pm-3am • mostly women • neighborhood bar • wheelchair access

Dick's Bar 192 2nd Ave. (12th St.) • 475-2071 • 2pm-4am • mostly gay men • videos

The Dugout 185 Christopher St. • 242-9113 • 4pm-2am, from noon Fri-Sun • mostly gay men • neighborhood bar • sports bar • Sun brunch

Eighty Eights 228 W. 10th St. • 924-0088 • 4pm-4am • gay-friendly • piano bar & cabaret • Sun brunch

Five Oaks 49 Grove St. • 243-8885 • 5pm-4am • gay-friendly • piano bar • also a restaurant • dinner (except Mon) • $15-20

Henrietta Hudson 438 Hudson (at Morton) • 243-9079 • 3pm-4am • mostly women • neighborhood bar • wheelchair access

Marie's Crisis 59 Grove St. • 243-9323 • 5pm-3am • popular • lesbians/gay men • piano bar from 9:30pm

Meow Mix 269 E. Houston St. • 254-1434 • clsd Mon • popular • mostly women • dancing/DJ • live shows

Mike's Club Cafe 400 W. 14th St. (at 9th) • 691-6606 • 2pm-4am • mostly gay men • neighborhood bar • live shows • food served

The Monster 80 Grove St. • 924-3557 • 4pm-4am • mostly gay men • dancing/DJ

Octopussy 35 E.13th St., 2nd flr. • 686-5592 • 9pm Sun • mostly women • dancing/DJ

Prospect Park 266 E. 10th St. (1st Ave.) • 677-1717 • 10pm Sun • mostly women • glamour girls

Pussin Boots 188 Ave A (12th St) • 777-6254 • 11pm Wed • lesbians/gay men • live shows

Rome 290 8th Ave (24th St) • 242-6969 • mostly gay men • live shows

Roxy 515 W. 18th St. • 645-5156 • roller-skating 8pm-2am Tue • dance floor Sat 11pm • popular • mostly gay men • alternative • live shows

Ruby Fruit Bar & Grill 531 Hudson St. • 929-3343 • 3pm-4am • mostly women • also a restaurant

She-Bang 631-1102 • 10pm Sat • mostly women • dancing/DJ • live shows • call for location

Shescape 686-5665 • women only • dance parties held at various locations throughout NYC area

Sound Factory (SFB) 12 W. 21st St. • 206-7770 • 11pm Fri • popular • mostly gay men • dancing/DJ

Stonewall Inn 53 Christopher St. • 463-0950 • 4pm-4am • mostly gay men • wheelchair access

Tunnel Bar 116 1st Ave. (7th St.) • 777-9232 • 2pm-4am • popular • mostly gay men • neighborhood bar

Wonder Bar 505 E. 6th. St. (Ave. A) • 777-9105 • 8pm-4am • lesbians/gay men • neighborhood bar • videos

WOW Wednesdays 248 W. 14th St. (7th Ave.) • 631-1102 • 9pm Wed • mostly women • dancing/DJ • live shows

RESTAURANTS & CAFES

Black Sheep 344 W. 11th St. • 242-1010 • popular • mostly gay men • fine dining w/ nostalgic country cooking • $16-25

Brunetta's 190 1st Ave. (11th) • 228-4030 • popular • lesbians/gay men • Italian • some veggie • $8-10

Cafe Tabac 232 E. 9th St. • 674-7072 • 6pm-3am • full bar

Chelsea Bistro & Bar 358 W. 23rd St. (9th Ave) • 727-2026 • trendy French • full bar

Circa 103 2nd Ave. (E. 6th St.) • 977-4120 • open late • popular • full bar • wheelchair access • women-owned/run

Claire 156 7th Ave. (19th St.) • 255-1955

Cola's 148 8th Ave. • 633-8020 • popular • Italian • some veggie • $8-12

Community Bar & Grill 216 7th Ave. (22nd St.) • 242-7900 • live shows

Empire Diner 210 10th Ave. (22nd St.) • 243-2736 • 24hrs • upscale diner

First 87 1st Ave (6th St.) • 674-3823 • late dining • hip crowd

Florent 69 Gansevoort St. • 989-5779 • 24hrs • popular • French diner • $10-15

Food Bar 149 8th Ave. (17th St.) • 243-2020 • popular

Global 33 93 2nd Ave. (5th St.) • 477-8427 • 5pm-midnight • int'l tapas • full bar • $8-15

Lucky Cheung's 24 1st Ave. (2nd St.) • 473-0516 • popular

Orbit Cafe 46 Bedford St. (7th) • 463-8717 • lunch & dinner, gospel brunch noon-5pm Sun, bar noon-2am, til 4am Fri-Sat • mid-scale American w/Latin accent • plenty veggie • full bar • wheelchair access • $9-20

Restivo 209 7th Ave. (22nd St.) • 366-4133 • gourmet • gay-owned/run

Sazerac House Bar & Grill 533 Hudson • 989-0313 • noon-midnight • Cajun • full bar • $8-20

Sung Tieng 343 Bleeker St. (10th St.) • 929-7800/924-8314 • popular • delivery

Universal Grill 44 Bedford St. • 989-5621 • lunch, dinner & Sun brunch • popular • lesbians/gay men

The Viceroy 160 8th Ave. (18th St.) • 633-8484 • popular • full bar

GYMS & HEALTH CLUBS

American Fitness Center 128 8th Ave. • 627-0065 • popular • mostly gay men

Archives Gym 666 Greenwich Ave. • 366-3725

Better Bodies 22 W. 19th St. • 929-6789 • lesbians/gay men

David Barton Gym 552 6th Ave. • 727-0004 • lesbians/gay men

BOOKSTORES & RETAIL SHOPS

A Different Light 151 W. 19th St. • 989-4850/(800) 343-4002 • 11am-11pm • lesbigay bookstore

Alternate Card & Gift Shop 85 Christopher St. • 645-8966 • noon-11pm

Bleeker Street Books 350 Bleeker St. • 10am-midnight

Don't Panic 98 Christopher St. • 989-7888

Greetings 45 Christopher St. • 242-0424 • 11am-10pm

▲ **Oscar Wilde Memorial Bookshop** 15 Christopher St. • 255-8097 • 11:30am-9pm • lesbigay

The Rainbows & Triangles 192 8th Ave. • 627-2166 • 11am-9pm • lesbigay

Soho Books 351 W. Broadway • 226-3395 • 10am-midnight

TRAVEL & TOUR OPERATORS

Empress Travel 224 W. 4th St., 2nd flr. • 206-6900/(800) 429-6969 • IGTA

Islander's Kennedy Travel 183 W. 10th St. • 242-3222/(800) 988-1181 • also Queens location: 267-10 Hillside Ave., Floral Park • (800) 237-7433 • IGTA

Wilderness Bridges 427 Washington St. • 802-9086 • lesbigay outdoor adventures

SEX CLUBS

Glove at The Vault 28 10th Ave. (13th St) • 255-6758 • 7pm-11pm 3rd Sun, doors close at 8:30pm • women only

EROTICA

Pleasure Chest 156 7th Ave. S. • 242-2158

N.Y.C. - Midtown   (212)

ACCOMMODATIONS

Central Park South B&B 586-0652 • lesbians/gay men • wheelchair access

Hotel Beverly 125 E. 50th St. • 753-2700/(800) 223-0945 • gay-friendly • food served • IGTA

Park Central Hotel 870 7th Ave. at 56th St. • 247-8000/(800) 346-1359 • gay-friendly • also a restaurant • wheelchair access

BARS

Bump 218 W. 47th St. • 869-6103 • 11pm-4am Sun • mostly gay men • dancing/DJ

Buster's 129 Lexington Ave. (at 29th) • 684-8832 • noon-4am • lesbians/gay men • neighborhood bar • transgender-friendly

Cleo's Saloon 656 9th Ave. (46 St.) • 307-1503 • 8am-4am • mostly gay men • neighborhood bar

Don't Tell Mama 343 W. 46th St. • 757-0788 • 4pm-4am • popular • gay-friendly • live shows

Edelweiss 580 11th Ave. (43rd St.) • 629-1021 • 4pm-4am • gay-friendly • dancing/DJ • live shows • fun mix of drag, transgender & everything else

The Greenhorn Saloon 818 10th Ave. • 582-5665 • noon-4am • mostly gay men • neighborhood bar • country/western • also 'Caroline's Oasis' from 8pm • dancing/DJ • transgender-friendly • live shows • patio

Her/She Bar 229 W. 28th St. (7th Ave.) • 631-1093 • 10pm Fri • mostly women • dancing/DJ

Julie's 204 E. 58th St., 3rd flr. • 688-1294 • 5pm-4am • mostly women • professional • live shows

S.O.S. 366 8th Ave. (28th St.) • 465-3122 • 10:30pm Sat • mostly women • dancing/DJ

South Dakota 405 3rd Ave. (29th St.) • 684-8376 • 3pm-4am • mostly gay men • neighborhood bar • wheelchair access

Twilo 530 W. 27th St. (10th Ave.) • 268-1600 • 11pm Fri-Sat • gay-friendly • dancing/DJ • live shows

The Web 40 E. 58th St. • 308-1546 • 4pm-4am • mostly gay men • mostly African-American • dancing/DJ

RESTAURANTS & CAFES

Cafe Un Deux Trois 123 W. 44th St. • 354-4148 • noon-midnight • popular • bistro • $12-24

Good Diner 554 42nd St. (at 11th Ave.) • 967-2661 • 24hrs • diner food, slightly upscale • $8-10

Mangia e Bevi 800 9th Ave. (53rd St.) • 956-3976 • Italian

Revolution 611 9th Ave. (43rd St.) • 489-8451 • trendy video dining

Rice & Beans 744 9th Ave. (50th St.) • 265-4444 • Latin/Brazilian • plenty veggie

Townhouse Restaurant 206 E. 58th (at 3rd) • 826-6241 • lunch & dinner, Sun brunch, late on wknds • popular • lesbians/gay men • eclectic & elegant • plenty veggie • live shows • $10-23

BOOKSTORES & RETAIL SHOPS

Eve's Garden 119 W. 57th St. Ste. 420 • 757-8651 • noon-7pm, clsd Sun • women's sexuality boutique

TRAVEL & TOUR OPERATORS

Our Family Abroad 459-1800/(800) 999-5500 • all-inclusive package & guided tours to Europe, Asia, Africa & S. America • IGTA

Pied Piper Travel 330 W. 42nd St. Ste. 1601 • 239-2412/(800) 874-7312 • IGTA

Stevens Travel Management 432 Park Ave. S., 9th flr. • 696-4300/(800) 275-7400 • IGTA

N.Y.C. - Uptown (212)

ACCOMMODATIONS

Malibu Studios Hotel 2688 Broadway • 222-2954/(800) 647-2227 • gay-friendly

New York B&B 134 W. 119th St. • 666-0559 • gay-friendly

BARS

Brandy's Piano Bar 235 E. 84th St. • 650-1944 • 4pm-4am • mostly gay men • wheelchair access

Candle Bar 309 Amsterdam (74th St.) • 874-9155 • 2pm-4am • popular • mostly gay men • neighborhood bar

Regents 317 E. 53rd St. • 593-3091 • noon-4am • mostly gay men • also a restaurant • Italian • plenty veggie • $7-17

N.Y.C. - Brooklyn (718)

INFO LINES & SERVICES

▲ **Dyke TV** Channel 34/67 • midnight 1st Fri • 'weekly half-hour TV show produced by lesbians, for lesbians'

BARS

Carry Nation 363 5th Ave., Park Slope • lesbians/gay men • neighborhood bar

Celebrity's 8705 3rd Ave., Bay Ridge • 745-9652 • 6pm-4am, from 4pm Sun, clsd Mon • lesbians/gay men • ladies night Tue

One Hot Spot 1 Front St. • 852-0139 • 9pm-3am, from 6pm Th, clsd Sun-Tue • lesbians/gay men • dancing/DJ • multi-racial • live shows • wheelchair access

The Roost 309 7th Ave. • 788-9793 • noon-2am • gay-friendly • neighborhood bar

Spectrum 802 64th St. • 238-8213 • 9pm-4am Wed-Sun • popular • lesbians/gay men • dancing/DJ • live shows

RESTAURANTS & CAFES

Kokobar Cybercafe & Bookstore 59 Lafayette Ave. (at Fulton) • 243-9040 • 7am-10pm, 10am-11pm Sat, til 10pm Sun • lesbians/gay men • wheelchair access

BOOKSTORES & RETAIL SHOPS

Community Book Store 143 7th Ave. • 783-3075 • 10am-9pm

TRAVEL & TOUR OPERATORS

Avalon Travel 9421 3rd Ave. • 833-5500 • IGTA

Deville Travel Service 7818 3rd Ave. • 680-2700 • IGTA

J. Bette Travel 4809 Ave. 'N' #279 • 241-3872 • IGTA

N.Y.C. - Queens (718)

INFO LINES & SERVICES

Q-GLU (Queens Gay/Lesbians United) PO Box 4669, 11104 • 1st Tue

BARS

The Boulevard 137-65 Queens Blvd., Briarwood • 739-2200 • 8pm-4am • mostly gay men

Krash 34-48 Steinway St., Astoria • 366-2934 • lesbians/gay men • more women Sat • dancing/DJ • multi-racial

Music Box 40-08 74th St. • 429-9356 • 4pm-4am • mostly gay men • multi-racial • leather

Stella's 12-21 Jackson Ave., Long Island City • 392-2132 • 11pm-4am • lesbians/gay men • live shows • ladies night Tue

N.Y.C. - Bronx   (212)

INFO LINES & SERVICES

BLUES (Bronx Lesbians United in Sisterhood) PO Box 1738, 10451 • 330-9196

▲ **Dyke TV** Channel 70 • 10pm Wed & Th • 'weekly half-hour TV show produced by lesbians, for lesbians'

N.Y.C. - Staten Island   (718)

INFO LINES & SERVICES

Lambda Associates of Staten Island PO Box 665, Staten Island • 876-8786

BARS

Legacy (Club Taboo) 23 Sands St. (Bay St.), Stapleton • 816-0713 • 9pm-4am • lesbians/gay men • dancing/DJ

Sand Castle 86 Mills Ave. • 447-9365 • 9am-4am • popular • lesbians/gay men • dancing/DJ • live shows • wheelchair access

Niagara Falls   (716)

INFO LINES & SERVICES

GALS (Gay/Lesbian Support) PO Box 1464, 14302 • mtg 2nd Sat

ACCOMMODATIONS

Old Niagara House B&B 610 4th St. • 285-9408 • gay-friendly

BARS

Club Alternate 492 19th St. (Ferry) • mostly gay men • dancing/DJ • inquire locally

Nyack   (914)

BARS

Barz 327 Rte. 9 W. • 353-4444 • 6pm-4am, from 2pm Sat & 1pm Sun, clsd Mon • lesbians/gay men • dancing/DJ • wheelchair access

Coven Cafe 162 Main St. • 358-9829 • noon-midnight, til 2am Fri-Sat, clsd Mon • gay-friendly • also a restaurant • cont'l w/ Southern accent • wheelchair access • $8-20

BOOKSTORES & RETAIL SHOPS

New Spirit Books & Beyond 128 Main St. • 353-2126 • noon-7pm, clsd Mon

Orange County   (914)

INFO LINES & SERVICES

Orange County Gay/Lesbian Alliance PO Box 1557, Greenwood Lake, 10925 • 782-1525 • 7:30pm Tue

RESTAURANTS & CAFES

Folderol II Rte. 284, Westtown • 726-3822 • noon-3pm & 5pm-9pm, til 11pm Fri-Sat, 3pm-9pm Sun, clsd Mon • French/farmhouse • some veggie • gay-owned/run • $13-23

Oswego   (315)

INFO LINES & SERVICES

SUNY Oswego Women's Center 243 Hewitt Union, 2nd flr. • 341-2967

Owego   (607)

TRAVEL & TOUR OPERATORS

Tioga Travel 189 Main St. • 687-4144 • IGTA

Plattsburg   (518)

BARS

Blair's Tavern 30 Marion St. • 561-9071 • 4pm-2am • lesbians/gay men • dancing/DJ • ladies night Th

Port Chester   (914)

BARS

Sandy's Old Homestead 325 N. Main St. • 939-0758 • 8am-4am • gay-friendly • food served • wheelchair access

Poughkeepsie   (914)

INFO LINES & SERVICES

Poughkeepsie GALA (Gay/Lesbian Association) PO Box 289, Hughsonville, 12537 • 431-6756 • 7:30pm Tue

Vassar Gay People's Alliance Box 271, 12601 • 437-7203

BARS

Congress 411 Main St. • 486-9068 • 3pm-4am, from 8pm Sun • lesbians/gay men • neighborhood bar • wheelchair access

TRAVEL & TOUR OPERATORS

Community Travel Connections 30 Griffen St., Poughquag • 227-4059/(800) 930-3011 • IGTA

SPIRITUAL GROUPS

Dignity-Integrity 15 Brandy St. (Christ Church) • 724-3209 • 8pm 3rd Fri

Rochester (716)

INFO LINES & SERVICES

AA Gay/Lesbian 232-6720 (AA#)

Finger Lakes Gay/Lesbian Social Group Box 941, Geneva, 14456 • 536-7753 • 1st Fri & 3rd Fri • ask for Sam Edwards

Gay Alliance 179 Atlantic Ave. • 244-8640 • 1pm-9pm, til 6pm Fri

BARS

Anthony's 522 Main St. E. • 325-1350 • noon-2am • lesbians/gay men • neighborhood bar

Atlantis 10-12 S. Washington St. • 423-9748 • call for events • mostly gay men • dancing/DJ

Avenue Pub 522 Monroe Ave. • 244-4960 • 4pm-2am • popular • mostly gay men • neighborhood bar • dancing/DJ

Chena's 145 E. Main St. • 232-7240 • 11am-2am • mostly women • neighborhood bar • food served • wheelchair access

Club Marcella 123 Liberty Pole Wy. • 454-5963 • clsd Mon-Tue • lesbians/gay men • dancing/DJ • live shows

Common Grounds 139 State St. • 262-2650 • 11am-2am • lesbians/gay men • neighborhood bar

Freakazoid 169 N. Chestnut St. • 987-0000 • call for events • gay-friendly • dancing/DJ • alternative

Muther's 40 S.Union • 325-6216 • 3pm-2am • lesbians/gay men • women's night 2nd & 3rd Th • live shows • also a restaurant • some veggie • patio • $5-18

Tara 153 Liberty Pole Wy. • 232-4719 • noon-2am • popular • lesbians/gay men • neighborhood bar • piano bar

RESTAURANTS & CAFES

Little Theatre Cafe 240 East Ave. • 258-0412 • 6pm-10pm, from noon wknds, til midnight Fri-Sat • popular • soups & salads • live shows • wheelchair access • $5-10

Slice of Life 742 South Ave. • 271-8010 • 11:30am-8pm, 10am-2pm Sun, clsd Mon-Tue • vegetarian

Triphammer Grill 60 Browns Race • 262-2700 • lunch & dinner, clsd Sun-Mon (dinner) • patio • full bar • $10-22

BOOKSTORES & RETAIL SHOPS

Borders 1000 Hylan Dr. • 292-5900 • general w/ lesbigay sections • cafe

The Pride Connection 728 South Ave. • 242-7840 • 10am-9pm, noon-6pm Sun • lesbigay

Rochester Custom Leathers 274 N. Goodman St. • 442-2323/(800) 836-9047 • 11am-9pm • popular

Silkwood Books 633 Monroe Ave. • 473-8110 • 11am-6pm, til 9pm Th-Fri, noon-5pm Sun, clsd Mon • women's/new age • wheelchair access

Village Green Books 766 Monroe Ave. • 461-5380 • 6am-11pm • also 1954 W. Ridge Rd. location • 723-1600

TRAVEL & TOUR OPERATORS

DePrez Travel 145 Rue De Ville • 442-8900 • ask for Ray • IGTA

Great Expectations 1649 Monroe Ave. • 244-8430/(800) 836-8110 • IGTA

Park Ave. Travel 25 Buckingham St. • 256-3080 • IGTA

SPIRITUAL GROUPS

Dignity/Integrity 17 S. Fitzhugh (St. Luke's/ St. Simon's Church) • 262-2170 • 5pm Sun

More Light Presbyterian 4 Meigs St. • 271-6513 • 10:30am Sun • wheelchair access

Nayim PO Box 18053, 14618 • 473-6459/442-3363 • lesbigay Jewish group

Open Arms MCC 875 E. Main St. • 271-8478 • 10:30am Sun • wheelchair access

PUBLICATIONS

Empty Closet 127 Atlantic Ave. • 244-9030

EROTICA

Dundalk News 561 State St. • 325-2248 • 24hrs

Saratoga Springs (518)

BOOKSTORES & RETAIL SHOPS

Nahani 482 Broadway • 587-4322 • 10am-6pm, noon-5pm Sun • wheelchair access

Schenectady (518)

ACCOMMODATIONS

Widow Kendall B&B 10 N. Ferry St. • (800) 244-0925 • gay-friendly • full brkfst • hot tub • fireplaces

BARS

Blythewood 50 N. Jay St. • 382-9755 • 9pm-4am • mostly gay men • neighborhood bar • wheelchair access

Clinton St. Pub 159 Clinton St. • 382-9173 • noon-4am • lesbians/gay men • neighborhood bar

Seneca Falls (315)

ACCOMMODATIONS

Guion House 32 Cayuga St. • 568-8129 • gay-friendly • full brkfst

RESTAURANTS & CAFES

Gene's Grille at the Gould 108 Fall St. • 568-4403 • lunch & dinner • bistro • full bar • wheelchair access • $4-15

Spring Valley (914)

BARS

Electric Dreams 302 N. Main St. • 362-4063 • lesbians/gay men • dancing/DJ

Stone Ridge (914)

ACCOMMODATIONS

Inn at Stone Ridge Rte. 209 • 687-0736 • gay-friendly • swimming • also a restaurant • regional American • full bar

Syracuse (315)

INFO LINES & SERVICES

AA Gay/Lesbian 463-5011

Gay/Lesbian Conference Hotline 422-5732

Lesbian Discussion Group (at Women's Center) • 7:30pm 2nd Fri

Lesbian Social Group 601 Allen St. (Women's Center) • 6:30pm 1st & 3rd Fri

Pride Community Center 446-4436 • newsletter

Syracuse Peace Council 924 Burnet Ave. • 472-5478 • also houses the 'Front Room Bookstore' • lesbigay • call for hours

Women's Information Center 601 Allen St. • 478-4636 • 10am-4pm Mon-Fri • wheelchair access

ACCOMMODATIONS

John Milton Inn Carrier Circle, Exit 35 • 463-8555/(800) 352-1061 • gay-friendly

BARS

Armory Pub 400 S. Clinton • 471-9059 • 8am-2am • mostly gay men • dancing/DJ • wheelchair access

Claudia's U.B.U. 1203 Milton Ave. • 468-9830 • 4pm-2am, from 7pm Sat, from noon Sun, clsd Mon-Tue • mostly women • dancing/DJ

Mr. T's 218 N. Franklin St. • 471-9026 • 3pm-2am, from noon Sun • popular • mostly gay men • neighborhood bar • dancing/DJ

My Bar 205 N. West St. • 471-9279 • 10am-2am, til 4am Fri-Sat •mostly women • dancing/DJ • food served (lunch,dinner & late night brkfst)

Ryan's Someplace Else 408-410 Pearl St. • 471-9499 • 8pm-2am, from noon Sun, clsd Mon-Wed • popular • mostly gay men • dancing/DJ • videos • wheelchair access

Trexx 319 N. Clinton St. • 474-6408 • 8pm-2am, til 4am Fri-Sat, clsd Mon-Wed • mostly gay men • dancing/DJ • live shows • wheelchair access

RESTAURANTS & CAFES

Happy Endings 317 S. Clinton St. • 475-1853 • 8am-11pm, 10am-2am Fri-Sat, 6pm-11pm Sun • lunch & coffeehouse • live shows • wheelchair access

Tu Tu Venue 731 Jay St. • 475-8888 • 4pm-1am, clsd Sun • popular • full bar • women-owned/run • $12-15

BOOKSTORES & RETAIL SHOPS

My Sister's Words 304 N. McBride St. • 428-0227 • 10am-6pm, til 8pm Th-Fri, clsd Sun (except Dec) • women's books • community bulletin board

SPIRITUAL GROUPS

MCC of Ray of Hope 326 Montgomery St. • 471-6618 • 6pm Sun • wheelchair access

PUBLICATIONS

Pink Paper PO Box 6462, 13217 • 476-5186

Utica (315)

INFO LINES & SERVICES

Greater Utica Lambda Fellowship PO Box 122, 13505

BARS

Carmen D's 812 Charlotte St. • 735-3964 • 4pm-2am, from 8pm Sat, clsd Sun • lesbians/gay men • neighborhood bar

Options 1724 W. Oriskany • 724-9231 • 5pm-2am, clsd Mon-Tue • lesbians/gay men • dancing/DJ

That Place 216 Bleecker St. • 724-1446 • 8pm-2am, from 4pm Fri • popular • mostly gay men • dancing/DJ • leather • wheelchair access

White Plains (914)

INFO LINES & SERVICES
Lesbian Line 949-3203 • 6pm-10pm

The Loft 200 Hamilton Ave. • 948-4922 • switchboard 1pm-4pm, 7pm-10pm • lesbi-gay community center • wheelchair access

BARS
Stutz 202 Westchester Ave. • 761-3100 • 5pm-4am, from 8pm wknds • popular • mostly gay men • dancing/DJ • live shows

Woodstock (914)

INFO LINES & SERVICES
Wise Women Center 246-8081 • retreat center • healing & herbal medicines

ACCOMMODATIONS
Woodstock Inn 38 Tannery Brook Rd. • 679-8211 • gay-friendly • swimming hole • wheelchair access

BOOKSTORES & RETAIL SHOPS
Golden Notebook 29 Tinker St. • 679-8000 • 10:30am-7pm, til 9pm summer • lesbigay section

Yonkers (914)

BARS
Harlee's 590 Nepperham Ave. • 965-6900 • 10pm-4am • lesbians/gay men • dancing/DJ

NORTH CAROLINA

Asheville (704)

INFO LINES & SERVICES
CLOSER (Community Liaison for Support, Education & Reform) 277-7815 • 7:30pm Tue (at All Souls Episcopal Church) • social/support group

Lambda AA 254-8539(AA#) • 8pm Fri (at All Souls Church, Biltmore Village)

OLOC (Older Lesbians Organizing for Change) PO Box 412, Fairview, 28730 • social/support group

OutFit 277-7815 • 1st & 3rd Sat • lesbigay youth support group

Phoenix PO Box 18332, 28814 • transgen-der support group • counseling & referrals avail.

ACCOMMODATIONS
27 Blake Street 27 Blake St. • 252-7390 • women only • Victorian home • $65

Apple Wood Manor Inn 62 Cumberland Cir. • 254-2244 • gay-friendly • full brkfst

The Bird's Nest 41 Oak Park Rd. • 252-2381 • lesbians/gay men • comfortable, secluded & quiet B&B • located on the sec-ond flr. of a turn-of-the-century home

Camp Pleiades 688-9201 (summer)/(904) 241-3050 (winter) • open Memorial Day-Halloween • women only • mountain retreat • cabins • swimming • food served

The Gate House 669-0507 • gay-friendly • large rental bungalow • women-owned/run

The Inn on Montford 296 Montford Ave. • 254-9569/(800) 254-9569 • gay-friendly • full brkfst • English cottage

Mountain Laurel B&B 139 Lee Dotson Rd., Fairview • 628-9903 • lesbians/gay men • full brkfst • 25 miles from Asheville

BARS
The Barber Shop/Hairspray Cafe 38 N. French Broad Ave. • 258-2027 • 7pm-2am • lesbians/gay men • dancing/DJ • live shows • private club • also 'Club Metropolis' • from 10pm Th-Sat

O'Henry's 59 Haywood St. • 254-1891 • 1pm-2am, from 11am Sat • lesbians/gay men • neighborhood bar • dancing/DJ • private club

Scandals 11 Grove St. • 252-2838 • 10pm-3am, clsd Sun-Wed • lesbians/gay men • dancing/DJ • live shows • 18+ Th • wheel-chair access • also 'Getaways' • quiet lounge • videos

Restaurants & Cafes

Grove Street Cafe 11 Grove St. • 255-0010 • 6pm-1am Wed-Sat (summer T-dance & BBQ 2pm-8pm Sun) • steaks/seafood • some veggie • full bar • patio • $10-15

Laughing Seed Cafe 40 Wall St. • 252-3445 • 11:30am-9pm, til 10pm Th-Sat, clsd Sun • vegetarian/vegan • beer/wine • patio • wheelchair access • $4-9

Laurey's 67 Biltmore Ave. • 252-1500 • 10am-6pm, til 4pm Sat, clsd Sun • popular • bright cafe w/ delicious salads & cookies • also dinners to-go • women-owned/run • wheelchair access

Bookstores & Retail Shops

Downtown Books & News 67 N. Lexington Ave. • 253-8654 • 8am-6pm, from 6am Sun • used books & new magazines

The Goddess Store 382 Montford Ave. • 258-3102 • noon-6pm, clsd Sun-Mon • lesbian/feminist gifts • divination tools • Wiccan items • call for class schedules • wheelchair access

Malaprop's Bookstore & Cafe 61 Haywood St. • 254-6734/(800) 441-9829 • 9am-8pm, til 10pm Fri-Sat, noon-6pm Sun • readings & performances

Rainbow's End 10 N. Spruce St. • 285-0005 • 10am-8pm • lesbigay

Travel & Tour Operators

Blue Ridge Travel 102 Cherry St., Black Mountain • 669-8681/(800) 948-3430 • lesbigay tours & cruises

Journeys, Inc. 8 Biltmore Ave., Pack Plaza • 232-0800/(800) 256-8235 • IGTA

Kaleidoscope Travel 120 Merrimon Ave. • 253-7777/(800) 964-2001

Spiritual Groups

The Cathedral of All Souls Biltmore Village • 274-2681 • 8am, 9am, 11am Sun & noon Wed • wheelchair access

MCC of Asheville 1 Edwin Pl. (Unitarian Universalist Church) • 259-3055 • 6:20pm Sun • wheelchair access

Unitarian Universalist Church of Asheville 1 Edwin Pl. • 254-6001 • 9am & 11am Sun (10am Sun during summer) • wheelchair access

WHISPER (Women's Holy Inspirational Performances, Events & Ritual) 258-3102 • weekly classes

Publications

Community Connections PO Box 18088, 28814 • 285-8861/285-9390

Erotica

Octopus' Garden 102 N. Lexington Ave. • 254-4980 • 11am-10pm, 1pm-6pm Sun

Bat Cave   (704)

Accommodations

Old Mill B&B Hwy 74, Box 252 • 625-4256 • gay-friendly • full brkfst

Blowing Rock   (704)

Accommodations

Stone Pillar B&B 144 Pine St. • 295-4141 • gay-friendly • full brkfst • wheelchair access

Boone   (704)

Spiritual Groups

MCC of the High Country 963-8582 • 7pm Sun

Cashiers   (704)

Accommodations

Jane's Aerie PO Box 1811, 28717 • 743-9002 • popular • mostly women • cottage in great mountain location

Chapel Hill   (919)

(See also **Durham** & **Raleigh**)

Info Lines & Services

B-GLAD (Bisexuals, Gay Men, Lesbians & Allies for Diversity) Box 39, Carolina Union CB#5210, 27599 • 962-4401 • call for events

Orange County Women's Center 210 Henderson • 968-4610 • 9am-7:30pm, til 5pm wknds • wheelchair access

Accommodations

Joan's Place 1443 Poinsett Dr. • 942-5621 • women only • shared baths • $45-48

Restaurants & Cafes

Crooks Corner 610 Franklin St. • 929-7643 • 6pm-10:30pm, Sun brunch • Southern • some veggie • full bar • wheelchair access • $20-25

Weathervane Cafe Eastgate Shopping Center • 929-9466 • lunch & dinner, Sun brunch • New American • some veggie • full bar • wheelchair access • $10-20

Bookstores & Retail Shops

Internationalist Books 405 W. Franklin St. • 942-1740 • 10am-8pm, til 6pm Sun • progressive/alternative • 'Movie Night' Fri

SPIRITUAL GROUPS
Community Church (Unitarian Universalist) 106 Purefoy Rd. • 942-2050 • 11am Sun

Jewish Gay/Lesbian/Bisexual Student Group 942-4057 • call for info

Charlotte (704)

INFO LINES & SERVICES
AA Gay/Lesbian 3200 Park Rd. (St. Luke's Lutheran Church) • 332-4387(AA#) • 8pm Tue

Charlotte Business Guild 565-5075 • networking group for lesbigay professionals

Gay/Lesbian Switchboard 535-6277 • 6:30pm-10:30pm

BARS
1800 West City View 1800 W. Morehead St. • 333-9769 • 10pm-4am, clsd Mon-Wed • lesbians/gay men • dancing/DJ • multi-racial clientele • African American • live shows • private club • wheelchair access

Brass Rail 3707 Wilkinson Blvd. • 399-8413 • 5pm-2:30am, from 3pm Sun • popular • mostly gay men • neighborhood bar • leather • private club • wheelchair access

Chaser's 3217 The Plaza • 339-0500 • 5pm-2am, from 3pm Sun • lesbians/gay men • dancing/DJ • live shows • videos • private club • wheelchair access

Liaisons 316 Rensselaer Ave. • 376-1617 • 4pm-1am • popular • lesbians/gay men • neighborhood bar • private club • women-owned/run

Mythos 300 N. College St. • 375-8765 • 10pm-3am, til 4am wknds • popular • gay-friendly • more gay Wed-Th • dancing/DJ • alternative • live shows • private club • wheelchair access

Oleen's Lounge 1831 South Blvd. • 373-9604 • 8pm-2am, from 3pm Sun • popular • lesbians/gay men • dancing/DJ • live shows • wheelchair access

Scorpio's Lounge 2301 Freedom Dr. • 373-9124 • 9pm-3:30am, clsd Mon • lesbians/gay men • dancing/DJ • country/western Tue • live shows • videos • private club • wheelchair access

RESTAURANTS & CAFES
300 East 300 East Blvd. • 332-6507 • 11am-11pm • new American • some veggie • full bar • $8-15

521 Cafe 521 N. College • 377-9100 • lunch Tue-Fri, dinner nightly • Italian • some veggie • wheelchair access • $8-15

Dikadees Front Porch 4329 E. Independence Blvd. • 537-3873 • 11am-10pm, til 11pm Fri-Sat • some veggie • full bar • wheelchair access • $6 & up

Dilworth Diner 1608 East Blvd. • 333-0137 • 7am-10pm, til 11pm Fri-Sat, 11am-5pm Sun • wheelchair access

El Gringo Grill & Cantina 3735 Monroe Rd. • 347-4241 • lunch Mon-Fri, dinner daily • Mexican • some veggie • full bar

Lupie's Cafe 2718 Monroe Rd. • 374-1232 • 11am-11pm, from noon Sat • homestyle • some veggie • $5-10

BOOKSTORES & RETAIL SHOPS
Paper Skyscraper 330 East Blvd. • 333-7130 • 10am-6pm, til 9pm Fri, noon-5pm Sun • books on art, contemporary fiction & gifts • wheelchair access

Rising Moon Books & Beyond 316 East Blvd. • 332-7473 • 10am-6pm • lesbigay & multicultural books • wheelchair access

Urban Evolution 1329 East Blvd. • 332-8644 • 11am-9pm, 1pm-6pm Sun • clothing & more

White Rabbit Books 834 Central Ave. • 377-4067 • 11am-9pm, 1pm-6pm Sun • lesbigay • also magazines, T-shirts & gifts

TRAVEL & TOUR OPERATORS
▲ **Damron Atlas World Travel/Pink Fairy Travel** 1409 East Blvd. Ste 6-A • 332-5545/(800) 243-3477 • IGTA

Mann Travels 9009-2 J.M. Keynes Dr. • (800) 849-2028 • IGTA

SPIRITUAL GROUPS
Lutherans Concerned 1900 The Plaza (Holy Trinity Church) • 651-4328 • 1st Sun

MCC Charlotte 4037 E. Independence Blvd. #300 • 563-5810 • 10:45am & 7:30pm Sun

New Life MCC 234 N. Sharon Amity Rd. (Unitarian Church) • (910) 784-0723 • 7pm Sun

PUBLICATIONS
▲ **The Front Page** PO Box 27928, Raleigh, 27611 • 829-0181

In Unison PO Box 8024, Columbia SC, 29202 • (803) 771-0804

Q Notes PO Box 221841, 28222 • 531-9988

Durham (919)
(See also **Chapel Hill** & **Raleigh**)

INFO LINES & SERVICES
Information Management & Presentation contact for women's business & professional organizations

Outright—Triangle Lesbian/Gay Youth
286-2396/(800) 879-2300 • 6pm-9pm info &
referrals, 2pm Sat mtg.

Steps, Traditions & Promises AA 2109 N.
Duke (Christ Lutheran) • 286-9499(AA#) •
7:30pm Tue

BARS

▲ **All About Eve** 711 Rigsbee Ave. • 688-3002
• 6pm-10pm, from 9pm Fri-Sat, 1pm-8pm
Sun • mostly women • dancing/DJ • private
club • deck & volleyball court • wheelchair
access

Boxers 5504 Chapel Hill Blvd • 489-7678 •
from 5pm • mostly gay men • alternative •
professional • videos

Power Company 315 W. Main St. • 683-
1151 • 9pm-? • lesbians/gay men • danc-
ing/DJ • live shows • private club • wheelchair access

RESTAURANTS & CAFES

Espress-O-Self 9th St. "Coffee Shack"
730 9th St. • 286-4885 • 9am-1am, til 2am
Fri-Sat, 10am-10pm Sun • live shows • art
gallery • wheelchair access

BOOKSTORES & RETAIL SHOPS

Lady Slipper, Inc. 3205 Hillsboro Rd.,
27705 • 683-1570 • distributor of women's
music & videos • also newsletter

Regulator Bookshop 720 9th St. • 286-
2700 • 9am-8pm, til 5pm Sun

PUBLICATIONS

The Newsletter PO Box 2272, 27702 • lesbian newsletter

Elizabethtown (910)

TRAVEL & TOUR OPERATORS

North & South Travel 118 W. Broad St. •
862-8557/(800) 585-8016

Fayetteville (910)

BARS

Millennium 2540 Gillespie St. • 485-2037 •
9pm-?, clsd Mon • mostly gay men • danc-
ing/DJ • also sports bar • live shows • private club • wheelchair access

Spektrum 107 Swain St. • 868-4279 • 5pm-
3am • lesbians/gay men • dancing/DJ • live
shows • patio

EROTICA

Priscilla's 3800 Sycamore Dairy Rd. • 860-
1776

Franklin (704)

ACCOMMODATIONS

Honey's Rainbow Acres PO Box 1367, 28734 • 369-5162 • mostly women • kitchen privileges • fireplace • great views • also private cottage

Gastonia (704)

TRAVEL & TOUR OPERATORS

Travel By Design 2333 Pine Haven Dr. • 864-0631 • IGTA

Greensboro (910)

INFO LINES & SERVICES

Gay/Lesbian Hotline 855-8558 • 7pm-10pm Sun, Tue-Th

Lesbian/Gay/Bisexual Resource Center Box 17725 Guilford College, 27410

Live & Let Live AA 2200 N. Elm (St. Pius Catholic Church) • 854-4278 • 8pm Tue

BARS

Babylon 221 S. Elm St. • 275-1006 • popular • lesbians/gay men • dancing/DJ • alternative • private club • call for events

The Palms 413 N. Eugene St. • 272-6307 • 9pm-2:30am • mostly gay men • dancing/DJ • live shows • private club

Warehouse 29 1011 Arnold St. • 333-9333 • 9pm-3am, clsd Mon-Tue • mostly gay men • dancing/DJ • live shows • private club

BOOKSTORES & RETAIL SHOPS

White Rabbit Books 1833 Spring Garden St. • 272-7604 • 11am-9pm, 1pm-6pm Sun • lesbigay • also magazines, T-shirts & gifts

TRAVEL & TOUR OPERATORS

Carolina Travel 2054 Carolina Circle Mall • 621-9000/(800) 289-9009 • IGTA

SPIRITUAL GROUPS

St. Mary's MCC 6720 W. Friendly Ave. • 297-4054 • 7pm Sun

Greenville (919)

BARS

Paddock Club 1008-B Dickinson • 758-0990 • 8pm-2:30am, clsd Mon-Tue • lesbians/gay men • dancing/DJ • alternative • live shows • private club • wheelchair access

Hickory (704)

BARS

Club Cabaret 101 N. Center St. • 322-8103 • 9pm-3am, clsd Mon-Wed • lesbians/gay men • dancing/DJ • live shows • private club • wheelchair access

SPIRITUAL GROUPS

MCC Hickory 109 11th Ave. NW (Unitarian Church) • 324-1960 • 7pm Sun & Tue

Hot Springs (704)

ACCOMMODATIONS

Deer Park Cabins Hwy. 209 • 622-3516 • gay-friendly • hot tub • gay-owned/run

The Duckett House Inn Hwy. 209 S. • 622-7621 • lesbians/gay men • Victorian farmhouse B&B w/ camping on Appalachian Trail • also a restaurant • vegetarian (reservations required)

Jacksonville (910)

BARS

Club Rebounds 200 Marine Blvd., Hwy 17 S. • 938-9431 • 8pm-?, clsd Mon • lesbians/gay men • dancing/DJ • live shows • food served

EROTICA

Priscilla's 113A Western Blvd. • 355-0765

Manteo (919)

PUBLICATIONS

Outer Banks GLC PO Box 1444, 27954 • 255-2073

Raleigh (919)

(See also **Chapel Hill** & **Durham**)

INFO LINES & SERVICES

AA Gay/Lesbian (Live & Let Live) 1601 Hillsboro St. (YMCA) • 783-6144 • 8pm

Gay/Lesbian Helpline of Wake County 821-0055 • 7pm-10pm

ACCOMMODATIONS

Oakwood Inn 411 N. Bloodworth St. • 832-9712 • gay-friendly • full brkfst

BARS

1622 Club 1622 Glenwood Ave. at Five Points • 832-9082 • 8pm-2am, from 5pm Sun, clsd Mon • lesbians/gay men • dancing/DJ • private club • wheelchair access

CC 313 W. Hargett • 755-9599 • 8pm-?, from 4pm Sun • mostly gay men • dancing/DJ • live shows • piano bar • 18+ • private club • wheelchair access

The Front Page

The Most Comprehensive Coverage of the Carolinas

Local, National and World News • Opinion
AIDS/HIV Coverage • Features • Cartoons
Film, Music & Book Reviews • Calendar
Community Resources • *Carolina Pulse*
Horoscope • Ms. Behavior • Classifieds

**To Send News, Letters, or Calendar Items
and for Advertising Information:**
Post Office Box 27928 • Raleigh, NC 27611
(919) 829-0181 • Fax: (919) 829-0830
E-mail: frntpage@aol.com

**Available Free Across the Carolinas
and by Subscription**

*Biweekly
26 issues per year*
$25 bulk rate
$45 first class mail
$2 sample copy

FREE Personals With Voice Mail

Serving the Gay and Lesbian Community Since 1979

Legends 330 W. Hargett St. • 831-8888 • 9pm-? • mostly gay men • more mixed crowd on wknds • dancing/DJ • private club • patio • wheelchair access

Restaurants & Cafes

Black Dog Cafe 208 E. Martin • 828-1994 • lunch & dinner, Sun brunch, clsd Mon • some veggie • full bar • wheelchair access • $6-17

Est • Est • Est Trattoria 19 W. Hargett St. • 832-8899 • 11am-10pm, clsd Sun • pasta • plenty veggie • full bar • $8-20

Irregardless Cafe 901 W. Morgan St. • 833-8898 • lunch & dinner, Sun brunch • plenty veggie • $9-15

Rathskeller 2412 Hillsborough St. • 821-5342 • 11am-11pm • some veggie • full bar • wheelchair access • $10-20

Bookstores & Retail Shops

Innovations 517 Hillsborough St. • 833-4833 • 11am-7pm, from 1pm Sun, clsd Mon-Tue • leather • fetish wear • piercings

Reader's Corner 3201 Hillsborough St. • 828-7024 • 10am-9pm, til 6pm Sat, 1pm-6pm Sun • used books

White Rabbit Books 309 W. Martin St. • 856-1429 • 11am-9pm, 1-6pm Sun • lesbi-gay • also magazines, T-shirts & gifts • wheelchair access

Travel & Tour Operators

Rainbow Travel 2801 Blue Ridge Rd. • 571-9054/(800) 633-9350 • IGTA

Spiritual Groups

Integrity 237-8825 • 6pm 2nd Sun • call for location

St. John's MCC 805 Glenwood Ave. • 834-2611 • 7:15pm Sun

Unitarian Universalist Fellowship 3313 Wade Ave. • 781-7635 • 9:30am & 11:15am Sun

Publications

▲ **The Front Page** PO Box 27928, 27611 • 829-0181

Spruce Pine   (704)

Accommodations

▲ **The Lemon Tree Inn** 912 Greenwood Rd. • 765-6161 • gay-friendly • also restaurant on premises • gay-owned/run

Spruce Ridge (704)

ACCOMMODATIONS
Shepherd's Ridge 765-7809 • open March-Nov • mostly women • cottage in the woods • sleeps 2-4 • $50

Wilmington (910)

INFO LINES & SERVICES
GROW Switchboard 341-11 S. College Rd. Ste. 182 • 799-7111 • 6pm-10pm

ACCOMMODATIONS
The Inn on Orange 410 Orange St. • 815-0035/(800) 381-4666 • gay-friendly • full brkfst • swimming • IGTA

Ocean Princess Inn 824 Ft. Fischer Blvd., South Kure Beach • 458-6712/(800) 762-4863 • gay-friendly • swimming • wheelchair access

The Taylor House Inn 14 N. 7th St. • 763-7581/(800) 382-9982 • gay-friendly • full brkfst • romantic turn-of-the-century house

BARS
Mickey Ratz 115-117 S. Front St. • 251-1289 • 5pm-2:30am • lesbians/gay men • dancing/DJ • live shows • private club

BOOKSTORES & RETAIL SHOPS
Rising Moon Books & Beyond 215-A Princess St. • 343-9106 • 10am-6pm, 1pm-5pm Sun • lesbigay & multicultural • lesbian-owned/run

PUBLICATIONS
Between Ourselves Newsletter 2148 Harrison St., 28401

Winston-Salem (910)

INFO LINES & SERVICES
Gay/Lesbian Hotline PO Box 4442, Greensboro, 27404 • 855-8558 • 7pm-10pm Sun, Tue-Th

LUNA (Lesbians Up for New Adventures) 788-1120 • 2nd Fri • social/support group

BARS
Bourbon Street 916 Burke St. • 724-4644 • 8pm-?, clsd Mon • lesbians/gay men • ladies' night Wed • dancing/DJ • live shows • private club • wheelchair access

NORTH DAKOTA

Fargo (701)

INFO LINES & SERVICES
The 10% Society PO Box 266, MSU, Moorhead MN • (218) 236-2200/236-5859 • confidential support group for lesbian/gay/bisexual students

Hotline 235-7335 • 24hrs • general info hotline (some lesbigay resources)

RESTAURANTS & CAFES
Fargo's Fryn Pan 300 Main St. • 293-9952 • 24hrs • popular • wheelchair access

Grand Forks (701)

INFO LINES & SERVICES
The UGLC (University Gay/Lesbian Community) 777-4321

EROTICA
Plain Brown Wrapper 102 S. 3rd St. • 772-9021 • 24hrs

OHIO

Akron (330)

INFO LINES & SERVICES
AA Intergroup 253-8181

ACCOMMODATIONS
Kimbilio Farm 6047 TR 501, Big Prairie • 378-2481 • women only • B&B • also cabin • swimming • 45 min from Akron • wheelchair access (cabin only)

BARS
Adams Street Bar 77 N. Adams St. • 434-9794 • 4:30pm-2:30am, from 3pm Sat, from 9pm Sun • popular • mostly gay men • dancing/DJ

Club 358 358 S. Main • 434-7788 • 5pm-2:30am • mostly gay men • wheelchair access

Gargoyles 271 S. Main • 384-1447 • 9pm-3am, clsd Tue • lesbians/gay men • dancing/DJ • live shows

Interbelt 70 N. Howard St. • 253-5700 • 9pm-2:30am, clsd Tue & Th • mostly gay men • dancing/DJ • live shows • videos

Roseto's 627 S. Arlington St. • 724-4228 • 6pm-1am • mostly women • dancing/DJ • country/western

RESTAURANTS & CAFES
Cheryl's Daily Grind 1662 Merriman Rd. • 869-9980 • 6:30am-7pm, til 9pm Th, til 11pm Fri-Sat, 8am-3pm Sun • lesbian-owned/run

The Sandwich Board 1667 W. Market St. • 867-5452 • 11am-8pm, clsd Sun • plenty veggie

TRAVEL & TOUR OPERATORS
Parkside Travel 3310 Kent Rd. Ste. 6, Stow • 688-3334/(800) 552-1647 • IGTA

SPIRITUAL GROUPS
Cascade Community Church 1196 Inman St. • 773-5298 • 2pm Sun

New Hope Temple 1215 Kenmore Blvd. • 745-5757 • 10am & 7pm Sun, 7pm Wed

PUBLICATIONS
Gay People's Chronicle PO Box 5426, Cleveland, 44101 • (216) 631-8646

Amherst (216)

INFO LINES & SERVICES
Gay/Lesbian Info Center 150 Foster Park Rd. (Deca Realty Bldg. lower level) • 988-5326/(800) 447-7163 • drop-in 6pm-9pm Wed

Athens (614)

INFO LINES & SERVICES
Open Doors (Gay/Lesbian/Bisexual Assoc.) 18 N. College St. OU • 594-2385 • mostly students

Canton (216)

BARS
540 Club 540 Walnut Ave. NE • 456-8622 • 9pm-2:30am, clsd Sun-Mon • mostly gay men • dancing/DJ • wheelchair access

Dar's Bar 1120 W. Tuscarawas • 454-9128 • 9pm-2:30am • lesbians/gay men • dancing/DJ

La Casa Lounge 508 Cleveland Ave. NW • 453-7432 • 10am-2:30am • mostly gay men • neighborhood bar • wheelchair access

Side Street Cafe 2360 Mahoning St. NE • 453-8055 • 3pm-1am, clsd Sun • mostly women • neighborhood bar • food served • wheelchair access

EROTICA
Tower Bookstore 219 12th St. NE • 455-1254

Cincinnati (513)

INFO LINES & SERVICES
AA Gay/Lesbian 861-9966

Alternating Currents WAIF FM 88.3 • 333-9243/961-8900 • 3pm Sat • lesbigay public affairs radio program • also 'Everywomon' • 1pm Sat

Cincinnati Youth Group PO Box 19852, 45219 • 684-8405/(800) 347-8336 • 24hrs info • mtg 6pm Sun at 103 William Howard (rear entrance)

Gay/Lesbian Community Switchboard 651-0070 • 6pm-11pm Sun-Fri, clsd holidays

Ohio Lesbian Archives 4039 Hamilton Ave. (above Crazy Ladies Books) • 541-1917 • Tue night & by appt.

People of All Colors Together PO Box 140856, 45250 • 395-7228 • social/support group • call for events

Women Helping Women 216 E. 9th St. • 381-5610 (crisis line)/977-5541 • 24hrs (hotline) • crisis center • support groups • lesbian referrals

ACCOMMODATIONS
Prospect Hill B&B 408 Boal St. • 421-4408 • gay-friendly • 1867 Italianate townhouse • full brkfst • smokefree • older kids ok by arr. • IGTA • gay-owned/run

Bars

Bullfish's 4023 Hamilton Ave. • 541-9220 • opens 7pm, from 6pm Sun • mostly women

Chasers 2640 Glendora • 861-3966 • 7pm-2:30am, clsd Mon • lesbians/gay men • dancing/DJ • live shows Th & Sun • free pizza Fri

The Dock 603 W. Pete Rose Wy. • 241-5623 • 4pm-2:30am, from 8pm Mon • popular • lesbians/gay men • dancing/DJ • live shows • volleyball court • patio • wheelchair access

Plum St. Pipeline 241 W. Court • 241-5678 • 4pm-2:30am • popular • mostly gay men • neighborhood bar • live shows • videos

Shirley's 2401 Vine St. • 721-8483 • 8pm-2:30am, from 4pm Sun, clsd Mon • mostly women • dancing/DJ • wheelchair access

Shooters 927 Race St. • 381-9900 • 4pm-2:30am • mostly gay men • dancing/DJ • country/western • lessons 8pm Tue & Th

Simon Says 428 Walnut • 381-7577 • 11am-2:30am, from 1pm Sun • popular • mostly gay men • neighborhood bar • wheelchair access

Spurs 326 E.8th St. • 621-2668 • 4pm-2:30am • popular • mostly gay men • leather • wheelchair access

The Subway 609 Walnut St. • 421-1294 • 6am-2:30am, from noon Sun • mostly gay men • neighborhood bar • dancing/DJ • live shows • food served

Restaurants & Cafes

Carol's Corner Cafe 825 Main St. • 651-2667 • 11am-1am (bar til 2:30am) • popular • some veggie • full bar • wheelchair access • $4-8

Kaldi's Cafe & Books 1204 Main St. • 241-3070 • 10am-1am, from 10am wknds • some veggie • full bar • live shows • wheelchair access

Mullane's 723 Race St. • 381-1331 • 11:30am-11pm, from 5pm Sat, clsd Sun • plenty veggie • beer/wine • wheelchair access • $5-12

Bookstores & Retail Shops

Crazy Ladies Bookstore 4039 Hamilton Ave. • 541-4198 • 10am-8pm, til 5:30pm Sat, noon-4pm Sun • women's

Fountain Square News 101 E. 5th St. • 421-4049 • 7:30am-6:30pm

LeftHanded Moon 48 E. Court St. • 784-1166 • 11:30am-7pm, clsd Sun • cards • gifts

Pink Pyramid 36-A W. Court • 621-7465 • 11am-10:30pm, til midnight Fri-Sat, clsd Sun • lesbigay bookstore & gifts

Travel & Tour Operators

Apache Travel 5017 Cooper Rd. • 793-5522 • ask for Laura

Victoria Travel 3330 Erie Ave. • 871-1100/(800) 626-4932 • ask for Dan • IGTA

Spiritual Groups

Dignity PO Box 983 • 557-2111 • 7:30pm 1st & 3rd Sat • mtg. at 690 Winding Wy. near Xavier U.

Integrity /Greater Cincinnati 65 E. Hollister (Church of Our Savior) • 242-7297 • 6:30pm 3rd Mon

New Spirit MCC 65 E. Hollister Ave. (Church of Our Saviour) • 241-8216 • 7pm Sun, 7pm Wed

Publications

Dinah PO Box 1485, 45201 • women's publication

The Ohio Word 225 E. N. St. Tower 1 Ste. 2800, Indianapolis IN, 46204 • (317) 579-3075

Cleveland   (216)

Info Lines & Services

AA Gay/Lesbian 241-7387

Blue Fish Production Company 3052 Meadowbrook Blvd., Cleveland Hts., 44118 • 371-9714 • producers/consultants for women's events

Buckeye Rainbow Society for the Deaf PO Box 6253, 44101

Cleveland Lesbian/Gay Community Center 1418 W. 29th St. • 522-1999 • 1pm-5pm Mon-Fri • call for events

Cleveland Lesbian/Gay Hotline 781-6736 • recorded info 24hrs

Daggin' Bitches 321-6295 • leatherwomen

GLOWS (Gay/Lesbian Older Wiser Seniors) 331-6302 • 7:30pm 2nd Tue

Hard Hatted Women 4207 Lorain Ave. • 961-4449 • non-profit group to support women in skill trades

Oven Productions PO Box 18175, Cleveland Hts., 44118 • 321-7799 • 'produces events to promote feminist culture'

Women's Center of Greater Cleveland 4828 Lorain Ave. • 651-1450/651-4357(helpline) • 9am-5pm Mon-Fri • some lesbian groups

BARS

Barbary Lane 2619 Noble Rd., Cleveland Hts. • 382-2033 • 3pm-1am, clsd Sun • lesbians/gay men • also a restaurant

Club Visions 1229 W. 6th • 566-0060 • 4pm-2:30am, til 4am Fri, from 6pm Sat • popular • mostly gay men • dancing/DJ • live shows • wheelchair access

Five Cent Decision (The Nickel) 4365 State Rd. • 661-1314 • 6pm-2:30am • mostly women • neighborhood bar

The Grid 1281 W. 9th • 623-0113 • 4pm-2:30am • popular • lesbians/gay men • more women Sun • neighborhood bar • dancing/DJ

Legends 11719 Detroit, Lakewood • 226-1199 • 11am-2:30am, from 7pm Sun • popular • mostly gay men • dancing/DJ • karaoke Mon & Wed

Metronome 1946 St. Clair Ave. • 241-4663 • 8:30pm-2:30am, 5pm-11pm Sun, clsd Mon-Tue & Th • mostly women • dancing/DJ • live shows • wheelchair access

MJ's Place 11633 Lorain Ave. • 476-1970 • 4pm-2:30am Mon-Sat • mostly gay men • women's night Th • neighborhood bar • karaoke • women very welcome

Muggs 3194 W. 25th St. • 661-5365 • noon-2:30am • lesbians/gay men • neighborhood bar • food served

Ohio City Oasis 2909 Detroit Ave. (at 29th St.) • 574-2203 • 8am-2:30am, from noon Sun • mostly gay men • leather • country/western Sun

Paradise Inn 4488 State Rd. (Rte.94) • 741-9819 • 11am-2:30am • lesbians/gay men • neighborhood bar

The Rec Room 15320 Brookpark Rd. • 433-1669 • 1pm-1am • mostly women • dancing/DJ • food served • wheelchair access • women-owned/run

Scarlet Rose's Lounge 2071 Broadview Rd. • 351-7511 • 5pm-2am, noon-8pm Sun • mostly women • neighborhood bar

U4ia 10630 Berea Rd. • 631-7111 • 9:30pm-2:30am Fri & Sun, til 4am Sat • popular • lesbians/gay men • dancing/DJ • live shows • wheelchair access

RESTAURANTS & CAFES

Billy's on Clifton 11100 Clifton Blvd. • 281-7722 • 11am-9pm, clsd Mon • some veggie • $5-12

Cafe Tandoor 2096 S. Taylor Rd., Cleveland Hts. • 371-8500/371-8569 • lunch & dinner • Indian • plenty veggie

Club Isabella 2025 University Hospital Rd. • 229-1177 • lunch & dinner, dinner only Sat, clsd Sun • Italian • full bar • live jazz • $15-25

Fulton Ave. Cafe 1835 Fulton Ave. • 522-1835 • 4pm-2:30am, from 8pm wknds • full bar

Cleveland   (216)

WHERE THE GIRLS ARE: Dancing downtown near Public Square, hanging out on State Rd. below the intersection of Pearl and Broadview/Memphis.

CITY INFO: 621-4110

ATTRACTIONS: Cleveland Metroparks Zoo. Coventry Road district. Cuyahoga Valley National Recreation Area. The Flats.

TRANSIT: Yellow-Zone Cab: 623-1500. AmeriCab: 881-1111.

The Inn on Coventry 2785 Euclid Heights Blvd., Cleveland Hts. • 371-1811 • 7am-9pm, 9am-3pm Sun • homestyle • some veggie • full bar • women-owned/run • $5-20

Lonesome Dove Cafe 3093 Mayfield Rd. • 397-9100 • 7am-6pm • some veggie • beer/wine • $5-7

Patisserie Baroque 1112 Kenilworth Ave. • 861-1881 • 8am-6pm, til 7pm Fri, from 10am Sat, clsd Sun-Mon • Euro-style pastry shop

Red Star Cafe 11604 Detroit Ave. • 521-7827 • 7am-11pm, til 1am Fri-Sat • lesbians/gay men • wheelchair access

Snickers 1261 W. 76th St. • 631-7555 • noon-10pm, 4pm-11pm Sat • some veggie • full bar • wheelchair access • $7-16

BOOKSTORES & RETAIL SHOPS
Bank News 4025 Clark • 281-8777 • 10:30am-8:30pm, clsd Sun

Cleveland

*C*leveland is making a comeback, after the recession and several economic facelifts. Actually, only some districts like 'the Flats' have had a beauty makeover. Other districts never lost the funky charm of this city that's home both to the Rock 'N Roll Hall of Fame and the Cleveland Symphony Orchestra.

Speaking of funky, flashback to the '60s with a trip down Coventry Road. University Circle is rumored to be another hangout of the avant garde, as is Murray Hill, known for its many galleries. While you're at it, make time for some serious art appreciation in the galleries of the world-famous Cleveland Museum of Art.

For the lesbian community, begin at **Gifts of Athena**, Cleveland's feminist bookstore. Here you can find out more about the ever-changing bar/coffeehouse scene in the **Gay People's Chronicle**, the local paper .

Be sure to contact **Oven Productions** about any events they're putting on for feminists.

For a wholesome meal, try the women-run **Snickers**, then head out to **Metronome**, a women's dance bar that also has live shows. For a more laid-back atmosphere, try **Five Cent Decision**.

Body Language 3291 W. 115th St. (at Lorain) • 251-3330 • noon-9pm, til 5pm Sun • "an educational store for adults in alternative lifestyles"

Bookstore on W. 25th St. 1921 W. 25th St. • 566-8897 • 10am-6pm, noon-5pm Sun • lesbigay section

Borders Bookshop & Espresso Bar 2101 Richmond Rd., Beachwood • 292-2660 • 9am-10pm, 11am-midnight Fri-Sat, 11am-9pm Sun • lesbigay section

The Clifton Web 11512 Clifton Rd. • 961-1120 • 10am-9pm, noon-5pm Sun • cards • gifts

Daily Planet News 1842 Coventry Rd. • 321-9973 • 6:30am-10pm • newspapers • magazines • gifts • wheelchair access

Gifts of Athena 2199 Lee Rd., Cleveland Hts. • 371-1937 • noon-7pm, 10am-6pm Sat, clsd Sun & Tue • women's bookstore

TRAVEL & TOUR OPERATORS

Flite II 23611 Chagrin Blvd., Beachwood • 464-1762/(800) 544-3881

Green Road Travel 2111 S. Green Rd., South Euclid • 381-8060

Playhouse Square Travel 1160 Henna Bldg./1422 Euclid Ave. • 575-0813/(800) 575-0813 • IGTA

Sun Lovers' Cruises & Travel 3860 Rocky River Rd. • 252-0900/(800) 323-1362 • IGTA

University Circle Travel 11322 Euclid Ave. • 721-9500/(800) 925-2339

SPIRITUAL GROUPS

Chevrei Tikva PO Box 18120, Cleveland Hts., 44118 • 932-5551 • 8pm 1st & 3rd Fri • lesbigay synagogue • call for events

Emmanuel Christian Fellowship Church 10034 Lorain Ave. • 651-0129 • 10:45am & 6:30pm Sun, 7:30pm Wed

Integrity-NE Ohio 18001 Detroit (St. Peter's Church) • 671-4946 • lesbigay Episcopalians

Presbyterians for Lesbian/Gay Concerns 932-1458 • 5:30pm 1st Sun • potluck & mtg.

PUBLICATIONS

Gay People's Chronicle PO Box 5426, 44101 • 631-8646

EROTICA

Laws Leather Shop 11112 Clifton Blvd • 961-0544 • 2pm-10pm, clsd Mon-Tue

Columbus   (614)

INFO LINES & SERVICES

AA Gay/Lesbian 253-8501

Bi-Lines PO Box 14773, 43214 • 341-7015 • call for events

Briar Rose PO Box 16235, 43216 • group for leather-oriented women

Crystal Club PO Box 287, Reynoldsburg, 43216 • 4th Sat • transgender social group

Dragon Leather Club PO Box 06417, 43206 • 258-7100 • pansexual leather group

Gay/Lesbian/Bi Alliance of OSU 340 Ohio Union, 1739 N.High St. • 292-6200 • student group

Nosotros 292-6200 • lesbigay Latina/o social group • call for time/location

Sisters of Lavender 93 W. Weisheimer (Unitarian Church) • 575-9646 • 7:30pm Wed • lesbian support group

Stonewall Union Hotline/Community Ctr. 1160 N. High St. • 299-7764 • 10am-7pm, 9am-5pm Fri, clsd Sat-Sun • wheelchair access

WOW (Women's Outreach for Women) 1950-H N. 4th St. • 291-3639 • 9am-5pm (meetings 5pm-8pm) • women's recovery center • wheelchair access

ACCOMMODATIONS

Columbus B&B 769 S. 3rd St. • 444-8888 • gay-friendly • referral svc. for German Village district • $55-65

Five Forty-Two B&B 542 Mohawk St. • 621-1741 • gay-friendly

The Gardener's House 556 Frebis Ave. • 444-5445 • lesbians/gay men only • spa • smokefree

Summit Lodge Resort & Guesthouse PO Box 951-D, Logan, 43138 • 385-3521 • popular • mostly gay men • camping avail. • hot tub • swimming • nudity • also a restaurant • wheelchair access

BARS

Blazer's Pub 1205 N. High St. • 299-1800 • 2pm-2:30am, 3pm-midnight Sun • mostly women • neighborhood bar

Club Deion 313 S. Fifth St. • 221-2804 • lesbians/gay men • dancing/DJ • mostly African-American

Clubhouse Cafe 124 E. Main • 228-5090 • 4pm-1am, clsd Mon • lesbians/gay men • food served

Downtown Connection 1126 N. High St. • 299-4880 • 3pm-2:30am • mostly gay men • sports bar

The Far Side 1662 W. Mound St. • 276-5817 • 5pm-1am, til 2:30am Fri-Sat, from 1pm Sun • lesbians/gay men • neighborhood bar

Garage Disco (at Trends Bar) • 461-0076 • 9pm-2:30am • popular • lesbians/gay men • dancing/DJ • alternative

Garrett's Saloon 1071 Parsons Ave. • 449-2351 • 11am-2:30am • mostly gay men • neighborhood bar

Havana Video Lounge 862 N. High • 421-9697 • open 4pm, from 3pm wknds • lesbians/gay men • popular • piano bar • videos • wheelchair access

Imagination Too 283 E. Spring St. • 224-2407 • gay-friendly • dancing/DJ

Outland 1034 Perry St. • 299-0300 • 6am-2:30am • lesbians/gay men • neighborhood bar • dancing/DJ

The Red Dog 196-1/2 E. Gay St. (rear) • 224-7779 • 4pm-2:30am • mostly gay men • live shows • wheelchair access

Remo's 1409 S. High St. • 443-4224 • 10am-2:30am, clsd Sun • lesbians/gay men • neighborhood bar • food served • pizza & subs • wheelchair access

Slammers Pizza Pub 202 E. Long St. • 469-7526 • 11am-2:30am, from 2:30pm wknds • lesbians/gay men • karaoke • wheelchair access

Summit Station 2210 Summit St. • 261-9634 • 4pm-2:30am • mostly women • neighborhood bar • dancing/DJ

Tabu 349 Marconi Blvd. • 464-2270 • 1pm-2:30am • mostly gay men • neighborhood bar • food served

Trends 40 E. Long St. • 461-0076 • 5pm-2:30am • popular • mostly gay men • dancing/DJ • wheelchair access

Union Station Cafe 630 N. High St. • 228-3740 • 1pm-2:30am • lesbians/gay men • food served • plenty veggie • $6-10

Wall Street 144 N. Wall St. • 464-2800 • 6pm-2:30am, clsd Mon • popular • mostly women • dancing/DJ • live shows • wheelchair access

RESTAURANTS & CAFES

The Coffee Table 731 N. High St. • 297-1177

Common Grounds 2549 Indianola Ave. • 263-7646 • 9am-midnight, til 11pm Sun, from 4pm Mon

Grapevine Cafe 73 E. Gay St. • 221-8463 • 5pm-1am, clsd Mon • lesbians/gay men • live shows • some veggie • full bar • wheelchair access • $7-15

Columbus   (614)

WHERE THE GIRLS ARE: Downtown with the boys, north near the University area, or somewhere in-between.

LESBIGAY PRIDE: June: 299-7764.

ANNUAL EVENTS: September - Ohio Lesbian Festival: 267-3953.

CITY INFO: 221-2489.

ATTRACTIONS: Columbus Zoo. Columbus Museum of Modern Art. German Village district. Ohio State University. Wexner Center for the Arts.

WEATHER: Truly midwestern. Winters are cold, summers are hot.

TRANSIT: Yellow Cab: 444-4444. Airport Shuttle: 478-3000. Central Ohio Transit Authority (COTA): 228-1776.

King Ave. Coffeehouse 247 King Ave. • 294-8287 • 11am-11pm, clsd Mon • popular • funky bohemian crowd • vegetarian • no alcohol • $3-7

L'Antibes 772 N. High St. (at Warren) • 291-1666 • dinner from 5pm, clsd Sun-Mon • French (vegetarian on request) • full bar • wheelchair access • from $16

Out on Main 122 E. Main • 470-1810/(888) 688-6246 • 5pm-10pm, til 11pm Fri-Sat, from 1pm Sun, clsd Mon • live shows • wheelchair access

BOOKSTORES & RETAIL SHOPS

ACME Art Company 737 N. High St. • 299-4003 • 1pm-7pm Wed-Sat • alternative art space • call for hours • also 'Cafe Ashtray' Fri

An Open Book 749 N. High St. • 291-0080 • 11am-10pm, from 10am wknds, til 6pm Sun • lesbigay • wheelchair access

The Book Loft of German Village 631 S. 3rd St. • 464-1774 • 10am-midnight • lesbigay

Hausfrau Haven 769 S. 3rd St. • 443-3680 • 10am-6:30pm, til 5pm Sun • cards • gifts • wine

Kukala's Tanning & Tees 636 N. High St. • 228-8337 • 11am-8pm, til 6pm wknds, from noon Sun • lesbigay novelties & gifts • women-owned/run

M.J. Originals 745 N. High St. • 291-2787 • 11am-7pm, til 6pm Sat, 1pm-5pm Sun • jewelry • gifts

Women's Words 3387 N. High St. • 447-0565 • 11am-7pm, noon-6pm wknds, clsd Mon • feminist bookstore • wheelchair access

TRAVEL & TOUR OPERATORS

Just Travel, Inc. 82 S. High St., Dublin • 791-9500/(800) 622-8660 • ask for Paul • IGTA

Ohio Division of Travel & Tourism (800) 282-5393

Travelplex East 555 OffiCenter Pl. Ste. 100 • 337-3155/(800) 837-9909 • IGTA

SPIRITUAL GROUPS

Dignity/Columbus 203 King Ave. (Presbyterian Church) • 451-6528 • 7pm 3rd Fri

Integrity/Columbus PO Box 292625, 43229 • 237-2844

Columbus

Although Columbus may not be a dyke mecca, there certainly must be something in the water, 'cuz we come out all over the place. Italian Village and Old Towne East are prime lesbian locations right next to (respectively) Victorian Village/Short North and German Village (which have great shopping and dining).

Columbus' lesbianville is Clintonville (affectionately known as Clitville), just north of the OSU campus. You will find the feminist bookstore/co-op, **Women's Words** (formerly Fan the Flames), where there is usually a woman-loving woman working the counter who can point you to the nearest fun stops like **Common Grounds** ("Where the girls are!"), **Moonspinners** or **Summit Station** (a.k.a. Jack's, a local watering hole). There you can also pick up the latest news as well as a calendar of events in **The Word Is OUT!**, our humble lesbian newszine, and also the **Gay People's Chronicle**, the **Stonewall Journal** (check out their "Guide" and calendar), Bar Trash and other "alterna-papers".

The Short North, the area on High St. just north of Downtown, is a funky, artsy neighborhood that hosts the Gallery Hop the first Saturday of every month when all the stores and galleries stay open till 10+. Nearby you will find **Blazer's Pub**, or try the Short North Pole; even if there aren't any girls there, there are fantastic ice cream concoctions. Girls also hang at the Coffee Table with lots of cruisin' boys.

The night before the Gallery Hop is First Friday at **Wall St.**, the downtown lesbian dance club, and every gay girl for a hundred miles shows up, starting early to catch the free buffet. If you can maintain a certain image, you can check out the very gay-friendly, very trendy **Mekka**, where you will be surrounded by gay boys and girls clad in vinyl or next to nothing.

If you're into the sports thang, check out Berliner Park, any season, to watch women's leagues of softball, volleyball, basketball, etc. Afterwards, head to the **Far Side**, the **Grapevine**, or **Slammers** and celebrate the victories or defeats with everyone else.

The best time of all is the Gay Pride March that always falls the same weekend in June as ComFest. This is the community festival at Goodale Park in Victorian Village which hosts a wide variety of merchants, food, information, and music, from local funk band Mary Adam 12 to Tribe 8.

— By Ada Kardos

(See back section on how to submit an essay about your favorite city.)

SOVEREIGNTY

FORMERLY SOVEREIGNTY FOR WOMAN

THE TIME IS NOW... TOGETHER WE CAN MAKE CHANGES.....

WERE NOT BUILDING BUSINESSES WE ARE BUILDING COMMUNITIES..

AN ALTERNATIVE MAGAZINE, FOCUSED ON THE LIGHTER SIDE OF THE GAY LESBIAN COMMUNITY.

FEATURING:

TRUE COMING OUT STORIES
HIGHLIGHTS OF EVENTS
UP COMING EVENTS
TRUE CONFESSIONS OF DRAG QUEENS
COMMUNITY CONTRIBUTIONS
ADVICE COLUMNS
AND MUCH MUCH MORE

SUBSCRIPTIONS ARE $18 A YEAR
SEND TO:
SOVEREIGNTY
P.O. BOX 259
BRICE OHIO 43109
FAX AND PHONE
614-833-2498
E-MAIL SFW1996@AOL.COM
HTT://MEMBERS.AOL.COM/SFW1996/SFW.HTM

The Jewish Group PO Box 06119, 43206 • informal Shabbat dinners

New Creation MCC 787 E. Broad St. • 224-0314 • 10:30am Sun

Spirit of the Rivers 1066 N. High St. • 470-0816 • 10:30am Sun • ecumenical service

St. Paul's Episcopal Church 787 E. Broad St. • 221-1703 • 5pm Sun • wheelchair access

St. Stephen's Episcopal Church 30 W. Woodruff • 294-3749 • 9:30am Sun

Publications

▲ **Sovereignty** PO Box 259, Brice, 43109 • 833-6468

The Stonewall Union Journal PO Box 10814, 43201 • 299-7764

Erotica

Bexley Art Theater & Video 2484 E. Main St. • 235-2341

Diablo Body Piercing 636 N. High St. • 228-8337 • clsd Tue

I.M.R.U. 235 N. Lazelle (above Eagle Bar) • 228-9660 • 11:30pm-2am Fri-Sat • leather

Piercology 874 N. High St. • 297-4743 • noon-7pm, til 6pm Sat, clsd Sun

Taboo Tattoos 636 N. High St. • 228-8337

Dayton (513)

Info Lines & Services

AA Gay/Lesbian 222-2211

Dayton Lesbian/Gay Center & Hotline 1424 W. Dorothy Ln. • 274-1776 • 7pm-11pm (hotline) • center 6:30pm Wed • coffeehouse 8pm Fri

Youth Quest PO Box 9343, 45409 • 275-8336 • lesbigay youth group 22 & under • call for time & location

Bars

1470 West 1470 W. Dorothy Ln., Kettering • 293-0066 • 8:30pm-2:30am, til 5am Fri-Sat, clsd Mon-Tue • popular • lesbians/gay men • live shows • videos • wheelchair access

Asylum 605 S. Patterson Blvd. • 228-8828 • 9pm-?, clsd Sun-Mon • gay-friendly • dancing/DJ • alternative • 18+

Down Under 131 N. Ludlow St. • 228-1050 • 11am-2pm for lunch, from 7pm, clsd Sun-Mon • mostly women • dancing/DJ • wheelchair access

Dugout 619 Salem Ave. • 274-2394 • 10am-2:30am • lesbians/gay men • neighborhood bar • dancing/DJ • food served

The Edge 1227 Wilmington • 294-0713 • 5pm-2:30am, clsd Sun • mostly gay men • dancing/DJ • country/western Tue • HiNRG Fri-Sat • wheelchair access

Jessie's After Dark 121 N. Ludlow • 223-2582 • 3pm-2:30am • popular • mostly gay men • dancing/DJ • karaoke • food served • wheelchair access

Right Corner 105 E. 3rd St. • 228-1285 • noon-2:30am • mostly gay men • neighborhood bar • wheelchair access

Rustic Cabin 2320 Wilmington Pike, Kettering • 253-7691 • 5pm-2:30am • mostly gay men • neighborhood bar • wheelchair access

Bookstores & Retail Shops

Books & Co. 350 E. Stroop Rd. • 298-6540 • 9am-11pm

Q Giftshop 121 N. Ludlow St. • 223-4438 • 10pm-1am, til 2:30am Fri, til 3am Sat • lesbigay

Spiritual Groups

Community Gospel Church 546 Xenia Ave. • 252-8855 • 10am Sun, 7:30pm Wed

MCC 1630 E. 5th St. (at McClure) • 228-4031 • 10am & 6:30pm Sun

Publications

The Ohio Word 225 E. N. St. Tower 1 Ste. 2800, Indianapolis IN, 46204 • (317) 579-3075

Rightfully Proud PO Box 3032, 45401-3032 • 274-1616

Erie (216)

Bars

Leeward Lounge 1022 Bridge St., Ashtabula • 964-9935 • 8pm-2am • lesbians/gay men • food served

Findlay (419)

Erotica

Findlay Adult Books & Video 623 Trenton Ave. • 422-1301 • 24hrs

Fremont (419)

Bars

Saloon Bar 531 W. State • 334-9340 • 1pm-2:30am, from 4pm wknds, clsd Mon • mostly gay men • neighborhood bar

Glenford (614)

ACCOMMODATIONS

Springhill Farm Resort 5704 Highpoint Rd., 43739-9727 • 659-2364 • mostly women • cabins & restored bar on 30 acres • hot tub • swimming

Guysville

ACCOMMODATIONS

Moon Ridge Rte 1, Box 240, 45735 • no phone • campground

Kent (216)

INFO LINES & SERVICES

Kent Lesbian/Gay/Bisexual Union KSU • 672-2068

RESTAURANTS & CAFES

The Zephyr 106 W. Main St. • 678-4848 • 8am-9pm, from 9am wknds, clsd Mon • live shows • vegetarian • wheelchair access • women-owned/run • $3-7

Lima (419)

BARS

Alternatives 138 W. 3rd St., Mansfield • 522-0044 • 7pm-2:30am, from 8pm Sun, clsd Mon • gay-friendly • dancing/DJ

Somewhere In Time 804 W. North St. • 227-7288 • 7pm-2:30am, from 8pm Fri-Sat • lesbians/gay men • dancing/DJ Fri-Sat • live shows

Logan (614)

ACCOMMODATIONS

Spring Wood Hocking Hills Cabins 15 miles NW of Logan • 385-2042 • lesbians/gay men • cabins • hot tub • smokefree • kids/pets ok • wheelchair access • $85-90

Lorain (216)

INFO LINES & SERVICES

Gay/Lesbian Info Center 150 Foster Park Rd. (Deca Realty Bldg. lower level), Amherst • 988-5326/(800) 447-7163 • drop-in 6pm-9pm Wed

BARS

Nite Club 2223 Broadway • 245-6319 • 8pm-2:30am, from 3pm Sun • mostly gay men • neighborhood bar • dancing/DJ • live shows • wheelchair access

Mentor (216)

INFO LINES & SERVICES

Hugs East PO Box 253, 44061 • 974-8909 • 7pm-9pm Wed, phone 24hrs • lesbigay info & referrals for Ashtabula, Geauga & Lake counties

Oberlin (216)

INFO LINES & SERVICES

Oberlin Lesbian/Gay/Bisexual Union Wilder Rm. 202 (Box 88), 44074 • 775-8179

Oxford (513)

INFO LINES & SERVICES

Miami University Gay/Lesbian/Bisexual Alliance 529-3823

Portsmouth (614)

ACCOMMODATIONS

1835 House B&B 353-1856 • gay-friendly • on the Ohio River • swimming • smokefree • kids/pets ok

Sandusky (419)

BARS

X-Centricities 306 W. Water St. • 624-8118 • 4pm-2:30am, from 1pm wknds (winter) • lesbians/gay men • dancing/DJ • live shows

BOOKSTORES & RETAIL SHOPS

City News 139 Columbus Ave. • 626-1265 • 7am-5:30pm

Springfield (513)

BARS

Chances 1912 Edwards Ave. • 324-0383 • 8:30pm-2:30am, clsd Tue • gay-friendly • dancing/DJ • live shows • patio

Steubenville (614)

EROTICA

Steubenville News 426 Market St. • 282-5842

Toledo (419)

INFO LINES & SERVICES

AA Gay/Lesbian 472-8242

Pro Toledo Info Line 472-2364 • 4pm-11pm

BARS

Blu Jean Cafe 3606 Sylvania Ave. • 474-0690 • 4pm-2:30am • popular • lesbians/gay men • more women Th • live shows • karaoke • food served

Bretz 2012 Adams St. • 243-1900 • 4pm-2:30am, til 4:30am Fri-Sat, clsd Mon-Tue • popular • mostly gay men • dancing/DJ • alternative • live shows • videos

Caesar's Show Bar 133 N. Erie St. • 241-5140 • 8pm-2:30am Th-Sun • lesbians/gay men • dancing/DJ • live shows • wheelchair access

Hooterville Station 119 N. Erie St. • 241-9050 • 5:30am-2:30am • mostly gay men • dancing/DJ • leather • wheelchair access

Scenic Bar 702 Monroe St. • 241-5997 • 1pm-2:30am • mostly women • dancing/DJ

RESTAURANTS & CAFES

Sufficient Grounds 3160 Markway (Cricket West Mall) • 537-1988 • 7am-11pm, til midnight Fri-Sat, from 10am Sun • wheelchair access • also 420 Madison • 243-5282

BOOKSTORES & RETAIL SHOPS

Tallulah's 6725 W. Central • 843-7707 • 11am-6pm, til 8pm Tue-Th, clsd Sun • feminist giftshop • wheelchair access

Thackeray's 3301 W. Central Ave. • 537-9259 • 9am-9pm, 10am-6pm Sun • wheelchair access

TRAVEL & TOUR OPERATORS

Great Ways Travel 4625 W. Bancroft • 536-8000/(800) 729-9297 • IGTA

Toledo Travel Club 4612 Talmadge Rd. • 471-2820/(800) 860-2820 • IGTA

SPIRITUAL GROUPS

MCC Good Samaritan 720 W. Delaware • 244-2124 • 11am Sun, (10am summers)

EROTICA

Adult Pleasures 4404 N. Detroit • 476-4587 • 24hrs

Tremont (216)

BARS

Hi & Dry Inn 2207 W. 11th St. • 621-6166 • 4pm-2am • lesbians/gay men • neighborhood bar • food served • plenty veggie • patio • $5-10

Warren (216)

BARS

The Alley 441 E. Market St. • 394-9483 • 2pm-2:30am • lesbians/gay men • dancing/DJ • live shows • wheelchair access

The Crazy Duck 121 Pine St. SE • 394-3825 • 4pm-2:30am • popular • lesbians/gay men • dancing/DJ • 18+ • wheelchair access

The Purple Onion 136 Pine St. • 399-2097 • noon-2:30am • lesbians/gay men • neighborhood bar • dancing/DJ • live shows

Wooster

INFO LINES & SERVICES

Lambda Wooster Box C-3166, College of Wooster, 44691

Yellow Springs (513)

INFO LINES & SERVICES

Gay/Lesbian Center Antioch College • 767-7331x601

RESTAURANTS & CAFES

Winds Cafe & Bakery 215 Xenia Ave. • 767-1144 • call for hours • vegetarian (organic) • full bar • wheelchair access • women-owned/run • $13-17

BOOKSTORES & RETAIL SHOPS

Epic Bookshop 232 Xenia Ave. • 767-7997 • 10am-6pm, til 9pm Fri, noon-6pm Sun

Youngstown (330)

INFO LINES & SERVICES

PACT (People of All Colors Together) PO Box 1131, 44501

BARS

Phil's Place 10 E. La Clede • 782-6991 • 4pm-2:30am • mostly women • neighborhood bar • patio • wheelchair access

Sophies 2 E. LaClede • 782-8080 • 4pm-2:30am • lesbians/gay men • neighborhood bar

Troubadour 2622 Market St. (enter back lot) • 788-4379 • 9pm-2:30am • lesbians/gay men • dancing/DJ • live shows • wheelchair access

OKLAHOMA

Claremore   (918)

TRAVEL & TOUR OPERATORS
International Tours of Claremore 608 W. Will Rogers Blvd. • 341-6866 • IGTA

El Reno   (405)

ACCOMMODATIONS
The Good Life RV Resort Exit 108 I-40, 1/4 mile S. • 884-2994 • gay-friendly • 31 acres w/ 100 campsites & 100 RV hookups • swimming

Lawton   (405)

BARS
Triangles 8-1/2 NW 2nd St. • 351-0620 • 9pm-2am, clsd Mon-Tue • lesbians/gay men • neighborhood bar • dancing/DJ • live shows • wheelchair access

Norman   (405)

BARS
Club Underground 1311 S. Jenkins • 329-9665 • 7pm-2am, clsd Mon-Tue • lesbians/gay men • more women Th • dancing/DJ • live shows

Oklahoma City   (405)

INFO LINES & SERVICES
AA Live & Let Live 3405 N. Villa • 947-3834 • noon, 5:30pm & 8pm

Gay/Lesbian Outreach 4400 N. Lincoln • 425-0399 • counseling for HIV affected • also substance abuse outreach • support groups for 14-20 yrs, 21-29+ yrs

Herland Sister Resources Inc. 2312 NW 39th St. • 521-9696 • 10am-5pm Sat, from 1pm Sun • women's resource center • wheelchair access

Oasis Resource Center 2135 NW 39th St. • 525-2437 • 7pm-10pm, til midnight Fri-Sat

ACCOMMODATIONS
America's Crossroads B&B 495-1111 • reservation service for private homes

▲ **Habana Inn** 2200 NW 39th St. • 528-2221 • popular • lesbians/gay men • swimming • also bars & restaurant on premises • wheelchair access

BARS
Angles 2117 NW 39th St. • 524-3431 • 9pm-2am, clsd Mon-Tue • popular • lesbian/gay men • dancing/DJ • wheelchair access

Bunkhouse 2800 NW 39th St. • 943-0843 • 1pm-2am • (restaurant 5pm-10pm, til 4am Fri-Sat) • popular • lesbians/gay men • dancing/DJ • country/western • leather • live shows • southern home cooking • wheelchair access • $3-7

Copa at Habana Inn Complex • 525-0730 • 9pm-2am • lesbians/gay men • dancing/DJ • live shows • wheelchair access

---

Oklahoma City (405)

ANNUAL EVENTS: May - Herland Spring Retreat: music, workshops, campfire. September - Herland Fall Retreat: 521-9696.

CITY INFO: 278-8912.

ATTRACTIONS: Myriad Garden's Crystal Bridge. National Cowboy Hall of Fame. National Softball Hall of Fame.

TRANSIT: Yellow Cab: 232-6161. Airport Express: 681-3311. Metro Transit: 235-7433.

The Habana Inn

We've Got It All!!!

Cable TV ★ Showtime
Free Local Phones ★ 200 Rooms

2200 NW 39th Expressway   Oklahoma City
405/528-2221   out of 405 area. call 1-800-988-2221

...and located in the Habana Inn Complex...

Gushers Restaurant
Your Finest Dining Choice in Oklahoma

FINISHLINE
For the Best COUNTRY & WESTERN Dancing in Town!

THE COPA

OKC's Premiere Show Bar and Dance Club

2200 NW 39th Expressway ♦ OKC ♦ 405/525-0730

Coyote Club 2120 NW 39th St. • 521-9533
• 5pm-2am, from 3pm Sun • mostly women • dancing/DJ • wheelchair access

▲ Finish Line (at Habana Inn) • 525-0730 • noon-2am • lesbians/gay men • dancing/DJ • country/western

Hi-Lo Club 1221 NW 50th St. • 843-1722 • noon-2am • lesbians/gay men • neighborhood bar • live shows

K.A.'s 2024 NW 11th • 525-3734 • 2pm-2am • mostly women • neighborhood bar • beer bar • Sun brunch

Park 2125 NW 39th St. • 528-4690 • 5pm-2am, from 3pm Sun • popular • mostly gay men • dancing/DJ • patio • wheelchair access

Roadhouse 4801 N. Lincoln Rd. • 525-8585/(800) 457-2582 • 4pm-2am • lesbians/gay men • 4 bar complex • neighborhood bar • dancing/DJ • wheelchair access

Tramps 2201 NW 39th St. • 521-9080 • noon-2am, from 10am wknds • popular • mostly gay men • dancing/DJ • wheelchair access

Tropical Heat 2805 NW 36th • 948-0572 • 5pm-2am, from 3pm wknds • clsd Mon-Tue • mostly women • Sun brunch

Wreck Room 2127 NW 39th St. • 525-7610 • 9pm-? Fri-Sat • popular • lesbians/gay men • dancing/DJ • juice bar • live shows • 18+

RESTAURANTS & CAFES

Grateful Bean Cafe 1039 Walker • 236-3503 • 8am-5pm, til midnight Fri, 10am-2pm Sun • live shows

▲ Gusher's Restaurant (at Habana Inn Complex) • 528-2221x411 • 11am-10:30pm, from 7am-3:30am Fri-Sat • wheelchair access

The Patio Cafe 5100 N. Classen • 842-7273

The Pinon Cafe 2124 NW 39th St. • 521-9202 • 5pm-3am, from 11am Th-Sun, clsd Mon • lesbians/gay men • southwest/Californian • some veggie • $7-9

BOOKSTORES & RETAIL SHOPS

Ziggyz 4005 N. Pennsylvania • 521-9999

TRAVEL & TOUR OPERATORS

Oklahoma Traveler Information (800) 652-6552

TLC Travel Professionals Inc. 1015 S. Meridian • 948-1740/(800) 852-1740 • IGTA

SPIRITUAL GROUPS

Dignity & Integrity NW 19th & Portland (Lighthouse MCC) • 636-4388 • 7:30pm 2nd & 4th Tue

Lighthouse MCC 3629 NW 19th • 942-2822 • 10:30am Sun, 7:30pm Wed

Oklahoma City Religious Society of Friends (Quakers) 312 SE 25th St. • 631-4174 • 10am Sun

PUBLICATIONS

Gayly Oklahoman PO Box 60930, 73146 • 528-0800

The Herland Voice 2312 NW 39th St., 73112 • 521-9696

Women's Yellow Pages of Oklahoma PO Box 54858 • 524-7020

EROTICA

Jungle Red (at Habana Inn) • 524-5733 • wheelchair access

Stillwater (405)

INFO LINES & SERVICES

Lesbigay Community Assoc. of OSU 744-5252

BARS

Snuffy's 2106 S. Main St. • 743-3659 • 6pm-2am, from noon wknds • clsd Mon-Tue • mostly gay men • dancing/DJ

Tulsa (918)

INFO LINES & SERVICES

Gay Info Line/TOHR 743-4297 • 8pm-10pm, women's supper club Wed

LesBiGay Alliance (at Tulsa University) • 583-9780

Rainbow Business Guild 665-5174

TULSA (Tulsa Uniform/Leather Seekers Assoc.) 838-1222

BARS

Bamboo Lounge 7204 E. Pine • 832-1269 • 11am-2am • mostly gay men • neighborhood bar • wheelchair access

Concessions 3340 S. Peoria • 744-0896 • 9pm-2am, clsd Mon-Wed • popular • lesbians/gay men • dancing/DJ • live shows • wheelchair access

Lola's 2630 E. 15th • 749-1563 • 4pm-2am, from 2pm wknds • lesbians/gay men • neighborhood bar • live shows

New Age Renegades/The Rainbow Room
1649 S. Main St. • 585-3405 • 2pm-2am •
popular • lesbians/gay men • neighborhood bar • live shows • patio • wheelchair
access

Silver Star Saloon 1565 S. Sheridan • 834-
4234 • 7pm-2am, clsd Mon-Tue • mostly
gay men • more women Sat • dancing/DJ •
country/western • wheelchair access

T.N.T. 2114 S. Memorial • 660-0856 • 6pm-
2am • popular • mostly women • danc-
ing/DJ

Restaurants & Cafes

Java Dave's 1326 E. 15th St. (Lincoln Plaza)
• 592-3317 • 7am-11pm • cafe

Samson & Delilah 10 E. 5th St. • 585-2221
• 11am-2pm, 5pm-10pm Fri-Sat • French •
plenty veggie

Wild Fork 1820 Utica Square • 742-0712 •
7am-10pm, clsd Sun • full bar • wheelchair
access • women owned/run • $10-20

Travel & Tour Operators

TLC Travel Professionals Inc. 6015 S.
Sheridan • 492-1852/(800) 290-6798 • IGTA

Spiritual Groups

Dignity-Integrity 5635 E.71st St. (church) •
298-4648 • 5pm 2nd Sat

Family of Faith MCC 5451-E S. Mingo •
622-1441

MCC of Greater Tulsa 1623 N. Maplewood
• 838-1715 • 10:45am Sun, 7pm Wed

Publications

Tulsa Family News PO Box 4140, 74159 •
583-1248

WOMEN'S TRAVELLER 1997

OREGON

Ashland (541)

INFO LINES & SERVICES

Womansource PO Box 335, 97520 • 482-2026 • feminist group • sponsors cultural activities like '1st Fri Coffeehouse' & annual Fall Gathering (wheelchair access) • also publishes 'Community News'

ACCOMMODATIONS

The Arden Forest Inn 261 W. Hersey St. • 488-1496 • gay-friendly • full brkfst • kids okay • wheelchair access • gay-owned/run • $65-105

Country Willows B&B Inn 1313 Clay St. • 488-1590/(800) 945-5697 • gay-friendly • full brkfst • swimming

Dandelion Garden Cottage 488-4463 • women only • retreat

Rogues Inn 600 E. Main St. • 482-4770/(800) 276-4837 • gay-friendly • apts.

Rose Cottage 272 N. 1st St. • (805) 684-5963 • seasonal • lesbians/gay men • secluded garden cottage • sleeps up to 6

The Royal Carter House 514 Siskiyou Blvd. • 482-5623/(800) 460-9053 • gay-friendly • full brkfst • swimming

Will's Reste 298 Hargadine St., 97520 • 482-4394 • lesbians/gay men • spa

BARS

Cook's Playbill Club 66 E. Main St. • 488-4626 • 5pm-2am • gay-friendly • more gay Th-Sat • dancing/DJ • live shows • wheelchair access

RESTAURANTS & CAFES

Ashland Bakery/Cafe 38 East Main • 482-2117 • 7am-8pm • plenty veggie • wheelchair access • $5-8

Geppetto's 345 East Main • 482-1138 • 8am-midnight • Italian • full bar • wheelchair access • $8-13

BOOKSTORES & RETAIL SHOPS

Bloomsbury Books 290 E. Main St. • 488-0029 • 8am-10pm, from 9am Sat, 10am-9pm Sun

Astoria (503)

ACCOMMODATIONS

Rosebriar Hotel 636 14th St. • 325-7427/(800) 487-0224 • gay-friendly • upscale classic hotel • full brkfst • wheelchair access

Baker City

INFO LINES & SERVICES

Lambda Eastern Oregon Association Box 382, 97814 • monthly mtgs.

Bend (541)

INFO LINES & SERVICES

Beyond the Closet 317-8966

Out & About PO Box 8427, 97701 • 388-2395 • sponsors socials & potlucks • newsletter

RESTAURANTS & CAFES

Cafe Paradiso 945 NW Bond St. • 385-5931 • 8am-11pm, til midnight wknds

Royal Blend 1075 NW Newport • 383-0873 • 7am-7pm • cafe

BOOKSTORES & RETAIL SHOPS

Curiosity Shoppe & Juice Bar 140 NW Minnesota • 382-3408

Corvallis (541)

INFO LINES & SERVICES

After 8 Club 101 NW 23rd • 752-8157 • 7pm 2nd Tue • lesbigay educational & support group

Lesbian/Gay/Bisexual Student Alliance-OSU 249 Snell, Memorial Union East • 737-6360 • 7pm Mon at Women's Center

BOOKSTORES & RETAIL SHOPS

Downtown Book Bin 2228 SW 3rd • 752-0040 • 7am-8pm, 9:30am-6pm Sat, from noon Sun • also 'Monroe Ave. Book Bin' • 2305 NW Monroe • 753-8398 • more text books

Grass Roots Bookstore 227 SW 2nd St. • 754-7668 • 9am-7pm, til 9pm Fri, til 5:30pm Sat, 11am-5pm Sun • wheelchair access • music section • espresso bar

Days Creek (541)

ACCOMMODATIONS

Owl Farm PO Box 133, 97429 • 679-4655 • women only • open women's land for retreat or residence • camping sites avail.

Eugene (541)

INFO LINES & SERVICES

Gay/Lesbian AA 342-4113 (AA#)

Lesbian/Gay/Bisexual Alliance-UO Ste. 319 EMU • 346-3360 • 9am-5pm • social 4pm-6pm Th • wheelchair access

TLC (The Lesbian Connection) 2360 Fillmore • 683-2793 • active lesbian social group

Women's Center University of Oregon • 346-4095/346-3327 • 8am-6pm (office) • some lesbian outreach

ACCOMMODATIONS

Campus Cottage B&B 1136 E. 19th Ave. • 342-5346 • gay-friendly • full brkfst • women-owned

River's Edge Inn 91241 Blue River Rd., Blue River • 822-3258/(800) 250-1821 • gay-friendly • 40 miles east of Eugene • full brkfst

BARS

Club Arena 959 Pearl St. • 683-2360 • 7pm-2:30am • popular • lesbians/gay men • dancing/DJ • live shows • videos

RESTAURANTS & CAFES

Keystone Cafe 395 W. 5th • 342-2075 • 7am-3pm • popular brkfst • plenty veggie

Perry's 959 Pearl St. • 683-2360 • 7am-9pm, clsd Sun • full bar til 2:30am • wheelchair access • $8-16

BOOKSTORES & RETAIL SHOPS

Hungry Head Bookstore 1212 Willamette • 485-0888 • 10:30am-6pm, noon-5pm Sun • progressive alternative titles

▲ **Mother Kali's Bookstore** 720 E. 13th Ave. • 343-4864 • 9am-6pm, from 10am Sat • lesbian/feminist & multi-racial sections • wheelchair access

Peralandra Books & Music 199 E. 5th Ave., Station Square • 485-4848 • 10am-6pm, clsd Sun • metaphysical titles

Ruby Chasm 152 W. 5th #4 • 344-4074 • 10am-6pm, noon-5pm Sun • goddess gifts & books • wheelchair access

TRAVEL & TOUR OPERATORS

Global Affair 285 E. 5th Ave. • 343-8595/(800) 755-2753 • IGTA • women-owned/run

SPIRITUAL GROUPS

MCC 23rd & Harris (1st Congregational Church) • 345-5963 • 4pm Sun

PUBLICATIONS

View Magazine PO Box 11067, 97440 • 302-6523 • 'chronicle of gay & lesbian life'

Womyn's Press PO Box 562, 97440 • 302-8146 • eclectic feminist newspaper since 1970

EROTICA

Exclusively Adult 1166 S. 'A' St., Springfield • 726-6969 • 24hrs

Grants Pass (541)

ACCOMMODATIONS
Womanshare 862-2807 • women only • cabin & campground • meals included • hot tub

Klamath Falls (541)

INFO LINES & SERVICES
HIV Resource Center 1112 Pine St. • 883-2437 • 11am-5pm

KALA (Klamath Area Lambda Association) LesBiGay Hotline PO Box 43, 97601 • 883-2437

La Grande

INFO LINES & SERVICES
GALA of Eastern Oregon State College Student Activities Office, Hoke College Center EOS, 97850 • 7pm 2nd & 4th Mon (Loso Hall #232)

Lincoln City (541)

ACCOMMODATIONS
▲ **Ocean Gardens Inn** 2735 NW Inlet • 994-5007/(800) 866-9925 • gay-friendly • spectacular views of the ocean • hot tub

RESTAURANTS & CAFES
Over the Waves 2945 NW Jetty Ave. • 994-3877 • 8am-10pm, lounge open til 2am wknds • live shows • $12-18

Medford (541)

INFO LINES & SERVICES
AA Gay/Lesbian 773-4848 (AA#)

BOOKSTORES & RETAIL SHOPS
Hands On Books 211 W. Main • 779-6990 • 10am-5:30pm, clsd Sun • general • some lesbigay titles

Newport (541)

ACCOMMODATIONS
Green Gables B&B (at Green Gables Bookstore) • 265-9141 • women only • ocean view • shared bath

BOOKSTORES & RETAIL SHOPS
Green Gables Bookstore 156 SW Coast St. • 265-9141 • 10am-5pm • women's • also used/children's books & women's music • also publishes 'Class' newsletter

Pacific City (503)

RESTAURANTS & CAFES
White Moon Cow Cafe 35490 Brooten Rd. • 965-5101 • 9am-6pm • wheelchair access • also bookstore • lesbian-owned

Bookstores & Retail Shops

Amazon Earthworks 392-3901 • matriarchal pottery images & sacred art • catalog avail.

Portland (503)

(See also **Vancouver, WA**)

Info Lines & Services

50+ Portland 281-4424/331-0415 • 3rd Sat • social group for lesbians 50+

Ample Opportunities 245-1524 • sponsors many activities for large women

Asian/Pacific Islander Lesbian/Gay/Bisexual Info Hotline 232-6408

Bad Girls PO Box 17254, 97217 • SM/leather/fetish org.

BiNet 299-4764 • meets 7pm 1st Tue at Laughing Horse Books

Cascade AIDS Project 620 SW 5th Ave. Ste. 300 • 223-5907/(800) 777-2437 • provides a variety of non-medical services

Gay Resource Center/Oregon AIDS Hotline 223-2437/(800) 777-2437 • 10am-9pm, noon-3pm wknds

Gay/Lesbian Archives of the Pacific Northwest PO Box 3646, 97208 • meet 1st Mon

Lesbian Community Project 223-0071 • multi-cultural political & social events

Live & Let Live Club 2400 NE Broadway, 2nd flr (MCC Portland) • 460-9404

Love Makes a Family PO Box 11694, 97211 • 228-3892 • many groups • call for locations • also radio show on KKEY 1150 AM • 7am Wed

Northwest Gender Alliance 646-2802 • 3rd Tue & 2nd Sat • transgender support group • newsletter

Phoenix Rising 620 SW 5th Ste. 710 • 223-8299 • sexual minority counseling center • wheelchair access

Pride Line 243-3424 • touchtone resource hotline

Reed College Queer Alliance 3203 SE Woodstock Blvd. #718, 97202

Accommodations

Holladay House B&B 1735 NE Wasco St. • 282-3172 • gay-friendly • full brkfst

Portland (503)

Where the Girls Are: Snacking granola while cycling (that's motorcycling) in the mountains, wearing boots and flannel. (Aw, hell, we don't know!)

Lesbigay Pride: July: 295-9788.

Annual Events: June- The Gathering: 482-2026, annual pagan camp in the Oregon Woods. September- Nothwest Women's Music Celebration, participatory event for musicians, songwriters & singers, NOT performance-oriented. The Fall Gathering: 482-2026. October - Living in Leather: (614) 899-4406, national conference for the leather, SM and fetish communities.

City Info: 222-2223. Oregon Welcome Ctr.: 285-1631.

Attractions: Microbreweries. Mt. Hood Festival of Jazz. Old Town. Pioneer Courthouse Square. Rose Festival. Wasington Park.

Best View: International Rose Test Gardens at Washington Park.

Weather: You'd better love your winters cold (low 30s at night), grey and WET! But all the rains give Portland its lush landscape that bursts into beautiful colors in the spring and fall. Summer brings sunnier days.
(Temperatures can be in the 50s one day and the 90s the next.)

Transit: Radio Cab: 227-1212.

Portland

Despite on-going harassment from the Oregon Citizen's Alliance, Oregon is still a haven for lesbians—just check out the proof: Portlandia, atop the Portland Building, is both city landmark and powerful Amazon icon—a lesbian for sure!

At the foot of Mt. Hood, sprawling along the Columbia River, you'll find this city that's home to rainy days, roses, lesbians, and the punk activist Riot Grrrls of 'zine & grunge fame. Nearby you can explore the Mount St. Helens National Volcanic Monument or the 5,000 acres of Macleay Park. And if you love jazz, head for the hills; the Mt. Hood Festival of Jazz brings the best of the jazz world to town every August.

Though you might expect blocks of women's bookstores and bars, lesbian life here focuses more on the outdoors and cocooning at home with small groups of friends. To get in touch, pick up a recent copy of **Just Out** or call the **Lesbian Community Project**.

Still, if your scene is the bars, Portland has two for women: **Choices Pub** and **Code Blue**. For a nourishing meal, hit **Old Wives Tales**, then pep up with java and art at **Espress It!** or the smoke-free **Cup & Saucer Cafe**.

Culturally minded visitors should drop by **In Other Words**, the only women's bookstore in town. They carry music along with a large selection of women's literature. **Powell's** is a huge new/used bookstore, and we've heard that the lesbian/gay section is a good meeting place on weekend nights—and they also have a little cafe. **It's My Pleasure** serves up erotica for women, and **In Her Image Gallery** shows women's art.

Hotel Vintage Plaza 422 SW Broadway • 228-1212/(800) 243-0555 • popular • gay-friendly • wheelchair access • $145-245

MacMaster House 1041 SW Vista Ave. • 223-7362/(800) 774-9523 • gay-friendly • historic mansion near the Rose Gardens

Sullivan's Gulch B&B 1744 NE Clackamas St. • 331-1104 • lesbians/gay men

BARS

Bar of the Gods 4801 SE Hawthorne • 232-2037 • 4pm-2:30am • gay-friendly • beer/wine • wheelchair access

Boxx's 1035 SW Stark • 226-4171 • 11:30am-2:30am • mostly gay men • videos • wheelchair access • also 'Brig' from 9pm • dancing/DJ

C.C. Slaughter's 1014 SW Stark St. • 248-9135 • 11am-2:30am • popular • mostly gay men • dancing/DJ • country/western on Wed & Sun • videos • food served

Candlelight Room 2032 SW 5th • 222-3378 • 10am-2:30am, from 11am wknds • gay-friendly • live shows • food served

Choices Pub 2845 SE Stark St. • 236-4321 • 1pm-1am, til 2:30am wknds • lesbians/gay men • dancing/DJ • wheelchair access

The City Nightclub 13 NW 13th Ave. • 224-2489 • 10pm-2am, til 4am Fri-Sat, clsd Mon-Tue • popular • lesbians/gay men • dancing/DJ • 18+ • live shows • no alcohol

Club Diva (at Choices Pub) • 227-1889 • 8pm-2am Sat only • mostly women • dancing/DJ

Code Blue (various locations) • 282-6979 • call for events • mostly women

Darcelle XV 208 NW 3rd Ave. • 222-5338 • 5pm-2:30am, clsd Sun • gay-friendly • live shows • food served • wheelchair access

Eagle PDX 1300 W. Burnside • 241-0105 • 4pm-2:30am • mostly gay men • leather

Egyptian Club 3701 SE Division • 236-8689 • noon-2:30am • mostly women • dancing/DJ • live shows • also a restaurant • pasta & more • some veggie • wheelchair access • $5-10

Embers Nightclub 110 NW Broadway • 222-3082 • 11am-2:30am • popular • gay-friendly • dancing/DJ • live shows • wheelchair access

Gail's Dirty Duck Tavern 439 NW 3rd • 224-8446 • 3pm-2:30am, from noon wknds • mostly gay men • neighborhood bar • leather • wheelchair access

Hobo's 120 NW 3rd Ave. • 224-3285 • open from 4pm daily • gay-friendly • live shows • also a restaurant • some veggie • wheelchair access • $5-20

La Luna 215 SE 9th Ave. • 241-5862 • 9pm-2am • gay-friendly • dancing/DJ • live shows • 18+

Melody Ballroom 615 SE Alder • 232-2759 • special events space • call for events

Panorama 341 SW 10th • 221-7262 • 9pm-4am Fri-Sat, til 2:30am Sun • popular • gay-friendly • dancing/DJ • beer/wine • wheelchair access

Silverado 1217 SW Stark St. • 224-4493 • 9am-2:30am • popular • mostly gay men • dancing/DJ • live shows • also full restaurant • wheelchair access

Squeezebox 214 SW Broadway (at Saucebox restaurant) • 241-3393 • 9pm-3am Sun only • popular • lesbians/gay men • dancing/DJ • live shows • wheelchair access

Starky's 2913 SE Stark St. (at 29th) • 230-7980 • 11am-2am • popular • lesbians/gay men • neighborhood bar • also a restaurant • some veggie • patio • $10-20

Three Sisters Tavern 1125 SW Stark St. • 228-0486 • 1pm-2:30am, clsd Sun • mostly gay men • neighborhood bar • dancing/DJ

RESTAURANTS & CAFES

Acapulco's Gold 2610 NW Vaughn • 220-0283 • popular • hearty Mexican

The Adobe Rose 1634 SE Bybee Blvd. • 235-9114 • 4pm-9pm, clsd Sun • New Mexican • some veggie • beer/wine • $5-7

Assaggio 7742 SE 13th • 232-6151 • 5:30-9:30pm • Italian • beer/wine

B.J.'s Brazilian Restaurant 7019 SE Milwaukie Ave. • 236-9623 • lunch & dinner, clsd Sun

Bastas Trattoria 410 NW 21st • 274-1572 • lunch & dinner • northern Italian • some veggie • full bar • $7-12

Bijou Cafe 132 SW 3rd Ave. • 222-3187 • 7am-3pm • popular • plenty veggie • $4-7

Brasserie Montmartre 626 SW Park • 224-5552 • lunch & dinner, Sun brunch • bistro • live jazz

Bread & Ink Cafe 3610 SE Hawthorne Blvd. • 239-4756 • 7am-9pm, 8am-10pm Sat, 9am-2pm & 5pm-9pm Sun • popular • wheelchair access

Cafe Lena 2239 SE Hawthorne Blvd. • 238-7087 • 8am-11pm • popular

Caffe Fresco 2387 NW Thurman • 243-3247 • 6:30am-4pm, from 8am wknds, til 2pm Sun • Italian

Caribou Cafe & Bar 503 W. Burnside • 227-0245 • noon-1am, from 5pm Sat, from 3pm Sun • diner • some veggie • full bar • $4-9

Coffee Cow 5204 NE Sacramento • 282-9910 • 7am-7pm, til 10pm Sat, 9am-5pm Sun

Coffee People 533 NW 23rd St. • 221-0235 • popular

Cup & Saucer Cafe 3566 SE Hawthorne Blvd. • 236-6001 • 7am-8pm • popular • full menu • smokefree

Esparza's Tex-Mex Cafe 2725 SE Ankeny St. • 234-7909 • 11:30am-10pm, clsd Sun-Mon • popular

Espress It! 1026 SW Stark • 227-2551 • 5pm-2:30am • lesbians/gay men • coffeehouse/sandwiches • also gallery

Fish Grotto 1035 SW Stark (at Boxx's bar) • 226-4171 • 11:30am-10:30pm, from 4:30pm wknds • popular • some veggie • full bar • $8-24

Genoa 2832 SE Belmont • 238-1464 • reservations only • clsd Sun • beer/wine • 7-course Italian dinner (prix-fixe) • $48

Gypsy Cafe 625 NW 21st • 796-1859 • 11am-1am, from 9am wknds • some veggie

Hamburger Mary's 3239 SW Broadway Dr. • 223-0900 • 7am-2am • popular • $7-11

Majas Tacqueria 1000 SW Morrison • 226-1946 • 11am-11pm

Marco's Cafe & Espresso Bar 7910 SW 35th, Multnomah • 245-0199 • 7am-9:30pm, from 8am wknds, til 2pm Sun • popular wknd brunch

Old Wives Tales 1300 E. Burnside St. • 238-0470 • 8am-10pm, til 11pm Fri-Sat • multi-ethnic vegetarian • beer/wine • wheelchair access • $7-14

Pizzacato 505 NW 23rd • 242-0023 • 11am-11pm, noon-9pm Sun • popular • plenty veggie

Ron Paul Charcuterie 1441 NE Broadway • 284-5439 • 8am-10pm, til midnight Fri-Sat, 9am-4pm Sun • fancy French deli

Santa Fe Taqueria 831 NW 23rd • 220-0406 • 11am-midnight, til 1am Fri-Sat • popular • Mexican • some veggie • patio • also full bar

Saucebox 214 SW Broadway • 241-3393 • 11:30am-2am clsd Sun-Mon • lesbians/gay men • multi-ethnic cafe • plenty veggie • full bar • $4-6

Shakers Cafe 1212 NW Glisan • 221-0011 • 7:30am-4pm, clsd Sun • homecooking • some veggie • beer/wine

Swagat Indian Cuisine 4325 SW 109th Ave., Beaverton • 626-3000 • 11am-3pm & 5pm-10pm

Vista Spring Cafe 2440 SW Vista • 222-2811 • 11am-10pm

Wildwood 1221 NW 21st Ave. • 248-9663 • 11am-9pm • popular • full bar

Zefiro 500 NW 21st • 226-3394 • lunch & dinner, clsd Sun • Mediterranean/Southeast Asian • some veggie • full bar

GYMS & HEALTH CLUBS

Inner City Hot Springs 2927 NE Everett St. • 238-4010 • 10am-11pm, 1pm-10pm Sun • gay-friendly • wellness center

Princeton Athletic Club 614 SW 11th Ave. • 222-2639 • 5am-10pm, 7am-7pm wknds • gay-friendly

BOOKSTORES & RETAIL SHOPS

In Her Image Gallery 3208 SE Hawthorne • 231-3726 • 10am-6pm, clsd Mon-Tue • wheelchair access

In Other Words 3734 SE Hawthorne Blvd. • 232-6003 • 10am-9pm, til 10pm Fri-Sat, til 5pm Sun • women's books • music • gallery • wheelchair access

The Jellybean 721 SW 10th Ave. • 222-5888 • 10am-6pm, clsd Sun • gifts • wheelchair access

Laughing Horse Bookstore 3652 SE Division • 236-2893 • 11am-7pm, clsd Sun • alternative/progressive • wheelchair access

Looking Glass Bookstore 318 SW Taylor • 227-4760 • 9am-6pm, from 10am Sat, clsd Sun

Powell's Books 1005 W. Burnside St. • 228-4651 • 9am-11pm, til 9pm Sun • new & used books • cafe • wheelchair access

Presents of Mind 3633 SE Hawthorne • 230-7740 • 10am-7pm, 11am-5:30pm Sun • jewelry, cards & unique toys • wheelchair access

Twenty-Third Ave. Books 1015 NW 23rd Ave. • 224-5097 • 9:30am-9pm, from 10am Sat, 11am-7pm Sun • general w/ lesbigay section • wheelchair access

TRAVEL & TOUR OPERATORS

Advantage Travel Service 812 SW Washington St. Ste. 200 • 225-0186 • IGTA

Gulliver's Travels & Voyages 514 NW 9th Ave. • 221-0013/(800) 875-8009 • IGTA

Hawthorne Travel Company 1939 SE Hawthorne Blvd. • 232-5944/(800) 232-5944 • IGTA

In Touch Travel 121 SW Morrison St. #270 • 223-1062/(800) 568-3246 • IGTA

J&M Travel 4370 NE Halsey Ste. 138 • 249-0305/(800) 875-0305 • IGTA

Mikuni Travel Service 1 SW Columbia St. Ste. 1010 • 227-3639/(800) 248-0624 • IGTA

Oregon Tourism Commission (800) 547-7842

Travel Agents International 917 SW Washington St. • 223-1100/(800) 357-3194 • ask for Rip • IGTA

Travel Corner 17175 SW T.V. Hwy., Aloha • 649-9867/(800) 327-0840 • IGTA • women-owned

Ultimate Travels 621 SW Morrison Ste. 435 • 220-8866/(800) 446-4117 • IGTA

SPIRITUAL GROUPS

Congregation Neve Shalom 246-8831 • 8:15pm Fri, 9am Sat • conservative synagogue w/ lesbigay outreach

Dignity/Portland 13th & SW Clay (St. Stephen's Episcopal Church) • 295-4868 • 7:30pm Sat

Integrity Columbia/Willamette 8147 SE Pine St. (Sts. Peter & Paul) • 288-5949

MCC Portland 2400 NE Broadway • 281-8868 • 10am Sun, 7pm Wed • wheelchair access

Pagan Info Line 650-7045 • also publishes 'Open Ways' newsletter

Reach Out! PO Box 1173, Clackamas, 97015 • support group for lesbigay Jehovah's Witnesses & Mormons

Sisterspirit 294-0645 • celebration w/ women sharing spirituality

PUBLICATIONS

Just Out PO Box 14400, 97214 • 236-1252

EROTICA

The Crimson Phoenix 1876 SW 5th Ave. • 228-0129 • 'sexuality bookstore for lovers' • wheelchair access

It's My Pleasure 4258 SE Hawthorne • 236-0505 • 10am-9pm, 11am-6pm Sun • sex toys & books for women

Leatherworks 2908 SE Belmont St. • 234-2697 • noon-6pm, clsd Sun-Mon

Spartacus Leather 302 SW 12th Ave. • 224-2604 • 10am-11pm, til 8pm Sun

Rockaway Beach (503)

ACCOMMODATIONS

Bear & Penguin Inn 421 N. Miller • 355-8610 • gay-friendly

Rogue River (541)

ACCOMMODATIONS

Whispering Pines B&B/Retreat 9188 W. Evans Creek Rd. • 582-1757/(800) 788-1757 • popular • lesbians/gay men • full brkfst • swimming • hot tub • $55-$65

Roseburg (541)

INFO LINES & SERVICES

Gay/Lesbian Switchboard PO Box 813, 97470 • 672-4126 • newsletter

BARS

Roma Cocktail Lounge & Restaurant 5096 Hwy. 99 S. • 679-7100 • 4pm-2am (kitchen closes at 10pm) • Italian • live shows

Salem (503)

INFO LINES & SERVICES

Mid-Oregon AIDS Support Service 494 State St. Ste. 256 • 363-4963 • 9am-2pm • wheelchair access

BARS

Sneakers Bar & Dance Club 300 Liberty St. SE • 363-0549 • 4pm-2:30am (restaurant clsd Sun-Mon) • lesbians/gay men • dancing/DJ • live shows • karaoke • also a restaurant • some veggie • wheelchair access • $10-20

RESTAURANTS & CAFES

Off Center Cafe 1741 Center St. NE • 363-9245 • 7am-2:30pm, from 8am wknds, 6pm-9pm Th-Sat • popular brkfst • some veggie • wheelchair access • $7-12

BOOKSTORES & RETAIL SHOPS

Rosebud & Fish 524 State St. • 399-9960 • 10am-7pm, noon-5pm Sun • alternative bookstore

SPIRITUAL GROUPS

Dignity 1020 Columbia St. (St. Vincent's Church) • 363-0006

Sweet Spirit MCC 363-6618 • 11am Sun

Unitarian Universalist Congregation of **Salem** 490 19th St. NE • 364-0932 • 9:30am & 11:15am Sun (10am only summers)

PUBLICATIONS

Community News PO Box 663, 97308 • 363-0006

Out & About Entertainer 3470 Donald St. NE • 375-3758

Tigard (503)

TRAVEL & TOUR OPERATORS

The Travel Shop 10115 SW Nimbus Ctr. Ste. 600 • 684-8533/(800) 285-8835 • ask for Mark • IGTA

Tiller (503)

ACCOMMODATIONS

Kalles Family RV Ranch 233 Jackson Creek Rd. • 825-3271 • lesbians/gay men • camping sites & RV hookups • btwn Medford & Roseburg

Waldport (541)

ACCOMMODATIONS

Cliff House B&B Yaquina John Point at 1450 Adahi St. • 563-2506 • gay-friendly • oceanfront • full brkfst • hot tub

RESTAURANTS & CAFES

Bumps & Grinds 225 SW Maple • 563-5769 • 7:30am-5pm • cafe • plenty veggie • patio w/view • wheelchair access • lesbian-owned • $3-6

Welches (503)

ACCOMMODATIONS

Cedar Grove Cottage 557-8292 • gay-friendly • secluded • near Sandy River • spa

Yachats (503)

ACCOMMODATIONS

Morningstar Gallery & B&B 95668 Hwy. 101 S. • 547-4412 • full brkfst • oceanfront • hot tub

Ocean Odyssey PO Box 491, 97498 • 547-3637/(800) 800-1915 • gay-friendly • vacation rental homes in Yachats & Waldport • women-owned/run • $75-125

The Oregon House 94288 Hwy. 101 • 547-3329 • gay-friendly • wheelchair access • smokefree

See Vue Motel 95590 Hwy. 101 S. • 547-3227 • gay-friendly

PENNSYLVANIA

Allentown (610)

INFO LINES & SERVICES

Gays/Lesbians of Reading & Allentown PO Box 1952, 18105 • 868-7183 • social group • newsletter

Lehigh Valley Lesbians 439-8755 (MCC) • 7pm 1st Tue

Your Turf 439-8755 (MCC) • 7pm Fri • lesbigay youth group • call for location

BARS

Candida's 247 N. 12th St. • 434-3071 • 11:30am-2am, from 2pm Fri-Sun • lesbians/gay men • neighborhood bar • food served

Moose Lounge/Stonewall 28-30 N. 10th St. • 432-0706 • 2pm-2am • popular • lesbians/gay men • dancing/DJ • live shows • videos • food served

RESTAURANTS & CAFES

Symphony Cafe 29 N. 6th St. • 432-6373 • brkfst & lunch • live shows • patio • wheelchair access

SPIRITUAL GROUPS

Grace Covenant Fellowship Church 247 N. 10th St. • 740-0247 • 10:45am Sun

Altoona (814)

INFO LINES & SERVICES

Gay/Lesbian/Bisexual Info 944-3583 • 8:30am-4:30pm Mon-Fri • ask for Melanie

Beaver Falls

BARS

A.S.S. (Alternative Subway Stop) 1204 7th Ave. (rear entrance) • 8pm-2am, clsd Sun • mostly gay men • dancing/DJ

Bethlehem (610)

BARS

Diamonz 1913 W. Broad St. • 865-1028 • 3pm-2am, from 2pm wknds • mostly women • dancing/DJ • live shows • also a restaurant • some veggie • wheelchair access • $7-13

SPIRITUAL GROUPS

MCC of the Lehigh Valley 424 Center St. (Unitarian Church) • 439-8755 • 6pm Sun

Bradford

INFO LINES & SERVICES

University of Pitt-Bradford BiGALA c/o Director of Student Activities 200 Campus Dr./235 Commons, 16701

Bridgeport (610)

BARS

The Lark 302 Dekalb St. (Rte. 202 N.) • 275-8136 • 8pm-2am, from 4pm Sun • mostly gay men • dancing/DJ • dinner served

Bristol (215)

EROTICA

Bristol News World 576 Bristol Pike (Rte. 13 N.) • 785-4770 • 24hrs

East Stroudsburg (717)

ACCOMMODATIONS

▲ **Rainbow Mtn. Resort & Restaurant** RD 8, Box 8174, 18301 • 223-8484 • popular • lesbians/gay men • B&B/deluxe stes. • cabins (seasonal) • swimming • also a restaurant • full bar • dancing/DJ Fri-Sat • piano bar • transgender-friendly • limited wheelchair access

Edinboro (814)

INFO LINES & SERVICES

Identity University Center, Edinboro UPenn, 16444 • 732-2000

Emlenton (412)

ACCOMMODATIONS

Allegheny House 214 River Ave. • 867-9636/(800) 547-8499 • gay-friendly • riverfront • full brkfst • smokefree

Ephrata (717)

TRAVEL & TOUR OPERATORS

Zeller Travel 4213 Oregon Pike • 859-4710/(800) 331-4359 • IGTA

Erie (814)

INFO LINES & SERVICES

Lambda Group AA 7180 New Perry Hwy. (Unitarian Universalist Church) • 452-2675 • 8pm Sun • wheelchair access

Trigon: Lesbian/Gay/Bisexual Coalition Reed Bldg., Penn State-Behrend • 898-6164

Womynspace 7180 New Perry Hwy. (Unitarian Universalist Church) • 7:30pm 1st Sat • alcohol/smokefree women's coffeehouse

ACCOMMODATIONS

Castle Great House 231 W. 21st St. • 454-6465 • lesbians/gay men • smokefree

Inn The Woods 436-7798/7343 • gay-friendly • 1hr SE of Erie • full brkfst

BARS

The Embers 1711 State St. • 454-9171 • 8pm-2am, clsd Sun • mostly gay men • dancing/DJ • piano bar • food served

Leeward Lounge 1022 Bridge St., Ashtabula OH • (216) 964-9935 • 8pm-2:30am • lesbians/gay men • food served

Lizzy Bordon's Part II 3412 W. 12th St. • 833-4059 • 9pm-2am, clsd Sun • popular • lesbians/gay men • dancing/DJ • wheelchair access

RESTAURANTS & CAFES

Cup-A-Ccinos Coffeehouse 18 N. Park Row • 456-1151 • 7:30am-9pm, til midnight Th-Sat, from 9am Sat, clsd Sun • live shows • wheelchair access

La Bella Bistro 556 W. 4th • 454-3616 • lunch & dinner, dinner only Sat, clsd Sun • BYOB • $9-20

Pie in the Sky Cafe 463 W. 8th St. • 459-8638 • 7:30am-2pm, dinner from 5pm Fri-Sat, clsd Sun • BYOB • wheelchair access

BOOKSTORES & RETAIL SHOPS

Perceptions 328 W. 6th • 454-7364 • 11am-7pm, til 5pm Sat, clsd Sun & Wed • metaphysical bookstore

TRAVEL & TOUR OPERATORS

Camelot Travel & Tours PO Box 3874, 16508 • 835-3434

SPIRITUAL GROUPS

Unitarian Universalist Congregation of Erie 7180 New Perry Hwy. • 864-9300 • 10:30am Sun

PUBLICATIONS

Erie Gay Community Newsletter PO Box 3063, 16501 • 456-9833

Gay Peoples Chronicle PO Box 5426, Cleveland OH, 44101 • (216) 631-8646

Gettysburg

INFO LINES & SERVICES

Gettysburg College Lambda Alliance Box 2256, Gettysburg College, 17325

Greensburg (412)

INFO LINES & SERVICES

Gay/Lesbian Outreach Coalition c/o Office of Student Life, Univ. of Pittsburgh, 15601

BARS

RK's Safari Lounge 108 W. Pittsburgh St. • 837-9948 • 9pm-2am, clsd Sun • popular • mostly gay men • dancing/DJ • patio • wheelchair access

Harrisburg (717)

INFO LINES & SERVICES

Gay/Lesbian Switchboard 234-0328

BARS

▲ **B-tls** 891 Eisenhower Blvd. • Th-Sat only • mostly women • dancing/DJ • videos • pool table • food served • women-owned/run

Neptune's Lounge 268 North St. • 233-3078 • 4pm-2am, from 2pm Sun • popular • mostly gay men • neighborhood bar • dinner 5pm-9pm Tue-Th

Stallions 706 N. 3rd St. (rear entrance) • 233-4681 • 4pm-2am, clsd Sun • popular • mostly gay men • dancing/DJ • karaoke • also a restaurant • dinner Th-Sat, Sun brunch • wheelchair access

Strawberry Cafe 704 N. 3rd St. • 234-4228 • 2pm-2am, clsd Sun • mostly gay men • neighborhood bar • videos • wheelchair access

RESTAURANTS & CAFES

Colonnade 300 N. 2nd St. • 234-8740 • 6am-8:30pm, from 7am Sat, clsd Sun • seafood • full bar • wheelchair access • $8-15

Paper Moon 268 North St. • 233-0581 • 5pm-9pm, til 11pm wknds • lesbians/gay men • $5-10

TRAVEL & TOUR OPERATORS

Pennsylvania Bureau of Travel (800) 847-4872

SPIRITUAL GROUPS

Dignity PO Box 297, 17108 • 232-2027

MCC of the Spirit 6th & Herr St. (Friends Meeting House) • 236-7387 • 7pm Sun

Indiana (412)

BOOKSTORES & RETAIL SHOPS

Josephine's 1176 Grant St. #2180 • 465-4469 • noon-5pm, til 8pm Th-Fri, clsd wknds • feminist

Johnstown (814)

BARS

Lucille's 520 Washington St. • 539-4448 • 9pm-2am, clsd Sun-Mon • lesbians/gay men • dancing/DJ • live shows

Kutztown (610)

ACCOMMODATIONS

Grim's Manor B&B 10 Kern Rd. • 683-7089 • gay-friendly • 200 yr. old stone farmhouse on 5 acres • full brkfst • older kids ok

Lancaster (717)

INFO LINES & SERVICES

Gay/Lesbian Helpline 397-0691 • 7pm-10pm Sun, Wed & Th

Pink Triangle Coalition PO Box 176, 17608 • 394-6260 • also youth mtgs.

ACCOMMODATIONS

Maison Rouge B&B 2236 Marietta Ave. • 399-3033 • gay-friendly • full brkfst

BARS

Sundown Lounge 429 N. Mulberry St. • 392-2737 • 8pm-2am, from 3pm Fri-Sat, clsd Sun • mostly women • dancing/DJ

Tally Ho 201 W. Orange • 299-0661 • 6pm-2am, from 8pm Sun • popular • lesbians/gay men • dancing/DJ (11pm-2am Wed-Sun)

RESTAURANTS & CAFES

Loft (above Tally Ho bar) • 299-0661 • lunch Mon-Fri, dinner Mon-Sat • French/American • $15-25

BOOKSTORES & RETAIL SHOPS

Borders Bookshop 940 Plaza Blvd. • 293-8022 • open til 11pm • some lesbigay titles

SPIRITUAL GROUPS

MCC Vision of Hope 130 E. Main St., Mountville • 285-9070 • 10am & 7pm Sun

Lancaster County (717)

ACCOMMODATIONS

DalEva Farms PO Box 6, Drumore, 17518 • 548-3163 • women only • smokefree • kids/pets ok • wheelchair access

Malvern (610)

ACCOMMODATIONS

Pickering Bend B&B RD 1, Box 121, Church Rd., Charlestown Village, 19355 • 933-0183 • gay-friendly • built in 1790 • 2 stes. • kitchen • fireplaces • kids/pets ok

Milford

ACCOMMODATIONS

K'saan (212) 663-2963 • women only • log house on 45 wooded acres • wknd or weekly rental only • sleeps 2-6 • swimming • $200-575

Monroeville (412)

EROTICA

Monroeville News 2735 Stroschein Rd. • 372-5477 • 24hrs

New Hope (215)

INFO LINES & SERVICES

AA Gay/Lesbian 862-0327/574-6900 (AA#)

ACCOMMODATIONS

The Fox & Hound B&B 246 West Bridge St. • 862-5082/(800) 862-5082 • gay-friendly • 1850s stone manor

The Lexington House 6171 Upper York Rd. • 794-0811 • lesbians/gay men • 1789 country home • swimming

The Raven 385 West Bridge St. • 862-2081 • popular • mostly gay men • swimming • also a restaurant • cont'l

The Victorian Peacock B&B 309 E. Dark Hollow Rd., Pipersville • 766-1356 • lesbians/gay men • swimming • spa • women owned/run

BARS

The Cartwheel 427 York Rd. (US 202) • 862-0880 • 5pm-2am • popular • lesbians/gay men • dancing/DJ • live shows • piano bar • also a restaurant • wheelchair access • $6-18

Ladies 2000 (609) 784-8341 • scheduled parties for women by women • call for times & locations

The Raven Bar & Restaurant (at Raven accommodations) • 862-2081 • 11am-2am • lesbians/gay men

RESTAURANTS & CAFES

Country Host 463 Old York Rd. (Rte. 202) • 862-5575 • 7am-10pm • full bar • wheelchair access • $7-12

Havana 105 S. Main St. • 862-9897 • 11am-midnight, bar til 2am • some veggie • live shows • $9-16

Karla's 5 W. Mechanic St. • 862-2612 • lunch & dinner, late night brkfst Fri-Sat • Italian • some veggie • full bar • live shows • $15-25

Mother's 34 N. Main St. • 862-5270 • 9am-10pm • some veggie • $10-20

Odette's South River Rd. • 862-3000 • 11am-10pm (piano bar & cabaret til 1am) • some veggie • wheelchair access • $15-25

Wildflowers 8 W. Mechanic St. • 862-2241 • noon-10pm, til 11pm Fri-Sat (seasonal) • outdoor dining • some veggie • BYOB • $8-15

BOOKSTORES & RETAIL SHOPS

▲ **Book Gallery** 19 W. Mechanic St. • 862-5110 • 11am-7pm (call for Feb-May hours) • feminist/lesbian

Ember'glo Gifts 27 W. Mechanic St. • 862-2929 • hours vary

TRAVEL & TOUR OPERATORS

Flight of Fancy, Inc. 408 York Rd. • 862-9665/(800) 691-1980 • IGTA

EROTICA

Grown Ups 2 E. Mechanic St. • 862-9304 • 11am-7pm, til 11pm Fri-Sat

New Milford (717)

ACCOMMODATIONS

Oneida Camp & Lodge PO Box 537, 18834 • 465-7011 • seasonal • mostly gay men • oldest gay-owned/operated campground dedicated to the lesbigay community • swimming • nudity

Norristown (610)

BARS

Doubleheader/Medusa's 354 W. Elm St. • 277-1070 • 8pm-2am, clsd Sun-Mon • lesbians/gay men • dancing/DJ • leather • videos

Philadelphia (215)

INFO LINES & SERVICES

AA Gay/Lesbian 574-6900

BiUnity 724-3663 • bisexual social/support groups for men & women

▲ **Dyke TV** Channel 54 • 9pm & midnight Th • 'weekly half-hour TV show produced by lesbians, for lesbians'

Female Trouble 928-5090 • social/educational woman-woman S/M group • 18+ • newsletter

Gay/Lesbian Radio WXPN-FM 88.5 • 898-6677 • 'QZine' 8pm Sun

Gay/Lesbian Switchboard 546-7100 • 7pm-10pm

Gay/Lesbian/Bisexual/Transgendered Commmunity Center 201 S. Camac St. (Penguin Place) • 732-2220 • 6pm-10pm Mon-Th, 11am-5pm Sat, 5pm-9pm Sun, Fri for special events • also 'Lesbigay Archives of Philadelphia'

Gender Transgressors c/o Ben Singer • 922-5943 • for people born female-bodied who have masculine gender expression • info • referrals • call for events

GROWP (Greater Roundtable of Women Professionals) PO Box 35010, 19128-0510 • (610) 789-4938 • lesbian social group

Open Home Lesbian Center 247-5545 • healing & services for women

Penn Women's Center 119 Houston Hall, 3417 Spruce St. • 898-3030

Philadelphia Transsexual Support Group 3637 Chestnut St. • 4pm 1st Sat

Sisterspace of the Delaware Valley 351 S. 47th St. # B-101, 19143 • 476-8856 • sponsors 'Sisterspace Pocono Weekend' & other events • newsletter

Tell-A-Woman Switchboard 1530 Locust St. #322 • 564-5810 • recorded info

Ujima 1207 Chestnut St. • 851-1958 • 6pm Wed • support group for African-American FTMs

Unity Inc. 1207 Chestnut St. • 851-1912 • 9am-5:30pm Mon-Fri, clsd wknds • lesbigay support/social services

ACCOMMODATIONS

Abigail Adams B&B 1208 Walnut St. • 546-7336 • gay-friendly • smokefree • kids ok

Antique Row B&B 341 S. 12th St. • 592-7802 • gay-friendly • 1820 townhouse in heart of gay community • full brkfst

Bag & Baggage B&B 338 S. 19th St. • 546-3807 • gay-friendly • kids ok

Glen Isle Farm 30 mi out of town, in Downington • (610) 269-9100/(800) 269-1730 • gay-friendly • full brkfst • smokefree • older kids ok (call first)

Sarah P. Wilson House 155 Main St., Phoenixville • (610) 933-0327 • gay-friendly • full brkfst • kids ok (call first)

Travelodge-Stadium 2015 Penrose Ave. • 755-6500/(800) 578-7878 • gay-friendly • swimming • full bar • wheelchair access

BARS

2-4 Club 1221 St. James St. • 735-5772 • from midnight Mon-Th, call for wknd hrs. • mostly gay men • dancing/DJ • private club • all-ages nights

247 Bar 247 S. 17th St. • 545-9779 • noon-2am • popular • mostly gay men • live shows • videos • also a restaurant

Bike Stop 204 S. Quince • 627-1662 • 4pm-2am, from 1pm Sat, from 3pm Sun • popular • mostly gay men • 4 flrs. • dancing/DJ • alternative • leather (very leather-women-friendly) • live shows • home of 'Female Trouble' • also cafe • some veggie • $6-16

Black Banana 205 N. 3rd • 925-4433 • 10pm-3am, from midnight wkdays • gay-friendly • dancing/DJ • alternative • wheelchair access

C.R. Bar 6405 Market St., Upper Darby • (610) 734-1130 • 8pm-2am, clsd Sun • mostly gay men • neighborhood bar

Key West 207 S. Juniper • 545-1578 • 4pm-2am, from 11am Sun • lesbians/gay men • dancing/DJ • live shows • also a restaurant • dinner Wed-Sat, Sun brunch • wheelchair access • $8-15

Ladies 2000 (609) 784-8341 • scheduled parties for women by women • call for times & locations

Milborn Social Club (upstairs at C.R. Bar) • (610) 734-1130 • from midnight Fri-Sat, 4pm-2am Sun • mostly gay men • dancing/DJ • private club

North Beach Resort 829-1500 • dancing/DJ • swimming • volleyball • entertainment complex

Port Blue 2552 E. Allegheny Ave., Port Richmond • 425-4699 • 6pm-2am, clsd Sun-Tue • gay-friendly • neighborhood bar

Raffles 243 S. Camac St. • 545-6969 • 4pm-2am • popular • lesbians/gay men • 3 bars • dancing/DJ • live shows • also a restaurant • $7-12

Rodz 1418 Rodman St. • 546-1900 • 5pm-11pm, til 2am Fri-Sat, from noon Sun • lesbians/gay men • dancing/DJ • piano bar • also 'Tyz' restaurant • some veggie • $10-12

Philadelphia (215)

WHERE THE GIRLS ARE: Partying downtown near 12th St., south of Market.

LESBIGAY PRIDE: June: 564-3332.

ANNUAL EVENTS: May-Pridefest Philadelphia: 790-7820: weekend of gay/lesbian film, performances, parties & more. Campfest Memorial Day Wknd: (609) 694-2037, in Oxford. June - Womongathering: (609) 694-2037, women's spirituality fest.

CITY INFO: 636-1666.

ATTRACTIONS: Academy of Natural Sciences Museum. Afro-American Historical and Cultural Museum. Betsy Ross' Home. National Museum Of American Jewish History. Norman Rockwell Museum. Philadelphia Museum of Art.

BEST VIEW: Top of Center Square, 16th & Market.

WEATHER: Winter temperatures hover in the 20°s. Summers are humid with temperatures in the 80°s and 90°s.

TRANSIT: Yellow Cab: 922-8400. Airport Shuttle: 969-1818. Transit Authority (SPTA): 580-7800.

Sisters 1320 Chancellor St. • 735-0735 • 4pm-2am • mostly women • dancing/DJ

Stars Too 1315 Samson St. • 545-4053 • 3pm-2am • gay-friendly • dancing/DJ • videos • food served

The Westbury 261 S. 13th • 546-5170 • 10am-2am • mostly gay men • neighborhood bar • also a restaurant • dinner til 10pm, til 11pm wknds • gourmet home-cooking • some veggie • wheelchair access • $9-14

Woody's 202 S. 13th St. • 545-1893 • 11am-2am • popular • mostly gay men • dancing/DJ • country/western • dance lessons • 18+ Wed • videos • food served • wheelchair access

RESTAURANTS & CAFES

10th Street Pour House 262 S. 10th St. • 922-5626 • 7:30am-11pm, from 9am Sat, 10am-8pm Sun • cafe

16th Street Bar & Grill 264 S. 16th St. • 735-3316 • 11:30am-11pm, bar open til 2am • Mediterranean • some veggie • full bar • $10-20

The Adobe Cafe 4550 Mitchell St., Roxborough • 483-3947 • 4:30pm-10:30pm • live shows • $9-12

Astral Plane 1708 Lombard St. • 546-6230 • 5pm-11pm • some veggie • full bar • $10-20

Backstage Bar & Restaurant 614 S. 4th St. • 627-9887 • 4pm-2am, dinner from 6pm-10pm, Sun brunch • $10-20

Philadelphia

*T*hough it's packed with sites of rich historical value, don't miss out on Philadelphia's multi-cultural present. To get a feel for it, browse the Reading Terminal Market, an ancient (for the US) and quaint farmer's market preserved within the new Convention Center. Here, smalltime grocers and farmers of many cultures sell their fresh food the Philadelphian way: old-fashioned.

A vital element in many of these cultures is the growing lesbian community. Stop by Penguin Place (the **Gay/Lesbian/Bisexual/Transgendered Community Center**), or check out **Sisters**, a new women's dance bar.

Giovanni's Room is the lesbian/gay bookstore, another good place to look for information on local goings-on of note; you can find the **Philadelphia Gay News** and **Au Courant** there as well as **Labyrinth**, the women's monthly.

Cafe on Quince 202 S. Quince St. • 592-1750 • 4:30pm-10pm • dinner & Sun brunch • women-owned/run

Cheap Art Cafe 260 S. 12th St. • 735-6650 • 24hrs

Circa 1518 Walnut St. • 545-6800 • lunch, dinner, Sun brunch • wheelchair access

Diner on the Square 1839 Spruce St. • 735-5787 • 24hrs • $7-10

Galileo's 1701 Spruce St. • 735-4611 • noon-10pm • lesbians/gay men • live shows • also 'Galileo's Observatory' • full bar • 4pm-2am

The Inn Philadelphia 251 S. Camac St. • 732-2339 • 4:30pm-10pm, til 9pm Sun • cont'l • some veggie • full bar • $12-26

Liberties 705 N. 2nd St. • 238-0660 • lunch & dinner, Sun brunch • full bar • live jazz wknds • $10-16

Makam's Kitchen 2401 Lombard • 546-8832 • 10am-10pm • live shows

Mont Serrat 623 South St. • 627-4224 • noon-midnight • some veggie • full bar • $6-15

My Thai 2200 South St. • 985-1878 • 5pm-10pm, til 11pm Fri-Sat • $10-20

Palladium/Gold Standard 3601 Locust Walk • 387-3463 • dinner, bar til 12:30am • some veggie • wheelchair access • $10-25

Rhino Coffee Roastery & Cafe 212 South St. • 923-2630 • 7am-midnight, from 8:30am wknds

Roosevelt's Pub 2222 Walnut • 636-9722 • lunch & dinner • some veggie • full bar • $5-12

Savoy Restaurant 232 S. 11th St. • 923-2348 • 24hrs • popular afterhours • $5-7

Shing Kee 52 N. 9th St. • 829-8983 • lunch & dinner • BYOB • gay-owned/run

Striped Bass 1500 Walnut St. • 732-4444 • lunch, dinner & Sun brunch • upscale dining

Waldorf Cafe 20th & Lombard Sts. • 985-1836 • dinner • some veggie • full bar • wheelchair access • $12-18

GYMS & HEALTH CLUBS

12th St. Gym 204 S. 12th St. • 985-4092 • 6am-11pm • gay-friendly

BOOKSTORES & RETAIL SHOPS

Afterwords 218 S. 12th St. • 735-2393 • 10am-midnight

Giovanni's Room 345 S. 12th St. • 923-2960 • call for hours, open 7 days a week • popular • lesbigay/feminist bookstore

Thrift for AIDS 633 South St. • 592-9014 • noon-9pm

Travelers Emporium 210 S. 17th St. • 546-2021 • 10am-6pm, clsd Sun

Urban Necessities 1506 Spruce St. • 546-6768 • 9am-9pm, til 6pm Sat • 'housewares fit for a queen'

TRAVEL & TOUR OPERATORS

Lambda Travel 21 S. 5th St. #545 • 925-3011/(800) 551-2240 • ask for Scott • IGTA

Philadelphia Convention & Visitors Bureau 16th St. & JFK Blvd. • (800) 225-5745 • publishes 'Philadelphia Gay & Lesbian Travel News' • IGTA

Sigmund Travel 262 S. 12th St. • 735-0090

Twin Travel 1101 Spruce St. • 923-2995

Will Travel 118 S. Bellevue Ave., Longhorn • 741-4492/(800) 443-7460 • IGTA

SPIRITUAL GROUPS

Beth Ahavah 8 Letitia St. • 923-2003 • 8pm 1st, 3rd & 5th Fri

Christ Episcopal Church 2nd above Market • 922-1695 • 9am & 11am Sun

Dignity 330 S. 13th St. (church) • 546-2093 • 7pm Sun

Integrity 1904 Walnut St. (church) • 382-0794 • 7pm 1st & 3rd Wed • pastoral counseling avail.

MCC 2125 Chestnut St. (First Unitarian Church) • 563-6601 • 7pm Sun

PUBLICATIONS

Au Courant News Magazine 2124 South St. • 790-1179

The Greater Philadelphia Lavender Pages 205 W. Mt. Pleasant Ave. Ste. 1 • 247-1018

Greater Philadelphia Women's Yellow Pages PO Box 1002, Havertown, 19083 • (610) 446-4747

Labyrinth PO Box 58489, 19102 • 546-6686 • women's newspaper

PGN (Philadelphia Gay News) 505 S.4th St. • 625-8501

EROTICA

Both Ways 201 S. 13th St. • 985-2344 • piercings • leather

Condom Kingdom 441 South St. • 829-1668 • condoms • toys

Infinite Body Piercing 626 S. 4th St. • 923-7335

The Pleasure Chest 2039 Walnut • 561-7480 • clsd Sun-Mon

Pittsburgh (412)

INFO LINES & SERVICES

AA Gay/Lesbian 471-7472

Asians & Friends Pittsburgh PO Box 16455, 15242 • 681-1556

Gay/Lesbian Community Center Phoneline 422-0114 • 6:30pm-9:30pm, 3pm-6pm Sat, clsd Sun

ISMIR (International Sexual Minorities Information Resource) PO Box 81869, 15217 • 422-3060 • monthly calendar of regional, national, int'l lesbigay events

TransFamily c/o Deni Scott, 962 Rockdale Rd., Butler, 16001 • 758-3578 (ask for Jan) • 2nd Tue, call for location • support for transgendered people, their families & friends

TransPitt PO Box 3214, 15230 • 224-6015 • social/support group for CD/TV/TS/TG

ACCOMMODATIONS

Brewers Hotel 3315 Liberty Ave. • 681-7991 • gay-friendly • residential

Camp Davis 311 Red Brush Rd., Boyers • 637-2402 • May-2nd wknd in Oct • 1 hr. from Pittsburgh • lesbians/gay men • adults 21+ only • pets on leash • call for events

The Inn on the Mexican War Streets 1606 Buena Vista St. • 231-6544 • lesbians/gay men • gay-owned/run

The Priory 614 Pressley • 231-3338 • gay-friendly • 24-rm. Victorian • kids ok • wheelchair access

BARS

Brewery Tavern (at Brewers Hotel) • 681-7991 • 10am-2am, from noon Sun • gay-friendly

C.J. Deighan's 2506 W. Liberty Ave., Brookline • 561-4044 • 9pm-2am, clsd Sun-Mon • lesbians/gay men • more women Th • dancing/DJ • live shows • food served • wheelchair access

Donny's Place 1226 Herron Ave. • 682-9869 • 5pm-2am, from 3pm Sun • popular • lesbians/gay men • dancing/DJ • country/western • live shows • food served

House of Tilden 941 Liberty Ave., 2nd flr. • 391-0804 • 10pm-3am • lesbians/gay men • dancing/DJ • private club

Huggs Restaurant & Lounge 704 Thompson Ave., McKees Rocks • 331-9011 • 4pm-2am, clsd Sun • lesbians/gay men • country/western • karaoke • food served

Images 965 Liberty Ave. • 391-9990 • 5pm-2am, from 9pm Sun • mostly gay men • karaoke • videos

Metropol 1600 Smallman St. • 261-4512 • 8pm-2am, clsd Mon-Tue • popular • gay-friendly • more gay Th • dancing/DJ • alternative • live shows • food served • wheelchair access

New York, New York 5801 Ellsworth Ave. • 661-5600 • 4pm-2am, from 11am Sun • popular • mostly gay men • piano bar Wed & Fri • karaoke Sun • also a restaurant • some veggie • wheelchair access • $9-15

Pegasus Lounge 818 Liberty Ave. • 281-2131 • 4pm-2am, from 8pm Sat, clsd Sun • popular • mostly gay men • dancing/DJ • live shows

Pittsburgh Eagle 1740 Eckert St. • 766-7222 • 8pm-2am, clsd Sun • mostly gay men • dancing/DJ • leather • wheelchair access

Real Luck Cafe 1519 Penn Ave. • 566-8988 • 3pm-2am • lesbians/gay men • neighborhood bar • food served • cafe menu • some veggie • wheelchair access • $5

RESTAURANTS & CAFES

Common Grounds Coffeehouse 5888 Ellsworth Ave. • 362-1190 • 10am-11pm, til 2am Fri-Sat, til 10pm Sun • lesbian-owned/run • wheelchair access

Rosebud 1650 Smallman St. • 261-2221 • lunch & dinner, clsd Mon • live shows • wheelchair access • $8-15

Sips 238 Shaddy Ave. • 361-4478 • 10am-midnight, til 4am wknds • Middle Eastern • live shows • wheelchair access • $3-6

BOOKSTORES & RETAIL SHOPS

The Bookstall 3604 5th Ave. • 683-2644 • 9:30am-5:30pm, til 4:30pm Sat, clsd Sun • general • wheelchair access

Getrude Stein Memorial Bookstore 1003 E. Carson St. • 481-9666 • 5:30pm-8pm Th-Fri, noon-6pm Sat, til 3pm Sun • women's

Slacker 1321 E. Carson St. • 381-3911 • noon-10pm, til 7pm Sun • magazines • clothing • leather • piercings • wheelchair access

St. Elmo's Books & Music 2214 E. Carson St. • 431-9100 • 9:30am-9:30pm, til 5pm Sun • progressive

True Colors PO Box 495, Carnegie, 15106 • 734-6650/(800) 285-3718 • rainbow designs • custom clothes • mail order

TRAVEL & TOUR OPERATORS

Alternative Travels 900 Penn Ave. • 279-8595

Bon Ami Travel Service 309 1st St., Apollo • 478-2000/(800) 426-6264 • IGTA

Cruises & Tours McKnight 1319 Boyle St. • 366-7678/(800) 992-7678 • ask for Frank • IGTA

Holiday Travel 5832 Library Rd., Bethel Park • 835-8747

Morgan Delfosse Travel 372-1846/(800) 538-2617

Pittsburgh Travel Service Station Square • 321-8511 • IGTA

SPIRITUAL GROUPS

Bet Tikvah PO Box 10140, 15232 • 682-2604 • 7:30pm 1st Fri • lesbigay shabbat

Dignity 100 N. Bellefield (5th Ave) • 362-5334 • 7:30pm Sun

First Unitarian Church Moorewood Ave. at Ellsworth • 621-8008 • 11am Sun (10am summers) • also 'Three Rivers Unitarian Universalists for Lesbigay Concerns' • 343-2523 • potluck last Fri

Integrity/Pittsburgh PO Box 3, Verona, 15147 • 734-8409 • 7:30pm 2nd Wed (call for summer schedule) • lesbigay Episcopalians

MCC of Pittsburgh 304 Morewood Ave. (church) • 683-2994 • 7pm Sun

PUBLICATIONS

Greater Pittsburgh Women's Yellow Pages PO Box 15330, 15237 • 561-5401

Out 747 South St. • 243-3350

EROTICA

Boulevard Videos & Magazines 346 Blvd. of the Allies • 261-9119 • 24hrs • leather • toys

Golden Triangle News 816 Liberty Ave. • 765-3790 • 24hrs

Iron City Ink Tattoo/Hellion House Body Piercing 1814 Penn Ave. • 391-2380 • noon-8pm, clsd Sun

Poconos   (717)

ACCOMMODATIONS

▲ **Blueberry Ridge** RR1 Box 67, Scotrun, 18355 • 629-5036 • women only • full brkfst • all meals on holidays • hot tub • smokefree • kids ok • $55-70

▲ **Rainbow Mtn. Resort** RD 8, Box 8174, East Stroudsburg, 18301 • 223-8484 • popular • lesbians/gay men • atop Pocono mtn. on 85 acres • (see ad under East Stroudsburg)

STONEY RIDGE

ENJOY THE CHARMING COMFORT OF THIS CEDAR LOG HOME POCONO GETAWAY

FOR RESERVATION INFORMATION CALL: PAT OR GRETA

717-629-6036

"OPEN YEAR ROUND"

Blueberry Ridge

PAT OR GRETA

717-629-5036

In the Pocono Mts. Tannersville, PA

Women's Guest House

"OPEN YEAR ROUND"

▲ **Stoney Ridge** RD 1, Box 67, Scotrun, 18355
• 629-5036 • women only • secluded log
home • kitchen • kids/pets ok • $250wknd/
$450 week

Quakerstown   (215)

EROTICA

Adult World 80 S. West End Blvd. (Rte.309)
• 538-1522

Reading   (610)

INFO LINES & SERVICES

Berks Gay/ Lesbian Alliance PO Box 417,
19603 • 373-0674 • mtg. 2nd Sun

Gays/Lesbians of Reading & Allentown
PO Box 1952, Allentown, 18105 • 868-7183
• social group • newsletter

BARS

Nostalgia 1101 N. 9th St. • 372-5557 •
9am-11pm, til 2am Fri-Sat • mostly women
• neighborhood bar • live shows

Rainbows 935 South St. (below Adams
Apple) • 373-7929 • 8pm-2am Fri-Sat only
• mostly women • dancing/DJ

Red Star 11 S. 10th St. • 375-4116 • 5pm-
2am, from 8pm Tue, clsd Mon • popular •
mostly gay men • dancing/DJ • food served

Scarab 724 Franklin • 375-7878 • 8pm-
2am, clsd Sun • popular • mostly gay men
• dancing/DJ

Scranton   (717)

BARS

The Buzz 400 Block of Spruce in Forest
Park • 969-0900 • 9pm-2am, clsd Sun-Mon
• lesbians/gay men • dancing/DJ • also
'Lounge' • wheelchair access

Silhouette Lounge 523 Linden St. • 344-
4259 • 10am-2am, clsd Sun • mostly gay
men • neighborhood bar • leather

RESTAURANTS & CAFES

Prufrock's 342 Adams Ave. • 963-0849 •
11am-6pm, clsd Sun • alternative cafe •
gallery • live shows

State College   (814)

INFO LINES & SERVICES

**Gay/Lesbian/Bisexual/Transgender
Switchboard** 237-1950 • info • peer counseling

Women's Resource Center 140 W. Nittany
Ave. • 2343-5050 (24hr hotline)/234-5222 •
9am-7pm Mon-Fri

BARS

Chumley's 108 W. College • 238-4446 •
4pm-2am, from 6pm Sun • popular • les-
bians/gay men • wheelchair access

Players 112 W. College Ave. • 234-1031 •
8pm-2am • gay-friendly • dancing/DJ •
videos

West Grove   (610)

BARS

Trib's Waystation 627 W. Baltimore Pike •
869-9067 • 11am-2am • gay-friendly • also
a restaurant • wheelchair access • $8-13

Wilkes-Barre   (717)

INFO LINES & SERVICES

Coming Home (AA) 97 S. Franklin Blvd.
(Pres. Church) • noon Th

BARS

Rumors Lounge 315 Fox Ridge Plaza • 825-
7300 • 5pm-2am, from 8pm Mon-Tue •
popular • lesbians/gay men • dancing/DJ •
also a restaurant • wheelchair access

Selections 45 Public Square, Wilkes-Barre
Ctr. • 829-4444 • 7pm-2am, clsd Sun • popular • lesbians/gay men • dancing/DJ • also
a restaurant • wheelchair access • $5-15

The Vaudvilla (The Vaude) 465 Main St.,
Kingston • 287-9250 • 9pm-2am, clsd Sun
• popular • lesbians/gay men • dancing/DJ
• live shows • videos

Williamsport   (717)

INFO LINES & SERVICES

**Gay/Lesbian Switchboard of North
Central PA** PO Box 2510, 17703 • 327-1411
• 6pm-3am • open 365 days

BARS

Peachie's Court 320 Court St. • 326-3611 •
10am-2am, clsd Sun • lesbians/gay men •
neighborhood bar

The Rainbow Room 761 W. 4th St. • 320-
0230 • 4pm-2am, clsd Sun • popular • les-
bians/gay men • dancing/DJ • live shows •
videos • food served

York   (717)

INFO LINES & SERVICES

York Area Lambda PO Box 2425, 17405 •
848-9142 • lesbigay social/educational
group • newsletter

BOOKSTORES & RETAIL SHOPS

Her Story Bookstore 2 W. Market St.,
Hallam • 757-4270 • 11am-7pm, 9am-5pm
Sat, noon-5pm Sun • women's books •
gifts • gourmet coffee • women-owned/run

RHODE ISLAND

Cranston   (401)

TRAVEL & TOUR OPERATORS

Anywhere Travel 1326 Plainfield St. • 943-3300/352-8947 • ask for Joe

Newport   (401)

ACCOMMODATIONS

Brinley Victorian Inn 23 Brinley St. • 849-7645 • gay-friendly • New England Victorian • lesbian following • non-smoking rms. avail. • older kids ok by arr.

Hydrangea House Inn 16 Bellevue Ave. • 846-4435/(800) 945-4667 • popular • lesbians/gay men • full brkfst • near beach

The Melville House Inn 39 Clark St. • 847-0640 • lesbians/gay men • full brkfst

BARS

David's 28 Prospect Hill St. • 847-9698 • 5pm-1am, from 2pm wknds • popular • lesbians/gay men • neighborhood bar • dancing/DJ • T-dance Sun

Pawtucket   (401)

INFO LINES & SERVICES

Women's Growth Center 97 Knowles St. • 728-6023 • 9am-9pm Mon-Fri

TRAVEL & TOUR OPERATORS

4 Seasons Travel 47 John St. • 722-5888

Providence   (401)

INFO LINES & SERVICES

AA Gay/Lesbian 438-8860 • call for various mtgs.

Enforcers RI PO Box 5770, 02903 • women & men into leather/SM/fetish

Gay/Lesbian Helpline of Rhode Island 751-3322 • 7pm-11pm (Mon-Fri only during summer)

Gay/Lesbian/Bisexual/Transgender Alliance PO Box 1930, SAO, Brown University, 02912 • 863-3062

Sarah Doyle Women's Center 185 Meeting St. (Brown University) • 863-2189 • referrals • also lesbian collective group

Triangle Center 645 Elmwood Ave. • 861-4590

BARS

Blinky's 125 Washington • 272-6950 • noon-1am, til 2am Fri-Sat • lesbians/gay men • live shows • videos • wheelchair access

Club In Town 95 Eddy St. • 751-0020 • noon-1am, til 2am Fri-Sat • popular • mostly gay men • piano bar • videos

Devilles 10 Davol Square (Simmons Bldg.) • 751-7166 • 4pm-1am, til 2am Fri-Sat, clsd Mon • popular • mostly women • neighborhood bar • dancing/DJ Wed-Sat • wheelchair access

Galaxy 123 Empire St. • 831-9206 • noon-1am • mostly gay men • dancing/DJ • live shows • karaoke • videos • wheelchair access

Generation X 235 Promenade St. • 521-7110 • 9pm-2am, clsd Mon-Tue • popular • mostly gay men • dancing/DJ • alternative

Gerardo's 1 Franklin Square • 274-5560 • 4pm-1am, til 2am Fri-Sat • lesbians/gay men • dancing/DJ • live shows • wheelchair access

Mirabar 35 Richmond St. • 331-6761 • 3pm-1am • mostly gay men • dancing/DJ • piano bar • wheelchair access

Union Street Station 69 Union St. • 331-2291 • noon-1am, til 2am Fri-Sat • mostly gay men • dancing/DJ • live shows • wheelchair access

RESTAURANTS & CAFES

Al Forno 577 South Main St. • 273-9760 • dinner • popular • Little Rhody's best dining experience • $13-24

Coffee Cafe 257 S. Main St. • 421-0787 • 7am-5pm, til midnight Fri-Sat, 10am-3pm Sun • patio • gay owned/run

Down City Diner 151 Weybosset St. • 331-9217 • lunch & dinner • popular Sun brunch (very gay) • full bar • wheelchair access

Julian's 318 Broadway • 861-1770 • 7am-3pm, clsd Mon

Rue de L'Espoir 99 Hope St. • 751-8890 • 11:30am-2:30pm lunch, 5pm dinner, clsd Mon • full bar • women-owned/run • $12-20

Troye's Southwestern Grill 404 Wickenden St. • 861-1430 • 5:30pm-9:30pm, til 10pm Fri-Sat, clsd Sun-Mon • BYOB

Turchetta's 312 Wickenden St. • 861-1800 • dinner only, clsd Mon • Italian • plenty veggie • wheelchair access • gay owned/run • $7-14

BOOKSTORES & RETAIL SHOPS

Books on the Square 471 Angell St. • 331-9097 • 9am-9pm, til 10pm Fri-Sat • some lesbigay titles

TRAVEL & TOUR OPERATORS

Travel Concepts 84 Lorimer Ave. • 453-6000/(800) 983-6900 • ask for Roger • IGTA

SPIRITUAL GROUPS

Bell St. Chapel (Unitarian Church) 5 Bell St. • 831-3794 • 10am Sun

Dignity PO Box 2231, Pawtucket, 02861 • 727-2657 • 2pm 2nd & 4th Sun • also 'Defenders' (leather/levi) chapter

Integrity 474 Fruit Hill Ave. (St. James Church) • 353-2079 • 4:30pm 2nd Sun • lesbigay Episcopalians

Morning Star MCC 231 Main St., Cherry Valley MA • 553-4320/(508) 892-4320 • 11am Sun, 7pm Wed

St. Peter's & Andrew's Episcopal Church 25 Pomona Ave. • 272-9649 • 8am &10am Sun, 7pm Wed (healing service)

PUBLICATIONS

Options PO Box 6406, 02940 • 831-4519

Smithfield (401)

BARS

The Loft 325 Farnum Pike • 231-3320 • 11am-1am, from 10am wknds & summer • lesbians/gay men • swimming • also a restaurant • Sun brunch • wheelchair access

Warwick (401)

BOOKSTORES & RETAIL SHOPS

Barnes & Noble 1441 Bald Hill Rd. • 828-7900 • 9am-11pm, 11am-7pm Sun • lesbigay section

Westerly (401)

ACCOMMODATIONS

The Villa 190 Shore Rd. • 596-1054/(800) 722-9240 • gay-friendly • close to beach • swimming • smokefree

Woonsocket (401)

BARS

Kings & Queens 285 Front St. • 762-9538 • 7pm-1am, til 2am Fri-Sat • lesbians/gay men • neighborhood bar • dancing/DJ

RESTAURANTS & CAFES

Monte's 104 Cass Ave. • 762-0088 • open 11:30am, from 4:30pm Sun, clsd Mon • New Orleans cuisine • full bar • $6-10

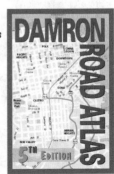

SOUTH CAROLINA

Anderson (864)

BARS

Europa 116 E. Benson St. • 225-6797 • 9pm-?, clsd Mon-Wed • lesbians/gay men • dancing/DJ • live shows • private club

Charleston (803)

INFO LINES & SERVICES

Acceptance Group (Gay AA) St. Stephen's Episcopal (Anson St.) • 762-2433 • 8pm Tue & 6:30pm Sat • also meets at MCC 8pm Th

LGLA (Lowcountry Gay/Lesbian Alliance) PO Box 98, 29402 • 720-8088 • info • referrals

ACCOMMODATIONS

1854 B&B 34 Montagu St. • 723-4789 • lesbians/gay men • Italianate antebellum dwelling in historic Charleston

65 Radcliff Street 65 Radcliff St • 577-6183 • lesbians/gay men

Charleston Beach B&B PO Box 41, Folly Beach, 29439 • 588-9443 • lesbians/gay men • unobstructed views of the Atlantic Ocean • full brkfst • swimming • nudity • 8-person spa • Sun BBQ

▲ **Charleston Columns** 8 Vanderhorst St. • 722-7341 • lesbians/gay men • intimate & hospitable antebellum lodging in historic district

Happy Landing Folly Beach • 588-6363 • gay-friendly • rustic log cabin • sleeps 6 • close to beach • swimming

BARS

The Arcade 5 Liberty St. • 722-5656 • 9:30pm-?, clsd Mon-Wed • popular • mostly gay men • dancing/DJ • alternative • karaoke • live shows • wheelchair access

Deja Vu II 445 Savannah Hwy. • 556-5588 • 5pm-3am • mostly women • dancing/DJ • live shows • private club • food served • wheelchair access

Dudley's Inc. 346 King St. • 723-2784 • 4pm-3am, from 2pm Sun • popular • mostly gay men • neighborhood bar • live shows • private club

RESTAURANTS & CAFES

Bear E. Patch 801 Folly Rd. • 762-6555 • 7am-8pm • cafe • patio • wheelchair access

Cafe Suzanne 4 Center St. • 588-2101 • 5:30pm-9:30pm, clsd Tue • live jazz • $10-15

Fanny's Diner 137 Market St. • 723-7121 • 24hrs • popular • gay owned/run

Johns Island Cafe 3406 Maybank Hwy., Johns Island • 559-9090 • breakfast & lunch Mon-Sat, dinner Wed-Sat • popular • Southern homecooking • beer/wine • $6-11

Vickery's of Beaufain Street 15 Beaufain St. • 577-5300 • 11am-3am • popular • Cuban influence • some veggie • $6-15

SPIRITUAL GROUPS

MCC Charleston 2010 Hawthorne Dr. Ste. 10 • 747-6736 • 11am Sun • wheelchair access

PUBLICATIONS

The Front Page PO Box 27928, Raleigh NC, 27611 • (919) 829-0181

In Unison PO Box 8024, Columbia, 29202 • 771-0804

Q Notes PO Box 221841, Charlotte NC, 28222 • (704) 531-9988

Columbia (803)

INFO LINES & SERVICES

AA Gay/Lesbian 254-5301 • call for times & locations

Bisexual, Gay & Lesbian Association PO Box 80098, 29225 • mtg Wed at USC Business Admin. Bldg.

South Carolina Gay/Lesbian Community Center/Info Line 1108 Woodrow St. • 771-7713 • 24hr message, 6pm-10pm, from 2pm Sat, clsd Sun-Mon

BARS

Affairs 712 Huger St. • 779-4321 • 4pm-2am • mostly gay men • neighborhood bar

Candy Shop 1903 Two Notch Rd. • mostly gay men • dancing/DJ • mostly African-American • private club

Capital Club 1002 Gervais St. • 256-6464 • 5pm-2am • mostly gay men • neighborhood bar • professional • private club • wheelchair access

Metropolis 1801 Landing • 799-8727 • 10pm-? • from 9pm Fri-Sun, clsd Mon • lesbians/gay men • dancing/DJ • live shows • private club

Pipeline 1109 Assembly • 771-0121 • 9pm-6am, clsd Sun-Tue • opens 4pm • lesbians/gay men • neighborhood bar • live shows • private club

Traxx 416 Lincoln St. • 256-1084 • mostly women • dancing/DJ • live bands • private club • wheelchair access

BOOKSTORES & RETAIL SHOPS

Intermezzo 2015 Devine St. • 799-2276 • 10am-midnight • general bookstore

Stardust Books 2805 Devine St. • 771-0633 • spiritual

TRAVEL & TOUR OPERATORS

B&A Travel Service 2728 Devine St. • 256-0547/(800) 968-7658 • IGTA

South Carolina Division of Tourism 734-0235

Travel Unlimited 612 St. Andrews Rd. #9 • 798-8122/(800) 849-2244 • IGTA

SPIRITUAL GROUPS

MCC Columbia 1111 Belleview • 256-2154 • 11am Sun

PUBLICATIONS

In Unison PO Box 8024, 29202 • 771-0804

Virago PO Box 11193, 29211 • 256-9090 • publishes lesbian newsletter

EROTICA

Chaser's 3128 Two Notch Rd. • 754-6672 • 24hrs

Greenville (864)

ACCOMMODATIONS

Ladyslipper Dell B&B 36 Dell Cir. • 834-0888 • wknds only • women only • full brkfst • $50

BARS

The Castle 8 Le Grand Blvd. • 235-9949 • 10pm-4am, clsd Mon-Wed • popular • lesbians/gay men • dancing/DJ • live shows • videos • private club • wheelchair access

New Attitude 706 W. Washington St. • 233-1387 • 10pm-? wknds • lesbians/gay men • mostly African-American • dancing/DJ

South Ramp 404 Airport Rd. • 242-0102 • 7pm-midnight Wed-Th, 7pm-2am Fri-Sat • lesbians/gay men • dancing/DJ • country/western • wheelchair access

SPIRITUAL GROUPS

MCC 37 E. Hillcrest Dr. (Unitarian Fellowship) • 233-0919 • 6:45pm Sun • also Th discussion group • wheelchair access

Hilton Head (803)

BARS

Moon Jammers 11 Heritage Plaza, Pope Ave. • 842-9195 • 8pm-2am • lesbians/gay men • neighborhood bar • dancing/DJ • alternative • live shows • private club • wheelchair access

Myrtle Beach (803)

BARS

Illusions 1012 S. Kings Hwy. • 448-0421 • 9pm-? • lesbians/gay men • women's night Th • dancing/DJ • live shows

Time Out 520 8th Ave. N. • 448-1180 • 6pm-?, til 2am Sat • popular • mostly gay men • neighborhood bar • dancing/DJ • private club • wheelchair access

Rock Hill (803)

BARS

Hideaway 405 Baskins Rd. • 328-6630 • 8pm-?, clsd Mon-Wed • lesbians/gay men • neighborhood bar • private club

Santee (803)

TRAVEL & TOUR OPERATORS

All Around Travel Network 1568 Village Square Blvd. • 854-2475/(800) 395-4255 • IGTA

Spartanburg (803)

BARS

Cheyenne Cattlemen's Club 995 Asheville Hwy. • 573-7304/(800) 428-9808 • 8pm-2am, til 4am Fri, from 3pm Sun • mostly gay men • dancing/DJ • live bands • live shows • private club

SOUTH DAKOTA

Pierre

TRAVEL & TOUR OPERATORS

South Dakota Dept. of Tourism 711 Wells Ave., 57501-3335 • (800) 952-3625 (in-state only)/(800) 732-5682 (out-of-state only)

Rapid City (605)

ACCOMMODATIONS

Camp Michael 13051 Bogus Jim Rd. • 342-5590 • lesbians/gay men • peaceful get-away in the woods of the Black Hills • full brkfst

EROTICA

Heritage Bookstore 912 Main St. • 394-9877

Sioux Falls (605)

INFO LINES & SERVICES

The Sioux Empire Gay & Lesbian Coalition PO Box 1716, 57101-1716 • 333-0603 • 24hrs • info • referrals

ACCOMMODATIONS

Camp America RR2 Box 201, Salem, 57058-1925 • 425-9085 • gay-friendly • 35 mi. west of Sioux Falls • camping • RV hook up • women-owned/run

RESTAURANTS & CAFES

Touchés 323 S. Phillips Ave. • 335-9874 • 8pm-2am • popular • lesbians/gay men • dancing/DJ • food served • wheelchair access

SPIRITUAL GROUPS

St. Francis & St. Clare MCC 1129 E. 9th St. • 332-3966 • 5:30pm Sun (7pm summers)

EROTICA

Studio One Book Store 311 N. Dakota Ave. • 332-9316 • 24hrs

TENNESSEE

Chattanooga (423)

INFO LINES & SERVICES

Gay AA at MCC • 629-2737 • 8pm Fri

BARS

Alan Gold's 1100 McCallie Ave. • 629-8080
• 4:30pm-3am • popular • lesbians/gay
men • dancing/DJ • live shows • food
served • wheelchair access

Chuck's II 27-1/2 W. Main • 265-5405 •
6pm-1am, til 3am Fri-Sat • lesbians/gay
men • neighborhood bar • dancing/DJ •
country/western • patio

Septembers 6005 Lee Hwy. • 510-6666 •
4pm-2am, clsd Mon • mostly gay men •
food served • live shows

SPIRITUAL GROUPS

Integrity 20 Belvior Ave. (Grace Church) •
629-2871 • 6pm 1st & 3rd Sun

MCC Chattanooga 1601 Foust St. • 629-
2737 • 6pm Sun • also women's mtgs. •
monthly

Gatlinburg (423)

ACCOMMODATIONS

Little Bell Cabin 320 Mayflower Dr.,
Knoxville, 37920 • 573-8572 • gay-friendly •
cabin • lesbian-owned/run

BOOKSTORES & RETAIL SHOPS

Blue Moon Signs 813 Glades Rd. • 436-
8733 • unique gifts designed & handcrafted
by women • custom redwood signs • wood
turnings

Haley (615)

RESTAURANTS & CAFES

Our House 389-6616/(800) 876-6616 • clsd
Mon • popular • fine dining • some veggie
• reservations only • wheelchair access •
$10-20

Jackson (901)

BARS

The Other Side 3883 Hwy. 45 N. • 668-
3749 • 5pm-?, from 7pm Sat, clsd Mon-Tue
• lesbians/gay men • live shows

Jamestown (615)

ACCOMMODATIONS

Laurel Creek Campground Rock Creek
Rte. Box 150 • 879-7696 • clsd Dec-April •
gay-friendly • camping • rentals • RV
hookups • horses • hiking • swimming

Johnson City (423)

BARS

New Beginnings 2910 N. Bristol Hwy. •
282-4446 • 9pm-2am, 8pm-3am Fri-Sat,
clsd Mon • popular • lesbians/gay men •
dancing/DJ • live shows • also a restaurant
• wheelchair access

SPIRITUAL GROUPS

MCC of the Tri-Cities Coast Valley
Unitarian Church • 926-4393 • 7pm Sun

Knoxville (423)

INFO LINES & SERVICES

AA Gay/Lesbian 3219 Kingston Pike (Tenn.
Valley Unitarian Church) • 522-9667 • 7pm
Mon & Fri

Gay/Lesbian Helpline 521-6546 • 7pm-
11pm

Lambda Student Union PO Box 8529,
37996 • 525-2335

Random Productions 688-3428 • women-
owned production company

BARS

Carousel II 1501 White Ave. • 522-6966 •
9pm-3am • popular • lesbians/gay men •
dancing/DJ • live shows

Old Plantations 837 N. 5th Ave. • 637-7132
• 8pm-3am, 10pm-6am Fri-Sun • lesbians/
gay men • neighborhood bar • live shows •
beer/wine & set-ups only • BYOB • wheelchair access

Trumps 4541 Kingston Pike • 584-4884 •
5pm-3am, from 9pm wknds • lesbians/gay
men • dancing/DJ • alternative • live shows
• wheelchair access

BOOKSTORES & RETAIL SHOPS

Chelsea Station News 103 W. Jackson Ave.
• 522-6390 • 9am-10pm, til 1am Fri-Sat •
alternative magazines & newspapers

Davis Kidd Bookstore The Commons, 113
N. Peters Rd. • 690-0136 • 9:30am-10pm,
10am-6pm Sun • general • wheelchair
access

Pandora's Books 133 S. Central Ave. • 524-
1259 • 11am-5pm, from 1pm Sun • alternative • wheelchair access

Violets & Rainbows 2426 Mineral Springs
• 687-5552 • noon-9pm, 10am-6pm Sat,
clsd Sun • lesbigay • wheelchair access

TRAVEL & TOUR OPERATORS

Bryan Travel, Inc. 5614 Kingston Pike,
Melrose Place • 588-8166/(800) 234-8166 •
IGTA

SPIRITUAL GROUPS

MCC Knoxville 934 N. Weisgarber Rd. (United Church of Christ) • 521-6546 • 6pm Sun

Memphis (901)

INFO LINES & SERVICES

Gay/Lesbian Switchboard 278-4297 • 7:30pm-11pm

Gay/Lesbian Switchboard 324-4297 • 7:30pm-11pm • counseling • referrals

Memphis Center for Reproductive Health 1462 Poplar • 274-3550 • non-profit feminist health clinic

Memphis Gay/Lesbian Community Center 1486 Madison Ave. • 726-5790

Memphis Lambda Center (AA) 1488 Madison • 276-7379 • 8pm nightly • meeting place for 12-Step groups

ACCOMMODATIONS

Talbot Heirs Guesthouse 99 S. 2nd St. • 527-9772/(800) 955-3956 • gay-friendly • funky decor • smokefree • kids ok • $150-250

BARS

501 Club 111 N. Claybrook • 274-8655 • noon-3am, til 6am Fri-Sat • mostly gay men • dancing/DJ • live shows • food served • wheelchair access

Amnesia 2866 Poplar • 454-1366 • 8pm-3am, clsd Mon-Wed • popular • lesbians/gay men • dancing/DJ • alternative • swimming • patio • dinner nightly • wheelchair access

Autumn Street Pub 1349 Autumn St. • 274-8010 • 1pm-3am, clsd Mon-Tue • lesbians/gay men • neighborhood bar • dancing/DJ • food served • patio • wheelchair access

Backstreet 2018 Court Ave. • 276-5522 • 8pm-3am, til 6am wknds • lesbians/gay men • more women Sun afternoon & Tue • dancing/DJ • beer & setups only • wheelchair access

Changes Bistro & Bar 2586 Poplar Ave. • 452-9100 • 11am-3am, from 3pm wknds • mostly women • live shows • patio

Crossroads 102 N. Cleveland • 725-8156 • noon-3am • lesbians/gay men • neighborhood bar • beer & set-ups only

David's 1474 Madison • 278-4313 • 3pm-3am, mostly gay men • neighborhood bar

One More 2117 Peabody Ave. • 278-8015 • 10am-3am, from noon Sun • gay-friendly • neighborhood bar • multi-racial • food served

Sunshine Lounge 1379 Lamar • 272-9843 • 7am-midnight, til 3am Fri-Sat • gay-friendly • neighborhood bar • beer & setups only • wheelchair access

Memphis (901)

WHERE THE GIRLS ARE: On Madison Ave., of course, just east of US-240.

CITY INFO: 543-5333.

ATTRACTIONS: Graceland, home and grave site of Elvis. Beale Street. Mud Island. Overton Square.

BEST VIEW: A cruise on any of the boats that ply the river.

WEATHER: Suth'n. H-O-T and humid in the summer, cold (30°s-40°s) in the winter, and relatively nice (but still humid) in the spring and fall.

TRANSIT: Yellow Cab: 526-2121. H.T.S. Airport Shuttle: 527-0100. MATA: 274-6282.

WKRB in Memphis 1528 Madison • 278-9321 • 5pm-3am • mostly women • dancing/DJ • live shows • beer & set-ups only • wheelchair access

X-scape 227 Monroe • 528-8344 • 10pm-3am, clsd Mon-Wed • mostly gay men • dancing/DJ • alternative • live shows

RESTAURANTS & CAFES

Alternative Restaurant 553 S. Cooper • 725-7922 • 11am-8pm, til midnight Fri-Sat, clsd Sun • homecooking • BYOB • gay-owned/run

Automatic Slim's Tonga Club 83 S. 2nd St. • 525-7948 • lunch & dinner Mon-Fri, dinner til 11pm Fri-Sat, clsd Sun • Caribbean & Southwestern • plenty veggie • full bar • wheelchair access

Cafe Society 212 N. Evergreen Ave. • 722-2177 • lunch & dinner, Fri-Sat til 11pm • full bar • wheelchair access

Coffee Cellar 3573 Southern • 320-7853 • 7am-midnight, 8am-8pm Sat • patio • wheelchair access

Memphis

*A*nother great city on the banks of the mighty Mississippi River, Memphis is a blend of 'Old South' and 'New South.'

Many people around the world know Memphis as the city of two musical phenomena: 'the blues' and 'the King.' The blues were born when W.C. Handy immortalized 'Beale St.,' and Elvis— well, he lived and died here. From everywhere on earth, people come to visit his home and gravesite at **Graceland** (800/238-2000).

Despite the stereotype of Southern cities as homophobic, Memphis has a strong lesbian community. There's **Meristem Women's Bookstore**, **WKRB in Memphis** women's bar, and **Changes Bistro & Bar**. For dancing, we've heard that **Amnesia** is the place to go.

For other info, check out the latest **Triangle Journal News**, or stop by the **Memphis Gay/Lesbian Community Center**.

Java Cabana/ Viva Memphis Wedding Chapel 2170 Young Ave. • 272-7210 • 1pm-11pm Sun & Tue-Th, 1pm-midnight Fri-Sat, clsd Mon • coffeehouse & wedding chapel • also art gallery • located in historic Cooper Young District

John Will's Barbecue Pit 5101 Sanderland Dr. • 761-5101 • 11am-9:30pm, wknds til 10:30pm • full bar

Maxwell's 948 S. Cooper St. • 725-1009 • 11am-3am Mon-Fri, 5pm-3am wknds • Mediterranean • full bar • wheelchair access

P&H Cafe 1532 Madison • 726-0906 • 11am-3am, from 5pm Sat, clsd Sun • beer/wine • wheelchair access

Saigon Le 51 N. Cleveland • 276-5326 • 11am-9:30pm, clsd Sun • Chinese, Vietnamese, Thai

BOOKSTORES & RETAIL SHOPS

Davis Kidd Booksellers 397 Perkins Rd. Ext. • 683-9801 • 9:30am-10pm, 10am-6pm Sun • general • lesbigay titles

Meristem Women's Bookstore 930 S. Cooper • 276-0282 • 10am-8pm, til 6pm Th & Sat, 1pm Sun, clsd Mon-Tue • wheelchair access

SPIRITUAL GROUPS

First Congregational Church 234 S. Watkins • 278-6786 • 11am Sun

Holy Trinity Community Church 1559 Madison • 726-9443 • 11am & 7pm Sun, 7:30pm Wed

Integrity 102 N. Second St. (Calvary Episcopal Church) • 525-6602 • 6pm 3rd Tue

PUBLICATIONS

Triangle Journal News Box 11485, 38111-0485 • 454-1411

Nashville (615)

INFO LINES & SERVICES

AA Gay/Lesbian 831-1050 • call for location & times

Center for Lesbian/Gay Community Services 703 Berry Rd. • 297-0008 • 5pm-10pm

Gay Cable Network Channel 19 • 9pm Tue & 10pm Sat

Nashville Women's Alliance PO Box 120834, 37212 • call Center for times & locations

ACCOMMODATIONS

Dancing Fish Lodge 627 Wisteria Ln., Waverly • 296-3533 • women only • country inn 70 mi. from Nashville • full brkfst • hot tub • $65-150

IDA 904 Vikkers Hollow Rd., Dowelltown • 597-4409 • lesbians/gay men • camping avail. May-Sept • private community 'commune' located in the hills • 1hr SE of Nashville

Savage House 167 8th Ave. N. • 244-2229 • gay-friendly • 1840s Victorian townhouse • full brkfst

---

Nashville (615)

WHERE THE GIRLS ARE: Just north of I-65/40 along 2nd Ave. S. or Hermitage Ave.

CITY INFO: 259-4700.

ATTRACTIONS: Country Music Hall of Fame and Museum. Grand Ole Opry.

BEST VIEW: Try a walking tour of the city.

WEATHER: See Memphis.

TRANSIT: Yellow Cab: 256-0101. Music City Taxi: 889-0038. Gray Line Airport Shuttle: 275-1180. MTA: 242-4433.

BARS

Chez Collette 300 Hermitage Ave. • 256-9134 • 4pm-3am • mostly women • neighborhood bar • women-owned/run

Chute Complex 2535 Franklin Rd. • 297-4571 • 5pm-3am • popular • mostly gay men • 5 bars • dancing/DJ • country/western • leather • live shows • also a restaurant • wheelchair access

Connection Nashville 901 Cowan • 742-1166 • opens 8pm, gift shop from 10pm • mostly gay men • dancing/DJ • live shows • also a restaurant • wheelchair access • $5-15

Gas Lite 167-1/2 8th Ave. N. • 254-1278 • 4:30pm-1am, til 3am Fri-Sat, from 3pm wknds • lesbians/gay men • food served

KC's Club 909 909 Church St. • 251-1613 • 6pm-3am, clsd Tue • mostly women • dancing/DJ • live shows • also a deli • wheelchair access

Ralph's 515 2nd Ave. S. • 256-9682 • 5pm-midnight, til 3am Fri-Sat • mostly women • wheelchair access • women-owned/run

The Triangle 1401 4th Ave. S. • 242-8131 • 8am-3am, from noon Sun • lesbians/gay men • neighborhood bar • food served • wheelchair access

Nashville

*T*here's only one 'Country Music Capital of the World' and that's Nashville. And there's no better place on earth to enjoy country and western music than at the Grand Ole Opry (889-6611). Be sure to plan ahead and get a performance schedule.

Many of the greats of country music have homes in Nashville, and there are plenty of bus tours to show you exactly where your favorite stars live. The Country Music Hall of Fame and Museum (255-5333) is also a favorite stop for those of us who are diehard country and western music fans.

After you've sat still listening to great music so long you can't stand it, get up and dance. Nashville has two women's bars— **Chez Collette** and **Ralph's**. Keep your star-gazing eyes open while you're cloggin' away on the floor; you never know who you might see! For more sedate activities, pick up a copy of **Query** at the **Center for Lesbian/Gay Community Services**.

If you're driving east, you'll pass through Knoxville—a small city with a quaint old town section and the main University of Tennessee. Call the **Gay/Lesbian Helpline** (521-6546) about local events, and stop by the **Carousel II** for dancing on Thursday nights.

Underground 176 2nd Ave. N. • 742-8909 • 9pm-3am • gay-friendly • dancing/DJ • alternative

Victor Victoria's 111 8th Ave. N. • 244-7256 • 11am-3am, from noon-3am Sun • mostly gay men • dancing/DJ • live shows • wheelchair access

RESTAURANTS & CAFES
Garden Allegro 1805 Church St. • 327-3834 • 8am-9pm, from 10am wknds • juice bar • plenty veggie • $4-7

The Mad Platter 1239 6th Ave. N. • 242-2563 • lunch, dinner by reservation only, clsd Sun-Mon • Californian • some veggie • wheelchair access • $20-30

Towne House Tea Room 165 8th Ave. N. (next to Gas Lite bar) • 254-1277 • lunch wkdays • American buffet • $5-10

World's End 1713 Church St. • 329-3480 • 4pm-1am, clsd Mon • American • $8-15

BOOKSTORES & RETAIL SHOPS
Davis-Kidd Booksellers 4007 Hillsboro Rd. • 385-2711 • 9:30am-10pm • general • lesbigay section

Tower Books 2404 West End Ave. • 327-8085 • 9am-midnight • large lesbigay section

TRAVEL & TOUR OPERATORS
Tennessee Tourist Development 741-2158

SPIRITUAL GROUPS
Integrity 419 Woodland St. (St. Ann's Church) • 383-6608 • 6:30pm 4th Tue

MCC 1808 Woodmont Blvd. • 262-0922 • 7pm Sun

PUBLICATIONS
Etc. PO Box 8916, Atlanta GA, 30306 • (404) 525-3821

Query PO Box 24241, 37202-4241 • 259-4135

Xenogeny PO Box 60716, 37206

Newport (423)
ACCOMMODATIONS
Christopher Place 1500 Pinnacles Wy. • 623-6555/(800) 595-9441 • gay-friendly • IGTA

Rogersville (423)
ACCOMMODATIONS
Lee Valley Farm 142 Drinnon Ln. • 272-4068 • lesbians/gay men • private retreat

Saltillo (901)
ACCOMMODATIONS
Parker House 1956 Tutwiller Ave. • 278-5844 • lesbians/gay men • Southern country house 2 hours outside Memphis • full brkfst • swimming • reservations only

Sewanee (615)
ACCOMMODATIONS
Boxwood Cottage B&B 333 Anderson Cemetery Rd. • 598-5012 • seasonal • lesbians/gay men • full brkfst • hot tub

TEXAS

Abilene (915)

BARS
Just Friends 201 S. 14th St. • 672-9318 •
7pm-midnight, til 1am Fri, til 2am Sat, clsd
Mon • lesbians/gay men • dancing/DJ • live
shows • wheelchair access

SPIRITUAL GROUPS
Exodus MCC 904 Walnut • 672-7922 •
10:45am & 6pm Sun

Amarillo (806)

INFO LINES & SERVICES
Amarillo Lesbian/Gay Alliance Info Line
373-5725 • 7:30pm 1st Tue • 'Queer Dinner
Club' meets twice monthly

BARS
Classifieds 519 E. 10th St. • 374-2435 •
noon-2am, clsd Mon • lesbians/gay men •
dancing/DJ • live shows • wheelchair
access

The Ritz 323 W. 10th Ave. • 372-9382 •
2pm-2am • popular • lesbians/gay men • dancing/DJ
• country/western • live shows

Sassy's 309 W. 6th St. • 374-3029 • 5pm-
2am • lesbians/gay men • dancing/DJ •
alternative

RESTAURANTS & CAFES
Italian Delight 2710 W. 10th • 372-5444 •
lunch & dinner, clsd Sun • some veggie •
beer/wine • wheelchair access • $5-10

SPIRITUAL GROUPS
MCC 2123 S. Polk St. • 372-4557 • 10:30am
& 6pm Sun

Arlington (817)

(See also **Fort Worth**)

INFO LINES & SERVICES
Tarrant County Lesbian/Gay Alliance
1219 6th Ave., Fort Worth • 877-5544 • info
line • newsletter

Women's Fellowship (at Trinity MCC) •
265-5454 • monthly social/support group

BARS
Arlington 651 1851 W. Division • 275-9651
• 4pm-2am • popular • mostly gay men •
dancing/DJ • karaoke • live shows • wheelchair access

SPIRITUAL GROUPS
Trinity MCC 609 Truman • 265-5454 •
9:30am Sun, 7:30pm Wed

Austin (512)

INFO LINES & SERVICES
Adventuring Outdoors 445-7216 • call for
newsletter

**ALLGO (Austin Latino/a Lesbian/Gay
Organization)** PO Box 13501, 78711 • 472-
2001 • 6:30pm Tue

Bound by Desire 473-7104 • 2nd Fri •
women's S/M group

Hotline 472-4357 • 24hrs • info • crisis
counseling

SapphFire 825 E. 53-1/2 St. Bldg. 'E' Ste.
103 • 450-0659 • 7pm 2nd & 4th Fri •
social/support group • monthly potlucks

Word of Mouth Women's Theatre PO Box
1175, 78767 • 837-9866

ACCOMMODATIONS
Driskill Hotel 604 Brazos St. • 474-
5911/(800) 527-2008 • gay-friendly • full bar
• wheelchair access

Omni Hotel 700 San Jacinto • 476-
3700/(800) 843-6664 • gay-friendly •
rooftop pool • health club • wheelchair
access

Park Lane Guest House 221 Park Ln. •
447-7460 • lesbians/gay men • kitchen •
kids ok • pets ok (call first) • $75-85 • also
cottage • wheelchair access • $110
($15/extra person) • women-owned/run

Summit House B&B 1204 Summit St. •
445-5304 • gay-friendly • full brkfst • reservation required

BARS
5th St. Station Saloon/Auntie Mame's 505
E. 5th St. • 478-6065 • 2pm-2am • les-
bians/gay men • dancing/DJ • country/west-
ern • live shows • wheelchair access

Area 52 404 Colorado • 476-8297 • 9pm-?,
clsd Mon-Tue • popular • lesbians/gay men
• dancing/DJ • alternative • 18+ • wheelchair access

Blue Flamingo 617 Red River • 469-0014 •
noon-2am • gay-friendly • neighborhood
bar • live shows • strong coffee served

'Bout Time 9601 N. IH-35 • 832-5339 •
2pm-2am • popular • lesbians/gay men •
neighborhood bar • transgender-friendly •
live shows • volleyball court • wheelchair
access

Casino El Camino 517 E. 6th St. • 469-
9330 • 4pm-2am, from 11am Sun • gay-
friendly • neighborhood bar • psychedelic
punk jazz lounge • great burgers

Kansas 213 W. 4th • 480-8686 • noon-4am
• lesbians/gay men • neighborhood bar •
dancing/DJ • wheelchair access

The Naked Grape 611 Red River • 476-3611 • 10am-2am • mostly gay men • dancing/DJ • live shows • patio • wheelchair access

O.H.M.S. 611 E. 7th • 472-7136 • 10pm-?, clsd Sun-Mon • gay-friendly • dancing/DJ • alternative • 18+

Oil Can Harry's 211 W. 4th • 320-8823 • popular • mostly gay men • dancing/DJ • alternative • wheelchair access

Proteus 501 6th St. • 472-8922 • 10pm-4am, clsd Sun-Tue • gay-friendly • dancing/DJ • alternative • theme nights • video lounge

Rainbow Cattle Company 305 W. 5th St. • 472-5288 • 2pm-2am • mostly gay men • dancing/DJ • country/western • food served

RESTAURANTS & CAFES

Bitter End Bistro & Brewery 311 Colorado St. • 478-2337 • wood-baked pizza

Eastside Cafe 2113 Manor Rd. • 476-5858 • lunch & dinner • some veggie • beer/wine • wheelchair access • $8-15

Katz's 618 W. 6th St. • 472-2037 • 24hrs • NY-style deli • full bar • wheelchair access • $8-15

Momma's Diner 314 Congress • 474-5730 • 24hrs • great homecooking

Romeo's 1500 Barton Springs Rd. • 476-1090 • Italian • some veggie • beer/wine • wheelchair access • $10-14

Soma 212 W. 4th St. • 474-7662 • 7am-midnight • til 4am Fri-Sat • espresso bar & cafe • some veggie

West Lynn Cafe 1110 W. Lynn • 482-0950 • vegetarian • beer/wine • $5-10

BOOKSTORES & RETAIL SHOPS

Book Woman 918 W. 12th. St. • 472-2785 • 10am-9pm, noon-6pm Sun • cards • jewelry • music • wheelchair access • women-owned/run

Celebration! 108 W. 43rd • 453-6207 • 10am-6:30pm, 12:30pm-5pm Sun • women's earth magic store • women-owned/run

Congress Avenue Booksellers 716 Congress Ave. • 478-1157 • 7:45am-8pm, 9am-6pm Sat, til 4pm Sun • lesbigay section

HighLife Cafe 407 E. 7th St. • 474-5338 • 8am-midnight, from 9am wknds • bistro fare

Lobo 3204-A Guadalupe • 454-5406 • 10am-10pm • lesbigay • wheelchair access

N8 1014-B N. Lamar • 478-3446 • 10am-9pm, noon-6pm Sun • designer/club clothes

Austin (512)

WHERE THE GIRLS ARE: Downtown along Red River St., or 4th/5th St. near Lavaca, or at the music clubs and cafes downtown and around the University.

ANNUAL EVENTS: May & Aug. - Splash Days: 476-3611, weekends of parties in clothing-optional Hippie Hollow. Sept-Austin G/L Int'l Film Festival: 472-3240.

CITY INFO: 478-0098. Greater Austin Chamber of Commerce: 478-9383.

ATTRACTIONS: Aqua Festival.

Elisabet Ney Museum. George Washington Carver Museum. Hamilton Pool. Laguna Gloria Art Museum. McKinney Falls State Park. Mount Bonnell. Museo del Barrio de Austin. Zilker Park.

BEST VIEW: State Capitol.

WEATHER: Summers are real scorchers (high 90°s - low 100°s) and last forever. Fall, winter and spring are welcome reliefs.

TRANSIT: Yellow-Checker: 472-1111. Various hotels have their own shuttles. Austin Transit: 474-1200.

Austin

*U*ntil the birth of the South By Southwest (SXSW) Music festival, Austin was Texas' best kept secret. A refreshing bastion of left-wing, non-confrontational radicalism, in many ways this most collegiate of cities seems to belong anywhere but the Lone Star State. Hard to believe it is actually the state capital, seat of the Texas Legislature.

When harried urbanites in Dallas and Houston want a quick getaway, many head to the natural beauty here in the Texas Hill Country. Just outside of the Capital City local boys and girls entertain themselves in the naturally cool (68° year round) waters of Barton Springs. The liberal attitudes at Hippie Hollow, site of the lesbigay **First** and **Last Splash Festivals**, has long been a favorite of the clothing-optional crowd.

In town, entertainment centers around the Mardi-Gras atmosphere of 6th Street downtown, where live and recorded music offerings literally run the gamut from hard-core punk to tear-jerkin' country-western. All of the bars tend to be mixed, female and male, but also mixed as in straight and gay. That's just how Austin is. Austin's lesbian culture currently only has one full-time womyn's bar, **Rainbow Cattle Company** (formerly Nexus). Leather dykes tend to mix it up at the mostly men's **Chain Drive**. Club kids dance, dance, dance at the progressive **Area 52** and the mostly male **Oil Can Harry's**.

The very popular bookstore, **Bookwomon**, is a great resource for connecting with like-minded womyn of every hue. They regularly schedule seminars, book signings and discussion groups and have details on all variety of events happening around town.

Austin Women's Rugby Club matches are very popular, as are Spring and Summer softball and volleyball leagues. Try Fans of Women's Sports (458-FANS) for the latest schedules and contacts.

Sadly, Austin's best lesbigay newsweekly, **The Texas Triangle**, is scheduled to cease publication in late '96, but the 'mainstream' Austin Chronicle lists events and organizations from all walks of life. You can also wire into the Austin Gay Friendly Online Directory (www.webcom.com/austin/)for listings of events, organizations, bars, etc.

—By Deirdre S. Green

(See back section on how to submit an essay about your favorite city.)

TRAVEL & TOUR OPERATORS

Capital of Texas Travel, Inc. 3006 Medical Arts St. • 478-2468/(800) 880-0068 • IGTA

Creative Travel Center 8650 Spicewood Springs Ste. 210 • 331-9560 • IGTA

Texas Tourist Division PO Box 5064, 78763-5064 • 462-9191/(800) 888-8TEX

West Austin Travel 2737 Exposition Blvd. • 482-8197/(800) 541-8583 • IGTA

SPIRITUAL GROUPS

Affirmation (Methodist) 7403 Shoal Creek Blvd. • 451-2329 • meets every other month

First Unitarian Church 4700 Grover Ave. • 452-6168 • 9:15am, 10:30am & 11:15am Sun • wheelchair access

Integrity 27th & University Ave. (church) • 445-6164 • 8pm 3rd Sun

MCC Austin 425 Woodward St. • 416-1170 • 9am, 11am & 7pm Sun • wheelchair access

Mishpachat Am Echad PO Box 9591, 78766 • 451-7018 • social group for Jewish lesbians/gays

PUBLICATIONS

Fag Rag PO Box 1034, 78767 • 479-9800 • gay boy party paper w/ occasional dish on the women's club scene

Texas Triangle 1615 W. 6th St. • 476-0576 • statewide

EROTICA

Forbidden Fruit 512 Neches • 478-8358 • also at 2001-A Guadalupe • 478-8542

Beaumont (409)

INFO LINES & SERVICES

Lambda AA 6300 College • 835-1508

BARS

Copa 304 Orleans St. • 832-4206 • 9pm-2am • popular • lesbians/gay men • dancing/DJ • live shows • wheelchair access

Sundowner 497 Crockett St. • 833-3989 • 4pm-2am • lesbians/gay men • dancing/DJ • live shows • beer/wine • BYOB

SPIRITUAL GROUPS

Spindletop Unitarian Church 1575 Spindletop Rd. • 833-6883 • 10:30am Sun

College Station (409)

INFO LINES & SERVICES

Gayline 847-0321 • Texas A&M Gay/Lesbian/Bisexual Student Services

BARS

Club 308 N. Bryan Ave., Bryan • 823-6767 • 9pm-2am • popular • lesbians/gay men • dancing/DJ • 18+ • live shows

Dudley's Draw 311 University • 846-3030 • 11am-1am • gay-friendly • neighborhood bar • wheelchair access

Corpus Christi (512)

INFO LINES & SERVICES

Lambda AA (at Christ's Temple MCC) • 882-8255

ACCOMMODATIONS

The Anthony's By The Sea 732 Pearl, Rockport • 729-6100/(800) 460-2557 • gay-friendly • quiet retreat • full brkfst • swimming

The Sea Horse Inn 1423 11th St., PO Box 426, Port Aransas, 78373 • 749-5221 • lesbians/gay men • Euro-style inn on dunes of Mustang Island & Port Aransas • swimming

BARS

Club Unity 4125 Gollihar • 851-1178 • 3pm-2am, from noon Sun • mostly women • dancing/DJ • live shows • women-owned/run

The Hidden Door 802 S. Staples St. • 882-5002 • 3pm-2am, from noon Sun • mostly gay men • leather • wheelchair access

The Hideout Leopard St. • 8pm-2am, clsd Mon • mostly gay men • neighborhood bar • Latino/a clientele • inquire locally

Mingles 512 S. Staples • 884-8022 • 8pm-2am, clsd Mon-Wed • mostly women • dancing/DJ

Numbers 1214 Leopard • 887-8445 • 4pm-2am • mostly gay men • dancing/DJ

UBU 511 Starr • 882-9693 • 9pm-2am Wed-Sun • gay-friendly • dancing/DJ • live shows • wheelchair access

SPIRITUAL GROUPS

Christ's Temple MCC 1315 Craig St. • 882-8255 • 11am Sun • wheelchair access

Dallas (214)

INFO LINES & SERVICES

Couples-Metro-Dallas PO Box 803156, 75380-3156 • 504-6775

Crossdressers/TV Helpline 264-7103

Crossroads Bar Hotline 380-3808 • 24hrs • info on 6 lesbigay bars

Dallas Gay Historic Archives (at Gay/Lesbian Center)

Dallas

Dallas' conservative reputation as the 'buckle of the Bible Belt' is well-deserved, but the city has mellowed a great deal since the economic meltdown of the late 1980s. Two openly gay men have been elected to the City Council and sexual orientation is included in the city's anti-discrimination policy.

Dallas is a relatively young city, but wealthy residents have created a legacy of art museums, historical sites and entertainment districts that will keep you busy. **The Arts District** in downtown is home to the Dallas Museum of Art (DMA) and a fabulous collection of modern masters, pre-Columbian artifacts, and the Reeves collection of Impressionist art and decorative pieces. The 6th Floor Museum, where Oswald allegedly perched while assassinating JFK, is a fascinating exploration of the facts and conspiracy theories. Old City Park recreates a pioneer village with original dwellings, period re-enactments, and exhibits. The West End, home of Planet Hollywood, the West End Marketplace and the Dallas World Aquarium offers a concentration of shops, restaurants and diversions in one spot.

East of downtown is **Deep Ellum**, one of Dallas' earliest African-American communities (Ellum is the way early residents pronounced Elm). Today it's live music central, with any of a number of clubs offering a host of local and national bands, 7 nights a week. Just about anything goes here, as long as it's left of center. Every segment of the population is represented in an ever-growing collection of off-beat bars, restaurants, shops, and tattoo parlors.

Further east is **Fair Park**, site of the State Fair of Texas every fall. Anytime of the year you can enjoy a wonderful day here touring the African American Museum, the Science Place and its IMAX theatre, Dallas Aquarium

Essay Contest • Women's Traveller

WT

Grand Prize Winner

(See back section on how to submit an essay about your favorite city.)

and Horticulture Center. The surrounding neighborhood is currently the local artists' habitué of choice with studios, showrooms, and gathering places along State and Parry streets. Millennium, at the corner of State and Parry, specializes in collectibles from the '40s to the '60s.

The Gay and Lesbian community in Dallas is thriving, concentrated in **Oak Lawn**, just north of downtown. Most of the businesses along the Cedar Springs Strip (Cedar Springs Road between Oak Lawn Avenue and Douglas) are gay-owned, and all are very lesbigay friendly. Same sex couples populate the sidewalks and restaurant tables day and night. Parking can be next to impossible on weekend nights, though, and caution should be taken if you decide to park on darkened side streets.

The local womyn's community is less visible than the gay men's, but you will find 3 full time womyns' bars: **Buddies II**, **Jugs** and **Sue Ellen's** and several active womyns' organizations. The community's churches and sports groups are popular meeting places for singles. Lesbian couples are concentrated in the suburbs of Oak Cliff or in Casa Linda, near White Rock Lake.

—By Deirdre S. Green

Dallas (214)

WHERE THE GIRLS ARE: Oak Lawn in central Dallas is the gay and lesbian stomping grounds, mostly on Cedar Springs Ave.

LESBIGAY PRIDE: September: 559-4190.

ANNUAL EVENTS: February- Black Gay/Lesbian Conference: 964-7820. June - Razzle Dazzle Dallas: 407-3553. Dance party & carnival benefits PWAs. September - Oak Lawn Arts Festival: 407-3553. Benefit in Lee Park for PWAs.

CITY INFO: (800) 752-9222.

ATTRACTIONS: Dallas Arboretum & Botanical Garden. Dallas Museum of Art. Dallas Theatre Center/ Frank Loyd Wright. Texas State Fair & State Fair Park.

BEST VIEW: Hyatt Regency Tower.

WEATHER: Can be unpredictable. Hot summers (90°s -100°s) with possible severe rainstorms. Winter temperatures hover in the 20°s through 40°s range.

TRANSIT: Yellow Cab: 426-6262. (817) 329-2000. Dallas Area Rapid Transit (DART): 979-1111.

Gay/Lesbian Community Center 2701 Reagan St. • 528-9254 • 9am-9pm, 10am-6pm Sat, from noon Sun • also credit union • wheelchair access

Gay/Lesbian Information Line 520-8781 • 7pm-9pm, 8pm-midnight Fri-Sat • info • crisis counseling

Lambda AA 2727 Oaklawn • 522-6259 • noon, 6pm, 8pm daily

Lesbian/Gay Welcome Wagon 2612 Bell St. • 979-0017 • community info for new arrivals

Lesbianas Latinas de Dallas 743-1644

SPROUTS 521-5342x256 • support/social group for women coming out or questioning their sexuality

TWIGS (The Womyn In Gay Society) 521-5342x269 • monthly social/discussion groups

Umoja Hermanas 943-8750 • group for lesbian & bisexual women of color

ACCOMMODATIONS

▲ **The Courtyard on the Trail** 8045 Forest Trail • 553-9700 • lesbians/gay men • full brkfst • swimming • gay-owned/run

▲ **The Inn on Fairmount** 3701 Fairmount • 522-2800 • lesbians/gay men • hot tub • gay-owned/run

Melrose Hotel 3015 Oaklawn Dr. • 521-5151/(800) 635-7673 • gay-friendly • historic hotel in Oak Lawn district • popular piano bar & lounge • 4-star restaurant

BARS

Anchor'Inn 4024 Cedar Springs • 526-4098 • 4pm-2am • mostly gay men • live shows • also 'Numbers' • 521-7861 • from 7am

Bamboleo's 5027 Lemmon St. • 520-1124 • 9pm-2am Fri-Sun • lesbians/gay men • dancing/DJ • Latino/a clientele • wheelchair access

Buddies II 4025 Maple Ave. at Throckmorton • 526-0887 • 11am-2am, from noon Sun • mostly women • country/western on wknds • live shows

Hideaway Club 4144 Buena Vista • 559-2966 • 8am-2am, from noon Sun • mostly gay men • professional • piano bar • patio

The Ice Factory 4117 Maple • 521-3154 • 2pm-2am, til 4am Fri-Sat • mostly gay men • dancing/DJ • leather

J.R.'s 3923 Cedar Springs Rd. • 528-1004 • 11am-2am • popular • mostly gay men • grill til 4pm • wheelchair access

Jugs 3810 Congress • 521-3474 • noon-2am • mostly women • dancing/DJ • multi-racial • live shows • wheelchair access • women-owned/run

Side 2 Bar 4006 Cedar Springs Rd. • 528-2026 • 10am-2am • lesbians/gay men • neighborhood bar • wheelchair access

Sue Ellen's 3903 Cedar Springs • 559-0707 • 3pm-2am, from noon wknds • popular • mostly women • live shows/bands • Sun BBQ • patio • wheelchair access

Village Station 3911 Cedar Springs Rd. • 526-7171 • 9pm-3am, from 5pm Sun • popular • mostly gay men • dancing/DJ • videos • Sun T-dance • also 'Rose Room' cabaret

RESTAURANTS & CAFES

Ali Baba Cafe 1905 Greenville Ave. • 823-8235 • lunch & dinner Tue-Sat, Sun lunch only, clsd Mon • Middle Eastern

Black-Eyed Pea 3857 Cedar Springs Rd. • 521-4580 • 11am-10:30pm • Southern homecooking • some veggie • wheelchair access • $5-10

Bombay Cricket Club 2508 Maple Ave. • 871-1333 • lunch & dinner • Indian

The Bronx Restaurant & Bar 3835 Cedar Springs Rd. • 521-5821 • lunch & dinner, Sun brunch, clsd Mon • some veggie • wheelchair access • gay-owned/run • $8-15

Cafe Society 4514 Travis St. • 528-6543 • 11am-11pm Mon-Th, 10am-midnight Fri-Sat, 10am-10pm Sun • women-owned/run

Cremona Bistro & Cafe 3136 Routh St. • 871-1115 • 11am-10:30pm • Italian • full bar

Dream Cafe 2800 Routh • 954-0486 • 7am-10pm Sun-Th, til 11pm Fri-Sat • popular • plenty veggie • wheelchair access • $7-12

Fresh Start Market and Deli 4108 Oak Lawn • 528-5535 • 8am-8pm Mon-Fri, 9am-6pm Sat, 11am-6pm Sun • organic • plenty veggie • wheelchair access • gay-owned/run

Hunky's 4000 Cedar Springs Rd. • 522-1212 • 11am-10pm • popular • grill • beer/wine • patio • wheelchair access • gay-owned/run • $5-10

La Familia 3851 Cedar Springs • 521-7079 • lunch & dinner • Mexican • full bar • patio • gay-owned/run • $5-10

Monica Aca Y Alla 2914 Main St. • 748-7140 • popular • Tex-Mex • full bar • live shows Fri-Sat • transgender-friendly • wheelchair access

The Natura Cafe 2909 McKinney Ave. • 855-5483 • lunch & dinner • healthy • full bar

Oak Cliff Coffee House 408 N. Bishop • 943-4550 • 7am-10pm • deli, salads • gay-owned/run

Spasso Pizza & Pasta Co. 4000 Cedar Springs • 521-1141 • some veggie • beer/wine • wheelchair access • gay-owned/run

Sushi on McKinney 4502 McKinney Ave. • 521-0969 • lunch & dinner, Fri-Sat til 11pm • full bar • wheelchair access

Thai Soon 2018 Greenville Ave. • 821-7666 • lunch & dinner, Fri-Sat til midnight

Vitto's 316 W. 7th St. • 946-1212 • lunch & dinner, Fri-Sat til 11pm • Italian • beer/wine • wheelchair access • gay-owned/run

Ziziki's 4514 Travis St., #122 in Travis Walk • 521-2233 • 11am-11pm, 11am-midnight Fri-Sat, clsd Sun • Greek • full bar • wheelchair access

GYMS & HEALTH CLUBS

Centrum Sports Club 3102 Oak Lawn • 522-4100 • gay-friendly • swimming

BOOKSTORES & RETAIL SHOPS

Crossroads Market 3930 Cedar Springs Rd. • 521-8919 • 10am-10pm, noon-9pm Sun • lesbigay bookstore • wheelchair access

Off the Street 3921 Cedar Springs • 521-9051 • 10am-9pm, noon-6pm Sun • lesbigay gifts

Shocking Gray 2851 Anode Ln., 75220 • 353-0882/(800) 344-4729

Tapelenders 3926 Cedar Springs Rd. • 528-6344 • 9am-midnight • lesbigay t-shirts • books • video rental • gay-owned/run

TRAVEL & TOUR OPERATORS

Planet Travel 3102 Maple Ave. #450 • 965-0800 • gay-owned/run

Strong Travel 8201 Preston Rd. Ste. 160 • 361-0027/(800) 747-5670 • IGTA

Travel Friends 8080 N. Central Expwy. Ste. 320 • 891-8833/(800) 862-8833 • IGTA

Travel With Us 6116 N. Central Expressway Ste. 175 • 987-2563/(800) 856-2563 • IGTA

White Heron Travel 4849 Greenville Ave. #173 • 692-0446 • ask for Mark Lee • IGTA

SPIRITUAL GROUPS

Affirmation (Methodist) at North Haven United Methodist • 528-4913 • 7:30pm 4th Mon

Cathedral of Hope MCC 5910 Cedar Springs • 351-1901 • 9am, 11am & 6:30pm Sun, 6:30pm Wed & Sat • wheelchair access

Congregation Beth El Binah 497-1591 • variety of services for lesbigay Jews

Dignity/Dallas 6525 Inwood Rd. (St. Thomas the Apostle) • 521-5342x832 • 5:30pm Sun (6:30pm summers) • wheelchair access

First Unitarian Church of Dallas 4015 Normandy • 528-3990 • 9am & 11am Sun (only 10am Sun summers)

Holy Trinity Community Church 4402 Roseland • 827-5088 • 11am Sun

Honesty/Texas PO Box 190869, 75219 • 521-5342x233 • call about monthly mtgs.

Integrity PO Box 190351, 75219 • 520-0912

White Rock Community Church 722 Tennison Memorial Rd. • 320-0043 • 9am, 10:30am & 7:30pm Sun, 7pm Wed

PUBLICATIONS

Dallas Voice 3000 Carlisle Ste. 200 • 754-8710

Lesbian Visionaries PO Box 191442, 75219 • 521-5342x844 • newsletter

TWT (This Week in Texas) 3300 Regan Ave. • 521-0622 • statewide

Women's Yellow Pages of Greater Dallas 18782 Vista Del Sol • 661-3364

EROTICA

Alternatives 1720 W. Mockingbird Ln. • 630-7071

Leather by Boots 2525 Wycliff Ste.124 • 528-3865 • noon-8pm, clsd Sun

Shades of Grey Leather 3928 Cedar Springs Rd. • 521-4739

Denison (903)

BARS

Goodtime Lounge 2520 N. Hwy. 91 N. • 463-9944 • 6pm-2am, from 2pm Sun • lesbians/gay men • more women Wed • private club

Denton (817)

INFO LINES & SERVICES

Denton County Lambda AA (at Harvest MCC) • 321-2332

BARS

Bedo's 1215 E. University Dr. • 566-9910 •
8pm-midnight, from 6pm Fri, til 1am Sat,
from 5pm Sun • lesbians/gay men • dancing/DJ • live shows • private club • wheelchair access • women-owned/run

SPIRITUAL GROUPS

Harvest MCC 5900 S. Stemmons • 321-2332 • 10:30am Sun

El Paso (915)

INFO LINES & SERVICES

Lambda AA 833-9544 (private home) •
7:30pm Mon

Lambda Line/Lambda Services PO Box
31321, 79931 • 562-4297 • 24hrs • info

Youth OUTreach (contact Lambda Line) •
562-4297

BARS

Briar Patch 204 E. Rio Grande St. • 546-9100 • noon-2am • lesbians/gay men •
neighborhood bar

The Old Plantation 301-309 S. Ochoa St. •
533-6055 • 8pm-2am, til 4am Th-Sat, clsd
Mon-Wed • popular • lesbians/gay men •
dancing/DJ • live shows • videos • wheelchair access

San Antonio Mining Co. 800 E. San
Antonio Ave. • 533-9516 • 3pm-2am • popular • lesbians/gay men • dancing/DJ •
videos • wheelchair access

U-Got-It 216 S. Ochoa • 533-9510 • 8pm-2am, clsd Sun-Tue • mostly gay men •
dancing/DJ • alternative • live shows •
wheelchair access

The Whatever Lounge 701 E. Paisano St. •
533-0215 • 3pm-2am • mostly gay men •
dancing/DJ • Latino/a clientele • beer/wine
• BYOB • wheelchair access

RESTAURANTS & CAFES

The Little Diner 7209 7th St., Canutillo •
877-2176

SPIRITUAL GROUPS

MCC 916 E. Yandell • 591-4155 • 6pm Sun,
7pm Wed

PUBLICATIONS

Lambda News PO Box 31321, 79931 • 562-4297

Fort Worth (817)

(See also **Arlington** & **Dallas**)

INFO LINES & SERVICES

Lambda AA 3144 Ryan Ave. • 921-2871 •
8pm daily • call for other mtgs.

Second Tuesday 877-5544 • lesbian social
group

Tarrant County Lesbian/Gay Alliance
1219 6th Ave. • 877-5544 • info line •
newsletter

ACCOMMODATIONS

Two Pearls B&B 804 S. Alamo St.,
Weatherford • 596-9316 • lesbians/gay men
• modernized 1898 home • full brkfst •
women-owned/run

BARS

651 Club Fort Worth 651 S. Jennings Ave. •
332-0745 • noon-2am • mostly gay men •
more women Fri-Sat • dancing/DJ • country/western • wheelchair access

Copa Cabana 1002 S. Main • 336-8911 •
mostly gay men

The Corral 621 Hemphill St. • 335-0196 •
11am-2am, from noon Sun • mostly gay
men • dancing/DJ • videos • patio • wheelchair access

Cowgirls Oasis 1263 W. Magnolia • 924-0224 • 5pm-2am, from 4pm Sun, clsd Mon-Tue • mostly women • BYOB

D.J.'s 1308 St. Louis St. • 927-7321 • 7pm-2am, til 3am Fri-Sat, clsd Mon-Tue • popular • lesbians/gay men • dancing/DJ • live
shows • also a restaurant

Neon Nights 1408 W. Magnolia • 870-0022
• 3pm-2am, clsd Mon • mostly gay men •
neighborhood bar • wheelchair access

TRAVEL & TOUR OPERATORS

Country Day Travel 6022 Southwest Blvd.
• 731-8551 • IGTA

SPIRITUAL GROUPS

Agape MCC 4516 SE Loop 820 • 535-5002
• 9am & 11am Sun • wheelchair access

First Jefferson Unitarian Universalist
1959 Sandy Ln. • 451-1505 • 11am Sun •
lesbigay group 7pm 1st Th • wheelchair
access

PUBLICATIONS

Alliance News 1219 6th Ave. • 877-5544

Galveston (409)

INFO LINES & SERVICES

Lambda AA ACCT office (23rd & Ursula) •
684-2140 • 8pm Th & 5pm Sun

ACCOMMODATIONS

Galveston Island Women's Guesthouse
763-2450 • women only • sundeck • jacuzzi
• smokefree • women-owned/run • $45-55

BARS

Evolution 2214 Ships Mechanic Rd. • 763-4212 • 4pm-2am, til 4am Fri-Sat • popular • lesbians/gay men • dancing/DJ • videos

Kon Tiki Club 312 23rd St. • 763-6264 • 4pm-2am, from 2pm wknds • popular • lesbians/gay men • dancing/DJ • live shows

Robert's Lafitte 2501 'Q' Ave. • 765-9092 • 10am-2am, from noon Sun • mostly gay men • live shows • wheelchair access

Groesbeck   (817)

ACCOMMODATIONS

Rainbow Ranch Rte. 2, Box 165, 76642 • 729-5847 • gay-friendly • camping • RV hook-up • on Lake Limestone halfway btwn. Houston & Dallas

Gun Barrel City   (903)

BARS

231 Club 231 W. Main St. (Hwy. 85) • 887-2061 • 6pm-midnight, til 1am Sat • gay-friendly • neighborhood bar • wheelchair access

Harlingen   (210)

BARS

Colors 703 N. Ed Carey • 440-8663 • 8pm-2am, til 3am Fri-Sat, clsd Mon-Tue • lesbians/gay men • dancing/DJ • live shows • wheelchair access

Zippers 319 W. Harrison • 412-9708 • 8pm-2am • lesbians/gay men • live shows • wheelchair access

Houston   (713)

INFO LINES & SERVICES

Gay/Lesbian Hispanics Unidos PO Box 70153, 77270 • 813-3769 • 7pm 2nd Wed

Gay/Lesbian Radio KPFT-FM 90.1 • 526-4000 • 'After Hours' midnight-4am Sat • 'Lesbian/Gay Voices' 6pm Fri

Gay/Lesbian Switchboard PO Box 66469, 77266 • 529-3211 • 3pm-midnight

Houston Area Women's Center/Hotline 1010 Waugh Dr. • 528-2121 • 9am-9pm, til noon Sat, clsd Sun • wheelchair access

Houston Outdoor Group PO Box 980893, 77098 • 526-7688 • monthly socials & camping

Lambda AA Center 1201 W. Clay • 521-1243 • noon-11pm, til 1am Fri-Sat • wheelchair access

LOAFF (Lesbians Over Age Fifty) 1505 Nevada (Houston Mission Church) • 661-1482 • 2pm 3rd Sun • call for info

ACCOMMODATIONS

The Lovett Inn 501 Lovett Blvd., Montrose • 522-5224/(800) 779-5224 • gay-friendly • historic home of former Houston mayor & Federal Court judge • swimming

---

Houston   (713)

WHERE THE GIRLS ARE: Strolling the Montrose district near the intersection of Montrose and Westheimer, or out on Buffalo Speedway at the Plaza.

LESBIGAY PRIDE: 529-6979.

CITY INFO: (800) 231-7799.

ATTRACTIONS: Allen's Landing & Old Market Square. Astrodome. Astroworld/ Waterworld. Bayou Bend Collection. Galleria Mall.

BEST VIEW: Spindletop, the revolving cocktail lounge on top of the Hyatt Regency.

WEATHER: Humid all year round—you're not that far from the Gulf. Mild winters, although there are a few days when the temperatures drop into the 30°s. Winter also brings occasional rainy days. Summers are very hot.

TRANSIT: Yellow Cab: 236-1111. Hobby Limousine: 644-8359 (runs between both airports). Metropolitan Transit Authority: 635-4000.

Houston

With mild winters and blazing summers, Houston is the hottest lesbian spot in the Southwest. From the Astrodome to San Jacinto, Houston welcomes sports fans, historians, and shoppers as well as "just look"-ers. We've got bars bigger than your hometown (like **Plaza 9220**) and as intimate as your best friend (**Bacchus II**), so you can dance the night away here.

Shop the emporiums devoted to women, from **Inklings** alternative bookstore and **Crossroads Market** with their hip coffee bar and periodicals, to **Lucia's**. Fine and casual dining among beautiful women takes place all over the cruisy Montrose (where lesbians are said to shop and party) and Heights neighborhoods. Try elegant **Baba Yega's** and **Java Java**. Take some time to admire the mansions of the Montrose and the elegant Victorian homes of the Heights.

For a change of scenery, check out the babes on Galveston Island beach, about a one hour drive south. While you're there, refresh yourself and dance at **Evolution**, the lesbigay bar.

After you've seen it all, collapse in your jacuzzi suite at the legendary **Lovett Inn** and listen to lesbian and gay radio, **"Afterhours"** on KPFT. Relax with a copy of the **Houston Voice** and know that Houston is *the* hottest queer place to vacation.

—By Esperanza Lavender Jazz Paz

Essay Contest
Women's Traveller
W

3rd Runner Up

(See back section on how to submit an essay about your favorite city.)

Rainbow's Inn 6830 Hansen, Groves • (409) 962-1497 • lesbians/gay men • rental home on Lake Sam Rayburn, approx. 2 1/2 hrs from Houston

BARS

Bacchus II 2715 Waughcrest • 523-3396 • 4pm-2am, from 2pm Sun • popular • mostly women • dancing/DJ • live shows

Backyard Bar & Grill 10200 S. Main • 660-6285 • 5pm-2am, from noon wknds • gay-friendly • volleyball courts • food served • dinner theater Fri-Sun • call for events • wheelchair access

The Berryhill II 12726 North Fwy. • 873-8810 • 6pm-2am • lesbians/gay men • neighborhood bar • dancing/DJ • live shows • wheelchair access • women-owned/run

Chances 1100 Westheimer • 523-7217 • 10am-2am • mostly women • dancing/DJ • live shows • wheelchair access

Cousins 817 Fairview • 528-9204 • 7am-2am • lesbians/gay men • neighborhood bar • live shows • wheelchair access

Gentry 2303 Richmond • 520-1861 • 2pm-2am, from noon wknds • popular • mostly gay men • neighborhood bar • live shows • wheelchair access

Heaven 810 Pacific • 521-9123 • 9pm-2am Wed-Sat, from 7pm Sun • popular • mostly gay men • dancing/DJ • 18+ Wed & Sat • live shows Th • videos

Incognito 2524 McKinney • 237-9431 • 9pm-2am, from 6pm Sun, clsd Mon-Tue • lesbians/gay men • ladies night Th • live shows

Inergy 5750 Chimney Rock • 666-7310 • 8pm-2am • popular • lesbians/gay men • dancing/DJ • multi-racial • leather • live shows

J.R.'s 808 Pacific • 521-2519 • 11am-2am, from noon Sun • popular • mostly gay men • more women Fri • live shows • videos • wheelchair access

Jo's Outpost 1419 Richmond • 520-8446 • 11am-2am • mostly gay men • neighborhood bar

Melas Tejano Country 1016 W. 19th St. • 880-1770 • 5pm-2am, clsd Mon-Tue • mostly gay men • multi-racial • leather

Palm Beach Club (at West Houston Hilton) 12401 Katy Fwy. (I-10) • 496-9090 • gay-friendly • dancing/DJ • Sat night 'Fantasy BBS' party • transgender-friendly

Past Time 617 Fairview • 529-4669 • 7am-2am • lesbians/gay men • neighborhood bar

The Ranch 9218 Buffalo Speedway. • 666-3464 • 4pm-2am, clsd Mon • popular • mostly women • 3 bars • dancing/DJ • country/western • volleyball court • wheelchair access

Steam 402 Lovett • 521-1450 • 1:30am-dawn, clsd Mon-Tue • mostly gay men

Tammy's Tavern 2915 Main St. • 521-9960 • 7pm-2am • mostly women • dancing/DJ • multi-racial • food served • BYOB

Trading Post Ice House 11410 S. Post Oak Dr. • 726-1963 • 11am-midnight, til 1am Sat, clsd Sun • lesbians/gay men • sports bar • beer/wine • wheelchair access

RESTAURANTS & CAFES

A Moveable Feast 2202 W. Alabama • 528-3585 • 9am-10pm • plenty veggie • also a health food store • wheelchair access • $7-12

Baba Yega's 2607 Grant • 522-0042 • 10am-10pm • popular • plenty veggie • full bar • patio • $5-10

Barnaby's Cafe 604 Fairview • 522-0106 • 11am-10pm, til 11pm Fri-Sat • popular • beer/wine • wheelchair access

Black-Eyed Pea 2048 W. Grey • 523-0200 • 11am-10pm • popular • Southern • wheelchair access • $5-10

Brasil 2604 Dunlavy • 528-1993 • 9am-2am • bistro • plenty veggie • full bar

Chapultepec 813 Richmond • 522-2365 • 24hrs • live shows • Mexican • some veggie • $8-15

Charlie's 1102 Westheimer • 522-3332 • 24hrs • lesbians/gay men • full bar • wheelchair access • $5-10

House of Pies 3112 Kirby • 528-3816 • 24hrs • popular • wheelchair access • $5-10

Jack Laurenzo's 5589 Richmond Ave. • 266-4191 • lunch & dinner • pasta/steak/seafood

Java Java Cafe 911 W. 11th • 880-5282 • popular

Ninfa's 2704 Navigation • 228-1175 • 11am-10pm • popular • Mexican • some veggie • $7-12

Ninos 2817 W. Dallas • 522-5120 • lunch & dinner, clsd Sun • Italian • some veggie • full bar • wheelchair access • $10-20

Pot Pie Pizzeria 1525 Westheimer • 528-4350 • 11am-11pm, clsd Mon • Italian • some veggie • beer/wine • $5-10

Q Cafe 2205 Richmond Ave. • 524-9696 • 4pm-2am • quesadillas & more • plenty veggie • full bar • wheelchair access

Rocky Java 220 Avondale • 521-7095 • 24hrs • patio • wheelchair access

Spanish Flower 4701 N. Main • 869-1706 • 24hrs • Mexican • some veggie • $7-12

Toopes Coffeehouse 1830 W. Alabama • 522-7662 • 6am-11pm, from 7am wknds • cafe • some veggie • beer/wine • patio • wheelchair access • lesbian-owned/run

GYMS & HEALTH CLUBS

Fitness Exchange 3930 Kirby Dr. Ste. 300 • 524-9932 • 6am-10pm, 10am-8pm wknds • popular • gay-friendly

YMCA Downtown 1600 Louisiana St. • 659-8501 • 5am-10pm, 8am-6pm Sat, from 10am Sun • gay-friendly • swimming

BOOKSTORES & RETAIL SHOPS

Basic Brothers 1232 Westheimer • 522-1626 • 10am-9pm, noon-6on Sun • lesbi-gay merchandise • wheelchair access

Crossroads Market Bookstore/Cafe 1111 Westheimer • 942-0147 • 9am-10pm, til 11pm Fri-Sat • lesbigay • wheelchair access

Hyde Park Gallery 711 Hyde Park • 526-2744 • lesbigay art gallery

Inklings: An Alternative Bookstore 1846 Richmond Ave. • 521-3369/(800) 931-3369 • 10:30am-6:30pm, noon-5pm Sun, clsd Mon • lesbigay/feminist • jewelry • music • videos

Lobo-Houston 3939 S. Montrose Blvd. • 522-5156 • 10am-10pm • lesbigay book-store • wheelchair access

Lucia's Garden 2942 Virginia • 523-6494 • 10am-10pm • spiritual herb center

TRAVEL & TOUR OPERATORS

Advance Travel 10700 NW Fwy. Ste. 160 • 682-2002/(800) 292-0500 • popular • IGTA

DCA Travel 1535 W. Loop S. Ste. 115 • 629-5377/(800) 321-9539

Woodlake Travel 1704 Post Oak Rd. • 942-0664/(800) 245-6180 • IGTA

SPIRITUAL GROUPS

Dignity/Houston 1307 Yale Ste. 8 • 880-2872 • 7:30pm Sat, 5:30pm Sun

Integrity 6265 S. Main (Autry House) • 432-0414 • 7pm 2nd & 4th Mon

Maranatha Fellowship MCC 3400 Montrose Ste. 600 • 528-6756 • 11am Sun

MCC of the Resurrection 1919 Decatur St. • 861-9149 • 9am & 11am Sun

Mishpachat Alizim PO Box 980136, 77298-0136 • 748-7079 • worship & social/support group for Jewish lesbians & gay men

PUBLICATIONS

Houston Voice 811 Westheimer Ste. 105 • 529-8490

OutSmart 3406 Audubon Pl., 77006 • 520-7237

TWT (This Week in Texas) 811 Westheimer St. • 527-9111 • statewide

EROTICA

Leather by Boots 2424 Montrose • 526-2668 • noon-8pm

Leather Forever 711 Fairview • 526-6940 • noon-8pm

Katy   (713)

TRAVEL & TOUR OPERATORS

In Touch Travel 1814 Powderhorn • 347-3596 • IGTA

Laredo   (210)

BARS

Discovery 2019 Farragut • 722-9032 • 6pm-2am Wed-Sun • lesbians/gay men • dancing/DJ • Latina/o clientele • live shows • beer/wine

Longview   (903)

BARS

Decisions 2103 E. Marshall • 757-4884 • 3pm-2am • lesbians/gay men • dancing/DJ • patio

Lifestyles 446 Eastman Rd. • 758-8082 • 11am-2am • lesbians/gay men • dancing/DJ • live shows • volleyball court

RESTAURANTS & CAFES

Brother's Coffee Bar & Gallery 302-A Spur 63 • 758-3707 • 7am-1am Mon-Th, 7am-3am Fri, 4pm-3am Sat, 4pm-1am Sun • sandwiches • open mike Mon • call for events

BOOKSTORES & RETAIL SHOPS

Newsland 301 E. Marshall • 753-4167 • 9am-6pm, clsd Sun

SPIRITUAL GROUPS

Church With A Vision MCC 420 E. Cotton St. • 753-1501 • 10am Sun • wheelchair access

Lubbock (806)

INFO LINES & SERVICES
AA Lambda 828-3316 • 8pm Fri at MCC

LLGA (Lubbock Lesbian/Gay Alliance) PO Box 64746, 79464 • 766-7184 • 7:30pm 2nd Wed • at Community Outreach Center

BARS
Captain Hollywood Main St. at Ave. X • 797-1808 • 8pm-2am • lesbians/gay men • dancing/DJ • live shows

Metro 1806 Clovis Rd. • 740-0006 • 7pm-2am, clsd Mon • lesbians/gay men • dancing/DJ

The Place 2401 Main St. • 744-4222 • 8pm-2am • mostly women • dancing/DJ • country/western • wheelchair access

SPIRITUAL GROUPS
MCC 4501 University Ave. • 792-5562 • 11am & 6pm Sun, 7:30pm Wed • wheelchair access

PUBLICATIONS
Dimensions PO Box 856, 79408 • 797-9647 • women's magazine covers TX,OK,NM & New Orleans, LA

McAllen (210)

BARS
Austin St. Inn 1110 Austin St. • 687-7703 • 8pm-2am, clsd Mon-Tue • lesbians/gay men • dancing/DJ • live shows

Just Tery's 1500 N. 23rd • 682-2437 • 7pm-2am, clsd Mon-Tue • mostly gay men • dancing/DJ • live shows • wheelchair access

P.B.D.'s 2908 Ware Rd. (at Daffodil) • 682-8019 • 8pm-2am • mostly gay men • neighborhood bar • wheelchair access

Tenth Avenue 1820 N. 10th St. • 682-7131 • 8pm-2am Wed-Sun • lesbians/gay men • dancing/DJ • Latina/o clientele • live shows • wheelchair access

Odessa/Midland (915)

INFO LINES & SERVICES
Free & Clean Lambda Group (Gay AA/AlAnon) 2535 E. Roper (The Basin) • 337-1436 • 7pm Fri & Sun

BARS
Mining Co. 409 N. Hancock • 580-6161 • 9pm-2am Wed-Sun • lesbians/gay men • dancing/DJ • live shows • beer/wine • BYOB • wheelchair access

Nite Spot 8401 Andrews Hwy. • 366-6799 • 8pm-2am, clsd Mon • popular • lesbians/gay men • dancing/DJ • live shows • videos • wheelchair access

SPIRITUAL GROUPS
Holy Trinity Community Church 402 E. Gist, Midland • 570-4822 • 11am Sun

Prodigal Ministries Community Church 1500 E. Murphy • 563-8880 • 10:30am Sun • wheelchair access

Port Aransas (512)

ACCOMMODATIONS
Port Aransas Inn 1500 11th St. • 749-5937 • gay-friendly • full brkfst • hot tub • swimming

Rio Grande Valley (210)

INFO LINES & SERVICES
Lesbigay Alliance 428-6800

San Angelo (915)

BARS
Silent Partners 3320 Sherwood Wy. • 949-9041 • 6pm-2am, clsd Mon • mostly women • dancing/DJ • country/western Wed • live shows • women-owned/run

San Antonio (210)

INFO LINES & SERVICES
▲ **Dyke TV** 'weekly half-hour TV show produced by lesbians, for lesbians' • call (212) 343-9335 for more info

Gay & Lesbian Community Center 923 E. Mistletoe • 732-4300 • noon-8pm, til 10pm Fri (movie night) • wheelchair access

The Happy Foundation 411 Bonham • 227-6451 • lesbigay archives

Lambda Club AA 8546 Broadway Ste. 255 • 824-2027 • 8:15pm daily

San Antonio Gay/Lesbian Switchboard 733-7300 • 7pm-11pm

Tuesday Night Discussion 8021 Pinebrook (Nexus) • 341-2818 • 7pm • 1st Tue: lesbian topic • 3rd Tue: lesbian/gay topic

ACCOMMODATIONS
Adelynne Summit Haus I & II 427 W. Summit Ave. • 736-6272/(800) 972-7266 • gay-friendly • full brkfst

Arbor House Hotel 339 S. Presa St. • 472-2005/(888) 272-6700 • gay-friendly • IGTA • gay-owned/run

Desert Hearts Cowgirl Club HC3 Box 650, Bandera, 78003 • 796-7446 • women only • 2-bdrm cabin on 30 acres • dinner served • kitchen • swimming • horseback riding • $168-238 (for 2) • lesbian-owned/run

Elmira Motor Inn 1123 E. Elmira • 222-9463 • gay-friendly

The Garden Cottage PO Box 12915, 78212 • (800) 235-7215 • gay-friendly • private cottage

▲ **The Painted Lady B&B** 620 Broadway • 220-1092 • popular • lesbians/gay men • private art deco suites • some w/ kitchenettes

San Antonio B&B 510 E. Guenther • 222-1828 • gay-friendly • full brkfst • hot tub

BARS

2015 Place 2015 San Pedro • 733-3365 • 2pm-2am • mostly gay men • neighborhood bar • live shows • patio

8th St. Restaurant & Bar 416 8th St. • 271-3227 • 4:30pm-midnight, til 2am Fri-Sat • gay-friendly • bar has lesbian following

B.B.'s Pub 5307 McCullough • 828-4222 • 2pm-? • lesbians/gay men • neighborhood bar • dancing/DJ • women-owned/run

The Bonham Exchange 411 Bonham St. • 271-3811 • 4pm-2am, from 8pm wknds, til 4am Fri-Sat • popular • gay-friendly • dancing/DJ • alternative • videos • 18+ on Wed • patio

Cameo 1123 E. Commerce • 226-7055 • 10pm-4am Fri-Sun • gay-friendly • dancing/DJ • beer/wine • underground mini-rave

Cowboy's 622 Roosevelt • 532-9194 • 4pm-2am, clsd Mon • lesbians/gay men • country/western

Lorraine's South Presa (at Military) • 532-8911 • 6pm-2am • gay-friendly • dancing/DJ • alternative

Mick's Hideaway 5307 McCullough • 828-4222 • 3pm-2am • lesbians/gay men • neighborhood bar • patio • wheelchair access

Miriam's 115 General Krueger • 308-7354 • 2pm-2am • lesbians/gay men • neighborhood bar • dancing/DJ • women-owned/run

New Ponderosa 5007 S. Flores • 924-6322 • 6pm-2am, from 3pm wknds • lesbians/gay men • dancing/DJ • Latina/o clientele • live shows

San Antonio

*A*lthough its moment of glory was more than 150 years ago, **The Alamo** has become a mythological symbol that still greatly influences San Antonians of today. Just to remind you, The Alamo was a mission in which a handful of Texans—including Davy Crockett and Jim Bowie—kept a Mexican army of thousands at bay for almost two weeks.

San Antonians are fiercely proud of this heritage, and maintain a rough-n-ready attitude just to prove it. This is just as true of the dykes in San Antonio as anyone else.

You'll find them at **Miriam's** or **Nexus** acting like cowgirls, or at **Textures** or **Q Bookstore** catching up on the latest. For shopping, try **Over the Rainbow**—but avoid tourist-trap River Walk unless you're a hardcore kitschaholic.

Don't miss the view from the deck of **The Painted Lady Bed & Breakfast**.

There's no gay ghetto in this spread-out city, but the lesbian-friendly businesses are clustered along various streets, including the 5000 blocks of S. Flores and McCullough, the 1400-1900 blocks of N. Main, and scattered along Broadway, San Pedro and elsewhere.

For sightseeing, there's always The Alamo, and the two-and-a-half mile Texas Star Trail walking tour that starts and ends there. The architecture in old San Antonio is quaint and beautiful—stop by **The Bonham Exchange** for just a taste.

Nexus SA (San Antonio) 8021 Pinebrook • 341-2818 • 6pm-2am, 7pm-4am Sat, clsd Mon • mostly women • dancing/DJ • country/western • wheelchair access • women-owned/run

Nite Owl 330 San Pedro Ave. • 223-6957 • 4pm-2am, from noon Sun • mostly gay men • more women weekdays • neighborhood bar • patio • wheelchair access

Red Hot & Blues 450 Soledad • 227-0484 • 4pm-2am • gay-friendly • dancing/DJ • videos • live shows • on the river walk • wheelchair access

The Saint 1430 N. Main • 225-7330 • 9pm-2am Fri, til 4am Sat only • mostly gay men • dancing/DJ • alternative • 18+ • live shows

Showcase 3625 West Ave. • 690-7727 • 10pm-3am • lesbians/gay men • dancing/DJ • alternative • 18+

Silver Dollar Saloon 1418 N. Main Ave. • 227-2623 • 2pm-2am • mostly gay men • dancing/DJ • country/western • videos • 2-story patio bar • 'Trash Disco' Sun • wheelchair access

Sparks 8011 Webbles St. • 653-9941 • 3pm-2am • mostly gay men • live shows • videos • karaoke Mon & Th

Woody's 826 San Pedro • 271-9663 • 2pm-2am • mostly gay men • videos

RESTAURANTS & CAFES

Giovanni's Pizza & Italian Restaurant 1410 Guadalupe • 212-6626 • 10am-7pm, clsd Sun • some veggie • $7-12

North St. Mary's Brewing Co. Pub & Deli 2734 N. St. Mary's • 737-6255 • 7pm-2am • live shows

BOOKSTORES & RETAIL SHOPS

On Main 2514 N. Main • 737-2323 • 10am-6pm, clsd Sun • gifts

Over the Rainbow CDs & Gifts 5301 McCullough • 822-6965 • 10am-6:30pm

Q Bookstore 2803 N. St. Mary's • 734-4299 • 10am-9pm, noon-6pm Sun • lesbigay

Textures Bookstore 805-8398 • 11am-6pm, til 5pm wknds, from 1pm Sun • feminist

TRAVEL & TOUR OPERATORS

Advantage Plus Travel 800 NW Loop 410 Ste. 306 S. • 366-1955/(800) 460-3755 • IGTA

SPIRITUAL GROUPS

Dignity St. Anne's St. & Ashby Pl. (St. Anne's Convent) • 558-3287 • 5:15pm Sun

MCC San Antonio 1136 W. Woodlawn • 734-0048 • 10:30am & 7pm Sun • wheelchair access

Re-Formed Congregation of the Goddess PO Box 12931, 78212 • 828-4601 • Dianic Wiccan group

River City Living MCC 202 Holland • 822-1121 • 11am Sun

PUBLICATIONS

Bar Talk PO Box 15568, 78291 • 737-7157

The Marquise PO Box 701204, 78232 • 545-3511

EROTICA

FleshWorks 2423 W. Wildwood • 731-8185 • clsd Tue & Sun • body piercing & alterations

Minx 1621 N. Main Ave. #2 • 225-2639 • piercing studio

Sherman (903)

TRAVEL & TOUR OPERATORS

About Travel 5637 Texoma Pkwy. • 893-6888/(800) 783-6481

San Antonio (210)

WHERE THE GIRLS ARE: Coupled up in the suburbs, or carousing downtown.

CITY INFO: 270-8748/(800) 447-3372.

BEST VIEW: From the deck of the Painted Lady Bed & Breakfast.

WEATHER: 90°s in the summer, 40°s in winter.

TRANSIT: Yellow Cab: 226-4242.

Temple (817)

Bars

Hard Tymes 313 S. 1st. St. • 778-9604 • 9pm-2am, clsd Mon • mostly gay men • military clientele

Texarkana (501)

Bars

The Gig 201 East St. (Hwy. 71 S.) • 773-6900 • 8pm-5am, from 3pm Sun, clsd Mon-Tue • lesbians/gay men • dancing/DJ • private club • live shows

Tyler (903)

Bars

Outlaws Hwy. 110 (4 miles S. of Loop 323) • 509-2248 • gay-friendly • dancing/DJ • 18+

Spiritual Groups

St. Gabriel's Community Church 13904 Country Rd. 193 • 581-6923 • 10:30am Sun • newsletter • wheelchair access

Waco (817)

Info Lines & Services

Gay/Lesbian Alliance of Central Texas PO Box 9081, 76714 • 752-7727/(800) 735-1122 (in state only) • info • newsletter • pride shop

Bars

David's Place 507 Jefferson • 753-9189 • 7pm-2am • lesbians/gay men • dancing/DJ • live shows • wheelchair access

Spiritual Groups

Central Texas MCC From the Heart 1601 Clay • 752-5331 • 10:45am Sun, 7:30pm Wed

Unitarian Universalist Fellowship of Waco 4209 N. 27th St. • 754-0599 • 10:45am Sun

Unity Church of the Living Christ 400 S. 1st, Hewitt • 666-9102 • 11am Sun

Wichita Falls (817)

Bars

Rascals 811 Indiana • 723-1629 • noon-2am • lesbians/gay men • dancing/DJ • live shows • BYOB

Spiritual Groups

MCC 1407 26th St. • 322-4100 • 11am Sun, 7pm Wed

UTAH

Bicknell (801)

Travel & Tour Operators

CowPie Adventures Boulder Mtn. • 297-2140 • camping trips

Escalante (801)

Accommodations

Rainbow Country B&B & Tours PO Box 333, 84726 • 826-4567/(800) 252-8824 • gay-friendly

La Sal (801)

Accommodations

Mt. Peale Resort B&B PO Box 366, 84530 • 686-2284 • gay-friendly • hot tub

Logan (801)

Info Lines & Services

Cache Valley Lesbian/Gay Youth Group Faith & Fellowship Center • 753-3135 • ask for Courtney • 8pm Th

Gay/Lesbian Alliance of Cache Valley 752-1129 • 7pm Mon

Spiritual Groups

MCC Briderland 1315 E. 700 N. • 750-5026 • 11am Sun

Ogden (801)

Info Lines & Services

Ogden Women's Group 625-1660 • lesbian social/support group • 7pm Fri

Bars

Brass Rail 103 27th St. • 399-1543 • 3pm-1am • lesbians/gay men • women's night Fri • dancing/DJ • private club

Ogden Iron Company 185 23rd St. • (888) 212-4766 • 5pm-1am, from 1pm Fri-Sun • lesbians/gay men • dancing/DJ • live shows • food served • private club

Spiritual Groups

MCC Ogden 255 32nd St. • 394-0204

Unitarian Universalist Society of Ogden 2261 Adams Ave. • 394-3338 • 10:30am Sun

Park City (801)

Bookstores & Retail Shops

A Woman's Place Bookstore 1890 Bonanza Dr. • 649-2722 • 10am-7pm, til 6pm Sat, noon-5pm Sun • women-owned/run

TRAVEL & TOUR OPERATORS

Resort Property Management PO Box 3808, 84060 • (800) 243-2932 • IGTA

Salt Lake City (801)

INFO LINES & SERVICES

AA Gay/Lesbian 539-8800 • call for times & locations

Bisexual Group Stonewall Center • 350-3915 • 7pm Fri • contact Brenda

Community Real Estate Referrals (800) 346-5592 • gay realtor at your service • no rentals

Concerning Gays & Lesbians KRCL 91 FM • 363-1818 • 12:30pm-1pm Wed

Fruits of Sobriety 363-1855 (Paul)/467-0558 (Howard) • lesbians/gay men • 12-step

Gay Helpline 243 W. 400 S. • 533-0927 • info • support

S/M Social and Support Group Stonewall Center • 7pm Th • pansexual

U of U Women's Resource Center 581-8030 • info • lesbian support group

Utah Gay/Lesbian Youth Group Utah Stonewall Center • 539-8800 • drop-in 5pm-7pm • mtg. 7pm Wed

Utah Stonewall Center 770 S. 300 W. • 539-8800 • 1pm-9pm, til 6pm Sat, clsd Sun • info • referrals • many mtgs.

ACCOMMODATIONS

Aardvark B&B 249 W. 400 S. • 533-0927/(800) 533-4357 • mostly gay men • call for reservations & info • non-profit • benefits helpline • full brkfst • smokefree • kids/pets ok • wheelchair access

Anton Boxrud B&B 57 S. 600 E. • 363-8035/(800) 524-5511 • gay-friendly

Peery Hotel 110 W. 300 S. • 521-4300 • popular • gay-friendly • also a restaurant • full bar • wheelchair access

Saltair B&B/Alpine Cottages 164 S. 900 E. • 533-8184/(800) 733-8184 • popular • gay-friendly • oldest continuously-operating B&B in Utah • cottages from 1870s

BARS

Bricks Tavern 579 W. 200 S. • 328-0255 • 9:30pm-2am, clsd Sun-Mon • popular • mostly gay men • very women-friendly • dancing/DJ • live shows • private club

Kings 108 S. 500 W. • 521-5464 • 10am-1am • lesbians/gay men • dancing/DJ • private club • wheelchair access

Paper Moon 3424 S. State St. • 466-8517 • 4pm-1am, 1pm-midnight Sun • mostly women • dancing/DJ • private club • wheelchair access

Radio City 147 S. State St. • 532-9327 • 11am-1am • mostly gay men • beer only • wheelchair access

The Sun 702 W. 200 S. • 531-0833 • noon-2am • lesbians/gay men • popular • dancing/DJ • food served • private club • patio • wheelchair access

The Trapp 102 S. 600 W. • 531-8727 • 11am-1am • lesbians/gay men • dancing/DJ • country/western • private club • wheelchair access

The Vortex 32 Exchange Pl. • 521-9292 • 9pm-2am, clsd Sun-Tue • gay-friendly • dancing/DJ • alternative

RESTAURANTS & CAFES

Baci Trattoria 134 W. Pierport Ave. • 328-1333 • lunch & dinner, clsd Sun • Italian • some veggie • full bar • wheelchair access • $6-25

Bill & Nadas Cafe 479 S. 600 E. • 359-6984 • 24hrs

Coffee Garden 898 E. 900 S. • 355-3425 • 7am-10pm • wheelchair access

Market St. Grill 50 Market St. • 322-4668 • lunch, dinner, Sun brunch • seafood/steak • full bar • wheelchair access • $15-30

Rio Grande Cafe 270 S. Rio Grande • 364-3302 • lunch & dinner • popular • Mexican • some veggie • full bar • $4-8

Santa Fe 2100 Emigration Canyon • 582-5888 • lunch & dinner, Sun brunch • some veggie • $10-12

BOOKSTORES & RETAIL SHOPS

A Woman's Place Bookstore 1400 Foothill Dr. Ste. 236 • 583-6431 • 10am-9pm, til 6pm Sat, noon-5pm Sun • wheelchair access • women-owned/run

Cahoots 878 E. 900 S. • 538-0606 • 10am-7pm, noon-5pm Sun • wheelchair access

Gypsy Moon Emporium 1011 E. 900 S. • 521-9100 • 11am-6pm, clsd Sun • metaphysical

TRAVEL & TOUR OPERATORS

Olympus Tours & Travel 311 S. State St. Ste. 110 • 521-5232/(800) 338-9661

Passage to Utah PO Box 520883, 84152 • 582-1896 • custom trips in the West

SPIRITUAL GROUPS

Restoration Church (Mormon) (800) 677-7252 • call for info

Sacred Light of Christ MCC 823 S. 600 E. • 595-0052 • 11am Sun

South Valley Unitarian Universalist Society 6876 S. 2000 E. • 944-9723 • 4pm Sun

Wasatch Affirmation (Mormon) PO Box 1152 (at Utah Stonewall Center), 84110 • 534-8693 • 5pm Sun

PUBLICATIONS

Labrys 2120 S. 700 E. Ste. H-233, 84106 • 486-6473 • monthly

The Pillar PO Box 57744, 84157 • 265-0066

EROTICA

All For Love 3072 South Main St. • 487-8358 • leather/SM boutique

Blue Boutique 2106 S. 1100 E. • 485-2072

Mischievous 559 S. 300 W. • 530-3100 • 10am-8pm

Video One 484 S. 900 W. • 539-0300 • also cult & art films

Springdale (801)

ACCOMMODATIONS

Red Rock Inn 998 Zion Park Blvd. • 772-3836 • gay-friendly • full brkfst • smokefree • wheelchair access • lesbian-owned/run • $65-135

Torrey (801)

ACCOMMODATIONS

Sky Ridge B&B Inn PO Box 750220, 84775 • 425-3222 • gay-friendly • full brkfst • hot tub • near Capitol Reef National Park

VERMONT

Andover (802)

ACCOMMODATIONS

The Inn At High View East Hill Rd. • 875-2724 • gay-friendly • full brkfst • swimming • sauna • ski trails • hiking • smokefree • IGTA

Arlington (802)

ACCOMMODATIONS

Candlelight Motel Rte. 7A, PO Box 97, 05250 • 375-6647/(800) 348-5294 • gay-friendly • swimming • IGTA

Hill Farm Inn RR #2, Box 2015, 05250 • 375-2269/(800) 882-2545 • gay-friendly • on 50 acres of farmland • full brkfst • dinner avail. Th-Sat

Bennington (802)

ACCOMMODATIONS

Country Cousin B&B Rte. 1B, Box 212, Shaftsbury, 05262 • 375-6985/(800) 479-6985 • lesbians/gay men • 1824 Greek Revival house in valley btwn. Taconic & Green Mts. • smokefree • older kids ok • pets by arr. • IGTA

Brattleboro (802)

INFO LINES & SERVICES

BAGL (Brattleboro Area Gays/Lesbians) PO Box 875, 05302 • 254-5947

Brattleboro Area Lesbian Center 71 Elliot St.

ACCOMMODATIONS

Mapleton Farm B&B RD 2 Box 510, Putney, 05346 • 257-5252 • gay-friendly • full brkfst • smokefree • kids 10+ ok • small pets by arr.

BARS

Rainbow Cattle Company Rte. 5, Dummerston • 254-9830 • 11am-2am • lesbians/gay men • 2 bars • dancing/DJ • country/western

RESTAURANTS & CAFES

Common Ground 25 Elliott St. • 257-0855 • lunch & dinner • popular • vegetarian/local fish • plenty veggie • beer/wine • $6-13

Peter Haven's 32 Elliott St. • 257-3333 • 6pm-10pm Tue-Sat • popular • cont'l

BOOKSTORES & RETAIL SHOPS

Everyone's Books 23 Elliott St. • 254-8160 • 10am-6pm, til 8pm Fri, 11am-4pm Sun • wheelchair access

Burlington (802)

INFO LINES & SERVICES

AA Gay/Lesbian St. Paul's Church on Cherry St. • 658-4221 • 7pm Th

Bi-Cycle c/o Micha Wolfgang, PO Box 8456, 05402 • support & penpal network for lesbigays & their kids • also Goddess/Pagan gatherings

Outright Vermont PO Box 5235, 05401 • 865-9677 • support/education for lesbigay youth • also hotline

Univ. of VT Gay/Lesbian/Bisexual Alliance B-163 Billings, UVM, 05405 • 656-0699 • 7pm Mon

Vermont Bisexual Network PO Box 8124, 05402

Vermont Gay Social Alternatives PO Box 237, 05402 • 865-3734

ACCOMMODATIONS

Allyn House B&B 16 Orchard Terr. • 863-0379 • gay-friendly • 1893 Victorian • full brkfst • smokefree • older kids ok

Howden Cottage B&B 32 N. Champlain St. • 864-7198 • lesbians/gay men • cozy lodging & warm hospitality • shared/private baths • smokefree • kids by arr.

BARS

135 Pearl 135 Pearl St. • 863-2343 • noon-2am • popular • lesbians/gay men • dancing/DJ • 18+ Fri • smokefree juice bar downstairs • wheelchair access

RESTAURANTS & CAFES

Alfredo's 79 Mechanics Ln. • 864-0854 • 4:30pm-10pm, from 3pm Sun • Italian • some veggie • full bar • wheelchair access • $6-12

Daily Planet 15 Center St. • 862-9647 • 11:30am-10:30pm • eclectic ethnic • plenty veggie • full bar • $6-15

Silver Palace 1216 Williston Rd. • 864-0125 • 11:30am-9:30pm • Chinese • some veggie • full bar • $10-15

BOOKSTORES & RETAIL SHOPS

Chassman & Bem Booksellers 81 Church St. Market Place • 862-4332 • 9am-9pm, til 5pm Sun

SPIRITUAL GROUPS

Dignity/Vermont PO Box 782, 05402 • 863-1377

Interweave G/L/B/T/S Unitarian Church 152 Pearl St., 05401

PUBLICATIONS

Out in the Mountains PO Box 177, 05402

East Cornith (802)

BOOKSTORES & RETAIL SHOPS
Heartland Books PO Box 1105-WT, East Corinth, 05040 • 439-5655 • catalog for lesbians

East Hardwick (802)

ACCOMMODATIONS
Greenhope Farm RFD Box 2260, 05836 • 533-7772 • women only • full brkfst • horseback-riding • near skiing • $45-75

Essex Junction (802)

RESTAURANTS & CAFES
Loretta's 44 Park St. • 879-7777 • lunch Tue-Fri, dinner Tue-Sat, clsd Sun-Mon • Italian • plenty veggie • take-out avail. • women-owned/run

Hartland Four Corners (802)

ACCOMMODATIONS
Twin Gables PO Box 101, 05049 • 463-3070 • gay-friendly • near outdoor recreation • smokefree • kids ok

Hyde Park (802)

ACCOMMODATIONS
Arcadia House PO Box 520, 05655 • 888-9147 • lesbians/gay men • swimming • smokefree

Killington (802)

ACCOMMODATIONS
Cortina Inn Rte. 4 • 773-3333/(800) 451-6108 • gay-friendly • hot tub • swimming • smokefree • kids/pets ok • food served • also tavern • wheelchair access

Manchester Center (802)

BOOKSTORES & RETAIL SHOPS
Northshire Bookstore Main St. • 362-2200 • 10am-5:30pm, til 9pm Fri, til 7pm Sat, clsd Sun

Middlebury

INFO LINES & SERVICES
MGLBA (Middlebury Gay/Lesbian/Bisexual Alliance) Drawer 8, Middlebury College, 05753

Montgomery Center (802)

ACCOMMODATIONS
Phineas Swann B&B PO Box 43, 05471 • 326-4306 • gay-friendly • full brkfst • near outdoor recreation • smokefree • kids ok

Montpelier (802)

INFO LINES & SERVICES
Vermont Coalition of Lesbians/Gays PO Box 1125, 05602 • political group

RESTAURANTS & CAFES
Julio's 44 Main St. • 229-9348 • lunch & dinner, from 4pm wknds • Mexican

Sarducci's 3 Main St. • 223-0229 • 11:30am-10pm • Italian • some veggie • full bar • wheelchair access • $8-15

BOOKSTORES & RETAIL SHOPS
Phoenix Rising 104 Main St. 2nd flr. • 229-0522 • 10am-5pm, 11am-3pm wknds • jewelry & gifts

Plainfield

INFO LINES & SERVICES
Lesbian/Gay/Bisexual Alliance Goddard College, 05667

St. Johnsbury (802)

INFO LINES & SERVICES
Game Ends 23 North Ave., 05819 • 748-5849 • social activities group

Umbrella Women's Center 1 Prospect Ave. • 748-8645 • lesbian support & resources

ACCOMMODATIONS
▲ **Highlands Inn** PO Box 118-WT, Bethlehem NH • (603) 869-3978 • women only • hot tub • kids/pets ok • wheelchair access (see ad page 1)

Stowe (802)

ACCOMMODATIONS
Buccaneer Country Lodge 3214 Mountain Rd. • 253-4772/(800) 543-1293 • popular • gay-friendly • country lodge near skiing • full kitchen suites • full brkfst • swimming • smokefree

Fitch Hill Inn RFD Box 1879, Hyde Park, 05655 • 888-3834/(800) 639-2903 • gay-friendly • antique-filled colonial farmhouse on a hill • full brkfst • dinner by arr. • swimming • older kids ok

Waterbury (802)

ACCOMMODATIONS
Grünberg House B&B RR 2, Box 1595, Rte. 100 S., 05676-9621 • 244-7726/(800) 800-7760 • gay-friendly • chalet in Green Mtns. • full brkfst • jacuzzi • sauna • smokefree • kids ok

EROTICA
Video Exchange 21 Stowe St. • 244-7004 •
clsd Sun

West Dover   (802)

TRAVEL & TOUR OPERATORS
New England Vacation Tours Rte. 100 Mt.
Snow Village • 464-2076/(800) 742-7669 •
IGTA

Winooski

INFO LINES & SERVICES
CRONES PO Box 242, 05404 • for women
40 & better

Woodstock   (802)

ACCOMMODATIONS
▲ **Country Garden Inn B&B** 37 Main St.,
Quechee • 295-3023 • gay-friendly • full
brkfst • swimming
Maitland-Swan House PO Box 72,
Taftsville, 05073 • 457-5181/(800) 959-1404
• gay-friendly • early-19th century home •
full brkfst • smokefree

Rosewood Inn 457-4485/(203) 829-1499 •
gay-friendly • full brkfst • smokefree • kids
ok

South View B&B PO Box 579 Rowe Hill
Rd., Brownsville, 05037 • 484-7934 • gay-
friendly • classic Vermont log home •
smokefree

Worchester   (802)

INFO LINES & SERVICES
Women of the Woods RFD 1 Box 5620,
05682 • 229-0109 • lesbian social group

B&B c. 1819. Quechee, VT. Elegant decor. Full 3-
course breakfast. All private baths. Walk to gourmet
dining, shopping. Privileges at the private Quechee
Resort, including 2 championship 18-hole golf
courses, tennis courts, pro shops, health club,
indoor-outdoor olympic size swimming pool.
Canoeing, hiking. Within 30 minutes of 8 major ski
areas for X/C and downhill and much more.

800-859-4191
37 Main Street • Box 404 • Quechee, VT 05059

VIRGINIA

Alexandria (703)

TRAVEL & TOUR OPERATORS
Just Vacations, Inc. 501 King St. • 838-0040

Uniglobe Direct Travel 1800 Diagonal Rd. Plaza D • 684-8824 • IGTA

Arlington (703)

INFO LINES & SERVICES
Arlington Gay/Lesbian Alliance PO Box 324, 22210 • 522-7660

ACCOMMODATIONS
Highgate House B&B 1594 Colonial Terr. • 524-8431 • gay-friendly • full brkfst

PUBLICATIONS
Woman's Monthly 1001 N. Highland St. Ste. PH, 22201 • 527-4881

Cape Charles (757)

ACCOMMODATIONS
Sea Gate B&B 9 Tazewell Ave. • 331-2206 • gay-friendly • near beach on quiet, tree-lined street • full brkfst • afternoon tea

Charlottesville (804)

INFO LINES & SERVICES
Gay AA (at Unitarian Church on Rugby Rd.) • 971-7720 • 7:30pm Th

Gay/Lesbian Information Service PO Box 2368, 22902 • 296-8783 • also contact for 'Piedmont Triangle Society' • active social group

Kindred Spirits 971-1555 • 2nd Fri • regional women's social clearinghouse

Women's Center 14th & University (UVA) • 982-2361 • 8:30am-5pm Mon-Fri

ACCOMMODATIONS
Intouch Women's Center Rte. 2 Box 1096, Kents Store, 23084 • 589-6542 • women only • campground & recreational area • wheelchair access

The Mark Addy Rte. 1, Box 375, Nellysford, 22958 • 361-1101/(800) 278-2154 • gay-friendly • full brkfst • swimming • wheelchair access

Thousand Acres B&B PO Box 758, Farmville, 23901 • 574-8807 • women only • 1 hr. S. of Charlottesville on a private river

BARS
Club 216 216 W. Water St. (rear entrance) • 296-8783 • 9pm-2am, til 4am Fri-Sat, clsd Sun-Wed • lesbians/gay men • dancing/DJ • live shows • private club • wheelchair access

RESTAURANTS & CAFES
Brasa 215 W. Water • 296-4343 • seafood • full bar

Eastern Standard/Escafe 102 Old Preston Ave. (W. end downtown mall) • 295-8668 • 5pm-midnight, til 2am Th-Sat, clsd Sun-Mon • lesbians/gay men • Asian/Mediterrean/nouvelle • some veggie • full bar • live shows • gay-owned/run • $8-16

SPIRITUAL GROUPS
Chavurah 982-2361 • lesbigay Jewish study group

MCC 717 Rugby Rd. (Thomas Jefferson Memorial Church) • 979-5206 • 6pm Sun

PUBLICATIONS
Lambda Letter PO Box 2191, 22902

Chesterfield (804)

ACCOMMODATIONS
Historic Bellmont Manor 6600 Belmont Rd. • 745-0106/(800) 809-9041x69 • gay-friendly • full brkfst • wheelchair access

Colonial Beach (804)

ACCOMMODATIONS
Tucker Inn 21 Weems St. • 224-2031 • seasonal • mostly women • beachside lodging • 75 miles SE of Washington, DC • full brkfst • women-owned/run • $55

Culpepper (703)

TRAVEL & TOUR OPERATORS
Culpepper Travel 763 Madison Rd. Ste. 208-B • 825-1258/(800) 542-4881 • IGTA

Falls Church (703)

ACCOMMODATIONS
Devonshire House B&B 7281 Lee Hwy. • 533-0874 • mostly women • swimming • patio

SPIRITUAL GROUPS
MCC of Northern VA Fairfax Unitarian Church • 532-0992 • 6pm Sun

Fredericksburg (540)

RESTAURANTS & CAFES

Merrimans 715 Caroline St. • 371-7723 • lunch & dinner, lounge til 2am, clsd Mon • popular • lesbians/gay men • dancing/DJ • fresh natural homemade • plenty veggie • full bar • $7-18

Luray (540)

ACCOMMODATIONS

Ruffner House Rte. 4 Box 620, 22835 • 743-7855 • lesbians/gay men • full brkfst • hot tub • swimming

Lynchburg (804)

INFO LINES & SERVICES

Lesbian/Gay Helpline PO Box 10511, 24506 • 847-5242

New Market (540)

ACCOMMODATIONS

A Touch of Country B&B 9329 Congress St. • 740-8030 • gay-friendly • full brkfst

Newport News (804)

BARS

Frank Corner Pocket 3516 Washington Ave. • 380-9875 • mostly gay men • neighborhood bar

BOOKSTORES & RETAIL SHOPS

Just For Us 9902-B Warwick Blvd. • 599-4070 • 11am-7pm, 10am-9pm Fri-Sat, clsd Sun (seasonal) • lesbigay • wheelchair access

Mr. D's Leather & Novelties 9902-A Warwick Blvd. • 599-4070 • 11am-7pm, til 8pm Fri-Sat, clsd Sun

Out of the Dark 530 Randolph Rd. • 596-6220 • 10am-6pm, til 8pm Fri-Sat, clsd Sun-Mon • Wiccan/pagan

Norfolk (804)

INFO LINES & SERVICES

AA Gay/Lesbian 1610 Meadow Lake Dr. (Triangle Services Center) • 622-3701

Mandamus Society PO Box 1325, 23501 • 625-6220 • active social group

BARS

Charlotte's Web 6425 Tidewater Dr. (Roland Park Shopping Center) • 853-5021 • 10am-2am • mostly women • dancing/DJ • country/western Th • Sun brunch • wheelchair access

Club Rumours 4107 Colley Ave. • 440-7780 • 11am-2am, clsd Mon-Wed • lesbians/gay men • dancing/DJ • more women Wed & Fri

The Garage 731 Granby St. • 623-0303 • 8am-2am, from 10am Sun • popular • mostly gay men • neighborhood bar • food served • wheelchair access • $3-9

Hershee Bar 6117 Sewells Pt. Rd. • 853-9842 • 4pm-2am, from noon wknds • mostly women • dancing/DJ • live shows • food served • some veggie • $2-7

Late Show 114 E. 11th St. • 623-3854 • midnight til dawn • popular • lesbians/gay men • dancing/DJ • food served • private club

Norfolk (804)

ANNUAL EVENTS: May - Virginia Women's Music Festival. July - July 4th Kickback. September - Wild Western Women's Weekend. All events: 589-6542.

CITY INFO: (800) 368-3097.

ATTRACTIONS: Douglas MacArthur Memorial. Norfolk Navy Base. St. Paul's Episcopal Church. The Chrysler Museum. Waterside Festival Marketplace.

TRANSIT: Yellow Cab: 622-3232. Norfolk Airport Shuttle: 857-1231. Tidewater Regional Transit: 627-9297.

Ms. P 6401 Tidewater Dr. • 853-9717 •
8pm-2am, clsd Mon-Wed • mostly women
• dancing/DJ

Nutty Buddys 143 E. Little Creek Rd. • 588-
6474 • 4pm-2am • popular • lesbians/gay
men • dancing/DJ • also a restaurant •
some veggie • live shows • wheelchair
access • $10-15

RESTAURANTS & CAFES

Charlie's Cafe 1800 Granby St. • 625-0824
• 7am-3pm • some veggie • beer/wine •
wheelchair access • $3-7

Mom's Diner 119 W. Charlotte St. • 627-
4491 • 6:30am-6pm, 7am-2pm wknds •
fresh fast food

Uncle Louie's 132 E. Little Creek Rd. • 480-
1225 • 11am-11pm, bar til 2am • Jewish
fine dining • live shows • wheelchair
access • $5-15

White House Cafe/Private Eyes 249 W.
York St. • 533-9290 • 11am-2am • grand
buffet Sun • some veggie • full bar • danc-
ing/DJ • live shows • wheelchair access •
$5-15

BOOKSTORES & RETAIL SHOPS

Lambda Rising 9229 Granby St. • 480-6969
• 10am-midnight • lesbigay • wheelchair
access

Leather & Lace 149 E. Little Creek Rd. •
583-4334 • 11am-9pm, clsd Sun

Phoenix Rising East 808 Spotswood Ave. •
622-3701/(800) 719-1690 • 11am-9pm, til
7pm Sun • lesbigay

Two of a Kind 6123 Sewells Pt. Rd. • 857-
0223 • 11am-9pm, til 11pm Wed-Th, til
2am Fri-Sat, 2pm-7pm Sun • lesbigay •
wheelchair access

TRAVEL & TOUR OPERATORS

Moore Travel Inc. 7516 Granby St. • 583-
2361 • IGTA

SPIRITUAL GROUPS

All God's Children Community Church
9229 Granby St. • 480-0911 • 10:30am Sun
& 7:30 pm Wed

Dignity 600 Tabbot Hall Rd. • 625-5337 •
6:30pm Sun

MCC New Life 1530 Johnston Rd. • 855-
8450 • 10:30am Sun

PUBLICATIONS

Our Own Community Press 739 Yarmouth
St. • 625-0700

Richmond (804)

INFO LINES & SERVICES

AA Gay/Lesbian 355-1212

Gay Info Line 967-9311

Richmond Lesbian Feminist 379-6422 •
community entertainment & educational
group

**Richmond Organization for Sexual
Minority Youth** PO Box 5542, 23220 • 353-
2077 • 3pm-8pm Mon & Wed

Virginians for Justice PO Box 342 Capital
Stn., 23202 • 643-4816 • statewide lesbigay
organization

BARS

Babe's of Carytown 3166 W. Cary St. • 355-
9330 • 11am-1am, til 2am Fri-Sat, from
8pm Sat, 9am-5pm Sun • mostly women •
dancing/DJ • food served • homecooking •
some veggie • wheelchair access • women-
owned/run • $4-7

Chaplin's Grill/Sanctuary Dance Club
2001 E. Franklin St. • 643-7520 • 6pm-2am,
from 9pm Sun, clsd Mon-Th • lesbians/gay
men • dancing/DJ • food served

Club Colors 536 N. Harrison St. • 353-9776
• 10pm-3am Fri-Sat • lesbians/gay men •
ladies night Fri • dancing/DJ • multi-racial
• food served • wheelchair access

Fielden's 2033 W. Broad St. • 359-1963 •
midnight-6am, clsd Mon-Wed • popular •
mostly gay men • dancing/DJ • BYOB • private club • wheelchair access

RESTAURANTS & CAFES

Broadway Cafe & Bar 1624 W. Broad St. •
355-9931 • 5pm-2am, from 6pm wknds •
wheelchair access • $7-10

Casablanca 6 E. Grace St. • 648-2040 •
11am-2am, from 3pm Sat • lesbians/gay
men • some veggie • full bar • wheelchair
access • $5-8

BOOKSTORES & RETAIL SHOPS

Carytown Books 2930 W. Cary St. • 359-
4831 • 9am-7pm, til 5pm Sun • lesbigay
section • wheelchair access

Phoenix Rising 19 N. Belmont Ave. • 355-
7939/(800) 719-1690 • 11am-7pm • lesbigay
bookstore • wheelchair access

TRAVEL & TOUR OPERATORS

Covington International Travel 4401
Dominion Blvd., Glen Allen • 747-
4126/(800) 922-9238

Virginia Division of Tourism (800) 847-
4882

SPIRITUAL GROUPS

Diginity-Integrity 815 E. Grace (St. Paul's Episcopal Church) • 355-0584 • 6:30pm Sun

MCC Richmond 2501 Park Ave. • 353-9477 • 9am, 10:45am & 6:30pm Sun

Roanoke   (540)

INFO LINES & SERVICES

The Supper Club/Blue Ridge Business Info Line PO Box 21391, 21391 • 772-5702 • lesbian social group & regional info

BARS

The Alternative Complex (Edge) 3348 Salem Trnpk. • 344-4445 • 9pm-? Fri-Sun • lesbians/gay men • dancing/DJ • food served • live shows

Back Street Cafe 356 Salem Ave. • 345-1542 • 7pm-2am, til midnight Sun • lesbians/gay men • neighborhood bar • food served

The Park 615 Salem Ave. • 342-0946 • 9pm-2am, clsd Mon-Tue & Th • popular • lesbians/gay men • dancing/DJ • live shows • videos • private club • wheelchair access

The Stag 9 W. Salem Ave. • 982-1668 • 2pm-2am, from 7pm Sun-Mon • lesbians/gay men • neighborhood bar

RESTAURANTS & CAFES

The Le Grande Dame 3348 Salem Trnpk. (at the Edge) • 344-4445 • 6pm-1am • lesbians/gay men • dinner & dancing • call for events

BOOKSTORES & RETAIL SHOPS

Out Word Connections 114 Kirk Ave. SW • 985-6886 • noon-8pm, til 9pm Fri-Sat • lesbigay bookstore

SPIRITUAL GROUPS

MCC of the Blue Ridge 2015 Grandin Rd. SW (Unitarian Church) • 344-4444 • 7pm Sun

Unitarian Universalist Church 2015 Grandin Rd. SW • 342-8888 • 11am Sun (10am summers)

PUBLICATIONS

Blue Ridge Lambda Press PO Box 237, 24002 • 890-6612 • covers western VA

Buddies PO Box 21201, 24018 • 989-1579 • entertainment & personals

Shenandoah Valley (540)

ACCOMMODATIONS

▲ **The Ruby Rose Inn** Rte. 2 Box 147, Stanley, 22851 • 778-4680 • gay-friendly • full brkfst • women-owned/run • $80-135

Virginia Beach (804)

BARS

Ambush 2838 Virginia Beach Blvd. • 498-4301 • 4pm-2am • mostly gay men • neighborhood bar

The Birdcage 4801 Shore Dr. (Bayside Shopping Ctr.) • 460-6336 • 4pm-2am • mostly gay men • dancing/DJ • food served • live shows

Danny's Place 2901 Baltic Ave. • 428-4016 • 5pm-2am • lesbians/gay men • dancing/DJ • food served • wheelchair access • $4-8

TRAVEL & TOUR OPERATORS

Alternative Adventures in Travel 6529 Auburn Dr. • 424-6362 • call collect • IGTA

Travel Merchants, Inc. 2232 Virginia Beach Blvd. #112 • 463-0014 .

PUBLICATIONS

Lambda Directory 198 S. Rosemont Rd. • 486-3546

Women's Yellow Pages Directory of Hampton Roads PO Box 64402, 23467 • 499-3545

WASHINGTON

Anacortes (360)

ACCOMMODATIONS
Blue Rose B&B 1811 9th St • 293-5175 • gay-friendly • full brkfst

Bellevue (206)

SPIRITUAL GROUPS
East Shore Unitarian Church 12700 SE 32nd St. • 747-3780 • 9:15am & 11:15am Sun (10am summer) • wheelchair access

Bellingham (360)

INFO LINES & SERVICES
Lesbian/Gay/Bisexual Alliance Western Washington University • 650-6120 • social/political group

BARS
Rumors 1317 N. State St. • 671-1849 • noon-2am • lesbians/gay men • dancing/DJ • multi-racial • beer/wine

Tony's Coffee 1101 Harris Ave. • 738-4710 • 7am-10pm • cafe • plenty veggie • patio • wheelchair access

BOOKSTORES & RETAIL SHOPS
Rainbow Bridge 304 W. Champion St. • 715-3684 • 10am-10pm Tue-Sun, clsd Mon • lesbigay bookstore • gifts • women-owned/run

Village Books 1210 11th St. • 671-2626 • 9am-10pm, til 8pm Sun

SPIRITUAL GROUPS
Song of Messiah MCC 929 N. State St. Ste. B • 671-1172 • 6pm Sun • wheelchair access

EROTICA
Great Northern Bookstore 1308 Railroad Ave. • 733-1650

Bremerton (360)

INFO LINES & SERVICES
West Sound Family 792-3960 • lesbigay social/support group

BARS
Brewski's 2810 Kitsap Wy. (enter off Wycuff St.) • 479-9100 • 11am-2am • gay-friendly • neighborhood bar • piano bar • food served • wheelchair access

Fandango Tavern 2711 6th St. • 373-9229 • 11am-2am • gay-friendly • neighborhood bar • beer/wine • 'Family Nights' Wed & Sun

Chelan (509)

ACCOMMODATIONS
Whaley Mansion 415 3rd St. • 682-5735/(800) 729-2408 • gay-friendly • full brkfst

Columbia River (509)

ACCOMMODATIONS
Sojourner Inn 142 Lyons Rd., Home Valley • 427-7070 • gay-friendly • full brkfst • wheelchair access

Ellensburg (509)

INFO LINES & SERVICES
Central Gay/Lesbian Alliance (CWU) 963-1391 • contact Sally Thelen for more info

Everett (206)

INFO LINES & SERVICES
AA Gay/Lesbian 2324 Lombard (church basement) • 252-2525 • 7pm Mon

BARS
Everett Underground 1212 California Ave. • 339-0807 • 3pm-2am • lesbians/gay men • dancing/DJ • multi-racial • live shows • karaoke • food served • wheelchair access

BOOKSTORES & RETAIL SHOPS
Orion at Twilight/Highlights 2934-B Colby Ave. • 303-8624 • metaphysical store • also publishes pagan newsletter

Gig Harbor (206)

ACCOMMODATIONS
Inn The Woods 4416 150th St. Court NW • 857-4954 • women only • brkfst in room • hot tub • massage • shared baths • $85

TRAVEL & TOUR OPERATORS
Blue Heron Sailing PO Box 173, 98335 • 851-5259 • women-owned/run

Index (206)

ACCOMMODATIONS
Bush House Country Inn 300 5th St. • 793-2312/(800) 428-2874 • gay-friendly • full brkfst • suite avail. • also restaurant & cocktail lounge

Wild Lily Ranch B&B PO Box 313, 98256 • 793-2103 • lesbians/gay men • riverside cabins • swimming • nudity • IGTA

Kirkland (206)

BOOKSTORES & RETAIL SHOPS
Magazine City 12063 124th Ave. NE • 820-9264

La Conner (360)

ACCOMMODATIONS
The Heron 117 Maple Ave., Mt. Vernon • 466-4626 • gay-friendly • full brkfst • hot tub • smokefree • pets ok • wheelchair access

The White Swan Guesthouse 1388 Moore Rd., Mt. Vernon • 445-6805 • gay-friendly • 1890s farmhouse • also cabin avail.

Langley (360)

ACCOMMODATIONS
The Gallery Suite B&B 302 First St. • 221-2978 • gay-friendly • condo rental on the water • art gallery/B&B

The Sea Haven II 3766 S. Bells Rd. • 730-3766 • gay-friendly • cottage on Whidbey Island w/ view of Cascade Mtns. • women-owned/run

The Whidbey Inn 106 1st St. • 221-7115 • gay-friendly • full brkfst • located on bluff over Saratoga Passage Waterway & Mtns.

Lopez Island (360)

ACCOMMODATIONS
The Inn at Swifts Bay Rte. 2 Box 3402, 98261 • 468-3636 • popular • gay-friendly • Tudor-style B&B on San Juan Islands • spa • fireplace • IGTA

Mt. Vernon (360)

RESTAURANTS & CAFES
Deli Next Door 202 S. 1st St. • 336-3886 • 9am-7pm, til 4pm Sun • healthy American • plenty veggie • wheelchair access • $4-6

BOOKSTORES & RETAIL SHOPS
Scott's Bookstore 121 Freeway Dr. • 336-6181

PUBLICATIONS
Northwest Gay Times 1500-A E. College Wy. #458 • 416-0498

Ocean Park (360)

ACCOMMODATIONS
Iris Guesthouse Box 72 Territory Rd., Oysterville • 665-5681 • mostly women • full kitchen privileges

Shakti Cove PO Box 385, 98640 • 665-4000 • lesbians/gay men • cottages

Olympia (360)

INFO LINES & SERVICES
Free at Last AA 11th & Washington (United Church) • 352-7344 • 7pm Th

Lesbian/Gay/Bisexual Support Services 943-4662 • 24hrs

Queer Alliance Evergreen State College • 866-6000x6544

BARS
Thekla 116 E. 5th Ave. • 352-1855 • 6pm-2am • gay-friendly • dancing/DJ • live shows • wheelchair access

RESTAURANTS & CAFES
Smithfield Cafe 212 W. 4th Ave. • 786-1725 • 7am-8pm • popular • lesbians/gay men • plenty veggie • wheelchair access • $4-7

BOOKSTORES & RETAIL SHOPS
Bulldog News 116 E. 4th Ave. • 357-6397 • 7am-9pm

SPIRITUAL GROUPS
Eternal Light MCC 219 'B' St. • 352-8157 • 7pm Sun

Port Townsend (360)

ACCOMMODATIONS
Bella Vista c/o L. Silverman 5590 Taft, Oakland CA, 94618 • (510) 655-5495 • vacation rental

Gaia's Getaway 4343 Haines St. • 385-1194 • lesbians/gay men • large studio apt. in small seaport village on Olympic peninsula

The James House 1238 Washington St. • 385-1238 • gay-friendly • smokefree • near tennis, golf & kayaking

Ravenscroft Inn 533 Quincy St. • 385-2784 • gay-friendly • seaport inn w/ views of Puget Sound • gourmet brkfst

Pullman (509)

INFO LINES & SERVICES
Washington State U. LesBiGay Group 335-6388

Seattle   (206)

INFO LINES & SERVICES

Aradia Women's Health Center 1300 Spring St. • 323-9388 • 10am-6pm, clsd Sun

Association of Lesbian Professionals PO Box 20424, 98102

Capitol Hill Alano 123 E. Boylston • 587-2838 (AA#)/322-9590 (club) • noon, 5:30pm, 8pm

Counseling Service for Sexual Minorities 1820 E. Pine • 323-0220 • noon-9pm Mon-Fri

▲ **Dyke TV** 'weekly half-hour TV show produced by lesbians, for lesbians' • call (212) 343-9335 for more info

FTM Outreach Phoneline Ingersoll Gender Center • 329-6651 • 6pm-8pm Wed • live one-on-one info/support for FTMs, by FTMs

GSBA (Greater Seattle Business Association) 2033 6th Ave. #804, 98121 • 443-4722 • publishes extensive directory

Lambert House 1818 15th Ave. • 322-2735 • 4pm-10pm, til midnight Fri-Sat • drop-in center for sexual minority youth

Lesbian Resource Center 1808 Bellevue Ave. Ste. 204 • 322-3953 • 2pm-7pm Mon-Fri

Partners Task Force for Gay/Lesbian Couples PO Box 9685, 98109 • 935-1206

Powersurge 1202 E. Pike St. #819 • 233-8429 • lesbian S/M conference

Seattle Bisexual Women's Network 517-7767 • active social/support organization

The TEN (The Eastside Network) 450-4890 • social/support group for Seattle's East Side

Transsexual Lesbians & Friends 292-1037 • call for info

ACCOMMODATIONS

Bacon Mansion/Broadway Guesthouse 959 Broadway E. • 329-1864/(800) 240-1864 • gay-friendly • Edwardian-style Tudor • IGTA

Capitol Hill Inn 1713 Belmont Ave. • 323-1955 • gay-friendly • full brkfst

Chambered Nautilus B&B 5005 22nd Ave. NE • 522-2536 • gay-friendly • full brkfst

The Country Inn 685 NW Juniper St., Issaquah • 392-1010 • gay-friendly • private estate • full brkfst • hot tub

▲ **Gaslight Inn** 1727 15th Ave. • 325-3654 • popular • gay-friendly • swimming

▲ **Hill House B&B** 1113 E. John St. • 720-7161/(800) 720-7161 • popular • lesbians/gay men • full brkfst

▲ **Landes House B&B** 712 11th Ave. E. • 329-8781 • lesbians/gay men • two 1906 houses joined by deck • hot tub • near Broadway

Pioneer Square Hotel 77 Yesler Wy. • 340-1234

Scandia House 2028 34th Ave. S. • 722-6216 • gay-friendly

The Shafer-Baillie Mansion 907 14th Ave. E. • 322-4654 • gay-friendly

Wild Lily Ranch B&B PO Box 313, Index, 98256 • (360) 793-2103 • lesbians/gay men • on Skykomish River • swimming • nudity • IGTA

BARS

C.C. Attle's 1501 E. Madison • 726-0565 • 6am-2am • popular • mostly gay men • neighborhood bar • videos • also 'Cadillac Grill Diner' • 323-4017 • 7am-4am, 24hrs wknds • some veggie • wheelchair access

Changes 2103 N. 45th St. • 545-8363 • noon-2am • mostly gay men • neighborhood bar • beer/wine • wheelchair access

The Cuff 1533 13th Ave. • 323-1525 • 2pm-2am • popular • mostly gay men • leather • uniform bar • 'Star Trek' night Tue • wheelchair access

Double Header 407 2nd Ave. • 624-8439 • 10am-1am • mostly gay men • neighborhood bar • one of the oldest gay bars in the US

The Easy 916 E. Pike • 323-8343 • 11am-2am, from 9am wknds • mostly women • dancing/DJ • live shows • food served • wheelchair access

Elite Tavern 622 Broadway Ave. E. • 324-4470 • 10am-2am • lesbians/gay men • neighborhood bar • beer/wine • wheelchair access

Elite Two 1658 E. Olive Wy. • 322-7334 • noon-2am, from 10am wknds • lesbians/gay men • neighborhood bar • beer/wine

Encore Restaurant & Lounge 1518 11th Ave. • 324-6617 • 11am-2am, from 8am wknds • lesbians/gay men • some veggie • wheelchair access • $5-15

Landes

House

BED & BREAKFAST

712 11th Ave. East   Seattle, WA 98102

(206) 329-8781

Seattle

*S*eattle's lush natural beauty—breathtaking views of Puget Sound and the Cascade Mountains—is actually more incredible than most let on. In addition, Seattle has small-town friendliness, as well as an international reputation for sophisticated cafe culture and for Grunge music and fashion.

The Space Needle is located in the Seattle Center, a complex that includes an opera house, Arena Coliseum and the Pacific Science Center. Another landmark is the quaint/touristy Pike Place Market (where all those commercials that feature mounds of fish are filmed).

For the perfect day trip, ferry over to the Olympic Peninsula and enjoy the fresh wilderness, or cruise by "Dykiki" a waterfront park on Lake Washington. Or sign up for an outdoor trip with one of the women-owned tour operators: **Adventure Associates** has trips listed in our Tours Operators section in the back.

For shopping, the **Broadway Market** in queer Capitol Hill is a multi-cultural shopping center. The **Pink Zone** lesbian-owned shop is here, and we're told that dyke-watching is best from the Market's espresso bar. If you've never been to a juice bar, check out the **Gravity Bar** at the Market—you can get almost any fruit or vegetable in liquid, shake or sandwich form here.

Speaking of coffee, Seattle's hazy days have nurtured a haute coffee culture here—so be careful to order your java correctly, or ask questions if you're unsure. The natives respect frank ignorance more than confused pretense. Lattés—one-third espresso, two-thirds milk—are the standard, and come iced or hot. Milk-intolerant coffee-lovers can even get Soy Lattés in some cafes!

Beyond the Closet is the local lesbigay bookstore where you can get a copy of the **Seattle Gay News**. Seattle's main women's bar, **Wildrose Tavern**, is for the 30+ crowd, while 20-somethings head for **The Easy** or to **Re-bar** on Thursdays. Big-boned gals line-dance at **Timberline**.

For sex toys, check out **Toys in Babeland** women's erotica. Pick up your safer sex supplies at the non-profit **Rubber Tree**, and those sex-inducing clothes at **Sin**.

Hana Restaurant & Lounge 1914 8th Ave. • 340-1536 • noon-2am • mostly gay men • piano bar • Japanese food • wheelchair access

HopScotch 332 15th Ave. E. • 322-4191 • gay-friendly • over 75 single malt scotches • food served

Kid Mohair 1207 Pine St. • 625-4444 • 4pm-2am • gay-friendly • women's night Wed • dancing/DJ • live shows • beer/wine

Neighbors Restaurant & Lounge 1509 Broadway (entrance on alley) • 324-5358 • 3pm-2am, til 4am Fri-Sat, clsd Mon • popular • mostly gay men • dancing/DJ • live shows • wheelchair access

The Palms Bar & Grill 420 E. Denny • 322-2555 • 11am-2am • lesbians/gay men • live shows • also a restaurant • wheelchair access • $7-25

R Place 619 E. Pine • 322-8828 • 2pm-2am • mostly gay men • neighborhood bar • videos • 3 stories • wheelchair access

Re-bar 1114 Howell (at Boren Ave.) • 233-9873 • 9pm-2am • popular • gay-friendly • dancing/DJ • 'Queer Disco' Th • live shows

Romper Room 106 1st Ave. N. • 284-5003 • 11pm-2am • gay-friendly • dancing/DJ • beer/wine

The Seattle Eagle 314 E. Pike St. • 621-7591 • 2pm-2am • mostly gay men • leather • patio • wheelchair access

Six Eleven Tavern 611 2nd Ave. • 345-9430 • noon-2am • lesbians/gay men • neighborhood bar

Tacky Tavern 1706 Bellevue Ave. • 322-9744 • 11am-2am, from 6am wknds • lesbians/gay men • transgender night Wed • neighborhood bar • beer/wine

Thumpers 1500 E. Madison St. • 328-3800 • 11am-2am • popular • mostly gay men • food served • more women in dining room • wheelchair access • $7-15

Timberline Tavern 2015 Boren Ave. • 622-6220 • 6pm-2am, from 4pm Sun, clsd Mon • lesbians/gay men • dancing/DJ • country/western • dance lessons 7:30pm Tue-Fri • beer/wine

The Vogue 2018 1st Ave. • 443-0673 • 9pm-2am • gay-friendly • dancing/DJ • live shows

Wildrose Tavern & Restaurant 1021 E. Pike St. • 324-9210 • 11am-midnight, til 2am Fri-Sat • mostly women • live shows • food served • some veggie • beer/wine • wheelchair access • $4-6

Seattle (206)

WHERE THE GIRLS ARE: Living in the Capitol Hill District, south of Lake Union, and working in the Broadway Market, Pike Place Market, or somewhere in between.

LESBIGAY PRIDE: 292-1035.

CITY INFO: 461-5800.

ATTRACTIONS: International District. Pike Place Market. Pioneer Square. Seattle Art Museum. Space Needle. Woodland Park Zoo.

BEST VIEW: Top of the Space Needle, but check out the World's Fair Monorail too.

WEATHER: Winter's average temperature is 50° while summer temperatures can climb up into the 90°s. Be prepared for rain at anytime during the year.

TRANSIT: Farwest: 622-1717. Broadway Cab: 622-4800. Airport Shuttle Express: 622-1424. Metropolitan Transit: 553-3000.

RESTAURANTS & CAFES

Addis Cafe 61224 E. Jefferson • 325-7805 •
8am-midnight • popular • Ethiopian • $3-7

Beyond the Edge Cafe 703 E. Pike St. •
325-6829 • 7am-10pm, til 3am Fri-Sat • live
shows

Black Cat Cafe 4110 Roosevelt Wy. NE •
547-3887 • 10am-10pm, til 7pm Sun, clsd
Mon • funky atmosphere • vegetarian •
wheelchair access • under $5

Cafe Illiterati 5327 Ballard NW • 782-0191
• 9am-5pm • wheelchair access • $4-7

Cafe Paradiso 1005 E. Pike • 322-6960 •
6am-1am, til 4am Fri-Sat • popular

Cafe Septieme 214 Broadway Ave. E. •
860-8858 • popular • lesbians/gay men

Cafe Vivace 901 E. Denny Wy. #100 • 860-
5869 • popular • very cute girls

Dahlia Lounge 1904 4th Ave. • 682-4142 •
lunch & dinner • some veggie • full bar •
$9-20

Frontier Restaurant & Bar 2203 1st Ave. •
441-3377 • 10am-2am • best cheap food in
town • full bar • wheelchair access

Giorgina's Pizza 131 15th Ave. E. • 329-
8118 • 11am-9pm, from 4pm Sat, clsd Sun

Gravity Bar 415 E. Broadway • 325-7186 •
9am-10pm • vegetarian/juice bar • also
downtown location • 448-8826 • wheelchair access

Jack's Bistro 405 15th Ave. E. • 324-9625 •
lunch & dinner • some veggie • full bar •
wheelchair access

Kokeb 9261 12th Ave. • 322-0485 • lunch &
dinner • Ethiopian • some veggie • full bar
• $5-10

Mae's Phinney Ridge Cafe 6410 Phinney
Ridge N. (at 65th) • 782-1222 • 7am-3pm •
brkfst menu • some veggie • 'Mud Room
Cafe' til 5pm • wheelchair access

Plaza Mexico 4116 University Wy. NE •
633-4054 • full bar

Queen City Grill 2201 1st Ave. • 443-0975 •
noon-11pm, from 5pm wknds • popular •
fresh seafood • some veggie • wheelchair
access

Sunlight Cafe 6403 Roosevelt Wy. NE •
522-9060 • 8am-3pm • vegetarian •
beer/wine • wheelchair access • $3-9

GYMS & HEALTH CLUBS

BQ Workout (in the Broadway Market) •
860-3070 • 6am-11pm, 9am-7pm Sun •
gay-friendly

BOOKSTORES & RETAIL SHOPS

Bailey/Coy Books 414 Broadway Ave. E. •
323-8842 • 10am-10pm, til 11pm Fri-Sat,
11am-8pm Sun • wheelchair access

Beyond the Closet Bookstore 518 E. Pike
• 322-4609 • 10am-10pm, til 11pm Fri-Sat •
lesbigay

Broadway Market 401 E. Broadway • popular • mall full of funky, queer & hip stores

Edge of the Circle 701 E. Pike • 726-1999
• 10am-8pm • alternative spirituality store

Fremont Place Book Company 621 N.
35th • 547-5970 • 11am-6pm, til 8pm Fri-
Sat • progressive bookstore

Metropolis 7220 Greenwood Ave. N. • 782-
7002 • cards & gifts

The Pink Zone 401 Broadway E. (B'way
Mkt.) • 325-0050 • lesbigay • tattooing &
piercing

Pistil Books & News 1013 E. Pike St. •
325-5401

Red & Black Books 432 15th Ave. E. •
322-7323 • 10am-8pm

The Rubber Tree 4426 Burke Ave. N. •
633-4750 • 10am-7pm, clsd Sun • non-profit safer sex supplies & referrals

Sin 616 E. Pine • 329-0324 • noon-8pm •
leather • piercings • wheelchair access

Sunshine Thrift Shops 1605 12th Ave. #25
• 324-9774 • noon-6pm, noon-7pm Sat •
non-profit for AIDS organizations • call for
details • wheelchair access

TRAVEL & TOUR OPERATORS

▲ **Adventure Associates** PO Box 16304,
98116 • 932-8352 • adventures for women
(see ad under Tour Operators)

Capitol Hill Travel Broadway Market 2nd
flr. • 726-8996/(800) 726-8996 • IGTA

It's Your World Travel 1411 E. Olive Wy. •
328-0616/(800) 955-6077 • IGTA

Passport Travel 6720 NE Bothell Wy. •
365-6755/(800) 373-6160 • IGTA

Progressive Travels 224 W. Galer Ste. C •
285-1987/(800) 245-2229 • IGTA

Sunshine Travel 519 N. 85th St. • 784-8141
• IGTA

Travel Solutions 4009 Gilman W. • 281-
7202/(800) 727-1616 • IGTA

SPIRITUAL GROUPS

Affirmation (Mormon) PO Box 23223,
98102 • 820-5729

Congregation Tikvah Chadashah 20th Ave. E. & E. Prospect (Prospect Cong. Church) • 329-2590 • 8:15pm 2nd & 4th Fri • shabbat services

Dignity Seattle 723 18th Ave. E. (St. Joseph's Church) • 325-7314 • 7:30pm Sun

Grace Gospel Chapel 2052 NW 64th St., Ballard • 784-8495 • 11am Sun

Integrity 1245 10th Ave. E. (Chapel of St. Mark's) • 525-4668 • 7pm Sun

MCC 2101 14th Ave. S. • 325-2421 • 11am Sun

PUBLICATIONS

Seattle's Alternative Guidebook 229 Broadway E. #22 • 726-9936

SGN (Seattle Gay News) 1605 12th Ave. Ste. 31 • 324-4297

The Stranger 1202 E. Pike #1225, 98122 • 323-7101 • alternative paper

Women's Yellow Pages of NW Washington PO Box 58876, Renton, 98058 • 726-9687

EROTICA

The Crypt 1310 E. Union St. • 325-3882

Fantasy Unlimited 102 Pike St. • 682-0167

Onyx Leather 328-1965 • by appt. only

Toys in Babeland 711 E. Pike • 328-2914 • noon-8pm, clsd Mon • women's sex toy store

Seaview (360)

ACCOMMODATIONS

Sou'wester Lodge Beach Access Rd. (38th Place) • 642-2542 • gay-friendly • inexpensive suites & cabins w/ kitchens

Spokane (509)

INFO LINES & SERVICES

AA Gay/Lesbian 224 S. Howard (upstairs) • 624-1442 • 6:30pm Mon

Lesbian/Gay Community Services Hotline 489-2266 • 24hrs

BARS

Dempsey's Brass Rail 909 W. 1st St. • 747-5362 • 3pm-2am, til 3:30am Fri-Sat • popular • lesbians/gay men • dancing/DJ • also a restaurant • beer/wine • wheelchair access • $5-12

Hour Place 415 W. Sprague • 838-6947 • 11am-2am • lesbians/gay men • dancing/DJ • also a restaurant • some veggie • wheelchair access • $5-8

Pumps II W. 4 Main St. • 747-8940 • 3pm-2am • lesbians/gay men • dancing/DJ • live shows • food served

BOOKSTORES & RETAIL SHOPS

Auntie's Bookstore & Cafe W. 402 Main St. • 838-0206 • 9am-9pm, 11am-5pm Sun • wheelchair access

Boo Radley's 5 N. Post • 456-7479 • 10am-6pm, noon-5pm • gift shop • wheelchair access

TRAVEL & TOUR OPERATORS

Edwards LaLone Travel S. 5 Washington • 747-3000/(800) 288-3788 • IGTA

The Travel Place W. 505 Parkade Plaza • 624-7434/(800) 727-9114 • women-owned/run

SPIRITUAL GROUPS

Emmanuel MCC 307 W. 4th • 838-0085 • 10:30am Sun • 7pm Wed (412 S. Bernard)

PUBLICATIONS

Stonewall News Spokane PO Box 3994, 99220 • 456-8011

Tacoma (206)

INFO LINES & SERVICES

AA Gay/Lesbian 209 S. 'J' St. (church) • 474-8897 • 7:30pm Mon & Fri

Oasis 596-2860 • lesbigay youth group run by Health Dept.

South Sound Alliance 924-1459

Tacoma Lesbian Concern PO Box 947, 98401 • 472-0422 • social events • resource list

ACCOMMODATIONS

Chinaberry Hill 302 Tacoma Ave. N. • 272-1282 • gay-friendly • full brkfst • hot tub • kids ok • very romantic • $85-125

Commencement Bay B&B 3312 N. Union Ave. • 272-1282 • gay-friendly • full brkfst • hot tub

BARS

24th Street Tavern 2409 Pacific Ave. • 572-3748 • noon-2am • lesbians/gay men • dancing/DJ • transgender-friendly • live shows • beer/wine • wheelchair access

733 Restaurant & Lounge 733 Commerce St. • 6pm-2am, clsd Sun-Mon • lesbians/gay men • dancing/DJ • transgender-friendly • live shows

The Gold Ball Grill & Spirits 2708 6th Ave. • 305-9861/627-0430 • 8am-2am, til 4am Fri-Sat • lesbians/gay men • neighborhood bar • dancing/DJ • transgender-friendly • live shows • beer garden • gambling

Goodfellows 5811 N. 51st. • 761-9802 • 4pm-2am • mostly gay men • neighborhood bar • karaoke • food served

Reflections 2405 Pacific Ave. • 593-4445 • 5pm-2am • mostly gay men • neighborhood bar

SPIRITUAL GROUPS
New Heart MCC 2150 S. Cushman • 272-2382 • 11am Sun, 7pm Wed

PUBLICATIONS
Tacoma Sounds PO Box 110816, 98411-0816 • 460-1308

Tri-Cities   (509)

SPIRITUAL GROUPS
River of Life MCC 619 W. Albany (Unitarian Church), Kennewick • 946-5250 • 6:30pm Sun

Vancouver   (360)
(See also **Portland, OR**)

BARS
North Bank Tavern 106 W. 6th St. • 695-3862 • noon-2am • lesbians/gay men • beer/wine • food served • wheelchair access

TRAVEL & TOUR OPERATORS
First Discount Travel 11700 NE 95th St. Ste. 110 • 896-6200/(800) 848-1926 • ask for Carl • IGTA

SPIRITUAL GROUPS
MCC of the Gentle Shepherd 4505 E. 18th St. (church) • 695-1480 • 6pm Sun • wheelchair access

Wenatchee

INFO LINES & SERVICES
North Central Washington Lesbian/Gay Alliance PO Box 234, 98807

WEST VIRGINIA

Berkeley (304)

EROTICA

Adam & Eve Adult Bookstore 2301 S. Fayette • 252-6733

Berkeley Springs (304)

EROTICA

Action Books & Video Rte. 522 S. • 258-2529

Charleston (304)

INFO LINES & SERVICES

COGLES (Community Oriented Gay/ Lesbian Events/Services) 1517 Jackson St. • 345-0491

West Virginia Lesbian/Gay Coalition PO Box 11033, 25339 • 343-7305

BARS

Broadway 210 Broad St. • 343-2162 • 4pm-3am, from 1pm wknds • mostly gay men • dancing/DJ • private club • wheelchair access

Grand Palace 617 Brooks St. • 342-9532 • noon-2:30am • mostly gay men • dancing/DJ • live shows • videos • private club

Tap Room 1022 Quarrier St. (rear entrance) • 342-9563 • 5pm-midnight, later wknds • mostly gay men • neighborhood bar • private club

RESTAURANTS & CAFES

Lee Street Deli 1111 Lee St. E. • 343-3354 • 11am-3pm, bar til 1am

TRAVEL & TOUR OPERATORS

West Virginia Tourism Division (800) 225-5982

Wild Wonderful Travel 1517 Jackson St. • 345-0491 • IGTA

PUBLICATIONS

Graffiti 1505 Lee St. • 342-4412 • mostly straight alternative entertainment guide

Elkins (304)

ACCOMMODATIONS

Retreat at Buffalo Run B&B 214 Harpertown Rd. • 636-2960 • gay-friendly

Huntington (304)

BARS

Driftwood Lounge 1121 7th Ave. • 696-9858 • 5pm-3am • lesbians/gay men • dancing/DJ • videos • wheelchair access • also 'Beehive' upstairs • open wknds • mostly gay men • live shows

Polo Club 733 7th Ave. (rear) • 522-3146 • 3pm-3:30am • lesbians/gay men • more women Tue • dancing/DJ • live shows • private club • wheelchair access

The Stonewall 820 7th Ave. (rear) • 528-9317 • 5pm-3:30am • popular • lesbians/gay men • more women Wed-Th • dancing/DJ

RESTAURANTS & CAFES

Calamity Cafe 1555 3rd Ave. • 525-4171 • 11am-10pm, til 3am wknds • live shows • Southern/Western • plenty veggie • full bar • wheelchair access • $10-15

EROTICA

Bookmark Video 1119 4th Ave. • 525-6861

House of Video 1109 4th Ave. • 525-2194

Lost River (304)

ACCOMMODATIONS

The Guesthouse Settlers Valley Wy. • 897-5707 • lesbians/gay men • full brkfst • swimming • steam & spa

Martinsburg (304)

EROTICA

Variety Books & Video 255 N. Queen St. • 263-4334 • 24hrs

Morgantown (304)

INFO LINES & SERVICES

Gay/Lesbian Switchboard PO Box 576, 26505 • 292-4292

BARS

Class Act 335 High St. (rear entrance) • 292-2010 • 8pm-3am, from 8pm Th-Sat, clsd Mon • lesbians/gay men • dancing/DJ • live shows • private club

EROTICA

Select Books & Videos 237 Walnut St. • 292-7714 • 24hrs

Parkersburg (304)

BARS

Different Strokes 604 Market St. • 485-5113 • 8pm-3am • lesbians/gay men • dancing/DJ

Stonewall Jackson Lake (304)

ACCOMMODATIONS

FriendSheep Farm Rte. 1 Box 158, Orlando, 26412 • 462-7075 • mostly women • secluded retreat w/ workshops • campsites • swimming • smokefree • kids/pets ok by arr.

Wheeling (304)

ACCOMMODATIONS

Row House Guest Quarters 718 Main St. • 232-5252/(800) 371-3020 • gay-friendly • apt w/ kitchen

BARS

Tricks 1429 Market St. (behind Market St. News) • 232-1267 • 9pm-2am, til 3am Fri, clsd Mon-Tue • lesbians/gay men • dancing/DJ • live shows

EROTICA

Market St. News 1437 Market St. • 232-2414 • 24hrs

WISCONSIN

Appleton (414)

BARS

Pivot Club 4815 W. Prospect Ave. • 730-0440 • 5pm-2am, from 7pm Sat, from 2pm Sun • lesbians/gay men • dancing/DJ • live shows • videos • wheelchair access

Rascals Bar & Grill 702 E. Wisconsin Ave. • 954-9262 • 5pm-2am, from noon Sun • lesbians/gay men • more women Fri • food served

Aztalan (414)

BARS

Crossroads Bar W. 6642 Hwy. B., Lake Mills • 648-8457 • 1pm-2am, clsd Mon • gay-friendly

Baileys Harbor (414)

ACCOMMODATIONS

Blacksmith Inn B&B PO Box 220, 54202 • 839-9222 • gay-friendly • fireplaces

Beloit (608)

BOOKSTORES & RETAIL SHOPS

A Different World 414 E. Grand Ave. • 365-1000 • 10am-8:30pm, til 5pm Mon, clsd Sun • women's & children's books

Eagle River (715)

ACCOMMODATIONS

Edgewater Inn 5054 Hwy. 70 W. • 479-4011 • gay-friendly • non-smoking rms avail. • kids ok

Eau Claire (715)

ACCOMMODATIONS

Back of the Moon Augusta • 286-2409 • women only • B&B-retreat • smokefree • wheelchair access

EROTICA

Adult Book & Novelty 129 N. Barstow • 835-7292

Adult Video Unlimited 1518 Bellinger St. • 834-3393

Green Bay (414)

INFO LINES & SERVICES

Gay AA/Al-Anon 494-9904/469-9999 • call for schedule

BARS

Brandy's II 1126 Main St. • 437-3917 • 1pm-2am • mostly gay men • neighborhood bar

Java's/Za's 1106 Main St. • 435-5476 •
8pm-2:30am • lesbians/gay men • dancing/DJ • videos • 18+ Sun

Napalese Lounge 515 S. Broadway • 432-9646 • 3pm-2am • mostly gay men • dancing/DJ • wheelchair access

Sass 840 S. Broadway • 437-7277 • 5pm-2am, from noon Sun (winters) • lesbians/gay men • dancing/DJ

SPIRITUAL GROUPS
Angel of Hope MCC PO Box 672, 54305 • 432-0830 • 11am Sun • services held at 614 Forest St.

PUBLICATIONS
Quest PO Box 1961, 54301

EROTICA
Adult Movieland 836 S. Broadway • 433-9640 • 24hrs

Main Attraction Book & Video/Nite Owl Motel 1614 Main • 465-6969 • 24hrs

Hayward   (715)

ACCOMMODATIONS
The Lake House 5793 Division on the Lake, Stone Lake • 865-6803 • gay-friendly • lakeside w/ sand beach • full brkfst • swimming • fireplaces • smokefree • kids ok by arr. • wheelchair access • lesbian-owned/run

Hazelhurst   (715)

BARS
Willow Haven Resort/Supper Club 4877 Haven Dr. • 453-3807 • gay-friendly • cabin rentals • also supper club • full bar • $8-16

Hixton   (715)

ACCOMMODATIONS
Inn at Pine Ridge Rte. 1, Box 28 • 984-2272 • women only • full vegetarian brunch • hot tub • sauna • lesbian-owned/run • $75-80

Kenosha   (414)

BARS
Club 94 9001 120th Ave. • 857-9958 • 7pm-2am, from 3pm Sun, clsd Mon • popular • lesbians/gay men • dancing/DJ • live shows • videos

Kimberly   (414)

RESTAURANTS & CAFES
Grand American Restaurant & Bar 800 Eisenhower Dr. • 731-0164 • 11:30am-2pm, 10:30am-2:30pm Sun (brunch) • some veggie • full bar • wheelchair access • $6-12

La Crosse   (608)

INFO LINES & SERVICES
Gay/Lesbian AA 126 N. 17th St. • 784-7560 • call for schedule

Gay/Lesbian Support Group 126 N. 17th St. • 784-7600 • 7:30pm Sun

ACCOMMODATIONS
Chela & Rose's B&B and Forest Camping Retreat 735-4829 • women only • camping on 35 acres of women's land • also 2 rms. avail. • full brkfst • sauna • kids/pets ok • lesbian-owned/run • $10/couple camping ($5 extra person) • $50 room

BARS
Cavalier 114 N. 5th • 782-9061 • 2pm-2am • gay-friendly • gay evenings only • wheelchair access

Rainbow's End 417 Jay St. • 782-9802 • opens 11am • lesbians/gay men • neighborhood bar

BOOKSTORES & RETAIL SHOPS
Rainbow Revolution 122 5th Ave. S. • 796-0383 • 10am-5:30pm, til 5pm Sat, noon-4pm Sun • alternative • wheelchair access

Red Oaks Books 323 Pearl St. • 782-3424 • 9am-8pm, til 9pm Fri, 10am-5pm wknds • lesbigay section

PUBLICATIONS
Leaping La Crosse PO Box 932, 54602 • 783-0069

La Farge   (608)

ACCOMMODATIONS
Trillium B&B Rte. 2, Box 121, 54639 • 625-4492 • gay-friendly • also cottages (sleep 5) • 35 miles from La Crosse • full brkfst

Lake Geneva   (414)

ACCOMMODATIONS
Eleven Gables Inn on the Lake 493 Wrigley Dr. • 248-8393 • gay-friendly • Victorian comfort in a spacious lakeside inn • full brkfst wknds • smokefree • wheelchair access

RESTAURANTS & CAFES

C.J. Wiz's 126 B East (Geneva Square Mall) • 248-1949 • casual dining • full bar

Laona (715)

ACCOMMODATIONS

Alexander's Guest House 5371 Beech • 674-2615 • gay-friendly • dorm-style/youth hostel rms • swimming

Madison (608)

INFO LINES & SERVICES

AA Gay/Lesbian 255-4297

Apple Island 849 E. Washington • 258-9777 • women's space • sponsors social events

Campus Women's Center 710 University Rm. 202 (University of Wisconsin) • 262-8093 • support programs

▲ **Dyke TV** Channel 4 • 8:30pm Mon • 'weekly half-hour TV show produced by lesbians, for lesbians'

Gay Line 255-4297 • 9am-9pm Mon-Fri

Lesbian Line 255-0743 • 9am-9pm Mon-Fri

LesBiGay Campus Center 510 Memorial Union • 265-3344 • drop-in 9am-4pm • social events • general info

Nothing to Hide cable Ch. 4 • 241-2500 • 8:30pm Wed • lesbigay TV show

The United 14 West Mifflin St. Ste. 103 • 255-8582 • 9am-5pm, 7pm-10pm Mon-Fri • drop-in center • library • newsletter • counseling (call ahead)

ACCOMMODATIONS

Prairie Garden B&B W. 13172 Hwy. 188, Lodi • 592-5187/(800) 380-8427 • lesbians/gay men • 30 min. from Madison • full brkfst • smokefree • kids/pets by arr.

BARS

Cardinal 418 E. Wilson St. • 251-0080 • 8pm-2am, clsd Mon • gay-friendly • dancing/DJ

Flamingo 636 State • 257-3330 • 11am-2pm (lunch), 8pm-2am (bar) • gay-friendly • food served

Geraldine's 3052 E. Washington Ave. • 241-9335 • 4pm-2am • lesbians/gay men • dancing/DJ

Green Bush 914 Regent St. • 257-2874 • 4pm-2am • gay-friendly • food served

R Place 121 West Main St. • 257-5455 • 4pm-2am, til 2:30am Fri-Sat • dancing/DJ • fireplace

Shamrock 117 W. Main St. • 255-5029 • 2pm-2am, from 11am Fri-Sat, from 5pm Sun • lesbians/gay men • dancing/DJ • also a grill • wheelchair access • $2-4

RESTAURANTS & CAFES

Monty's Blue Plate Diner 2089 Atwood Ave. • 244-8505 • 7am-10pm, til 9pm Sun-Tue, from 7:30am wknds • some veggie • beer/wine • wheelchair access • $5

Wild Iris 1225 Regent St. • 257-4747 • 11:45am-10pm, from 9am wknds • Italian/Cajun • some veggie • beer/wine • $8-12

BOOKSTORES & RETAIL SHOPS

A Room of One's Own 317 W. Johnson St. • 257-7888 • 9:30am-8pm, 10am-6pm Tue, Wed & Sat, noon-5pm Sun • women's books & music

Borders Book Shop 3416 University Ave. • 232-2600 • 9am-11pm, til 8pm Sun • lesbigay section • also espresso bar

Going Places 2860 University Ave. • 233-1920 • travel-oriented books

Mimosa 212 N. Henry • 256-5432 • 9:30am-6pm, noon-5pm Sun • alternative

Pic-A-Book 506 State St. • 256-1125 • 9am-8pm, til 5pm Sun

We Are Family 524 E. Wilson (at the Wilson Hotel) • 258-9918 • pride gifts • espresso

TRAVEL & TOUR OPERATORS

Dan's Travel The Gateway, 600 Williamson St. • 251-1110/(800) 476-0305 • IGTA

Wisconsin Division of Tourism (800) 432-8747

SPIRITUAL GROUPS

Integrity & Dignity 1001 University Ave. (St. Francis Episcopal) • 836-8886 • 7:30pm 2nd & 4th Sun (Sept-May)

James Reeb Unitarian Universalist Church 2146 E. Johnson St. • 242-8887 • 10am Sun (summer) • call for winter hours

PUBLICATIONS

Of a Like Mind PO Box 6677, 53716 • women's newsletter of pagan spirituality

Solitary PO Box 6091, 53716 • 244-0072 • lesbigay pagan journal

EROTICA

Piercing Lounge 520 University Ave. #120 • 284-0870

Red Letter News 2528 E. Washington • 241-9958 • 24hrs

Maiden Rock (715)

ACCOMMODATIONS

Eagle Cove B&B PO Box 65, 54750 • 448-4302/(800) 467-0279 • gay-friendly • 6 acre country retreat w/ panoramic views of Lake Pepin & the Mississippi River Valley • hot tub • smokefree • pets ok • wheelchair access

Mauston (608)

ACCOMMODATIONS

CK's Outback W. 5627 Clark Rd. • 847-5247 • camping • near outdoor recreation

Milwaukee (414)

INFO LINES & SERVICES

AA Galano Club 2408 N. Farwell Ave. • 276-6936 • 12-step social group • call after 5pm for extensive mtg. schedule

AA Gay/Lesbian 771-9119

Black Gay Conciousness Raising 933-2136 • 7:30pm 3rd Mon • call for info

Counseling Center of Milwaukee 2038 N. Bartlett • 271-2565 • various support groups for women

DAMES (Dykes Against Minority Erotic Suppression) PO Box 1272, 53201 • leatherdyke group

Gay Information & Services 444-7331 • 24hr referral service

Gay People's Union Hotline 562-7010 • 7pm-10pm

Gay Youth Wisconsin Hotline 272-8336/(888) 429-8336 (outside Milwaukee) • 7pm-11pm Fri-Sat • queer youth operators

Gemini Gender Group PO Box 44211, 53214 • 297-9328 • 2nd Sat • transgender support • call for location

Lesbian Alliance PO Box 93323, 53203 • 264-2600

LOC (Lesbians of Color) 351-4549 • call for activities

People of All Colors Together PO Box 93127, 53203 • 871-3048 • 3rd Sun • newsletter

SAGE Milwaukee PO Box 92482, 53202 • 271-0378 • for older lesbigays • call after 4pm

Ujima PO Box 92183, 53202 • 272-3009 • African-American social/support group

ACCOMMODATIONS

Park East Hotel 916 E. State St. • 276-8800/(800) 328-7275 • gay-friendly • smokefree • also a restaurant • some veggie • wheelchair access • $10-15

BARS

1100 Club 1100 S. 1st St. • 647-9950 • 7am-2am • mostly gay men • dancing/DJ • dinner served • $4-15

The 3B Bar 1579 S. 2nd St. • 672-5580 • 3pm-2am, from noon wknds • lesbians/gay men • more women wknds • dancing/DJ • country/western

Milwaukee (414)

WHERE THE GIRLS ARE: In East Milwaukee south of downtown, spread out from Lake Michigan to S. Layton Blvd.

ANNUAL EVENTS: June - Pagan Spirit Gathering: (608) 924-2216, summer solstice celebration in Mt. Horeb.

CITY INFO: 273-3950.

ATTRACTIONS: Annunciation Greek Orthodox Church. Breweries. Grand Avenue. Mitchel Park Horticultural Conservatory. Summerfest. Pabst Theatre.

BEST VIEW: 41st story of First Wisconsin Center. Call 765-5733 to arrange a visit to the top floor observatory.

WEATHER: Summer temperatures can get up into 90°s. Spring and fall are pleasantly moderate but too short. Winter brings snows, cold temperatures and even colder wind chills.

TRANSIT: Yellow Cab: 271-6630. Milwaukee Transit: 344-6711.

Milwaukee

*M*ilwaukee was settled, and named, by the local Native American tribe of Mahanawakee-Seepe, for whom Milwaukee means 'gathering place by the waters'. The French and English colonized the area in the 1800s, and were followed by settlers from many cultures. This multi-cultural flavor is still evident in the city's architecture, cultural institutions, and numerous ethnic fairs and festivals.

For Frank Lloyd Wright fans, the Annunciation Greek Orthodox Church was the last building he designed. And for you beer lovers, the smell of malt permeates the air and leads even the most discriminating nose to the Miller, Pabst, and Sprechers breweries.

Speaking of breweries, Laverne & Shirley may have been closeted, but Milwaukee's lesbian community is not! (We know what that "L" on Laverne's shirt stood for.)

For you woman-identified women, Milwaukee has women's groups, bars, and more. The bars here are relaxed: **The 3B Bar** is a country/western dance bar with more women on weekends, **Fannie's** is a beer-garden with a dancefloor, **Station 2** is more intimate. **Club 219** is a mixed lesbian/gay bar with dancing, shows and a multi-racial clientele. **AfterWords** is the lesbigay bookstore, and it's got an espresso bar to boot!

Women of color can hook up with others via the social group, **Lesbians of Color**. For other groups, scan one of the local papers, or call the **Counseling Center of Milwaukee**.

Just an hour-and-a-half west of Milwaukee is **Madison**—home of the University of Wisconsin, and a hotbed of "cultural feminism." That includes dyke separatism and feminist spirituality, as well as anti-violence and anti-pornography activism. If that branch of feminism interests you, call the **Lesbian Line** or **Apple Island** for current events, and stop by **A Room of One's Own** for local publications **Solitary** or **Of A Like Mind**, excellent resources for pagan and women's spiritual information.

Cafe Melange 720 N. 3rd St. • 291-9889 • 11am-2am • gay-friendly • dancing/DJ • live shows • food served • some veggie • wheelchair access • $10 & up

Club 219 219 S. 2nd St. • 271-3732 • 4pm-2am • lesbians/gay men • dancing/DJ • multi-racial • live shows

Fannie's 200 E. Washington St. • 643-9633 • 7pm-2am, from 4pm Sun • popular • mostly women • wheelchair access

Gargoyles 354 E. National • 225-9676 • 2pm-2am • mostly gay men • leather • live shows • wheelchair access

Grubb's Pub & Le Grill 807 S. 2nd St. • 384-8330 • 9pm-3:30am • lesbians/gay men

Henry's Pub at Coffee Trader 2625 N. Downer Ave. • 332-9690 • noon-2am • lesbians/gay men • full menu • wheelchair access

Just Us 807 S. 5th St. • 383-2233 • 4pm-2am, from 1pm Sun • lesbians/gay men • dancing/DJ • transgender-friendly

La Cage (Dance, Dance, Dance) 801 S. 2nd St. • 383-8330 • 9pm-2am • popular • mostly gay men • more women wknds • dancing/DJ • live shows • food served • wheelchair access

M&M Club 124 N. Water St. • 347-1962 • 11am-2am • mostly gay men • more women wknds • live shows • food served • some veggie • wheelchair access • $5-10

The Nomad 1401 E. Brady St. • 224-8111 • noon-2am • gay-friendly • sponsors 'Women's Music Week'

Station 2 1534 W. Grant • 383-5755 • 5pm-midnight Mon, Wed-Th, til 2:30am Fri-Sat, clsd Tue • mostly women • neighborhood bar • dancing/DJ • sports bar

Walker's Point Marble Arcade 1101 S. 2nd St. • 647-9430 • 3pm-2am • lesbians/gay men • bowling alley • live shows • food served • wheelchair access

RESTAURANTS & CAFES

Cafe Knickerbocker 1030 E. Juneau Ave. • 272-0011 • 6:30am-10pm, til 11pm Sat-Sun • popular • some veggie • full bar • wheelchair access • $8-15

La Perla 734 S. 5th St. • 645-9888 • 10:30am-10pm, til 11:30pm Fri-Sat • Mexican • $7-14

Mama Roux 1875 N. Humboldt • 347-0344 • 3pm-2am • Cajun • full bar • wheelchair access

Walkers Point Cafe 1106 S. 1st St. • 384-7999 • 10am-4am

BOOKSTORES & RETAIL SHOPS

AfterWords Bookstore & Espresso Bar 2710 N. Murray • 963-9089 • 10am-10pm, til 11pm Fri-Sat, noon-6pm Sun • lesbigay • wheelchair access

Peoples' Books 3512 N. Oakland Ave. • 962-0575 • 10am-7pm, til 6pm Sat, noon-5pm Sun

Schwartz Bookstore 209 E. Wisconsin Ave. • 274-6400 • 9:30am-5:30pm, clsd Sun

TRAVEL & TOUR OPERATORS

Horizon Travel N. 81 W. 15028 Appleton Ave., Menomonee Falls • 255-0704/(800) 562-0219 • IGTA

Trio Travel 2812 W. Forest Home Ave. • 384-8746/(800) 417-4159 • IGTA

SPIRITUAL GROUPS

Dignity 2506 Wauwatosa Ave. (St. Pius X Church) • 444-7177 • 6pm Sun

First Unitarian Society 1342 N. Astor • 273-5257 • 9:30am Sun

Integrity 914 E. Knaap, 53211 • 276-6277

Lutherans Concerned 2460-A S. Kinnickinnic Ave. • 5pm 3rd Sun

Milwaukee MCC 924 E. Juneau (Astor Hotel) • 332-9995 • 11am & 7pm Sun

St. James Episcopal Church 833 W. Wisconsin Ave. • 271-1340 • 10:30am Sun • call for weekday schedule

PUBLICATIONS

In Step 225 S. 2nd St. • 278-7840

Q Voice PO Box 92385, 53202 • 278-7524

Quest PO Box 1961, Green Bay, 54301

Wisconsin Light 1843 N. Palmer St. • 372-2773

Women's Yellow Pages of Greater Milwaukee PO Box 13827, 98058 • 789-1346

EROTICA

Popular News 225 N. Water St. • 278-0636 • toys • B&D videos

Mineral Point   (608)

ACCOMMODATIONS

The Cothren House 320 Tower St. • 987-2612 • gay-friendly • full brkfst • gay-owned/run

RESTAURANTS & CAFES

Chesterfield Inn/Ovens of Brittany 20 Commerce St. • 987-3682 • open May-Oct • Cornish/American • some veggie • full bar • $10-16

Oshkosh (414)

EROTICA
Pure Pleasure 1212 Oshkosh Ave. • 235-9727

Racine (414)

BARS
JoDee's International 2139 Racine St. (S. Hwy. 32) • 634-9804 • 7pm-2am • lesbians/gay men • dancing/DJ • live shows • courtyard

What About Me? 600 6th St. • 632-0171 • 7pm-2am, from 3pm Tue & Fri • lesbians/gay men • neighborhood bar

EROTICA
Racine News & Video 316 Main St. • 634-9827

Shawano (715)

ACCOMMODATIONS
Prince Edward B&B 203 W. 5th St. • 526-2805 • gay-friendly • full brkfst

Sheboygan (414)

BARS
The Blue Lite 1029 N. 8th St. • 457-1636 • 2pm-2am, til 2:30am Fri-Sat • mostly gay men • more women wknds early • neighborhood bar

Somerset (715)

ACCOMMODATIONS
Country Guesthouse 1673 38th St. • 247-3520 • women only • rental home on 20 wooded acres in St. Croix River Valley • kitchen

Stevens Point (715)

INFO LINES & SERVICES
Women's Resource Center 1209 Fremont (University of Wisconsin Nelson Hall) • 346-4242x4851 • 10am-4pm Mon-Fri • some lesbian outreach

BARS
Platwood Club 701 Hwy. 10 W. • 341-8862 • 9pm-? Th-Sat • lesbians/gay men • dancing/DJ • wheelchair access

Sturgeon Bay (414)

ACCOMMODATIONS
Chadwick Inn B&B 25 N. 8th Ave. • 743-2771 • fireplaces

The Chanticleer B&B 4072 Cherry Rd. • 746-0334 • gay-friendly • swimming • smokefree • kids ok • wheelchair access

Superior (715)

BARS
JT's Bar & Grill 1506 N. 3rd St. • 394-2580 • 4pm-2am, from 1pm wknds • lesbians/gay men • dancing/DJ • wheelchair access

The Main Club 1813 N. 3rd St. • 392-1756 • 3pm-2am, til 2:30am Fri-Sat • popular • lesbians/gay men • dancing/DJ

Molly & Oscar's 405 Tower Ave. • 394-7423 • 3pm-2am, til 2:30am Fri-Sat • gay-friendly • neighborhood bar

Trio 820 Tower Ave. • 392-5373 • 1pm-2am • mostly women • neighborhood bar • grill menu • wheelchair access

Wascott (715)

ACCOMMODATIONS
Wilderness Way PO Box 176, 54890 • 466-2635 • women only • resort property w/ cottages, camping & RV sites • swimming • wheelchair access • camping $10-14 • cottages $44-68

Wausau (715)

BARS
Mad Hatter 320 Washington • 842-3225 • 7pm-2am, from 3pm Sun • lesbians/gay men • dancing/DJ • wheelchair access

West Allis (414)

EROTICA
Booked Solid 7035 W. Greenfield Ave. • 774-7210

Willard (715)

ACCOMMODATIONS
The Barn B&B N. 7890 Bachelors Ave. • 267-3215 • gay-friendly • hot tub • smokefree • wheelchair access

Winter (715)

ACCOMMODATIONS
Flambeau Forest Resort Star Rte. 67, Box 65, 54896 • 332-5236 • gay-friendly • wheelchair access

WYOMING

Casper (307)

INFO LINES & SERVICES
Central Wyoming Gender Support Group PO Box 1301, Evansville, 82636 • 265-3123 • contact Bernadette

Cheyenne (307)

INFO LINES & SERVICES
United Gay/Lesbians of Wyoming PO Box 2037, Laramie, 82070 • 632-5362 • info • referrals • also newsletter

EROTICA
Cupid's 511 W. 17th • 635-3837

Etna (307)

BOOKSTORES & RETAIL SHOPS
Blue Fox Studio & Gallery 107452 Hwy. 89 • 883-3310 • open 7 days • hours vary • pottery & jewelry studio • local travel info

Jackson (307)

ACCOMMODATIONS
Bar H Ranch PO Box 297, Driggs ID, 83422 • (208) 354-2906 • seasonal • gay-friendly • also women-only horseback riding trips in Grand Tetons (see 'WomanTours' or 'Bar H Ranch' under Tour Operators section)

Fish Creek Lodging PO Box 833, Ashton ID, 83420 • 652-7566 • lesbians/gay men • private log cabin • kitchen • kids ok • women-owned/run

Redmond Guest House 110 Redmond St. • 733-4003 • seasonal • lesbians/gay men • house rental • smokefree • kids/pets ok • women-owned/run

Spring Creek Resort 733-8833/(800) 443-6139 • popular • gay-friendly • swimming • non-smoking rms. avail. • food served • wheelchair access

Three Peaks Inn 53 S. Hwy. 33, Driggs ID • (208) 354-8912 • gay-friendly • full brkfst • near outdoor recreation • shared/private baths • kids ok • women-owned/run

RESTAURANTS & CAFES
Sweetwater 85 King St. • 733-3553 • lunch & dinner • full bar • $7-12

BOOKSTORES & RETAIL SHOPS
Valley Books 125 N. Cache • 733-4533

Riverton (307)

RESTAURANTS & CAFES
Country Cove 301 E. Main • 856-9813 • 6am-4pm, clsd Sun • plenty veggie • wheelchair access • women-owned/run • $4-6

Thermopolis (307)

ACCOMMODATIONS
Out West B&B 1344 Broadway • 864-2700 • gay-friendly • near world's largest natural hot spring • full brkfst • smokefree • kids ok • gift shop • gay-owned/run

Looking for Dorothy?

PREMIER EDITION
ISSUE No. 1

THE RAINBOW CHOICES DIRECTORY

NORTH AMERICAN

GAY & LESBIAN ENTERTAINMENT & BUSINESS

DIRECTORY 1997

Find her in the Rainbow!

The Rainbow Choices Directory is your lesbian and gay entertainment & business source which will reach more than a quarter of a million lesbian and gay shoppers. Don't miss out on this exciting opportunity!

Book your ad today!
(416) 762-1320
Fax (416) 762-3600

THE RAINBOW CHOICES DIRECTORY IS A WHOLLY OWNED DIVISION OF RAINBOW DIRECTORY INC.

PROUDLY GAY OWNED AND OPERATED

CANADA

CARIBBEAN

MEXICO

ALBERTA

Calgary (403)

INFO LINES & SERVICES

Front Runners AA 777-1212 • 7:30pm Fri-Sat, 8:30pm Mon-Th

Gay Line & Center 223 12th Ave. SW #206 • 234-8973 • 7pm-10pm, call for other hours • many groups including 'Of Color' & 'Queer Youth' • women's drop-in 7pm Sun

Illusions Social Club Box 2000, 6802 Ogden Rd. SE, T2C 1B4 • 236-7072 • transgender club

Lesbian Information Line 223 12th Ave. SW #211 • 265-9458 • 7:30pm-9:30pm Mon & Wed

Southern Alberta Assoc. for Fetish/Fantasy Exploration 42014 Acadia PO, T2J 7A6 • social & educational group

ACCOMMODATIONS

Black Orchid Manor B&B 1401 2nd St. NW • 276-2471 • lesbians/gay men • leather-friendly

Westways Guest House 216 25th Ave. SW • 229-1758 • lesbians/gay men • full brkfst • hot tub • $45-88

BARS

Arena 310 17th Ave. SW • 244-8537 • 9pm-3am Th-Sat • gay-friendly • dancing/DJ

Loading Dock/Detour 318 17th Ave. SW • 244-8537 • 3pm-3am • mostly gay men • neighborhood bar • dancing/DJ

Money Penny's 111 15th Ave. SW • mostly women

Rooks 112 16th Ave. NW • 277-1922 • 11am-2am • mostly women • dancing/DJ

Trax 1130 10th Ave. SW • 245-8477 • 4pm-2am • mostly gay men • dancing/DJ • country/western • live shows • videos • private club

The Warehouse 731 10th Ave. SW (alley entrance) • 264-0535 • 9pm-3am, clsd Sun & Tue • gay-friendly • dancing/DJ • private club

RESTAURANTS & CAFES

Andrews Pizza 719 Edmonton Trail NE • 230-4202 • 11am-1am • more gay weeknights • full bar • wheelchair access

Cafe Beano 1613 9th St. SW • 229-1232 • 7am-midnight • some veggie • wheelchair access

Folks Like Us 110 10th St. NW • 270-2241 • 11am-10pm, til 8pm Sat, til 5pm Sun, clsd Mon • lesbians/gay men • bistro menu • plenty veggie • beer/wine • lesbian-owned/run • $4-7

Grabbajabba 1610 10th Ave. SW • 244-7750 • 7am-11pm • lesbians/gay men • cafe • some veggie • wheelchair access • $2-7

The Koop Cafe 211-B 12th Ave. SW • 269-4616 • 11am-1am

Max Beanie's Coffee Bar 1410 4th St. SW • 237-6185 • 9am-10pm, clsd Sun • food served • wheelchair access

Victoria's 306 17th Ave. SW • 244-9991 • lunch, dinner, wknd brunch • homecooking • some veggie • full bar • wheelchair access • $6-10

Wicked Wedge Pizza 618 17th Ave. SW • 228-1024

BOOKSTORES & RETAIL SHOPS

A Woman's Place 1412 Centre St. S. • 263-5256 • 10am-6pm, clsd Sun • women's bookstore • large lesbigay section • wheelchair access

B&B Leatherworks 6802 Ogden Rd. SE • 236-7072 • 10am-6pm Tue-Sat • drag/fetish items

Books 'n Books 738-A 17th Ave. SW • 228-3337 • 10am-6pm, til 9pm Th-Fri • wheelchair access

Daily Globe 1004 17th Ave. SW • 244-2060 • periodicals

With the Times 2212-A 4th St. SW • 244-8020 • 8:30am-11pm

TRAVEL & TOUR OPERATORS

Fletcher/Scott Travel 803 8th Ave. SW • 232-1180/(800) 567-2467 (in Canada only) • IGTA

Leisure Life Vacations 333 11th Ave. SW Ste. 1100 • 264-2604

Let's Talk Travel Worldwide Ltd. 4428 16th Ave. NW • 247-0600 • IGTA

Uniglobe Swift Travel 932 17th Ave. SW #220 • 244-7887

SPIRITUAL GROUPS

Integrity/Calgary Box 23093 Connaught PO, T2S 3B1 • meets 1st Sun in Old Y Common Room • write for more info

PUBLICATIONS

Perceptions Box 8581, Saskatoon SK, S7K 6K7 • (306) 244-1930 • covers the Canadian prairies

EROTICA

Angelheart Tattoo Studio 6130 1A St. SW #52 • 259-5662

Tad's Bookstore 1217-A 9th Ave. SE • 237-8237 • wheelchair access

Edmonton (403)

INFO LINES & SERVICES
AA Gay/Lesbian 424-5900

Gay Line 486-9661 • voice-mail for local groups & services

Gay/Lesbian Community Centre 10112 124th St. • 488-3234 • 7pm-10pm Mon-Fri • also youth group

Gay/Lesbian Info Line 988-4018 • recorded info & event listing

Northern Chaps 10342 107th St. #216, T5J 1K2 • 486-9661x2 • 9pm 1st & 3rd Fri at 'Boots' • mixed SM group

Womonspace 9930 106th St. (basement) • 425-0511 • meetings • social events

ACCOMMODATIONS
Northern Lights B&B 8216 151st St. • 483-1572 • lesbians/gay men • full brkfst • swimming • $45-55

BARS
The Bar at the Crockery 4005 Calgary Trail N. • 435-4877 • 7pm-2am • mostly women

Boots 'N Saddle 10242 106th St. • 423-5014 • 3pm-2am • mostly gay men • private club • wheelchair access

Rebar 10551 Whyte Ave. • 433-3600 • 8pm-3am • gay-friendly • dancing/DJ • wheelchair access

The Roost 10345 104th St. • 426-3150 • 8pm-3am • mostly gay men • dancing/DJ • live bands

RESTAURANTS & CAFES
Boystown Cafe 10116 124th St. • 488-6636 • 11am-midnight • lesbians/gay men • beer/wine • wheelchair access • also 'Buddy's' bar (upstairs)

Jazzberry's 9965 82nd Ave. • 433-2039

BOOKSTORES & RETAIL SHOPS
Audrey's Books 10702 Jasper Ave. • 423-3487 • 9am-9pm, 9:30am-5:30pm Sat, noon-5pm Sun

Divine Decadence 10441 82nd Ave. • 439-2977 • 10am-9pm • hip fashions • accessories

The Front Page 10846 Jasper Ave. • 426-1206 • 8am-6pm • periodicals

Greenwood's Bookshoppe 10355 82nd Ave. • 439-2005 • 9:30am-9pm, til 5:30pm Sat, clsd Sun

Orlando Books 10640 Whyte Ave. • 432-7633 • 10am-6pm, til 9pm Th-Fri, noon-4pm Sun • women's • lesbigay section • wheelchair access

Varscona Books 10309 Whyte Ave. • 439-4195 • 10am-6pm, til 9pm Th, clsd Sun

SPIRITUAL GROUPS
Dignity PO Box 55, T5J 2G9 • 469-4286

MCC—Edmonton 10086 MacDonald Dr. • 429-2321 • 7:15pm Sun • also 'Wayward Daughters' women's group • 431-2128

Grand Prairie (403)

INFO LINES & SERVICES
Peace Gay/Lesbian Association Box 1492, T8V 4Z3 • 539-3325 • 7:30pm-9:30pm Tue-Sat • drop-in center

BARS
Touché 8502 112th St. #201 • 538-9998 • 9pm-3am, from 2pm Sun • lesbians/gay men • neighborhood bar • dancing/DJ • private club

Lethbridge (403)

INFO LINES & SERVICES
GALA (Gay/Lesbian Association of Lethbridge) Box 2081, T1J 4K6 • 329-4666 • 7pm-10pm Wed • social group

Lighthouse Social Club PO Box 24003, T1J 1T7 • 380-4257 • monthly dances & weekly events for lesbians/gays

Millet (403)

ACCOMMODATIONS
Labyrinth Lake Lodge RR 1 Site 2, Box 3 • 878-3301 • mostly women • retreat • swimming

Red Deer (403)

INFO LINES & SERVICES
Gay/Lesbian Association of Central Alberta PO Box 1078, T4W 5E9 • 340-2198 • 7pm-9pm Wed

BARS
The Other Place Bay #3-4, 5579 47th St., T4N 1A1 • 342-6440 • 4pm-3am, til 11pm Sun • lesbians/gay men • dancing/DJ • wheelchair access

Rocky Mtn. House (403)

ACCOMMODATIONS
Country Cabin B&B Box 1916, T0M 1T0 • 845-4834 • gay-friendly • cabins • hot tub • swimming • pets ok

BRITISH COLUMBIA

Birken   (604)

ACCOMMODATIONS

Birkenhead Resort Box 369, Pemberton, V0N 2L0 • 452-3255 • gay-friendly • cabins • campsites • hot tub • swimming • also a restaurant • gourmet homecooking • some veggie • full bar

Blind Bay   (604)

ACCOMMODATIONS

The Sunset B&B 3434 McBride Rd., Box 168, V0E 1H0 • 675-4803 • gay-friendly • near outdoor recreation • shared baths • smokefree

Courtenay   (604)

INFO LINES & SERVICES

Women's Resource Center 3205 S. Island Hwy. • 338-1133 • 10am-4am Mon-Th

Cranbrook   (604)

INFO LINES & SERVICES

Cranbrook Women's Resource Center 20-A 12th Ave N. • 426-2912 • 9am-4pm, from noon Th, til 1pm Fri

Duncan   (604)

INFO LINES & SERVICES

Island Gay/Lesbian Society of Duncan 748-7689

Fort Nelson   (604)

INFO LINES & SERVICES

Women's Resource Center 5004 52nd Ave. W. • 774-3069 • 8:30am-noon, 1pm-4pm

Gokten   (604)

INFO LINES & SERVICES

Golden Women's Resource Center Box 2343, V0A 1H0 • 344-5317 • 9am-4pm Mon-Th, 11am-3pm Fri

Kelowna   (604)

INFO LINES & SERVICES

Kelowna Women's Resource Center 347 Leon #107 • 762-2355 • 9am-4pm, til 7pm Wed, clsd Fri-Sun

Okanagan Rainbow Coalition PO Box 711 Stn. A, V1Y 7P4 • 860-8555 • sponsors dances & coffeehouse • women's group Wed

ACCOMMODATIONS

The Flags B&B 2295 McKinley Rd., RR1 Site 10 C2 • 868-2416 • seasonal • lesbians/gay men • mini-resort • full brkfst • hot tub • swimming • nudity • $40-65

Nanaimo   (604)

RESTAURANTS & CAFES

Olde Firehall Coffee Roastery 34 Nichol St. Ste. 2 • 754-7733 • 9am-midnight, til 1am Fri-Sat • cafe • vegetarian • $5

Nelson   (604)

INFO LINES & SERVICES

Nelson Women's Center 507 Hall St. • 352-9916 • noon-4pm Tue, Wed, Fri

West Kootaney Gay/Lesbian Line Box 725, V1C 4C7 • 354-4297 • social group

ACCOMMODATIONS

Hestia's RR #3, S41, C23, V1L 5P6 • 229-5325 • women only • quiet retreat • all meals (vegetarian) • swimming • pets ok (call first)

Prince George   (604)

INFO LINES & SERVICES

GALA North 562-6253 • recorded info • social group

Teen Crisis Line 564-8336 • 4pm-11pm

ACCOMMODATIONS

Hawthorne B&B 829 P.G. Pulp Mill Rd. • 563-8299 • gay-friendly • full brkfst • $60-70

Prince Rupert   (604)

INFO LINES & SERVICES

Prince Rupert Gay Info Line 627-8900

Quesnel   (604)

INFO LINES & SERVICES

Women's Resource Center 690 Mclean St. • 992-8472 • 9am-4pm Mon-Fri

Revelstoke

INFO LINES & SERVICES

Lothlorien Box 8557, V0E 3G0 • info & referrals

Saltspring Island   (604)

ACCOMMODATIONS

The Blue Ewe 1207 Beddis Rd. • 537-9344 • lesbians/gay men • private on 5-1/2 acres • full brkfst • hot tub w/ ocean view • nudity ok

Green Rose Farm B&B 346 Robinson Rd., Ganges • 537-9927 • gay-friendly • heritage farm house • full brkfst • $95

Saltspring Driftwood Bed & Brunch 1982 N. End Rd. • 537-4137 • gay-friendly • miniature farm for art & animal lovers • kids/pets ok

Summerhill Guesthouse 209 Chu-An Dr. • 537-2727 • lesbians/gay men • on the water • full brkfst • $75-95

Sunnyside Up B&B 120 Andrew Pl. • 653-4889 • lesbians/gay men • panoramic views • full brkfst • hot tub • deck • $85

Tofino (604)

ACCOMMODATIONS

West Wind Guest House 1321 Pacific Rim Hwy. • 725-2224 • lesbians/gay men • private hideaway retreat • 5 min. from beach • hot tub • $105-125

Vancouver (604)

INFO LINES & SERVICES

AA Gay/Lesbian 434-3933/434-2553 (TDD)

The Gay and Lesbian Library 1170 Bute St. • 684-5309 • 7:30pm-9:30pm, from 4:30pm Mon, 3pm-6pm Wed • lending library at the Gay & Lesbian Centre

Vancouver Gay/Lesbian Centre 1170 Bute St. • 684-6869 • 11am-5pm, 7pm-10pm

Vancouver Lesbian Centre 876 Commercial Dr. • 254-8458 • 11am-6pm Th-Fri, noon-5pm Sat

Vancouver Women's Health Collective 1675 W. 8th Ave. Ste. 219 • 736-5262 • hours vary

Women & Sobriety 3080 Prince Edward St. • 434-3933 • 8pm Sun

ACCOMMODATIONS

The Albion Guest House 592 W. 19th Ave. • 873-2287 • lesbians/gay men • full brkfst • hot tub

Beach House 5834 Morgan Rd., Mirror Lake • 353-7676 • gay-friendly • private house on Lake Kootenay • weekly rental • near outdoor recreation • some shared baths • smokefree

Vancouver (604)

WHERE THE GIRLS ARE: In the West End, between Stanley Park and Gastown, or exploring the beautiful scenery elsewhere.

LESBIGAY PRIDE: August: 684-2633.

CITY INFO: Vancouver Travel Info Center: 683-2000.

ATTRACTIONS: Stanley Park. Gastown. Chinatown. Capilano Suspension Bridge. Wreck Beach (great gay beach).

BEST VIEW: Biking in Stanley Park, or on a ferry between peninsulas and islands. Atop one of the surrounding mountains.

WEATHER: Cold and wet in winter (30°s-40°s); absolutely gorgeous in summer (60°s-70°s)!

TRANSIT: Yellow Cab: 681-1111. Vancouver Airporter: 244-9888. A Visitors' Map of all bus lines is available through the tourist office listed below. B.C. Transit 521-0400.

The Buchan Hotel 1906 Haro St. • 685-5354/(800) 668-6654 • gay-friendly

Colibri B&B 1101 Thurlow St. • 689-5100 • gay-friendly • full brkfst • $85-120

Columbia Cottage 205 W. 14th Ave. • 874-5327 • gay-friendly • 1920s Tudor • full brkfst • IGTA • $70-110

Dufferin Hotel 900 Seymour St. • 683-4251 • gay-friendly • also restaurant • German/Canadian • 7am-2pm & 5pm-9pm • wheelchair access

French Quarter B&B 2051 W. 19th Ave. • 737-0973 • gay-friendly • cottages • full brkfst • swimming • gym • smokefree • French spoken

Heritage House Hotel 455 Abbott St. • 685-7777 • lesbians/gay men • 3 bars on premises • live shows

The Johnson House 2278 W. 34th Ave. • 266-4175 • gay-friendly • full brkfst • some shared baths • smokefree

Mountain B&B 258 E. Balmoral Rd. • 987-2725 • gay-friendly • full brkfst

Nelson House B&B 977 Broughton St. • 684-9793 • lesbians/gay men • full brkfst • jacuzzi en suite • IGTA • $78-140

River Run Cottages 4551 River Rd. W., Ladner • 946-7778 • gay-friendly • on the Fraser River • limited wheelchair access

Rural Roots 4939 Ross Rd. • 856-2380 • mostly gay men • full brkfst • swimming • wheelchair access • $30-50

▲ **The West End Guest House** 1362 Haro St. • 681-2889 • gay-friendly • 1906 historic Victorian • full brkfst • some veggie • $99-190

BARS

Celebrities 1022 Davie St. • 689-3180 • 9pm-2am, til midnight Sun • mostly gay men • women's night Sun • dancing/DJ

Chuck's Pub (at Heritage House Hotel) • 685-7777 • 11am-1:30am • lesbians/gay men • dancing/DJ • live shows • also 'Uncle Charlie's' • mostly gay men • live shows • beer/wine

Denman Station 860 Denman • 669-3448 • 7pm-2am, til midnight Sun • mostly gay men • more women Sun • neighborhood bar • dancing/DJ • live shows • karaoke • videos

Fly Girl 1545 W. 7th Ave. • 875-9907 • 9pm-2am every other Sat • popular • mostly women • dancing/DJ

Vancouver

J ust three hours north of Seattle, Vancouver is literally one of the most beautiful cities in the world. When the European colonizers charted the waters around Vancouver in 1792, these densely forested inlets were inhabited by Native American peoples whose distinctive art and cultural heritage still influence the city's character.

You can get a feel of how Vancouver used to be with a trip to **Stanley Park**, the largest park in North America. There you can enjoy the Aquarium, Zoo and famous carved Native American totem poles. **Gastown**, where Vancouver began in the 1860s, is now a lively, historic area with boutiques, antique shops, and a vast array of restaurants. Dining and shopping in this city are excellent, as are sailing, boating, and women-watching.

Dyke dancing machines should check out the women's nights at the city's many mixed bars—start out Friday at the **Lotus Club** women's night. Sundays are hot at **Celebrities**, **Denman Station**, and on alternate Sundays, try the **Riley Cafe** or **Fly Girl**.

Book-loving lesbians will be happy to know that one of the world's most beautiful cities has a women's bookstore, **Women in Print**, a lesbian/gay bookstore, **Little Sister's**, and several bookstores with lesbian studies sections. While you're at one, pick up a copy of **Kinesis**, the women's newsmagazine, **Xtra! West**, the local gay paper, or the aptly named **Lezzie Smut**. Speaking of smut, check out **Womyns' Ware** for all your erotica needs. The owners also organize women's dungeon parties; call the store for info on the next **Muffs & Cuffs** event.

Latté-lovers will enjoy the many cafes and vegetarians will fare well at **La Quena** co-op, or **O-Tooz**, the only vegetarian fast food place we know of. Those who love touring the potluck/support group circuit are also in luck. Vancouver has a good range of lesbian-friendly services, so inquire at the **Vancouver Gay/Lesbian Centre** for help in finding the perfect activity. And ask about their annual Lesbian Pride Week!

Lotus Club (at Heritage House Hotel) • 685-7777 • lesbians/gay men • women's night Fri • dancing/DJ

Ms. T's Cabaret 339 W. Pender St. • 682-8096 • 8pm-2am • lesbians/gay men • dancing/DJ • transgender-friendly • karaoke

Muffs & Cuffs 254-2543 • women only • dungeon play parties • call for dates & locations

Numbers 1042 Davie • 685-4077 • 8pm-2am, til midnight Sun • mostly gay men • dancing/DJ • live shows • videos

The Odyssey 1251 Howe St. • 689-5256 • 9pm-2am • popular • mostly gay men • dancing/DJ • alternative

Papa's Place 1025 Granville St. (at Royal Hotel) • 685-5335 • 11am-11pm • mostly gay men • neighborhood bar • live bands Wed-Sat

Shaggy Horse 818 Richards St. • 688-2923 • 8pm-2am, clsd Sun-Mon • lesbians/gay men • women's night Wed • dancing/DJ • leather on wknds

Twilite Zone 7 Alexander St. • 682-8550 • gay-friendly • more gay Tue & Sat • dancing/DJ • alternative • leather

RESTAURANTS & CAFES

The Alabaster 1168 Hamilton St., Yaletown • 687-1758 • Italian

Cafe S'il Vous Plaît 500 Robson St. • 688-7216 • 9am-10pm, clsd Sun • homecooking • plenty veggie • wheelchair access • $3-6

D.D.'s on Denman 1030 Denman • 688-6264 • noon-10pm, from 10am wknds • vegetarian • beer/wine • $6-10

Delilah's 1906 Haro St. • 687-3424 • 5:30pm-midnight • some veggie • wheelchair access • $16-26

Friends Cafe 1221 Thurlow St. • 685-0995 • 11am-11pm • lesbians/gay men

Hamburger Mary's 1202 Davie St. • 687-1293 • 6am-4am • neighborhood bar • some veggie • full bar • $5-10

Harry's 1716 Charles St. • 253-1789 • 8am-11pm Mon-Sat • 10am-11pm Sun • cafe • deli • wheelchair access

Isadora's 1540 Old Bridge St., Granville Island • 681-8816 • 9am-9pm • plenty veggie • beer/wine • cooperatively run

La Quena 1111 Commercial Dr. • 251-6626 • 11am-11pm • vegetarian • wheelchair access • $3-5

Lola's at the Century House 432 Richards St. • 684-5652 • great menu & atmosphere • full bar

Luxy Bistro 1235 Davie St. • 681-9976 • 9am-11pm • some veggie • wheelchair access

O-Tooz 1068 Davie St. • 689-0208 • 7am-midnight • lowfat vegetarian fast food

The Oasis 1240 Thurlow St. (upstairs) • 685-1724 • dinner, Sat & Sun brunch • int'l cuisine • piano bar • patio

Riley Cafe 1661 Granville St. • 684-3666 • 10:30am-11pm • BBQ • some veggie • full bar • also 'Riley T' • alternative lesbigay social night 1st & 3rd Sun • wheelchair access • $5-12

The Second Cup 1184 Denman • 669-2068 • 7am-midnight • pastries • wheelchair access

BOOKSTORES & RETAIL SHOPS

D&R Clothing 1112 Davie St. • 687-0937 • clubwear & underwear

Little Sister's 1238 Davie St. • 669-1753/(800) 567-1662 (in Canada only) • 10am-11pm • lesbigay

Return to Sender 1076 Davie St. • 683-6363 • 11am-9pm, noon-6pm Sun • cards & gifts • wheelchair access

Spartacus Books 311 W. Hastings • 688-6138 • 10am-8:30pm, noon-6pm wknds • progressive

State of Mind 1100 Davie St. • 682-7116 • designer queer clothes

Women in Print 3566 W. 4th Ave. • 732-4128 • 10am-6pm, noon-5pm Sun • women's • wheelchair access

TRAVEL & TOUR OPERATORS

English Bay Travel 1267 Davie St. • 687-8785 • IGTA

Progressive Travel Inc. 1120 Davie St. • 687-3837 • IGTA

Super Natural Adventures 626 West Pender St., Main flr. • 683-5101 • hiking & helicopter-hiking trips in Western & Northern Canada

Travel Clinic 669-3321/(800) 705-7454

SPIRITUAL GROUPS

Dignity PO Box 3016, V6B 3X5 • 432-1230

Integrity PO Box 2797, V6B 3X2 • 432-1230

MCC 3214 W. 10th (St. James) • 739-7959

PUBLICATIONS

Angles 1170 Bute St. #4-B • 688-0265

Diversity Magazine PO Box 47558, Coquitlam, V3K 6T3 • 937-7447 • pansexual fetish/fantasy zine

Kinesis 1720 Grant St. #301, V5L 2Y6 • 255-5499 • women's newsmagazine

Lezzie Smut 1027 Davie St. Box 364, V6E 4L2 • 252-6299 • lesbian erotica for all North America

▲ **Rainbow Choices Directory** 56 McMurray Ave., Toronto OT, M6P 2T1 • (416) 762-1320 • lesbigay entertainment & business directory for Canada

Xtra! West 1033 Davie St. #501 • 684-9696

EROTICA

Love's Touch 1069 Davie St. • 681-7024

Mack's Leathers 1043 Granville • 688-6225 • 11am-7pm

Next Body Piercing 1068 Granville St. • 684-6398

Womyns' Ware 896 Commercial Dr. • 254-2543 • hours vary, clsd Mon • toys • fetish wear

Vernon (604)

INFO LINES & SERVICES

Rural Lesbian Association Box 1242, V1T 6N6 • 542-7531

ACCOMMODATIONS

Rainbows End RR 3, Site 11, Box 178, V1T 6L6 • 542-4842 • lesbians/gay men • full brkfst • hot tub • some shared baths • pets ok • wheelchair access

Victoria (604)

INFO LINES & SERVICES

Gay/Lesbian AA 383-7744

Hot Flashes Women's Coffeehouse 106 Superior St. • 598-4900 • 8pm 3rd Fri

Island Gay/Lesbian Association Phone Line 598-4900 • 6pm-10:30pm

Prime Timers Victoria PO Box 45030, Mayfair PO, V8Z 7G9 • 727-6669 • 3pm 3rd Sun • group for gays 30+

ACCOMMODATIONS

The Back Hills 4470 Leefield • 478-9648 • women only • 30 min. from Victoria in the Metchosin Hills • full brkfst • near outdoor recreation • fireplaces • smokefree • pets ok • women-owned/run • $50

Claddagh House B&B 1761 Lee Ave. • 370-2816 • gay-friendly • full brkfst • $55-85

Hospitality Exchange 562 Simcoe St. #205, V8V 1L8 • 385-4945

Lavender Link 136 Medana St. • 380-7098 • gay-friendly • renovated 1912 character home • smokefree • kids 4+ yrs ok • wheelchair access • $60-75

Oak Bay Guest House 1052 Newport Ave. • 598-3812 • gay-friendly • beaches nearby

The Weekender B&B 10 Eberts St. • 389-1688 • June-Sept (wknds only Nov-May) • lesbians/gay men • seaside • smokefree • $80-95

BARS

BJ's Lounge 642 Johnson (enter on Broad) • 388-0505 • noon-1am • lesbians/gay men • lunch daily

BOOKSTORES & RETAIL SHOPS

Everywoman's Books 635 Johnson St. • 388-9411 • 10:30am-5:30pm, clsd Sun

Whistler (604)

ACCOMMODATIONS

The Whistler Retreat B&B 8561 Drifter Wy. • 938-9245 • lesbians/gay men • spacious alpine home • outdoor hot tub • sauna • mtn. views

Winfield (604)

ACCOMMODATIONS

Willow Lane 11571 Turtle Bay Ct. • 766-4807 • lesbians/gay men • full brkfst • near outdoor recreation

MANITOBA

Brandon   (204)

INFO LINES & SERVICES

Gays/Lesbians of Western Manitoba PO Box 22039, R7A 6Y9 • 727-4297 • 7pm-9pm Fri

Winnipeg   (204)

INFO LINES & SERVICES

Coming Out cable channel 11 • 9pm Fri

Gay/Lesbian Resource Center 1-222 Osborne St. • 284-5208 • office 1pm-4:30pm, info line 7:30pm-10pm Mon-Fri • French language info Wed

Lesbian Social Discussion Group (at Gay/Lesbian Resource Center) • call for time

New Freedom AA Group 300 Hugo at Mulvey (St. Michael & All Angels) • 942-0126 • 8:30pm Th, 3:30pm Sun

Prairie Rose Gender Group Box 3, Group 4, RR#1, Dugald, R0E 0K0 • 257-2759 • transgender social/support group

Women's Center 515 Portage Ave., U of Winnipeg, Graham Hall, 4th flr. • 786-9788 • drop-in resource center

Women's Resource Center 1088 Pembina Hwy. • 477-1123 • 9am-noon, 1pm-4:30pm Mon-Fri

ACCOMMODATIONS

Winged Ox Guest House 82 Spence St. • 783-7408 • gay-friendly • turn-of-the-century brick home • full brkfst • some veggie • smokefree • kids ok • pets ok (call first) • $35-50

BARS

Club 200 190 Garry St. • 943-6045 • 4pm-2am, clsd Sun • lesbians/gay men • dancing/DJ • live shows • dinner served • some veggie • $7-11

Gio's 272 Sherbrooke St. • 786-1236 • 9pm-2am, clsd Sun • mostly gay men • dancing/DJ • live shows • private club

Happenings 274 Sherbrooke St. (upstairs) • 774-3576 • 9pm-2am, til 3am Sat, clsd Sun • lesbians/gay men • dancing/DJ • live shows • private club

Heartland Social Club 298 Fort St. • 957-0591 • mostly gay men • food served • private club

Ms. Purdy's Women's Club 226 Main St. • 989-2344 • 8pm-2am, clsd Sun-Mon • women only • men welcome Fri • dancing/DJ • live shows • private club • women-owned/run

RESTAURANTS & CAFES

Times Change Blues Cafe 234 Main • 957-0982 • from 8pm Th-Sun • some veggie • live shows • under $6

BOOKSTORES & RETAIL SHOPS

Dominion News 263 Portage Ave. • 942-6563 • 8am-9pm, noon-6pm Sun • some gay periodicals

McNally Robinson 100 Osborne St. S. (at River) • 453-2644 • 9:30am-9:30pm, til 6pm Sat, noon-5pm Sun • some gay titles

SPIRITUAL GROUPS

Affirm 452-2853

Dignity PO Box 1912, R3C 3R2 • 772-4322 • 7:30pm 1st & 3rd Th • call for events

MCC St. Stephen's (on B'way & Kennedy) • 661-2219 • 7:30pm Sun

PUBLICATIONS

Perceptions PO Box 8581, Saskatoon SK, S7K 6K7 • (306) 244-1930 • covers the Canadian prairies

EROTICA

Unique Boutique 561 Portage Ave. • 775-5435 • 10am-midnight, til 10pm wknds

NEW BRUNSWICK

Fredericton   (506)

INFO LINES & SERVICES
Fredericton Gay Line 457-2156 • 6pm-9pm Mon & Th

BARS
Kurt's Dance Warehouse/Phoenix Rising 377 King St., 3rd flr. • 453-0740 • 8pm-1am • lesbians/gay men • dancing/DJ • wheelchair access

SPIRITUAL GROUPS
New Hope MCC 749 Charlotte St. (Unitarian Fellowship House) • 455-4622 • 7pm Sun

Miramichi   (506)

ACCOMMODATIONS
Fourth Generation B&B Box 126, Newcastle, E1U 3M3 • 622-3221/244-4411 • gay-friendly • dinner avail. • health retreat packages • deck • French spoken

Moncton

BARS
La Cave/Dans L'Fond 234 St. George St./Alexander (unverified for '97)
Triangles 234 St. George St. • 857-8779 • clsd Mon • lesbians/gay men • dancing/DJ

Sackville   (506)

ACCOMMODATIONS
Georgian House RR #3 • 536-1481 • seasonal • gay-friendly • 1840 home in quiet country setting • $45-50

St. John   (506)

ACCOMMODATIONS
Mahogany Manor 220 Germain St. • 636-8000 • gay-friendly • turn-of-the-century home • smokefree • $55-65

BARS
Bogarts 9 Sydney St. • 652-2004 • 8pm-2am, clsd Sun-Tue

NEWFOUNDLAND

Corner Brook   (709)

INFO LINES & SERVICES
Women's Resource Centre 2 West St. Box 373 • 639-8522

St. John's   (709)

INFO LINES & SERVICES
Gay/Lesbian Info Line 753-4297 • 7pm-10pm Th
Women's Centre 83 Military Rd. • 753-0220 • 9am-5pm Mon-Fri

BARS
Schroders Piano Bar 10 Bates Hill • 753-0807 • 4pm-1am, til 2am Fri-Sat, til midnight Sun • gay-friendly • also 'Zapata's' restaurant downstairs • Mexican • some veggie
Zone 216 216 Duckworth St. • 754-2492 • 8pm-2am, til midnight Sun • lesbians/gay men • dancing/DJ • wheelchair access

Stevenville   (709)

INFO LINES & SERVICES
Bay St. George Women's Centre 54 St. Clare Ave. • 643-4444

NOVA SCOTIA

Bear River (902)

ACCOMMODATIONS
Lovett Lodge Inn 1820 Main St. • 467-3917/(800) 341-6096 (in Canada only) • seasonal • 1892 Victorian doctor's residence • full brkfst • smokefree • kids ok • $40-44

Cheticamp (902)

ACCOMMODATIONS
Seashell Cabins Box 388 Cheticamp Beach Rd. • 224-3569 • seasonal • gay-friendly • housekeeping units on the ocean • lesbian-owned/run

Halifax (902)

INFO LINES & SERVICES
Gay/Lesbian/Bisexual Line 423-7129 • 7pm-10pm Th-Sat • also gay AA info
Queer News CKDU (97.5FM) • 494-6479

ACCOMMODATIONS
Centretown-ville B&B 2016 Oxford St. • 422-2380 • lesbians/gay men • 1920s style bungalow w/ front veranda • smokefree • French spoken
Fresh Start B&B 2720 Gottingen St. • 453-6616 • gay-friendly • small Victorian mansion near center of city • $45-70
Peggy's Cove c/o 107 Westwood Ave., Cranston RI, 02905 • (401) 461-4533 • seasonal • rental home • $500 wk

BARS
Reflections Cabaret 5184 Sackville St. • 422-2957 • noon-3:30am, from 4pm Sun • lesbians/gay men • dancing/DJ • food served • live shows • wheelchair access
The Stonewall Inn 1566 Hollis St. • 425-2166 • 11:30am-2am • lesbians/gay men • neighborhood bar • food served
The Studio Lounge 1537 Barrington St. • 423-6866 • 4pm-2am, 6pm-1am Sun • mostly gay men • dancing/DJ

RESTAURANTS & CAFES
The Daily Grind 5686 Spring Garden Rd. • 429-6397 • 7am-11pm • cafe & newsstand
Le Bistro 1333 South Park • 423-8428 • lunch & dinner • some veggie • full bar • wheelchair access • $7-13

BOOKSTORES & RETAIL SHOPS
Entitlement Book Sellers Lord Nelson Arcade • 420-0565 • 9:30am-10pm, noon-6pm Sun

Frog Hollow Books 5640 Spring Garden Rd., 2nd flr. • 429-3318
Red Herring Book Store 1578 Argyle St. • 422-5087 • 10am-6pm, til 9pm Th-Fri • lesbigay section
Schooner Books 5378 Inglis St. • 423-8419 • 9:30pm-6pm, til 9pm Fri, til 5:30pm Sat, clsd Sun • large selection of women's titles
Smith Books 5201 Duke St. (Scotia Sq.) • 423-6438 • 9:30am-6pm, til 9pm Th-Fri
Trident Booksellers & Cafe 1570 Argyle St. • 423-7100 • 8:30am-9pm

SPIRITUAL GROUPS
Safe Harbour MCC 5500 Inglis St. (church) • 453-9249

PUBLICATIONS
Wayves PO Box 34090 Scotia Sq., B3J 3S1 • 429-2661

EROTICA
Atlantic News 5560 Morris St. • 429-5468

Lunenburg (902)

ACCOMMODATIONS
Brook House 3 Old Blue Rocks Rd. • 634-3826 • gay-friendly • quiet retreat in Canada's oldest German town • $45-55

Shelburne (902)

ACCOMMODATIONS
The Toddle Inn 163 Water St. • 875-3229/(800) 565-0000 • seasonal • gay-friendly • restaurant & bar on premises • $50-70

Sydney (902)

INFO LINES & SERVICES
Women's Unlimited Feminist Association PO Box 368, B1P 4T1 • 564-5926

Yarmouth (902)

ACCOMMODATIONS
Murray Manor B&B 225 Main St. • 742-9625 • gay-friendly • early 19th century home • full brkfst

Ontario

Bancroft (613)

ACCOMMODATIONS

Greenview Guesthouse Box 1192, K0L 1C0 • 332-3922 • women only • country retreat • full brkfst & dinner • plenty veggie • hot tub • sauna

Brighton (613)

ACCOMMODATIONS

Butler Creek B&B RR 7, Hwy. 30, K0K 1H0 • 475-1248 • gay-friendly

Cambridge (519)

BARS

Robin's Nest 26 Hobston St. (in Farmers Bldg., Galt St. entrance) • 621-2688 • Tue, Fri-Sat only • mostly women • country/ western

Dutton (519)

ACCOMMODATIONS

Victorian Court B&B 235 Main St. • 762-2244 • lesbians/gay men • restored Victorian • smokefree • wheelchair access • $45-75

Fort Erie (905)

ACCOMMODATIONS

Whistle Stop Guesthouse 871-1265 • women only • all-inclusive weekends only • $125

Grand Valley (519)

ACCOMMODATIONS

Manfred's Meadow Guest House RR #1, L0N 1G0 • 925-5306 • lesbians/gay men • all meals included • swimming • sauna • spa • smokefree • $78-99

Guelph (519)

INFO LINES & SERVICES

Gay Line 836-4550

Guelph Queer Equality Box 773, N1H 6L8 • 824-4120x8575

BOOKSTORES & RETAIL SHOPS

Bookshelf Cafe 41 Quebec St. • 821-3311 • 9am-9pm, til 10pm Fri-Sat, 10:30am-3pm Sun (bar noon-1am) • popular • gay-friendly • also cinema & restaurant • some veggie • $5-10

Hamilton (905)

ACCOMMODATIONS

The Cedars Tent & Trailer Park 1039 5th Concession Rd. RR2, Waterdown • 659-3655/659-7342 • lesbians/gay men • private campground • swimming • also social club • dancing/DJ • karaoke • wknd restaurant • some veggie

BARS

Cafe 121 121 Hughson St. N. • 546-5258 • noon-1am • lesbians/gay men • 3 bars • dancing/DJ • also a restaurant • some veggie • $3-10

The Embassy Club 54 King St. E. • 522-7783 • 9pm-3am Fri-Sat • mostly gay men • dancing/DJ

Windsor Hotel 31 John St. N. • 522-5990 • 11am-1am • gay-friendly • lunch daily • some veggie • karaoke

BOOKSTORES & RETAIL SHOPS

The Women's Bookstop 333 Main St. W. • 10:30am-7pm, til 5pm Sat, clsd Sun

Jasper (613)

ACCOMMODATIONS

Starr Easton Hall PO Box 215 RR #3, K0G 1G0 • 283-7497 • gay-friendly • B&B-inn • full breakfast • also a restaurant • int'l fine dining • some veggie • full bar • live shows • wheelchair access • $60-80

Kingston (613)

INFO LINES & SERVICES

Lesbian/Gay/Bisexual Phoneline & Directory 531-8981 • 7pm-9pm Mon-Fri

BARS

Robert's Club Vogue 477 Princess St. • 547-2923 • 4pm-1am, til 3am Fri-Sat • popular • lesbians/gay men • dancing/DJ • alternative • food served

RESTAURANTS & CAFES

Chinese Laundry Cafe 291 Princess St. • 542-2282 • 10am-midnight, til 2am Fri-Sat • popular • cafe food & desserts • some veggie • $4-8

Kitchener (519)

BARS

Club Renaissance 24 Charles St. N. • 570-2406 • 9pm-3am • lesbians/gay men • dancing/DJ • food served • live shows

Club XTC 1 Queen St. N • 743-3016 • 9pm-1am • lesbians/gay men • dancing/DJ • wheelchair access

TRAVEL & TOUR OPERATORS

TCB Travel 600 Doon Village Rd. • 748-0850 • ask for Linda

London (519)

INFO LINES & SERVICES

AA Gay/Lesbian 649 Colborne (at Halo Club) • 7pm Mon & Wed • also at Bishop Cronin Church (downstairs) • 8pm Fri • mostly women

Gay Line 433-3551 • live 7pm-10pm Mon, Tue & Th

UW Out 432-3078 • 7:30pm-10pm Mon • lesbigay student group

BARS

52nd Street 347 Clarence St. • 679-4015 • 2pm-2am • lesbians/gay men • dancing/DJ • patio in summer • wheelchair access

Halo Club (Gay/Lesbian Community Center) 649 Colborne St. • 433-3762 • 7pm-midnight, 9pm-2am wknds • lesbians/gay men • last Fri women only • dancing/DJ • live shows • private club • wheelchair access • call for community center events • also monthly newsletter

The Junction 722 York St. • 438-2625 • 24hrs • mostly gay men • cabaret

RESTAURANTS & CAFES

Blackfriars Cafe 46 Blackfriars • 667-4930 • 10am-10pm • popular • lesbians/gay men • plenty veggie • full bar • $4-10

BOOKSTORES & RETAIL SHOPS

Mystic Book Shop 616 Dundas St. • 673-5440 • 11am-6pm, clsd Sun • spiritual

Womansline Books 573 Richmond St. • 679-3416 • 10am-5:30pm, til 6pm Fri, clsd Sun • lesbian/feminist

SPIRITUAL GROUPS

Dignity London PO Box 1884 Stn. A, N6A 5J4 • 686-7709 (evenings) • 7:30pm 2nd Mon • meets at Halo Club, 2nd flr.

Holy Fellowship MCC 442 Williams St. • 645-0744 • 7:20pm Sun

Maynooth (613)

ACCOMMODATIONS

Wildewood Guesthouse Box 121, K0L 2S0 • 338-3134 • lesbians/gay men • on 20 acres • all meals included • hot tub • swimming • kids ok by arr. • wheelchair access

North Bay (705)

INFO LINES & SERVICES

Gay/Lesbian/Bisexual North Bay Area Box 1362, P1B 8K5 • 495-4545 • 7pm-9pm Mon • social & support group • newsletter

Oshawa (905)

BARS

Club 717 7-717 Wilson Rd. S. • 434-4297 • 2am-2am Sat only • also referral service

Ottawa (613)

(See also **Hull, PQ**)

INFO LINES & SERVICES

237-XTRA 237-9872 • touch-tone lesbigay visitors' info

Gayline/Télégai 238-1717 • 7pm-10pm • French & English spoken

Lambda Line 233-8212 • business/professional group

Pink Triangle Services 71 Back St. (above McD's) • 563-4818 • many groups & services

Women's Place 241 Bruyere St. • 789-2155 • 9am-4pm Mon-Fri • drop-in center

ACCOMMODATIONS

Gabrielle's Guesthouse 40 Gilmour St. • 237-0829 • women only • smokefree • reservations required

Rideau View Inn 177 Frank St. • 236-9309/(800) 268-2082 • gay-friendly • full brkfst • $55-75

The Stonehouse B&B 2605 Yorks Corners • 821-3822 • lesbians/gay men • $60

BARS

Camp B Tavern/Pride Disco 363 Bark St. • 237-0708 • 11am-2am, disco from 9pm • lesbians/gay men • neighborhood bar • dancing/DJ • food served

Centretown Pub 340 Somerset St. W. • 594-0233 • 2pm-1am • lesbians/gay men • dancing/DJ • food served • videos • leather bar upstairs • piano bar downstairs • Th-Sat

Coral Reef Club 30 Nicholas • 234-5118 • Fri-Sat only • more women Fri • dancing/DJ

Icon 366 Lisgar St. • 8pm-3am, clsd Sun-Wed • lesbians/gay men • neighborhood bar • dancing/DJ • also a restaurant

Le Club 77 Wellington, Hull PQ • (819) 777-1411 • 10pm-3am • popular • lesbians/gay men • dancing/DJ

Market Station 15 George St. (downstairs) • 562-3540 • noon-1am, from 11am Sun (brunch) • gay-friendly

RESTAURANTS & CAFES

Alfonsetti's 5830 Hazeldern, Stittsville • 831-3008 • noon-11pm, from 5pm Sat, clsd Sun • Italian • plenty veggie • $12-22

Blue Moon Cafe 311 Bank • 230-1239 • 10am-midnight • French • veggie on request • $5-15

Cafe Deluxe 283 Dalhousie St. • 241-4279 • 4pm-1am, from noon wknds

Manfred's 2280 Carling Ave. • 829-5715 • 5pm-10pm • European • some veggie • full bar • $10-16

The News 284 Elgin • 567-6397 • noon-midnight • some veggie • wheelchair access • $6-18

BOOKSTORES & RETAIL SHOPS

After Stonewall 105 4th Ave., 2nd flr. • 567-2221 • 10am-6pm, til 7pm Fri, noon-4pm Sun • lesbigay bookstore

Food for Thought Books 103 Clarence St. • 562-4599 • 10am-10pm

Mags & Fags 286 Elgin St. • 233-9651 • gay periodicals

Mother Tongue Books/Femmes de Parole 1067 Bark St. • 730-2346 • women's

Octopus Books 798 Bank St. • 235-2589 • 10am-6pm, til 9pm Th-Fri, noon-5pm Sun • progressive

Ottawa Women's Bookstore & Gift Gallery 272 Elgin St. • 230-1156 • 10am-6pm, til 9pm Th-Fri, noon-5pm Sun

SPIRITUAL GROUPS

Dignity Ottawa Dignité 386 Bank St. • 746-7279

MCC of Ottawa Somerset & Elgin (St. John's Anglican Church) • (800) 786-6622 • 4pm Sun

PUBLICATIONS

Capital Xtra! 303-177 Nepean St. • 237-7133

▲ **Rainbow Choices Directory** 56 McMurray Ave., Toronto, M6P 2T1 • (416) 762-1320 • lesbigay entertainment & business directory for Canada

Peterborough   (705)

ACCOMMODATIONS

Windmere Selwyn RR#3, Lakefield, K0L 2H0 • 652-6290/(800) 465-6327 • gay-friendly • full brkfst • sauna

Port Sydney   (705)

ACCOMMODATIONS

Divine Lake Resort RR1, Box XD3, P0B 1L0 • 385-1212/(800) 263-6600 • lesbians/gay men • resort • also cottages • brkfst & dinner included • swimming • nudity • also restaurant • some veggie • wheelchair access • IGTA • US$72-96

Sault Ste. Marie   (705)

BARS

The Warehouse 196 James St. • 759-1903 • 4pm-2:30am • lesbians/gay men • dancing/DJ • live shows • afterhours

Stratford   (519)

ACCOMMODATIONS

Anything Goes B&B 107 Huron St. • 273-6557 • gay-friendly • full veggie brkfst • smokefree • kids ok by arr. • $45-90

Burnside Guest Home 139 William St. • 271-7076 • gay-friendly • on Lake Victoria • full brkfst • hot tub • $25-65

The Maples of Stratford 220 Church St. • 273-0810 • gay-friendly • smokefree • $50-90

BARS

Old English Parlour 101 Wellington St. • 271-2772 • 11:30am-1am, from 10:30am Sun (brunch) • gay-friendly • some veggie • wheelchair access • $10-16

RESTAURANTS & CAFES

Down the Street 30 Ontario St. • 273-5886 • noon-11pm • Mediterranean/Mexican • full bar • live shows • $10-12

BOOKSTORES & RETAIL SHOPS

Fanfare Books 92 Ontario St. • 273-1010 • 9:30am-8pm, til 5:30pm Mon, til 5pm Sun

Sudbury   (705)

BARS

D-Bar 83 Cedar St. • 670-1189 • 8pm-1am • lesbians/gay men • dancing/DJ • live shows

Thunder Bay   (807)

INFO LINES & SERVICES

Northern Women's Center 184 Camelot St. • 345-7802 • 9:30am-5pm Mon-Fri

Toronto (416)

INFO LINES & SERVICES

519 Church St. Community Center 519 Church St. • 392-6874 • 9:30am-10:30pm, noon-5pm wknds • location for numerous events • wheelchair access

925-XTRA 925-9872 • touch-tone lesbigay visitors' info

AA Gay/Lesbian 487-5591 • extensive schedule

Canadian Lesbian/Gay Archives 86 Temperance St. • 777-2755 • 7:30pm-10pm Tue-Th

Durham Alliance Association PO Box 914, Oshawa, L1H 7H1 • 434-4297 • info • also 'Club 717' social group

Flashline 462-7540 • DJ Denise Benson's women's event line

Lesbigay Youth Line 962-9688/(800) 268-9688

Toronto Area Gay/Lesbian Phone Line 964-6600 • 7pm-10pm Mon-Sat • counseling

Transsexual Transition Support Group 519 Church St. • 925-9872x2121 • 7pm-10pm 2nd & 4th Fri • for all members of the gender community & their significant others

Two-Spirited People of the First Nations 2 Carlton St. Ste. 1006 • 944-9300 • lesbi-gay Native group

Women's Center 49 St. George St. (Univ. of Toronto) • 978-8201 • pro-lesbian center • call for times

Women's Counseling Referral Center 525 Bloor St. W. • 534-7501

ACCOMMODATIONS

Acorn House B&B 255 Donlands Ave. • 463-8274 • mostly gay men

Allenby B&B 223 Strathmore Blvd. • 461-7095 • gay-friendly

Amblecote B&B 109 Walmer Rd. • 927-1713 • lesbians/gay men • reservations required • full brkfst • smokefree • IGTA • $55-65

Catnaps Guesthouse 246 Sherbourne St. • 968-2323/(800) 205-3694 • lesbians/gay men

▲ **Dundonald House** 35 Dundonald St. • 961-9888/(800) 260-7227 • lesbians/gay men • full brkfst • hot tub

Hotel Selby 592 Sherbourne St. • 921-3142/(800) 387-4788 • lesbians/gay men • popular • Victorian tourist class hotel • swimming • IGTA • from $50

Toronto (416)

LESBIGAY INFO: 519 Church St. Community Center: 392-6874. Toronto Area Gay/Lesbian Phone Line: 964-6600, 7pm-10pm Mon-Sat. Xtra! Gay/Lesbian Info Line: 925-9872 (touchtone info).

LESBIGAY PAPER: Xtra!: 925-6665.

WHERE THE GIRLS ARE: On Parliament St. or elsewhere in "The Ghetto," south of Bloor St. W., between University Ave. and Parliament St.

LESBIGAY AA: AA Gay/Lesbian: 487-5591.

LESBIGAY PRIDE: July: 214-0232.

CITY INFO: 203-2500.

ATTRACTIONS: Eaton Square. CN Tower. Nation Phillips Square. Royal Ontario Museum.

BEST VIEW: Sightseeing air tour or a three-masted sailing ship tour.

WEATHER: Summers are hot (upper 80°s-90°s) and humid. Spring is gorgeous. Fall brings cool, crisp days. Winters are cold and snowy just like you imagined they would be in Canada!

TRANSIT: Metro Cab: 364-8161. Grey Coach: 393-7911. Transit Informa-tion: 393-4636.

Huntley House 65 Huntley St. • 923-6950 • gay-friendly

Mike's on Mutual 333 Mutual St. • 944-2611 • mostly gay men • B&B-private home • full brkfst • smokefree • $50-65

Palmerston B&B 322 Palmerston Blvd. • 920-7842 • gay-friendly • popular • IGTA • $45-65

Seaton Pretty 327 Seaton St. • 972-1485 • gay-friendly • full brkfst

▲ **Ten Cawthra Square B&B** 10 Cawthra Sq. • 966-3074/259-5474 • lesbians/gay men • in heart of gay Toronto • shared baths • fireplaces • smokefree • pets ok • gay owned/run

Toronto

*T*oronto, the capital city of Ontario, is the cultural and financial center of eastern Canada. Though it's not far from Buffalo, New York and Niagara Falls, Toronto has a European ambiance fostered by its eclectic architecture and peaceful diversity of cultures.

Restaurants and shops from Asia, India, Europe, and many other points on the globe attract natives and tourists alike to the exotic Kensington Market (buy your fresh groceries here), the malls of **Eaton Centre**, and the crafts and antiques available at the Harbourfront. Toronto's Chinatown is just north of funky shops and artsy cafes on Queen St. West.

For intrepid shoppers, Toronto has a lot to offer. **Out in the Street** carries lesbigay accessories. Big, beautiful femmes can check out **Take a Walk on the Wild Side** for larger-size finery. The **Omega Centre** is the place for metaphysical literature and supplies.

Toronto is also well-known for its repertory film scene, so try not to miss the two-week Lesbian/Gay Film Fest in the spring, or the film Festival of Festivals in September. In April, Toronto has two weeks of leather pride events, culminating in the Ms. & Mr. Leather Toronto contest. On Christmas Eve, get a seat at the MCC's annual service—the largest in the city!

Any other time of year, you'll find the women hanging out at **Tango** or at **Rose Cafe**—unless it's Friday night, when they might be at **Oz**. To find out about the latest women's nights, check out the weekly **Xtra!**, available at the **Toronto Women's Bookstore**, among other places.

Toronto B&B 588-8800 • gay-friendly • contact for various B&Bs

Winchester Guesthouse 35 Winchester St. • 929-7949 • lesbians/gay men

BARS

Aztec/Tango 2 Gloucester St. • 975-8612 • 11am-2am • lesbians/gay men • dancing/DJ • food served • 'Aztec' dance club Th-Sun • 'Tango' women's bar open from 4pm

Bar 501 501 Church • 944-3163 • 11am-1am • lesbians/gay men • more women Sun & Tue • neighborhood bar

Barn 83 Granby • 977-4684 • 9pm-1am, til 4am Fri-Sat • popular • mostly gay men • dancing/DJ • leather • also 'Stables' • 977-4702 • 8pm-1am, til 4am Fri-Sat • mostly gay men • women's night Th • food served

The Black Eagle 459 Church St. (upstairs) • 413-1219 • 4pm-1am, from 2pm Sat, from noon Sun (brunch) • mostly gay men • leather • theme nights • also a restaurant

Blue Atlantis Bar & Cafe 2318 Danforth Ave. • 422-0766 • 4pm-1am • lesbians/gay men

Bulldog Cafe 457 Church St. • 923-3469 • noon-2am • lesbians/gay men • neighborhood bar • also a restaurant • homecooking • $8-12

Catch 22 379 Adelaide St. W. • 703-1583 • 9pm-3am, clsd Sun-Tue • gay-friendly • dancing/DJ

Crews/Ghetto Fag 508 Church • 972-1662 • noon-3am • mostly gay men • food served • wheelchair access

El Convento Rico 750 College St. • 588-7800 • 8pm-4am Wed-Sun, clsd Mon • mostly gay men • dancing/DJ • Latin/salsa music • mostly Latino-American • live shows

Jax 619 Yonge St., 2nd flr. • 922-3068 • 11am-1am • mostly gay men • neighborhood bar

Oz/Emerald City 15 Mercer St. • 506-8686 • lesbians/gay men • women's night Fri • dancing/DJ • 18+

The Playground 11-A St. Joseph St. • 923-2595 • 12:30am-4am, from 11pm Fri-Sat, clsd Mon • lesbians/gay men • dancing/DJ

Queen's Head Pub 263 Gerrard St. E. • 929-9525 • 3pm-1am • gay-friendly • neighborhood bar • food served • patio • wheelchair access

Rose Cafe 547 Parliament • 928-1495 • 5pm-1am • mostly women • dancing/DJ • live shows • food served • some veggie • women-owned/run • $5-10

Trax V 529 Yonge St. • 963-5196 • 11am-1am • popular • mostly gay men • dancing/DJ • piano bar • live shows • food served • wheelchair access

Whiskey Saigon 250 Richmond • 593-4646 • 10pm-2am Th-Sun • gay-friendly • dancing/DJ • live shows

Woody's 467 Church • 972-0887 • noon-2am • popular • mostly gay men • neighborhood bar • wheelchair access

RESTAURANTS & CAFES

Archer's 796 St. Clair Ave. W. • 656-7335 • 5:30pm-10pm, clsd Mon • fixed cont'l menu • $15 & up

The Babylon 553 Church St. • 923-2626 • til 4am, 11am-4pm Sun (brunch)

Bistro 422 422 College St. • 963-9416 • 4pm-midnight

Byzantium 499 Church St. • 922-3859 • 5:30pm-1am • eastern Mediterranean • full bar

Cafe Diplomatico 594 College • 534-4637 • 8am-1am • popular • brkfst • in the center of Little Italy

Cafe Jambalaya 501 Yonge St. • 922-5262 • Cajun, Caribbean & vegetarian

Cafe Volo 587 Yonge St. • 928-0008 • 11am-10pm, bar til 1am • Italian • some veggie • $9-13

The Courtyard (at Hotel Selby) • 921-0665 • open May-Sept • full bar • patio

Il Fornello 1560 Yonge • 920-8291 • Italian • plenty veggie • also 486 Bloor W. • 588-9358 • also 576 Danforth Ave. • 466-2931

La Hacienda 640 Queen W. • 703-3377 • lunch & dinner • Mexican • sleazy, loud & fun

The Living Well 692 Yonge St. • 922-6770 • noon-1am, til 3am Fri-Sat • plenty veggie • full bar • $8-12

The Mango 580 Church St. • 922-6525 • 11am-1am • popular • lesbians/gay men • also Sun brunch

Pints 518 Church St. • 921-8142 • 11:30am-1am • plenty veggie • neighborhood bar • $6-8

PJ Mellon's 489 Church St. • 966-3241 • 11am-11pm • Thai/cont'l • some veggie • wheelchair access • $7-12

Rivoli Cafe 332 Queen St. W. • 597-0794 • 11:30am-11pm, bar til 1am • int'l • some veggie • $8-12

The Second Cup 548 Church St. (Wellesley) • 964-2457 • 24hrs • popular • coffee/desserts

Trattoria Al Forno 459 Church St. • 944-8852

BOOKSTORES & RETAIL SHOPS

A Different Booklist 746 Bathurst St. • 538-0889 • 10am-10pm • multi-racial titles & authors

Ex Libris 467 Church St., 2nd flr. • 975-0580 • 11am-9pm, til 6pm Wed, from 10am Sat, from noon Sun • new & used lesbigay books

Glad Day Bookshop 598-A Yonge St. • 961-4161 • 10am-9pm, noon-8pm Sun • lesbigay

The Omega Centre 29 Yorkville Ave. • 975-9086/(888) 663-6377(in Canada) • 10am-9pm, til 5pm wknds • metaphysical books & supplies

Out in the Street 551 Church St. • 967-2759/(800) 263-5747 • lesbigay accessories

Take a Walk on the Wide Side 161 Gerrard St. E. • 921-6112 • 10am-7pm, til 11pm Sat • drag emporium

This Ain't The Rosedale Library 483 Church St. • 929-9912 • 10am-7pm

Toronto Women's Bookstore 73 Harbord St. • 922-8744 • 10:30am-6pm, til 7pm Fri, noon-6pm Sun

Volumes 74 Front St. E. • 366-9522 • large selection of int'l periodicals

TRAVEL & TOUR OPERATORS

La Fabula Travel & Tours Inc. 551 Church St. • 920-3229/(800) 667-2475

Talk of the Town Travel 565 Sherbourne St. • 960-1393 • IGTA

Toronto Convention & Visitors Association PO Box 126, 207 Queen's Quay W., M5J 1A7 • (800) 363-1990

SPIRITUAL GROUPS

Christos MCC 353 Sherbourne St. (St. Luke's United Church) • 925-7924 • 7pm Sun

Congregation Keshet Shalom 925-9872x2073/925-1408 • call for events

Dignity Toronto Dignité 11 Earl St. • 925-9872x2011 • 6:30pm 2nd & 4th Sat

Integrity Toronto PO Box 873, Stn. F, M4Y 2N9 • 925-9872x2050/(905) 273-9860 • monthly mtgs • call for time/location

MCC Toronto 115 Simpson Ave. • 406-6228 • 9am, 11am & 7pm Sun

PUBLICATIONS

Fab 25 Wood St. Ste. 104, M4Y 2P9 • 599-9273

The Pink Pages 392 King St. E. • 864-9132 • annual lesbigay directory

▲ **Rainbow Choices Directory** 56 McMurray Ave., M6P 2T1 • 762-1320 • lesbigay entertainment & business directory for Canada

▲ **Sorority Magazine** 1170 Bay St. Ste. 110 • 324-2225 • lesbian publication for Canada & US (see ad in front color section)

Women's Press 517 College St. Ste. 233 • 921-2425 • lesbian/feminist book publisher • catalog avail.

Xtra! 100 Wellesley St. E. #104 • 925-6665

EROTICA

Allure 357-1/2 Yonge St. • 597-3953 • leather • toys • magazines

Doc's Leather & Latex 726 Queen • 504-8888 • call for appt • fetish clothes • toys • fantasy equipment

North Bound Leather 19 St. Nicholas St. • 972-1037 • 10am-7:30pm, noon-5pm Sun • toys • clothing • wheelchair access

Passage Body Piercing 473 Church St. • 929-7330 • 11am-7pm • tattoos • piercing • scarification

Priape 465 Church St. • 586-9914 • 11am-7pm, til 9pm Th-Sat • lesbigay toys • leather

Studio Auroboros 580 Yonge St. • 962-7499 • noon-8pm • body ornaments & piercing

Trenton   (613)

ACCOMMODATIONS

Devonshire House B&B RR #4 (Hwy. 2 West), K8V 5P7 • 399-1851 • gay-friendly • Italianate-style red brick farmhouse ca. 1875 • full brkfst • $38-48

Whitby   (905)

BARS

The Bar 110 Dundas St. W. • 666-3121 • 8pm-3am, clsd Mon-Wed • lesbians/gay men • dancing/DJ

Windsor   (519)

INFO LINES & SERVICES

Lesbian/Gay/Bisexual Phone Line 973-4951 • 8pm-10pm Th-Fri

BARS

Club Happy Tap Tavern 1056 Wyandotte St. E. • 256-8998/256-2737 • 2pm-1am, from 4pm Sun • lesbians/gay men • more women Sun • dancing/DJ • live shows

Silhouettes 1880 Wyandotte St. E. • 252-0887 • 4pm-1am, from 11am wknds • lesbians/gay men • neighborhood bar • different meaty entrees nightly & Sun brunch

SPIRITUAL GROUPS

MCC Windsor 977-6897 • 7pm Sun • call for location

PRINCE EDWARD ISLAND

Charlottetown   (902)

INFO LINES & SERVICES

Women's Network Box 233, C1A 7K4 • 368-5040 • also publishes feminist magazine 'Common Ground'

ACCOMMODATIONS

Blair Hall Vernon Bridge • 651-2202/(800) 268-7005 • gay-friendly • home w/ Old World charm on Orwell Bay • 15 min. outside of town • $45-50

Charlottetown Hotel PO Box 159, C1A 7K4 • 894-7371 • gay-friendly • swimming • also a restaurant • cont'l/seafood • lounge clsd Sun • $10-25

BARS

Baba's Lounge 81 University Ave. • 892-7377 • 5pm-2am • gay-friendly • also a restaurant • opens 11am • Canadian/Lebanese • some veggie

Doc's Corner 185 Kent St. • 566-1069 • 11am-2am • gay-friendly • also 'Hillard's Dining Room' • some veggie • live shows • wheelchair access

BOOKSTORES & RETAIL SHOPS

Book Mark 172 Queen St. (in mall) • 566-4888 • 8:30am-9pm • will order lesbian titles

PUBLICATIONS

Gynergy Books/Ragweed Press Box 2023, C1A 7N7 • 566-5750 • feminist press

Summerside   (902)

INFO LINES & SERVICES

East Prince Women's Info Center 75 Central St. • 436-9856 • 9am-4pm Mon-Fri

PROVINCE OF QUEBEC

Chicoutimi (418)

BARS

Bar Rosco 70 W. rue Racine • 698-5811 • 3pm-3am • mostly gay men

Drummondville (819)

INFO LINES & SERVICES

Women's Resource (Maison des Femmes) 102 rue St-George • 477-5957 • some lesbian info

ACCOMMODATIONS

Motel Alouette 1975 Boul. Mercure • 478-4166 • gay-friendly

Hull (613)

(See also **Ottawa, OT**)

BARS

Le Pub de Promenade 175 Promenade de Portage • 771-8810 • 11am-3am • popular • lesbians/gay men • neighborhood bar • dancing/DJ

Joliette (514)

ACCOMMODATIONS

L'Oasis des Pins 381 boul. Brassard, St. Paul de Joliette • 754-3819 • gay-friendly • swimming • camping April-Sept • restaurant open year-round

Laval (514)

INFO LINES & SERVICES

Comité des Gaies/Lesbiennes Montmorency 475 boul. de L'Avenir, N74 5H9

EROTICA

Boutique Carrefour du Sexe 1735 Blvd. Labelle • 688-6969

Mont-Tremblant (819)

ACCOMMODATIONS

Versant Ouest B&B 110 Chemin Labelle • 425-6615/(800) 425-6615 • lesbians/gay men • country home near skiing • full brkfst • $56-80

Montréal (514)

INFO LINES & SERVICES

AA Gay/Lesbian 4024 Hingston Ave. (church) • 376-9230 • 7pm Tue & 7:30pm Th

FACT (Federation of American & Canadian Transsexuals) C.P. 293 Succ., Côte des Neiges, H3S 2S6

Gai Ecoute 521-1508 • gay info line 'en français' • 7pm-11pm

Gay Line 990-1414 • 6:30pm-10pm

Gay/Lesbian Community Center of Montréal 2035 Amherst St. • 528-8424 • 9am-9pm, clsd wknds

Women's Center of Montréal 3585 St-Urbain • 842-4780 • 9am-5pm Mon, Wed-Fri, til 9pm Tue • wheelchair access

ACCOMMODATIONS

Angelica B&B 1074 Ste-Dominique • 875-5270 • gay-friendly

Au Bon Vivant Guest House 1648 Amherst • 525-7744 • popular • lesbians/gay men • IGTA • $49-79

Auberge de la Fontaine 1301 Rachel St. est • 597-0166/(800) 597-0597 • gay-friendly • full brkfst • wheelchair access • $89-175

Auberge Encore 53 rue Milton • 483-0834 • lesbians/gay men

Canadian Accommodations Network Box 42-A Stn. M, H1Z 3L6 • 254-1250 • accommodation reservation service

Chateau Cherrier 550 Cherrier St. • 844-0055/(800) 816-0055 • lesbians/gay men • full gourmet brkfst • $50-75

Ginger Bread House 1628 St-Christophe • 597-2804 • mostly gay men • IGTA

Hébergement touristique du Plateau Mont-Royal 1301 Rue Rachel est • 597-0166/(800) 597-0597 • gay-friendly • B&B network/reservation service

Home Suite Hom PO Box 762 Succ. C, H2L 4L6 • 523-4642 • home exchange

Hotel Américain 1042 St-Denis • 849-0616 • gay-friendly • kitchen • private/shared bath • gay-owned/run

Hotel du Parc 3625 Parc Ave. • 288-6666 • gay-friendly • IGTA

Hotel Kent 1216 rue St-Hubert • 845-9835 • gay-friendly

Hotel Le St-Andre 1285 rue St-Andre • 849-7070 • lesbians/gay men

Hotel Lord Berri 1199 rue Berri • 845-9236 • gay-friendly • also a restaurant • Italian/cont'l • wheelchair access

Hotel Manoir des Alpes 1245 rue St-André • 845-9803 • gay-friendly

Hotel Pierre 169 Sherbrooke est • 288-8519 • gay-friendly

Hotel Vogue 1425 rue de la Montagne • 285-5555/(800) 465-6654 • popular • gay-friendly • full service upscale hotel • also a restaurant

King of Diamonds 1637 Amherst, M2L 3L4 • lesbians/gay men • shared/private baths • patio • skylight • antiques • gay owned/run

La Douillette 7235 de Lorimier St. • 376-2183 • women only • full brkfst • cat on premises • $40-60

Le Chasseur Guest House 1567 rue St-André • 521-2238 • mostly gay men • 1920s European townhouse • summer terrace

Le Pension Vallieres 6562 de Lorimer St. • 729-9552 • women only • full brkfst • $60

Lesbian/Gay Hospitality Exchange International PO Box 612, Stn. C, H2L 4K5 • 523-1559 • membership accommodations exchange

Lindsey's B&B 3974 Laval Ave. • 843-4869 • popular • women only • full brkfst • $55-75

Ronnie's B&B 781 rue Guy • 939-1443 • women only

Turquoise B&B 1576 rue Alexandre de Sève • 523-9943 • gay-friendly • shared baths • $50-60

Bars

Bistro 4 4040 St-Laurent (Duluth) • 844-6246 • 9am-midnight, til 2am wknds • lesbians/gay men • food served • cafe

Cabaret Sapho 2017 Frontenac St. • 523-0292 • 9pm-3am • mostly women • live shows

Cafe Fetiche 1426 Beaudry • 523-3013 • noon-3am • mostly women

Campus 1111 Ste-Catherine est, 2nd flr. • 526-9867 • 7pm-3am • mostly gay men • women's night Sun • live shows

Citibar 1603 Ontario est • 525-4251 • 11am-3am • lesbians/gay men • neighborhood bar

City Pub 3820 St-Laurent • 499-8519 • 11am-3am • gay-friendly • beer/wine • food served

Club Date 1218 Ste-Catherine est • 521-1242 • 3pm-3am • gay-friendly • neighborhood bar

Montréal   (514)

Lesbigay Info: Centre Communitaire des Gais et Lesbiennes: 528-8424. Women's Center of Montréal: 842-4780, 9am-5pm. Gay Info Line: 990-1414 (English), 521-1508 (French).

Lesbigay Paper: Fugues/Gazelle: 848-1854.

Where the Girls Are: In the popular Plateau Mont-Royal neighborhood, or in the bohemian area on Ste-Catherine est.

Lesbigay AA: 376-9230.

Lesbigay Pride: July: 285-4011.

City Info: Province of Québec Visitors Bureau: (800) 363-7777.

Attractions: Latin Quarter.

Montréal Museum of Fine Arts. Old Montréal & Old Port. Olympic Park. Underground City.

Best View: From a *caleche* ride (horse-drawn carriage), or from the patio of the old hunting lodge atop Mont Royal (the mountain in Parc du Mont-Royal).

Weather: It's north of New England so winters are for real. Beautiful spring and fall colors. Summers get hot and humid.

Transit: Diamond Cab: 273-6331. Aero-bus (airport shuttle): 476-1100. Montréal Urban Transit: 280-5100. Autobus: 288-6287.

K.O.X. 1450 Ste-Catherine est • 523-0064 • 3pm-3am • popular • lesbians/gay men • dancing/DJ • live shows

L' Exit 4297 St-Denis • 2pm-2am • women only • neighborhood bar • beer only

La California 1412 Ste-Elizabeth • 843-8533 • 3pm-1am • popular • lesbians/gay men • neighborhood bar • also a restaurant • patio

Le St-Sulpice 1680 St-Denis • 844-9458 • noon-3am • gay-friendly • dancing/DJ

Lézard 4177 St-Denis & Rachel, 2nd flr. • 289-9819 • 11pm-3am • gay-friendly • more gay Tue • dancing/DJ

Max 1166 Ste-Catherine est • 598-5244 • 3pm-3am • popular • mostly gay men • dancing/DJ

Montréal

*M*ontréal is the world's second-largest French-speaking city, and Canada's most cosmopolitan city.

There is much to see and do here. You'll discover the Place Ville-Marie, an immense underground shopping promenade. Theatre, dance and music companies as well as a celebrated symphony orchestra all thrive in this historic city. You should also visit the **Latin Quarter** and Old Montréal, or come during the World Film Festival (end of August), or bike the cycling paths along the river banks.

Montréal also has a strong women's community, with three women's guesthouses, several women's bars, a lesbian/gay bookstore and a variety of women's services through the **Women's Center**. Montréal is home to many women's bars: **Cabaret Sapho, P-Town, ♀' Side, Sisters**, and women-only **L'Exit**. You can't help but have a wonderful time in this city.

Just remember that the people of Québec are proud of their French heritage and language. So brush up on your high school French before you go, if you want to make friends and avoid embarrassment. If you don't speak any French, your first question to any natives should be, "Do you speak English?"

Meteor 1661 Ste. Catherine est • 523-1481 • 11am-3am • lesbians/gay men • dancing/DJ • food served

♀ **Side** 4075-B St-Denis • 849-7126 • 1pm-2am • women only • neighborhood bar • also a restaurant

P-Town 1364 Ste-Catherine, 2nd flr. • 524-1584 • 2pm-3am • popular • mostly women • neighborhood bar • dancing/DJ • patio

Paco Paco 451 Rachel est • 499-0210 • 4pm-3am • lesbians/gay men • neighborhood bar

Playground/Groove Society 1296 rue Amherst • 284-2266 • 2am-10am Sun • 'Groove Society' 10pm Th only • mostly gay men

Pub du Village 1366 Ste-Catherine est • 524-1960 • 9am-3am • popular • lesbians/gay men • food served

Sister's 1456 Ste-Catherine est • popular • mostly women • dancing/DJ • live shows

Sky 1474 Ste-Catherine est • 10pm-3am • popular • lesbians/gay men • more women Th • dancing/DJ • alternative

Taverne Plateau 71 Ste-Catherine est • 843-6276 • 9am-midnight • gay-friendly

RESTAURANTS & CAFES

Après le Jour 901 Rachel est • 527-4141 • Italian/seafood

Cafe Titannic 445 St-Pierre • 849-0894 • 7am-5pm, clsd wknds • popular • salad & soup

Callipyge 1493 Amherst • 522-6144 • 5pm-11pm, clsd Mon-Tue • Québécois cuisine • popular Sun brunch

Cantarelli 2181 Ste-Caterine est • 521-1817 • Italian

Chablis 1639 St-Hubert • 523-0053 • Spanish/French • some veggie • full bar • patio

Chez Better 1310 De Maisonneuve • 525-9832 • European sausages/great french fries • beer/wine • patio

Commensal 400 Sherbrooke est (St-Denis) • vegetarian

Da Salossi 3441 St-Denis • 843-8995 • Italian • some veggie • beer/wine

Jardin du Me-Kong 1330 Ste-Catherine • 523-6635 • Vietnamese • some veggie

L'Ambiance (Salon De Thé) 1874 Notre-Dame ouest • 939-2609

L'Anecdote I 801 Rachel est • 526-7967 • 8am-10pm • burgers • some veggie

L'Exception 1200 St-Hubert • 282-1282 • vegetarian

L'Express 3927 St-Denis • 845-5333 • 8am-3am • popular • French bistro & full bar • great pâté

L'Un & L'Autre 1641 rue Amherst • 597-0878 • 11am-1am, from 5pm wknds • bistro • full bar

La Campagnola 1229 rue de la Montagne • 866-3234 • popular • Italian • great eggplant! • some veggie • beer/wine • $12-20

La Paryse 302 Ontario est • 842-2040 • 11am-11pm • lesbians/gay men • burgers/sandwiches

Le Crystal 1140 Ste-Catherine est • 525-9831 • 7pm-5am • popular • Greek/American

Napoléon 1694 Ste-Catherine est • 523-2105 • French

Paganini 1819 Ste-Catherine • 844-3031 • 11:30am-midnight • popular • fine Italian • some veggie

Piccolo Diavolo 1336 Ste-Catherine est • 526-1336

Pizzédélic 1329 rue Ste-Catherine est • 526-6011 • noon-midnight • pizzeria • some veggie • also 3509 boul. St-Laurent • 282-6784 • also 370 Laurier ouest • 948-6290

Saloon Cafe 1333 Ste-Catherine est • 522-1333 • 11am-1am, til 3am Fri-Sat • popular • burgers

GYMS & HEALTH CLUBS

Colonial Bath 3963 Colonial • 285-0132 • men only Wed-Mon • women only Tue

Physotech 1657 Amherst • 527-7587 • lesbians/gay men

BOOKSTORES & RETAIL SHOPS

L'Androgyne 3636 boul. St-Laurent • 842-4765 • 9am-6pm, til 9pm Th-Fri • popular • lesbigay bookstore • wheelchair access

TRAVEL & TOUR OPERATORS

M.A.P. Travel 410 St-Nicholas Ste. 118 • 287-7446/(800) 661-6627 • IGTA

Voyages Alternative 42 Pine Ave. W. Ste. 2 • 845-7769 • IGTA

PUBLICATIONS

Fugues/Gazelle/Village 1212 St-Hubert, H2L 3Y7 • 848-1854 • monthly

Homo Sapiens C.P. 8888 succ.A (U du Q), H3C 3P8 • 987-3000

Le Guide Gai du Québec/Insiders Guide to Gay Quebec 915 Stn. C., H2L 4Z2 • 523-9463 • annual guide book

▲ **Rainbow Choices Directory** 56 McMurray Ave., Toronto OT, M6P 2T1 • (416) 762-1320 • lesbigay entertainment & business directory for Canada

EROTICA

Cuir Plus 1321 Ste-Catherine est • 521-7587 • 11am-6pm • leather • sex toys • wheelchair access

Priape 1311 Ste-Catherine est • 521-8451 • open 10am, from noon Sun • popular • erotic gay material

Pointe au Pic   (418)

ACCOMMODATIONS

Auberge Mona 212 rue du Quai • 665-6793 • lesbians/gay men • full brkfst • women-owned/run

Prevost   (514)

BARS

Le Secret 3029 boul. Labelle (at Hotel Up North, Rte. 117 N.) • 224-7350 • 9pm-3am • lesbians/gay men • dancing/DJ • live shows

Québec   (418)

ACCOMMODATIONS

727 Guest House 727 rue d'Aiguillon, Québec • 648-6766 • lesbians/gay men

Auberge Montmorency Inn 6810 boul. Ste-Anne, L'Ange-Gardien • 822-0568 • gay-friendly

Bed & Breakfast in Old Québec City 35 rue des Ramparts • 655-7685 • gay-friendly • restored monastery w/ apts. avail. • full brkfst

Hotel la Maison Doyon 109 rue Ste-Anne • 694-1720 • gay-friendly • $50-110

L'Auberge Du Quarter 170 Grande Allée ouest, Québec • 525-9726 • gay-friendly

Le Coureur des Bois Guest House 15 rue Ste-Ursule • 692-1117 • lesbians/gay men

BARS

Bar L' Eveil 710 rue Bouvier Ste. 120 • 628-0610 • 11am-3am • lesbians/gay men • neighborhood bar

Fausse Alarme 161 rue St-Jean • 529-0277 • 4pm-3am (from 11am summers) • mostly gay men • neighborhood bar

L'Amour Sorcier 789 Côte Ste-Genevieve • 523-3395 • 11:30am-3am • popular • lesbians/gay men • neighborhood bar • videos • terrace

La Ballon Rouge 811 rue St-Jean • 647-9227 • 9pm-3am • popular • mostly gay men • dancing/DJ

Le Bol Vert 2470 Chemin Ste-Foy • 650-6525 • mostly women • dancing/DJ

Pub du Carré 945 rue d' Aiguillon • 692-9952 • 8am-midnight, clsd Sun • mostly gay men • neighborhood bar • beer only

Studio 157 157 Chemin Ste-Foy • 529-9958 • 10pm-3am Wed-Sat • popular • mostly women • dancing/DJ • live shows

Taverne Le Draque 815 rue St-Augustin • 649-7212 • 8am-3am • popular • mostly gay men • neighborhood bar • live shows • beer/wine • wheelchair access

RESTAURANTS & CAFES

Kookening Kafe 565 rue St-Jean • 521-2121

Le Commensal 860 rue St-Jean • 647-3733 • vegetarian

Le Hobbit 700 rue St-Jean • 647-2677 • opens 7:30am • some veggie

Restaurant Diana 849 rue St-Jean • 524-5794 • 8am-1am, 24hrs Fri-Sat • popular

Zorba Grec 853 St-Jean • 525-5509 • 8am-5pm • Greek • wheelchair access

BOOKSTORES & RETAIL SHOPS

L'Accro Librairie 845 rue St-Jean • 522-9920 • lesbigay

Rimouski   (418)

INFO LINES & SERVICES

Maison des Femmes de Rimouski 78 Ste-Marie #2 • 723-0333 • 9am-noon, 3pm-7pm Mon-Fri • women's resource center

Rivière Du Loupe   (418)

BARS

Disco Jet rue Lafontaine • 862-6308 • 3pm-3am, clsd Mon-Tue • lesbians/gay men • dancing/DJ

Sherbrooke   (819)

BARS

Les Dames de Coeur 54 rue King est • 821-2217 • 4pm-2am, clsd Mon-Tue • lesbians/gay men

RESTAURANTS & CAFES

Au Pot au Vin 40 rue King est • 562-8882 • lunch & dinner

St-Donat   (819)

ACCOMMODATIONS

Havre du Parc Auberge 2788 Rte. 125 N., St. Donat • 424-7686 • gay-friendly • quiet lakeside inn • food served

St-Hyacinthe (514)

BARS

Bistrot Mondor 1400 Cascades ouest •
773-1695 • 8am-3am • mostly women •
neighborhood bar

Trois Rivières (819)

INFO LINES & SERVICES

Gay Ami CP 1152, G9A 5K1 • 373-0771 •
lesbigay social contacts

ACCOMMODATIONS

Le Gité Du Huard 42 rue St-Louis • 375-
8771 • gay-friendly

BARS

La Maison Blanche #3 767 St-Maurice •
379-4233 • 9pm-3am • lesbians/gay men •
dancing/DJ • live shows

Le Lien 1572 rue Royal • 370-6492 • mostly women

Verdun (514)

INFO LINES & SERVICES

Centre des Femmes de Verdun 4255 rue
Wellington • 767-0384 • 9am-noon, 1pm-
4pm • general women's center • limited
lesbian info

SASKATCHEWAN

Moose Jaw (306)

INFO LINES & SERVICES

Lesbian/Gay Committee 692-2418 •
social/support group

Ravenscrag (306)

ACCOMMODATIONS

Spring Valley Guest Ranch Box 10, S0N
0T0 • 295-4124 • popular • gay-friendly •
1913 character home, cabin & tipis • also a
restaurant • country-style • $30-50

Regina (306)

INFO LINES & SERVICES

Pink Triangle Community Services 24031
Broad St. • 525-6046 • 8:30pm-11pm Tue &
Fri

Regina Women's Community Center 2505
11th Ave. #306 • 522-2777 • 9am-4:30pm
Mon-Fri

BARS

Oscar's 1422 Scarth St. • 522-7343 •
8:30pm-2am • lesbians/gay men • live
shows

SPIRITUAL GROUPS

Dignity Regina Box 3181, S4P 3G7 • 569-
3666 • 6:30pm 3rd Sun

Koinonia 3913 Hillsdale Ave. • 525-8542 •
7pm 2nd & 4th Sun • interfaith worship

Saskatoon (306)

INFO LINES & SERVICES

Gay/Lesbian AA 665-6727 • also call
Gay/Lesbian Line for schedule

Gay/Lesbian Line 665-1224 • noon-4:30pm
& 7:30pm-10:30pm, til 5:30pm Sat

ACCOMMODATIONS

Brighton House 1308 5th Ave. N. • 664-
3278 • gay-friendly • smokefree • kids ok •
wheelchair access

BARS

Diva's 220 3rd Ave. S. Ste. 110 (alley
entrance) • 665-0100 • 8pm-2am, clsd Mon
• lesbians/gay men • dancing/DJ • private
club

BOOKSTORES & RETAIL SHOPS

Cafe Browse 269-B 3rd Ave. S. • 664-2665
• 10am-11pm, from 12:30pm Sun

Out of the Closet 241 2nd Ave S., 3rd flr. •
665-1224 • lesbigay materials

TRAVEL & TOUR OPERATORS

Jubilee Travel 108-3120 8th St. E. • 373-
9633 • ask for Mike • IGTA

SPIRITUAL GROUPS

Affirm PO Box 7518, S7K 6K7 • 653-1475 •
1st Sun • for gays & lesbians in the United
Church

PUBLICATIONS

Perceptions Box 8581, S7K 6K7 • 244-1930
• covers the Canadian prairies

YUKON

Whitehorse (403)

INFO LINES & SERVICES

**Gay/Lesbian Alliance of the Yukon
Territory** PO Box 5604, Y1A 5H4 • 667-7857

Victoria Faulkner Women's Center 404-A
Ogilvie • 667-2693 • call for hours

Yukon Gays/Lesbians PO Box 5604, Y1A
5H4 • 667-7857

COSTA RICA

Manuel Antonio (506)

ACCOMMODATIONS

El Parador (800) 451-4398 • gay-friendly • large resort • swimming

▲ **Hotel Casa Blanca** apdo. 194 Entrada La Mariposas, Quepos, 6350 • 777-0253 • lesbians/gay men • walking distance to gay beach • swimming

Makanda by the Sea 777-8201 • gay-friendly • private oasis • swimming

Si Como No (800) 237-8207 • gay-friendly • popular • swimming

Villas Mar y Sol Inn PO Box 256-6350, Quepos, • 777-0307 • gay-friendly • food served • $45-65

BARS

Arco Iris behind iron bridge at the waterfront, Quepos • gay-friendly

Kamuk Pub at Katuk Hotel, downtown, Quepos • gay-friendly • open til 4am

Mar y Sombra 1st Beach • popular • lesbians/gay men • dancing/DJ • food served

Vela Bar 1st Beach • 777-0413

RESTAURANTS & CAFES

El Barba Roja Quepos • popular • great sunset location

El Gran Escape Quepos • clsd Tue • Tex-Mex

Karola's Quepos • clsd Wed • great brkfst w/ a view

The Plinio (in the Hotel Plinio) • 777-0055 • Italian

Tico Rico paved road to national park, Quepos • lunch & dinner includes use of pool bar

TRAVEL & TOUR OPERATORS

Costa Rica Connection 975 Osos St., San Luis Obispos CA, 93401 • (805) 543-8823/(800) 345-7422

Puntarenas (506)

ACCOMMODATIONS

Casa Yemaya 661-0956 • women only • travel planning avail. • Spanish classes • lesbian-owned/run

BARS

La Deriva gay-friendly

San Jose (506)

INFO LINES & SERVICES

Centro Feminista de Intercambio Cultural (at Casa Yemaya) • 223-3652

ACCOMMODATIONS

Amstel Amon (800) 575-1253 • gay-friendly • modern hotel • quiet location

Cariari Hotel & Country Club (800) 227-4274 • gay-friendly • luxury resort w/ great golfing • swimming

Colours—The Guest Residence El Triangulo, Blvd. Rohrmoser • 32-35-04/(800) 934-5622/(305) 532-9341 • lesbians/gay men • premier full-service accommodations w/ tours & reservation services throughout Costa Rica • swimming • IGTA

Don Carlos B&B 221-6707 • popular • gay-friendly

Hotel L'Ambiance 949 Calle 27 • 23-15-98 • gay-friendly • no visitors allowed in rooms • also restaurant & bar • courtyard

Joluva Guesthouse Calle 3 B, Aves. 9 & 11 #936 • 223-7961/(800) 298-2418 • lesbians/gay men

Scotland Apartments Ave. 1 Calle 27 • 23-08-33 • gay-friendly • rental apts

BARS

Antros Ave. 14 (btwn. Calle 7 & 9) • gay-friendly

Cantabrico Ave. 6 (btwn. Calles Central & 2nd) • lesbians/gay men

De Ja Vu Calle 2 (btwn. Ave. 14 & 16) • 8pm-?, from 9pm Fri-Sat, clsd Mon-Th • popular • lesbians/gay men • dancing/DJ • live shows • take taxi to avoid bad area

El Churro Español Calle 11 (btwn. 8 & 10—knock on the door) • lesbians/gay men

La Avispa Calle 1 (btwn. Ave. 8 & 10, #834—no name outside of pink house) • clsd Mon & Th • mostly women Wed

La Esmeralda Ave. Segunda (btwn. Calles 5 & 7) • gay-friendly • food served • live shows

La Taberna Calle 1 (btwn. Ave. 7 & 9) • 6pm-midnight • mostly gay men • on 1st & 2nd flr. (no sign)

Los Cucharones Ave. 6 btwn Calles Central & 1st (no name outside, listen for music) • opens 8pm, clsd Mon-Tue • mostly gay men

Monte Carlo Ave. 4 & Calle 2 (on corner) • gay-friendly

RESTAURANTS & CAFES

Cafe de Teatro National National Theatre • 223-4488 • lunch

La Cocina de Lena El Pueblo area • 5 min. from downtown • Costa Rican • $12

La Perla Calle Central Ave. 2 (on corner)

La Piazetta Paseo Colon • Italian • $18

Machu Pichu off Paseo Colon • just outside downtown area • Peruvian seafood • $18

Nimbe suburb of Escazu • 281-1739

Vishnu Vegetarian Restaurant Ave. 1 (btwn. Calle 3 & 1) • popular • $5

TRAVEL & TOUR OPERATORS

Amatirasu Tours 257-8529 • tours & reservation service

DOMINICAN REPUBLIC

Puerto Plata (787)

ACCOMMODATIONS

Purple Paradise Cabarete • 571-0637 • women only • swimming • $55

Santo Domingo (787)

ACCOMMODATIONS

Hotel David Arzobispo Novel 308, Zona Colonial • 688-8538 • gay-friendly

BARS

Pariguayso Calle Padre Billini #412 • 682-2735 • lesbians/gay men

The Penthouse Calle Saibo & 20th St. (difficult to find) • Th-Sat • popular • lesbians/gay men • dancing/DJ

RESTAURANTS & CAFES

Cafe Coco Calle Sanchez 153 • 687-9624 • noon-10pm • small English restaurant • full bar • live shows

Le Pousse Cafe 107 19 de Marzo • lesbians/gay men • popular • dancing/DJ

DUTCH WEST INDIES

Aruba (297)

BARS

Cafe the Paddock 94 L.G. Smith Blvd., Oranjestad • 83-23-34 • gay-friendly • neighborhood bar

The Cellar 2 Klipstraat, Oranjestad • 82-64-90 • 3pm-5am • gay-friendly • popular • neighborhood bar • also 'The Penthouse' • from 11pm • lesbians/gay men • dancing/DJ • alternative

Jewel Box Revue La Cabana Resort & Casino, Oranjestad • 87-90-00 • gay-friendly • live shows

Jimmy's Waterweg & Middenweg, Oranjestad • 82-25-50 • afterhours • popular • gay-friendly • neighborhood bar • food served

Paradiso 16 Wilhelminastraat, Oranjestad • opening fall '96 • inquire locally

RESTAURANTS & CAFES

Grand Cafe Cobra 60 L.G. Smith Blvd. (Marisol Bldg.), Oranjestad • 83-31-03

FRENCH WEST INDIES

St. Barthelemy (596)

ACCOMMODATIONS

Hostellerie des 3 Forces Vitet • 27-61-25/(800) 932-3222 • gay-friendly • mountaintop new age/metaphysical retreat/inn • swimming • food served • IGTA • $120-170

Hotel Normandie 27-62-37 • gay-friendly

St. Bart's Beach Hotel Grand Cul de Sac • 27-60-70 • gay-friendly

Village St. Jean 27-61-39/(800) 633-7411 • gay-friendly

BARS

American Bar Gustavia • gay-friendly • food served

Le Sélect Gustavia • 27-86-87 • gay-friendly • more gay after 11pm

RESTAURANTS & CAFES

Eddie's Ghetto Gustavia • Creole

Newborn Restaurant Anse de Caye • 27-67-07 • French Creole

St. Martin (590)

BARS

Pink Mango at Laguna Beach Hotel, Nettle Bay • 87-59-99 • 6pm-3am • popular • lesbians/gay men • dancing/DJ

PUERTO RICO

Aguada (787)

ACCOMMODATIONS

San Max PO Box 1294, 00602 • 868-2931 • lesbians/gay men • guesthouse & studio apt on the beach • weekly rentals

BARS

Johnny's Bar Carretera 115 • lesbians/gay men • inquire at 'San Max' accommodations for directions

Bayamón (787)

BARS

Gilligan's Betances D-18 Hnas. Davila • 786-5065 • gay-friendly • live shows • private club

Yabba Dabba Pub Rd. 110 • open daily

Cabo Rojo (787)

BARS

Village Pub Cafe HCO 1 Box 13819 • 851-6783

Caguas

BARS

Villa Camito Country Club off old Hwy. 3 (turn right at Cafe de los Pisos) • opens 6pm Sat • popular • lesbians/gay men • food served • live shows

Coamo (787)

ACCOMMODATIONS

Parador Baños de Coamo PO Box 540, 00630 • 825-2186/825-2239 • gay-friendly • resort • mineral baths • also a restaurant • full bar • kids ok • public baths open 24 hrs • men only late nights

Hato Rey

BARS

Choices 70 Eñasco • open wknds • gay-friendly • dancing/DJ

Isabela

BARS

Paradise Cocktail Lounge Hacia La Playa de Jobos, Carr. 466, KM.06.3 • 9pm-? • clsd Mon-Tue

Villa Ricomar 8 Calle Paz, Carretera 459, Barrio Jobos • opens 9pm Fri-Sat, from 6pm Sun • lesbians/gay men • dancing/DJ • live shows

Mayaguez

BARS

Roma Calle de Diego 151 • open Th-Sun • lesbians/gay men • dancing/DJ • private club

Ponce

BARS

The Cave Barrio Teneria #115 • gay-friendly • live shows

San German

BARS

Norman's Bar Carretera 318, Barrio Maresúa • 6pm-1am • lesbians/gay men • dancing/DJ • salsa & merengue

The World Rd. 360 km. 1 • 264-2002 • 10pm-7am Th-Sat • gay-friendly • dancing/DJ

San Juan (787)

INFO LINES & SERVICES

CONCRA 112 Ave. Universidad, Santa Rita, Rio Piedras • 753-9443 • STD/HIV clinic • health care & referrals

Madres Lesbianas PO Box 1103, Old San Juan Station, 00902 • 722-4838 • lesbian mothers group

Telefino Gay PO Box 11003, Estación Viejo San Juan • 722-4838/(800) 981-9179

ACCOMMODATIONS

Atlantic Beach Hotel 1 Calle Vendig, Condado • 721-6900 • popular • lesbians/gay men • swimming • also a restaurant • full bar • IGTA

Casablanca Guest House 57 Caribe St., Condado • 722-7139 • popular • gay-friendly • 1 blk to beach

Condado Inn 6 Condado Ave. • 724-7145 • lesbians/gay men • guesthouse w/ terrace restaurant & lounge • near beach

El Canario Inn 1317 Ashford Ave., Condado • 722-3861/(800) 742-4276

Embassy Guest House 1126 Seaview, Condado • 725-8284 • across the street from beach

Glorimar Guesthouse 111 University Ave., Rio Piedras • gay-friendly • rms & apts

Gran Hotel El Convento 100 Christo St., Old San Juan • 723-9020/(800) 468-2779 • popular • gay-friendly • swimming

Hotel Iberia 1464 Wilson Ave., Condado • 722-5380 • lesbians/gay men • European-style hotel • also a restaurant • gay-owned/run

L' Habitation Beach Guesthouse 1957
Calle Italia, Ocean Park • 727-2499 • les-
bians/gay men • on the beach • also a
restaurant • salads & sandwiches • full bar
• $4-7

Numero Uno on the Beach 1 Calle Santa
Ana, Ocean Park • 726-5010 • gay-friendly •
swimming • also bar & grill • wheelchair
access

▲ **Ocean Park Beach Inn** Calle Elena # 3,
Ocean Park • 728-7418/(800) 292-9208 •
lesbians/gay men • skyline & sea views •
swimming • IGTA • wheelchair access •
gay-owned/run

▲ **Ocean Walk Guest House** 1 Atlantic Place,
Ocean Park • 728-0855/(800) 468-0615 •
gay-friendly • Spanish-style home on the
beach near Condado • swimming • IGTA

BARS

Abbey Disco Calle Cruz #251 (Lazer Bar) •
725-7581 • gay-friendly • gay Sun & Th •
dancing/DJ

Bebo's Playa Pinones • 253-3143/269-3429
• 3pm-? Wed-Sat • lesbians/gay men •
dancing/DJ • live shows

Boccacio Muñoz Rivera, Hato Rey (across
from Fire Dept. on dead end street) • les-
bians/gay men • popular • dancing/DJ •
live shows

Cups Calle San Mateo #1708, Santurce •
268-3570 • clsd Mon • lesbians/gay men

El Danuvio Azul Calle San Juan #613,
Santurce • 8pm-4am, clsd Sun •
lesbians/gay men

Junior's Bar 602 Calle Condado, Santurce •
6pm-2am, til 4am Fri-Sat • lesbians/gay
men • neighborhood bar • dancing/DJ •
salsa & merengue

Krash 1257 Ponce de Leon, Santurce • 722-
1131 • 9pm-4am, clsd Mon • popular •
lesbians/gay men • dancing/DJ • live shows
• videos

La Laguna Night Club 53 Calle
Barranquitas, Condado • from 10pm • popular • mostly gay men • dancing/DJ • live
shows • private club

Taboo Calle Loiza #1753, Santurce • 728-
5906 • 8pm-?, clsd Sun • lesbians/gay men
• dancing/DJ • private club

Tia Maria's Jose de Diego, Stop 22, Ponce
de Leon, Santurce • gay-friendly • popular
• liquor shop & bar

RESTAURANTS & CAFES
809 Cafe 1 Vendig St., Condado • 721-6900
• Caribbean

Amanda's Cafe 424 Norzagaray, Old San Juan • 722-1682 • 11am-2am, til 4am Fri-Sat

Cafe Amadeus Calle San Sebastian • 722-8635 • popular

Cafe Berlin 407 Calle San Francisco, Old San Juan • 722-5205 • popular • espresso bar

Golden Unicorn 2415 Calle Laurel • 728-4066 • 11am-11pm • Chinese

La Bombonera 259 San Francisco St., Old San Juan • 722-0658 • popular

Panache 1127 Calle Seaview, Condado • 725-2400 • dinner only • popular • French

Sam's Patio 102 San Sebastian, Old San Juan

The Terrace Restaurant 6 Condado Ave. • 724-7145 • dinner, clsd Tue • $14

TRAVEL & TOUR OPERATORS

Travel Maker International Tours San Claudio Mail Stations, Box 224, Rio Piedras, 00926 • 755-5878 • ask for Ruben • IGTA

PUBLICATIONS

Puerto Rico Breeze Castillo del Mar #1397, Isla Verde, 00979 • 282-7184

EROTICA

Condom Mania 353 San Francisco St., Old San Juan • 722-5348 • toys

Vieques Island   (787)

ACCOMMODATIONS

Connections, Inc. PO Box 358, Vieques, 00765 • 741-0023/(800) 772-3050 • gay-friendly • villa rentals • easy access to San Juan

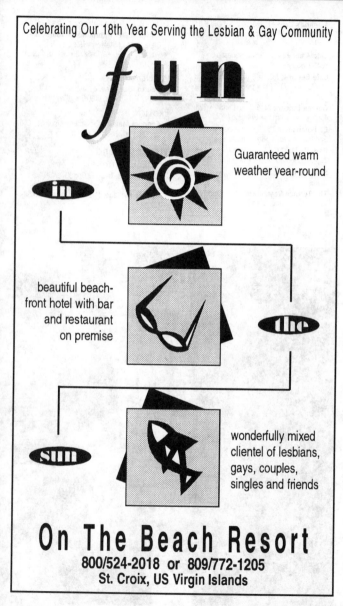

VIRGIN ISLANDS

St. Croix (809)

ACCOMMODATIONS

King Christian Hotel 59 Kings Wharf, Christiansted • 773-2285 • gay-friendly • swimming • also a restaurant

▲ **On The Beach Resort** 127 Smithfield Rd., Frederiksted • 772-1205/(800) 524-2018 • beachfront resort • swimming • also a restaurant • full bar

Prince Street Inn 402 Prince St., Frederiksted • 772-9550

BARS

The Last Hurrah King St., Frederiksted • 772-5225 • gay-friendly

St. John (809)

ACCOMMODATIONS

Gallows Point Suite Resort Cruz Bay • 776-6434 • gay-friendly • beachfront resort • all suites • swimming • kitchens • also a restaurant • full bar

Maho Bay & Harmony V.I. National Park • 776-6240/(800) 392-9004 • gay-friendly • camping & environmentally aware resort

Oscar's Guest House Estate Pastory #27 • 776-6193/(800) 854-1843 • gay-friendly • near outdoor recreation

Sunset Pointe 773-8100 • rental residences

TRAVEL & TOUR OPERATORS

Sail Ananda Cruz Bay • 776-6922 • private charters

St. Thomas (809)

ACCOMMODATIONS

Blackbeard's Castle PO Box 6041, 00801 • 776-1234/(800) 344-5771 • popular • gay-friendly • small intimate hotel on historic site overlooking town & harbor • swimming • also a restaurant

Danish Chalet Guest House PO Box 4319, 00803 • 774-5764/(800) 635-1531 • gay-friendly • overlooking harbor • spa • deck • limited wheelchair access

Hotel 1829 PO Box 1567, 00804 • 776-1829/(800) 524-2002 • gay-friendly • swimming • full bar

Pavilions & Pools Hotel 6400 Estate Smith Bay • 775-6110/(800) 524-2001 • gay-friendly • one-bdrm villas each w/ its own private swimming pool • wheelchair access

RESTAURANTS & CAFES

Fiddle Leaf Restaurant Government Hill • dinner only, clsd Sun • popular

TRAVEL & TOUR OPERATORS

Journeys by the Sea, Inc. 6501 Redhook Plaza, Ste. 201 • 775-3660/(800) 825-3632 • yacht vacation • day sails • IGTA

Tortola (809)

ACCOMMODATIONS

Fort Recovery Estate Village Box 239, Road Town, British VI • 495-4354/(800) 367-8455 • gay-friendly • swimming • kids ok

MEXICO

Acapulco (52-74)

ACCOMMODATIONS

Casa Condesa 125 Bella Vista • 84-1616 • mostly gay men

Casa Le Mar Lomas Del Mar 32-B • 84-1022 • mostly gay men • full brkfst • swimming • maid & cook avail.

Fiesta American Condesa Costera Miguel Aleman • 84-2355/(800) 223-2332 • gay-friendly • swimming

Las Brisas 84-1580/(800) 223-6800 • gay-friendly • popular • luxury resort • rms w/ private pools

Royale De Acapulco & Beach Club Calle Caracol 70, Fraccion Amiento Farallón • 84-3707 • gay-friendly • swimming • food served

Villa Costa Azul 555 Fdo. Magallanes • 84-5462 • lesbians/gay men • swimming • IGTA

BARS

Demas Privada Piedra Picuda #17 (behind 'Carlos & Charlie's') • opens 10pm • popular • lesbians/gay men • dancing/DJ

La Melinche Picuda 216 (behind Plaza Condesa) • mostly gay men • live shows

Relax Calle Lomas de Mar 7 • 84-0421 • 9pm-5am, clsd Mon-Wed • mostly gay men • dancing/DJ • live shows

RESTAURANTS & CAFES

Beto's Beach Restaurant Condesa Beach • lesbians/gay men

Chicken Choza Benito Juárez St. (1/2 blk off Zócalo) • lesbians/gay men • full bar • gay-owned/run

Jovitos Costera (across from the Fiesta Americana Condesa) • traditional fare • plenty veggie

Kookaburra Carretera Escénica (at Marina Las Brisas) • 84-1448 • popular • int'l • $20-25

La Guera de Condesa Condesa Beach

La Tortuga Calle Lomas del Mar 5-A • noon-2am • full bar

Le Bistroquet Andrea Doria #5, Fracc. Costa Azul • 84-6860 • popular • lesbians/gay men • turn off the costera at the Oceanic Park

Su Casa/La Margarita Ave. Anahuac 110 • 84-4350 • traditional cuisine • great views

Aguascalientes

BARS

Merendero Kikos Calle Arturo J. Pani 132 • closes at 11pm • gay-friendly • food served

RESTAURANTS & CAFES

Restaurant Mitla Calle Madero 220

Restaurant San Francisco Plaza Principal

Cabo San Lucas (52-11)

BARS

The Rainbow Bar & Grill Blvd. de la Marina #39-C • 43-1455 • popular • lesbians/gay men • dancing/DJ • patio

Cancun (52-98)

ACCOMMODATIONS

Caribbean Reef Club 20 mi. S. in Puerto Morelos • (800) 322-6286 • popular • gay-friendly • swimming • food served

BARS

Caramba Ave. Tulum 87 • 84-0032 • 10pm-? • gay-friendly • dancing/DJ

Picante Bar Avenida Tulum 20 (east of Ave. Uxmal) • 9:30pm-4am • popular • mostly gay men

Ta' Güeno Ave. Yaxachilián 15 • 9pm-4am • mostly gay men • dancing/DJ • live shows

GYMS & HEALTH CLUBS

Shape Calle Conoco (1 blk from San Yaxchen) • gay-friendly

Ciudad Juárez (52-16)

ACCOMMODATIONS

Hotel de Luxe 300 S. Lerdo Ave., PO Box 1061, El Paso TX, 79946 • 15-0202 • gay-friendly • restaurant & bar • inexpensive

Plaza Continental Ave. S. Lerdo de Tejada 112 • 12-2610 • gay-friendly • also restaurant

BARS

Club La Madelon Calle Santos Degollado 771 N. • lesbians/gay men • popular wknds • dancing/DJ • live shows

Nebraska Mariscal #251 Centro • closes at midnight • popular • lesbians/gay men

Ritz 1/2 block N. & 1/2 block E. of Hotel de Luxe • 14-2291 • open til 2am • mostly gay men • neighborhood bar

RESTAURANTS & CAFES

El Coyote Invalido Ave. Lerdo Sur • 24hrs

Cozumel (52-98)

ACCOMMODATIONS

La Perla Beach & Diving Resort Playa Paraíso • 72-0188/(800) 852-6404 • gay-friendly • swimming

Sol Cabañas del Caribe beachfront • 72-0017/0072/(800) 336-3542 • gay-friendly • food served

Cuernavaca (52-73)

ACCOMMODATIONS

Casa Aurora B&B Calle Arista 12 (antes 303) • 18-6394 • gay-friendly • Spanish classes can be arranged • $18-24

Hotel Narajeva Sonora 1000 Col. Vista Hermosa • gay-friendly

BARS

Shadee Avenida Adolfo Lopez Mateos • 12-4367 • 9pm-4am • popular • mostly gay men • food served • live shows

Durango (52-18)

BARS

Bar Country 122 Constitución Norte • lesbians/gay men • food served

Buhós Restaurant & Bar 615 5 de Febero • 12-5811 • gay-friendly

Eduardos 805 20 de Noviembre Pte. • lesbians/gay men

Ensenada (52-68)

BARS

Club Ibis Blvd. Costero at Ave. Sagines • Fri-Sat only • gay-friendly • dancing/DJ

Coyote Club 1000 Blvd. Costero #4 & 5 at Diamante • 47-3691 • 9pm-3am clsd Mon-Tue • popular • lesbians/gay men • dancing/DJ • patio

Ola Verde Calle Segunda 459-A • popular late night • lesbians/gay men • food served

RESTAURANTS & CAFES

Mariscos California Calle Ruiz & Segunda • 9am-9pm, clsd Mon • seafood

TRAVEL & TOUR OPERATORS

Gay Baja Tours Alvarado 143, Local 7J • 48-3676/(888) 225-2429

Guadalajara (52-36)

ACCOMMODATIONS

Hotel Calinda Roma Ave. Juárez 170 • (800) 228-5151 • gay-friendly • food served

Travel Recreation International 1875 Ave. Libertad, Local-C, Sec Juárez • 26-3398 • gay-friendly • IGTA

BARS

Candilejas 961 Ave. Niños Héroes (near Hotel Carlton) • 8pm-4am, clsd Mon • gay-friendly • dancing/DJ • live shows

La Malinche 1230 Alvaro Obregón St. at Calle 50, Libertad District • 8pm-3am • popular late night • mostly gay men • dancing/DJ • live shows • food served

Monica's Disco Bar 1713 Alvaro Obregón St., Libertad District • 43-9544 • 9pm-3am, clsd Mon • popular • dancing/DJ • live shows

Pancho's 179 Calle Maestranza Centro • 11am-midnight • gay-friendly • food served

SOS Club 1413 Ave. La Paz, Hidalgo District • 11pm-3am, clsd Mon • popular lesbian hangout • lesbians/gay men • dancing/DJ • live shows

RESTAURANTS & CAFES

Brasserie 1171 Prisciliano Sanchez St., downtown Juárez District

Copa de Leche 414 Juárez Ave., Juárez District • 14-5347 • 7am-10pm • live shows

Sanborn's Juárez Ave. at 16 de Septiembre St.

Sanborn's Vallarta 1600 Vallarta Ave., downtown Juárez District

Guanajuato (52-47)

ACCOMMODATIONS

Castillo Santa Cecilia Camino a La Valenciana • 32-0477 • excellent food

Hotel Museo Posada Sante Fe downtown • 32-0084

BARS

El Incendio Calle Cantarranas 15 • 32-1372 • gay-friendly

Jalapa

BARS

La Mansion take a cab towards Bandarilla, 20 min. NW of town • Fri-Sat only • lesbians/gay men • live shows

La Paz (52-11)

ACCOMMODATIONS

Casa La Paceña Calle Bravo 106 • 25-2748/(707) 869-2374 (off-season) • open Nov-June • gay-friendly

Gran Baja near harbor Mariano Abasolo • gay-friendly

Hotel Perla 1570 Ave., Alvaro Obregón • 22-0777x131 • gay-friendly

BARS

Bar Intimo Calle 16 de Septiembre • lesbians/gay men

Manzanillo   (52-33)

ACCOMMODATIONS

Pepe's c/o 2698 Pacific Ave., San Francisco CA, 94115 • 33-0616/(415) 346-4734 • gay-friendly • food served

Matamoros

BARS

Montezuma Lounge St. 6 Gonzalez • gay-friendly

Mr. Lee Disco Ave. de las Rosas, Col. Jardin • gay-friendly • dancing/DJ

Mazatlan   (52-69)

BARS

Pepe Toro Ave. de las Garzas 18, Zona Dorado • 14-4167 • 8pm-4am, from 9pm Fri-Sat • lesbians/gay men • dancing/DJ • lunch daily • not busy til midnight

Valentino's Ave. Camarón Sabalo • gay-friendly • dancing/DJ

RESTAURANTS & CAFES

Panama Restaurant Pasteleria Ave. del las Garzas & Cammarron Sabalo • lesbians/gay men • cafe

Restaurante Rocamar Ave. del Mar, Zona Costera • 81-6008 • popular

Señor Frogs Ave. del Mar, Zona Costera • gay-friendly • dancing/DJ • upscale seafood

Merida (52-99)

ACCOMMODATIONS

Casa Exilio B&B Calle 68, N. 495 between. 57 & 59 • 28-2505 • gay-friendly

Gran Hotel Parque Hidalgo, Calle 60 #496 • 24-7622 • gay-friendly • food served

BARS

Ciudad Maya Calle 84 #506 • 24-3313 • lesbians/gay men

Kabuki's Calle 60 & 53 • lesbians/gay men • dancing/DJ • many bars in the area come & go—follow the crowd

Romanticos Piano Bar Calle 60 #461 • 9pm-3am • lesbians/gay men • live shows

RESTAURANTS & CAFES

Cafe Express Calle 60 (across from Hidalgo Park)

La Bella Epoca Calle 69 #447 (Hotel de Parque) • 28-1928 • 6pm-1am • Yucatean cuisine

Mexicali

BARS

Copacabana Ave. Tuxtla Gutierrez at Baja California St. • mostly women • neighborhood bar

El Taurino Calle Zuazua 480 (at Ave. José Maria Morelos) • popular • lesbians/gay men

Los Panchos Ave. Juárez 33 • popular • lesbians/gay men • oldest gay bar in Mexicali

Shaflarelo's Bar Ave. de la Reforma at Calle Mexico • open late • gay-friendly • live shows

Tare Calle Uxmal & Ave. Jalisco • mostly gay men

México City (52-5)

INFO LINES & SERVICES

Calamo Gay Center 118 Culiacán (3rd flr.) • support & social group

Casa de la Sal A.C. Córdoba 76, Roma Sur • 207-8042

Gay/Lesbian AA 123 Culiacán Atlas, Colonia Hipodromo Condessa • 8pm Mon-Sat, 6pm Sun

Voz Humana A.C. 530-2873/2592

ACCOMMODATIONS

Aristos Paseo de la Reforma #276 • 211-0112/(800) 527-4786 • gay-friendly • swimming

Hotel Casa Blanca Lafragua #7 • 566-3211/(800) 448-8355 • gay-friendly • swimming • food served

Hotel Krystal Rosa Liverpool #155 • 221-3460/(800) 231-9860 • gay-friendly • swimming • food served

Hotel Michelangelo Calle Rio Amazonas 78 • 566-9877 • gay-friendly • kitchen • $40

Marco Polo 27 Amberes, Pink Zone • 207-1893/(800) 223-0888 • gay-friendly • upscale hotel

Westin Galeria Plaza Hamburgo #195 • 211-0014/(800) 228-3000 • gay-friendly • swimming • food served

BARS

33 Ave. Lázaro Cárdenas & Republica del Perú • mostly gay men • neighborhood bar

Butterfly Disco Calle Izazaga 9 at Ave. Lazaro Cárdenas Sur • 9pm-4am, clsd Mon • popular • lesbians/gay men • live shows

Caztzi Calle Carlos Arellano 4, Ciudad Satélite • lesbians/gay men • dancing/DJ • live shows

Dandy's Le Club 118 Martin del Campo • 9pm-4am

El Don 79 Tonalá St. • 9pm-4am • lesbians/gay men • dancing/DJ • live shows

El Taller Ave. Florencia 37-A • lesbians/gay men • dancing/DJ • live shows

Enigma Calle Morelia 111 • more women Th

L' Baron Ave. Insurgentes Sur 1231 • popular • mostly gay men • dancing/DJ

Los Rosàles Calle Pensador Mexicano 11 • mostly gay men • dancing/DJ • live shows

Privata Ave. Universidad 1901 Col. Copilco • 661-5939 • mostly gay men • dancing/DJ

Spartacus 8 Cuauhtémoc Ave., Nezahualcóyotl City • 9pm-5am • popular • mostly gay men • live shows

Tom's Leather Bar Ave. Insurgentes Sur 357 • mostly gay men • leather

RESTAURANTS & CAFES

El Hábito 13 Madrid St., Coyoacan District • gay-friendly • avante-garde theater

La Fonda San Francisco Calle Velázquez de Leon 126 • 546-4060 • noon-1am • lesbians/gay men • live shows

La Opera Calle 5 de Mayo 10 • 1pm-midnight, clsd Sun • mostly gay men

Vip's Hamburgo 126 Calle Hamburgo, Zona Rosa • also at Paseo de la Reforma & Florencia (near Independence Angel Statue) • also Niza & Hamburgo

Casa Camelinas

❦

A Unique Bed & Breakfast in Historic Morelia, Michoacan, Mexico, Catering to Women

You will love this colonial city only 3½ hours from Mexico City. Our women-owned B&B is also a great jumping-off point for sightseeing in nearby quaint towns specializing in wonderful arts and crafts. For the authentic Mexico, clean, safe, lovely surroundings and, if you wish, Spanish tutoring by a tenured teacher right on our premises, come to Casa Camelinas. Call or fax us for a brochure at: 415-661-5745.

❧

Also see our web page at
http://www.cimarron.net/
mexico/camelinas.html

Telephone: +52-43-140963
E-Mail: Camelinas@aol.com

BOOKSTORES & RETAIL SHOPS

El Angel Azul 64 Londres A&B • periodicals • clothing

Sueños Salvajes 177 E. Zapata, Col. Portales

TRAVEL & TOUR OPERATORS

The Gay Travel Club Ave. Mexico 99-PB Col. Hipodromo, 06170

Stag Travel & Tours Hamburgo 214-31 Col. Juárez, 06600 • 525-4658 • IGTA

PUBLICATIONS

Ser Gay 534-3804

Monterey

BARS

Charaos Calle Isaac Garza Oriente (at Zaragoza) • open late, clsd Sun • gay-friendly • dancing/DJ

Fridas Calle Padre Mier Poniente • lesbians/gay men • live shows

Obelisco Ave. Juán Ignacio Ramón 333 Pte., 3rd flr. • 10pm-2am, clsd Sun-Tue • popular • lesbians/gay men • dancing/DJ • live shows

Vongole Blvd. Pedrera 300 • 336-0335 • 10pm-3am, clsd Sun-Tue • mostly gay men • dancing/DJ • live shows

BOOKSTORES & RETAIL SHOPS

Revisteria Johnny Calle Aramberri 807 Poniente

Morelia   (52-43)

ACCOMMODATIONS

▲ **CasaCamelinas B&B** PO Box 2154, San Francisco CA, 94126-2154 • 14-0963/(415) 661-5745 • mostly women • 3-1/2 hours from Mexico City

BARS

Los Ebines Ave. Madero Pte. at Guadalajara 5039 • gay-friendly • dancing/DJ • live shows

No Que No Ave. Campestre at Rincón de los Compadres • 10pm-3am, clsd Mon • mostly gay men • dancing/DJ • live shows

RESTAURANTS & CAFES

Cafe Bizare 90 Ignacio Zaragoza (inside Posada dela Soledad Hotel) • 12-1818

Cafe Catedral Portal Hidalgo 23

Las Mercedes Calle Leon Guzmán 47 • 12-6113 • popular

Oaxaca (52-95)

ACCOMMODATIONS

Mission de los Angeles Hotel Calzada Porfirio Diaz 102 • 15-1500/1000/(800) 221-6509 • gay-friendly • food served • swimming

Stouffer Presidente 300 Ave. 5 de Mayo • (800) 468-3571 • gay-friendly • 4-star hotel • food served • swimming

BARS

Bar Jardin Portal de Flores • 16-2092 • lesbians/gay men • food served

Coronita Bustamante at Xochitc • gay-friendly

La Cascada Bustamente, N. of Periferico • popular • mostly gay men • food served

RESTAURANTS & CAFES

El Asador Vasco Portal de Flores (upstairs) • 16-9719 • great views

Pátzcuaro (52-45)

ACCOMMODATIONS

Hotel Posada San Rafael Plaza Vasco de Quiroga • 42-0770 • gay-friendly • food served

RESTAURANTS & CAFES

Doña Pala Calle Quiroga

Puebla

BARS

Keops Disco Calle 14 Poniente 101, Cholula • 10pm-3am Fri-Sat only • popular • lesbians/gay men • dancing/DJ • live shows

La Cigarra 5 Poniente & 7 Sur, Centro • popular • lesbians/gay men

La Fuente Hermanos Serdán 343 • gay-friendly • dancing/DJ

Puerto Vallarta (52-32)

ACCOMMODATIONS

Casa de los Arcos Apto 239-B, 48300 • 22-5990 • gay-friendly • vacation rental near beach • swimming

Casa dos Comales Calle Aldama 274 • 23-2042 • gay-friendly • $75-125

Casa Panoramica B&B Carretera a Mismaloya, Apt postal #114, 48300 • 22-3656/(800) 745-7805 • gay-friendly • overlooking Bandares Bay & old downtown Puerto Vallarta • full brkfst • swimming • IGTA

Jungle Nancy Villa (800) 936-3646 • gay-friendly • lesbian-owned/run

Paco Paco Descanso del Sol 583 Pino Suarez • 23-2077/(800) 936-3646 • popular

Vallarta Cora 174 Pilitas • 23-2815 • gay-friendly • apartments • swimming

Villa Felíz PO Box 553, 48300 • 22-0798/(714) 752-5456 x277 • (416) 925-9621 (Canada only) • lesbians/gay men • full brkfst

BARS

Blue Chairs (Tito's) southern Los Muertos Beach • lesbians/gay men • food served

Club Paco Paco Ignacio L. Vallarta 278 • 22-1899 • 3pm-4am • popular • lesbians/gay men • dancing/DJ

Gerardo's Party Pad Calle Venustiano 268 • lesbians/gay men • live shows

Los Balcones 182 Juárez, upstairs (at Libertad) • 10pm-3am • mostly gay men • dancing/DJ

Studio 33 Avenida Juárez 728 • closed Mon • gay-friendly • dancing/DJ • live shows

Zotano 101 Morelos by Plaza Rio • gay-friendly • dancing/DJ

RESTAURANTS & CAFES

Adobe Cafe 252 Basilio Badillo • southwestern

Bombo's 327 Corona • gourmet int'l

Cafe Sierra Insurgentes 109 • 22 -2748 • 9am-11pm • lesbians/gay men • full bar

Cuiza Isla Rio Cuale, West Bridge • 22-5646 • lesbians/gay men

De Claire's 269 Basilio Badillo

La Palada Los Muertos Beach (near Pier)

Le Bistro Jazz Cafe Isla Ria Cuale #16-A • popular • expensive & touristy

Memo's Casa de los Hotcakes 289 Basilio Badillo • popular

Papaya 3 169 Abasalo • natural food/sandwiches

Santos Francisca Rodriquez 136 • 22-5670 • clsd Mon • lesbians/gay men • full bar

Sego's 625 Aguiles Serdán • popular • steaks/Mexican

BOOKSTORES & RETAIL SHOPS

Safari Accents 244 Olas Altas

Studio Rustiko Basilo Badillo 300 • gay-owned/run

TRAVEL & TOUR OPERATORS

Amadeus Tours 23-2815

Doin' It Right Travel (415) 621-3576/(800) 936-3646 • Puerto Vallarta gay travel specialist • IGTA

Queretaro

Bars

La Iguana at Hotel Maria Teresa (Ave. Universidad 308) • gay-friendly • dancing/DJ • live shows

San Luis Potosí (52-48)

Bars

Sheik Calle Prolongación Zacatecas 347 • 12-7457 • 10pm-4am Fri-Sat • lesbians/gay men • dancing/DJ • live shows

San Miguel De Allende (52-46)

Accommodations

Aristos San Miguel De Allende 30 Calle Ancha de Santonio • 52-0149/(800) 223-0880 • gay-friendly • full-service hotel

Casa de Sierra Nevada 35 Calle Hospicio • 52-0415/(800) 223-6510 • gay-friendly

Bars

El Ring 25 Calle Hidalgo • 10pm-4am Fri-Sat • gay-friendly • dancing/DJ

Tampico

Bars

Bilbao W. of Calle Francisco I. Madero Oriente & A. Serdan Sur • lesbians/gay men

Tropicana Bar Calle de General López de Lara Sur • lesbians/gay men

Tepic (52-32)

Restaurants & Cafes

Cafe La Parroquia Calle Amado Nerro 18 (upstairs) • 12-6772

Wendy's Ave. México, Norte 178 • (not burgers)

Tijuana (52-66)

Info Lines & Services

Gay/Lesbian Info Line 88-0267

Accommodations

Fiesta Americana Hotel 4558 Blvd. Agua Caliente • 81-7000/(800) 343-7821 • gay-friendly • expensive rates

La Villa De Zaragoza 1120 Ave. Madero • 85-1832 • gay-friendly

Palacio Azteca Hotel Ave 16 de Septiembre • 86-5401 • gay-friendly

Plaza De Oro Hotel 2nd St. at Ave. 'D' • 85-1437 • gay-friendly

Bars

Caramba Ave. Revolución (near 'Mike's Disco') • gay-friendly • dancing/DJ

El Taurino Bar 198 Niños Héroes Ave. (btwn. 1st St. & Coahuila) • 85-2478 • 10am-3am, til 6am wknds • popular • lesbians/gay men • live shows

Emilio's Cafe Musical 1810-11 Calle Tercera (3rd St.), downtown • 88-0267 • from dusk til 3am • popular • gay-friendly • live shows • food served • beer/wine • also coffeehouse

Jardin de Alá btwn. Calle 4 & 5, 2nd flr. • lesbians/gay men • live shows • food served

Los Equipales 2024 7th St. (opposite Jai Alai Palace) • 88-3006 • opens 9pm, clsd Mon-Tue • popular • lesbians/gay men • dancing/DJ • live shows

Mi Kasa Calle 4 #1923 • noon-3am • gay-friendly • dancing/DJ • live shows

Mike's 1220 Revolución Ave. & 6th St. • 85-3534 • 9pm-6am Mon-Tue • popular • lesbians/gay men • dancing/DJ • live shows

Noa Noa Calle Primera & 154 'D' Miguel F. Martinez Ave. • 81-7901 • opens 9pm, clsd Mon • popular • lesbians/gay men • dancing/DJ • live shows

Terraza 9 Calle 5 at Ave. Revolución • 85-3534 • 8pm-2am • lesbians/gay men

Publications

Frontera Gay A.P. 3302, 22000 • 88-0267

Toluca

Bars

Bar El Conde 201-E Passaje Curi Norte • gay-friendly • food served

Bar El Jardin 100-D Ave. Hildalgo Ote. • gay-friendly

Cafe del Rey Portal 20 de Noviembre • gay-friendly • food served

Vip's Toluca Paseo Tollocán y Boulevard Isidoro Fabela • lesbians/gay men

Tuxtla Guiterrez

Bars

Sandy's Bar Calle 9 Sur at 8 Poniente (inquire in 'Via Fontana') • gay-friendly • transgender-friendly

Veracruz (52-29)

Accommodations

Hotel Imperial Plaza de Armas • 32-8788 • gay-friendly • food served • expensive

BARS

Deeper Calle Icazo 1005 (Victoria & Revillagigedo) • 35-0265 • lesbians/gay men • dancing/DJ

Hippopotamos Fracc. Costa Verde • 9pm-6am, clsd Mon-Wed • gay-friendly • dancing/DJ • live shows

Sotano's Bar Calle 1 (corner of Olmedo) • 37-0444 • 10pm-5am Th-Sat • mostly gay men • dancing/DJ

Villahermosa   (52-93)

ACCOMMODATIONS

Hotel Don Carlos Ave. Madero 418 centro • 12-2499 • gay-friendly • food served

Hyatt Villahermosa 106 Juarez Ave. • 13-4444/(800) 233-1234

BARS

Yardas 1318 Ave. 27 de Febrero • 13-4362 • lesbians/gay men

Zacatecas   (52-49)

ACCOMMODATIONS

Quinta Real Zacatecas Ave. Rayon 434 • 22-9104/(800) 878-4484 • gay-friendly • 5-star hotel

BARS

La Toma Calle Juárez 116 • clsd Sun-Tue • gay-friendly • dancing/DJ

RESTAURANTS & CAFES

Cafe Acropolis Ave. Hidalgo

Zihuatanejo

BARS

La Cambina del Captain Calle Vincente Guerrero at Nicolas Bravo, 2nd flr. • gay-friendly

La Casita Camino escenico a Playa 'La Ropa' (across from 'Kontiki' restaurant) • gay-friendly

Roca Rock Calle 5 de Mayo • gay-friendly • dancing/DJ

RESTAURANTS & CAFES

Splash Calle Ejido & Calle Vincente Guerrero • popular • lesbians/gay men

THE NAMES PROJECT CHAPTERS (U.S.)

California
Bay Area	415/863-1966
Inland Empire	909/784-2437
Long Beach	310/434-0021
Los Angeles	213/653-6263
Orange County	714/490-3880
Sacramento	916/484-5646
San Diego	619/492-8452
Ventura County	805/650-9546

Connecticut
Central Connecticut	203/591-1886

District of Columbia
National Capital Area	202/296-2637

Hawaii
Honolulu	808/948-1481

Iowa
Cedar Valley	319/266-7903

Illinois
Chicago	312/472-4460

Indiana
Indianapolis	317/920-1200

Massachusetts
Boston	617/262-6263

Maine
Maine	207/774-2198

Michigan
Detroit	313/371-9599
Thumb Area	810/982-6361

Minnesota
Twin Cities	612/373-2468
Missouri	
Metro St. Louis	314/997-9897 #43

North Carolina
Charlotte	704/376-2637

New Jersey
New Jersey	908/739-4863

New Mexico
New Mexico	505/466-2211

New York
Long Island	516/477-2447
New York City	212/226-2292
Syracuse	315/425-8695

Oklahoma
Tulsa Area	918/748-3111

Oregon
Portland	503/650-7032

Pennsylvania
Philadelphia	215/735-6263
Susquehanna Valley	717/234-0629
Pittsburgh	412/343-9846

Rhode Island
Rhode Island	401/847-7637

Texas
Dallas	214/520-7397
Fort Worth/Tarrant County	817/336-2637
Houston	713/526-2637

Utah
Salt Lake City	801/487-2323

Virginia
Central Virginia	804/346-8047

Washington
Seattle	206/285-2880

West Virginia
Upper Ohio Valley	304/242-9443

THE NAMES PROJECT
AIDS Memorial Quilt

TRAVEL

AND

TOURS

NOTE: Sites primarily for women are *italicized*.

UNITED STATES
Alaska

FAIRBANKS   (907)

Billie's Backpackers Hostel 2895 Mack Rd. • 457-2034 • gay-friendly • hostel & campsites • kids ok • food served • women-run • $15-20

Arizona

COTTONWOOD   (520)

Mustang B&B 4257 Mustang Dr. • 646-5929 • lesbians/gay men • full brkfst • one RV hookup • movie theater • $45-65

Arkansas

EUREKA SPRINGS   (501)

Greenwood Hollow Ridge B&B Rte 4, Box 155, 72632 • 253-5283 • exclusively gay • on 5 quiet acres • full brkfst • near outdoor recreation • shared/private baths • kitchens • RV hookups • $45-65

California

CLEARLAKE   (707)

Sea Breeze Resort 9595 Harbor Dr., Glenhaven • 998-3327 • gay-friendly • cottages • RV hookups • swimming • kids ok • gay-owned/operated • $55-85

GARBERVILLE   (707)

Giant Redwoods RV & Camp PO Box 222, Myers Flat, 95554 • 943-3198 • gay-friendly • campsites • RV • located off the Avenue of the Giants on the Eel River • shared baths • kids/pets ok • $16-22

PLACERVILLE   (209)

Rancho Cicada Retreat PO Box 225, Plymouth, 95669 • 245-4841 • lesbians/gay men • secluded riverside retreat in the Sierra foothills w/ two-person tents & cabin • swimming • nudity • $100-200, lower during wk

RUSSIAN RIVER   (707)

Faerie Ring Campground 16747 Armstrong Woods Rd., Guerneville • 869-2746/869-4122 • gay-friendly • on 14 acres • RV spaces • near outdoor recreation • pets ok • $20-25

Fife's Resort PO Box 45, Guerneville, 95446 • 869-0656/(800) 734-3371 • lesbians/gay men • cabins • campsites • also a restaurant • some veggie • full bar • $10-20 • IGTA • $50-215

Redwood Grove RV Park & Campground 16140 Neely Rd., Guerneville • 869-3670 • gay-friendly

Riverbend Campground & RV Park 11820 River Rd., Forestville • 887-7662 • gay-friendly • kids ok • wheelchair access

Schoolhouse Canyon Park 12600 River Rd. • 869-2311 • gay-friendly • campsites • RV • private beach • kids/pets ok

The Willows 15905 River Rd., Guerneville • 869-2824/(800) 953-2828 • lesbians/gay men • old-fashioned country lodge & campgound • smokefree • $49-119

Florida

CRESCENT CITY   (904)

Crescent City Campground Rte. 2 Box 25, 32112 • 698-2020/(800) 634-3968 • gay-friendly • tenting sites • RV hookups • swimming • laundry • showers • $15 day, $90 week, $200 month

LAKELAND   (941)

Sunset Motel & RV Resort 2301 New Tampa Hwy. • 683-6464 • gay-friendly • motels, apts, RV hookups & private home on 3 acres • swimming • wheelchair access

MIAMI   (305)

Something Special 7762 NW 14th Ct. (private home) • 696-8826 • noon-9pm, 2pm-7pm Sun • women only • vegetarian • plenty veggie • also tent space

Georgia

DAHLONEGA (706)

Swiftwaters Rte. 3 Box 379, 30533 • (706) 864-3229 • seasonal • women only • on scenic river • hot tub • deck • women-owned/run • $60-75 (B&B) • $40 (cabins) • $10 (camping)

Hawaii

HAWAII (BIG ISLAND) (808)

Kalani Honua Seaside Retreat RR2 Box 4500, Beach Rd., Pahoa, 96778 • 965-7828/(800) 800-6886 • gay-friendly • coastal retreat • conference center & campground w/in Hawaii's largest conservation area • swimming • food served • IGTA

Wood Valley B&B Inn PO Box 37, Pahala, 96777 • 928-8212 • mostly women • plantation home B&B • tent sites • veggie brkfst • sauna • nudity • women-owned/run • $35-55

MAUI (808)

Camp Kula - Maui B&B PO Box 111, Kula, 96790 • 878-2528 • popular • lesbians/gay men • on the slopes of Mt. Haleakala • HIV+ welcome • wheelchair access • $35-78

Maine

CAMDEN (207)

The Old Massachusetts Homestead Campground PO Box 5 Rte. 1, Lincolnville Beach • 789-5135 • open May-Nov • gay-friendly • cabins, tentsites & RV hookups • swimming

SEBAGO LAKE (207)

Maine-ly For You RR2 Box 745, Harrison • 583-6980 • gay-friendly • cottages • campsites

Massachusetts

MARTHA'S VINEYARD (508)

Webb's Camping Area RFD 3 Box 100, 02568 • 693-0233 • open May-Sept • gay-friendly • women-owned/run

Michigan

OWENDALE (517)

Windover Resort 3596 Blakely Rd. • 375-2586 • women only • campsites • swimming • $20

SAUGATUCK (616)

Camp It Rte. 6635 118th Ave., Fennville • 543-4335 • seasonal • lesbians/gay men • campsites & RV hookups

Minnesota

KENYON (507)

Dancing Winds Farm 6863 Country 12 Blvd. • 789-6606 • lesbians/gay men • B&B on working dairy farm • tentsites • full brkfst • work exchange avail. • women-owned/run

Mississippi

OVETT (601)

Camp Sister Spirit PO Box 12, 39462 • 344-2005 • mostly women • 120 acres of camping & RV sites • $10-20

Missouri

NOEL (417)

Sycamore Landing Drawer H, Hwy. 59 S., 64854 • 475-6460 • open May-Sept • campsites & canoe rental

Montana

BOULDER (406)

Boulder Hot Springs Hotel & Retreat PO Box 930, 59632 • 225-4339 • gay-friendly • spiritual/recovery retreat • camping avail. • food served • smokefree • call for info

RONAN (406)

North Crow Vacation Ranch 2360 North Crow Rd. • 676-5169 • seasonal • lesbians/gay men • cabins • tipis • 80 mi. S. of Glacier Park • hot tub • nudity

North Carolina

ASHEVILLE   (704)

Camp Pleiades 688-9201 (summer)/(904) 241-3050 (winter) • open Memorial Day-Halloween • women only • mountain retreat • cabins • swimming • food served

HOT SPRINGS   (704)

The Duckett House Inn Hwy. 209 S. • 622-7621 • lesbians/gay men • Victorian farmhouse B&B w/ camping on Appalachian Trail • also a restaurant • vegetarian (reservations required)

Ohio

COLUMBUS   (614)

Summit Lodge Resort & Guesthouse PO Box 951-D, Logan, 43138 • 385-3521 • popular • mostly gay men • camping avail. • hot tub • swimming • nudity • also a restaurant • wheelchair access

GUYSVILLE

Moon Ridge Rte. 1, Box 240 • no phone • campground

Oklahoma

EL RENO   (405)

The Good Life RV Resort Exit 108 I-40, 1/4 mile S. • 884-2994 • gay-friendly • 31 acres w/ 100 campsites & 100 RV hookups • swimming

Oregon

DAYS CREEK   (541)

Owl Farm PO Box 133, 97429 • 679-4655 • women only • open women's land for retreat or residence • camping sites avail.

EUGENE   (541)

Campus Cottage B&B 1136 E. 19th Ave. • 342-5346 • gay-friendly • full brkfst • women-owned

GRANTS PASS   (541)

Womanshare 862-2807 • women only • cabin & campground • meals included • hot tub

TILLER   (503)

Kalles Family RV Ranch 233 Jackson Creek Rd. • 825-3271 • lesbians/gay men • camping sites & RV hookups • btwn. Medford & Roseburg

Pennsylvania

NEW MILFORD   (717)

Oneida Camp & Lodge PO Box 537, 18834 • 465-7011 • seasonal • mostly gay men • oldest gay-owned/operated campground dedicated to the lesbigay community • swimming • nudity

PITTSBURGH   (412)

Camp Davis 311 Red Brush Rd., Boyers • 637-2402 • May-2nd wknd in Oct • 1 hr. from Pittsburgh • lesbians/gay men • adults 21+ only • pets on leash • call for events

South Dakota

RAPID CITY   (605)

Camp Michael 13051 Bogus Jim Rd. • 342-5590 • lesbians/gay men • peaceful getaway in the woods of the Black Hills • full brkfst

SIOUX FALLS   (605)

Camp America RR2 Box 201, Salem, 57058-1925 • 425-9085 • gay-friendly • 35 mi. west of Sioux Falls • camping • RV hook up • women-owned/run

Tennessee

JAMESTOWN   (615)

Laurel Creek Campground Rock Creek Rte. Box 150 • 879-7696 • clsd Dec-April • gay-friendly • camping • rentals • RV hookups • horses • hiking • swimming

NASHVILLE   (615)

IDA 904 Vikkers Hollow Rd., Dowelltown • 597-4409 • lesbians/gay men • camping avail. May-Sept • private community 'commune' located in the hills • 1hr SE of Nashville

Texas

GROESBECK (817)

Rainbow Ranch Rte. 2, Box 165, 76642 • 729-5847 • gay-friendly • camping • RV hook-up • on Lake Limestone halfway btwn. Houston & Dallas

Virginia

CHARLOTTESVILLE (804)

Intouch Women's Center Rte. 2 Box 1096, Kents Store, 23084 • 589-6542 • women only • campground & recreational area • wheelchair access

West Virginia

STONEWALL JACKSON LAKE (304)

FriendSheep Farm Rte. 1 Box 158, Orlando, 26412 • 462-7075 • mostly women • secluded retreat w/ workshops • campsites • swimming • smokefree • kids/pets ok by arr.

Wisconsin

LA CROSSE (608)

Chela & Rose's B&B and Forest Camping Retreat 735-4829 • women only • camping on 35 acres of women's land • also 2 rms. avail. • full brkfst • sauna • kids/pets ok • lesbian-owned/run • $10/couple camping ($5 extra person) • $50 room

MAUSTON (608)

CK's Outback W. 5627 Clark Rd. • 847-5247 • camping • near outdoor recreation

WASCOTT (715)

Wilderness Way PO Box 176, 54890 • 466-2635 • women only • resort property w/ cottages, camping & RV sites • swimming • wheelchair access • camping $10-14 • cottages $44-68

CANADA
British Columbia

BIRKEN (604)

Birkenhead Resort Box 369, Pemberton, V0N 2L0 • 452-3255 • gay-friendly • cabins • campsites • hot tub • swimming • also a restaurant • gourmet homecooking • some veggie • full bar

Ontario

HAMILTON (905)

The Cedars Tent & Trailer Park 1039 5th Concession Rd. RR2, Waterdown • 659-3655/659-7342 • lesbians/gay men • private campground • swimming • also social club • dancing/DJ • karaoke • wknd restaurant • some veggie

Province of Québec

JOLIETTE (514)

L'Oasis des Pins 381 boul. Brassard, St. Paul de Joliette • 754-3819 • gay-friendly • swimming • camping April-Sept • restaurant open year-round

Saskatchewan

RAVENSCRAG (306)

Spring Valley Guest Ranch Box 10, S0N 0T0 • 295-4124 • popular • gay-friendly • 1913 character home, cabin & tipis • also a restaurant • country-style • $30-50

CARIBBEAN
Virgin Islands

ST. JOHN (809)

Maho Bay & Harmony V.I. National Park • 776-6240/(800) 392-9004 • gay-friendly • camping & environmentally aware resort

NOTE: Tour Operators offering trips for **"women only"** or **"mostly women"** are italicized.

A Friend in New York
Gay/Lesbian

260 7th St., Hoboken, NJ 07030 • (201) 656-7282 • personalized excursions tailored to your budget and schedule

Above All Travel
Gay/Lesbian

(602) 946-9968 • worldwide lesbian/gay cruises & tours

Activities

336 Via Lido, Ste. E, Newport Beach, CA 92663 • (714) 675-6200/(800) 876-8708 • custom-designed private women's tours and meetings in unique locations

▲ *Adventure Associates*

PO Box 16304, Seattle, WA 98116 • (206) 932-8352 • co-ed and women-only outdoor adventures • member IGTA

> January—17-20—Cross-Country Ski British Columbia, CDN - women only
> January—26-Feb 1—Cross-Country Ski Yellowstone Park - women only
> January—11-26—Costa Rica Adventure
> January—11-Feb 2—Safari East Africa
> February—14-17—Cross-Country Ski North Cascades, WA - women only
> February—16-28—Trek Copper Canyon, MX
> February—TBA—Copper Canyon Adventure, MX - women only
> February—TBA—Sea Kayak Baja
> March—TBA—Sea Kayaking Baja - women only
> March—TBA—Trek Nepal / Himalayas
> May—TBA—Women's Challenge Personal Discovery Retreat
> June—6-8—Whale Watch Sea Kayak Weekend - women only & coed
> June—13-15—Whale Watch Sea Kayak Weekend - women only & coed
> June—20-22—Whale Watch Sea Kayak Weekend - women only & coed
> June—27-29—Whale Watch Sea Kayak Weekend - women only & coed
> June—21-23—Women's Solstice Ocean Retreat - women only
> June—TBA—Raft Deschutes River, OR - women only
> June—TBA—East Africa Safari
> July—TBA—Sea Kayak San Juan Islands, WA - women only
> July—TBA—Fly Fish the Tetons, ID - women only
> July—TBA—Backpack Wilderness Coast, WA - women only
> July—TBA—Lodge-based Hiking No. Cascades, WA - women only
> July—TBA—Llama Trek Olympic Mountains, WA - women only
> July—TBA—Mt. Rainier Women's Wilderness Retreat
> July—TBA—Climb (Snow School) Mt. Baker, WA - women only
> August—TBA—Wilderness Gourmet / Basecamp Hiking Cascades, WA - women only
> August—TBA—Sea Kayak San Juan Islands, WA - women only
> August—TBA—Backpack Tetons - women only
> August—TBA—Sail the Northern Aegean, Greece - women only
> August—TBA—Multi-Sport San Juan Islands, WA - women only
> August—TBA—Lodge-based Hiking Olympic Mountains / Coast - women only
> September—TBA—Bali / Lombok with Thalia Zepato
> October—TBA—Trek Nepal Himalayas
> Nov / Dec—TBA—Explore New Zealand - women only
> Nov / Dec—TBA—Cruise Galapagos / Explore Ecuador
> Nov / Dec—TBA—Costa Rica Tropical New Year's
> December—26-Jan 2—Cross-country Ski New Year's, Cascades, WA - women only

Adventures for Women

PO Box 515, Montvale, NJ 07645 • (201) 930-0557 • hiking, canoeing & cross-country skiing in the Adirondacks

African Pride Safaris Gay/Lesbian
673 NE 73rd St., Miami, FL 33138 • (305) 751-5216/(800) 237-4225 • group and individual tours to Africa • member IGTA

March—14—African Pride
March—14—Kenya Explorer
March—19—Pride of Africa
March—29—Out in Africa
April—22—Kenya Explorerr
May—10—Okavango
July—19—Camp Tanzani
August—9—Okavang
August—22—African Pride
August—22—Kenya Explorer
August—23—Pride of Africaa
September—26—Kenya Explorer
September—27—Out in Africa
October—24—Gambia Roots
November—14—Kenya Explore
December—5—African Prideo
December—27—Out in Africa (New Year's Party)

Ahwahnee Whitewater Expeditions Mixed Gay/Straight
PO Box 1161, Columbia, CA 95310 • (209) 533-1401 • women-only, co-ed & charter rafting • member IGTA

Alaska Women of the Wilderness Foundation
PO Box 773556, Eagle River, AK 99577 • (907) 688-2226/(800) 770-2226 (AK only) • year-round wilderness & spiritual empowerment programs for women

All About Destinations Gay/Lesbian

Gallery 3 Plaza, 3819 N. 3rd St., Phoenix, AZ 85012-2074 • (602) 277-2703/(800) 375-2703 • member IGTA

> January—10-17—Cruise Los Angeles to Acapulco
> May—12-19—Cruise Acapulco to San Francisco
> August—29-Sept 1—Labor Day Community Cruise to Baja, Mexico

Allegro Travel Gay/Lesbian

900 West End Ave. #12C, New York, NY 10025 • (212) 666-6700/(800) 666-3553 • 22 departures yearly to Russia, Italy, Egypt & Scandinavia

Alyson Adventures Mostly Gay/Lesbian

PO Box 181223, Boston, MA 02118 • (617) 247-8170/(800) 825-9766 • member IGTA

Amazon Tours & Cruises Gay/Lesbian

8700 W. Flagler #190, Miami, FL 33174 • (800) 423-2791 • weekly cruises, includes upper Amazon • member IGTA

Another Way

RFD5 Box 290-B1, Webster, NH 03303 • (603) 648-2751 • comfortable lesbian camping tours in New England, Canada & Florida • member IGTA

Arizona Adventure Straight/Gay

(602) 204-2422 • 3-day hikes, horse rides & tours

Artemis Sailing Charters

PO Box 931, Driggs, ID 83422 • (208) 354-8804/(800) 838-7783 • sailing adventures worldwide

> February—1-10—Sail Tahiti
> April—4-11—Sail Tonga, South Pacific
> November—8-15—Sea of Cortez
> November—16-27—Sea of Cortez

Artemis Wilderness Tours

PO Box 1574, El Prado, NM 87529 • (505) 758-2203 • whitewater boating and rafting in New Mexico and Colorado

Atlas Travel Service Mixed Gay/Straight

8923 S. Sepulveda Blvd., Los Angeles, CA 90045 • (310) 670-3574/(800) 952-0120 • member IGTA

Bar H Ranch

PO Box 297, Driggs, ID 83422 • (208) 354-2906 • guesthouse and summer horseback trips in Wyoming's Tetons • near Jackson Hole, WY

Call of the Wild Wilderness Trips

2519 Cedar St., Berkeley, CA 94708 • (510) 849-9292 • hiking & wilderness trips for all levels in Western US

Cloud Canyon Backpacking

411 Lemon Grove Lane, Santa Barbara, CA 93108 • (805) 969-0982 • seasonal wilderness backpacking in Utah and the Sierra Nevadas

▲ *Club Le Bon*

PO Box 444, Woodbridge, NJ 07095 • (908) 826-1577/(800) 836-8687 • tours for lesbians, and for gay/lesbian parents & kids

> January—10-18—Amazon Rainforest
> February—TBA—Assam, Northeast India
> April—19-26 — 'Kool Kids' gay family program to Isla Mujeres, Mexico
> May—3-10—Isla Mujeres, Mexico
> October—4-11—Isla Mujeres, Mexico
> November—15-22—Barbados

▲ **Club Skirts**

Dinah Shore Women's Weekend parties • Dinah Shore hotline: 310-281-1715 • hot gathering of women Labor Day weekend in Monterey • Monterey hotline: 415-337-4962

March—28-30—Dinah Shore Women's Weekend
August—29-31—Club Skirts Monterey Bay Women's Weekend

▲ *Common Earth Wilderness Trips*

PO Box 1191, Fairfax, CA 94978 • (415) 455-0646 • non-profit women-owned • sliding scale • multicultural • cross-country skiing, backpacking & kayaking in California, the Southwest, and Alaska

Connections Tours   Gay/Lesbian

169 Lincoln Rd., Ste. 302, Miami Beach, FL 33139 • (305) 673-3153/(800) 688-8463 (OUT-TIME) • local arrangements in Florida • member IGTA

Cow Pie Adventures   Straight/Gay

(801) 297-2140 • camping • hiking • biking • fishing

Cruise Express   Gay/Lesbian

1904 3rd Ave., Ste. 900, Seattle, WA 98101 • (206) 467-0467/(800) 682-1988 • cruises & tours • member IGTA

We are a women owned and operated non-profit, specializing in quality, memorable back packing and kayaking treks in California, the Southwest and Alaska!

MULTICULTURAL · SLIDING-SCALE
EXPERT GUIDES · CUSTOMIZED TRIPS

P.O. BOX 1191 • FAIRFAX, CA 94978
(415) 455-0646

There Are a Number of Things to Know About Lesbian Travel...Fortunately, You Have Only One Number to Remember:

1-800-448-8550

Cruises
Tours
Resorts

No matter where you want to go, how you want to get there or where you want to stay, The International Gay Travel Association's worldwide network of over 1000 gay & lesbian community-based travel agents will professionally guide you with the latest information on all the hot, new travel opportunities. For an IGTA travel agent or IGTA accommodations worldwide call today!

International Gay Travel Association

Opening Doors To Gay & Lesbian Travel & Adventure

Home Page: http://www.rainbow-mall.com/igta
AOL: Gay/Lesbian forum

Cruisin' the Castro Gay/Lesbian

375 Lexington St., San Francisco, CA 94110 • (415) 550-8110 • guided walking tour of the Castro • member IGTA

Custom Cruises International

482 Great House Dr., Milpitas, CA 95035 • (408) 945-8286

Different Strokes Tours Gay/Lesbian

1841 Broadway Ste. 607, New York, 10023 • (212) 262-3860/(800) 688-3301 • gay cultural safaris to worldwide destinations • member IGTA

Doin' It Right Tours & Travel Gay/Lesbian

1 St. Francis Pl. Ste. 2106, San Francisco, CA 94107 • (415) 621-3576 • gay cultural exchange tours & SF accommodations • member IGTA

Earth Walks Straight/Gay

(505) 988-4157 • guided tour of American Southwest & Mexico

February—9-16—Yoga Retreat, Oaxaca, Mexico

Eco-Explorations Mostly Gay/Lesbian

(408) 335-7199 • scuba and kayak adventures in Monetery Bay, CA and worldwide

Executive Tour Associates Gay/Lesbian

PO Box 42151, Mesa, AZ 85274 • (602) 898-8853/(800) 382-1113 • deluxe motorcoach tours of the Southwest • member IGTA

Fiesta Travel Gay/Lesbian

323 Geary St. #619, San Francisco, CA 94102 • (415) 986-1134/(800) 200-0582 • tours to Latin America for New Year's and Carnival in Rio

Florida Adventures

PO Box 677893, Orlando, FL 32867 • (407) 677-0655

GAYVentures Gay/Lesbian

2009 SW 9th St., Miami, FL 33135 • (305) 541-6141/(800) 940-7757 • Puerto Rico tours • member IGTA

Great Canadian Ecoventures Mixed Gay/Straight

1896 W. Broadway, Vancouver, BC V6J-1Y9 • (604) 730-0704/(800) 667-9453 • wildlife photography tours

Hawk, I'm Your Sister

PO Box 9109-WT, Santa Fe, NM 87504 • (505) 984-2268 • women's wilderness canoe trips and writing retreats in the Americas and Russia

Her Wild Song

PO Box 515, Brunswick, ME 04011 • (207) 721-9005 • spiritually aware wilderness journeys for women

International Gay Rodeo Association Gay/Lesbian

(303) 832-4472

International Tours & Cruises Gay/Lesbian

1235 N. Main St., Madisonville, KY 42431 • (502) 821-0025/(800) 844-2072 • worldwide tours, ask for Art Nance

International Tours of New Orleans

615 Baronne St. Ste. 205, New Orleans, LA 70113 • (504) 558-9001/(800) 522-6811

▲ *Joani Weir Productions & Klub Banshee*

(310) 281-7358 • all-inclusive hotel & entertainment package for women during Dinah Shore Weekend

Kenai Peninsula Guided Hikes

HCR 64 Box 468, Seward, AK 99664 • (907) 288-3141 • guided day hikes

L'Arc en Ciel Voyages Gay/Lesbian

PO Box 234, Wayne, PA 19087-0254 • (610) 964-7888/(800) 965-LARC (5272) • custom-designed tour programs for the gay & lesbian community

> February—12-18—Valentines Day in Paris
> February—25-Mar 8—Christian Pilgrimmage to Israel
> April—25-May 3—Queen's Day in Amsterdam
> May—31-June 8—The G.I. Favorite: WWII History Tour, London, Normandy, Paris
> August 1998—1-8—Amsterdam Gay Games: Pre-Registration, Tour Programs available

Lost Coast Llama Caravans

77321 Usal Rd., Whitehorn, CA 95489 • women-led pack trips

Lotus Land Tours Straight/Gay

1251 Cardero St., Ste. 1251, Vancouver, Canada, BC V6G 2H9 • (604) 684-4922 • day paddle trips, no experience necessary.

Mangrove Mistress

Murray Marine, 5710 U.S. 1, Key West, FL 33040 • (305) 294-4213 • snorkeling • nature exploring • sunset cruises • ceremonies

▲ *Mariah Wilderness Expeditions*

PO Box 248, Port Richmond, CA 94807 • (510) 233-2303/(800) 462-7424 • woman-owned • whitewater rafting in California and Central America

Maui Surfing School

PO Box 424, Puunene, HI 96784 • (808) 875-0625

McNamara Ranch

4620 County Rd. 100, Florissant, CO 80816 • (719) 748-3466 • horseback tours for 2-3

Merlyn's Journeys

PO Box 277, Altaville, CA 95221 • (209) 736-9330/(800) 509-9330 • relaxing & adventurous getaways for women

Mountain Madness

(206) 937-8389

Multi-Travel & Tours Gay/Lesbian

855 Washington Ave., Miami Beach, FL 33139 • (305) 672-4600/(800) 762-3688 • ski tours and more

New Dawn Adventures Gay/Lesbian

PO Box 1512, Vieques, PR 00765 • (809) 741-0495 • Caribbean retreat • bunkhouse and campground

New England Vacation Tours Gay/Lesbian

PO Box 571 - Rte. 100, West Dover, VT 05356 • (802) 464-2076/(800) 742-7669 • fall foliage and party weekend • gay/lesbian tours conducted by a mainstream tour operator

Northern Alternative

202 W. Sheridan St., Ely, MN 55731 • (218) 365-2894/(800) 774-7520 • wilderness adventures including skiing, snow shoeing, dog sledding and ice fishing

Ocean Voyager Gay/Lesbian

404 1/2 Henry St., Brooklyn, NY 11201 • (718) 624-3063/(800) 435-2531 • Cruise Consultants, LTD

> December—21-Jan 4 1997—Christmas Cruise
> February—14-17—Key West Cruise
> March—15-22—East Caribbean Cruise
> April—19-27—Transatlantic Crossing
> May—24-June 1—Grandeur of the Seas, East Caribbean Cruise
> July—11-18—Alaska Cruise

OceanWomyn Kayaking

620 11th Ave. E., Seattle, WA 98102 • (206) 325-3970 • guided sea kayaking adventures

> February—20-27—Baja del Sur Mexico: Sea of Cortez
> March—3-10—Baja del Sur Mexico: Sea of Cortez
> August—10-16—British Columbia: West Vancouver Island
> August—20-26—British Columbia: West Vancouver Island

▲ **Olivia Cruises**

4400 Market St., Oakland, CA 94608 • (510) 655-0364/(800) 631-6277 • huge cruises to Alaska, Caribbean, Mediterranean, Club Med Ixtapa

> February—15-22—Tahiti Cruise
> March—16-23—Club Med Ski Adventure, Copper Mountain, CO
> April—14-21—Mexican Caribbean Cruise
> July—4-11—Greek Isles / Turkey Cruise
> October—25-Nov 1—Huatulco, Mexico, Club Med Resort

Our Family Abroad Gay/Lesbian

40 W. 57th St., New York, NY 10019 • (212) 459-1800/(800) 999-5500 • all-inclusive package and guided motorcoach tours in Europe, Asia, Africa and South America

Out 'n Arizona / Cowgirls N' Ghost Towns Gay/Lesbian

Dept. 215, PO Box 22333, Tempe, AZ 85285 • (602) 234-1168/(800) 897-0304 • fall & winter van tours

Outdoor Vacations for Women Over 40

PO Box 200, Groton, MA 01450 • (508) 448-3331

Outland Adventures Straight/Gay

PO Box 16343, Seattle, WA 98116 • (206) 932-7012 • ecologically sensitive cultural tours • snorkeling and biking in Central America, Canada, Alaska and Washington State

OutWest Adventures Gay/Lesbian

PO Box 8451, Missoula, MT 59807 • (406) 543-0262/(800) 743-0458 • specializing in active Western vacations

> January—25-Feb 1—Big Sky Gay Ski Tour
> February—22-Mar 1—Big Sky Gay Ski Tour
> March—15-22—Big Sky Gay Ski Tour

Paddling South & Saddling South Straight/Gay

4510 Silverado Trail, Calistoga, CA 94515 • (707) 942-4550 • horseback, mountain biking, and sea kayak trips in Mexico • call for complete calendar

> January—19-25—Coastal Springs Ride
> January—25-Feb 1—X-Peninsula & Whale Watch—biking
> February—8-16—Sea to Sea & Whales—hiking
> February—15-23—X-Peninsula & Whale Watch—biking
> March—9-15—Candy & Flower Gardens—hiking
> March—2-9—Kayak Baja—women only
> March—30-Apr 6—Kayak Baja—women only
> April—6-12—Mt. Ranch & Swimmin' Holes—hiking
> May—4-11—Kayak Baja—women only

▲ **Pangaea Expeditions**

PO Box 5753, Missoula, MT 59806 • (406) 721-7719 • river rafting in Montana • call for complete calendar

Parkside Travel　　　　Gay/Lesbian

3310 Kent Rd. Ste. 6, Stowe, OH 44224 • (216) 688-3334/(800) 552-1647 • also Gay Travel Cub membership and discounts

Passage to Utah　　　　Straight/Gay

PO Box 520883, Salt Lake City, UT 84152 • (801) 582-1896 • custom trips in the West • hiking • horseback riding • river riding

Passport Travel & Tours　Gay/Lesbian

415 E. Golf Rd. #111, Arlington Heights, IL 60005 • (708) 364-0634/(800) 549-8687 • upscale tours to Europe incorporating local gay history and culture

Personal Maui

(808) 572-1589/(800) 326-5336 • guide & driver for tours of the hidden Maui

Pink Triangle　　　Mostly Gay/Lesbian

743-A Addison St., Berkeley, CA 94710 • (510) 843-0181 • once-yearly worldwide country/western and square-dancing oriented tours.

February—17-March 3—Pink Triangles Down Under: Australia

July—15-26—Pink Triangles in Green & Plaid: Ireland & Scotland

Progressive Travels

Mostly Gay/Lesbian

224 W. Galer Ste. C, Seattle, WA 98119 • (206) 285-1987/(800) 245-2229 • luxury and standard walking and biking tours of Europe and the Pacific Northwest • member IGTA

Rainbow Country Tours/B&B

Straight/Gay

PO Box 333, Escalante, UT 84726 • (800) 252-8824 • gay-friendly hiking in Utah • B&B • custom tours available

Rainbow Tours　　　　Gay/Lesbian

87-3203 Road Guava, Kona Paradise, Captain Hook, HI 96704 • (808) 328-8406 • kayaking & snorkeling off black sand beaches of Kona Coast.

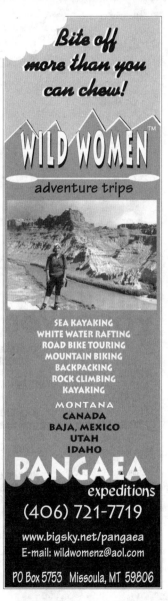

Rainbow Ventures

1520 N.E. 26th Ave., Fort Lauderdale, FL 33304 • (800) 881-4814 • women only B&B and commitment ceremonies

Regency Travel

1075 Duval St. #19, Key West, FL 33040 • (305) 294-0175/(800) 374-2784

Rockwood Adventures   Straight/Gay

1330 Fulton Ave., West Vancouver, Canada, BC V7T 1N8 • (604) 926-7705 • rain forest walks • all levels • free hotel pick up

Sail Alaska   Straight/Gay

PO Box 20348, Juneau, AK 99802 • (907) 463-3372 • experience the pristine beauty of southeast AK with lesbian guides

Sea Safaris Sailing   Mixed Gay/Straight

12060 Carver Ave., New Port Richey, FL 34654 • (813) 671-4611/(800) 497-2508 • some women-only charter sail trips and cruises to the Caribbean

Sea Sense

25 Thames St., New London, CT 06320 • (203) 444-1404/(800) 332-1404 • custom sailing courses in Florida, Lake Michigan, New England and the Virgin Islands

Skunk Train California Western

299 E. Commercial St., Willits, CA • (707) 459-5248

▲ **Skylink**

2460 W. Third St. Ste. 215, Santa Rosa, CA 95401 • (707) 570-0105/(800) 225-5759 • low-cost, air-included tours worldwide for women in couples or single

February—Mardi Gras in Sydney, Australia

South Carolina Division of Tourism

(803) 734-0235

Spirit International Travel Club

(800) 823-4784

Super Natural Adventures   Straight/Gay

626 West Pender St., Main Fl., Vancouver, BC V6B 1V9 • (604) 683-5101 • hiking and helicopter-hiking trips in Northern and Western Canada

T.R.I.P. Tours LTD.   Gay/Lesbian

11 Grace Ave., Great Neck , NY 11021 • (516) 487-9400/(800) 553-7494 • Holidays at Sea: Cruise with Congenial Companions • member IGTA

February—14-17—Valentine's Day: S. Caribbean on the Nordic Empress
February—15-22—Presidents' Week: W. Caribbean on the Sun Princess
February—15-22—Presidents' Week: S. Caribbean on the Windward

TBI Tours

787 Seventh Ave. #1101, New York, NY 10015 • (212) 489-1919/(800) 223-0266 • tours to Asia

Tennessee Tourist Development

(615) 741-2158

Texas Tourist Division

(512) 462-9191/(800) 888-8TEX

▲ *Thanks Babs*

(888) WOW-BABS • "the vacation expert for women"

Tropical Tune-ups

PO Box 390847, Kailua-Kona, HI 96739 • (800) 587-0405 • small group retreats for women

Underseas Expeditions   Gay/Lesbian

PO Box 9455, Pacific Beach, CA 92169 • (619) 270-2900/(800) 669-0310 • warm-water diving and scuba trips worldwide • member IGTA

February—15-22—Dive Saba aboard Caribbean Explorer
March—12-22—Dive Palau aboard Sun Dancer
March—23-30—Dive Truk, wrecks from WWII Japanese fleet
August—TBA—Dive Fiji aboard Fiji Aggressor

Venus Adventures

PO Box 167-X, Peaks Island, ME 04108 • (207) 766-5655 • goddess-oriented tours for women to sacred sites in England and Ireland

Voyages & Expeditions   Mostly Gay/Lesbian

8323 Southwest Freeway #800, Houston, TX 77074 • (713) 776-3438/(800) 818-2877 • group and individual deluxe cruises

Water Sport People   Mixed Gay/Straight

(305) 296-4546 • scuba-diving instruction, group charters

Whelk Women

PO Box 1006-D, Boca Grande, FL 33921 • (813) 964-2027 • custom boat tours for women • outfitted camping • accommodations

Wild Women Expeditions

PO Box 145, Stn. B, Sudbury, ON P3E 4N5 • (705) 866-1260 • Canada's only women-run canoe excursions, all equipment supplied, riverside basecamp on the Spanish River, sauna

Woman Tours

PO Box 931, Driggs, ID 83422 • (800) 247-1444 • bicycle tours for women

March—2-8—Cycle New Zealand
March—8-21—Cycle New Zealand
May—24-31—Bike and Hike Zion / Bryce
June—7-15—Cycle Yellowstone / Grand Tetons
August—30-Sept 5—Cycle Canadian Rockies, Banff Jasper
September—6-14—Cycle Canadian Rockies, Hot Springs & Lakes
September—20 -28—Cycle Zion / Bryce / Grand Canyon
October—11-19—Cycle Mississippi, Natchez Trace
October—27-31—Cycle California: Sonoma / Napa Valley Vineyards to Waves

Women for Sail

1035 W. Belden #3, Chicago, IL 60614 • (800) 346-6404 • learn to sail while on vacation in the Carribean & other exotic destinations

Women in the Wilderness

566 Ottawa Ave., St. Paul, MN 55107 • (612) 227-2284 • teaches outdoor skills & nature study

January—TBA—Dogsledding in Minnesota
February—TBA—Dogsledding in Minnesota
February—TBA—Whale watching, sea-kayaking, Baja, California
February—TBA—Snowshoe/ski retreat for cancer survivors
March—3-9—Writers' workshop with Carol Bly, with snowshoeing and dogsledding in northern MN
March—TBA—Sail Virgin Islands
March—TBA—Whitewater raft/jungle study Honduras
April—TBA—Greece in high flowering season
May—TBA —Whitewater canoeing, Wisconsin
June—TBA—Solo canoeing, Minnesota
June—TBA—Sailing, Apostle Islands, Wisconsin
June—TBA—Canoeing, hiking on Lake Superior, Pukaskwa Nat'l Park, Ontario, Canada
July—TBA—Mother/daughter canoeing, Minnesota
July—TBA—Hiking, paddling retreats, Northwoods, Minnesota
August—TBA—Sailling Apostle Islands, Wisconsin
August—TBA—Canoeing Mississippi headwaters
August—TBA—Canoeing Finnish Lapland
August—TBA —Outdoor leadership training, Minnesota
August—17-23—Canoeing Vermilion River, Minnesota
September—5-8—Hiking, canoeing retreats, Minnesota
September—11-14—Sailing Apostle Islands, Wisconsin
September—27-Oct 14—Hiking among Anasazi ruins, Utah & Colorado
October—4-11—Canoeing Labrynth Canyon, Green River, Utah
October—2-5—Canoeing Northern Minnesota
October—16-19—Writers' retreat, Northern Minnesota
November—TBA—Amazon rainforest nature study

Women on the Water

PO Box 502, Key West, FL 33041 • (305) 294-4213 • sunset sails • day sails • snorkeling

Women's EcoScapes

PO Box 1408, Santa Cruz, CA 95061 • (408) 479-0473 • coral reef ecology • snorkeling, kayaking, sailing • well-dolphin whale encounters • Key West, California, Hawaii and Bahamas

Women's Outdoor Challenges

40 Winn Hill Rd., Sunapee, NH 03782 • (603) 763-5400 • outdoor adventure programs for women of all ages

Woodswomen

25 W. Diamond Lake Rd., Minneapolis, MN 55419 • (612) 822-3809/(800) 279-0555 •
non-profit tour operator • outdoor adventures • domestic and international

January—2-13—Galapagos Island Cruise, Ecuador
January—29-Feb 3—Dogsledding in the Northland, Minnesota
February—13-17—Dogsledding in the Northland, Minnesota
February—15-Mar 2—New Zealand Bicycle Tour
February—19-23—Dogsledding in the Northland, Minnesota
February—22-Mar 1—Cycling Hawaii: The Big Island
March—1-7—Yellowstone Ski Extravaganza, Wyoming
March—9-23—Red Sea Diving & Touring Israel
March—13-22—Exploring Costa Rica, Wildlife viewing, hiking
March—15-21—Vacation in Cozumel, Mexico, Snorkeling, bicycling, sightseeing
March—22-29—Joshua Tree Rock Climbing, California
March—22-29—Leadership in Joshua Tree, Rock climbing & leadership skills
May—2-4—St. Croix Spring Hike, Wisconsin
May—9-11—Namekagon River Odyssey, Wisconsin
May—11-17—Desert Slickrock Backpack, Utah
May—16-18—Whitewater School, Wisconsin, learn paddling skills
May—30-June 1—Learn to Bicycle Tour, Wisconsin
June—7-14—Cataract Canyon Rafting, Utah
June—7-14—BWCA Creative Dynamics, Minnesota, Canoeing & leadership skills
June—13-16—Horsepacking in Wisconsin
June—20-22—Red Cedar Trail Festival, Wisconsin
July—5-11—Mountaineer & Glacier Travel, Washington
July—6-12—Northern Lakes Loop, Canoeing in northern Minnesota
July—13-19—Lakes, Rivers, and Pictographs, Canoeing in northern Minnesota
July—13-19—Cracks, Crevasses & Volcanoes, Washington, mountaineering & leadership skills
July—20-26—Rainbow Island Retreat, Minnesota, Canoeing, rustic cabin lodging
July—20-26—Olympic Nat'l Park Backpack, Washington
July—26-31—Kenai Fjords Sea Kayak, Alaska
July—27-Aug 2—Northern Lakes Loop, Canoeing in northern Minnesota
August—2-8—Hiking in Denali Park, Alaska
August—3-9—Mt. Rainier Backpack, Washington
August—3-15—Bicycling in Tuscany, Italy
August—3-16—Canadian Wilds Canoe Journey
August—10-16—Hiking in Denali Park, Alaska
August—17-23—Isle Royale Backpack, Michigan
August—22-25—Horsepacking in Wisconsin
August—24-28—San Juan Sea Kayak, Washington
August—31-Sept 6—Autumn Canoe Excursion, Minnesota
September—11-14—Northshore Hike, Minnesota
September—20-26—Grand Canyon Leadership, Arizona
September—28-Oct 4—Grand Canyon Backpack, Arizona
September—28-Oct 3—California Wine Country Bicycling
October—3-9—Autumn in Provincetown, Cape Code, MA, Whale watching, bicycling
November—1-8—SCUBA in Roatan

Zeus Tours

(800) 447-5667

GiRL BAR
Los Angeles
& **club Skirts**
San Francisco

proudly present

The Dinah Shore Weekend '97

March 27th-30th
Easter Weekend

Palm Springs, California

The Riviera Resort & Racquet Club
For Hotel Reservations
1(800) 444-8311

or

The Wyndham Hotel
For Hotel Reservations
1(619) 322-6000

Both Hotels Exclusively Ours!

You must mention the DINAH SHORE WEEKEND to receive our Group Rates

ABSOLUT VODKA

For More information:
Call Toll Free 888-44-DINAH
(34624)

NOTE:
- Events for *"mostly women"* or *"women only"* are italicized.
- **TBA** means that the actual event dates have yet '**to be announced**'.

January

25-Feb 1: **Aspen Gay Ski Week** Aspen, CO
c/o Aspen Gay/Lesbian Community, Box 3143, Aspen, CO 81612 • (970) 925-9249
• gay/lesbian • 2000+ attendees

31-Feb 2: **Pantheon of Leather** New Orleans, LA
c/o The Leather Journal, 7985 Santa Monica Blvd. 109-368, W. Hollywood, CA
90046 • (213) 656-5073 • annual SM community service awards • mixed
gay/straight

February

2-9: **Whistler Gay Ski Week: Altitude '97** Whistler, BC
c/o Out On The Slopes Productions, PO Box 1370, Whistler, BC V0N 1B0 • (604)
938-0772/(604) 816-6710 • popular ski destination 75 mi. north of Vancouver •
gay/lesbian

11: **Mardi Gras** New Orleans, LA
c/o New Orleans Convention & Visitors Bureau, 1520 Sugarbowl Dr., New
Orleans, LA 70112 • (504) 566-5011 • North America's rowdiest block party •
mixed gay/straight

13-17: **Black Gay/Lesbian Conference** Dallas, TX
c/o Nat'l Black Gay/Lesbian Leadership Forum, 1219 S. La Brea Ave., Los
Angeles, CA 90019 • (213) 964-7820 • gay/lesbian

14-17: **Pantheocon** Oakland, CA
c/o Ancient Ways, 4075 Telegraph Ave, Oakland, CA 94609 • (510) 653-3244 •
Pagan convention at the Red Lion Hotel, Starhawk ritual, Reclaiming collective
• mixed gay/straight

March

7-10: **Gay Ski East '97: The Winter Games at Lake Placid, NY** Lake Placid, NY
c/o Eclectic Excursions, 2045 Hunters Glen Dr. Ste. 502, Dunedin, FL 34698 •
(813) 734-1111 • gay/lesbian • 200+ attendees

24-30: *Nabisco Dinah Shore Golf Tournament* Palm Springs, CA
(619) 324-4546 • see Club Skirts or Joani Weir Productions under Tour Operators
for party & accommodation info • mostly women

27-30: *Dinah Shore Women's Weekend* Palm Springs, CA
c/o Club Skirts & Girl Bar • (310) 281-1715 • huge gathering of lesbians for pool
parties, dancing and yes, some golf-watching • women only

28-31: *Gulf Coast Womyn's Festival at Camp SisterSpirit* New Orleans, LA
c/o Camp SisterSpirit, PO Box 12, Ovett, MS 39464 • (601) 344-1411 • They won
their lawsuit - so go support a celebration of womyn's land in the South! • 2 1/2
hours from New Orleans, LA • entertainment & politics • mostly women

April

9: **AIDS Dance-a-thon San Francisco**   San Francisco, CA
   c/o Miller Zeitchik Publicity, PO Box 193920, San Francisco, CA 94119 • (415)
   392-9255 • AIDS benefit dance at the Moscone Center • mixed gay/straight •
   7000+ attendees • $75+ pledges

TBA: **Readers/Writers Conference**   San Francisco, CA
   c/o A Different Light • (415) 431-0891 • 3rd annual weekend of workshops &
   roundtables with queer writer & readers, at the Women's Building

27: **AIDS Dance-a-thon L.A.**   Los Angeles, CA
   c/o AIDS Walk LA, PO Box 933005, Los Angeles, CA 90093 • (213) 466-9255 •
   AIDS benefit at Universal Studios • mixed gay/straight • $75+ pledges

May

2-4: *Russian River Women's Wknd*   Guerneville, CA
   (707) 869-4522//(800) 253-8800 • 2 hrs north of San Francisco • mostly women

9-11: *Pridefest '97*   Philadelphia, PA
   c/o Pridefest, 200 S. Broad St., Philadelphia, PA 19102 • (215) 732-3378 • 70
   events capped by Saturday night party • gay/lesbian

16-18: *A Gathering of Priestesses*   Bagley, WI
   c/o Of a Like Mind, Box 6677, Madison, WI 53716 • (608) 244-0072 • women's
   spirituality conference • mostly women

21-26: *Campfest Memorial Day Wknd*   Oxford, PA
   PO Box 559, Franklinville, NJ 08322 • (609) 694-2037/(301) 598-9035 (TTY) • 'The
   Comfortable Womyn's Festival' • women only • 1400+ attendees • $200

23-25: *Wiminfest*   Albuquerque, NM
   c/o Women in Movement in New Mexico (WIMINM), PO Box 80204,
   Albuquerque, NM 87198 • (505) 255-7274 • music, comedy, art, recreation &
   dances • mostly women

30: **Lambda Literary Awards**   Chicago, IL
   c/o Lambda Book Report, 1625 Connecticut Ave. NW, Washington, DC 20009 •
   (202) 462-7924 • the 'Lammies' are the Oscars of lesbigay writing & publishing •
   gay/lesbian

TBA: **Ancient Ways Festival**   Harbin Hot Springs, CA
   c/o Ancient Ways, 4075 Telegraph Ave., Oakland, CA 94609 • (510) 653-3244 •
   annual 4-day mixed gender/orientation spring festival in May or June of pan-
   pagan rituals, workshops and music w/ lesbian/gay campsite • mixed
   gay/straight

TBA: *Herland Spring Retreat*   Oklahoma City, OK
   c/o Herland, 2312 NW 39th, Oklahoma City, OK 73112 • (405) 521-9696 • music,
   workshops, campfire events & potluck • boys under 10 only • $15-60 sliding
   scale registration • mostly women

June

May 30-June 1: **Virginia Women's Music Festival**
c/o Intouch, Rte. 2, Box 1096, Kent's Store, VA 23084 • (804) 589-6542 • women only • 600 attendees • $85

May 29 - June 4: **National Women's Music Festival** Bloomington, IN
PO Box 1427-WT, Indianapolis, IN 46206 • (317) 927-9355/(317) 253-9966 (Dreams & Swords Bookstore #) • mostly women

May 29-June 3: **Springfest Maine®** Lincolnville, ME
c/o CPJ Productions, PO Box 5682, Augusta, ME 04332 • (207) 993-2177 • 'gentle, apolitical' festival on Maine coast (between Belfast & Camden) with sports, concerts & self-help workshops • featuring Suede and Alix Dobkin • wheelchair access • ASL interpreter on request • women only • 550+ attendees • $40

13-22: **San Francisco International Lesbian/Gay Film Festival** San Francisco, CA
c/o Frameline, 346 9th St., San Francisco, CA 94103 • (415) 703-8650

15-22: **Pagan Spirit Gathering** Mt. Horeb, WI
c/o Circle Sanctuary, PO Box 219, Mt. Horeb, WI 53572 • (608) 924-2216 • summer solstice celebration in Wisconsin, primitive camping, workshops, rituals • mixed gay/straight

19-22: **Womongathering** Pocono Mtns, PA
PO Box 559, Franklinville, NJ 08322 • (609) 694-2037/(301) 598-9035 (TTY) • women's spirituality fest • women only • 300+ attendees • $200

July

3-9: **WomenFest** Key West, FL
201 Coppitt Rd. #106A, Key West, FL 33040 • (305) 296-4238 • concerts, dances, theater, fair, film festival, seminars and more • mostly women

4-6: **July 4th Kickback** Kent's Store, VA
c/o Intouch, Rte. 2, Box 1096, Kent's Store, VA 23084 • (804) 589-6542 • watergames • women only • 80 attendees • $75

17-20: **International Ms. Leather Contest** San Diego, CA
c/o Bare Images, 4332 Browne St., Omaha, NE 68111 • (402) 451-7987 • contest • workshops • parties • mostly women

26-30: **Lesbian/Gay Health Conference** Atlanta, GA
c/o Nat'l L/G Health Assoc., 1407 'S' St. NW, Washington, DC 20009 • (202) 994-4285 • health and AIDS/HIV issues facing our communities

WomenFest '97

September 3rd – 9th, 1997

Wine Tasting Dinners
Cocktail Parties & Picnics
Sunset Cruises & Snorkeling
Sisters for Brothers Blood Drive
Authors' Booksignings & Readings
The WomenFest Experience at La Te Da
Tour Key West on the Old Town Trolley
The WomenFest Street Fair on Duval Street
Backcountry Kayaking with Mosquito Coast
Water & Sand Volleyball at the Fairfield Inn
The SKYY Ball at the Mel Fisher Maritime Museum
Two Nights of Comedy at Holiday Inn Beachside
The WomenFest Brunch Fashion Show at Alexander's
The Infamous Wet T-Shirt Contest at Atlantic Shores Resort
The WomenFest Tennis Tournament at Holiday Inn Beachside

Information:
Please send SASE to 201 Coppitt Road, #106A
Key West, FL 33040 • (305) 296-4238

August

TBA: **Halstead St. Fair** Chicago, IL
c/o North Halstead St. Merchants Assoc. • (312) 883-0500

8-10: **Guys & Gals** Kent's Store, VA
c/o Intouch, Rte. 2, Box 1096, Kent's Store, VA 23084 • (804) 589-6542 • live
country/western music & dancing • gay/lesbian • 80 attendees • $40

12-17: **Michigan Womyn's Music Festival** Walhalla, MI
PO Box 22, Walhalla, MI 49458 • (616) 757-4766 • music, performances, videos,
movies and more • self-help, creative, spiritual, political and other workshops •
childcare • ASL interpreting • differently-abled resources • women only

TBA: **Women Celebrating Our Diversity** Luisa, VA
c/o Twin Oaks Community, Rte. 4, Box 169, Luisa, VA 23093 • (540) 894-5126 •
usually last wknd in Aug • camping • ASL interpreting • mostly women

29-31: **Club Skirts Monterey Bay Women's Wknd** Monterey, CA
c/o MT Productions, 584 Castro St., San Francisco, CA 94114 • (415) 337-4962 • 3
huge dance parties • golf tournament benefiting the Human Rights Campaign •
live comedy night • celebrity guests • book early! • mostly women

TBA: **Wigstock** New York, NY
c/o Lesbian/Gay Community Services Center • (212) 620-7310 • outrageous
wig/drag/performance festival in Tompkins Square Park in the East Village •
gay/lesbian

TBA: **National Gay Softball World Series** San Diego, CA
c/o NAGAAA, 1014 King Ave., Pittsburgh, PA 15206 • (412) 362-1247 • gay/lesbian

September

Aug 29-Sept 11: **Austin Gay/Lesbian International Film Festival** Austin, TX
(512) 472-3240/(512) 476-2454 • gay/lesbian

TBA: **AIDS Walk L.A.** Los Angeles, CA
c/o AIDS Walk LA, PO Box 933005, Los Angeles, CA 90093 • (213) 466-9255 •
AIDS benefit at Universal Studios • mixed gay/straight • $75+ pledges

4-7: **Fallfest Maine**
c/o CPJ Productions, PO Box 5682, Augusta, ME 04332 • (207) 377-3992 • 3-day
women's festival, 'gentle, apolitical' • mostly women

5-7: **The Fall Gathering** Ashland, OR
PO Box 335, Ashland, OR 97520 • (503) 482-2026 • annual women's camp in the
Oregon woods • women only • 150+ attendees

TBA: **Northern Lights Womyn's Music Festival**
c/o Aurora Northland Lesbian Center, 32 E. 1st St. Ste. 104, Duluth, MN 55802 •
(218) 722-4903 • day-long festival in Minnesota wilderness • mostly women

26-28: **Russian River Women's Wknd** Guerneville, CA
(707) 869-4112/(800) 253-8800 • mostly women

TBA: **Iowa Women's Music Festival**
c/o Prairie Voices Collective, 130 N. Madison, Iowa City, IA 52242 • (319) 335-
1486 • mostly women

TBA: **Cruise with Pride** San Juan, PR
c/o Cruiseworld, 901 Fairview Ave. N. #A150, Seattle, WA 98126 • (800) 340-0221
• Pride Foundation fundraiser in the Greek Islands, 6 days • gay/lesbian • 50+
cabins attendees

October

3-12: **Pride Film Festival Tampa**   Tampa, FL
   1222 Dale Mabry Ste. 602, Tampa, FL 33629 • (813) 837-4485 • gay/lesbian

TBA: *Provincetown Women's Week*   Provincetown, MA
   (800) 637-8696 • very popular—make your reservations early! • mostly women

11: **National Coming Out Day**
   c/o National Coming Out Day, PO Box 34640, Washington, DC 20043-4640 •
   (800) 866-6263 • gay/lesbian • free

TBA: *Film Festival*   Chicago, IL
   c/o Chicago Filmmakers, 1543 W. Division, Chicago, IL 60622 • (312) 384-5533 •
   gay/lesbian • 7-10,000 attendees • $75

31: *Halloween Spiral Dance*   East Bay, CA
   c/o Women's Spirituality Forum, PO Box 11363, Oakland, CA 94611 • (510) 893-
   3097 • mostly women

November

TBA: **AIDS Dance-a-thon New York**   New York, NY
c/o Gay Men's Health Crisis, PO Box 10, Old Chelsea Stn. , New York, NY 10113-0010 • (212) 807-9255 • AIDS benefit • mixed gay/straight • 6000+ attendees • $75+ pledges

6-9: **Heart of the West V**   Las Vegas, NV
c/o PLUS (People Like Us) Productions, PO Box 103, Lakeside, CA 92040 • (800) 438-7587 (GET PLUS)/(619) 390-9889 • 5th annual women's extravaganza • workshops, crafts, music and dancing • at majestic Stardust resort & casino

TBA: **Santa Barbara Lesbian/Gay Film Festival**   Santa Barbara, CA
c/o Gay/Lesbian Resource Center, 126 E. Haley Ste. A-17, Santa Barbara, CA 93101 • (805) 963-3636 • gay/lesbian

21-23: **Gay & Lesbian Weekend**   Catskill Mtns., NY
c/o Pines Resort Hotel • (800) 367-4637 • two nights of entertainment and gay events • meals included • gay/lesbian • $269

December

7-14: **Wahine Week in Wailea**   Maui, HI
c/o Remote Possibilities, PO Box 1851, Wailuku, Maui, HI 96793 • (800) 511-3121 • 7-day resort in Maui • tennis, golf, sailing, windsurfing, kayaking • women only

TBA: **Gay Day at Disneyland**   Anaheim, CA
c/o Odyssey Adventures, PO Box 923094, Sylmar, CA 91392 • (818) 893-2777 • gay/lesbian • $32-37

Did we miss something?

Do you know of a women's event (national/regional in scope) we haven't listed? Or a lesbian-friendly campground or RV lot?

Send us information (including the address and phone number) so we can list it in our next guide—if you're the first reader to inform us, we'll send you a *free copy of the 1998 Women's Traveller*.

Mail: **Women's Traveller**
PO Box 422458
San Francisco, CA 94142

Fax: **(415) 703-9049**   Email: **Update@Damron.com**

By now, you've probably heard about DYKE TV's

bi-weekly television show,

but did you know we now air in nearly

60 cities nation-wide

and have the potential to reach

6 million house-holds

all over the USA?

Plus...we offer

free video production workshops

for lesbians who'd like to begin producing their own work. We also create

educational videos

alone and with other community organizations. We also maintain an extensive

video archive library

with hours of dyke herstory on tape!

If you want

more info,

and your very own

DYKE TV sticker or button,

mail us your name and address. Or, visit our Web site at

www.dyketv.org

or call

(212) 343-9335

Check our listing under "Info Lines & Services"

What time is DYKE TV on? in your city or town in the Damron Women's Traveller!

MAIL ORDER
SECTION

A Different Light Bookstores (800) 343-4002 • books • cards • calendars • videos • catalog

After Midnight Collection PO Box 13176, Scottsdale, AZ 85267 • sexual supplies for women • send $5 for catalog

Avalon Herbaly PO Box 69, Euless, TX 76039 • handmade herbal soaps & natural bath products

Avena Botanicals 219 Mill St., Rockport, ME 04856 • organically grown herbal products for women • catalog

Bande Designs 7102 Castor Ave., Philadelphia, PA 19149 • womyn's jewelry • send $1 for catalog

Banshee Designs 923 SE 37th Ave., Portland, OR 97214 • 'garments for goddesses of every size' • adult sizes to 8X • send SASE with 55c postage for catalog

Bookwoman Books PO Box 67, Media, PA 19149 • (601) 566-2990 • books • videos • posters • free catalog

Brigit Books (813) 522-5775 • lesbian & feminist titles • catalog

Brookside Soap Company PO Box 55638, Seattle, WA 98155 • (206) 363-3701 • all-natural soaps handmade by women

Cleis Press (800) 780-2279 • publishes 'provocative books in lesbian and gay studies, sexual politics, and literature' • catalog

Different Voices (800) 824-3915 • gifts • T-shirts • pridewear • free catalog

Dreams & Swords 6503 Ferguson St., Indianapolis, IN 46220 • (317) 253-9966/(800) 937-2706 • women's books • music • videos • T-shirts • pride accessories • catalog

Dykes to Watch Out For c/o Alison Bechdel, PO box 215, Dept. LC, Jonesville, VT 05466 • send a stamp for catalog

Eve's Garden 119 W. 57th St. Ste. 420, New York, NY 10019 • (212) 757-8651 • sex toys • books • videos • all from the first sexuality boutique created by women for women • send $3 for catalog

Good Vibrations 1210 Valencia St., San Francisco, CA 94110 • (415) 974-8990/(800) 289-8423 • lesbian-made erotica • sex toys • books • videos • send $2 for catalog

Heartland Books PO Box 1105-N, East Corinth, VT 05040 • (800) 535-3755 • lesbian & feminist titles carefully selected by lesbians who love reading • free catalog

Herspective PO Box 8977, Emeryville, CA 94662 • (510) 653-2523 • t-shirts • gifts • catalog

♀♀♀♀♀♀♀♀♀♀♀♀♀

♀♀♀♀♀♀♀♀♀♀♀♀♀

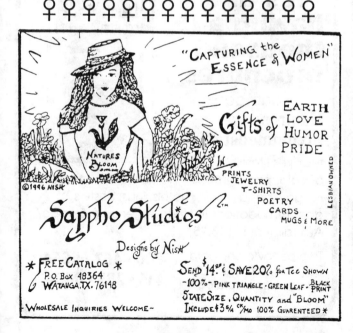

▲ **Jewelry By Ponce** (800) 969-RING • lesbian/gay commitment rings & assorted jewelry

Lady Slipper, Inc. 3205 Hillsboro Rd., Durham, NC 27705 • (919) 683-1570/(800) 634-6044 • women's music • videos

Lammas (800) 955-2662 • women's books • music • jewelry • much more

Lavana Shurtliff Jewelry 1119 E. Gaylord St., Mt. Pleasant, MI 48858 • (517) 773-3801 • flame-worked glass jewelry • catalog

Lesbian Book Club (800) 798-5828 • buy 3 & get 1 free • no membership or additional purchases • free catalog

Lielin West Jewelers PO Box 733, Benicia, CA 94510 • (707) 745-9000 • women's imagery in precious metals

Lizzie Brown/Pleiades PO Box 389, Brimfield, MA 01010 • (413) 245-9484 • woman-identified jewelry

Mama Bears (800) 643-8629 • women's books and more

Music for the Masses PO Box 90272, San Jose, CA 95109 • T-shirts • photos • posters • videos • songbooks • all of your favorite women recording artists • send two 32-cent stamps for catalog

Naiad Press, Inc. PO Box 10543, Tallahassee, FL 32302 • (904) 539-5965/ (800) 533-1973 • lesbian books & videos

New Herizons PO Box 405, Lancaster, MA 01523 • (508)365-4340 • books • videos • jewelry • free catalog

Pleasure Chest (800) 753-4536 • for all your erotic needs • catalog

Pleasure Place (800) 386-2386 • erotic gifts • toys • catalog

▲ **Sappho Studios** PO Box 48365, Watauga, TX 76148 • jewelry • gifts • cards • free catalog • see display ad

Snake & Snake Productions 511 Scott King Rd., Durham, NC 27713 • (919) 544-2028 • goddess t-shirts up to 4XL

Socket Science 4014 24th St. #187-1194, San Francisco, CA 94114 • (415) 587-7459 • sex toys designed by and for women

Sumiche PO Box 428, Waterville, OR 97489 • (541) 896-9841 • custom jewelry • commitment rings

T-shirts by Stephanie PO Box 605, Farmington, NH 03835 • (603) 755-2926 • feminist T-shirts • catalog

Third Side Press 2250 W. Farragut, Chicago, IL 60625 • (800) 471-3029 • lesbian press • fiction • erotica • health • free catalog

▲ **Tico Joe** (888) TICO-JOE • gourmet Costa Rican coffee

We'moon Calendar c/o Mother Tongue Ink PO Box 1395-C, Estacada, OR 97023

Wildfire Glass 2235 Latcha Rd., Millbury, OH 43447 • (419) 836-2294 • womyn-owned glass studio • catalog

Wimmins' Creations c/o K. Parker, 1335 Taylor, Ft. Wayne, IN 46802 • (219) 422-9353 • crafts by several women artisans • catalog

Wolfe Video PO Box 64, New Almaden, CA 95042 • (408) 268-6782/(800) 438-9653 • video productions by lesbians

Womankind Books 5 Kivy St., Huntington Stn., New York, NY 11746 • (516) 427-1289/(800) 648-5333 • over 5,000 books & videos • free catalog

Xandria Collection PO Box 31039, San Francisco, CA 94131 • sexual products from around the world • send $4 for catalog

Favorite City

Hey writers! See your work published in the next *Women's Traveller*! Win prizes! Show your friends! Write up the local lesbian scene in your favorite city (150-500 words) and send it to us—if our editors like it, we'll include it in the next edition of the *Women's Traveller*, with your name! Plus we'll send you prizes.*

SUGGESTIONS

Keep it short! A few well-placed adjectives are preferable to long sentences describing the ambiance of each café or bar.

Emphasize the diversity your city offers. Include events and places for women of color, differently abled women, older women, young women, large women and women of different backgrounds (such as transgendered, bisexual, butch, femme, leather, separatist, etc).

Tell us about it! Don't just list places and events. Compose a witty, entertaining short essay that highlights popular lesbian gathering places as well as those that are unique-but-not-well-known.

Pretend you're just visiting. Think about your city in terms of a woman just coming through town for a few days—what would be most interesting or valuable? Where do you take friends who stay with you for a few days?

RULES

Deadline: Entries must be received by June 15, 1997.

*Prizes: *Women's Traveller* T-Shirt and latest editions of the *Women's Traveller*, *Damron Road Atlas* and *Damron Accommodations*. Prize winners will be notified by mail and/or phone.

Eligibility: Open to anyone over 18 years of age, except employees of Damron Company, their affiliates and agencies. Void where prohibited or restricted by law. All federal, state and local laws apply.

No purchase necessary.

Mail to: The *Women's Traveller* Favorite City Contest
PO Box 422458, San Francisco, CA 94142-2458

Email: WomenTravl@aol.com

Fax: (415) 703-9049

Entries become the property of The Damron Company and may be edited.

Please take a few minutes to fill out this survey and mail it back to us. *We want our Damron books to remain the best travel guides for the gay lesbian and gay community for many years to come—and we need your input! Thanks for your time.*

1. **Gender:** ❑ Male ❑ Female ❑ MTF ❑ FTM

2. **Race:** ❑ Asian ❑ African-American ❑ Latino
   ❑ Native American ❑ Euro-American/White ❑ Other

3. **Age:** ❑ under 21 ❑ 21-25 ❑ 26-32
   ❑ 33-39 ❑ 40-49 ❑ 50+

4. **Sexual Identity:** ❑ Lesbian ❑ Gay Male
   ❑ Bisexual ❑ Heterosexual

5. **Personal Income:**
   ❑ under $15K ❑ $15-20K ❑ $2-25K
   ❑ $25-35K ❑ $35-50K ❑ $50-75K or more

6. **Total Household Income:**
   ❑ under $15K ❑ $15-20K ❑ $2-25K
   ❑ $25-35K ❑ $35-50K ❑ $50-75K
   ❑ $75-100K ❑ $100-150K ❑ $150K or more

7. **Type of Residence:**
   ❑ Own Home ❑ Rent Home
   ❑ Rent Apt/Flat ❑ Live with Family

8. **Where do you live?** (City, State, Country)
   _____

9. **Education:**
   ❑ High School Graduate ❑ Some College
   ❑ Associate Degree ❑ Technical Certificate
   ❑ College Graduate ❑ Post-Graduate Studies
   ❑ Master's/Doctorate ❑ None of above

10. **Employment Status:**
    ❑ Unemployed ❑ Employed
    ❑ Retail Sales/Service ❑ Artist/Craftperson
    ❑ Skilled Labor ❑ Clerical
    ❑ Military ❑ Not Employed

11. **Events you plan to attend in the future:**
    ❑ Dinah Shore/Palms Springs Events
    ❑ Women's Weekend-Provincetown
    ❑ Women's Music Festival City: _____
    ❑ Lesbian cruises Specify: _____
    ❑ Other_____

12. Own or Use a Computer: ❑ Yes ❑ No (skip to 19)

13. What Make & Model: _____

14. How Much Memory: RAM _____ Hard Drive ____

15. Peripherals You Use: ❑ Modem: Speed: _____
                    ❑ CD-Rom: Speed: _____
                    ❑ Newton/PDA

16. Online Services You Use:
    ❑ America Online   ❑ Compuserve
    ❑ Prodigy   ❑ GayNet
    ❑ Other:_____

17. Internet Access:
  ❑ Email Only ❑ Web ❑ Full Access ❑ None

18. Services You Would Use for Gay Travel Info:
    ❑ CD-Rom   ❑ Floppy Disks
    ❑ Website   ❑ Bulletin Board
    ❑ Mailing List   ❑ Chat Forum
    ❑ Newton/PDA program
    ❑ Other:_____

19. Familiarity with the Women's Traveller:
    ❑ This is the first copy I've looked at
    ❑ I've used previous editions

20. Other Damron Publications You Have Used:
    ❑ Damron Road Atlas
    ❑ Damron Accommodations
    ❑ Damron Address Book
    ❑ None

21. Please Comment on the Women's Traveller (compared to other travel guides):

_____
_____
_____
_____

To get on our mailing list, please fill in:

Name _____

Address _____

City/State/Zip _____

Please Mail To: Women's Traveller Survey
                  PO Box 422458
                  San Francisco, CA 94142